The Welsh Language
before the Industrial Revolution

Editor

GERAINT H. JENKINS

**CARDIFF
UNIVERSITY OF WALES PRESS
1997**

© University of Wales, 1997
   reprinted, 2001

All rights reserved. No part of this book may be reproduced, stored in a retrieval system, or transmitted, in any form or by any means, electronic, mechanical, photocopying, recording or otherwise, without clearance from the University of Wales Press, 6 Gwennyth Street, Cardiff, CF24 4YD.
www.wales.ac.uk/press

British Library Cataloguing-in-Publication Data
A catalogue record for this book is available from the British Library.

ISBN 0–7083–1418–X

The financial assistance of the Board of Celtic Studies towards the publication of this book is gratefully acknowledged.

Typeset at the University of Wales Press, Cardiff.
Printed in England by Bookcraft, Midsomer Norton, Avon.

'. . . having discharged . . . what I conceived to be a part of my duty to my mother tongue, and pay'd a small tribute to the pre-eminence of my native language, I shall not hesitate to profess to the world, that I prefer *this* to any of the languages ancient or modern, that I have any acquaintance with.'

John Walters, *A Dissertation on the Welsh Language* (1771)

Contents

	List of Contributors	ix
	Preface	xi
	List of Abbreviations	xiii
	Introduction *Geraint H. Jenkins*	1
1.	The Welsh Language before 1536 *Llinos Beverley Smith*	15
2.	The Welsh Language in Early Modern Wales *Geraint H. Jenkins, Richard Suggett and Eryn M. White*	45
3.	Tudor Legislation and the Political Status of 'the British Tongue' *Peter R. Roberts*	123
4.	The Welsh Language and the Court of Great Sessions *Richard Suggett*	153
5.	The Welsh Language in Local Government: Justices of the Peace and the Courts of Quarter Sessions *c.* 1536–1800 *J. Gwynfor Jones*	181
6.	Unity of Religion or Unity of Language? Protestants and Catholics and the Welsh Language 1536–1660 *Glanmor Williams*	207
7.	The Established Church, Dissent and the Welsh Language *c.*1660–1811 *Eryn M. White*	235
8.	Humanist Learning, Education and the Welsh Language 1536–1660 *William P. Griffith*	289
9.	Popular Schooling and the Welsh Language 1650–1800 *Eryn M. White*	317

10. The Welsh Language in Scholarship and Culture 1536–1660
    R. Geraint Gruffydd   343

11. The Cultural Uses of the Welsh Language 1660–1800
    Geraint H. Jenkins   369

12. The Celtic Languages of Britain
    Brynley F. Roberts   407

    Index   441

Maps

Principal language zones *c.*1750   49

Non-Celtic place-names before 1715   52

Principal language zones *c.*1750: parishes with at least one school
    1738–77   327

Contributors

Dr William P. Griffith, Lecturer, School of History and Welsh History, University of Wales, Bangor

Professor Emeritus R. Geraint Gruffydd, Honorary Senior Research Fellow, University of Wales Centre for Advanced Welsh and Celtic Studies

Professor Geraint H. Jenkins, Director, University of Wales Centre for Advanced Welsh and Celtic Studies

Professor J. Gwynfor Jones, School of History and Archaeology, University of Wales, Cardiff

Dr Brynley F. Roberts, Former Librarian, National Library of Wales

Dr Peter R. Roberts, Lecturer, School of History, University of Kent at Canterbury and Honorary Fellow, University of Wales Centre for Advanced Welsh and Celtic Studies

Dr Llinos Beverley Smith, Senior Lecturer, Department of History and Welsh History, University of Wales, Aberystwyth

Mr Richard Suggett, Investigator, Royal Commission on the Ancient and Historical Monuments of Wales

Dr Eryn M. White, Lecturer, Department of History and Welsh History, University of Wales, Aberystwyth

Sir Glanmor Williams, Professor Emeritus, Department of History, University of Wales, Swansea

Preface

There has emerged of late a growing recognition that far more attention needs to be paid to the social history of language. 'It is high time for a social history of language, a social history of speech, a social history of communication', wrote Peter Burke in 1987, and it is a great pleasure, therefore, to introduce the first volume in a collaborative, multi-volume scholarly enterprise which will survey the social history of the Welsh language in modern times. The projected series on 'The Social History of the Welsh Language' – the fruits of the second major research project of the Centre for Advanced Welsh and Celtic Studies – will provide an authoritative and challenging account of the fortunes of the Welsh language from the Acts of Union to the present day. The research strategy of the Centre is based on collaborative work between research fellows at the Centre and scholars within the constituent institutions of the University of Wales and elsewhere, and the proposed volumes will draw widely on the expertise of demographers, geographers, geolinguists, anthropologists and sociolinguists, as well as social historians. The present volume includes contributions from Professor Emeritus R. Geraint Gruffydd and Dr Peter R. Roberts, both of whom are Honorary Fellows of the Centre, and it should also be noted that, prior to her appointment to a lectureship in the Department of History and Welsh History at the University of Wales Aberystwyth, Dr Eryn M. White spent two extremely fruitful years as a research fellow at the Centre working on the Welsh language in early modern Wales.

Although the present team of research fellows at the Centre – Dr David Llewelyn Jones, Mrs Dot Jones, Dr Marion Löffler, Dr Gwenfair Parry, Dr Dylan Phillips, Dr Robert Smith and Ms Mari Williams – have been appointed to work on the social history of the Welsh language in the nineteenth and twentieth centuries, this volume has benefited from their valuable and constructive advice. I also offer my sincere thanks to members of the Advisory Committee associated with this project – Professor Emeritus Harold Carter, Professor Emeritus Ieuan Gwynedd Jones, Dr Brynley F. Roberts, Professor J. Beverley Smith and Professor Emeritus J. E. Caerwyn Williams – for their helpful and supportive collaboration. I am deeply indebted to Mrs Glenys Howells for her patient editorial scrutiny and to Mrs Aeres Bowen Davies and Ms Siân Lynn Evans for their untiring help in the preparation of successive drafts. Many of the footnotes were verified by Mr Hywel Befan Owen and I must also record my gratitude to Mr William H. Howells for preparing the index. I am indebted to the following either for preparing or for their generous permission to reproduce maps in this volume: Professor John Aitchison and Professor Emeritus Harold Carter; Royal Commission on the Ancient and Historical Monuments of Wales; Mr Ian Gulley, Design Office, Institute of Earth Studies, University of Wales, Aberystwyth; Mr John Hunt, Project Officer (Cartography), Faculty of Social Sciences, The Open University; and Dr W. T. R. Pryce, the Open University in Wales. It is a pleasure to thank the staff of the National Library of Wales for their unfailing readiness to place their manuscripts and printed books at our disposal, and to the staff of the University of Wales Dictionary for many valuable suggestions and references. The Centre is also deeply grateful to the Board of Celtic Studies of the University of Wales and to the Catherine and Lady Grace James Foundation for making grants towards the preparation and publication of this volume. The staff of the University of Wales Press, especially Susan Jenkins, Ceinwen Jones and Richard Houdmont, have shown great kindness and forbearance, and it is our good fortune to launch this ambitious series on the occasion of the seventy-fifth anniversary of this invaluable press.

Since the social history of the Welsh language is such a massive and intimidating field of study, it would be foolish to pretend that this series will tell the whole chequered story, but all those associated with this seminal venture hope that its findings will interest and intrigue the general public as well as specialists in the field. The primary function of the historian of language is to communicate and explain, and those diverse and complex factors which have determined the fortunes of the Welsh language in modern times deserve to be understood by as wide a range of people as possible.

February 1997   *Geraint H. Jenkins*

Abbreviations

AC	*Archaeologia Cambrensis*
ALM	Hugh Owen (ed.), *Additional Letters of the Morrises of Anglesey (1735–1786)* (Parts 1–2, London, 1947–9)
BBCS	*Bulletin of the Board of Celtic Studies*
BIHR	*Bulletin of the Institute of Historical Research*
BLJ	*British Library Journal*
CA	*The Carmarthen[shire] Antiquary*
CAR	*Cambrian Register*
CCHMC	*Cylchgrawn Cymdeithas Hanes y Methodistiaid Calfinaidd*
CLR	*Cambrian Law Review*
CMCS	*Cambridge Medieval Celtic Studies*
Companion	Meic Stephens (ed.), *The Oxford Companion to the Literature of Wales* (Oxford, 1986)
DWB	*The Dictionary of Welsh Biography down to 1940* (London, 1959)
EA	*Efrydiau Athronyddol*
EFC	*Efrydiau Catholig*
EHR	*English Historical Review*
FHSJ	*Flintshire Historical Society Journal*
FHSP	*Flintshire Historical Society Publications*
GH	*Glamorgan Historian*
GPC	*Geiriadur Prifysgol Cymru*
HR	*Historical Research*
HRO	Herefordshire Record Office
HT	*History Today*
JAH	*Journal of American History*
JEH	*Journal of Ecclesiastical History*
JHG	*Journal of Historical Geography*
JHSCW	*Journal of the Historical Society of the Church in Wales*
JMEH	*Journal of Medieval History*
JMHRS	*Journal of the Merioneth Historical and Record Society*
JWBS	*Journal of the Welsh Bibliographical Society*

Libri Walliae	Eiluned Rees, *Libri Walliae: A Catalogue of Welsh Books and Books Printed in Wales, 1546–1820* (Aberystwyth, 1987)
LlC	*Llên Cymru*
LlLlG	Thomas Parry and Merfyn Morgan (eds.), *Llyfryddiaeth Llenyddiaeth Gymraeg* (Caerdydd, 1976)
*LlLlG*²	Gareth O. Watts (ed.), *Llyfryddiaeth Llenyddiaeth Gymraeg. Cyfrol 2 1976–1986* (Caerdydd & Aberystwyth, 1993)
MA	*Monmouthshire Antiquary*
MC	*Montgomeryshire Collections*
ML	John H. Davies (ed.), *The Letters of Lewis, Richard, William and John Morris, of Anglesey, (Morrisiaid Môn) 1728–1765* (2 vols., Aberystwyth, 1907–9)
MLR	*Modern Language Review*
MP	*Modern Philology*
NLW	Manuscript at the National Library of Wales
NLWJ	*National Library of Wales Journal*
NMS	*Nottingham Medieval Studies*
OED	*The Oxford English Dictionary*
Owen, *Description*	George Owen, *The Description of Penbrokshire*, ed. Henry Owen (4 vols., London, 1892–1936)
PBA	*Proceedings of the British Academy*
PCC	Prerogative Court of Canterbury
PH	*Pembrokeshire Historian*
PP	*Past and Present*
PRO	Public Record Office
SC	*Studia Celtica*
SRO	Shropshire Record Office
SS	*Scottish Studies*
TAAS	*Transactions of the Anglesey Antiquarian Society and Field Club*
TCBS	*Transactions of the Cambridge Bibliographical Society*
TCHBC	*Trafodion Cymdeithas Hanes Bedyddwyr Cymru*
TCHS	*Transactions of the Caernarvonshire Historical Society*
TDHS	*Transactions of the Denbighshire Historical Society*
THSC	*Transactions of the Honourable Society of Cymmrodorion*
TLWNS	*Transactions of the Liverpool Welsh National Society*
TRHS	*Transactions of the Royal Historical Society*
UWBL	University of Wales Bangor Library
WHR	*Welsh History Review*

Introduction

GERAINT H. JENKINS

ALTHOUGH it is unlikely that any of the contributors to this volume would endorse the sweeping view expressed in the historical introduction to the famous Report *Welsh in Education and Life* (1927) that 'the history of Wales is the history of the Welsh language', it is nevertheless certain that none of them would hesitate to assert that the Welsh language was integral to the collective identity of the Welsh people in early modern Wales. Monoglot Welsh speakers formed a substantial proportion of the population and the mother tongue was inextricably woven into the fabric of society. Among the common people, most of whom were insulated from other tongues, there were no fears for the future of Welsh as an everyday medium. Only erudite scholars and cultural patriots, who cherished their literary inheritance, believed there were reasons for alarm and that large-scale endeavour was required to raise the status and esteem of the Welsh language in order to remove the stigma placed upon it by the celebrated 'language clause' of 1536. In the aftermath of the Union legislation, initiatives towards strengthening the language – both in its spoken and printed form – were mainly the work of cultured middling sorts who, sustained to a greater or lesser degree by cultural atavism, religious piety and utilitarian values, took their responsibilities seriously and ensured that by the end of the period under study the Welsh language was not only in good fettle but also poised to play a decisive role in the shaping of modern Wales. This book is principally concerned with the processes of social change which brought this about.

Although this volume deals mainly with the period between the Acts of Union and the Industrial Revolution, the first chapter by Llinos Beverley Smith is devoted to the history of the Welsh language in the Middle Ages from the period when memoranda in Welsh were recorded in the margins of the Book of St Chad to the so-called 'language clause' in the first Act of Union of 1536. Welsh was the language of the overwhelming majority and it flourished as the medium of daily discourse. The language was a patchwork of local accents and dialects, and social intercourse was heavily dependent on speaking and listening. Of crucial importance was the fact that Welsh was the language of learning and culture. The poets, in their capacity as the nation's remembrancers, were successful in preserving and fostering ancient traditions orally and in deepening the pride of their fellow-countrymen in them. The Gogynfeirdd – the court poets of Wales between *c.*1100 and *c.*1300 – sang memorable odes of eulogy and elegy to the princes, and when their golden age ended the *cywydd* became the principal Welsh verse-form from the middle of the fourteenth century onwards. Since the bardic system was so powerful and influential, the nobility were more than happy to sustain it and, on the whole, they themselves were familiar with the wealth of language embodied in the poetic tradition. The same period also produced prose literature noteworthy for its precision and clarity of expression, and also a splendid corpus of legal texts which demonstrated beyond any doubt that the Welsh language possessed all the necessary attributes to deal with a host of complex and technical subjects and terms.

The Welsh language encompassed a remarkably wide geographical area in medieval times and it succeeded in casting its net still further to include places where Saxons and Normans had taken root. Welsh was commonly to be heard in Shropshire, Cheshire and Herefordshire, and it is evident that no overriding linguistic significance was attached to the old boundary of Offa's Dyke. In the same way, extensive parts of the Vale of Glamorgan and some of the most obdurately Anglicized towns had become Cymricized by the end of the fifteenth century. From the twelfth century onwards, however, Welsh had to compete for its place, especially in the fields of politics and law, against other languages and cultures, including Latin, French and English. Among the gentry families who laid claim to connections with the English and who were familiar with their language, and also among officials hungry for office under the Crown, the English language was accorded a higher status than Welsh. By the fifteenth century there was a growing trend towards drawing up documents such as wills, settlements, land transactions, marriage contracts, petitions and letters in English. Welsh was not considered an appropriate language for use in documents, statutes and government, and the 'language clause' which came into effect in 1536 did no more than give formal recognition to social and economic trends which had been under way for several generations.

The extensive chapter on 'The Welsh Language in the Early Modern Period' written by Geraint H. Jenkins, Richard Suggett and Eryn M. White, is divided into three sections. The first, a survey of the geographical distribution of Welsh, reveals that by the time of the first census in 1801 there were more speakers of the language (around half a million) than ever before. On the eve of the Industrial Revolution seven out of ten people were still monoglot Welsh speakers, and the craggy mountains and rudimentary roads of the country formed a robust dividing wall which insulated the monoglot inhabitants of the north and west against English influences. Apart from the traditional Englishries where the English language reigned, the most obvious signs of language erosion were to be found in the border counties. Several Welsh-speaking communities in the Marches were lost to England as a result of the administrative restructuring which followed the Acts of Union, and although the loss of Welshness in those areas was a slow process it was not easy to withstand the strength and influence of the English language. By the eighteenth century the English language was penetrating more vigorously than ever before through the border counties, and those who had business contacts with England inevitably borrowed and adapted English words and expressions. Even so, it cannot be overemphasized that Welsh, and Welsh alone, was undeniably the language of the great mass of the population.

The second section considers the status of the Welsh language in the home and the workplace, and also seeks to show how it gained a foothold in such fields as politics, administration and law, where it was officially proscribed. Although the Act of Union of 1536 had contrived to disfranchise those who would have liked to use Welsh as the medium of law and administration, there is no reason to believe that those in power had deliberately set their minds on destroying the language. Except in religion, however, nothing was done officially to accord Welsh greater respect and dignity. Indeed, the 'language clause' encouraged the English to disregard and despise Welsh and caused the monoglot Welshman to feel inadequate in his own land. Yet it soon became evident that effective administration was not possible without extensive informal use of Welsh in election campaigns, court cases and political discussions. Among radical and unconventional groups Welsh was used to express hostility towards oppressive landowners who were also becoming Anglicized as the period unfolded. The gentry benefited substantially from the Union legislation and as a consequence they increasingly distanced themselves from the multitude and abandoned their traditional duty of patronage to poets and musicians. Moreover, since English was the language of trade and commerce, a growing proportion of the mobile population could not fail to learn English words and phrases through their dealings with those who lived in the Anglicized border towns and beyond Offa's Dyke. On the other hand, many of these influences were counteracted by the success of the campaign to enthrone the Welsh language in the religious life of the people. The growing influence of the printing press and, in particular, the

Welsh translation of the Bible, brought about a shift from the image to the word, and as zealous middling sorts acquired a taste for pious reading material and spellbinding sermons they were irresistibly drawn towards the evangelical religion. At the popular level, too, large numbers acquired reading skills which encouraged biblical literacy in the native tongue. Thanks to the tireless efforts of cultured middling sorts in the eighteenth century, the status of Welsh as a language of scholarship was restored, and institutions and channels of communication were established which enabled not only men of letters but also the articulate populace to defend the language against the scorn and hostility of the English.

The third section is an attempt to listen closely to the voices of people in early modern Wales. If, as the novelist L. P. Hartley has suggested, they 'do things differently' in the foreign country which is the past, by the same token they must also have spoken and written differently. On the whole, Welsh historians have devoted surprisingly little attention to the manner of speech of the people about whom they write, and this section is designed, at least partly, to remedy that defect. For this period, sources for the social historian and the sociolinguist are far more substantial than anything which is available for the Middle Ages. An appreciable proportion of the output of the Welsh press has survived, together with the massive and invaluable archive of the Court of Great Sessions and the records of the ecclesiastical courts. In addition, scholars and antiquarians have preserved words, sayings, idioms, aphorisms and proverbs that would otherwise have been lost or forgotten. This section, therefore, sheds new light on Welsh as a spoken language, including ways in which people blessed, greeted, insulted, maligned, slandered, nicknamed and cursed one another. Despite the growing influence of the Welsh Bible from 1588 onwards, it appears that dialects and non-standard (though remarkably rich) patterns of speech continued to flourish, and that Welsh, especially from 1660 onwards, became more vulnerable to the influx of English words and phrases. But although there were undeniable signs of linguistic contamination, the general impression is that the language of the articulate populace continued to be exceptionally correct, robust and colourful.

Since the terms of the Acts of Union (1536-43), together with their consequences, heavily influenced the fortunes of the Welsh language, three chapters have been devoted to a study of Tudor legislation, the functions of the Court of Great Sessions, and the activities of the justices of the peace in the Court of Quarter Sessions. Peter R. Roberts analyses the political and social considerations which formed the background to the 'language clause' in the Act of 1536, a clause which has been bitterly attacked by modern nationalists. At that time it was generally supposed that the law of England was the key to 'friendly concord and union', and the aim of Henry VIII was to establish administrative uniformity throughout the kingdom. It had become patently obvious by then that gentry families were anxious to secure the same political and legal privileges as the English and to identify themselves with the Tudors by occupying administrative posts where English was an essential qualification. The king and his chief minister, Thomas Cromwell, were motivated less by a cold machiavellian desire to eliminate the Welsh language than by the need to establish uniform and efficient administration. The fact that there was no vociferous protest at the time against the 'language clause' strongly suggests that the gentry were in favour of the legislation and that the rest of the population, especially monoglot Welsh speakers, had not fully appreciated the far-reaching administrative, legal and linguistic consequences. That exceptionally learned and assiduous humanist William Salesbury was convinced that the legislation would not imperil the language and initially he was in favour of urging the Welsh people to learn English. By the reign of Edward VI, however, Salesbury and others were deeply troubled by the strong likelihood that the printing press would facilitate the adoption of English as the official medium of public worship throughout Wales. Salesbury knew only too well that only a small proportion of Welsh people were likely to learn English and he believed that it was the duty of leading Protestants to ensure that monoglot speakers of Welsh had the Holy Scriptures in their own language. It should be borne in mind that there was considerable prejudice against the Welsh language among those who believed that uniformity in language, as well as in religion and administration, was essential to the socio-political well-being of the kingdom. Had the political situation not been so vulnerable at the beginning of Elizabeth's reign, it is entirely feasible that she and her advisers would have resisted the fervent appeal of leading Welsh humanists for legislation which would have sanctioned the production of the Book of Common Prayer and the Bible in Welsh. That is why the act of parliament of 1563, which ordered the translation of the Scriptures into Welsh, was of seminal importance for the survival of the language. From the point of view of the status of Welsh, it could be argued that the beneficial effects of the Act of 1563 counteracted (although without negating) the damaging influence of the 'language clause' in the Act of Union of 1536.

It is one thing to introduce legislation; to implement it effectively and in accordance with the wishes of the legislators is another matter. In his chapter on 'The Welsh Language and the Court of Great Sessions', Richard Suggett reveals the way in which Welsh was used in the chief royal court in Wales in spite of the fact that the 'language clause' had enacted that English should prevail. Although his portrait is essentially satirical, Ellis Wynne, writing in 1703, conveys something of the hubbub which occurred whenever the Court of Great Sessions assembled: '. . . a drove of assize-men, with devils carrying the train of half a dozen justices, followed by a myriad of their tribe, such as pleaders, attorneys, notaries, recorders, bailiffs, catchpoles and Curse of the Courts' ('gyrr o wŷr y Sesiwn, a diawliaid yn cario cynffonnau chwech o ustusiaid, a myrdd o'u sil, yn gyfarthwyr, twrneiod, clarcod, recordwyr, beiliaid, ceisbyliaid, a Checryn y Cyrtiau'). Outside the court, most people would discuss, quarrel and upbraid one another in Welsh, but once they ventured into the lion's den Welsh speakers soon realized that their monoglottism placed them under a grave disadvantage. Almost without exception, the judges who attempted to administer justice could neither speak nor understand Welsh and those who served on juries, especially grand juries, were expected to understand English. Defendants were expected to plead in English and if they knew no English they were permitted to repeat the English words after the clerk of the court. Translators, who were generally of mixed ability, were employed to interpret the evidence of monoglot Welsh defendants and witnesses, and the judge not only directed the jury in English but also expected to hear the verdict in English. Not surprisingly, therefore, there were occasions when court proceedings were reduced to a farce. Monoglot Welsh speakers must have felt deprived, if not inferior, under such a system, and it is easy to appreciate why many of them preferred to avail themselves of less formal methods outside the court, such as arbitration, compurgation and compensation, since they were able to do so in their own language. Nevertheless, for entirely practical reasons, the Welsh language could not be wholly excluded from the court, and among the main features of this chapter are the striking examples of defamatory language in Welsh and the manner in which disaffected or rebellious people impugned the political and religious order by uttering blasphemous, treasonable and revolutionary words.

Although the Act 27 Henry VIII, c.5, namely the Act for conferring office upon Justices of the Peace in Wales, did not stipulate in what language justices should hear cases in the Quarter Sessions (created under the terms of the second Act of Union in 1543), the new officials must have known full well that English would be the lingua franca, and this was confirmed when the first Act of Union was passed in April 1536. But although English would henceforth be the language of law and administration, J. Gwynfor Jones shows in his chapter that there was no possible way for these courts to operate justly and efficiently without allowing monoglots to use Welsh in public. The records of the Quarter Sessions are peppered with examples of everyday spoken Welsh which were so spicy and robust that those who translated and recorded the evidence formally had great difficulty in conveying accurately what was said. Fortunately, most justices of the peace in Wales (at least up to 1660) knew Welsh and were aware that they were expected to establish a good relationship with the common people, especially their own tenants, if they were to maintain law and order. It is not hard to believe that a 'thoughtful, just magistrate' ('ustus cofus cyfiawn') could more easily win the respect and trust of the people by using his mother tongue in arbitrating and reconciling within his territory. Having guarded the correctness of the Welsh language for so long, poets always appreciated those who honoured their native language and literature, especially in a period when the professional bardic system was allowed to fall into desuetude. Time after time they would remind the gentry that it was the duty of the county chieftain ('penadur') to serve his community by administering the law of England impartially and fairly through the medium of Welsh. But as the eighteenth century unfolded, the tendency grew stronger among the most affluent Welsh families to flaunt their wealth and to distance themselves from the nation's indigenous language and culture, and to entrust the task of sustaining the native heritage to the minor gentry. By the end of the period under study, no longer did every landowner openly acknowledge that the Welsh language lay at the heart of good government and community.

The next two chapters consider the complex, and sometimes controversial, relationship between religion and language. When the church liturgy was reformed in the reign of Edward VI, prophets of doom argued that the future belonged to the English language and that Welsh could not be saved 'from everlasting oblivion' ('rhag difancoll tragyfythawl'). An English Prayer Book was placed in every church in Wales in 1549 and thereafter English was the only language to be heard in places of worship. At a critical time in the nation's history, however, a small group of Protestant humanists, steeped in their native language and armed with powerful arguments, stepped into the breach to persuade the authorities that only through the medium of Welsh could the precious souls of their fellow-countrymen be saved, and that religious unity was infinitely more important than linguistic unity. Those who were familiar with the development of the Reformed Faith in Europe knew that Protestantism could never flourish in Wales unless its doctrines were disseminated in Welsh. Glanmor Williams maintains that establishing the principle that Welsh speakers possessed the right to hear and read the Bible in their own language ensured that Protestantism would establish itself and that Welsh would not degenerate into a patchwork of undignified and despised minor dialects. Nor should the contribution of

Welsh-speaking Catholics in exile on the Continent during the Elizabethan period be underestimated. Although those who sought to restore the Old Faith to Wales were fighting against the odds, their literary output and their pride in their spiritual heritage were far from negligible. Nevertheless, buttressed by the full power of the state, Protestantism prevailed, and in the course of time the Welsh would come to refer with affection to the *Ecclesia Anglicana* as 'the Mother Church'.

From 1563 onwards Welsh was in principle the language of public worship in Wales, and following the publication of the New Testament and Prayer Book (1567) and of the Bible (1588), Welsh speakers who attended church (as they were obliged to do) were able to listen to the Gospel in Welsh every Sunday. The thrill which they experienced on hearing the Word of God in the language learnt at their mother's knee can well be imagined. Without William Morgan's excellent Welsh Bible and the revised edition by Richard Parry and John Davies in 1620, it is more than likely that in time the language would have disappeared. But although the early Protestant reformers were determined to see Welsh owned and used regularly in the churches, by the eighteenth century supporters of the language were convinced that a plot was afoot to Anglicize the established Church. In a chapter based on the voluminous records of the church, Eryn M. White reveals how the Welsh were outraged by the conduct of alien English bishops who displayed gross favouritism towards non-Welsh-speaking clerics and induced them to hold services in the English language. As the discreditable and often bizarre saga of 'The Arrant Englishman' ('Y Sais Brych') highlighted, from time to time Welsh-speaking parishioners were provoked to righteous anger, and there were frequent complaints about clergymen who practised their affected English in the pulpit in order to please a handful of gentry or the occasional judge. Such behaviour made light of the twenty-fourth article of the Church of England, which prohibited the conduct of services 'in a tongue not understood of the people'. Yet, in spite of the fears expressed at the time, the 'Anglo Bishops' ('Yr Esgyb Eingl') did not come close to realizing their ambition of banishing Welsh from the churches. The overwhelming majority of the clergy were Welsh speakers who faithfully discharged their commitments by communicating efficiently and well with their parishioners.

The rich evidence contained in visitation returns confirms that Welsh was the language of worship throughout much of Wales in the eighteenth century. Only in the eastern counties was serious evidence of linguistic decline detectable, and this was attributable to stronger commercial and industrial contacts with England and also to the inclination of bishops to appoint to those parishes clergymen who gave precedence to the English language. In the north-east and in mid-Wales the number of Sunday services held alternately in Welsh and in English became more frequent, and in Radnorshire, east Breconshire and east Monmouthshire the number of bilingual or wholly English services increased as the eighteenth century progressed. English was the language of the church in the Englishries, but in the Vale of Glamorgan the two languages fought so fiercely for supremacy that extremely varied and complex linguistic patterns emerged. It is hard not to sympathize with clergymen who were obliged to provide the means of grace in bilingual communities. If they failed to provide adequately for the spiritual and linguistic needs of their parishioners, the latter would defect to Dissenting chapels or Methodist societies, where in general there was a more cordial welcome for speakers of Welsh as well as a more serious concern for the spiritual well-being of the individual. In the long run, the result was to strengthen the traditional ties between religion and the mother tongue, and to reinvigorate efforts to extend the life of the language.

If, as the poet Gwenallt wrote, the Welsh language became 'one of the dialects of God's Revelation' ('un o dafodieithoedd Datguddiad Duw'), no parallel attempt was made to stake a claim for the language in the field of education during the Tudor and Stuart period. Since it was not possible to acquire any office of importance under the Crown or in commerce without a thorough education and a knowledge of English, sons of the gentry and the middle class attended grammar schools, the universities, and the inns of court, none of which gave formal recognition to the Welsh language. Indeed, it was forbidden to speak Welsh in the grammar schools of Wales, and the main emphasis was placed on teaching Latin and Greek and promoting the English language. Welsh-speaking students at the universities found it hard not to ride the crest of fashion and, as the chapter by William P. Griffith shows, by adopting the vocabulary, idiom and accent of their English counterparts, they forfeited the opportunity of creating a special sense of identity. As they became more familiar with English manners and learning, they saw less virtue in their native language and culture. On the other hand, the fact that the brightest among them studied the classics and fell under the spell of the cultural values embodied in the Renaissance and the Reformation enriched their knowledge of Europe and enabled them to interpret the needs of Wales in a wider context. It is worth remembering that the leading prose writers in Wales in the period before 1660 were university graduates and that they delighted in the range and quality of Welsh as a language of high scholarship. William Morgan's translation of the Scriptures would have lacked much of its lustre but for the classical and biblical grounding he had received at St John's College, Cambridge.

The next chapter by Eryn M. White focuses on the campaign to teach the common people to read. It need hardly be said that the majority of them had had no opportunity to read or understand the ideas and learned debates of the humanists, and when the influence of the Renaissance waned Puritan reformers believed that the time was ripe for them to embark on a God-given evangelical mission. Since Wales, even in the mid-seventeenth century, was still reckoned to be one of the darkest corners of the kingdom, English philanthropists believed that the most effective means of remedying ignorance and illiteracy was by setting up a network of schools, financed mainly by private charity. The old argument that it was more important to protect political and religious union than to maintain the Welsh language perversely reasserted itself and, as a result, the English language held sway in the charity schools founded between 1650 and 1740. Unsurprisingly, little success was achieved. Many religious reformers in Wales were angered by the contemptuous attitude of the charitable societies towards the Welsh language and by the lukewarm approach of schoolmasters to the needs and aspirations of monoglot Welsh speakers. It is no exaggeration to claim that had this misguided policy persisted throughout the eighteenth century the Welsh language would have languished and declined. But Griffith Jones and Thomas Charles, two evangelists of thundering eloquence and censoriousness, realized that the anti-Welsh animus of the charitable organizations posed as much a threat to the future of the Protestant religion as to the well-being of the Welsh language. Impelled by an intense desire to save every 'sad wounded soul' ('enaid clwyfus trist') from eternal damnation, they founded hundreds of Welsh-medium circulating schools and Sunday schools throughout the land which had the effect of transforming the prospects and the status of the language. One of the most remarkable features of the eighteenth century was the manner in which humble and underprivileged people struggled to learn to read the Scriptures and master the catechism by utilizing every spare minute or by burning their candles late into the night. By the end of the century, more than half the population of Wales had acquired the reading habit. In terms of safeguarding the Welsh language, this achievement was of incalculable significance.

Changes in the cultural domain were no less sweeping in the eighteenth century, although the early initiatives of littérateurs in the Renaissance period were also of considerable significance. Our guide in this field is R. Geraint Gruffydd. When the incomparable Dr John Davies of Mallwyd produced his grammar of the Welsh language in 1621, he claimed that only in the bardic tradition of the Middle Ages could be found the kind of linguistic standard, consistency and correctness that were worth bringing to the attention of the world. Following the death of Tudur Aled in 1526, however, the bardic tradition entered a period of decline. As the years rolled by, those who feared for the future of Welsh learning had greater cause than ever before to bemoan the plight of the poets. By this stage, gentry families, who were gradually becoming Anglicized, were extremely reluctant to support professional poets, to invite them to sing their praises (with unctuous flattery), and to entertain them in their fashionable mansions. Nor were the poets themselves blameless. The neglectful and slothful among them continued to trade in falsehoods and flattery, thereby rejecting the many-sided ideals implicit in humanist learning. As a result, the standard of their poetry declined and by around 1660 the age of the *penceirddiaid* (chief poets) had passed. Numerous though they were, the able and enthusiastic amateurs who sought to take their place and who produced a spate of poems in the strict metres failed to achieve a sufficient standard of skill and polish to compensate for the lost art of the classical poets. And although the new free-metre verse, together with traditional oral rhymes, proved extremely popular among the peasantry, the work of such poets was often riddled with colloquialisms and English expressions.

The response of sixteenth-century prose writers to the wealth of culture which was spreading from Europe was more encouraging. All of them agreed that the printing press held the key, but since Catholic authors in exile on the Continent were at a disadvantage in this respect, it fell mainly to Protestant prose writers to use Gutenberg's invention to protect the Welsh language and its culture. To some extent, therefore (and there was every justification for it at the time), the pristine ideals of the new liberal humanism were sacrificed on the altar of the Protestant mission. Since Protestant humanists were keenly aware of the spiritual needs of their fellow-countrymen, they gave priority to the task of translating religious works. While much of this commendable endeavour resulted in the production of several literary treasures, with the Welsh Bible as the crowning achievement, the price which was paid was the neglect of other many-faceted and innovative subjects which lay at the heart of the Renaissance ethos. Nevertheless, it must be acknowledged that the humanists succeeded in drawing attention to the ancient and learned lineage of the Welsh language (especially its supposed relationship with the three languages universally recognized as learned, namely Latin, Greek and Hebrew), in developing and refining its vocabulary, in awakening interest in the historical past of the nation, and in strengthening the faith of learned and sentient Welsh people in the intrinsic value and resources of Welsh as a language of learning. From the point of view of the translation and interpretation of the Scriptures, the marriage between the Renaissance and the Reformation proved extremely effective, and the standard literary language of the Welsh Bible of 1588 and 1620 became a lantern to light the way for prose writers in the centuries which followed. Although it could be said that the ambitions of the humanists, notably their desire to create a varied body of learned prose, exceeded their achievements, in the circumstances it is not surprising that the harvest proved leaner than they had expected.

In spite of these achievements, confidence in the language as a literary medium was low in the late seventeenth century, and prophets of doom still insisted that Welsh was not conducive to truly learned discussion or sufficiently attuned to the fashions and sensibilities of the age. However, as the chapter by Geraint H. Jenkins reveals, this sense of cultural crisis paradoxically ushered in a period of vigorous activity. A host of poets, prose writers, antiquarians, lexicographers, almanackers, philologists, interlude-writers and romantics began to use old and new means of rekindling interest in the literary traditions of the nation and to highlight the role of the Welsh language in the spiritual, cultural, and recreational life of the common people. One of the main characteristics of the age was the blight which struck the vernacular languages of Europe. While the peasantry clung to Occitan in Languedoc, the nobility and the middle class adopted French. In Bohemia Czech ceased to be the language of those who supposed German to be the language of advancement, and in Norway gentry families spoke Danish rather than their native tongue. Such was the pattern in Wales also. In the wake of the Anglicization of the gentry and their disparaging attitude to the Welsh language, poets feared that Wales had become a country with no one at its helm. It was natural in these circumstances to seek leadership from among scholars at Oxford or from among affluent London-Welshmen. Although this quest was not entirely in vain, it must be emphasized that the energy and vivacity which made the eighteenth century such a rich and exuberant period came from within Wales itself.

The establishment of printing presses in Wales provided the opportunity to publish and distribute an abundance of books which not only educated and brought saving knowledge to pious and literate farmers and craftsmen but also encouraged them to respect their mother tongue as the language of learning, religion and popular culture. The culture of print helped to disseminate knowledge, create new perspectives and shape expectations. The bardic tradition was given a new lease of life, albeit in a different guise. A new form of strict metres was devised, the *cywydd* and the *awdl* were given a place of honour in popular almanacks as well as in the activities of the Morris Circle, and the demand for ballads and other popular verses and rhymes was insatiable. A remarkable stream of religious books was published, some of them by the greatest masters of Welsh prose, and the language became increasingly identified with the growth of the evangelical and Dissenting religion. The extraordinary labours of Edward Lhuyd inspired scholars to study and revere their Celtic inheritance, and antiquarians succeeded in rescuing, copying and bringing to light many hidden treasures in the form of chronicles and manuscripts. In spite of their shortcomings and follies, the romantics took the initiative and began to appeal to the imagination of the Welsh and to use institutions like the Eisteddfod and the Gorsedd of the Bards of the Isle of Britain as vehicles to rally support for the native language. In the process, Welsh became an indispensable part of the cultural self-image of the Welsh people.

In the final chapter, Brynley F. Roberts analyses the fortunes of the other Celtic languages of Britain and highlights the fact that the overriding aim of successive governments was to persecute, reduce and annihilate such 'barbaric' and 'bestial' tongues and to uphold the supremacy of the English language. Largely because of the apathy of the native people and their inability to arrest the irreversible influence of English, the Cornish language perished at the end of the eighteenth century. The prospects for Manx were also fragile, and it faded rapidly as a spoken language. 'Civilizing' and 'Anglicizing' was the policy adopted in Scotland, and anti-Gaelic educational and religious policies were pursued so energetically that the common people were conditioned to believe that their mother tongue was synonymous with illiteracy and that its proper place was the dung-heap. In Ireland, too, dispossession, discrimination and persecution were at work. From 1534 onwards the Irish language was banished from every sphere of influence, and power was concentrated in the hands of landowners and a middle class whose language and attitudes alike were English. Catholics were fiercely hounded and a substantial proportion of the land of Ireland fell into the hands of Protestant planters from Britain. As a result, Irish became the language of the disfranchised and the dispossessed, and the poetry of Ó Bruadair and Ó Rathaille gave poignant expression to the manner in which the Irish were robbed of their cultural identity. The Papist (and subsequently Jacobite) bogeyman aroused such terror in those who believed that Protestantism was the only true faith and that the British Constitution was the most glorious the world had ever seen, that no status could be conferred upon the Gaelic or Irish languages. In short, the Celts were believed to be irredeemably reprobate and their languages beneath contempt.

Of all the Celtic countries in Britain, only Wales was granted legislation (the Act of 1563 which decreed the translation of the Bible and Prayer Book into Welsh) which dignified its native language with any kind of status. Thus the importance of having the Scriptures in Welsh, together with the flow of printed books which followed, can hardly be overemphasized. Without proof that the nation possessed a learned language and a divine mission, the task of preserving the Welsh language in a country devoid of libraries, universities and museums would have depended almost entirely on the ability of the common people to empower their local dialects and withstand the growing influence of the English language. The experience of the other Celtic countries reveals that they could not have done so and that the fate of the Welsh language would have been (as William Salesbury feared) to waste away and decay 'as the Brythonic of Cornwall in this island, and that of Brittany across the sea, became full of corrupt speech and well-nigh perished' ('fel ydd aeth Britanneg Kernyw yn yr ynys hon, a Brytannaeg Brytaniet Llydaw yn y tir hwnt tra mor, yn llawn llediaeth ac ar ddivancoll hayachen'). That such a tragedy was averted bears irrefutable witness to the unwillingness of the Welsh people to lose the principal badge of their identity, namely their language.

1
The Welsh Language before 1536

LLINOS BEVERLEY SMITH

THE EARLIEST example of written syntactical Welsh so far identified is a marginal entry inscribed on a page of an eighth-century gospel book, although it is possible that vernacular texts in Old Welsh or its precursor had been committed to writing in an earlier period. The text, known from its opening Latin verb as the *Surexit* memorandum, appears in the Gospel Book of St Chad which, after its sojourn at the church of St Teilo, was later removed to the cathedral of Lichfield. Dated to the first half of the ninth century, the memorandum records the settlement of the dispute between two landed proprietors, Tudfwlch ap Llywyd and Elgu ap Gelli, about their respective right to the land known as 'Tir Telych', now plausibly identified and located to the west of the river Cothi in a region noted since Roman times and even before as rich in deposits of gold. For all its terseness and brevity, the entry is of the utmost importance, not only for the emergence of Welsh as a distinctive language, but for its social history in the medieval centuries. For here is revealed a language which was already a written vernacular, one worthy to be inscribed on the most hallowed of sacred relics and, moreover, one which was already a vehicle for legal, technical use in a secular record of solemn and lasting importance.[1]

---

[1] Dafydd Jenkins and Morfydd E. Owen, 'The Welsh Marginalia in the Lichfield Gospels', *CMCS*, 5 (1983), 37–66 and ibid., 7 (1984), 91–120; Glanville R. J. Jones, 'Tir Telych, the Gwestfau of Cynwyl Gaeo and Cwmwd Caeo', *SC*, XXVIII (1994), 81–95. Important studies suggesting a possible early manuscript tradition are to be found in John T. Koch, 'When Was Welsh Literature First Written Down?', *SC*, XX–XXI (1985–6), 43–66; David N. Dumville, 'Palaeographical Considerations in the Dating of Early Welsh Verse', *BBCS*, XXVII, part 2 (1977), 246–51 and idem, 'Early Welsh poetry: problems of historicity' in Brynley F. Roberts (ed.), *Early Welsh Poetry. Studies in the Book of Aneirin* (Aberystwyth, 1988), pp. 1–16; Patrick Sims-Williams, 'The Emergence of Old Welsh, Cornish and Breton Orthography, 600–800: The Evidence of Archaic Old Welsh', *BBCS*, XXXVIII (1991), 20–86. For the development of Welsh as a distinct language, Kenneth H. Jackson, *Language and History in Early Britain* (Edinburgh, 1953) remains a standard work. For an authoritative survey of more recent scholarship, see D. Ellis Evans, 'Insular Celtic and the Emergence of the Welsh Language' in Alfred Bammesberger and Alfred Wollmann (eds.), *Britain 400–600: Language and History* (Heidelberg, 1990), pp. 149–77 and the comments of Patrick Sims-Williams, 'Dating the Transition to Neo-Brittonic: Phonology and History, 400–600', ibid., pp. 217–61.

But medieval Wales, in common with many other frontier or peripheral regions of Europe, was also a land of rich and creative linguistic diversity.[2] Even if we must now regard with a measure of scepticism the claims made for a substantial and permanent Viking settlement in pre-Norman Wales, the presence and impact of peoples of different cultures and speech cannot be doubted.[3] In the ninth and tenth centuries the impressive and long-lasting monastic tradition of Latin learning was sustained, in some scriptoria at least, by Welsh and Irish monks for whom, almost certainly, Latin was the medium of contact. Ireland, a rich and exuberant source of settlers and cultural influence in the earlier centuries, continued to energize the towns and rural hamlets of late-medieval Wales and beyond with its people.[4] The Irish, according to George Owen, a perceptive observer of Pembrokeshire society in the sixteenth century, were so 'powdered' among the inhabitants of Roose and Castlemartin 'that every third, fourth and fifth householder was Irish'. Although the increased influx of Irishmen was, according to Owen, a recent phenomenon and the language they used a rude English tongue, men *de Hibernia* or bearing the sobriquet *Gwyddel* or labelled by toponymical surnames had long been evident in Welsh urban and rural society.[5] Saxon colonists had extended well beyond Offa's Dyke to the river Clwyd in the north, to the regions of Knighton, Radnor and Knucklas in the middle March, and perhaps to the coastal plains of Gwent and Glamorgan in the south.[6] Subsequent colonizations in the wake of the Norman invasions introduced English, French and Flemish settlers into Welsh towns and villages, and Latin and French as the language of administration and government. Although the linguistic geography of Welsh, its standard in speech and in writing and the domains of its use will

---

[2] Robert Bartlett, *The Making of Europe. Conquest, Colonization and Cultural Change 950–1350* (London, 1993), pp. 197–221.

[3] K. L. Maund, *Ireland, Wales and England in the Eleventh Century* (Woodbridge, 1991), pp. 156–82 and the sources cited; B. G. Charles, *Old Norse Relations with Wales* (Cardiff, 1934); G. O. Pierce, 'The Evidence of Place-names' in Hubert N. Savory (ed.), *Glamorgan County History, Vol. II, Early Glamorgan* (Cardiff, 1984), pp. 456–92.

[4] See, in general, D. Simon Evans, 'The Welsh and the Irish before the Normans – contact or impact', *PBA*, LXXV (1989), 143–61 and the sources cited; A. Harvey, 'The Cambridge Juvencus Glosses: Evidence of Hiberno-Welsh literary interaction?' in P. Sture Ureland and George Broderick (eds.), *Language Contact in the British Isles. Proceedings of the Eighth International Symposium on Language Contact in Europe, Douglas, Isle of Man, 1988* (Tübingen, 1991), pp. 181–98.

[5] Owen, *Description*, I, pp. 40–1. For Irish settlers in late-medieval Wales, although the evidence relates in the main to individuals and families rather than to substantial migrations, see, e.g., A. D. Carr, *Medieval Anglesey* (Llangefni, 1982), pp. 164–5, Ralph A. Griffiths, 'Aberystwyth' in idem (ed.), *Boroughs of Medieval Wales* (Cardiff, 1978), pp. 38–9.

[6] R. R. Davies, *Conquest, Coexistence, and Change. Wales 1063–1415* (Oxford, 1987), pp. 4–11. But see also Paul Courtney, 'The Norman invasion of Gwent: a reassessment', *JMEH*, 12, no. 4 (1986), 297–313.

be the main concerns of this chapter, some attempt must also be made to evaluate the status of Welsh alongside Latin and the vernacular languages in use in the period before the incorporation of Wales into the English state and the enactment of the 'language clause' of the Act of Union of 1536, and to identify some of the main determinants of language attitudes within a land and society where, in these early centuries, several languages were both spoken and written.

There can be little doubt that, in geographical terms, the Welsh language was far more widely disseminated in the medieval centuries than was true of later periods. Indeed, there is good reason to believe that the language had been able to survive, or even to re-establish its strength, in areas which had been won for the Saxons and for the Norman invaders. Carrying his power into Tempsiter, or Dyffryn Tefeidiad in 1263, Llywelyn ap Gruffudd occupied, albeit temporarily, the western parts of the lordship of Clun, an area long subject to alien rule and colonization but which, as the place-names indicate, had seen extensive Welsh resettlement.[7] In the area to the north, between Clun and Montgomery, it was claimed in 1307 that the residents of the three townships of Aston, Chestrock and Mutton, habitations long in dispute between the bishops of Hereford and St Asaph, had command only of the Welsh language, so much so that Thomas Cantilupe, when he was bishop of Hereford, was obliged to make use of an interpreter when he preached in the region.[8] In the course of an episcopal visitation of the same see in 1397, the parishioners of Garway in Archenfield maintained that their priest was unable adequately to minister to their needs for he knew no Welsh and many of them had no knowledge of English.[9] These border lands and, indeed, some regions within the county of Hereford were evidently ones where settled, Welsh-speaking inhabitants were to be found. But by the Later Middle Ages, if not earlier, they were regions of high population mobility, as newcomers were drawn from the villages and rural settlements of Wales. When the records of the ecclesiastical courts of the diocese of Hereford become available from c.1440 onwards, they reveal the presence, not only in the border parishes of the deaneries of

---

[7] For the survival of Welsh customs and terminology there, see R. R. Davies, 'The Survival of the Bloodfeud in Medieval Wales', *History*, 54 (1969), 338–57 and SRO 552/1/45 m. 1v, for the use of terms such as 'estyn cadw' and 'nawdd' in the fifteenth century. See also John Rhŷs, 'The Welsh Inscriptions of Llanfair Waterdine', *Y Cymmrodor*, XXVI (1916), 88–114.

[8] Michael Richter, *Sprache und Gesellschaft im Mittelalter* (Stuttgart, 1979), p. 196. See also R. G. Griffiths and W. W. Capes (eds.), *The Register of Thomas de Cantilupe Bishop of Hereford (A D., 1275–1282)* (Hereford, 1906), esp. pp. 103–4.

[9] A. T. Bannister, 'Visitation Returns of the Diocese of Hereford in 1397', *EHR*, XLIV (1929), 289.

Leominster, Ludlow, Weobley and Clun but also in the more thoroughly English parts of the diocese, of a number of migrant and transient Welshmen and women who may well have been harvest workers drawn to the ripening crops of lowland England. Men and women from Carmarthen, Cedewain, Arwystli and even distant Edeirnion were resident in the diocese, and at least two Welsh poets, whose compositions survive, can be shown to have sojourned there at the end of the fifteenth century. However brief their stay in the region, the presence of substantial numbers of Welsh speakers must have created a demand for a spiritual ministry in Welsh and would have accustomed the permanent settlers to the speech and culture of their Welsh neighbours.[10] No better illustration can be provided than the evidence given at the inquiry conducted when the canonization of Thomas Cantilupe, bishop of Hereford, was at issue. Not only was it maintained that, through the bishop's intercession, a young man born without the power of speech had been able to speak in both English and Welsh but a canon of Hereford, speaking in support of the bishop's canonization, was able to report that the youth had uttered the words 'Argluth deu e seint Thomas' (Lord God and Saint Thomas) giving also, for good measure, the Latin translation *domine Deus et Sancte Thomas*.[11]

Further to the north, a similar impression of a Welsh language, vibrant and prevalent at all social levels, is conveyed by our sources. In the lordship of Oswestry, for instance, the earlier Anglo-Saxon predominance had been all but overturned during the course of the twelfth century when the region was recolonized by a Welsh population.[12] By the fifteenth century the town of Oswestry, now graced with the Welsh name

---

[10] The records consulted are HRO O/1–38 and I/1–6. From among the numerous examples of men and women who, on the evidence of locational names, hailed from Welsh communities, see, e.g., O/3, p. 31; O/4, p. 4; O/18, p. 187. A brief description of the ecclesiastical courts of the diocese and a discussion of the appearance of the poets Ieuan Dyfi and Bedo Brwynllys before the bishop's tribunals may be found in Llinos Beverley Smith, 'Olrhain Anni Goch' in J. E. Caerwyn Williams (ed.), *Ysgrifau Beirniadol XIX* (Dinbych, 1993), pp. 107–26.

[11] See the evidence given at the canonization proceedings of Thomas Cantilupe, based on MS Vat. Cod. Lat. 4015, in Richter, *Sprache und Gesellschaft*, pp. 173–217. For discussion of the proceedings and references to further manuscript and printed sources, see Patrick H. Daly, 'The Process of Canonization in the Thirteenth and Early Fourteenth Centuries' in Meryl Jancey (ed.), *St Thomas Cantilupe Bishop of Hereford. Essays in His Honour* (Hereford, 1982), pp. 125–35 and R. C. Finucane, 'Cantilupe as Thaumaturge: Pilgrims and their "Miracles"', ibid., pp. 137–44.

[12] See, in general, L. O. W. Smith, 'The Lordships of Chirk and Oswestry, 1282–1415' (unpubl. University of London PhD thesis, 1970), pp. 16–25, 262–9, and the valuable study by B. G. Charles, 'The Welsh, their Language and Place-names in Archenfield and Oswestry' in Henry Lewis (ed.), *Angles and Britons* (Cardiff, 1963), pp. 85–110; Melville Richards, 'The Population of the Welsh Border', *THSC* (1970), 77–100.

of 'Croesoswallt' or 'Y Fynachlog Wen' (L. *Album Monasterium*), was addressed, in Welsh, by several major Welsh poets. Described as the 'London of Wales' ('Llundain gwlad Owain'), the town's English street-names were now rendered into their Welsh equivalents. Oswestry's Black Gate, for instance, was known to Tudur Aled (*fl.*1480–1526) as 'Y Porth Du', and the same poet exulted in the welcome accorded him by the people of 'Stryd y Betris' (Beatrice Street) and the quiet dignity of Stryd y Llan or Chirton.[13] Property deeds, likewise, testify to the regular use of Welsh names or elements – Tir Ithel Dda, Crofftydd y Castell, Maes y Clawdd Ucha – as markers of closes and fields within the town's liberties.[14] More generally in both Shropshire and Cheshire, field names suggest the areas where Welsh linguistic influences were strong. In the manor of Aston, divided between the abbey of Haughmond and the earl of Arundel as a constituent part of his lordship of Oswestry, despite the continuing usage of English place-names and field names, parcels of land were commonly identified in Welsh in deeds of the thirteenth century and later. Where English place-names were not rendered partly or entirely into a Welsh equivalent, they might be convincingly transformed into names of apparent Welsh origin by the replacement of English sounds by Welsh. In the lordship of Whittington, the OE. township name of Porkington emerged as the seemingly Welsh name of Brogyntyn, while OE. Sulatun was rendered into Selattyn.[15] Although a case for a stable linguistic frontier, on the basis of place-name evidence, may be convincingly made for some areas, for others there is compelling evidence for the extension of Welsh settlement and language in the Late Middle Ages.[16]

---

[13] T. Gwynn Jones (ed.), *Gwaith Tudur Aled* (2 vols., Caerdydd, 1926), I, pp. 261–4; for a *cywydd* by Guto'r Glyn, see John Llywelyn Williams and Ifor Williams (eds.), *Gwaith Guto'r Glyn* (Caerdydd, 1939), pp. 183–5 and D. J. Bowen, 'Croesoswallt y Beirdd', *Y Traethodydd,* 135 (1980), 137–43. For the history of the town in the medieval period, see Llinos Beverley Smith, 'Oswestry' in Griffiths, *Boroughs of Medieval Wales,* pp. 219–42. For place-name evidence, see J. McN. Dodgson, *The Place-names of Cheshire* (5 vols., London, 1970–81) and H. D. G. Foxall, *Shropshire Field-names* (Shropshire Archaeological Society, 1980).

[14] See, e.g., NLW Aston Hall, 2520, 1779, 2192 and Charles, 'Archenfield and Oswestry', pp. 96–110. The same paper contains valuable evidence for the Welsh complexion of Archenfield in Herefordshire.

[15] Ibid., p. 107. See also Melville Richards, 'Welsh Influence on some English place-names in North-east Wales' in F. Sondgren (ed.), *Otium et Negotium: Studies in Onomatology and Library Science Presented to Olaf von Feilitzen* (Stockholm, 1973), pp. 216–20.

[16] Pembrokeshire, for which, see B. G. Charles, 'The English Element in Pembrokeshire Welsh', *SC,* VI (1971), 103–37 and Brian S. John, 'The Linguistic Significance of the Pembrokeshire Landsker', *PH,* 4 (1972), 7–29, and the Radnorshire border may be suggested as examples.

Just as indicative of the Welsh texture of many of the border settlements is the fact that several of the poets of the fourteenth and fifteenth centuries were regular visitors to homes in the area. Owain ap Llywelyn ab y Moel was one for whom Offa's Dyke, once the acknowledged boundary between the Welsh and the English, held little significance. Although he referred to the dyke in his *cywyddau*, his patrons were to be found on either side of the traditional line. At Churchstoke, according to the poet, the court of Gruffudd ap Hywel ap Dafydd nestled in the very shadow of the dyke ('dan Gaer Offa'); at Chirbury, so the same poet avowed, lay the seat of Dafydd Llwyd Fychan whose court 'gave pleasure to many of our language' ('a lawenhâi lu o'n hiaith'), while Caus Castle itself, for all its self-consciously Norman nomenclature, was, by the fifteenth century, 'a court which fostered the language' ('llys erioed yn llesáu'r iaith') under the kindly tutelage of its master, Wiliam ap Dafydd ap Gruffudd. Likewise, in Lewys Glyn Cothi's view, to penetrate the March between England and Wales was to enter a region where he was welcomed and honoured. At Brilley (Brulhai), a parish set on the border of Elfael and Huntington, he was received by Philpot ap Rhys 'the best Welshman and speaker of Welsh', just as Sion ap Hywel ap Tomas of Ewias Lacy — 'the lock of Longtown' ('Clo'r Dre-hir') — could be ranked among Lewys's patrons.[17]

Indeed, rightly or wrongly, the impression conveyed by the evidence is of a distinct resurgence of the Welsh language within several communities in the course of the fifteenth century. Whether such a renaissance resulted from an absolute increase or, rather, a redistribution of existing Welsh speakers in areas and social milieux where the language was unknown at an earlier date is an important but unanswerable question. What may be said with some confidence, however, is that regions like the Vale of Glamorgan, whose speech had been preponderantly English or Anglo-Norman in earlier centuries, were, by the eve of the Union, regaining the Welsh language as a normal medium of social discourse. Several gentle families like those of Turberville, Bassett, Gamage and Stradling were, by then, evincing an interest and a respect for the native culture, even if we cannot be sure that they themselves had mastered the language.[18] An

---

[17] Eurys Rolant (ed.), *Gwaith Owain ap Llywelyn ab y Moel* (Caerdydd, 1984), pp. 2, 5, 14; Dafydd Johnston (ed.), *Gwaith Lewys Glyn Cothi* (Caerdydd, 1995), pp. 274–5. For the Welsh character of Churchstoke, see the property deeds of fifteenth and sixteenth century date in BL Add Charter 41194–41295. But see the comments on the implications of the poets' itineraries by A. Cynfael Lake, 'Goblygiadau Clera a Golwg ar Ganu Guto'r Glyn' in J. E. Caerwyn Williams (ed.), *Ysgrifau Beirniadol XX* (Dinbych, 1995), pp. 125–48, and esp. pp. 135–6.

[18] Brian Ll. James, 'The Welsh Language in the Vale of Glamorgan', *Morgannwg*, XVI (1972), 16–36; Ceri W. Lewis, 'The Literary Tradition of Morgannwg down to the Middle of the Sixteenth Century' in T. B. Pugh (ed.), *Glamorgan County History, Vol. III, The Middle Ages* (Cardiff, 1971), pp. 449–554 and idem, 'Syr Edward Stradling

influx of Welsh tenants into the lowland manors of the lordship of Ogmore may likewise suggest new advances made by the language, and it may be significant that, by the early sixteenth century, the poet Thomas ab Ieuan, while noting the English speech of the dwellers of the village of Wick (Y Wig), was nevertheless prepared to take in his stride the manors of Laleston, Llangewydd and Ogmore on his begging itinerary.[19] Just as the gentry families of Glamorgan had absorbed important elements of the Welsh cultural tradition, so, too, in north-east Wales, a similar process was at work. Immigrant families, through intermarriage with Welsh native stocks and through a long process of naturalization, were opening their homes and purses to poets. Members of the Salusbury family, for instance, not only provided staunch patronage to several fifteenth-century poets, but, by the end of the century, were possibly using the Welsh language for their personal business accounts.[20] Among town-dwellers, too, it may well be that the Welsh language was more regularly and consciously used by the end of our period. 'Brig y dref foneddigaidd' (the head of the gentle town) was how Lewys Glyn Cothi addressed Hywel Prains of Cowbridge in the Vale of Glamorgan and although Dafydd ap Gwilym (fl.1320–70) had noted the 'lediaith lud' (persistent alien speech) of Elen, the English wife of Robin Nordd of Aberystwyth, a century later the town's population was overwhelmingly Welsh.[21] Although the circumstances which encouraged the spread of the Welsh language in the fifteenth century are still poorly understood, the fact of its rejuvenation seems clear enough.[22]

What may be said of the standards of the written and spoken language and the domains of its use? In so far as the spoken language is concerned, the existence of strong local dialects is attested by several early observers. In one of the most fascinating and revealing passages of his *Descriptio Kambriae*, Gerald of Wales comments as follows: 'It is thought that the Welsh language is richer, more carefully pronounced and preferable in all

---

(1529–1609), Y "Marchog Disgleirlathr" o Sain Dunwyd' in J. E. Caerwyn Williams (ed.), *Ysgrifau Beirniadol XIX* (Dinbych, 1993), pp. 139–207; Matthew Griffiths, 'The Vale of Glamorgan in the 1543 Lay Subsidy Returns', *BBCS*, XXIX, part 4 (1982), 746–7.

[19] Dafydd H. Evans, 'Thomas ab Ieuan a'i "Ysgowld o Wraig"' in J. E. Caerwyn Williams (ed.), *Ysgrifau Beirniadol XIX* (Dinbych, 1993), pp. 86–106.

[20] See below, p. 25.

[21] *Gwaith Lewys Glyn Cothi*, pp. 239–42 (the origin of the name is briefly discussed on p. 575); Thomas Parry (ed.), *Gwaith Dafydd ap Gwilym* (Caerdydd, 1952), p. 266; Griffiths, 'Aberystwyth' in idem, *Boroughs of Medieval Wales*, p. 39.

[22] For comment on the disappearance from the lordship of Gower of several families of non-Welsh origin by the early sixteenth century, see W. R. B. Robinson, 'The Landowners of the Englishry of Gower in the Early Sixteenth Century', *BBCS*, XXIX, part 2 (1981), 301–19.

respects in north Wales, for the area has far fewer foreigners. Others maintain that the speech of Ceredigion in south Wales is better articulated and more to be admired, since it is in the middle and the heartland of Wales.'[23] The alleged distinctiveness of the speech of Ceredigion is uncorroborated by the comments of any other observer, but the poet Dafydd Benfras (*fl.c.*1220–58) also commented on his own 'Venedotian' Welsh (*y Wyndodeg*), and later, Casnodyn (*fl.*1320–40) referred to his Gwentian speech (*Gwenhwyseg*).[24] Less easily identified from the medieval evidence are class accents or social nuances in vocabulary and expression even though both twelfth and thirteenth-century poets and those of a later age might take particular and admiring note if the language were spoken with dignity and refinement. But variegated as the dialects of spoken Welsh may have been, its written standard had achieved a remarkable degree of orthographic and morphological uniformity at an early period. It may well be that a 'northern written standard' was already exerting its influence on the written standards of other regions in the medieval period. But the task of identifying the geographical associations of medieval Welsh texts on the basis of their linguistic variants has proved difficult and elusive, although new methodological and analytical approaches are beginning to uncover interesting dialectological perspectives.[25] In general, however, and most certainly in comparison with the fortunes of English in the thirteenth and fourteenth centuries, it is the standardization not the dialectical variants of the written Welsh language which deserves emphasis, even if, as is possible, the surviving prose texts of the fifteenth century show some deterioration from the standards of an earlier period.[26]

If the written language had achieved a remarkable degree of homogeneity in the medieval centuries, the domains of its use were many

---

[23] James F. Dimock (ed.), *Giraldi Cambrensis Opera* (8 vols., London, 1861–91), V, p. 177. Cf. the comments of David Burnley, 'Lexis and Semantics' in Norman Blake (ed.), *The Cambridge History of the English Language, Vol. II, 1066–1476* (Cambridge, 1992), pp. 414–15 on medieval views about language purity and linguistic borrowing.

[24] Gerald Morgan, 'Nodiadau ar Destun Barddoniaeth y Tywysogion yn Llsgr. NLW 4973', *BBCS*, XXI, part 2 (1965), 149–50; Dafydd Benfras's *œuvre* is now definitively edited by Y Chwaer Bosco et al., *Gwaith Dafydd Benfras ac Eraill o Feirdd Hanner Cyntaf y Drydedd Ganrif ar Ddeg* (Caerdydd, 1995). The *awdl* is to be found on p. 445. For Casnodyn's assertion, see *Glamorgan County History, Vol. III*, p. 483.

[25] See the important study and the refined methodology suggested by Peter Wynn Thomas, 'Middle Welsh Dialects: Problems and Perspectives', *BBCS*, XL (1993), 17–50. For comment on the implications of standardization, see R. A. Lodge, 'Language Attitudes and Linguistic Norms in France and England in the Thirteenth Century' in P. R. Coss and S. D. Lloyd (eds.), *Thirteenth Century England IV: Proceedings of the Newcastle Upon Tyne Conference 1991* (Woodbridge, 1992), pp. 73–83.

[26] The spoken dialects and the great diversity in writing of Middle English are discussed and sources cited by James Milroy, 'Middle English Dialectology' in Blake (ed.), *Cambridge History of the English Language*, II, pp. 156–206.

and varied. In addition to the abundant corpus of creative vernacular poetry and prose, increasingly written down, a rich harvest of functional prose texts, both works of translation and original compositions, may be identified. Despite claims made of the difficulty of rendering texts into the vernacular (a common enough topos of the medieval translator), they reveal a supple and plastic language capable of sophisticated scientific and philosophical expression. Indeed, the domain of the language, it has been well said, 'was not purely that of Celtic romance and magic, of archaic legalism, heroic praise poetry and love lyrics, but a complex mixture of philosophy, religion, science, music and grammar which underlay and enriched the native literary genres traditionally associated with the period'.[27] Historical writing in Welsh of which *Brut y Tywysogyon* (The Chronicle of the Princes), a translation into Welsh of a now lost Latin original, is the outstanding example, shows not only how a profound national consciousness was sustained in the post-conquest period but also how Welsh had become, in the monastic scriptorium, a medium as worthy as Latin for preserving the nation's history for posterity. A major and invaluable corpus of twelfth and thirteenth-century court poetry written in Welsh has been convincingly shown to have been the product of the scriptorium of the Cistercian house of Strata Florida and likewise evinces the elevated status of Welsh within the cloisters of a Latin monastic order.[28] Encouraged by the pastoral emphasis placed by ecclesiastical authorities on the use of the vernacular and responding to the demand of literate lay men and women for religious literature in their own native tongue, several devotional and didactic texts, both original works and translations, were produced. Equally, the tastes of a textual community were reflected in the texts of creative prose – native tales and romances – to be found in manuscripts of the fourteenth and fifteenth centuries. Nor was the monastic scriptorium the only locus of literate activity in the vernacular, for Llyfr Coch Hergest, a prodigious compendium of Welsh prose and poetry, is a prime example of a codex

---

[27] For an excellent introduction in English to the texts of functional prose, see Morfydd E. Owen, 'Functional Prose: Religion, Science, Grammar, Law' in A. O. H. Jarman and G. R. Hughes (eds.), *A Guide to Welsh Literature Volume I* (Cardiff, 1992), pp. 248–76, and the extensive bibliography in the volume.

[28] Thomas Jones (ed.), *Brut y Tywysogyon or the Chronicle of the Princes: Red Book of Hergest Version* (Cardiff, 1955); idem, 'Historical Writing in Medieval Welsh', *SS*, 12 (1968), 15–27; Brynley F. Roberts, 'Testunau Hanes Cymraeg Canol' in Geraint Bowen (ed.), *Y Traddodiad Rhyddiaith yn yr Oesau Canol* (Llandysul, 1974), pp. 274–302. The associations of Llawysgrif Hendregadredd with the house of Strata Florida are examined in the important study by Daniel Huws, 'Llawysgrif Hendregadredd', *NLWJ*, XXII, no. 1 (1981), 1–23.

compiled at lay instigation and at a lay scriptorium at the end of the fourteenth century.[29]

In the sphere of legal literature, the use of Welsh had long been established, and the surviving texts, which date from the middle of the thirteenth century onward, constitute one of the most impressive examples of the use of the vernacular among the medieval nations of Europe. Although a number of thirteenth-century Latin texts exist, it is clear that the production of Welsh texts such as Llyfr Cyfnerth and Llyfr Iorwerth reflect an activity in which both lay and clerical practitioners and redactors had long participated. The texts reveal rich resources in technical terms and a capacity for precise legal expression. Pleading in Welsh was taken for granted (as is shown by the tractate on pleading incorporated in thirteenth-century redactions), while, by the sixteenth century, the rich technical vocabulary of the law texts had extended far beyond the courts of law.[30] It has been shown, for instance, that included in the luxuriant lexis in the marginal entries of William Salesbury's translation of the New Testament in 1567 is a substantial number of terms derived from the medieval Welsh lawbooks, of which one Peniarth MS 30 (Llyfr Colan) was liberally annotated in Salesbury's hand.[31] The wide-ranging written use of the Welsh language in the medieval period, perhaps even more so than the surviving texts reveal, is also reflected in materials such as agricultural treatises like *Llyfr Hwsmonaeth*, a translation of Walter of Henley's *Book of Husbandry*, or a brief tract on milling, both of which reveal the concerns of the landowner and farmer. A treatise on hunting, which, although probably a mid-sixteenth-century confection, incorporates older traditional material in Welsh and in English, and a treatise on heraldry, reveal the technical language of the gentleman's recreations and his delight in lineage. The speech of princes and peasants, of gentry and artisans, the broad social dimensions of Welsh are also

---

[29] For the impulses which lay behind the religious texts, see Glanmor Williams, *The Welsh Church from Conquest to Reformation* (Cardiff, 1962), pp. 81–114, and for the texts, Jarman and Hughes, *A Guide to Welsh Literature* and the bibliography cited. For the Red Book of Hergest, see Gifford Charles-Edwards, 'The Scribes of the Red Book of Hergest', *NLWJ*, XXI, no. 3 (1980), 246–56.

[30] For a good introduction to the texts, see T. M. Charles-Edwards, *The Welsh Laws* (Cardiff, 1989), and for more specialized studies, see Morfydd E. Owen, 'Y Cyfreithiau' in Bowen, *Y Traddodiad Rhyddiaith*, pp. 196–244. Pleading is studied by T. M. Charles-Edwards, '*Cynghawsedd*: Counting and Pleading in Medieval Welsh Law', *BBCS*, XXXIII (1986), 188–98; Aled Rhys Wiliam, 'Llyfr Cynghawsedd', ibid., XXXV (1988), 73–85. The use of French in the law courts of England in the period is examined by George E. Woodbine, 'The Language of English Law', *Speculum*, XVIII (1943), 395–436 and for the position in Wales in the Later Middle Ages see below, n. 83.

[31] Christine James, 'Bann wedy i dynny: Medieval Welsh Law and Early Protestant Propaganda', *CMCS*, 27 (1994), 61–86; Dafydd Ifans, *William Salesbury and the Welsh Laws* (Aberystwyth, 1980).

reflected in the concerns and preoccupations revealed by the written word.[32]

There is also some evidence in the late-medieval centuries which strongly suggests that Welsh was, if not a language of documentary literacy, at least used to commit private financial accounts and personal memoranda to writing. In this context one late-fifteenth-century manuscript, hitherto little regarded, deserves particular attention.[33] It is a volume which is mainly concerned with the purchases and rents of one Rhys ab Einion Fychan in the townships of the lordship of Denbigh between 1490 and 1495. According to the later testimony of Sir John Wynn of Gwydir, a large part of Rhys's inheritance (which in Wynn's estimation was worth as much as a thousand marks per annum) fell to Robert Salusbury, following his marriage to Gwenhwyfar, daughter of Rhys ab Einion and, from the frequent mention of both Robert and Rhys in the volume, it is reasonable to suppose that the accounts and memoranda were set down in writing by them or at their behest.[34] What is especially relevant, however, is that the volume was written entirely in Welsh. It provides a detailed list of tenants and their dues, and includes also a substantial number of property deeds, likewise rendered in Welsh. Reference is made to 'the money due from Mathebrwd for pasture at Pentecost' ('arian porfa y sulgwyn o faethebyrwt'), to the payment of 'this year's tithe' ('degwm yleni') and to the payment of 'ebediw' (heriot) on behalf of one of the tenants. Of outstanding interest are the numerous property deeds written in Welsh, a fact of especial significance in view of the total absence of such examples from the many estate collections which have survived from the fourteenth and fifteenth centuries. In almost all instances, moreover, they conform to the normal diplomatic conventions of contemporary property deeds. 'Bid hysbys achydnabyddus i bawb', records one example of a *prid* deed or mortgage, 'bod Res ap Jollyn yn dwyn xxs. gan Res ap Eignion Vyghan yn brid ar i dir ovewn tre varroc o vewn kymwd uwchaled hyd ymhenn y pedair blynedd ac velly ovewn y pedair blynedd bygilydd oni gollynger a dechre Nosswyl Bawl a

---

[32] Ifor Williams and Gwilym Peredur Jones, 'Hen Draethawd ar Hwsmonaeth', *BBCS*, II, parts 1 and 2 (1923–4), 8–16, 132–4; Iorwerth C. Peate, 'Traethawd ar Felinyddiaeth', ibid., VIII, part 4 (1937), 295–301; William Linnard, 'The Nine Huntings: A Re-examination of *Y Naw Helwriaeth*', ibid., XXXI (1984), 119–32. For comment on the significance of vernacular texts which reflect gentle pursuits to the social history of the English language, see Burnley, *Cambridge History of the English Language*, II, p. 457.

[33] Cardiff MS 51. The volume deserves more attention than is possible in this present study. For a brief description, see J. Gwenogvryn Evans, *Report on Manuscripts in the Welsh Language* (2 vols., London, 1898–1902), II, pp. 253–4.

[34] John Wynn, *The History of the Gwydir Family and Memoirs*, ed. J. Gwynfor Jones (Llandysul, 1990), pp. 18, 30–2, 34.

Dwynwenn yny vlwyddyn oed ir iesse mil a ccclxxxxi [1491]. Yn wybyddiaid ar hynn Meredith ap Llewelin, Ieuan ap Gruffith ap Hoell, Ieuan ap Wilkoc adigon am benn hynny' (Be it known to all men that Res ap Jollyn takes a *prid* of xxs. from Res ap Eignion Vyghan on his land within tre varroc in the commote of uwchaled for the term of four years and thus from four years to four years unless redeemed beginning on the vigil of St Paul and St Dwynwen in the year of Our Lord one thousand and ccclxxxxi [1491]. In witness thereof Meredith ap Llewelin, Ieuan ap Gruffith ap Hoell, Ieuan ap Wilkoc and many others).[35] At about the same period, and from the neighbouring lordship of Chirk, an important volume of records and memoranda was compiled by John Edwards, a notable landowner and bureaucrat of the area.[36] This, too, is a volume which comprises a number of vernacular texts. It includes Welsh versions of the Latin and French charters granted by Richard Arundel to his tenants of the lordship of Chirk in the fourteenth century as well as copies, also in Welsh, of *cydfodau* or agreements between the tenants of contiguous lordships relating to matters of common concern. Most interesting of all is a brief legal memorandum, recording practice and dicta of the courts of the region, where loanwords such as *ysgutor* (executor) or *yndeintur* (indenture) or *gweithred ffi-tail* (a deed of fee tail) appear cheek by jowl with native, vernacular terms such as *tremyg* and *cynhysgaeth* and where the forms of action of English common law – even terms like *novel disseisin* which never achieved an English equivalent – are felicitously rendered into Welsh. While the contribution of the north-east March to the conservation of literary and documentary materials of the medieval past is quite outstanding, the same readiness to commit matters of personal account to writing in Welsh is also evident in other areas. In south-west Wales, for instance, the owners of the nascent Edwinsford estate recorded particulars of their landed property in a document written in Welsh. 'Llyma bridie Willym ap Rees ap Eynon' (These are the prid lands of Willym ap Rees ap Eynon) is the heading bestowed upon one of the records in the family's papers, which goes on to describe in detail William's 'right inheritance by descent from his father' ('iawn etiveddiaeth

---

[35] Cardiff MS 51, ff. 9, 32, 151. The fact that several of the *prid* deeds are struck through perhaps suggests that they were redeemed by the gagor. The close correspondence between the Welsh formulae and contemporary Latin deeds (e.g. the words 'Bid hysbys a chydnabyddus i bawb' and 'a digon am ben hynny' correspond, respectively, to the Latin 'pateat universis per presentes' and 'multis aliis') suggests that the Welsh examples in the volume may be translations of a Latin original.

[36] BL Add MS 46846. See also Llinos Beverley Smith, 'The Grammar and Commonplace Books of John Edwards of Chirk', *BBCS*, XXXIV (1987), 174–84. For the Edwards family, see D. J. Bowen, 'I Wiliam ap Siôn Edwart, Cwnstabl y Waun' in J. E. Caerwyn Williams (ed.), *Ysgrifau Beirniadol XVIII* (Dinbych, 1992), pp. 137–59.

Res ap William oblegid y dad'). In north-west Wales a document in Welsh recorded the partition of the lands of Hywel ap Gruffudd Fychan of Aber-erch in Llŷn, while arbitration awards drawn up in both the lordship of Denbigh and in the county of Carmarthen reflect the use of Welsh in bringing disputes to conclusion.[37] In all of these instances, chance survivals from a body of evidence which was once, perhaps, substantial, the Welsh language emerges not as an archaic and cumbersome medium but as one with a capacity to express contemporary technical concepts and as a language of thorough practical use.

For all the massive presence of Welsh, medieval Wales was also a linguistically mixed society. Some attempt must therefore be made to identify the social and geographical milieux of the languages, which, in addition to Welsh, imparted a measure of linguistic pluralism to the period from c.1100 onwards. The following discussion will be devoted mainly to the use of English and French. Although Gerald of Wales testified to the use of the Flemish speech among the Flemish settlers of south Pembrokeshire, and although the possible persistence of their distinctive speech in the sixteenth century has been suggested, the chronicler John Trevisa, writing at the end of the fourteenth century, could assert how 'the Flemmynges that woneth in the weste side of Wales haueth i-left her straunge speche and speketh Saxonliche i-now'.[38] On the other hand, there is convincing evidence of an early and continuing knowledge of French. While we cannot be certain what language was spoken by people described in charters as *Franci*, the presence of French speakers is amply confirmed in a number of sources.[39] The aristocratic penchant for French is clearly revealed in the valuable linguistic indicators to be found in the canonization proceedings of Thomas Cantilupe in 1307. Lady Mary de Braose, first in a deputation from Swansea to testify to the miraculous recovery of one William ap Rhys, made her depositions in French (*deposuit in Gallico vulgariter*). Her son William, described as baron and knight (*baro et miles*), likewise gave evidence *in vulgari Gallico*. But other members also had knowledge of French. Two priests gave their evidence *in Gallico*. One was, by his own admission, not a native of Wales and had left the town soon after the alleged miracle and, indeed, was described in

---

[37] NLW Edwinsford 3366; also 3228, 3367; UWBL Mostyn 786; NLW Trovarth and Coedcoch 573. The arbitration concerning land at Llwyn Gwyn in Carmarthenshire is published and discussed by T. Jones Pierce, 'The Law of Wales – The Last Phase', *THSC* (1963), 7–32. See also below, p. 44.

[38] Lauran Toorians, 'Wizo Flandrensis and the Flemish Settlement in Pembrokeshire', *CMCS*, 20 (1990), 99–118; C. Babington (ed.), *Polychronicon Ranulphi Higden Monachi Cestrensis* (9 vols., London, 1865–86), II, p. 159.

[39] On the use of the term *Franci*, see Bartlett, *Making of Europe*, pp. 102–3.

1307 as the rector of a living in the diocese of Chichester. The other, however, Thomas Marescalh by name, explicitly claimed to have been brought up in Swansea (*de qua fuerat oriundus*) and had known of the events associated with William ap Rhys since boyhood (*a puericia ipsius testis in villa predicta*), but he nevertheless chose to give testimony in French. One layman, described as steward of the household (*senescallus hospicii*) of William de Braose, likewise gave evidence in French, the only lay deponent (apart from the Braoses) to do so. From the same canonization proceedings, a precious glimpse is afforded of the languages spoken in Conwy. There, too, the small delegation consisted of French speakers, including the chief witness, Gervase, described as the cook of the castle constable, William de Sigons (himself a Burgundian knight), whose two-year-old son had been brought back to life through Cantilupe's intercession. Although of native Welsh origin (*est oriundus de Wallia*), Gervase was apparently sufficiently competent in French to testify in that language. Likewise, of four other burgesses who bore witness in French, two may have been Welsh or may have been resident in Wales while, of the two clerical deponents, one gave his evidence in French and the other in Latin. It has been suggested, moreover, that in the new colonial foundation of Conwy French was used as a true lingua franca at the end of the thirteenth century and knowledge of French may even have been, in practice, a precondition for professional or occupational advancement.[40] Although the small sample provided both by Swansea and Conwy is valuable it nevertheless precludes rash generalizations about the linguistic balance of the urban population of Wales in the years after the conquest of 1282. Moreover, the absence of any comment on the use of Welsh by deponents makes it difficult to assess to what extent the Welsh language flourished or languished in the urban environment in the period.

    Just as a measure of professional necessity helped to determine the linguistic competence of town-dwellers, so, too, did royal and seigniorial administrations create a ready demand for a knowledge of French. Documents, both public and private, written in French were common by the fourteenth century. The charter granted by the earl of Arundel to his tenants of the lordship of Chirk in 1334 was written in French; Llywelyn ap Llywelyn, likewise of Chirk, bestowed dower rights on his wife by the custom of England (*a la coustumez d'Angleter*) by means of a document drawn up in French, while a charter which remained in the custody of John Owen of Ystumcegid in the sixteenth century was described by Sir John Wynn as 'being in French with the duke's [John of Gaunt] seal and arms'.

---

[40] Richter, *Sprache und Gesellschaft*, pp. 197–201.

In the same period, the practice of addressing petitions to kings and to seigniorial authorities in French would have encouraged the need for Francophone bureaucrats.[41] A fourteenth-century poet may well have had one such in mind when he addressed an *awdl* in praise of his patron's 'good, brilliant and unaccented French' ('ffrangec da loewdec diletyeith').[42] Likewise, the poet Ieuan ap Rhydderch, if he were indeed the son of Rhydderch ab Ieuan Llwyd, hailed from precisely the social and learned milieu in which a knowledge of French would be encouraged. In one of his *cywyddau* he, too, boasted how he had acquired the 'expansive French' ('eang Ffrangeg') and recommended it as a key to education and a 'good, fair language' ('da iaith deg').[43] Indeed, diplomatic intercourse may long have demanded a knowledge of French. Already in the thirteenth century, members of the princely entourages were sent on diplomatic missions to the court of the king of England and encountered royal representatives, who were themselves not infrequently Welshmen of the March, at meetings held at Rhyd Chwima, on the Severn at Montgomery.[44] By the fourteenth century, war-service in France was exposing Welshmen of all social levels to new linguistic vistas, although, of course, we cannot establish to what extent any practical competence had been gained by these means.[45]

[41] Llinos Beverley Smith, 'The Arundel Charters to the Lordship of Chirk in the Fourteenth Century', *BBCS*, XXIII, part 2 (1969), 153–66; BL Add Charter 74382; Wynn, *History of the Gwydir Family*, p. 21; William Rees, *Calendar of Ancient Petitions Relating to Wales* (Cardiff, 1984), passim. For a review of the documents written in French which emanate from Wales, see D. Trotter, 'L'Anglo-Français au Pays de Galles: Une Enquête Préliminaire', *Revue de Linguistique Romane*, 58 (1994), 461–87, and for comment on the quality of Anglo-Norman in the remoter parts of the realm, see W. Rothwell, 'Language and Government in Medieval England', *Zeitschrift für französische Sprache und Literatur*, 93 (1983), 258–70. Cf. the experiences of Orderic Vitalis who claimed that, as an oblate, the French spoken in the cloisters of his Norman monastery had not been understood by him. M. Chibnall (ed.), *The Ecclesiastical History of Orderic Vitalis* (6 vols., Oxford, 1969–78), VI, p. 554.
[42] J. Gwenogvryn Evans (ed.), *The Poetry in The Red Book of Hergest* (Llanbedrog, 1891), p. 63.
[43] Henry Lewis, Thomas Roberts and Ifor Williams (eds.), *Cywyddau Iolo Goch ac Eraill* (Caerdydd, 1937), p. 228. For Rhydderch ab Ieuan Llwyd, see below, p. 35.
[44] Envoys of the king were sometimes churchmen, such as Bishop Richard of Bangor or Master Madog ap Philip. Among the laymen often engaged were Ednyfed Fychan and Einion Fychan, who acted for Llywelyn ap Iorwerth, and Einion ap Caradog and Dafydd ab Einion, who negotiated the treaty of Montgomery for Llywelyn ap Gruffudd. See David Stephenson, *The Governance of Gwynedd* (Cardiff, 1984), pp. 205–28 and J. Beverley Smith, *Llywelyn ap Gruffudd* (Caerdydd, 1986), pp. 54, 70, 155–7, 226–7. For the meetings of arbitrators (*dictatores*) at the ford of Montgomery and elsewhere, see ibid., pp. 114–15.
[45] A. D. Carr, 'Welshmen and the Hundred Years' War', *WHR*, 4, no. 1 (1968), 21–46 and idem, *Owen of Wales* (Cardiff, 1991). Among the many references to soldiers returning from war-service in Gascony and parts of France, see, e.g. PRO SC 2/217/12, m. 2; SC 2/217/14, m. 22v. (references are to the court rolls of the lordship of Dyffryn Clwyd).

French loanwords had entered the Welsh language, even though the means of transmission, in some cases, may have been English.[46] A taste for original or translated French literary texts, the *Roman de la Rose*, the *Chanson de Roland*, the *Bestiaire d'Amour* or the *Queste del Saint Graal*, had been cultivated among Welsh men and women. Even earlier, in the March of Wales, an original Anglo-Norman creation, the legend of *Fouke le Fitz Waryn*, took as its setting and hero the lordship and seigneur of the small lordship of Whittington.[47]

Yet, in the justified emphasis placed on the French language in Wales, we must doubt whether French was ever the mother tongue of a substantial number of speakers. On the contrary, the fortunes of the language in Wales can hardly have differed from its experience in England where, according to the best available authorities, a competence in French was, by the thirteenth century, a social and professional accomplishment acquired by deliberate intent and persistence, even by divine intervention. By then, textbooks and teaching manuals were being produced, aimed at both children and adults, and designed to inculcate a basic knowledge of French or to equip the businessman and the commercial entrepreneur with the necessary phrases needed to negotiate his transactions.[48] By contrast, the English language was, in Wales, even in the twelfth century and possibly earlier, a natural mother tongue. Indeed, George Owen of Henllys, admittedly a late witness, was firmly of the opinion that 'the greatest parte of these people that came into Pembrokshere with these

[46] From among studies of French loanwords, see Morgan Watkin, 'The French Linguistic Influence in Mediaeval Wales', *THSC* (1918–19), 146–222; Marie E. Surridge, 'Words of Romance origin in the works of the Gogynfeirdd', *BBCS*, XXIX, part 3 (1981), 528–30 and eadem, 'The Number and Status of Romance Words Attested in *Ystorya Bown de Hamtwn*', ibid., XXXII (1985), 68–78.

[47] Ceridwen Lloyd-Morgan, 'French Texts, Welsh Translators' in Roger Ellis (ed.), *The Medieval Translator II* (London, 1991), pp. 45–63 and eadem, 'Rhai Agweddau ar Gyfieithu yng Nghymru yn yr Oesoedd Canol' in J. E. Caerwyn Williams (ed.), *Ysgrifau Beirniadol XIII* (Dinbych, 1985), pp. 134–45; Annalee C. Rejhon, *Cân Rolant: The Medieval Welsh Version of the Song of Roland* (Berkeley, 1984); G. C. G. Thomas, *A Welsh Bestiary of Love being a Translation into Welsh of Richard de Fornival's 'Bestiaire d'Amour'* (Dublin, 1988); E. J. Hathaway, P. T. Ricketts, C. A. Robson and A. D. Wiltshire (eds.), *Fouke le Fitz Waryn* (Oxford, 1975). For a religious poem in Anglo-Norman French composed by a canon of Carmarthen priory in the thirteenth century, see F. G. Cowley, *The Monastic Order in South Wales 1066–1349* (Cardiff, 1977), pp. 152–3.

[48] From the substantial literature now available, see, e.g., R. M. Wilson, 'English and French in England 1100–1300', *History*, 28 (1943), 37–60; Helen Suggett, 'The Use of French in England in the Later Middle Ages', *TRHS*, XXVIII (1946), 61–83; W. Rothwell, 'The Teaching of French in Medieval England', *MLR*, 63 (1968), 37–46; idem, 'The Role of French in Thirteenth-Century England', *Bulletin of the John Rylands Library*, 58 (1975), 445–66; I. Short, 'On Bilingualism in Anglo-Norman England', *Romance Philology*, 33, no. 4 (1980), 467–79; Glanville Price, *The Languages of Britain* (London, 1984). See also the remarks of Burnley, *Cambridge History of the English Language*, II, pp. 423–32, 456–7.

[Norman] Earles were Saxons and Englishmen', adding that 'manye of them yf not *maior pars* were Saxons, for otherwise the Englishe tongue had not ben theire comon and mother speache as it was'.[49] Moreover, there is some evidence to suggest that such early settlers were reinforced in the twelfth and thirteenth centuries by successive waves of new colonists who braved the perils of the Severn Sea and set down their roots in south Pembrokeshire and the Vale of Glamorgan. Following the conquest of Edward I, yet more newcomers, attracted to the nascent castle-boroughs of Wales and, in some instances, to the rural townships of the north-eastern lordships, imparted a distinctively English flavour to the parts where they settled.[50] English words, such as *yarnwindle*, *barncloit*, *alestake*, and *pursekeruer*, appear in the records, while manorial accounts, although written in Latin, commonly used words such as *lathnail*, *bordnail*, *waturwalk* and *fflodyetes* in recording expenditure.[51] Town fields, houses and street names were often rendered in English. By the fifteenth century, the English ambience of the town of Caernarfon was so firmly established that one of Sir John Wynn's ancestors had been sent there to school where, in addition to acquiring a knowledge of Latin, he 'learnt the English tongue'.[52] Little can be deduced, however, about the nature of that 'English tongue' learned by Maredudd ab Ieuan ap Robert. Although settlers were often drawn from regions of strong and contrasting dialectal diversity (Yorkshiremen, such as Hugh de Smethynton of Ruthin, who kept in touch with his relatives in Rothwell, intermingled with settlers from the counties of Shropshire, Hereford, Northampton and Bedford), the linguistic effects of such mixing on the language spoken and written in medieval Wales still awaits detailed investigation.[53]

---

[49] Owen, *Description*, I, pp. 36–7. For reference made by Gerald of Wales to English spoken by a knight of the Cardiff region in the twelfth century, see A. B. Scott and F. X. Martin (eds.), *Expugnatio Hibernica. The Conquest of Ireland by Giraldus Cambrensis* (Dublin, 1978), p. 110. See also *Giraldi Cambrensis Opera*, VI, p. 64.

[50] R. R. Davies, 'Colonial Wales', *PP*, 65 (1974), 3–23; D. Huw Owen, 'The Englishry of Denbigh: An English Colony in Medieval Wales', *THSC* (1975), 57–76; R. I. Jack, 'Welsh and English in the Medieval Lordship of Ruthin', *TDHS*, 18 (1969), 23–49.

[51] From the numerous examples, I have selected the following: NLW Chirk Castle, D.9, D.40; PRO SC 2/220/9, m. 61; SC 2/216/6, m. 20; SC 2/216/11, m. 3v. For their meanings, see *OED*, s.v.

[52] For evidence of English place-names within towns, see, e.g., NLW Ruthin Lordship Records 103, 1139, 110 (Ruthin); NLW Llanfair and Brynodol D. 932, 924, 920 (Caernarfon); Wynn, *History of the Gwydir Family*, p. 49.

[53] For a useful discussion of the issues involved in the context of the English language in Ireland, see A. Bliss, 'Language and Literature' in James Lydon (ed.), *The English in Medieval Ireland* (Dublin, 1984), pp. 27–45 and Jeffrey L. Kallen, 'English in Ireland' in Robert Burchfield (ed.), *The Cambridge History of the English Language, Vol. V* (Cambridge, 1994), pp. 148–96. For a general overview of the English language in Wales, see Alan R. Thomas, 'English in Wales', ibid., pp. 94–147, esp. pp. 107–10. For Hugh de Smethynton, see PRO SC 2/218/7, m. 5v.

Ni wybûm erioed medru Saesneg,
Ni wn ymadrawdd o ffrawdd Ffrangeg.

(I was never able to speak English, I do not know a single phrase of passionate French.)

So claimed the Welsh poet, Dafydd Benfras as he fashioned his *awdl* to prince Dafydd ap Llywelyn. Dafydd Benfras was by no means unique. The language divide is clearly evinced by the fact that, from an early date, agents of secular and ecclesiastical authority deemed it expedient, indeed essential, to make use of interpreters or latimers. In the March of Wales men might hold land in return for services as latimers between the Welsh and the English; at several points in his discussion, Gerald of Wales refers to the need to make use of interpreters in preaching the crusade among Welsh communities, while in the early fourteenth century interpreters had to be sent to receive the homage of the men of the lordship of Brecon 'because the people there did not know how to do homage in English'. 'He knows no language other than his father's language' ('Ni ŵyr iaith ond iaith ei dad'), remarked the poet Guto'r Glyn of Dafydd Llwyd, the fifteenth-century lord of Abertanad, adding that English noblemen of 'northern speech' ('ogleddiaith') showed him respect even though he had not mastered their language.[54]

Equally suggestive is the evidence presented at Swansea in the course of the canonization proceedings to which reference has already been made. William ap Rhys, a convicted felon whose miraculous survival through the bishop's intercession had prompted the enquiry and who hailed from Llanrhidian, a village situated on the very border of two linguistic and cultural zones, not only gave his evidence in Welsh through interpreters and was specifically described as one who knew no Latin (*nesciebat loqui litteraliter*), no French and no English, but had confessed his sins to a Welsh-speaking priest 'because he knew not how to speak English' (*quia . . . nesciebat loqui Anglicum*). Moreover, it is possible, although here the evidence is not quite as conclusive, that some of the deponents in Swansea

---

[54] Morgan, 'Nodiadau ar Destun Barddoniaeth y Tywysogion', 150; H. Hall (ed.), *Red Book of the Exchequer II* (R.S., 1896), p. 454 (*per serjanteriam ut sit latimerus inter Anglos et Walenses*); *Giraldi Cambrensis Opera*, VI, pp. 14, 55, 126. On the contrast between the image of Wales presented by Gerald in his *Descriptio* and *Itinerarium*, see M. Richter, *Giraldus Cambrensis. The Growth of the Welsh Nation* (Aberystwyth, 1972) and the suggestive article by Huw Pryce, 'In Search of a Medieval Society: Deheubarth in the Writings of Gerald of Wales', *WHR*, 13, no. 3 (1987), 265–81; *Calendar of Inquisitions Miscellaneous*, I, p. 508; *Gwaith Guto'r Glyn*, pp. 197–9. It is significant that the profoundly Welsh character of the lordship of Brecon is noted by the poet Siôn Cent, *Iolo Goch ac Eraill*, p. 269.

knew only English, three of them testifying in English because they had no knowledge of Latin or French.[55] Several centuries later, the profound linguistic dichotomy of Pembrokeshire was vividly described by George Owen in a celebrated and compelling passage:

> And nowe this diversitie of speeches breedeth some inconveniences, soe that often tymes it is founde at the Assises, that in a Iurye of xii men there wilbe the one half that cannot vnderstand the others wordes; and yett must they agree upon the truth of the matter, before they departe: and I have seene two tryers sworne for tryall of the rest of the pannell, the on meere Englishe, the other not vnderstandinge anye worde of Englishe, have lasted out three daies vpon the matter: the on not able to speake to the other.[56]

In an equally interesting and suggestive passage, he contended that the 'meaner sort' did not normally join together in marriage nor engage in commercial transactions with one another. Indeed, even when mixed marriages and commercial interchange can be securely documented, it may well be that their consequence was to reinforce the existence of linguistically homogenous communities such as those found in parts of late-medieval Hungary where bilingualism at this social level was relatively rare, and where it was rather the tendency for discrete language groups to assimilate the speakers of other tongues.[57] Encounters between monoglot Welshmen and uncomprehending English ladies, and the comic potential implicit in such a scenario, were wickedly and deliciously exploited by late-medieval poets. 'Gad i'r llaw dan godi'r llen / Dy glywed, ddyn deg lawen' ('Let my hand lift up your skirt / and feel you, fair merry girl'), exclaims an ardent lover in Tudur Penllyn's celebrated *cywydd*; 'I am not Wels, thow Welsmon, / Ffor byde the, lete me alone', retorts the object of his unwelcome advances. Similarly, Thomas ab Ieuan described the vain attempts of his shrewish wife to prepare him for his begging itinerary

---

[55] Richter, *Sprache und Gesellschaft*, pp. 197–201. Competence in Welsh is not mentioned in the depositions.
[56] Owen, *Description*, I, p. 40.
[57] Ibid., p. 39; Janos M. Bak, '"Linguistic Pluralism" in Medieval Hungary' in M. A. Meyer (ed.), *The Culture of Christendom* (Hambledon, 1993), p. 278. In 1558 a Pembrokeshire defendant at the Court of Great Sessions maintained that he had lived in Wales since his childhood and knew no English. Richard Suggett, 'Slander in Early-Modern Wales', *BBCS*, XXXIX (1992), 124.

by priming him with some choice English phrases, only to find that her husband's tongue could not encompass the strange, foreign words.[58]

Yet the language cleavage, despite its significance, was by no means unbridgeable. In the sixteenth century George Owen testified to the existence of an important bilingual element in Pembrokeshire society. Writing of the near-equal division of monoglot Welsh and English speakers within the county, he also showed how the inhabitants of around six parishes on the border between the Englishry and the Welshry spoke both English and Welsh.[59] Corroborative indications of a measure of bilingualism in the medieval centuries is more readily forthcoming for individuals than for entire communities, but the evidence is nevertheless suggestive. Apart from the linguistic repertoire of interpreters and translators, whose skills were a matter of professional necessity and pride, it may well be that the acquisition of skills in French and possibly in English had been growing apace in the period of princely rule. The presence at the thirteenth-century princes' courts of princesses and ladies of royal and baronial dynasties of England and the March suggests some use of French, while several leading servants of Prince Llywelyn ap Gruffudd such as Tudur ab Ednyfed and Einion Fychan spent long periods in England as prisoners or servants of the king. Many more members of important lineages were sent to England as hostages, often at an early age, and opportunities to learn the tongue of their captors must have been many.[60] Commercial intercourse, of which the cattle-trade and itinerant labour are prime examples, likewise facilitated increased language skills. By the late fifteenth and early sixteenth centuries, the poetry of Tudur Penllyn (reputedly a drover by profession), or the free verse of Thomas ab Ieuan, suggests familiarity with English on the part of the authors themselves and, perhaps, on the part of their audience. Likewise, it has

---

[58] The *cywydd*, although attributed to various poets, is included in the canon of Tudur Penllyn's works, Thomas Roberts (ed.), *Gwaith Tudur Penllyn ac Ieuan ap Tudur Penllyn* (Caerdydd, 1958), pp. 53–4 (a translation of the *cywydd* is included in Dafydd Johnston (ed.), *Medieval Welsh Erotic Poetry* (Cardiff, 1991), p. 75); Evans, 'Thomas ab Ieuan a'i "Ysgowld o Wraig"', *Ysgrifau Beirniadol XIX*, p. 96.

[59] Owen, *Description*, I, p. 48.

[60] For the use of interpreters, see above, p. 17; Richter, *Sprache und Gesellschaft*, pp. 177–9; C. Bullock-Davies, *Professional Interpreters and the Matter of Britain* (Cardiff, 1966). For the detention of prominent Welshmen in England and, in Tudur's case, subsequent service to the king, see Stephenson, *Governance of Gwynedd*, pp. 106–7, 211, 218–19 and Smith, *Llywelyn ap Gruffudd*, pp. 54, 114, 227. It is a point of some interest that although references are made to the use of interpreters in the course of diplomatic negotiations in documents of the twelfth century, references to interpreters in the more voluminous records of the thirteenth century are exiguous, which may suggest an increasing linguistic competence on the part of prominent Welshmen. Latimers continued to be employed by seigniorial administrations in their dealings with Welsh communities in the Later Middle Ages.

been plausibly argued that the fourteenth-century poet Iolo Goch, whose opus displays a large number of English loanwords, many making their only recorded appearance in his work, had learned English through contact with English settlers, and, from the evidence of his first-hand knowledge of at least one English poem, he was clearly conversant with contemporary English literary tastes.[61] More explicit still is the linguistic competence shown by the poet Ieuan ap Hywel Swrdwal, a name which is itself redolent of the vibrant and creative syncretism which could be achieved. His ode to the Blessed Virgin, a *cywydd* conforming in all respects to the disciplines imposed by the strict-metre *cynghanedd*, whatever the precise circumstances of its compositions, shows a complete and consummate mastery of the English language.[62] Moreover, in the March between England and Wales, there were families whose members, according to poetic evidence, were competent in English and Welsh. The fifteenth-century poet Bedo Brwynllys specifically commended his patron, Thomas ap Rosier of Hergest, scion of an exceptionally distinguished and cultured lineage, for cultivating two languages in his home, just as Lewys Glyn Cothi, in a *cywydd* addressed to the same lineage, reflected the bilingualism of his patron's household. 'Doeth ieithydd teg' (a fair and wise linguist) was how the poet Tudur Aled addressed John Edwards of Chirk and we may be sure that English was included in the linguistic repertoire so fulsomely praised by the poet. In remoter Cardiganshire, at a still earlier date, Rhydderch ab Ieuan Llwyd, a learned and cultured jurist and patron, may have been knowledgeable in both English and French, and conversant with the new, popular anthologies of French and English literature. In a *cywydd* addressed to one of Rhydderch's descendants, the poet Dafydd Nanmor (fl.c.1410–80) referred to the command of three languages which many a gentleman ('ysgwier') of his time could exhibit.[63]

Indeed, it so happens that an unusually clear indication both of the linguistic skills of one late-fifteenth-century Welsh family and the medium of their instruction can be established. A handsome and well-executed grammar book, almost certainly written in the hand of John

---

[61] David Johnston, 'Iolo Goch and the English: Welsh Poetry and Politics in the Fourteenth Century', *CMCS*, 12 (1986), 73–98.
[62] E. J. Dobson, 'The Hymn to the Virgin', *THSC* (1954), 70–124 and Williams, *Welsh Church*, p. 424.
[63] F. G. Payne, *Crwydro Sir Faesyfed* (Llandybïe, 1966), p. 33; *Gwaith Lewys Glyn Cothi*, p. 285; *Gwaith Tudur Aled*, II, p. 254; Daniel Huws, 'Llyfr Gwyn Rhydderch', *CMCS*, 21 (1991), 17; Thomas Roberts and Ifor Williams (eds.), *The Poetical Works of Dafydd Nanmor* (Cardiff, 1923), p. 71. Cf. the 'four languages' ('bedeirieith') in the *awdl* mentioned above in n. 42. For the English works of a distinguished descendant of a Welsh marcher family, see V. J. Scattergood, *The Works of Sir John Clanvowe* (Cambridge, 1975).

Edwards of Chirk, survives.[64] Along with the stalwart Latin literary texts, such as the Eclogue of Theodolus or Cato's Distychs and the popular Latin poem on etiquette, entitled *Stans puer ad mensam*, favoured by the medieval grammar-masters, there is much material of essential linguistic interest in the volume. A discourse on orthography and a tract on prosody derived from the *Doctrinale* of Alexander de Villa Dei, worthy and well-known works of the medieval Latin curriculum, find place in the volume. Also included are several *vocabula* or *vulgaria* – vocabularies of Latin words, bringing together all the words of one signification such as parts of the body, food, buildings and dress, and a short treatise on heretoclite nouns. There is, moreover, a tract, intended to inculcate the elementary principles of Latin grammar, which may be attributed with confidence to John Leyland, a well-known Oxford grammarian, who taught there at the end of the fourteenth century. From the point of view of our present inquiry, however, it is the copious use of English as the medium of instruction which deserves our attention. The Latin vocabularies are interlineated with their English equivalents, while the treatise on heretoclite nouns, although it outlines the rules in Latin, is accompanied by illustrations in English. John Leyland's grammar is likewise inscribed in the volume in English, and key Latin phrases are rendered in English. A like volume of grammar, whose use by Thomas Pennant, abbot of Basingwerk, seems well-established, also contains material of a similar nature, the two volumes together strongly suggesting that when young boys of the social background of John Edwards of Chirk were taught the rudiments of Latin grammar, they were taught through the medium of English.[65] Within this sophisticated, lettered and cultured social milieu, a knowledge of English was clearly essential for their formal instruction as well as professional advancement.

If education and training, career prospects as well as a closer integration, through marriage and the camaraderie of a shared social universe, encouraged the use of English at this social level, a measure of linguistic contact among the lower orders can also be assumed. Admittedly, little direct information concerning the language and speech patterns of peasants and artisans has as yet been uncovered. Actions of slander, a rich and suggestive source for later periods, are disappointingly reticent in the late-medieval centuries, and defamatory words were normally rendered in the relevant court rolls only in Latin.[66] Some indices that a process of

---

[64] NLW 423D. I have discussed the volume in *BBCS*, XXXIV (1987), 179–82.

[65] NLW Peniarth 356B. The volume is described in D. Thomson, *A Descriptive Catalogue of Middle English Grammatical Texts* (New York, 1979), pp. 114–32.

[66] Suggett, 'Slander in Early-Modern Wales', 119–53; cases of slander came before both the secular and ecclesiastical tribunal. Very few of the records of cases which came to the

linguistic adaptation was at work in some Welsh communities may, nonetheless, be suggested. Geographical mobility which brought Welsh speakers into contact with the English tongue is an obvious and well-documented phenomenon. Equally deserving of emphasis, however, is that a sojourn *in Anglia* was often followed by a return to the native heath. Seasonal, migrant agricultural labour was a practice which may be copiously illustrated in several upland communities and presumably the time spent abroad must have left some permanent impact on the individual's linguistic repertoire. Evidence from Dyffryn Clwyd reveals several examples of tenants who had returned to the lordship and to their family lands after working for a considerable time in England. Conversely, Englishmen living in Wales might well have acquired some knowledge of Welsh.[67] A Hereford witness at Cantilupe's canonization proceedings in 1307 argued that it was entirely possible that the bilingual skills so miraculously exhibited by the healed youth could be explained by natural means since he had been exposed to a Welsh language community from his childhood.[68] Naming conventions using proper names and craft, even if they do not provide absolute proof of the languages spoken, suggest cultural interchange across the language divide. Simultaneous binomialism, a well-documented phenomenon, shows the easy passage of individuals between linguistic groups, just as the adoption of English names and naming practices by the Welsh, and of Welsh ones by the English, betoken the mutual adaptation which might be achieved. Occupational labels such as *saer* or cooper, *eurych* or goldsmith, *cigydd* or flesewer, *cribwraig* or kempster were used interchangeably, and if this reflects colloquial usage as well as scribal practice, a measure of bilingualism among artisans and town-dwellers is possible.[69]

What significance, therefore, was attached to the Welsh language in the medieval centuries and what were the main determinants of attitudes towards language and of linguistic behaviour? For the Welsh, as for other peoples and ethnic groups, there were criteria besides language through which a sense of distinctive identity might be conveyed. 'A folk of strange origin and custom' ('diadnabydus herwyd kenedlaeth a moeseu') was how

---

secular jurisdictions give the words in any vernacular; they are given in English, but never, as far as I am aware, in Welsh in the courts of the diocese of Hereford. For examples, see HRO O/21, p. 237; O/27, p. 222; O/32, p. 102. For examples (also in English) of alleged heretical statements, see ibid., O/22, p. 222; O/24, p. 249. For an instance of a petition in English from the parishioners of Hyssington, see O/29, p. 109b.

[67] See, e.g., PRO SC 2/221/9, m. 20 and SC 2/221/10, m. 13.
[68] Richter, *Sprache und Gesellschaft*, p. 196.
[69] See the following illustrative examples taken from the court rolls of the lordship of Dyffryn Clwyd: PRO SC 2/220/9, m. 1v; SC 2/217/12, mm. 26v, 27; SC 2/218/3, mm. 14v, 15.

a native Welsh chronicler described the intrusive Flemings; to the chronicler Ranulph Higden, writing in Chester, the Welsh were a people characterized by their dress, manners, diet, and indolent habits, while George Owen, although he made frequent reference to the Welsh language spoken in Pembrokeshire, also noted the surnames, buildings, diet and husbandry practices which distinguished the Welsh from the English.[70] Of especial importance was law, a critical and often sensitive criterion, not only as a politicized symbol of national identity, but also in areas where ethnic groups intermingled.[71] For the English chronicler, Matthew Paris, Prince Llywelyn ap Gruffudd's assertion of power was made on behalf of his people's customs and laws. In the mixed societies of some marcher lordships in the fourteenth century, a separate law, even sometimes a separate legal forum, was one of the clearest ways of distinguishing between the Welsh and the English. Moreover, it is equally well-known that peoples among whom a common language was absent might often display the most trenchant marks of unity and identity. In Scotland the Gaelic tradition regarded the men of the Lowlands, despite their difference in speech, as indubitably 'Albannaich' and never questioned the integrity of the kingdom of Scotland. In late-medieval Brittany, likewise, a distinctive regional identity was nurtured on the basis of political allegiance to the ducal court.[72]

Yet although a sense of identity might be expressed in numerous ways, the sense of belonging to a language community was also a critical defining characteristic. In Welsh, the word *iaith* was invested with precisely the same conceptual nuances as was accorded the Latin word *lingua* or the West Slav word *jazyk*, which denoted both language and people.[73] Likewise, the word *cyfiaith* (common language) was used to denote a fellow-countryman or compatriot, while the stranger or *estron*, was, by the same token, *anghyfiaith* (without the language) and his

[70] Jones, *Brut y Tywysogyon*, p. 52; Owen, *Description*, I, pp. 38–41.
[71] For sensitive comment on the importance of law (*lex*), see R. Bartlett, 'The Conversion of a Pagan Society in the Middle Ages', *History*, 70 (1985), 185–201, esp. 190–2; idem, *Making of Europe*, pp. 197–220. For Wales, see R. R. Davies, 'Law and National Identity in Thirteenth-Century Wales' in R. R. Davies et al. (eds.), *Welsh Society and Nationhood. Historical Essays Presented to Glanmor Williams* (Cardiff, 1984), pp. 51–69.
[72] Glanmor Williams, *Religion, Language and Nationality in Wales* (Cardiff, 1979), pp. 1–34, 127–48; V. H. Galbraith, 'Nationality and Language in Medieval England', *TRHS*, XXIII (1941), 113–28; J. MacInnes, 'The Gaelic Perception of the Lowlands' in William Gillies (ed.), *Gaelic and Scotland* (Edinburgh, 1989), pp. 92, 96; Michael Jones, '"Mon Pais et ma Nation": Breton Identity in the Fourteenth Century' in C. T. Allmand (ed.), *War, Literature, and Politics in the Late Middle Ages* (Liverpool, 1976), pp. 144–68. For the Breton language, see L. Fleuriot, 'Breton et Cornique à la fin du Moyen Age', *Annales de Bretagne*, 76 (1969), 701–21.
[73] *Gwaith Guto'r Glyn*, p. 142. For similar concepts in the languages of eastern Europe, see Bartlett, *Making of Europe*, pp. 201–2.

language sometimes derided as a raucous, discordant speech.[74] Indigenous Welsh rulers, although they made use of a wide range of criteria in their attempt to convey a sense of their people's identity, also made much of the difference in language. The imposition of alien prelates and priests – strangers to the speech of their flock – was widely viewed as a challenge to a people's distinctiveness. Prince Llywelyn ap Iorwerth expressed his concerns that the church of the Welsh (*ecclesia Walensica*) was served by men who knew nothing of the customs or language [of the Welsh] and who were unable to preach or to hear confession except through interpreters, and Owain Glyndŵr, excoriating the 'fury of the barbarous Saxons' pressed for the presentation to Welsh livings of clergy 'who know our own language' (*scientibus lingua nostra*).[75] Such protests occasionally elicited a positive response. In 1284 it was maintained that one of the three chaplains who were to serve in the church of Conwy should be 'an honest Welshman . . . because of the difference of language', and in 1366 careful investigation was ordered into the linguistic skills of Alexander Dalby, dean of Chester and a contender for the see of Bangor, as to whether or not he was capable of preaching in Welsh. 'The land of Wales lies in a corner and differs in language and manners (*mores*) from the other people in the realm', declared King Richard III, adding that for that reason it needed its particular lord under the royal authority.[76]

Such overt recognition by an English king of the claims of a language community to a measure of political autonomy, even if it may be only fleetingly glimpsed, counsels caution in making any attempt to portray the post-conquest period as one in which the use of Welsh was suppressed. True, it was in the Late Middle Ages that the myth of linguistic proscription took root in many European communities. It was in the late thirteenth century, for instance, that a Polish chronicler recorded how the Teutonic knights had intended to exterminate the Polish language (*conantes exterminare ydyoma Polonicum*). In England the Croyland

---

[74] For the use of *cyfiaith* for people or nation, see, e.g., K. A. Bramley et al. (eds.), *Gwaith Llywelyn Fardd ac Eraill* (Caerdydd, 1994), p. 378. From among many examples of the word *anghyfiaith*, see Nerys Ann Jones and Ann Parry Owen (eds.), *Gwaith Cynddelw Brydydd Mawr I* (Caerdydd, 1992), p. 158 where *agkyfyeith* is explicitly translated as foreigner (*estron*), and Rhian M. Andrews et al. (eds.), *Gwaith Bleddyn Fardd a Beirdd Ail Hanner y Drydedd Ganrif ar Ddeg* (Caerdydd, 1996), pp. 243 n. 118, 290. See also GPC s.v.

[75] J. Conway Davies (ed.), *Episcopal Acts and Cognate Documents Relating to Welsh Dioceses 1066–1272* (2 vols., Cardiff, 1946–8), I, p. 324; T. Matthews, *Welsh Records in Paris* (Carmarthen, 1910), pp. 53–4.

[76] *Calendar of Chancery Rolls, Various, 1277–1326*, p. 287; *Calendar of Papal Registers 1362–1404*, p. 25. Richard III's charter creating his son Prince of Wales in 1483 is quoted in Peter R. Roberts, 'The Union with England and the Identity of "Anglican" Wales', *TRHS*, 22 (1972), 59 from PRO, Charter Roll no. 198, m. 3.

Chronicler expressed the belief that English had once been imperilled by the Normans, who had been intent on its destruction (*ipsum . . . idioma tantum abhorrebant*) and had ordained the use of French in all writings, charters and books and in the promulgation of law. Indeed, in the fourteenth century, the low esteem in which the English language was held was regretfully outlined by Osbert Bokenham who, in his translation of Higden's *Polychronicon*, related how, by the conqueror's decree, 'lordis sonys and alle nobylle and worthy mennys children were set to lyrnyn and speken ffrenssch', with the result that 'the rurales, that they myghte semyn the more worschipfulle . . . leftyn hure modre-tounge and labouryd to kunne spekyne ffrenssche'.[77] Nor were such fears always misplaced. Alarmed at the progressive Gaelicization of the English settler families in Ireland, it was ordained that no one of English descent was to converse with other Englishmen in the Irish tongue, a measure which formed part of a broader, draconian attempt to curtail the adoption of Irish habits and customs by the *advenae* and to preserve a knowledge of English among them. Men who had no knowledge of English might be imprisoned and would be released only under the strict proviso that they would learn the language. Apprentices, unless they were of 'Inglish aray, habite and speche', might be denied admission to urban liberties. Likewise, in Poland at the end of the fifteenth century, a German bishop ordered the inhabitants of one of his villages to learn German on pain of expulsion.[78] Measures of such severity and intensity, whatever their practical consequences may have been, were rarely encountered in Wales. Although intermarriage with Welsh women or the sending of children to be fostered among Welsh families was, occasionally, forbidden to Englishmen, evidence of a clearly articulated policy of language proscription is elusive.[79] Urban charters, such as that granted to Welshpool in 1406, might sometimes decree that pleading in the courts of the town should be allowed only in English or French, while Adam of Usk, in his *Chronicon*, revealed how the common people of Cardigan, erstwhile adherents of Owain Glyndŵr, deserted his cause and returned to their homes 'being permitted to use the Welsh tongue, although its destruction had been determined on by the English' (*lingua Walicana uti permissi, licet*

---

[77] P. Knoll, 'Economic and Political Institutions on the Polish-German Frontier in the Middle Ages: Action, Reaction, Interaction' in Robert Bartlett and Angus MacKay (eds.), *Medieval Frontier Societies* (Oxford, 1989), p. 169; Burnley, *Cambridge History of the English Language II*, pp. 423–4.

[78] For the position in Ireland, see Lydon, 'The Middle Nation' in idem (ed.), *The English in Medieval Ireland*, pp. 1–26 and Bartlett, *Making of Europe*, pp. 203–4 and the sources cited for Poland, ibid.

[79] For the prohibition of intermarriage and fostering, see H. Ellis (ed.), *Registrum Vulgariter Nuncupatum 'The Record of Caernarvon'* (Rec. Comm., 1838), p. 240.

ejus destruccio per Anglos decreta fuisset). His assertion, however, rests on doubtful authority and, indeed, by his own clear admission, the 'decree' (*decretum*) was revoked by Divine intervention and the prayer and cry of the oppressed.[80]

More important to the fortunes of the Welsh language than any explicit proscriptive decree were the silent influences at work within Welsh society. During the course of the fifteenth century the steadily increasing prominence of English as a medium of documentary literacy in England was mirrored also in Wales, even though the Welsh language was itself fully capable of expressing all the precision and technical rigour required of the formal documentary register. Despite the continuing importance of Latin as a language of record, it is evident that English, rather than Welsh, had begun to encroach on its sphere. Property deeds written in English survive from this period, while marriage settlements, arbitration decrees and wills, when they were not drawn up in Latin, were normally committed to writing in English.[81] Moreover, if the testimony of George Owen is to be credited, the pernicious habit, familiar enough among literate Welshmen and women of a much later age, of penning their personal correspondence in English was already firmly established. Noting the low prestige accorded the English tongue in the wake of the Norman conquest of England and the preference among English speakers then for writing in French, he referred to the same tendency at work within Wales: '[Welshmen] allthoughe they vsuallye speacke the welshe tongue, yett will they writte eche to other in Englishe, and not in the speache they vsuallye talke.' While Owen's assertion can scarcely be put to the test in view of the pitifully small number of letters which survive from this period, it is noteworthy that the extant examples are, indeed, written in English and conform punctiliously to the English epistolary style. Likewise, the formularies of documents and deeds in use, like that

---

[80] The Welshpool charter of 1406, which specifies that neither English nor Welsh are to plead in the town court 'nisi in gallicis verbis vel in anglicis', may be found in M. C. Jones, 'The Feudal Barony of Powys', *Powysland Club*, I (1868), 307. For Adam of Usk's statement, see E. M. Thompson (ed.), *Chronicon Adae de Usk A.D. 1377–1404* (London, 1876), pp. 68–9. Less certain is the reference in BL Add Charter 51498 which allows an English tenant in the lordship of Moldsdale to be tried 'per Anglicos et linguam Anglicanam et non Wallensem'.

[81] See, e.g., NLW Brogyntyn 3450 (a marriage agreement between John Owen ap John ap Maredudd and Lowri daughter of Madog ap Ieuan ap Gruffudd); UWBL, Baron Hill 476 (a *prid* deed in English) and for arbitration awards written in English, see Llinos Beverley Smith, 'Disputes and Settlements in Medieval Wales: The Role of Arbitration', *EHR*, CVI (1991), 835–60. Conditional bonds, increasingly popular by the late fifteenth century, are commonly endorsed in English. For wills written in English, see Helen Chandler, 'The Will in Medieval Wales to 1540' (unpubl. University of Wales MPhil thesis, 1991), pp. 233–63. Numerous petitions in English are to be found in the court rolls of the lordship of Dyffryn Clwyd in the fifteenth century.

associated with Edward ap Rhys, a prominent bureaucrat of the north-east March, show how models written in English were being included alongside the Latin exemplars.[82]

Moreover, although the Welsh language was extensively spoken at all social levels and was a vibrant and resonant medium for creative literature and functional prose, a vehicle for private and public devotion and perhaps even for pleading in the legal forum, it was not, in so far as can now be established, a normal medium of formal documentary literacy.[83] Of the numerous property deeds of fourteenth- and fifteenth-century date which survive, not a single example was written in Welsh and although, as we have noted above, landowners might have had recourse to the vernacular in recording particulars of their landed estates, such documents as we have bear the hallmarks of compilations intended for private, personal use rather than ones to be proffered as proofs of title in the public domain.[84] Likewise, of the three hundred and fifty or so wills so far discovered, although nearly a half were written partly or entirely in English, only a few brief sentences interspersed in a Latin will of early-sixteenth-century date survive in the native vernacular.[85] The use of English was clearly proceeding apace in Wales several decades before the 'language clause' of the Act of Union of 1536 ratified its enhanced primacy and prestige in the domain of royal administration and justice.

The burgeoning importance of English in fifteenth-century Wales need occasion little surprise. The language of literacy, so we are told, bears no

---

[82] Owen, *Description*, I, p. 36; NLW Peniarth 354. A brief description of the volume may be found in *BBCS*, XXXIV (1987), 182–3. A letter written in English by an early-fifteenth-century outlaw Gruffudd ap Dafydd ap Gruffudd to Reginald de Grey, lord of Ruthin, is printed in J. Beverley Smith, 'The Last Phase of the Glyndŵr Rebellion', *BBCS*, XXII, part 3 (1967), 257. Grey's response may be found ibid., 258–9 and in Douglas Gray (ed.), *The Oxford Book of Late Medieval Verse and Prose* (Oxford, 1985), pp. 34–5. For the epistolary style, see J. Taylor, 'Letters and Letter Collections in England, 1300–1420', *NMS*, 24 (1980), 57–70.

[83] There is little direct evidence for the linguistic conventions of the law courts of the period before the Union and the language in use has been the subject of much speculation. Evidence of insistence on pleading in English and French is noted above, p. 40 and n. 80. For evidence that proclamations for the holding of sessions were made both in English and Welsh, see Peter R. Roberts, 'The Welsh Language, English Law and Tudor Legislation', *THSC* (1989), 33. See also J. Goronwy Edwards, 'The Language of the Law Courts in Wales: Some Historical Queries', *CLR*, 6 (1975), 5–9. For the position in other regions of Europe, see Bartlett, *Making of Europe*, pp. 212–14.

[84] See above, pp. 25–7.

[85] The calculations have been made from the list provided by Chandler, 'The Will in Medieval Wales', pp. 233–63. Only one example written in French has so far been identified. The will of Rhys ap Hywel ap Rhys of Llanidan (proved 24 January 1539), which contains some Welsh, is transcribed from PCC 17 Crumwell on pp. 231–2.

necessary correlation to the speech used by the majority of the people.[86] Already redolent of authority and high social status, English was the language of lordship and power, of social aspiration and economic advancement. Itself enlarged and adorned for the services of national and civic bureaucracies, the English language, now increasingly standardized even before the advent of print, was, likewise, assuming its role as a vehicle for administrative procedures and processes in Wales.[87] A class of professional scriveners (*scriptores*), well versed in the conveyancing practices of Latin and English property deeds, and linked with the urban milieux of royal and seigniorial administrations, was emerging. At Caernarfon, the Foxwist dynasty, whose skills may well have been passed down from father to son, possessed an extensive scribal practice at the turn of the fifteenth century, as is shown by the very considerable geographical range of the property deeds which they penned. Small wonder indeed that the memorial brass erected in the church of Llanbeblig to the memory of Richard Foxwist, a man in whom 'the glory of writing outshone many' (*in quo pre multis scribendi gloria fulsit*), was embellished with the tools of his craft, an inkhorn and penner. Although much work remains to be done on the identities and training of these humble but indispensable practitioners, their role in the dissemination and enhancement of English as a language of documentary literacy seems clear.[88]

By the same token the low prestige of the Welsh language in the administrative and documentary domain may also be readily explained. For one thing, it is questionable whether the formal enrolment in writing of property transactions had ever formed part of the native legal tradition. George Owen of Henllys, once again an illuminating source for the practice and customs of earlier centuries, provides significant comment. Observing the remarkable absence of deeds of pre-Union date from the counties of Cardigan and Carmarthen, he maintained that before 1536 the

---

[86] M. T. Clanchy, *From Memory to Written Record* (London, 1979), pp. 173–4. The position in Wales was already approximating more closely to one of diglossia, for which see Lodge, 'Language Attitudes', pp. 73–5 and the suggestive comments by Price, *The Languages of Britain*, pp. 120–1.

[87] The words 'enlarged and adorned' appear in the Brewers' Abstract Book of the early fifteenth century, quoted in John H. Fisher, 'Chancery and the Emergence of Standard Written English in the Fifteenth Century', *Speculum*, LII, no. 4 (1977), 898. On the influences which encouraged the development of a written standard in English, see also M. Richardson, 'Henry V, the English Chancery, and Chancery English', ibid., LV, no. 4 (1980), 726–50 and Burnley, *Cambridge History of the English Language, II*, pp. 409–96.

[88] The scriveners are discussed in Llinos Beverley Smith, 'Inkhorn and Spectacles in Late-medieval Wales' in Huw Pryce (ed.), *Literacy in Medieval Celtic Societies* (Cambridge, forthcoming). For the memorial brass of Richard Foxwist, see J. M. Lewis, *Welsh Monumental Brasses. A Guide* (Cardiff, 1974), pp. 40–1.

practice was to pass 'all lands . . . by surrender in the Lords Courte accordinge to the lawes of *Howell dha*', a custom confirmed also by later witnesses, who likewise made note of how bond and free lands were 'passed . . . allwayes in the lords courte by ye Rodde' whereof a record was kept by the lord.[89] Moreover, bereft of the stimulus to bureaucratic activity in Welsh which indigenous lordship might have provided in the post-conquest period, Welsh communities were increasingly being exposed to the written registers of French and English. Nor were the English rulers of Wales confronted with a clearly articulated demand for the use of the native tongue in the spheres of administration and government, as was the case in the lands of Brabant and Flanders, where a dominant Burgundian regime, for which French was the language of rule, nonetheless sanctioned the use of Flemish in several important respects, and where the use of Netherlandish was closely identified with the defence of urban and indigenous interests.[90] While the legislative intentions and the principles which informed the 'language clause' of the first Act of Union may be open to debate, it is clear that 'the use and exercise' of English had long exerted a formative influence on the role and prestige of the Welsh language in Wales.

Seven centuries after the agreement between Tudfwlch ap Llywyd and Elgu ap Gelli regarding 'Tir Telych' was recorded in Welsh in the Book of St Chad, a dispute arose over another parcel of land in the same neighbourhood. In a document dated the 'eighth day of June in the thirty second year of Henry VIII' (1540) two judges declared their decision concerning the land of Llwyn Gwyn in the commote of Caeo.[91] Written entirely in Welsh and made in accord with the precepts of native Welsh law, the Llwyn Gwyn arbitration displays not only a continuing recourse to Welsh legal practice but also a capacity to express a legal decision in a robust and richly nuanced vernacular that was both clear and precise. If the influences which favoured the use of English in Wales were increasingly evident by the time of the Union, it is equally clear that the Welsh language remained a resilient and dignified medium fully capable of responding to the manifold needs of Welsh society.

[89] Owen, *Description*, I, pp. 169–70, and for the observation that feoffments had usually been made 'in Latine and sometimes in Frenche', ibid; W. Rees, *A Survey of the Duchy of Lancaster Lordships in Wales, 1609–1613* (Cardiff, 1953), pp. xxiv–v, 251–2. The practice is attested also in the lordship of Dyffryn Clwyd in the fourteenth and fifteenth centuries.

[90] C. A. J. Armstrong, 'The Language Question in the Low Countries: the Use of French and Dutch by the Dukes of Burgundy and their Administration' in J. R. Hale, J. R. L. Highfield and B. Smalley (eds.), *Europe in the Late Middle Ages* (London, 1965), pp. 386–409. It is an important, although unanswerable, question whether the Welsh versions of the documents mentioned above were compiled from practical considerations or antiquarian interests.

[91] See above, n. 37.

2

The Welsh Language in Early Modern Wales

GERAINT H. JENKINS, RICHARD SUGGETT
and
ERYN M. WHITE

ON THE TITLE-PAGE of his celebrated dictionary, published in 1632, the lexicographer Dr John Davies, Mallwyd, drew attention to the rich and diverse ways of referring to the Welsh language in early modern Wales: *Antiquae Linguae Britannicae, Nunc vulgò dictae Cambro-Britannicae, A suis Cymraecae vel Cambricae, Ab aliis Wallicae . . . Dictionarium Duplex.*[1] His modern successors – the staff of the Dictionary of the University of Wales – have assembled a rich profusion of references to 'iaith' (language), 'heniaith' (the old language), 'mamiaith' (the mother language), 'Brutaniaith' (the language of the Britons) and 'Cymraeg' (Welsh) found in the manuscripts and printed books of the early modern period.[2] This evidence reflects several crucial factors: the territorial domination of the Welsh language; the extent to which daily discourse at virtually all levels was conducted in the vernacular; and the preoccupation of poets, authors and scholars with the well-being of the native tongue. This chapter focuses on three major themes: the geographical distribution of the Welsh language and the linguistic shifts which occurred; the status and practical use of the Welsh language in the domains of politics, law, economic and social life, religion, education, and culture; and finally, spoken modes of communication in everyday life.

Distribution

It is important to emphasize at the outset that, over the whole of the period under study, the majority, probably the overwhelming majority, of the inhabitants of Wales were monoglot Welsh speakers. Welsh was the dominant tongue and in most agricultural communities it was the sole vehicle of verbal communication. In a country which possessed no

---

[1] John Davies, *Antiquae Linguae Britannicae . . . Dictionarium Duplex* (London, 1632), title-page.
[2] *GPC* 1950– .

separate institutions of nationhood, the native tongue was the most distinctive and widely recognized badge of the collective identity of the Welsh people and one of the few unifying factors within Wales. Language was a central element which set the Welsh apart from the English. To the Welsh people, Wales was *Cymru*, the Welsh language *Cymraeg*, while England was *Lloegr* and the English language *Saesneg*. As a spoken language, Welsh was neither beleaguered nor imperilled in this period; no one believed that it might not survive. Its existence as the daily, face-to-face means of communication for up to nine of every ten inhabitants was not under threat and there was no obvious struggle (except for some communities in the border counties in the eighteenth century) for supremacy between the Welsh and the English languages.[3] Although the most powerful sections of society might deride or despise the Welsh language, there was no reason at the time not to suppose that it would continue to flourish. It was an intrinsic part of the social fabric of 'the world we have lost' and even the hostile author of the squib *Wallography* (1682) conceded that it was 'near and dear to the Folk that utter it'.[4]

It is logical to begin with numbers. Unfortunately, the first official population census enumeration was not conducted until 1801, and no data on the actual distribution of the Welsh language was recorded until the census of 1891. All demographic estimates for the early modern period (including the census of 1801) must be treated with extreme caution since they contain substantial margins of error.[5] In spite of heroic attempts by demographers to marshal and interpret skimpy material contained in lay-subsidy rolls, parish registers, hearth-tax returns and church visitation records, it is clear that the data is deficient and unreliable.[6] Nevertheless, the long-term trend is patently clear: the population of Wales more than doubled between *c.*1545 and 1801. It increased from about 250,000 in

---

[3] W. H. Rees, 'The Vicissitudes of the Welsh Language in the Marches of Wales, with special reference to its territorial distribution in modern times' (unpubl. University of Wales PhD thesis, 1947); W. Ogwen Williams, 'The Survival of the Welsh Language after the Union of England and Wales: the First Phase, 1536–1642', *WHR*, 2, no. 1 (1964), 67–93; W. T. R. Pryce, 'Welsh and English in Wales, 1750–1971', *BBCS*, XXVIII, part 1 (1978), 1–36.

[4] William Richards, *Wallography; or the Britton describ'd* (London, 1682), p. 123.

[5] For a discussion of the shortcomings of census material, see E. A. Wrigley and R. S. Schofield, *The Population History of England 1541–1871. A Reconstruction* (London, 1981).

[6] David Williams, 'A Note on the Population of Wales, 1536–1801', *BBCS*, VIII, part 4 (1937), 359–63; Leonard Owen, 'The Population of Wales in the Sixteenth and Seventeenth Centuries', *THSC* (1959), 99–113; W. T. R. Pryce, 'Parish Registers and Visitation Returns as Primary Sources for the Population Geography of the Eighteenth Century', *THSC* (1973), 271–93; idem, 'Wales as a Culture Region: Patterns of Change 1750–1971', ibid. (1978), 229–61.

1545–63 to 587,245 in 1801, i.e. an increase of 135 per cent.[7] It is a fair assumption, therefore, that quantitatively there were twice as many Welsh speakers by around 1800 than had been the case at the time of the Acts of Union. By 1801 there were 279,407 males (47.6 per cent) and 307,838 females (52.4 per cent) living in the thirteen counties of Wales and perhaps as many as 90 per cent of them spoke Welsh. When the census figures of 1801 were published, Iolo Morganwg mischievously seized the opportunity to remind the people of Gwynedd that the highest proportion of Welsh speakers lived in south Wales. Never a slave to accuracy, he cleverly massaged the figures in order to celebrate the contribution of his beloved Glamorgan to the cause of the Welsh language.[8] But although his calculations were not entirely accurate, it was nonetheless true that there were 334,460 inhabitants in the seven counties of Brecon, Cardigan, Carmarthen, Glamorgan, Monmouth, Pembroke and Radnor, as opposed to 252,785 in the six counties of Anglesey, Caernarfon, Denbigh, Flint, Merioneth and Montgomery. Even when the substantial numbers of monoglot English speakers who dwelt in Englishries such as south Pembrokeshire and Gower are subtracted, the balance of Welsh speakers still favoured the southern half of Wales.

These bald figures, however, do not tell the whole story. The percentage increase over the period as a whole reveals that the most striking growth in numbers (183 per cent) had occurred in the six counties of north Wales. It is also important to remember that at least until 1670 (if evidence based on hearth-tax returns can be relied upon) the population of the six counties of north Wales was greater than that of the seven counties of south Wales.[9] Moreover, although the average population density increased from around 40 per cent in the Tudor period to around 73 per cent in 1801, these figures mask substantial differences between the relatively small number of people who inhabited remote upland parishes and the much higher concentration of people in the fertile valleys, coastal plains, market towns and marcher shires.

At this stage it is worth drawing attention to the relative numerical strength of the Welsh language *vis-à-vis* its Celtic partners by *c.*1800.[10] Welsh was clearly strong in comparison with Cornish, Manx and Scottish Gaelic. Dolly Pentreath, allegedly the last native speaker of Cornish, had died in 1777 and Cornish could no longer claim to be a living language by

---

[7] John Williams, *Digest of Welsh Historical Statistics* (2 vols., The Welsh Office, 1985), I, p. 7; Pryce, 'Welsh and English in Wales', 25–35.
[8] NLW MS 13128A, ff. 66–7.
[9] Owen, 'The Population of Wales', 102.
[10] For the background, see V. E. Durkacz, *The Decline of the Celtic Languages* (Edinburgh, 1983) and Peter Trudgill, *Language in the British Isles* (Cambridge, 1984).

the end of the eighteenth century.[11] There were only 20,000 speakers of Manx in the mid-eighteenth century and their numbers were declining.[12] A combination of political stratagem and religious bigotry had gravely weakened Scottish Gaelic. It was inextricably associated with popery, Jacobitism and disloyalty, and following the cataclysmic Highland Clearances from the 1780s onwards the language was driven to the marginal north and western coasts and to the Hebrides. By 1806 the number of Gaelic speakers had dwindled to 297,823, i.e. 18.5 per cent of the total population of 1,608,420 in 1801.[13] Conversely, although the Irish people had begun the complex process of abandoning their language, the Irish-speaking population numbered 2,400,000 in 1799 and only in parts of Ulster and in small pockets along the east coast was it completely extinct.[14] Numerically, too, the Breton language seemed well-placed: the best part of a million people spoke Breton in 1807.[15] But the fact that they constituted only 4 per cent of the population of France was an expression of the relative weakness of the language. In many respects, however, the Welsh language was alive and well. It was spoken habitually by over half a million people, many of whom were more than ready to rally in defence of 'the fine old mother tongue' ('yr hen-famiaith odidog').[16]

Possibly as many as 70 per cent of the inhabitants were still monolingual Welsh by 1800.[17] Even as late as 1891 the census returns reveal that more than 30 per cent of the population were monoglot Welsh speakers. Monolingualism was historically a distinctive feature not only of much of the Welsh heartland (where it was relatively easy to remain impervious to English speech, manners and behaviour) but also of the eastern and southern fringe and even parts of Herefordshire. Much of the evidence relating to monolingualism is anecdotal, but the records of the Court of Great Sessions and other courts provide, *inter alia*, specific examples of monolingualism in different areas and contexts. Evidence of the presence

---

[11] Glanville Price, *The Languages of Britain* (London, 1984), p. 136; idem, 'Cornish Language and Literature' in Glanville Price (ed.), *The Celtic Connection* (Gerrards Cross, 1992), pp. 301–14.

[12] Price, *The Languages of Britain*, p. 75; Robert L. Thomson, 'Manx Language and Literature' in Price, *The Celtic Connection*, pp. 154–70.

[13] Charles W. J. Withers, *Gaelic in Scotland 1698–1981* (Edinburgh, 1984), p. 83.

[14] Reg Hindley, *The Death of the Irish Language* (London, 1990), p. 15. See also Brian Ó Cuív, 'The Irish Language in the Early Modern Period' in T. W. Moody, F. X. Martin and F. J. Byrne (eds.), *A New History of Ireland, III, Early Modern Ireland 1534–1691* (Oxford, 1976), pp. 509–45.

[15] R. D. Grillo, *Dominant Languages. Language and Hierarchy in Britain and France* (Cambridge, 1989), p. 25.

[16] Samuel Williams, *Amser a Diwedd Amser* (Llundain, 1707), sig. A2v–A3v. For similar sentiments, see Garfield H. Hughes (ed.), *Rhagymadroddion 1547–1659* (Caerdydd, 1951), pp. 47–8, 63–73, 111–13, 118–19.

[17] Pryce, 'Wales as a Culture Region', p. 230.

THE WELSH LANGUAGE IN EARLY MODERN WALES 49

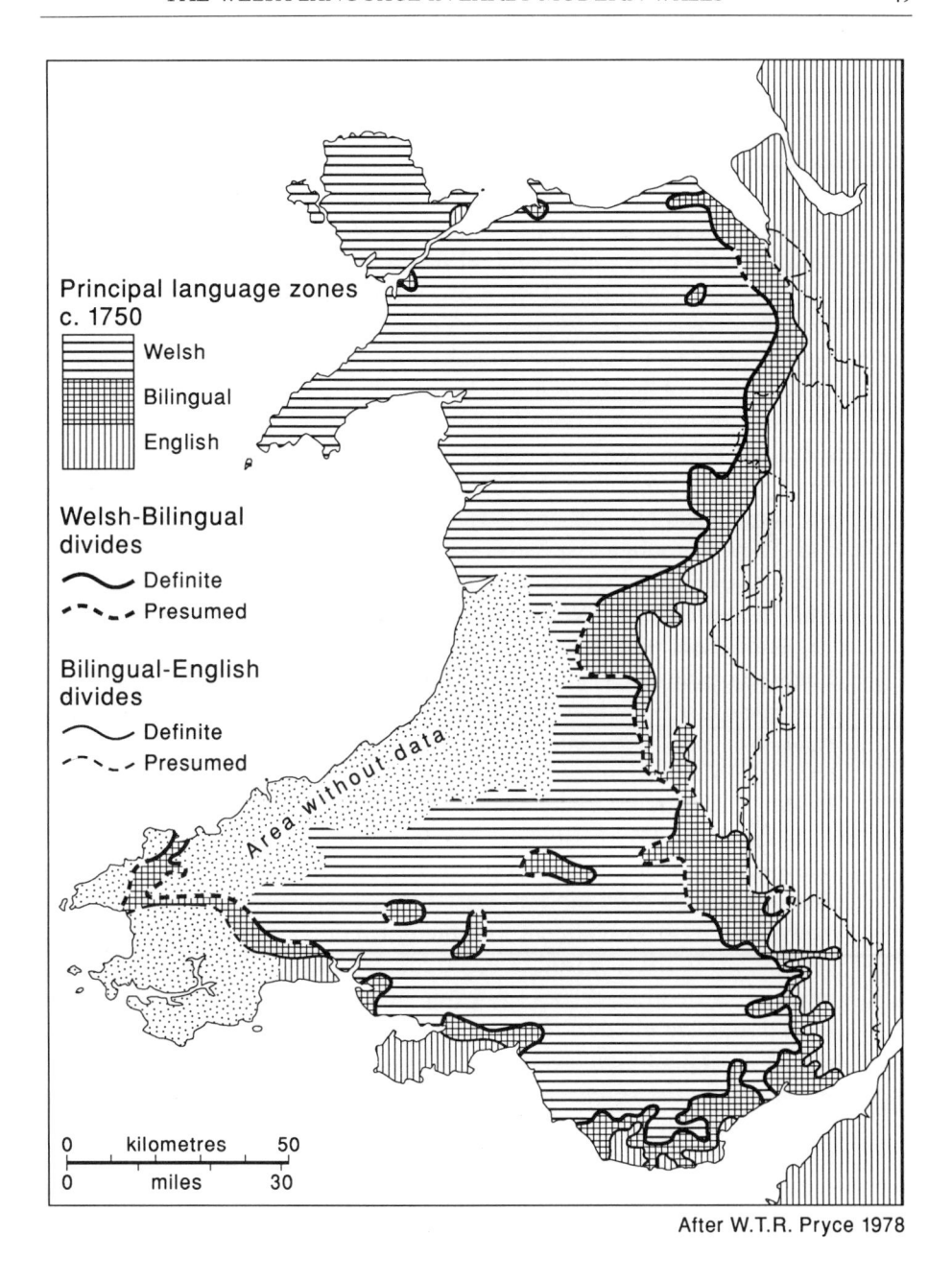

Principal language zones c.1750

After W.T.R. Pryce 1978

of monoglot Welsh speakers in north-east Wales near the Chester border is provided by a group of mid-seventeenth-century petitions in which the petitioners, poor freeholders from the Whitford area in Flintshire, asked to be discharged from jury service because of their inability to understand English.[18] The deposition of witnesses also provides instances of monoglot Welsh speakers. In Pembrokeshire in 1656 David Lewis of Little Newcastle 'did not understand what was spoken in the English tongue' and, similarly, William Meylor of St David's 'was not able to render himself sufficiently in English'.[19] Since many rural inhabitants had few opportunities to acquire any English, those who wanted to do business in Wales were obliged to learn Welsh. William Copeland, a Scottish packman selling linen cloth, claimed in 1683 that he understood 'many words' of Welsh. When he was robbed at Llanfyllin in Montgomeryshire, he made 'great complaint' in 'broaken Welsh' and English, but his English was understood by only one person.[20] Communication between English and Welsh monoglot speakers gave rise to difficulties. In 1617 the evidence of Edward Gruffydd ap Ednyfed of Garthgarmon, Denbighshire, who had encountered William Rogers, Sir John Wynne's warrener and a suspected thief, was limited since it was said that 'hee can [speak] no English nor the other noe Welsh'.[21] When Jonathan Swift was marooned in Anglesey in 1727, he felt like an intruder among local monoglot Welsh speakers,[22] and since none of the forty passengers who accompanied the traveller William Hutton on the Tal-y-foel ferry in 1799 could speak English, he sat in glum silence.[23]

As far as the Welsh language is concerned, the most critical constant historical factor deciding its fortunes has been the topography of Wales. Throughout the early modern period the geographical nature of the land exercised a powerful influence on the distribution of the Welsh-speaking population. Wales — a land of 8,000 square miles — is broadly rectangular in shape, with a longer axis stretching broadly from north to south. The most distinctive physical feature — the central massif where craggy peaks, rolling plateaux, high aggregates of rainfall, acidic soils and isolation accounted for the slender size of the population — served as a powerful and seemingly impregnable impediment to the westward movement of the English language. Signs of linguistic erosion were fewest in the north-west and west of Wales, precisely in those counties shielded by the central core

---

[18] NLW, Great Sessions 13/46/3. See also p. 157 below.
[19] NLW, Great Sessions 4/792/5/46, 58.
[20] NLW, Great Sessions 4/162/4/43–6.
[21] NLW, Great Sessions 4/16/4/17.
[22] Helen Ramage, *Portraits of an Island: Eighteenth Century Anglesey* (Llangefni, 1987), p. 56.
[23] William Hutton, *Remarks upon North Wales* (Birmingham, 1803), p. 179.

of craggy mountains and best able to retain their linguistic cohesion and sociocultural mores.

Sealed off by rugged mountains, people living in the counties of Anglesey, Caernarfon, Merioneth, Cardigan and, to a lesser extent, Carmarthen, were better able to preserve a high proportion of monoglot Welsh speakers. When the scholar Moses Williams claimed in 1714 that there were upwards of 500 parishes in Wales 'in which the generality of the People understand no other Language',[24] he was referring chiefly to north and west Wales, where the physical configuration of the mountains and the wretched state of communications encouraged social isolation and monoglottism, and blunted any threat to the territorial dominance of the Welsh language. 'We have whole parishes in the mountainous parts of Wales', wrote Lewis Morris in 1761, 'where there is not a word of English spoke.'[25] Around the same time John Jones, a barrister-at-law of Llynon in Anglesey, estimated that not more than one in forty people in north Wales understood the English language,[26] and there are grounds for believing that his calculation heavily overestimated the penetration of the English tongue. Tens of thousands of people spoke only Welsh, insisted Walter Davies (Gwallter Mechain) in 1795, and in the most sequestered parts of north Wales 'the impregnable fortress of the Welsh language . . . dwells as commander in chief'.[27] Even as late as 1931, one in five of the inhabitants of the counties of Anglesey, Caernarfon and Merioneth were recorded as monoglot Welsh speakers.[28] A familiar litany rings out in the visitation returns for the diocese of Bangor in the eighteenth century – 'Welsh – the only language understood in my parishes', 'They know no language but the Welsh', 'Welsh – the only language spoke in the Parish'[29] – and it is easy to appreciate why so many English travellers and tourists found this a hostile and impenetrable world. In these counties there were no fears for the future of the language as an oral medium since Welsh was intimately bound up with home, worship and workplace. People were not exposed daily to Anglicizing influences and they were under no pressure to become bilingual. Indeed, they had no experience of bilingualism. According to Thomas Llewelyn, a child born in north-west

---

[24] Moses Williams, *Proposals for reprinting the Holy Bible and Common Prayer Book in the British or Welsh Tongue* (London, 1714).
[25] *ALM*, II, p. 511.
[26] John Jones, *Considerations on the illegality and impropriety of preferring clergymen who are unacquainted with the Welsh Language, to benefices in Wales* (2nd ed., London, 1768), p. 14.
[27] Walter Davies, 'A Statistical Account of the Parish of Llanymyneich, in Montgomeryshire', *CAR*, I (1795), 280.
[28] D. Trevor Williams, 'Linguistic Divides in North Wales: a Study in Historical Geography', *AC*, XCI (1936), 207.
[29] NLW, Records of the Church in Wales, B/QA/5; B/QA/6; SA/RD/26.

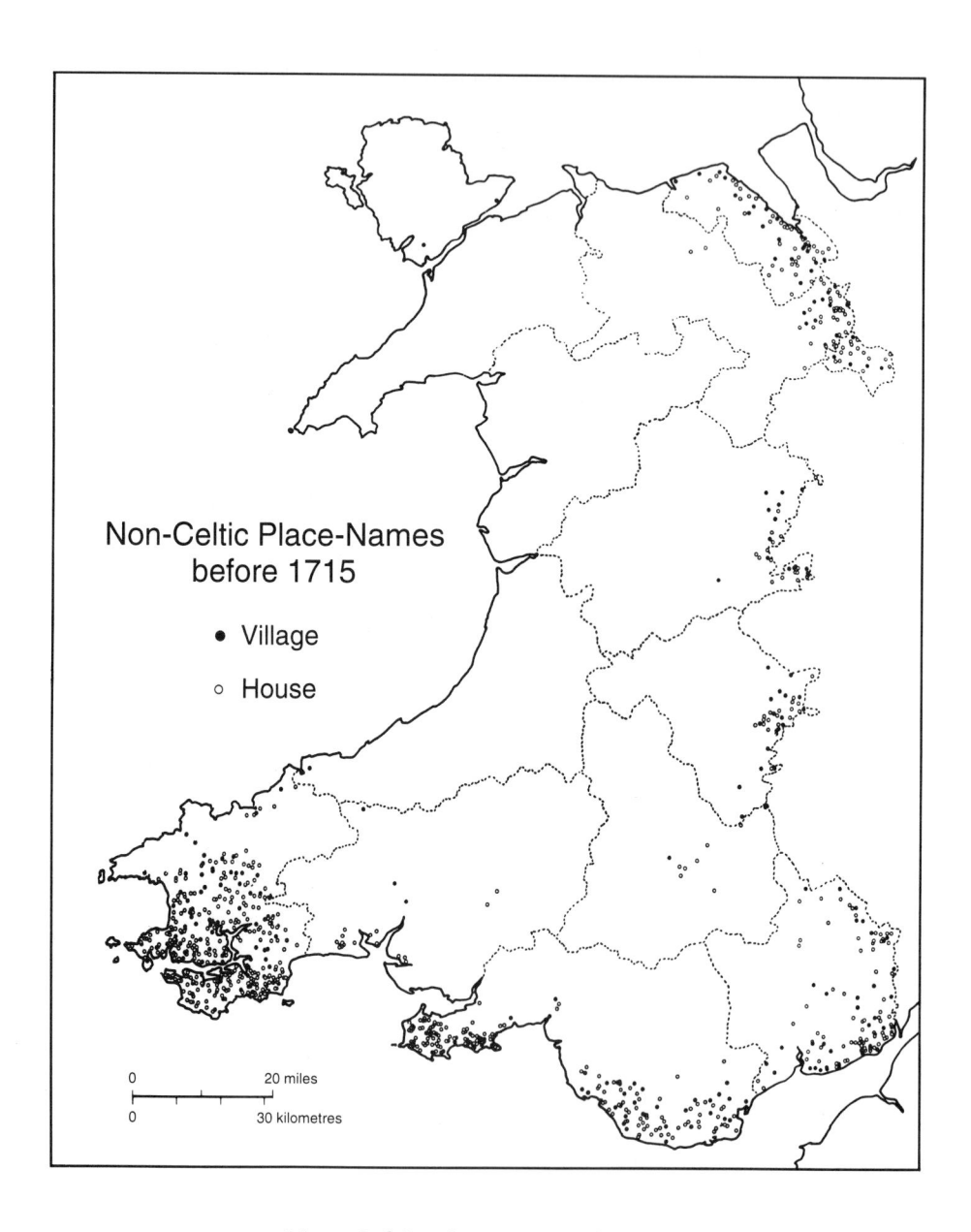

Non–Celtic place-names before 1715

Wales acquired the language of his parents and neighbours 'as naturally and as innocently, as he sucks his mother's breasts, or breathes the common air'.[30] The King's English, he continued, was of no more consequence to them 'than to the inhabitants of Mesopotamia or Patagonia',[31] except perhaps when it arrived in the person of an exciseman, a land-surveyor, an inquisitive English traveller, or an egregious sinecurist. Dr John Davies ventured to claim in 1621 that in such strongholds the Welsh language was 'in a thoroughly healthy condition, almost totally unblemished and uncorrupted' ('yn gwbl iach ei chyflwr, bron yn hollol ddianaf a dilwgr').[32]

Although the physical geography of Wales clearly helped to protect the Welsh language, it would be unwise to paint a simple picture of socially isolated agricultural communities. All areas were linked to markets and there was considerable seasonal migration both within Wales and to England. Seasonal harvesters, drovers, soldiers and sailors spent appreciable time in England and in every community there were well-travelled men (more rarely women) with a knowledge of English and sometimes other languages. We now know that the agricultural population was far more mobile than was once thought, and they must have acquired some English words and idioms as they overheard snatches of gossip in country houses and taverns and as they listened to tales told by members of the armed forces or by unscrupulous drovers returning from the fairs and markets of London. Nevertheless, in spite of the presence of English speakers, speech communities remained Welsh since the everyday domains of language use were Welsh.

Although topography is fundamental to understanding the fortunes of the Welsh language, a simple linear geographical and chronological perspective of the steady retreat of the Welsh language must be modified by considerations of language maintenance, class and occupation. Unlike the nineteenth and twentieth centuries, early modern Wales did not experience a remorseless, dispiriting erosion of the Welsh language. Language communities and boundaries were far more durable and the westward progress of the English language was less a march than a sluggish plod which could, and often did, grind to a halt or even retreat. Although there were clear signs of dynamic linguistic instability in the border counties of Wales,[33] the territorial regression of the Welsh language

---

[30] Thomas Llewelyn, *An Historical Account of the British or Welsh Versions and Editions of the Bible* (London, 1768), p. 76.
[31] Ibid., p. 71.
[32] NLW MS 21299D, f. 68.
[33] G. J. Lewis, 'The Geography of Cultural Transition: The Welsh Borderland 1750–1850', *NLWJ*, XXI, no. 2 (1979), 131–44; W. T. R. Pryce, 'Approaches to the Linguistic Geography of Northeast Wales, 1750–1846', *NLWJ*, XVII, no. 4 (1972), 343–63.

should not be exaggerated. It was a slow, uneven process which did not gather pace until the eighteenth century, and linguistic shifts were nowhere near as striking as those which fragmented and undermined Welsh-speaking communities in the second half of the nineteenth century.

Another vital factor of historical and geographical significance was the presence within Wales of well-established, well-defined and extremely robust Englishries whose inhabitants set little if any store by Welsh. Since the Anglo-Norman conquest of Wales in the eleventh century, the descendants of the original soldiers and settlers had occupied the fertile lowlands of south Pembrokeshire and peninsular Gower, thereby giving rise to enduring differences of language and culture between the Englishries and Welshries.[34] The most compelling account of the maintenance of the differences between Englishries and Welshries, including language, was written by George Owen of Henllys at the end of the Elizabethan period. He described how the English and Welsh in Pembrokeshire differed in language and custom, including 'maners, diett, buildinges, and tyllinge of the lande'. The two nations kept apart so that 'the meaner sorte of people, will not nor doth not vsually joyne together in mariadge . . . no comerce or buye but in open faires'. This division was so well defined that one could find in a border parish 'a pathe waye, parteinge the welshe and Englishe, and the on side speake all Englishe, the other all welshe, and differringe in tyllinge and in measuringe of theire lande and diuerse other matters'. The county was almost exactly divided between the Welsh in the north and the English in the south. Seventy-four parishes were English-speaking, sixty-four were Welsh-speaking, and the six remaining parishes spoke both languages 'beinge as it were the marches betweene both those Nations'.[35] Whenever a Welshman summoned sufficient courage to cross the divide into 'Little England beyond Wales', he invited derisive cries of 'looke there goeth a Welshman', though it has recently been pointed out that Owen's evidence in this instance more probably referred to the heart of the English hundreds of Roose and Castlemartin rather than parishes located on the linguistic border.[36]

The linguistic situation in Pembrokeshire was further complicated in the late sixteenth century by the in-migration of many Irish people. According to George Owen, a third to a fifth of all householders in Roose and Castlemartin were Irish, and some parishes were wholly inhabited by

---

[34] Brian S. John, 'The Linguistic Significance of the Pembrokeshire Landsker', *PH*, no. 4 (1972), 7–29.
[35] Owen, *Description*, I, pp. 39–40, 47–8.
[36] Ibid., I, p. 47; B. G. Charles, *The Place-names of Pembrokeshire* (2 vols., Aberystwyth, 1992), I, p. liv.

the Irish, leaving 'not one Englishe or Welshe but the parson of the parish'. It is probable that there had always been an Irish presence in south-west Wales and possibly an Irish-speaking community. Nevertheless, Owen was convinced that the Irish in his county reinforced the English-speaking communities because 'for the moste parte [they] speake and vse here the English tongue'.[37]

The *Landsker* remained a long-standing linguistic and cultural divide between the Welsh-speaking north and the English-speaking south. Even in 1804 Benjamin Malkin was deeply struck by the marked social, economic and cultural differences between the two peoples, and seven years later Richard Fenton observed that 'the barrier line is to this day strictly preserved, and a brook or a footpath is known to separate the languages'.[38] Social and economic intercourse between the two people was minimal and even as late as 1893 it was observed that ancient prejudice precluded free intermarriage between the English and the Welsh in Pembrokeshire.[39]

Gower was another area where the linguistic and cultural division between English and Welsh was strongly marked. An accurate picture of the Englishries and Welshries was supplied for the benefit of Edward Lhuyd by the Revd. Isaac Hamon at the end of the seventeenth century. In west Gower the parishes were English-speaking. English speakers in the southern part pronounced their words 'something like the West of England', while in the north they 'inclined more to the Welsh pronunciation and mixed some Welsh words amongst their old English'.[40] The language boundaries were evidently stable, but Hamon also provided valuable evidence of changes in vocabulary and pronunciation in *Gower Anglicana*. The Welsh and English parts of Gower remained robustly different from each other and in the late eighteenth century the Revd. John Evans went so far as to claim that they had 'an utter aversion for each other'.[41] Whenever a bemused traveller in the Englishry sought to locate a person living in the Welsh part of Gower he was likely to be told with ill-concealed contempt – 'I danna knaw, a lives

---

[37] Owen, *Description*, I, p. 40.
[38] Benjamin H. Malkin, *The Scenery, Antiquities, and Biography, of South Wales* (London, 1804), p. 432; Richard Fenton, *A Historical Tour through Pembrokeshire in 1811* (London, 1811), p. 203.
[39] David W. Howell (ed.), *Pembrokeshire County History, Vol. IV. Modern Pembrokeshire 1815–1974* (Haverfordwest, 1993), p. 455.
[40] D. Trevor Williams, 'Gower: A Study in Linguistic Movements and Historical Geography', *AC*, LXXXIX (1934), 302–27, F. V. Emery, 'Edward Lhuyd and some of his Glamorgan Correspondents: a view of Gower in the 1690s', *THSC* (1965), 59–114.
[41] John Evans, *Letters written during a Tour through South Wales in the Year 1803* (London, 1804), p. 195.

somewhere in the Welshery' – as though non-English speakers were rather less than human.[42]

The geographical distribution of the Welsh language (particularly in the border counties) had also been complicated in an interesting way by arbitrary political decisions. The Act of Union of 1536, which defined the new Welsh counties, treated linguistic communities with brutal disregard. There were profound consequences for the linguistic and cultural environment of the inhabitants of communities who had hitherto spoken Welsh but who now found themselves casualties of major boundary changes. The most arbitrary changes were the transfer of the Archenfield region and the lordship of Clun to the respective counties of Hereford and Shropshire.[43] The severance from Wales of substantial communities of this kind meant that 'the Welsh toong', according to the Tudor historian David Powel, 'is commonlie vsed and spoken Englandward'.[44] At a stroke, artificial boundaries had been created which consigned a not inconsiderable number of Welsh speakers to life in the counties of Gloucestershire, Herefordshire and Shropshire, where they found themselves in intensified contact with English influences. The detailed story of the survival of Welsh in these communities is irrecoverable, but it is clear they did not abandon their native tongue overnight. The decision made in 1563 to include the bishop of Hereford among the Welsh bishops made responsible for ensuring the translation of the Bible and the Book of Common Prayer into Welsh suggests that considerable numbers still spoke Welsh in parts of Herefordshire a generation after the first Act of Union.[45] Humphrey Llwyd claimed that Welsh was widely spoken in the lordships of Ewias Harold and Ewias Lacy in the Elizabethan period.[46] Evidence from litigation in the eighteenth century reveals that Welsh-speaking areas in west Herefordshire, adjoining Breconshire and Monmouthshire, had survived. Of nine cases of defamation in the Clodock area (including Craswell, Longtown and Llanveynoe) between 1712 and 1774, eight were in Welsh.[47] Other cases of Welsh defamation occurred at Dulas in 1738 and Ewias Harold in 1728–9, although the adjoining parish of St Margarets seems to have been English-speaking.[48] The Welsh-speaking enclaves in Herefordshire were not necessarily bilingual, as might have been expected. Lewis Jenkins of

[42] Anon., 'Cursory Remarks on Welsh Tours or Travels', *CAR*, II (1796), 438.
[43] B. G. Charles, 'The Welsh, their Language and Place-names in Archenfield and Oswestry' in Henry Lewis (ed.), *Angles and Britons* (Cardiff, 1963), pp. 85–110.
[44] David Powel, *The historie of Cambria* (London, 1584), p. 5.
[45] Melville Richards, 'The Population of the Welsh Border', *THSC* (1970), 95.
[46] B. G. Charles, 'The Welsh', p. 95.
[47] NLW, Consistory Court Records, Archdeaconry of Brecon, SD/CCB/59, 143, 145, 147, 149, 152, 153, 154; SD/CC/G/693, 714.
[48] NLW, SD/CCB/59, 148, 235; SD/CC/G/987.

Michaelchurch Escley, aged nineteen in 1757, revealed in his testimony to the Consistory Court that he was 'a stranger to the English tongue [not] able to speak or understand but very few words'.[49]

The apparent vitality of the Welsh language in west Herefordshire strongly suggests that the Anglicization of the eastern March was by no means a straightforward or inevitable process. Nevertheless, for geographical reasons, counties lying east of the mountain uplands were less well placed than the western counties to resist the territorial advance of the English language.[50] As we have seen, intimidating mountains and long stretches of bleak moorland were highly effective insulating barriers. But because of the presence of rivers flowing in a south-easterly direction along relatively fertile, low-lying valleys, counties located on the eastern borders were vulnerable to language shifts. They provided routeways for in-migrants, cross-border trade, intermarriage and settlement. Similarly, counties with south-facing coastal plains, where the climate was milder and soils more easily cultivated, provided greater access to traders, merchants, settlers and travellers. As a result, pockets of bilingualism and English-only zones were bound to develop, particularly as economic ties were strengthened in the post-Union period. River valleys such as the Dee, Severn, Wye and Usk, and to a lesser degree the Arrow, Lugg and Vyrnwy, provided gateways for the English tongue. By the eighteenth century topography and commerce were reshaping linguistic patterns. In 1770, for instance, the inhabitants of upland Flintshire were still strongly Welsh-speaking and deeply suspicious of English-speaking interlopers, while those who dwelt in the more fertile lowlands were bilingual and so well endowed with 'English manner and customs' that they could easily be described as 'natives of different countries and climates'.[51] A clearly identifiable bilingual zone was beginning to travel from north-east Flintshire in a southerly direction. In both east Denbighshire and east Montgomeryshire there were growing challenges to the strength of the native tongue, and as the English language seized its opportunity to penetrate along well-established lines of commercial interdependence many communities began to display a considerable degree of linguistic complexity.[52] By the second half of the eighteenth century, what constituted 'a Welsh-speaking parish' in such parts was a teasing question.

---

[49] NLW, SD/CCB/59, 153c.
[50] E. G. Bowen (ed.), *Wales. A Physical, Historical and Regional Geography* (London, 1957); idem, *Daearyddiaeth Cymru fel Cefndir i'w Hanes* (London, 1964); Harold Carter (ed.), *National Atlas of Wales* (Cardiff, 1980–9).
[51] Joseph Cradock, *Letters from Snowdon* (London, 1770), p. 14.
[52] A. H. Dodd, 'Welsh and English in East Denbighshire: A Historical Retrospect', *THSC* (1940), 34–65; W. T. R. Pryce, 'Welsh and English', 10–15; Lynn Davies, 'Linguistic Interference in East Montgomeryshire', *MC*, 62 (1971), 183–94.

In the south-eastern counties English was undoubtedly gaining ground at the expense of Welsh, but here, too, physical configurations were key factors. In Breconshire the farmer and his labourer who dwelt on small upland farms were proudly Welsh and Welsh-speaking even in the late eighteenth century, but the 'vile English jargon'[53] (as Theophilus Jones indelicately called it) had entrenched itself in communities which opened out onto the English borders. A similar situation existed in the more sparsely populated county of Radnorshire.[54] Upland inhabitants spoke Welsh which was, at least to the ears of Lewis Morris, as pure and correct as that heard in north Wales, but the language was clearly receding westwards as the eighteenth century progressed.[55] Moreover, by around the 1750s Welsh had ceased to be the language of worship in the market towns and villages on the eastern side of the county. Historians may have exaggerated the speed with which Radnorshire became Anglicized, but there is little doubt that the Welsh language rapidly vanished from the lips of the young in the eighteenth century. With slight regret, Jonathan Williams, the first to compile a history of Radnorshire, wrote of 'the growing disuse of Welsh' in the county.[56] A similar pattern was detected in Monmouthshire by two observant travellers – William Coxe in 1801 and Benjamin Malkin in 1804. In the upland west, country folk doggedly clung to the vernacular and sullenly shunned visitors who spoke the unfamiliar Saxon tongue.[57] A bilingual zone had established itself in the middle portion of the county, and the inhabitants of the eastern lowlands spoke English. As early as 1651 John Edwards, rector of Tredynog and translator of *Madruddyn y difinyddiaeth diweddaraf*, had confessed that his translation was more prone to error and infelicity because he had been raised on the banks of the Severn in Gwent 'where the English language is stronger than the Welsh language' ('lle y mae'r saesoniaith yn drech n'ar Brittanniaith').[58] Within a century the decay of Welsh in eastern Monmouthshire was well advanced and would gather pace in the wake of greater economic prosperity.

The process of language shift in the early modern period, however, was by no means a uniform process and it is valuable to contrast the differing

---

[53] Theophilus Jones, *A History of the County of Brecknock* (2 vols., Brecknock, 1805–9), II, p. 270.

[54] Llywelyn Hooson-Owen, 'The History of the Welsh Language in Radnorshire since 1536' (unpubl. University of Liverpool MA thesis, 1954).

[55] *ML*, II, p. 237; *ALM*, I, pp. 108–14, 117.

[56] Jonathan Williams, *A General History of the County of Radnor* (Brecknock, 1905), p. 168. For interesting evidence regarding the parishes of Abaty Cwm-hir and Clyro, see NLW, Church in Wales Records, SD/QA/190.

[57] William Coxe, *An Historical Tour in Monmouthshire* (2 vols., London, 1801), I, p. 2; Malkin, *The Scenery*, p. 210.

[58] John Edwards, *Madruddyn y difinyddiaeth diweddaraf* (Llundain, 1651), sig. A5r.

experiences of the counties of Radnor and Glamorgan. In the former, the Welsh language was maintained until the early eighteenth century when it began to retreat westwards. In the latter, the Welsh language overwhelmed English-speaking communities in the seventeenth and eighteenth centuries and a vigorous Welsh-language culture flourished.

The mapping of slander cases between 1550 and 1650 reveals that Welsh was spoken throughout Radnorshire, apart from an entirely English-speaking enclave of eight parishes (around Presteigne) on the eastern side which lay historically within the diocese of Hereford. It is possible that Welsh actually gained ground in the early seventeenth century. The earliest cases of slander from Gladestry are in English, but cases became Welsh at the beginning of the seventeenth century. By the early eighteenth century, however, English was again advancing in Gladestry and adjacent parishes. The parson of Gladestry commented in 1720 that the 'English tongue does . . . daily get ground here'.[59] Defamation cases suggest that the use of English was increasing in the east and north of the county in the early eighteenth century, and church visitation returns for 1733 and 1750 note the increasing use of English within parish churches. Nevertheless, the continued resilience of Welsh in the south and west of the county in the eighteenth century is noteworthy, although Lewis Morris suggested that the country people were essentially bilingual. Slander cases from parishes like Glascwm and Aberedw, only a few miles from the Herefordshire border, were invariably in Welsh from the sixteenth century to the mid-eighteenth century.[60] The county was not effectively Anglicized until the early nineteenth century and not until 1870 was the death of the last Welsh-speaking native of Clyro recorded.[61]

The case of Glamorgan is more complicated and reveals that the forward march of English was not inexorable. Welsh was extensively spoken by the so-called 'mountain folk' in the remote and inhospitable farmsteads and villages of the *Blaenau*, but there were strong enclaves of English speakers in the early sixteenth century along the fertile coastal lowlands from Cardiff to St Brides Major.[62] The little-known early-sixteenth-century 'Cân Cymhortha' (Begging Song) by Thomas ap Ieuan ap Rhys illustrates the linguistic situation. The poet described his journey from upland Glamorgan to the Vale in search of corn. Since the English from Llanilltud to Ewenni Priory and around Wick would not understand

---

[59] Bodleian Library, Oxford, Willis MS 37, f. 136.
[60] NLW, Radnorshire plea rolls, Great Sessions 26/54, m. 7; 26/74, m. 27d.; 26/109, m. 21; 26/109, m. 33; 26/115, m. 30; NLW, SD/CCB/59/1–5, 250–2.
[61] William Plomer (ed.), *Kilvert's Diary 1870–1879* (3 vols., London, 1973–7), I, p. 347.
[62] Gwynedd O. Pierce, *The Place-names of Dinas Powys Hundred* (Cardiff, 1968); Brian Ll. James, 'The Welsh Language in the Vale of Glamorgan', *Morgannwg*, XVI (1972), 16–36.

his Welsh, his wife taught him an English entreaty: 'I prau jow syr, ffor lov maestyr'. To the response 'kom hom syre', the poet was to say, 'Il kwm to yow, god redward yow'.[63] Slander cases in the Elizabethan period confirm that English was spoken along the coast west of Cardiff at Cogan, St Andrews (Dinas Powys) and Llantwit Major, and by the end of the seventeenth century trading contacts with West Country ports were having adverse effects on the spoken Welsh of inhabitants of some parishes on the coastal fringe of the Vale. By the early Stuart period, however, Ewenni and Wick seem to have become entirely Welsh-speaking. Six Welsh slander cases arose from St Brides Major and Wick between 1602 and 1638, and three from Ewenni in the period 1592–1641.[64] Defamation cases show that English-speaking enclaves in the Vale of Glamorgan had disappeared by the eighteenth century, apart from the exceptional case of Llantwit Major which is discussed below. As Iolo Morganwg confidently declared in the late eighteenth century, 'the *vernaculum*' in the Vale was Welsh.[65] At a time when Welsh was retreating in Radnorshire, it was expanding in English-speaking areas in Glamorgan in both town and countryside. One of the most striking features of linguistic shifts in eighteenth-century Wales is the manner in which the inhabitants of the Vale of Glamorgan became more consciously and publicly Welsh-speaking.

Finally there remains those who spoke Welsh but who did not, for a variety of reasons, dwell in Wales. Exactly how many people settled in England on a short-term or permanent basis cannot be determined with any degree of certainty simply because no statistics exist. It has been tentatively estimated, however, that the number of Welsh inhabitants living in London doubled from 6,000 in the early Stuart period to 12,000 by the end of the eighteenth century.[66] The Welsh were quite widely dispersed in Stuart London, but by the eighteenth century they clustered more heavily in the Clerkenwell area, where the Welsh school founded

---

[63] L. J. Hopkin James and T. C. Evans (eds.), *Hen Gwndidau, Carolau, a Chywyddau* (Bangor, 1910), pp. 25–7.

[64] NLW, Glamorgan plea rolls, Great Sessions 22/90, m. 20d.; 22/110, m. 15d.; 22/125, m. 39d.; 22/132, m. 17d.; 22/135, mm. 21d., 49d.; 22/158, m. 24; 22/160, m. 27d.; 22/181, m. 23; 22/187, last m.

[65] G. J. Williams, *Iolo Morganwg* (Caerdydd, 1956), p. 99; W. T. R. Pryce, 'Language Areas and Changes, c.1750–1981' in Prys Morgan (ed.), *Glamorgan County History, Vol. VI, Glamorgan Society 1780–1980* (Cardiff, 1988), pp. 265–313. See also Owen J. Thomas, 'Caerdydd a'r Iaith Gymraeg 1550–1850' (unpubl. University of Wales MA thesis, 1991), pp. 51, 54.

[66] Emrys Jones, 'The Welsh in London in the Seventeenth and Eighteenth Centuries', *WHR*, 10, no. 4 (1981), 466; R. T. Jenkins and H. M. Ramage, *A History of the Honourable Society of Cymmrodorion* (London, 1951), p. 137.

by the Society of Antient Britons was located.[67] Those who regularly frequented London-Welsh societies in the eighteenth century were at least partly impelled by a desire to speak Welsh with their fellow countrymen, to demonstrate their cultural distinctiveness, and to promote the interests of their native tongue. Growing numbers of Welsh people also settled in Bristol (which served as the economic capital of south-east Wales) and the eighteenth-century diarist William Thomas believed that as the English went abroad from ports like Bristol 'ye Welch men fills England in their stead'.[68] Outside England, the largest numbers of Welsh speakers who had been born in Wales were located in Pennsylvania, notably in the Welsh Tract colonized by Quaker emigrants from the 1680s onwards. By Moses Williams's reckoning, there were 6,000 Welsh speakers living in Pennsylvania and other parts of America by 1714.[69] Quakers made strenuous, but unavailing, efforts to maintain their linguistic exclusivity by worshipping in Welsh and publishing Welsh books, and the Baptist Abel Morgan achieved the considerable feat of compiling the first Welsh concordance, which was published posthumously in Philadelphia in 1730.[70] A Welsh Society, founded in Philadelphia in 1729, encouraged Welsh settlers to assemble on St David's Day to hear a sermon 'in the old British language', but as the English language began 'swallowing up' the Welsh tongue, enclaves of Welsh-speaking emigrants became increasingly fragmented.[71] The number of Welsh speakers clearly declined as the century unfolded, and when the intrepid John Evans of Madog fame visited the Welsh Tract in 1792 he discovered that although aged people could still speak Welsh fluently, their children were monolingual English.[72] When a tide of new Welsh-speaking emigrants crossed the Atlantic in the 1790s, one of their leaders, Morgan John Rhys, was so disturbed by the declining numbers of Welsh speakers that he

---

[67] Peter Clark and David Souden (eds.), *Migration and Society in Early Modern England* (London, 1987), p. 274; Meurig Owen, *Tros y Bont. Hanes Eglwys Falmouth Road Llundain* (Llundain, 1989), pp. 14–15.

[68] Cardiff MS 4.877 (Transcript of the Diary of William Thomas, Michaelston-super-Ely), f. 29. See also *The Diary of William Thomas of Michaelston-super-Ely, near St Fagans, Glamorgan, 1762–1795*, abridged and edited by R. T. W. Denning (South Wales Record Society, 1995).

[69] BL Add MS 14952, f. 8; C. H. Browning, *Welsh Settlement of Pennsylvania* (Philadelphia, 1912), pp. 18–19.

[70] Abel Morgan, *Cyd-Gordiad Egwyddorawl o'r Scrythurau* (Philadelphia, 1730); W. Williams, 'The First Three Welsh Books Printed in America', *NLWJ*, II, nos. 3 and 4 (1942), 109–19.

[71] E. G. Hartmann, *The Welsh Society of Philadelphia 1729–1979* (Philadelphia, 1980), p. 3; B. S. Schlenther, '"The English is Swallowing up their Language": Welsh Ethnic Ambivalence in Colonial Pennsylvania and the Experience of David Evans', *The Pennsylvania Magazine of History & Biography*, CXIV, no. 2 (1990), 224.

[72] NLW MS 21281E, f. 158.

interrogated an American well versed in Indian speech in order to ascertain whether the Padoucas really did exist and whether Welsh words and idioms resembled the language of the descendants of Madog.[73] Like his forebears, Rhys learnt the hard lesson that sustaining the Welsh language in a foreign land was an enterprise doomed to failure.

Domains

We now turn to consider the extent to which the Welsh language, in the face of considerable opposition or sheer apathy, established itself in some of the major social domains in the early modern period. The first is the practice of politics in the wake of the administrative and legal structure established by the Tudor settlement of 1536–43. Since unity, uniformity and administrative efficiency within all parts of the realm were central to the strategies devised by Tudor administrators, it was perhaps inevitable that English should become the official language of government, law and administration in Wales.[74] The seminally important 'language clause' included in the Act of Union of 1536 declared that no Welsh speaker could hold public office unless he was able to 'use and exercise the English Speech or Language'.[75] Ambitious gentlemen could not aspire to the office of justice of the peace, sheriff, escheator, *custos rotulorum*, lord lieutenant or member of parliament without achieving fluency in English. This clause, whatever may have been the intent behind it, undoubtedly had an adverse effect on the Welsh language since it robbed it of political status in its own land and offered irresistible inducements to the gentry to acquire English as soon as possible. English became the language of opportunity and advancement to all those who entered or aspired to enter the new world of Tudor citizenship. The need to impart a wider knowledge of English was implicit in the Union legislation, and by excluding Welsh monoglots from public office and access to power the highest possible premium was placed on the English language. To use the terminology of sociolinguists, English was a High language, a language of prestige and dominance.[76] It was the language of public life and the professions, of commerce and progress, of prosperity and advancement.

---

[73] NLW MS 13222C, ff. 461–4; G. J. Williams, 'Letters of Morgan John Rhys to William Owen [-Pughe]', *NLWJ*, II, nos. 3 and 4 (1942), 131–41.

[74] Peter R. Roberts, 'The Welsh Language, English Law and Tudor Legislation', *THSC* (1989), 19–75.

[75] Ivor Bowen (ed.), *The Statutes of Wales* (London, 1908), p. 87.

[76] Suzanne Romaine, *Language in Society. An Introduction to Sociolinguistics* (Oxford, 1994), pp. 46–7.

Even so, it should not be inferred that the state actively sought to eradicate the Welsh language. In Ireland, political conquest and the suppression of the Irish language were inextricably connected,[77] but there is no evidence of an overt and concerted effort by Tudor, Stuart or Hanoverian governments to dig a grave for the Welsh language. Cultural genocide was simply not on the political agenda in early modern Wales and we can discount the exaggerated view, advanced in 1801 by Iolo Morganwg, that since the days of the Union 'all that could decently, and with saving-appearances, be done, was attempted, to suppress and annihilate it [i.e. Welsh]'.[78] Although the *questione della lingua* greatly exercised Welsh humanists in the sixteenth century and cultural patriots in the eighteenth century, the language issue was not really a matter of profound concern to the state, particularly since Wales was increasingly viewed as a loyal, even deferential, province within the nation-state. It was axiomatic that one tongue – 'the King's English' – should enjoy power and authority in government, law and administration, and a proposal made in the House of Lords in 1730 that the proceedings of parliament should be translated into Welsh was derided.[79] Only in retrospect (notably in the twentieth century) did the language clause of 1536 become controversial. In its own times it occasioned, as far as we can tell, no anguished breast-beating or acute sense of guilt. Even the most ardent champions of Welshness were happy to admit that 'congruency of opinion' rather than 'that mistaken tye of unity in language' was the most potent binding force within the state.[80]

Nevertheless, the fact remains that throughout this period the Welsh language lived in the shadow of a dominant political language and, as Peter Burke has reminded us, 'like other forms of social history, the social history of language cannot be divorced from questions of power'.[81] The subordinate status conferred upon Welsh was bound to have significant effects on the Welsh people, especially those who were monoglot Welsh speakers. 'For it is very obvious', wrote William Gambold in 1727, 'that the Language of such, must as well give way to the Language of the Conquerors; as the Necks of the Inhabitants must truckle under the yokes

---

[77] Maureen Wall, 'The Decline of the Irish Language' in Brian Ó Cuiv (ed.), *A View of the Irish Language* (Dublin, 1969), pp. 81–90.
[78] William Owen Pughe et al. (eds.), *The Myvyrian Archaiology of Wales* (3 vols., London, 1801–7), I, p. x.
[79] W. Charles Townsend, *Memoirs of the House of Commons from the Convention Parliament of 1688–9 to 1832* (2 vols., London, 1844), II, p. 87.
[80] Jenkins and Ramage, *History of Cymmrodorion*, p. 19.
[81] Peter Burke and Roy Porter (eds.), *The Social History of Language* (Cambridge, 1987), p. 13. Cf. George Steiner, *After Babel. Aspects of Language and Translation* (London, 1975), p. 32.

of their Subduers.'[82] The 'language clause' had important consequences for the self-identity of the Welsh, for men of breeding and education increasingly prevailed on them to abandon their native tongue, gain a thorough grounding in English, and become 'of one speech'. The result, in many cases, was a crippling sense of inadequacy or inferiority, and it is no accident that the stock music-hall figure known as *Dic Siôn Dafydd* should have entered the historical stage in the immediate post-Union period.[83] *Dic Siôn Dafydd* was a quaint, rather effete, pseudo-gentleman who affected an English accent in the futile hope that this transformation would render him more socially acceptable beyond Offa's Dyke. Filled with self-loathing, he associated his native language with penury, illiteracy and backwardness, and he was only too glad to set aside his native tongue when he espied the river Severn or the spires of Shrewsbury and heard an Englishman say 'Good Morrow'.[84] Renaissance scholars as well as ballad-mongers and almanackers developed a fine sardonic line in satirizing the contrived accent and broken Welsh-English speech patterns of such turncoats.

The union legislation also deeply influenced English perceptions of the Welsh and their language. As the preamble to the 1536 act made plain, Welsh was 'a Speech nothing like, nor consonant to the natural Mother Tongue used within this Realm',[85] and this set the tone for a spate of lampoons, squibs and parodies of the language designed presumably to pander to the tastes of Anglophiles. The common stereotype of the Welsh in the early modern period is of a patriotic, impulsive, credulous, mendacious people who wore coarse frieze, devoured leeks, toasted cheese and flummery, quaffed metheglin, strummed harps, and kept flea-ridden goats and sheep. The 'Welsh manner' of speaking English – mixing the tenses of verbs and using 'she' and 'her' as catch-all pronouns[86] – invited derision, and the penchant of the likes of Shinkin ap Morgan and Taffy William Morgan for tedious storytelling ('Like the Welshman', wrote the Puritan Samuel Young, 'tell a tale, and begin it again')[87] provoked ridicule.[88] It was no surprise to the English that a people whom they considered 'rude and indigested Lumps' should speak an

[82] William Gambold, *A Welsh Grammar* (Carmarthen, 1727), sig. A2r.
[83] Bobi Jones, 'The Roots of Welsh Inferiority', *Planet*, 22 (1974), 53–72.
[84] Hughes, *Rhagymadroddion*, p. 47.
[85] Bowen, *Statutes*, p. 75.
[86] Richards, *Wallography*, p. 82; Andrew Borde, *The Fyrst Boke of the Introduction of Knowledge*, ed. F. J. Furnivall (London, 1870), pp. 125–6; W. J. Hughes, *Wales and the Welsh in English Literature* (Wrexham, 1924), chapter 2; Peter Lord, *Words with Pictures* (Planet, 1995), pp. 33–52.
[87] W. M. Lamont, *Richard Baxter and the Millennium* (London, 1979), p. 57.
[88] See, for instance, *The Welch-man's Life, Teath and Periall* (London, 1641) and *The Welsh Man's Inventory* (London, 1641).

incomprehensible tongue akin to the 'uncouth lingua' of Cherokee Indians.[89] Summarizing English animadversions of his native tongue, Dr John Davies listed the following censures: 'difficilis, impedita, confragosa, iniucunda, illepida, insulsa' ('rough, difficult, tied up, hard to be understood, unpleasant, without delectation, hath no pleasant fashion in words').[90] Not all Englishmen, of course, poked fun at the Welsh language. William Camden employed a Welsh servant in order to master the language and Ben Jonson learnt Welsh and penned a masque 'For the Honour of Wales' in 1619.[91] But these were exceptions to the rule. Baffled and irritated by the consonantal mutations and repelled by the unpronounceable spirant *ch* and the liquid *ll*, English writers were prone to set Welsh 'barbarity' alongside English 'civility' and English travellers treated natives from 'the dark corners' as quaint 'specimens'. Satirists claimed that Welsh resembled 'the Gobling of Geese, or Turkeys' and that only throats incorporating nutmeg graters could produce such harsh, guttural sounds.[92] In Tobias Smollett's first novel, *The Adventures of Roderick Random* (1748), the speech and song of Mr Morgan, the Welsh first mate on board the man-of-war 'Thunder', was accompanied by 'a thousand contortions of face and violent gestures of body'.[93] To Joseph Hucks, the Welsh tongue was redolent of 'the ravishing sounds of a cat-call, or the musical clack of a flock of geese when highly irritated'.[94] Prejudices of this kind were repeated uncritically in scores of publications and nurtured an attitude of disparagement and contempt towards the Welsh language among English speakers.

Although the English language was enthroned as the official language in the domain of public administration and political life, the need to communicate political information effectively meant that, in certain circumstances, Welsh was a *sine qua non*. Common sense often prevailed. In the Elizabethan period the Council in the Marches of Wales ordered justices in the remote and overwhelmingly Welsh-speaking county of Merioneth to read and publish 'in the Welsh tonge' instructions for the

[89] Richards, *Wallography*, p. 82; NLW MS 13121B, f. 486.
[90] NLW MS 21299D, f. 68; John Davies, *Antiquae Linguae Britannicae* (London, 1621), sig. C1r.
[91] Andrew Clark (ed.), '*Brief Lives*', *chiefly of Contemporaries, set down by John Aubrey* (2 vols., London, 1898), I, pp. 145–6; Roland Mathias, *Anglo-Welsh Literature. An Illustrated History* (Bridgend, 1986), p. 26.
[92] Ned Ward, *A Trip to North-Wales* (London, 1701), p. 3. Cf. Richard Blome, *Britannia: Or, A Geographical Description of the Kingdoms of England, Scotland, and Ireland* (London, 1673), p. 59; Henry Wigstead, *Remarks on a Tour to North and South Wales in the Year 1797* (London, 1799), p. 14.
[93] Tobias Smollett, *The Adventures of Roderick Random*, ed. Paul-Gabriel Boucé (Oxford, 1981), pp. 146–7, 176.
[94] Joseph Hucks, *A Pedestrian Tour through North Wales* (London, 1795), p. 135.

suppression of felonies in the county.[95] At Denbigh in March 1603, William Morgan, bishop of St Asaph, read the proclamation declaring the accession of James I in Welsh to the inhabitants 'whoe well applauded the same'.[96] Lusty-voiced town criers perambulated the streets, declaiming in both languages the content of proclamations, news-sheets and letters. On market day at Builth in 1746 the local crier doffed his hat, bellowed 'O Yea' thrice, addressed the throng in Welsh and then in English, and wound up his theatrical performance with the cry, 'God bless the King and the Lord of the Manor'.[97] Welsh almanacks and ballads – often read or sung aloud within the domestic circle – also kept common people informed of turbulent public affairs both at home and abroad.

Political campaigners during critical county or borough elections were also obliged at least to pay lip-service to the Welsh language. Posing as the champion of the native tongue could bring rich dividends to a local gentleman whenever his opponent happened to be either a carpetbagger or an avowed critic of things Welsh. When, during the Monmouthshire county election in 1771, Valentine Morris of Piercefield had the temerity to publish his electoral address not only in English but also 'in the Language of my forefathers who were originally Natives and People of property in this County for Hundreds of Years', John Morgan of Tredegar replied in kind and even commissioned an election song in Welsh by William Williams – *The Antient British Bard's Toast. Ffwrdd Ddieithryn* (Hence Stranger) – who loudly denounced the 'upstart Creole' for presuming to challenge the might of the Tredegar family.[98] The appeal of Welshness was often employed in campaigns against the arbitrary power of absentee landowners. In 1774 William Vaughan of Corsygedol bitterly chastized one of his neighbours for breaking ranks by promising his vote to 'strangers whom you know nothing about and who care not how soon we (the old people) go to the devil once their purpose is served' ('estroniaid na wyddoch ddim amdannut ag na waeth gan Rhain mae gyntem yr elom ni (hên bobl) i ddawl [sic] gwedi iddunt gael i pwrpas').[99] When the French Revolution began to cast its shadow over Britain, the freeholders of Glamorgan were reminded in Welsh that a vote for Thomas Wyndham, the local candidate, rather than for the reviled absentee

---

[95] Peter R. Roberts, 'Elizabethan "Overseers" in Merioneth', *JMHRS*, IV, part 1 (1961), 7–8.
[96] 'Robert Parry's Diary', *AC*, XV (1915), 127–8.
[97] Anon., *A Journey to Llandrindod Wells* (2nd ed., London, 1746), p. 54.
[98] NLW, Tredegar Park MSS 66/45, 72/58, 72/84, 53/290, 53/29, 72/54. For a Welsh circular by John Myddelton, published during the Denbighshire election of 1741, see NLW, Chirk Castle MS 39C and MS F4724–5.
[99] Martin Davis, 'Hanes Cymdeithasol Sir Feirionnydd 1750–1859' (unpubl. University of Wales MA thesis, 1988), p. 258.

Thomas Windsor, would be fully in tune with the message of the old Welsh proverb 'Trech Gwlad nag Arglwydd' (A Country is mightier than a Lord).[100]

There were also other groups, usually representing minority interests, who were adept at circumventing the growing prevalence of English in official political circles. The Welsh language proved a positive asset to Catholic recusants whose deep-rooted resistance to the government and religion of the day made them marked men. For priests, fugitives, spies and sympathisers, Welsh was a vehicle for secrecy. Having lost his native tongue during his sojourn in Elizabethan London, the Abergavenny-born Catholic priest, Father Augustine Baker, relearnt Welsh 'and used to writ downe in it such as he would not have every one, that should looke on his papers, understand'.[101] The recusant spy, Hugh Owen of Plas Du, Llanarmon – a man of considerable political acumen and bravery – corresponded with fellow Welsh conspirators in his native tongue in order to mystify their enemies on the Continent.[102] Similarly, Hugh Owen of Gwenynog, Anglesey, a devout Catholic who could write in French, Spanish, Dutch and Italian, wrote in Welsh whenever pressing matters relating to the cause of the Counter-Reformation called for the attention of his countrymen.[103]

Robust and stubborn plebeians, located on the fringes of political life, evidently used Welsh as a political vehicle during periods of revolutionary upheaval. Some of these freeborn Welshmen became acutely aware of the symbolic significance of their native tongue in an age of rhetoric, hyperbole and scepticism. In 1647 the self-styled prophet Arise Evans of Llangelynnin, Merioneth, who plagued the great and the godly in strife-torn London, baffled Newgate gaolers by discussing radical politics and millennial doctrines (over English beer!) in Welsh with his fellow countryman, Christopher Love of Cardiff.[104] When a bailiff's son addressed the Quaker George Fox in Hebrew in Scarborough prison, he responded in Welsh and 'bid him fear God'.[105] Not least among the curious traits of Quakers was a capacity to cope with linguistic challenges by claiming an unusually wide verbal repertoire, even to the extent of surmounting the barrier of natural languages. By flouting age-old conventions and violating codes of deference, Quakers invited attention

---

[100] NLW, Tredegar Park MSS 72/83, 72/84.
[101] J. McCann and H. Connolly (eds.), *Memorials of Father Augustine Baker* (Catholic Record Society, vol. XXXIII, London, 1933), p. 58.
[102] J. Henry Jones, 'John Owen, *Cambro-Britannus*', *THSC* (1940), 139.
[103] Emyr Gwynne Jones, 'Hugh Owen of Gwenynog', *TAAS* (1938), 42–9.
[104] Arise Evans, *An Eccho to the Voice from Heaven* (London, 1652), p. 65.
[105] John L. Nickalls (ed.), *The Journal of George Fox* (Cambridge, 1952), p. 505.

and opprobrium. Their plain language, and especially their use of the personal pronoun of address ('ti', 'tithe'; 'thee', 'thou'), offered a linguistic as well as a religio-political challenge to authority. They revelled in their self-appointed roles as speakers of 'pure' language and celebrated the moral and symbolic significance of silence.[106] 'Plain' or 'pure' language, couched in Welsh, served as an insulating device which enabled Quakers to survive in a hostile environment. No better example could be cited of the manner in which Quakers could marry an appeal to precedent and language than the occasion when Richard Davies of Cloddiau Cochion met the Welsh-born Sir Leoline Jenkins, Secretary of State, in his chambers at Whitehall. Jenkins sought to discomfit the Quaker by challenging him to provide the Welsh word for Quaker. Davies swiftly rejoined: '*Crynwr, Crynwyr*, it being the Singular and Plural Number', before adding crushingly, 'I am sorry that one of the Stock of the Ancient Britains, who first received the Christian Faith in England, should be against those who have received the true Christian Faith in this Day.'[107]

The intellectual ferment inspired by the American and French Revolutions in the late eighteenth century also produced hard-hitting radical spokesmen who viewed the Welsh language as a political tool. During William Pitt's notorious 'Reign of Terror' in the 1790s, leading Welsh radicals like Thomas Evans (Tomos Glyn Cothi) and Iolo Morganwg used coded messages in Welsh in order to shield themselves from the wrath of the authorities.[108] Evans and his friends would often toast Iolo's name in Welsh and drink pure 'republican' water. In the heart of rural Montgomeryshire, William Jones of Llangadfan – 'The Welsh Voltaire' – proclaimed his support for *sans-culottes*, Jacobins and followers of Tom Paine so loudly that local postmasters were instructed to intercept and open letters sent to and from his home at Dolhywel. Undeterred, Jones continued to correspond with fellow radicals in Welsh and devised a peculiar form of stenography which bewildered government spies. 'I have a method', he cried gleefully, 'of writing letters which no human being can decipher without a key.'[109]

Nor should it be forgotten that common people were capable of making political statements concerning language. Some of them clearly

---

[106] Richard Bauman, *Let your Words be Few. Symbolism of speaking and silence among seventeenth-century Quakers* (Cambridge, 1983), p. 27; Geraint H. Jenkins, *Protestant Dissenters in Wales 1639–1689* (Cardiff, 1992), p. 35.

[107] Richard Davies, *An Account of the Convincement, Exercises, Services, and Travels of ... Richard Davies* (London, 1710), pp. 220–2.

[108] NLW MS 21281E, ff. 167, 172, 174. See also Olivia Smith, *The Politics of Language 1791–1819* (Oxford, 1986).

[109] NLW MS 1806E, ff. 782, 786; Geraint H. Jenkins, '"A Rank Republican [and] a Leveller": William Jones, Llangadfan', *WHR*, 17, no. 3 (1995), 372–4.

nursed a deep-seated animus against the English language. The *Morris Letters* refer to 'iaith plant Alis y biswail' (the language of Alice the dung)[110] and there were poets like Huw Jones of Llangwm who had 'a natural aversion to Saxons and Normans and to all languages but his own'.[111] It was not uncommon for peasants to be sullen, truculent or even abusive towards inquisitive or overbearing travellers and tourists. 'Dim Saissonick', 'Dim Sassenach', 'Dim Sarsenic' were the misspelt and laconic replies recorded in the journals of flummoxed and exasperated strangers.[112] 'Hang me!' cried Old Townley, a character in a farce penned by Thomas Dibdin, 'if I ask but a simple question, the answer is "Dim Saesneg".'[113] Artful countrymen were not above using their monoglottism to mystify heavy-handed tax collectors or brusque stewards and agents. Some parents taught their children the phrase 'Give me a penny' and urged them to put it to good use whenever travellers pressed them for information.[114] In a variety of ways, therefore, the Welsh language was not only an insulating medium but also a means of expressing the undercurrent of popular hostility towards outsiders as well as to the notion that only the swift and permanent dissemination of the English language would create 'amicable Concord and Unity' between Welsh speakers and English speakers.[115]

The second domain which became something of a citadel for English speaking was the legal structure. The Act of Union of 1536 brought the whole of Wales – both Principality and March – under a single uniform law which was enforced in the courts through the medium of the English language. From 1543 to 1732 the official language for the records of the courts was Latin, although English was used during the Commonwealth period 1651–60 and also from 1733 onwards.[116] In practice, however, the administration of the law in Wales could never have operated effectively without the informal and frequent use of the Welsh language in the courts. It proved impossible to outlaw the use of the native tongue within the courts, both great and small.[117] Monoglot Welsh-speaking defendants

---

[110] *ML*, II, p. 390; *ALM*, II, p. 643.
[111] *ALM*, II, p. 534.
[112] Richards, *Wallography*, p. 123; Hucks, *A Pedestrian Tour*, p. 108; Arthur Aikin, *Journal of a Tour through North Wales* (London, 1797), p. ix; Tegwyn Jones, 'A Walk through Glamorgan, 1819', *GH*, XI (1975), 116; W. H. Rees, 'Vicissitudes', pp. 313–14.
[113] Hughes, *Wales and the Welsh*, p. 106.
[114] Wigstead, *Remarks on a Tour*, p. 17.
[115] Bowen, *Statutes*, p. 76.
[116] J. A. Andrews and L. G. Henshaw, *The Welsh Language in the Courts* (Aberystwyth, 1984), p. 3; John Rowlands et al. (eds.), *Welsh Family History. A Guide to Research* (Association of Family History Societies of Wales, 1993), p. 191.
[117] W. Ogwen Williams (ed.), *Calendar of the Caernarvonshire Quarter Sessions Records, vol. 1, 1541–1558* (Caerns. Hist. Soc., 1956), p. xx.

and witnesses were only able to give evidence in their mother tongue, and some justices and lawyers presumably resorted to Welsh on occasions in order to emphasize crucial points while addressing Welsh-speaking juries. In spite of these concessions, however, Welsh-speaking litigants, witnesses and jurors were evidently placed under a grave disadvantage. It is likely that fewer than ten of the 217 judges appointed to serve on the Court of Great Sessions between 1543 and 1830 were able to speak or understand Welsh.[118] Travellers from England noted how Assize judges embarked on elegant perorations to members of the jury, none of whom understood a single syllable but still huddled together dutifully 'to determine a matter of which they were totally ignorant'.[119] Just as the use of Latin and Norman-French proved unintelligible to the layman in England and antagonized seventeenth-century Levellers,[120] so did the use of English in the courts of Wales mystify, bewilder and intimidate Welsh speakers. It was common for poets to animadvert on the treachery and corruption of attorneys who deliberately confused or hoodwinked monoglot Welsh defendants and witnesses,[121] baffling them with impenetrable procedural jargon like 'a writ of error', 'judgement by Default', 'a non process', 'a bail bond', 'bills of cost' and 'the hallowed touch of a Bum-Bailiff'.[122]

On the whole, the standard of translations undertaken in the courts was probably lamentable. Translators received no professional training and were so inadequately paid that they were vulnerable to bribery and corruption. One suspects that most of them were incompetent rather than venal, and only the harshest historians would blame them for failing unerringly to convey the exact meaning of oral testimony delivered by nervous or tongue-tied witnesses. But incompetence inevitably led to errors and misunderstandings which, in turn, generated miscarriages of justice. In 1575, Sir William Gerard, a strong believer in effective administration, noted that palpable injustices occurred regularly in the

---

[118] Dewi Watkin Powell, 'Y Llysoedd, yr Awdurdodau a'r Gymraeg: Y Ddeddf Uno a Deddf yr Iaith Gymraeg' in T. M. Charles-Edwards, Morfydd E. Owen and D. B. Walters (eds.), *Lawyers and Laymen* (Cardiff, 1986), p. 291; Hywel Moseley, 'Gweinyddiad y Gyfraith yng Nghymru', *THSC* (1972–3), 17. For an excellent introduction to the records of the Courts of Great Sessions, see Glyn Parry, *A Guide to the Records of Great Sessions in Wales* (Aberystwyth, 1995).

[119] Cradock, *Letters from Snowdon*, pp. 121–3.

[120] H. N. Brailsford, *The Levellers and the English Revolution* (London, 1961), pp. 121–3, 650–1.

[121] For some examples, see Dafydd Huw Evans, 'Cywydd i ddangos mai uffern yw Llundain' in J. E. Caerwyn Williams (ed.), *Ysgrifau Beirniadol XIV* (Dinbych, 1988), pp. 148–9; Dafydd Manuel, *Dwy o Gerddi Difrifol* [n.d.]; Anon., *Pedwar o Gywyddeu* (Bala, 1761), pp. 4–8.

[122] Thomas Roberts, *Cwyn yn erbyn Gorthrymder* (Llundain, 1798), pp. 17–18; Malkin, *The Scenery*, p. 324.

Courts of Great Sessions: 'many times the Evidence is tolde accordynge to the mind of the interpreter whereby the Evidence is expounded contrarie to that which is said by the Examynate and so the Judge gyveth a wronge charge'.[123] At the end of the eighteenth century, the prickly radical John Jones (Jac Glan-y-gors) memorably recounted the manner in which William Evans, an aged and forgetful translator at Caernarfon Assizes, occasioned mystification and mirth in equal proportions when he offered 'the hilt of a thief' as a translation of 'carn lleidr' (an arch-thief), thereby prompting Thomas Roberts, Llwyn'rhudol, to remark: 'that which smelleth sweet in the one tongue stinketh when it is translated literally into another'.[124]

Since common people were rarely able to register their views about the legal system, it is difficult to judge how far it was viewed as unjust, alien and corrupt. Some brave defendants were moved to challenge the meaning of words, partly in order to save their own skins but also to expose the incompetence and deceit which characterized the proceedings of the civil and ecclesiastical courts. Monoglottism could be employed to evade or soften the rigours of the law. At the Great Sessions in Haverfordwest in 1558 the monoglot Welsh speaker Gruffith Adam vigorously denied having uttered certain scandalous English words against John Jankyn Gwyn on the grounds that Welsh was his sole language since birth.[125] At Brecon in 1727 it was mischievously claimed that since an allegation of defamation in Welsh centred on the use of the words 'whôr, whôr, yr whŵr', rather than the pertinent Welsh word 'putain', there was no case to answer.[126] It is surely significant that Welsh Quaker emigrants who settled in Pennsylvania in the 1680s fully expected that civil and legal matters within the so-called Welsh Tract would be determined by officers and jurors 'of our language'.[127] When Jenkyn Morgan, a Congregationalist minister at Rhos-meirch, Anglesey, was accused of keeping an unlicensed school, he doggedly refused to defend himself in the English language – a symbolic gesture redolent of the tactics employed by seventeenth-century Levellers against the use of 'Norman French' in English courts.[128]

In matters relating to probate, too, there were heartening signs by the eighteenth century that Welsh was being more widely used in the making

---

[123] Powell, 'Y Llysoedd', p. 293.
[124] O. M. Edwards (ed.), *Gwaith Glan y Gors* (Llanuwchllyn, 1905), pp. 79–81; Roberts, *Cwyn yn erbyn Gorthrymder*, p. 20.
[125] NLW, Great Sessions 13/27/1; Richard Suggett, 'Slander in Early-Modern Wales', *BBCS*, XXXIX (1992), 123–4.
[126] NLW, SD/CCB/58, 80.
[127] Browning, *Welsh Settlement*, p. 19.
[128] NLW, BCC/G/29.

of wills. Until the end of the seventeenth century, the number of wills written in Welsh was tiny. In his study of probate records in Caernarfonshire from 1630 to 1690, Gareth H. Williams read over a thousand wills and inventories, but discovered only four (two wills and two inventories) which contained material in Welsh.[129] Nuncupative (or oral) wills were invariably couched in Welsh but were recorded in English, normally by the local clergyman, in accordance with the demands of the law. The general practice was for the recorder to translate the English document into Welsh at the bedside of the terminally ill testator in order to ensure that the content was correct. In 1614, for instance, Ieuan David Lloyd Oliver, curate of Gwnnws in Cardiganshire, recorded the oral testimony of Rees Thomas 'and the next day he came again to the said testator and did repeat and interprete in the Welshe tounge the will and testament uppon Recorde remayninge'.[130] From the mid-eighteenth century onwards, however, the number of wills written in Welsh either by yeomen, corvisors, joiners, labourers and widows or on their behalf by local clergymen increased appreciably in the dioceses of Bangor and St Asaph.[131] This development, probably associated with higher levels of literacy and an enhanced sense of Welshness, emboldened Welsh speakers to defy the letter of the law.

When writers like Morgan Llwyd, Ellis Wynne, Twm o'r Nant and a host of almanackers, ballad-mongers and scribblers painted unflattering portraits of pettifogging lawyers 'smiling at one another forty times', the animus against court officials was at least partly coloured by their manifest contempt for the Welsh language.[132] People must have automatically associated the legal system with the English tongue. It did not pass unnoticed that whenever judges, lawyers and other 'persons of Distinction' attending legal circuits frequented places of worship, English-

[129] Gareth H. Williams, 'A Study of Caernarfonshire Probate Records 1630–1690' (unpubl. University of Wales MA thesis, 1972), pp. 445–8.

[130] NLW, Archdeaconry of Cardigan P.R.1614. We owe this reference to Mr Gerald Morgan.

[131] *Bangor Probate Index 1750–1858* (NLW, 1992), Welsh Documents, pp. 1–25; *St Asaph Probate Index 1750–1858* (NLW, 1993), Probate Records (Welsh), pp. 1–5. See also Gerald Morgan, 'Ewyllysiau Cymraeg 1539–1858' in Geraint H. Jenkins (ed.), *Cof Cenedl XII* (Llandysul, 1997), pp. 33–67. It is worth noting, too, that the number of Welsh *englynion* carved on gravestones begin to multiply in the second half of the eighteenth century. See J. Elwyn Hughes, *Englynion Beddau Dyffryn Ogwen* (Llandysul, 1979); G. T. Roberts, *Llais y Meini* (Caernarfon, 1979); Gomer M. Roberts, *Detholiad o Englynion y Beddau* (Abertawe, 1980); Gwilym G. Jones, *Meini sy'n Llefaru* (Y Bala, 1980); M. Euronwy James, *Englynion Beddau Ceredigion* (Llandysul, 1983).

[132] NLW Brogyntyn MS 131; T. E. Ellis (ed.), *Gweithiau Morgan Llwyd o Wynedd*, I (Bangor, 1899), pp. 236–7; Ellis Wynne, *Gweledigaetheu y Bardd Cwsc* (Llundain, 1703), pp. 20, 62, 121; Isaac Foulkes (ed.), *Detholion o Weithiau Thomas Edwards (Twm o'r Nant)* (Liverpool, 1861), pp. 62, 103.

medium services were arranged for their benefit by pliant clerics.[133] In 1745 Griffith Jones, Llanddowror, encountered a churchwarden on his way to the triennial visitation court of the bishop of Llandaff to testify to the virtuous character of his clergyman. The churchwarden privately admitted to Jones that the presentment was untruthful and that the clergyman's character was far from unspotted. But since he would be obliged to swear an oath in English (a language foreign to him) and in view of the fact that the clergyman was 'a Bottle-Companion to the top Gentry' and vengeful by nature, he preferred to keep silent.[134] All in all, if there was such a person as the freeborn Englishman in the early modern period, he most certainly possessed greater rights in the eyes of the law than the Welsh-speaking Welshman. 'There never will be truth where there are many poets', wrote Ellis Wynne, 'nor justice where there are many lawyers.' ('Ni cheir byth Wir lle bo llawer o Feirdd, na Thegwch lle bo llawer o Gyfreithwyr.')[135] By the end of the eighteenth century attitudes towards the legal system and its practitioners had hardened considerably and Iolo Morganwg summed up the general feeling of hostility:

> Oh! spare us a while from the vultures of Law,
> That feed on man's blood with insatiable maw,
> Till to some foreign desart [*sic*] we safely withdraw
> Spare us good Lord.[136]

We turn now to the language of trade, commerce and economic life in general. Economic changes in the post-Union period meant that the English language became more accessible, more attractive and better-known. It is significant that records of estate administration, including rentals, surveys, leases, wills, marriage settlements, tax returns, manorial records, household account books, commonplace books and bills of sale were almost invariably written in English. So, too, were parochial records like parish registers (which were kept either in Latin or English between 1538 and 1733 and in English thereafter),[137] vestry minutes, rate assessments, trade and poor apprenticeships, taxation records and bonds of indemnity. Only a handful of manuscripts couched in Welsh – a Crown rental survey, some manorial records, abstracts of rents, a tax return,

---

[133] For some examples, see NLW, Church in Wales Records, SA/QA/6; SA/QA/8; SA/RD/26; Ll/QA/10; SA/RD/21; SA/RD/23.
[134] Griffith Jones, *A Letter to a Clergyman* (London, 1745), pp. 51–2.
[135] Wynne, *Gweledigaetheu*, p. 63.
[136] NLW MS 21401E, f. 3.
[137] R. W. McDonald, 'The Parish Registers of Wales', *NLWJ*, XIX, no. 4 (1976), 399–429.

accounts of wages paid to farm-servants, tithe charges, bills, a few deeds, churchwardens' returns, documents concerning the payment of ship money – have survived, and it is clear that for official purposes English was the language of trade and commerce.[138] Closer and more durable social and economic ties with England and the replacement of customary law by English law had important implications for Welsh words and phrases relating to agricultural tenure and property. Greater mobility also directly affected the language of trade. As opportunities for internal and cross-border trade expanded in order to meet the needs of the growing population, English became more widely mastered by middling groups such as merchants, drovers and hosiers as well as by the gentry.

The sociocultural importance of drovers merits special attention. Resourceful and hard-headed cattle dealers and drovers were responsible for driving substantial herds of cattle, sheep and pigs along roads, trackways and moorland to fattening pastures in the English Midlands and to the principal fairs and markets of London. In order to conduct their business transactions efficiently and bargain fluently with their streetwise and sometimes unscrupulous counterparts in England, Welsh drovers needed to speak English reasonably well. Edward Morris of Perthillwydion, who died in Essex in 1689, penned stanzas in English and Dafydd Jones of Caeo (d.1777) was sufficiently well-versed in English to translate the hymns of Isaac Watts into Welsh.[139] Most drovers returned to Wales armed not only with golden sovereigns for penurious farmers but also a rich variety of catchy songs and ballads acquired in inns and taverns in England. Alehouses, inns and taverns were important foci for the activities of drovers and merchants on both sides of the border and by

---

[138] Among the miscellaneous manuscript material couched in Welsh are the following. There is a Crown rental survey, compiled in 1549, relating to groups of *gwelyau* in Anglesey: UWBL, Baron Hill MS 1436. See T. Jones Pierce, 'An Anglesey Crown Rental of the Sixteenth Century', *BBCS*, X, part 2 (1940), 156–76. A Welsh contract and accounts form part of rent rolls in UWBL, Penrhyn Estate, uncatalogued rentals, May 1595 and 1614. There is an early-sixteenth-century rental in NLW, Edwinsford 3228, and an early-seventeenth-century example in R. J. Thomas, 'Rhòl Rent Meisgyn a Chlwn', *NLWJ*, XVII, no. 3 (1972), 249–68. Rent rolls of Plas-y-ward in 1575–6 were written in Welsh by the poet Simwnt Fychan. E. D. Jones, 'Simwnt Fychan a Theulu Plas y Ward', *BBCS*, VII, part 3 (1934), 141–2. For account books recording miscellaneous payments and agricultural produce, see NLW MSS 2770A, 4471A, 4533B, and Hugh Owen, 'The Diary of Bulkeley of Dronwy, Anglesey, 1630–1636', *TAAS* (1937), 26–172. For bills, see NLW, W. Evans George and Son MSS 3684, 3737. For deeds, see E. D. Jones, 'Pethau nas Cyhoeddwyd', *NLWJ*, III, nos. 1 and 2 (1943), 23–8. For churchwardens' returns, see UWBL Bangor MS 8861–2 (for Llangefni 1771 and 1774) and NLW MS 3128B (for Llanfair-iuxta-Harlech in 1748).

[139] NLW MS 37B, f. 119; Gwenllian Jones, 'Bywyd a Gwaith Edward Morris, Perthi Llwydion' (unpubl. University of Wales MA thesis, 1941), p. 482; Gomer M. Roberts, *Dafydd Jones o Gaeo* (Aberystwyth, 1948), pp. 39–67; Richard Colyer, *The Welsh Cattle Drovers* (Cardiff, 1976), p. 46.

serving in Wales as centres for gossip, anecdotes and songs they enabled English words and phrases to enter common discourse. Labourers who worked at harvest time in English counties, weeders who spent periods of time in London, as well as travelling pedlars, hawkers and colporteurs, brought growing numbers of Welsh-speaking people into contact with English words, idioms and manners.

Welsh towns, especially those blessed with administrative facilities, good communications and lively trade, were the focus for buying and selling. In old borough towns like Beaumaris, Caernarfon and Pembroke, the colonizing dominance of English prevailed among people of taste and discernment. Watering places, tourist resorts, commercial entrepôts and administrative centres were more likely than most other communities to boast bilingual or English-only speakers, and many of them radiated 'to their surrounding rural areas Anglicising influences in ever-widening circles'.[140] 'There is never a market towne in Wales', wrote John Penry with unblushing exaggeration in 1587, 'where English is not as rife as Welsh.'[141] Regular social and economic intercourse with thriving border towns exposed Welsh farmers to English influences. Shrewsbury was a principal magnet for cloth traders and farmers in mid-Wales,[142] and prosperous fairs and markets held at Oswestry and Ludlow tempted Welsh speakers to settle in the vicinity. Wrexham offers a striking example of a town which lost its Welshness as its trading capacity increased. Norden's survey of the town in 1620 reveals that the bulk of the inhabitants were Welsh and that every place (save one field) bore a Welsh or semi-Welsh name. Following the upheavals of the civil war and the Interregnum, however, things changed rapidly. In the wake of brisk commercial activity, English surnames like Baker, Dutton, Platt, and Weld replaced the traditional Welsh patronymics in the parish registers of the town, and street names (Church, Charles, Chester, Lambpit and Mount) were posted in English.[143] By the late Stuart period Wrexham was the principal urban centre in north Wales. Noted for its 'Politeness, Taste, and Hospitality', it became by 1770, at least in the eyes of Joseph Cradock, a town 'perfectly

---

[140] W. H. Rees, 'Vicissitudes', p. 80. See Harold Carter, *The Towns of Wales* (Cardiff, 1965), chapter 3; Matthew Griffiths, '"Very Wealthy by Merchandise"? Urban Fortunes' in J. Gwynfor Jones (ed.), *Class, Community and Culture in Tudor Wales* (Cardiff, 1989), pp. 197–235.

[141] John Penry, *A Treatise containing the Aeqvity of an Humble Supplication* (Oxford, 1587), p. 52.

[142] Percy Enderbie, *Cambria Triumphans* (London, 1661), p. 193; Daniel Defoe, *A Tour through the whole island of Great Britain*, ed. G. D. H. Cole and D. C. Browning (2 vols., London, 1962), I, pp. 76–7.

[143] A. N. Palmer, *History of the Town of Wrexham* (Wrexham, 1893), p. 6; A. H. Dodd, *A History of Wrexham* (Wrexham, 1957), pp. 45–66.

Englished'.[144] Elsewhere on the border, towns like Knighton and Presteigne in Radnorshire looked eastwards for their prosperity. Even in south-west Wales, where counties like Cardiganshire and Carmarthenshire were reckoned to be 'entirely Welch',[145] market and administrative centres such as Carmarthen, Cardigan, Llandeilo and Aberystwyth were enclaves of bilingualism, especially among trading groups where fluency in English was an economic asset of the highest importance.

Nevertheless, it is probable that many towns which had been English enclaves were becoming more Welsh in the early modern period. In late-sixteenth-century Glamorgan, it was claimed that English speakers 'inhabite either the Townes, or in the lowe Country neere the Sea Side',[146] but Cowbridge and Cardiff were becoming essentially bilingual towns and the English dialect of the Vale was disappearing. Further east, at Abergavenny in Monmouthshire, 'the main or principall language was the Welsh or Brittish tongue', a fact which prompted some of its prominent citizens to dispatch their sons to London to improve their command of the English language.[147] Hugh Thomas, the late-seventeenth-century historian of Brecon, perceived the 'wonderful great Scouts and Judgements of God' in the undoing of the English character of the town. By around 1700 the 'language of this place is Generally Welsh' and 'that as good as most in Wales'. Families of 'English Names and Descent' had 'dwindled away to nothing', while the names of the 'best livers' in the town were for the most part Welsh.[148]

Before the eighteenth century the flow of migrants from England into Wales was relatively small and insignificant. Individuals or migrant families were easily absorbed, though local resentments did surface whenever the influx of settlers threatened to dislocate traditional patterns of work, social relationships and general harmony. English families sometimes acquired farms in Wales, particularly in the eastern counties, and disputes involving them gave rise to overt racism. Following a fatal assault in 1592 on Humphrey Curton, an English settler in Guilsfield, Montgomeryshire, Ieuan ap David was said to have remarked with a click of his fingers: 'What nedes all this adooe, hit ys but on Englyshe man out of the waye and yf he do dye I do not waye hit of a fyllip.'[149] Prior to assaulting an English settler in an adjoining parish, a Welshman was alleged to have

---

[144] Palmer, *Wrexham*, p. 274n.; Cradock, *Letters from Snowdon*, p. 106.
[145] Mary Clement (ed.), *Correspondence and Minutes of the S.P.C.K. Relating to Wales 1699–1740* (Cardiff, 1952), p. 82.
[146] Rice Merrick, *A Booke of Glamorganshires Antiquities*, ed. J. A. Corbett (London, 1887), p. 42.
[147] G. Dyfnallt Owen, *Elizabethan Wales* (Cardiff, 1964), p. 93.
[148] *Hugh Thomas' Essay Towards the History of Brecknockshire 1698* (Brecon, 1967), pp. 21, 27.
[149] NLW, Great Sessions 4/135/1/15.

said: 'It is an ill time . . . when John Jervis an English man master or controls us in Castell [Caereinion].'[150]

Much depended on how many migrant workers arrived and where they settled. In traditional Welsh-speaking communities they could seldom hope to remain wholly insulated from their neighbours. Even in the mid-eighteenth century the Cornish miners who inhabited the Ogwen Valley and Aberglaslyn, and the Irish and Scottish miners who settled at Drws-y-coed, were relatively easily absorbed and in many cases Cymricized.[151] But the story was rather different in the border counties. Substantial numbers of coal miners and lead workers settled in the lowland regions of east Denbighshire and east Flintshire in the early eighteenth century and formed English-speaking 'colonies'. Robert Roberts, vicar of Chirk, published bilingual religious tracts designed for 'a People of Two different Nations under Heaven. Parthians and Medes',[152] and as Welsh began to retreat westwards attitudes towards English-speaking workers hired on relatively short-term contracts began to harden. When managers (bearing names like Moore, Paynter, Roose and Shelton) and skilled labour from Cornwall, Derbyshire and Northumberland were imported into the lead industry in Montgomeryshire, the rural dean of Pool noted in 1710 that the lead miners who had settled in the parish of Llangynog were 'all English and the parish all Welsh'.[153] Although the local curate was anxious to oblige the newcomers by arranging alternate Welsh and English services, once the practice had been established it proved difficult to dislodge even after the contingent of lead miners had departed. Similar sociolinguistic tensions surfaced in the Neath area when, at the turn of the seventeenth century, Sir Humphrey Mackworth employed handpicked, skilled miners from Cornwall, Derbyshire and Shropshire whose language and customs prompted local inhabitants to dub them 'the Men of Mera'.[154] The Iron Kings in the second half of the eighteenth century brooked no opposition to their political and linguistic imperialism.[155] At Merthyr Tydfil, the cradle of the industrial revolution and, by 1801, the

[150] NLW, Great Sessions 4/140/2/38. See also Geraint H. Jenkins, *Hanes Cymru yn y Cyfnod Modern Cynnar 1530–1760* (Caerdydd, 1983), pp. 5–6.
[151] T. M. Bassett and B. L. Davies (eds.), *Atlas of Caernarvonshire* (Gwynedd Rural Council, 1977), p. 151.
[152] Robert Roberts, *A Sacrament Catechism. Sacrament Gatechism* (no imprint, 1720); idem, *A Du-Glott-Exposition of the Creed* (Shrewsbury, 1730).
[153] NLW, SA/RD/5; SA/RD/26; W. J. Lewis, *Lead Mining in Wales* (Cardiff, 1967), p. 262.
[154] R. M. Thomas, 'A Linguistic Geography of Carmarthenshire, Glamorgan and Pembrokeshire from 1750 to the present day' (unpubl. University of Wales MA thesis, 1967), p. 8.
[155] Chris Evans, '*The Labyrinth of Flames*'. *Work and Social Conflict in Early Industrial Merthyr Tydfil* (Cardiff, 1993), chapter 9.

largest town in Wales, the erection of major iron-making furnaces and forges, and the importation of English-speaking managers and agents, led to the introduction of English prayers and sermons on alternate Sundays in the parish church.[156] In the world of commerce, English had unquestionably become the language of advancement.

We must now turn to the association of the landed gentry with the Welsh language. Although the traditional rulers of Welsh society constituted only a small percentage of the total population, they exercised an enormous influence in their respective counties. Since Wales could not boast a university or a college, a court, a museum, an academy, a major library, a cultural capital like Dublin or Edinburgh, or any other similar talismans of national identity, Welsh authors pinned their hopes on the patronage of the traditional landowning families. Some of the more optimistic writers believed that it might be possible to enlist the support of the Crown as a champion of the Welsh language. Robert Holland, who translated James I's *Basilikon Doron* (1604), believed that the newly enthroned Scottish king 'doth allow & like the language' and that his son Henry, Prince of Wales, should resolve to acquire 'a taste of the tongue' in order to enable him to establish a rapport with the Welsh people.[157] In the preface to his famous dictionary in 1632, Dr John Davies urged the two-year-old Charles, Prince of Wales and heir to King Charles I, to learn 'the antient Language of this Island',[158] and a century later Griffith Owens of Pwllheli believed that the Welsh language wanted for nothing 'to make it famous save a King to speak it'.[159] These yearnings were at best over-optimistic and at worst thoroughly impractical. Few Tudor and Stuart monarchs ventured into Wales for any length of time and successive Princes and Princesses of Wales have no real claims on the attention of posterity.

As the principal local beneficiaries of the Union legislation, the Welsh gentry were best placed to take full advantage of the material rewards which public office and enhanced social standing entailed. Although it is undoubtedly true that the majority of the Welsh gentry spoke English long before the 1536 act reached the statute book, the union legislation encouraged them to become active Anglicizing influences. In their eyes, English had become the language of advancement and enrichment. Post-Union Wales offered growing opportunities to seek fame and fortune, and

---

[156] NLW, Ll/QA/4–6. In 1804 Malkin emphasized: 'the workmen of all descriptions at these immense iron works are Welshmen. The language is almost entirely Welsh.' Malkin, *The Scenery*, p. 179.
[157] Robert Holland, *Basilikon Doron* (London, 1604), sig. (a)1v, A2v.
[158] Davies, *Antiquae*, Epistola Dedicatoria.
[159] UWBL, Bangor MS 421, f. 331.

the attractions of life beyond Offa's Dyke and especially in London encouraged many of them to jettison their native language and culture. They corresponded with one another in English, penned their diaries in English, and sent their sons to learn 'English manners' at Bedford, Eton, Westminster and Winchester, or to grammar schools in Wales where no place was given to instruction in Welsh.[160] It would be foolish, however, to believe that all Welsh landowners deserted the traditional Welsh culture by shunning poets and writers. Not all of them by any means were antipathetic to Welsh. Sir William Herbert, earl of Pembroke (d.1570), was more fluent in Welsh than English and insisted on speaking Welsh to his fellow countrymen in the Tudor court. Hailed by Dafydd Benwyn as 'the grace of his age, and the terror of the Saxons' ('Y by ras oeswr, a bw ar Saysonn'), he epitomized those whom Siôn Dafydd Rhys called 'Ieithymgeleddwyr' (guardians of the language).[161] Sir Edward Stradling of St Donat's (d.1609) was an extraordinarily bountiful 'Golden Knight' ('Marchog Euraid') who spoke Welsh with his wife Agnes, welcomed poets, heralds and copyists to his splendid library, and bore the printing and publishing costs of Siôn Dafydd Rhys's Welsh grammar in order to advance the cause and prestige of 'the British tongue'.[162] In Elizabethan Wales it was not unusual for Welsh gentlemen to invite poets to compose poems in honour of their families, and also to compose fairly modest *cywyddau* and *englynion* themselves.[163] Hospitality was offered to roving bards, scholars and minstrels, and in Merioneth, where the tradition of supporting poets persisted longest, as many as twenty gentry homes continued to welcome bards and minstrels until the end of the eighteenth century.[164] Landowners were obliged to retain some Welsh in order to communicate effectively with tenants, servants and other dependants. When Lord Herbert of Chirbury was nine (in 1591), he was despatched by his parents to Plas-y-ward in Denbighshire to learn Welsh so that he could 'treat with those of my friends & tenants who understood no other language'.[165] In the late Stuart period Sir Robert Owen of Porkington, near Oswestry, still spoke Welsh fluently and even the Glamorgan gentry

---

[160] R. Brinley Jones, '*Certain Scholars of Wales*'. *The Welsh Experience in Education* (Llanwrda, 1986), p. 51.
[161] Michael P. Siddons, *The Development of Welsh Heraldry* (3 vols., Aberystwyth, 1991–3), I, p. 170; Henry Lewis (ed.), *Hen Gyflwyniadau* (Caerdydd, 1948), p. 3.
[162] Ceri W. Lewis, 'Syr Edward Stradling (1529–1609), Y "Marchog Disgleirlathr" o Sain Dunwyd' in J. E. Caerwyn Williams (ed.), *Ysgrifau Beirniadol XIX* (Dinbych, 1993), pp. 139–207; Nesta Lloyd (ed.), *Blodeugerdd Barddas o'r Ail Ganrif ar Bymtheg (Cyfrol 1)* (Cyhoeddiadau Barddas, 1993), pp. 38–41.
[163] Jones, *Class, Community and Culture*, p. 69.
[164] Davis, 'Hanes Cymdeithasol Sir Feirionnydd', pp. 181–2.
[165] C. H. Herford (ed.), *The Autobiography of Edward Lord Herbert of Cherbury* (Gregynog Press, 1928), p. 13.

were able to exchange Welsh pleasantries with their tenants in the early eighteenth century.[166]

In general, however, it is true to say that by the early Stuart period the Welsh gentry were far less zealous in defence of their mother tongue than their forebears had been. The life and language of England offered so many new and exciting avenues of advancement that their lives began to change swiftly. The career, lifestyle and interests of the Wynn family of Gwydir epitomize the dual identities which characterized the lives of gentry families in post-Union Wales. Essentially a home-loving man, Sir John Wynn (d.1627) took pride in his reputation as 'chief master of the county' ('pen meistr y sir') and as a patron of bards and minstrels, but his son Sir Richard Wynn (d.1649) was so seduced by the glitter of London that Welsh poets could not find it in their hearts to praise him. His wife, Ann Darcy, showed no interest in the Welsh language and she and her husband aspired to 'mirror the splendours of England' in their sociocultural life.[167] By the eve of the civil wars, the quality of bardic verse had declined alarmingly, the *cwrs clera* (the bardic circuit) was much more circumscribed, and the increasingly Anglicized gentry no longer deemed themselves the privileged custodians of Welsh culture.[168] Poets became insecure and pessimistic as the *awdl* and *cywydd* lost their appeal. In lamenting the general loss of Welshmen in gentry circles, Gruffudd Phylip (d.1666) cried: 'Mae'n rhoddion mawrion a'n maeth?' (Where are our bounteous gifts and nourishment?)[169]

Worse was to follow. From the Restoration onwards convulsive socio-economic changes occurred which had profound implications for the Welsh language and its culture. Wholesale changes in the disposition of landed property and the structural composition of the gentry led to the demise of the small landowner, and, as a result, community structures were seriously undermined. By the mid-eighteenth century the fulcrum of economic power had shifted decisively in favour of a small ruling clique of great estate owners sometimes referred to by contemporaries as the Great Leviathans.[170] The rise of powerful, absentee landowners, akin in some ways to the English and Scottish 'planters' in Ireland, ushered in

---

[166] NLW, Brogyntyn Letters and Papers 1023; Philip Jenkins, *The Making of a Ruling Class. The Glamorgan Gentry 1640–1790* (Cambridge, 1983), p. 209.

[167] J. Gwynfor Jones, 'Priodoleddau Bonheddig yn Nheulu'r Wyniaid o Wedir: Tystiolaeth y Beirdd', *THSC* (1978), 123.

[168] Idem, *Concepts of Order and Gentility in Wales 1540–1640* (Llandysul, 1992), pp. 248–57.

[169] Glenys Davies, *Noddwyr Beirdd ym Meirion* (Dolgellau, 1974), p. 210. See also Gwyn Thomas, 'Y Portread o Uchelwr ym Marddoniaeth Gaeth yr Ail Ganrif ar Bymtheg' in J. E. Caerwyn Williams (ed.), *Ysgrifau Beirniadol VIII* (Dinbych, 1974), pp. 110–29.

[170] J. P. Jenkins, 'The Demographic Decline of the Landed Gentry in the Eighteenth Century: A South Wales Study', *WHR*, 11, no. 1 (1982), 31–49.

complex socio-economic pressures which also had cultural implications. Among the 'new' proprietors, prejudice, ill will and hostility towards the Welsh language were common. Just as minority languages like Basque, Breton and *la langue d'oc* were deemed 'barbarous', 'contemptible' and 'primitive' by the upper classes of Europe, so was the Welsh language viewed as impure, slovenly and subordinate by the 'behemoths' of Wales.[171] In their eyes, English was the language of polite speech, elegance and breeding, whereas Welsh, spoken in the main by penurious and ignorant mountain dwellers, was not in any way a suitable vehicle for political discourse, administrative matters, high culture or polite social life. 'Our Chief Men here', wrote Lewis Morris in 1754, 'have forgot their Native Tongue, to their Shame and Dishonour be it spoken.'[172] The speech of upper-class gentry, in the presence of inferiors, reflected their status and power, and as they exerted influence through hard-headed and sometimes brutal stewards (few of whom spoke Welsh) and implemented a tenurial system which deprived tenants of long-term security, rural society became markedly polarized between the English-speaking 'haves' and the Welsh-speaking 'have-nots'. By the end of the eighteenth century the growth of multiple landed estates had been achieved at the expense of much of the respect and loyalty of tenants, and part of this alienation stemmed from the inability of the gentry class to speak Welsh and their determination to exercise dominance over their inferiors through the medium of an alien tongue.[173] William Jones of Llangadfan was convinced that the gentry believed that vulgar sorts should be seen and not heard, for they could 'scarcely be distinguished from brutes . . . and our language [is] but an incoherent jargon'.[174]

Force of circumstances conspired, however, to ensure that the Welsh language achieved a dominant position in the religious life of Wales and this vital domain must now be considered. From the mid-sixteenth century onwards it became ominously clear to the small but determined band of Welsh Protestant humanists that the Reformation was unlikely to make significant progress in a land where few people spoke or understood English. The English Prayer Books, which had officially replaced Latin as the language of public worship and which had been introduced into Wales in 1549, 1552 and 1559, were probably less intelligible, and

---

[171] Thomas Jones, *The British Language in its Lustre, Or a Copious Dictionary of Welsh and English* (London, 1688), sig. A2v–A4r; Gambold, *A Welsh Grammar*, 'To the Reader'.
[172] *ALM*, I, p. 254; ibid., II, p. 440. See also Thomas Richards, *Antiquae linguae Britannicae thesaurus* (Bristol, 1753), p. xv, and John Evans, *Letters written during a Tour through North Wales* (3rd ed., London, 1804), pp. 386–7.
[173] Geraint H. Jenkins, *The Foundations of Modern Wales: Wales 1642–1780* (Oxford, 1987), p. 265.
[174] NLW MS 13221E, f. 377.

certainly less familiar, than Latin had been before the Reformation. Utilizing a foreign tongue was scarcely likely to prove the most productive means of winning the minds and hearts of a people whose popular religion was still essentially Catholic. The dilemma confronting ardent Welsh Protestants was stark. Was the reformed religion necessarily and inextricably associated with the English language or could the interests of unity and uniformity be served by granting official recognition to more than one language? Put another way, either the Welsh were to be left an easy prey to popery and its inevitable consequences or they were to be furnished with God's Word in their native tongue. In the event, representations at the highest political level by Bishop Richard Davies, Humphrey Llwyd and William Salesbury helped to undermine the school of thought which believed that introducing English Bibles and Prayer Books would have the effect of compelling the Welsh to learn English. They eloquently pleaded the case for the right of the Welsh people to have the Bible in their own tongue, and, as a result, Elizabeth's closest advisers were persuaded (largely for political reasons) that 'the true religion' of Protestantism could best be advanced in Wales through the medium of the Welsh language.[175]

The epoch-making act of 1563 declared that the Bible and Prayer Book should be translated into Welsh and thereafter used in public worship in those parishes 'where the Welsh tongue is commonly used'.[176] This legislation was a significant milestone in the history of the Welsh language because it halted – or at least delayed – the seemingly remorseless drive towards uniformity which the Henrician revolution of the 1530s had begun. By granting official recognition to Welsh in matters relating to religion, the act to some degree compensated for the lack of prestige possessed by the Welsh language in the realm of politics and administration, spheres which bore less heavily on the daily lives of the peasantry. Without this high-status domain associated with the native tongue, it is hard to see how the Welsh language could have survived, let alone prospered. From the Elizabethan period to late Victorian times the contents of the Scriptures, Prayer Book and Psalms, regularly recited with dignity and solemnity in Sunday services throughout virtually the whole of Wales, embedded themselves in the minds and hearts of churchgoers. Protestantism thus became associated with the mother tongue. Moreover, Welsh itself gained a new and lasting importance in the learned culture of Wales. In 1588 William Morgan's classic Welsh Bible rescued the

[175] Glanmor Williams, *The Welsh and their Religion* (Cardiff, 1991), pp. 37–8; idem, 'Iaith, Llên a Chrefydd yn yr Unfed Ganrif ar Bymtheg', *LlC*, 19 (1996), 29–40.
[176] See A. Owen Evans, *A Memorandum on the Legality of the Welsh Bible and the Welsh Version of the Book of Common Prayer* (Cardiff, 1925).

language from the bizarre 'Latinisms' and orthographical archaisms which had sullied William Salesbury's translation of the New Testament and Prayer Book in 1567. Although he did not reject out of hand current forms of spoken and living Welsh, Morgan relied heavily on the dignified language of the classical *cywydd*-writers who had nourished the tongue with consummate care in the traditional bardic schools. His labours not only set the highest possible literary standard for future generations of scholars and writers to emulate but also enabled Welsh-speaking clergy to conduct services in an intelligible and attractive manner.[177]

Unlike the law, there was a sense in which religion was a contested domain of language use. Since most parishioners were monoglot Welsh speakers and could not read, it was imperative that the medium of religious instruction should be in the vernacular. Attempts to use English could provoke protest and disorder. At Trefeglwys in Montgomeryshire in 1593 the English sermon of John Gwyn, a licensed public preacher, was interrupted by several parishioners who attempted to drag him from the pulpit. In the meantime, one John Jones, clerk, strode up and down reading in Welsh from a tattered book before proceeding to the chancel where he read the service in Welsh so loudly that the English sermon was inaudible.[178] Whenever vernacular Bibles and Prayer Books were unavailable, clergymen found great difficulty in placating parishioners who demanded intelligible services. Richard Pigot of Denbigh was forced to explain 'the chapters in Welsh upon the English bible' because a Welsh Bible was unavailable and as a result he was suspected of doctrinal irregularity in 1615.[179] In 1688 eighty-four parishioners of Llandaff and Whitchurch in Glamorgan pleaded for the removal of their vicar, Thomas Andrews, 'a mere stranger to the Welsh tongue' whose 'unreasonable and arbitrary appointment' was causing 'great danger and discomfort' to their souls.[180] Confrontations of this kind became even more frequent when English bishops appointed non-Welsh incumbents to key livings.

For these and many other reasons, the initial progress of the Protestant faith proved much slower than many had anticipated and it was left to English Puritanism to release powerful new spiritual energies in the so-called penurious and barren corners of the land. Like early Protestantism, however, Puritanism was equated with 'Englishness' and this is not surprising given that its Welsh origins lay in bilingual or even English border

---

[177] See Isaac Thomas, *William Morgan a'i Feibl. William Morgan and his Bible* (Cardiff, 1988) and Prys Morgan, *A Bible for Wales* (National Committee to celebrate the four hundredth anniversary of the Welsh Bible, 1988).
[178] NLW, Great Sessions 4/136/2/25–27.
[179] NLW, Great Sessions 4/16/3/6–7.
[180] Bodleian Library, Tanner MS 146, ff. 160–3.

communities like Llanfaches, Cnwclas, Olchon and Brampton Bryan.[181] It was common knowledge that English Puritans, many of whom were anxious to preach and instil the merits of the 'civilized' English world in conservative, pro-royalist rural backwaters, had little good to say of the Welsh language. While discussing the desirable, but remote, possibility of converting the Jewish people to Christianity, Richard Baxter wrote: 'Halfe their age must be spent in learning to speake: And when they have done, men will laugh at them for their ill accented broken language, as we do at foreigners and Welshmen.'[182] It was noticed that Puritanism thrived best in bilingual urban communities. At Wrexham, for instance, Morgan Llwyd's congregation, which comprised lesser gentry, merchants, tradesmen and shopkeepers, was largely English-speaking, and in many similar towns Puritanism was the preserve of the 'industrious sorts'.[183] It is significant that John Myles, a native of Herefordshire, chose to establish the first Baptist church in Wales in Anglicized Gower.[184] Puritan gospellers like Richard Blinman, William Erbery and (on many occasions) Vavasor Powell preached in English, and it has been suggested that several Welsh Puritan radicals suffered from 'an inferiority complex' concerning their cultural roots.[185] The two celebrated Joneses – Colonels John and Philip – both spoke Welsh, but seldom conversed or wrote in their native tongue. The brisk and often over-zealous efficiency of English-speaking tax-collectors and tithe-gatherers associated with the Propagation of the Gospel in Wales in the early 1650s did not endear the Puritan faith to the Welsh and it was scant wonder that Major-General Charles Fleetwood came to believe that they possessed 'envenomed hearts against the wayes of God'.[186] The English-medium schools established by the Puritan propagators and subsequently by the Welsh Trust meant that Puritan morality and self-improvement became associated in the public mind with Anglicization. The formal records of the Society of Friends, kept with loving care and attention, were couched in English and the Dissenting registers of Baptist and Congregationalist chapels were also normally written in English until the latter part of the nineteenth century.[187]

[181] Jenkins, *Protestant Dissenters*, pp. 10–11.
[182] Lamont, *Richard Baxter*, p. 56.
[183] A. H. Dodd, 'A Remonstrance from Wales, 1655', *BBCS*, XVII, part 4 (1958), 284, 286–92.
[184] D. Rhys Phillips, 'Cefndir hanes Eglwys Ilston, 1649–60', *TCHBC* (1928), 1–107; T. M. Bassett, *The Welsh Baptists* (Swansea, 1977), pp. 18–19.
[185] Stephen Roberts, 'Welsh Puritanism in the Interregnum', *HT*, March 1991, 38.
[186] Thomas Richards, *Religious Developments in Wales (1654–1662)* (London, 1923), p. 147.
[187] The records of the Society of Friends relating to Wales are in the custody of the Glamorgan Record Office and Friends' House Library, London. For Welsh Dissenting registers, see Dafydd Ifans (ed.), *Cofrestri Anghydffurfiol Cymru. Nonconformist Registers of Wales* (Aberystwyth, 1994).

It would be foolish, however, to portray Puritanism as a movement entirely hostile to Welshness and antipathetic to the Welsh language. Although Rees Prichard's *Canwyll y Cymru* (The Welshmen's Candle), a work which ran through fifty-two editions between 1658 and 1820, was riddled with more than 600 English borrowings, the songs were widely read, recited and sung.[188] Puritans like Oliver Thomas and Evan Roberts mapped out the new discipline and morality implicit in Calvinism in Welsh manuals. Most of all, Morgan Llwyd of Cynfal explored in memorable (if sometimes opaque) Welsh prose the complex and intriguing connection between the language of God and human language.[189] Llwyd was a conscious stylist who delighted in juxtaposing allegorical, mystical, spiritual and sectarian language in such an enigmatic way that he sometimes mystified even his most learned and devoted colleagues. 'Rwyti yn scrifennu yn rhŷ dywyll, ni fedr nêb mo'th ddeall' (You write too obscurely, no one can understand you),[190] he wrote of himself, and as a result his ability to convey divine truths to the common man was seriously impaired. Nonetheless, his writings revealed the capacity of the Welsh language to express ideals which lay at the heart of the Puritan and radical tradition in the years when the world was turned upside down.

The school of thought which believed that unity and uniformity could only be realized and maintained throughout the realm by compelling the use of the English language took on a new lease of life after the Restoration. There was a very real danger that Puritanism and Dissent would become tainted by their supposed 'Englishness' and these fears were strengthened by the determination of the founders of the Welsh Trust (1674–81) to ensure that teachers within charity schools concentrated on instilling the three Rs through the medium of the English language. This prompted Stephen Hughes, 'the Apostle of Carmarthenshire', to rouse his fellow Dissenters to greater zeal in the cause of Welshness. He strongly believed that the imperative of bringing scriptural knowledge to the monoglot vulgar sorts demanded the use of

---

[188] Ivor James, *The Welsh Language in the 16th and 17th Centuries* (Cardiff, 1887), p. 12; D. Simon Evans, 'Yr Hen Ficer a'i Genhadaeth (1579–1644)' in J. E. Caerwyn Williams (ed.), *Ysgrifau Beirniadol XIX* (Dinbych, 1993), pp. 212–15; Nesta Lloyd (ed.), *Cerddi'r Ficer, Detholiad o Gerddi Rhys Prichard* (Cyhoeddiadau Barddas, 1994), pp. xviii, xxi, 177–214; eadem, 'Sylwadau ar Iaith Rhai o Gerddi Rhys Prichard', *NLWJ*, XXIX, no. 3 (1996), 257–80.

[189] Nigel Smith, *Perfection Proclaimed. Language and Literature in English Radical Religion 1640–1660* (Oxford, 1989), pp. 217–25; M. Wynn Thomas, *Morgan Llwyd: Ei Gyfeillion a'i Gyfnod* (Caerdydd, 1991), pp. 51–69.

[190] *Gweithiau Morgan Llwyd*, I, p. 260; N. H. Keeble and G. F. Nuttall (eds.), *Calendar of the Correspondence of Richard Baxter* (2 vols., Oxford, 1991), I, p. 218.

Welsh. Always the pragmatist, he poured scorn on cultural imperialists: 'yn barnu nad da printio math yn y byd o lyfrau cymraeg i gynnal y iaith i fynu; ond ei fod yn weddus i'r bobl golli ei iaith, a dysgu saesneg. Digon da. Ond cofied y cyfryw, mai Haws dywedyd mynydd na myned trosto' (Some people think that printing Welsh books to sustain the language is not a good thing and that it is becoming for the people to lose their language and learn English. Very good. But let us remember that it is easier to say mountain than to cross it).[191] By systematically organizing the dissemination of didactic and devotional books, Hughes helped to ensure that the literate common people became the custodians of the vernacular.[192] Instilling the reading habit helped to foster independent thinking and also meant that ministers of religion and common people established a bond which enabled them to 'support the [Welsh] tongue, and retain the customs and traditions and principles, and proverbs of their ancestors'.[193]

By the eighteenth century, however, there were clear signs that Welsh bishops had pledged themselves to promote the wider use of English by every means in their power. As early as 1703 it was claimed that the Anglican mission was vitiated by the appointment 'of perfect strangers to our country, and language'.[194] Known as 'Yr Esgyb Eingl' (the Anglo Bishops),[195] such prelates resolved to make explicit the underlying assumption in the language clause of 1536 that the total assimilation of Wales within England should be hastened. Richard Newcome, bishop of Llandaff (1755–61), loudly declared that 'there should be no distinction between an Englishman and a Welshman in our days',[196] and some of his colleagues were so hostile to the Welsh language that conscientious clergymen succumbed either to fits of melancholy or bouts of rage. At St Asaph, Bishop Robert Hay Drummond touched a raw nerve by ordering that Welsh copies of the New Testament and Prayer Book be locked in church chests,[197] and when an English-speaking advocate publicly declared in the Court of Arches that 'Wales is a conquered country, it is proper to introduce the English language, and it is the duty of the bishops

---

[191] Stephen Hughes (ed.), *Gwaith Mr Rees Prichard* (Part IV, Llundain, 1672), sig. A3v.
[192] G. J. Williams, 'Stephen Hughes a'i Gyfnod', *Y Cofiadur*, 4 (1926), 5–44; Geraint H. Jenkins, 'Apostol Sir Gaerfyrddin: Stephen Hughes c. 1622–1688' in *Cadw Tŷ mewn Cwmwl Tystion: Ysgrifau Hanesyddol ar Grefydd a Diwylliant* (Llandysul, 1990), pp. 1–28.
[193] Thomas Jones, *Of the Heart and its Right Soveraign* (London, 1678), p. 243.
[194] Lambeth Palace Library MS 930, f. 33.
[195] See the vitriolic comments of Evan Evans (Ieuan Fardd) in NLW MS 2009B.
[196] *ALM*, I, p. 322; C. L. S. Linnell (ed.), *The Diaries of Thomas Wilson D.D. 1731–37 and 1750* (London, 1964), p. 235.
[197] *ML*, I, pp. 236–7, 288; *ALM*, II, p. 666. See also Robert Hay Drummond, *A Sermon preached before the Incorporated Society for the Propagation of the Gospel in Foreign Parts* (London, 1754), p. 22.

to promote the English, in order to introduce the language',[198] many came to believe that a grand strategy had been devised to deCymricize the established Church.

Such was the antipathy of some prelates towards the Welsh language that the common bond which had existed between parson and parishioner since Elizabethan times was gravely imperilled. Although the mass of the clergy remained thoroughly Welsh, there emerged a growing number of clerics, usually 'planted' in key livings by non-Welsh prelates, who were determined to 'civilize' or 'enlighten' their flocks by introducing English services, thereby undermining the spirit of the act of 1563 which had declared that the language of parochial worship should be appropriate to the needs of the inhabitants. Thomas Collins of Swansea believed that the perpetuation of the Welsh language kept the people in ignorance of matters relating to religious and civil life, while John Catlyn, the Hull-born vicar of Kerry in Montgomeryshire, sought to please his bishop by imparting a 'just and necessary knowledge' of English to his Welsh-speaking parishioners.[199] The poet, Goronwy Owen, encountered a young curate in Montgomeryshire who airily claimed that Welsh literature was beneath contempt and that the encroachment of the English tongue was so irresistible that the Welsh language would assuredly be dead and buried within a hundred years.[200] Such clergymen pandered to the whims of English-speaking gentry families, danced attendance upon judges and lawyers associated with the Courts of Great Sessions, and employed poorly paid Welsh-speaking curates to minister to their flocks. In towns like Oswestry and Newport they increasingly pressed influential English families to petition for fewer Welsh services and, whenever large numbers of visitors or tourists arrived, ad hoc arrangements were made to supply them with English sermons.[201]

The erosion of confidence in the governors of the established Church and their inability to provide for the spiritual and linguistic needs of the Welsh-speaking populace were partly responsible for the rise of the Methodist movement. Although almost all their energies were focused on their individual spiritual experiences and the fate of the souls of others, Methodist preachers and exhorters were not unaware of the need to cultivate the Welsh language, and by means of powerful sermons and tight-knit society meetings they enabled their native tongue to acquire a new and enhanced status as the language of evangelical fervour, soul-saving and

---

[198] *The Depositions, Arguments and Judgment in the Cause of the Church-Wardens of Trefdraeth, in the County of Anglesea, against Dr. Bowles* (London, 1773), p. 59.
[199] Clement, *Correspondence ... of the S.P.C.K.*, pp. 34, 48, 53, 77.
[200] J. H. Davies (ed.), *The Letters of Goronwy Owen (1723–1769)* (Cardiff, 1924), p. 67.
[201] NLW Ll/QA/5 (Newport); SA/QA/6 (Abergele); SA/QA/12 (Oswestry).

intimate spiritual discourse.[202] Unlike university-trained clergymen, Methodist preachers could discourse extempore for several hours and their tongues, so they claimed, were moved according to the dictates of the Holy Spirit. As they groped for words to express profound spiritual fervour, they helped to deepen the understanding of the importance of inward experience. They bared their souls within their letters, hymns, books and society reports, and were often extravagantly rhetorical and incantatory in their modes of speech as they strove to rescue benighted sinners from the fires of eternal damnation. Welsh Methodism's most celebrated spokesman was William Williams, Pantycelyn, whose memorable prose works and hymns touched the lives of thousands of Welsh people.[203] In a wide range of publications Williams endeavoured to convey the wonders of the creation, to impart current scientific knowledge, and to offer new insights into the psychology of sex and marriage. In so doing, he not only kindled a new spirit of inquiry among worshippers and readers but also widened the parameters of the Welsh language. Moreover, his shrewd and successful use of colloquial 'market Welsh' (together with many English forms) was deliberately designed to make hymnody accessible to common people and enable them to articulate a wide range of emotions and feelings.[204]

The conventional and still dominant view is that there was nothing intrinsically Welsh about Methodism and that the sole motivation of its leaders was to promote the cause of salvation rather than to protect the interests of the native language. Cultural patriots in the eighteenth century certainly believed that evangelical leaders were instruments of Anglicization. Although Howel Harris, the mercurial leader of Welsh Methodism, invariably wrote in English, he admitted that most Society members 'understand no English';[205] therefore, he not only consciously associated the movement with support for the Welsh language as an oral medium, but also made public declarations to that effect, especially during the latter years of his life. At Pontfaen, near Fishguard, in May 1770, he informed hearers 'that God is a Welchman can talk Welsh has s^d. to many in Welch Thy sins are forgiven thee'. A year later he deplored the manner in which pride and luxury, transferred from England into Wales, had persuaded many to 'learn English to our children before that ancient

---

[202] The best introduction is Derec Llwyd Morgan, *The Great Awakening in Wales*, translated by Dyfnallt Morgan (London, 1988).
[203] Gomer M. Roberts (ed.), *Y Pêr Ganiedydd* (2 vols., Aberystwyth, 1949, 1958); Gomer M. Roberts and Garfield H. Hughes (eds.), *Gweithiau William Williams Pantycelyn* (2 vols., Caerdydd, 1964, 1967).
[204] Glyn Tegai Hughes, *Williams Pantycelyn* (Cardiff, 1983), pp. 116–19.
[205] Gomer M. Roberts (ed.), *Selected Trevecka Letters (1742–1747)* (Caernarfon, 1956), p. 177.

Language which God has given us in this shew a folly madness that no other Nation in ye World but our selves do shew'.[206] Monoglot Welsh exhorters, however, were often frustrated by their inability to spread the gospel as widely as possible. In Anglicized parts of Glamorgan John Richard was filled with a deep sense of inadequacy on 'discovering valuable lambs' ('gwerthfawr ŵyn') yearning for spiritual sustenance which he was unable to satisfy.[207] John Wesley, who possessed no Welsh, deplored 'the Confusion of Tongues' as he vainly sought to preach the virtues of Arminian Methodism. His brand of evangelism appealed mainly to bilingual 'genteel hearers' in towns like Abergavenny, Bridgend, Builth and Cardiff, and elsewhere he was normally obliged to rely on translators to convey the substance of his message.[208] In most Methodist circles in Wales, the language of spiritual experience was Welsh, and therein lay part of its success.

In the field of popular education, too, saving souls and stiffening the language went hand in hand in the eighteenth century. It swiftly became clear that the predominantly English-medium schools established by the SPCK (1699–1737) had failed to win the respect, let alone the affection, of Welsh people. Progress was so slow and uneven that no amount of publicity could disguise the fact that monoglot Welsh-speaking pupils continued to emerge from long periods of English tuition unable to comprehend relatively straightforward passages of scripture and parts of the catechism. Learning by rote, cramming and a rigid adherence to the principle of the 'three Rs' had failed to serve the needs of a rural-based, Welsh-speaking population.[209] By contrast, the remarkably successful network of Welsh circulating schools launched by Griffith Jones, Llanddowror, in the 1730s offered a much more effective and flexible system of education based on instilling into adults and children alike a firm grasp of Welsh letters, syllables and words.[210] It has been established that increased levels of literacy enrich and stabilize a language, and the rudimentary but easily accessible instruction offered in peripatetic schools undoubtedly enhanced the standard of spoken Welsh as well as improving and extending reading ability. In the long run, this helped to create what

---

[206] NLW, CM Archives, Howel Harris's Diary 262, 24 May, 3 July 1770; Diary 264, 31 August 1771.
[207] NLW, CM Archives, Trevecka Letters I, no. 1284. See also Gomer M. Roberts, 'Adroddiadau John Richard i'r Sasiwn', *CCHMC*, XXVIII, no. 1 (1943), 1–9.
[208] A. H. Williams (ed.), *John Wesley in Wales 1739–1790* (Cardiff, 1971), pp. 16–17, 25, 27, 36, 40, 55, 85, 96.
[209] NLW MS 17B, ff. 12–13; Griffith Jones (ed.), *The Welch Piety* (London, 1740), pp. 29–62.
[210] Geraint H. Jenkins, '"An Old and Much Honoured Soldier": Griffith Jones, Llanddowror', *WHR*, 2, no. 4 (1983), 449–68.

William Owen Pughe rather quaintly called 'a community of literary rustics'.[211]

Although Griffith Jones shared the aversion of so-called 'improvers' towards the other Celtic languages (probably because the Irish and Scottish Gaelic tongues were associated with popery, disloyalty and rebellion), his veneration for his own native tongue was boundless, so much so that he constructed a much more advanced and persuasive appreciation of the social, educational and cultural value of Welsh than any of his Protestant predecessors. In his annual publication, *The Welch Piety*, Jones assembled a thesis which was a subtle blend of sentiment and pragmatism. To him, the language was an old and honourable tongue, copious, pure, felicitous and elegant: 'She has not lost her *Charms*, nor *Chasteness*, remains unalterably the same, is now perhaps the same She was *Four thousand Years* ago; still retains the *Beauties* of *her Youth*, grown *old in Years*, but *not decayed*.'[212] This was not mawkishness on his part or simply lip-service to notions popularized by Paul Pezron and Theophilus Evans, for he firmly believed that 'the decrees of Heaven' favoured the preservation of Welsh. The native tongue, moreover, was of vital importance to the spiritual and moral well-being of the Welsh people in so far as it acted as a bulwark against the alien tide of infidelity, obscenity, and deism. Providing instruction through the medium of English might encourage labourers and tenant farmers to desert their callings and seek a new life across the seas, thereby impoverishing the Welsh economy. No right-thinking person, he argued, would set up French charity schools in England and take the risk of permitting thousands of ignorant souls to fall into 'the dreadful Abyss of Eternity'. 'Welsh is still the vulgar tongue and not English', he reminded potential donors, and experience had shown that a Welsh-medium education was the swiftest and most cost-effective means of bringing basic instruction and literacy to thousands of people.[213] Moreover, the acquisition of reading skills in the mother tongue provided a valuable vehicle for the subsequent acquisition of the English language, a view which was shared by Thomas Charles, founder of the Welsh Sunday schools. He strongly believed that imparting religious knowledge in the mother tongue increased the desire to acquire a 'stock of ideas' and a facility in English. 'I can vouch for the truth of it', he maintained, 'that there are *twenty* to *one* who can read English to what could when the

---

[211] William Owen Pughe, *A Dictionary of the Welsh Language* (2 vols., London, 1803), I, Introduction, sig. c1v.
[212] *The Welch Piety* (London, 1740), p. 51.
[213] Ibid., pp. 32, 37–49.

Welsh was entirely neglected.'[214] Griffith Jones's remarkably successful educational campaign created an army of Welsh readers by the latter half of the eighteenth century, and by providing substantial numbers of farmers, labourers, servants and young children with the opportunity to learn to read, he enhanced the prestige-value of the Welsh language and strengthened people's attachment to it.

Since many of these profound changes were closely bound up with the printing press and new cultural values, we must now consider the literary culture of the period and its contribution to the remodelling of the Welsh language. In 1547 William Salesbury, the most gifted Welsh scholar of his day, issued a salutary warning to his countrymen: 'unless you bestir yourselves to cherish and mend the language before the present generation is no more, it will be too late' ('a nyd achubwch chwi a chweirio a pherfeithio r iaith kyn daruod am y to ysydd heddio, y bydd rhyhwyr y gwaith gwedy').[215] He was, of course, referring to the language as a vehicle of high culture rather than as an everyday medium. Among such scholars there were understandable fears that, as a result of the penchant of the gentry for things English and the irrevocable disintegration of the bardic order, the 'old British tongue' was likely to deteriorate into a host of rustic dialects lacking dignity, status and correctness.[216] Although most Renaissance scholars in Wales were avowed admirers of the English language and ardent supporters of the Union legislation, they also took pride in their role as *vetustae linguae custodes*.[217] In the Middle Ages, the word *iaith* had been used to denote 'nation' and Welsh scholars were aware that the native tongue was a fundamental badge of the Welshman's self-awareness if not of his nationality. They were conscious that 'men of affairs' born in Wales or of Welsh ancestry believed that Welsh was marginal to serious intellectual study and that scholarship and learning could only be sought and acquired outside Wales. Although their ideals and goals were spurned by those who chose to write creatively in English, Renaissance scholars like William Salesbury, Richard Davies, Siôn Dafydd Rhys and John Davies remained convinced that the Welsh language possessed enormous untapped potential, so much indeed that it should not be allowed to become 'the

---

[214] D. E. Jenkins (ed.), *The Life of the Rev. Thomas Charles of Bala* (3 vols., Denbigh, 1908–10), III, p. 367.

[215] William Salesbury, *Oll Synnwyr pen Kembero ygyd* (London, 1547), sig. Aiiir.

[216] R. Brinley Jones, *The Old British Tongue: the Vernacular in Wales, 1540–1640* (Cardiff, 1970); idem, '"Yr Iaith sydd yn Kychwyn ar Dramgwydd", Sylwadau ar y Gymraeg yng nghyfnod y Dadeni Dysg' in J. E. Caerwyn Williams (ed.), *Ysgrifau Beirniadol VIII* (Dinbych, 1974), pp. 43–69.

[217] See Ceri Davies (ed.), *Rhagymadroddion a Chyflwyniadau Lladin 1551–1632* (Caerdydd, 1980) and idem, *Latin Writers of the Renaissance* (Cardiff, 1981).

language only of the farmyard and the market-place'.[218] In their eyes, it had every right to be considered a fitting medium for cultured conversation and study, and their faith in the language prompted them to devote much time and energy to publishing valuable treatises on grammar, spelling and rhetoric, as well as dictionaries, in order to embellish, enrich and standardize it and strengthen its ailing status as a cultivated tongue.

As a consequence, the printed word played a major role in creating new interest in the Welsh language and enabling it to acquire 'a new fixity which made it appear more permanent and hence (by an optical illusion) more "eternal" than it really was'.[219] Although the shift from script to print and from the ear to the eye was a relatively slow process in Tudor and early Stuart Wales, a printed book culture had certainly emerged by the Restoration period. Over 2,500 Welsh books (this figure does not include ephemera) were published in the eighteenth century, most of them religious works designed to instil the fundamental doctrines of the Christian faith, to encourage Bible-reading, and to assist the individual's quest for assurance.[220] But many works, too, sought to stiffen 'the old and most excellent British language'.[221] Even the most cursory reader of eighteenth-century printed books cannot fail to be impressed by the considerable affection lavished upon the native tongue by lexicographers, grammarians, churchmen and Dissenters, almanackers and ballad-mongers, and this must surely have had a direct or indirect effect on the attachment of the growing book-reading public towards the Welsh language. There were welcome signs, too, that major gaps in subject literature in Welsh were being filled. Religious reformers had always acknowledged the special blessing which God had conferred upon the Welsh nation by means of the printing press, and the development of native presses from 1718 onwards helped to stabilize the language and encourage the habit of book-reading.[222] Different and wider tastes were catered for. The first publication legally printed on Welsh soil – at Trerhedyn in south Cardiganshire in 1718 – was a song on tobacco,[223] and in the same year Simon Thomas's *Hanes y Byd a'r Amseroedd* disseminated a wide range of miscellaneous information on astronomy, astrology, geography and science. Thomas Durston of Shrewsbury published

---

[218] Glanmor Williams, *Religion, Language, and Nationality in Wales* (Cardiff, 1979), pp. 131–2.
[219] Eric Hobsbawm, *Nations and Nationalism since 1780* (2nd ed., Cambridge, 1992), p. 61.
[220] *Libri Walliae*.
[221] Thomas Jones, *Almanac am y Flwyddyn 1681* (Llundain, 1681), sig. A2r.
[222] Geraint H. Jenkins, *Literature, Religion and Society in Wales, 1660–1730* (Cardiff, 1978), pp. 255–304.
[223] Alban Thomas, *Cân o Senn iw hen Feistr Tobacco* (Trerhedyn, 1718).

Cyfarwyddiad i Fesurwyr (1715), the first technical work on numbers and measurements designed for carpenters, joiners, stonemasons, sawyers and slaters, and Lewis Morris translated a treatise on japanning and varnishing for the benefit of Welsh craftsmen.[224] Dafydd Lewys's path-breaking work *Golwg ar y Byd* (1725) was the first Welsh book devoted specifically to scientific subjects, a theme which William Williams, the Methodist hymnologist and prose writer, pursued with some success. *Llyfr Meddyginiaeth a Physygwriaeth* (c.1740) was an admirable attempt to revive or invent words relating to plants, herbs and medicine, and to assist in the preparation and cooking of birds, fish and meat. There were also, of course, intriguing titbits of information available in Welsh almanacks and ballads. By the end of the eighteenth century virtually every town of any consequence in Wales could boast at least one printing press, and as books became cheaper and more accessible to literate farmers, tradesmen, craftsmen and artisans, the cumulative effects for the Welsh language were of critical importance. Writing at the turn of the eighteenth century, William Owen Pughe rightly acknowledged what had been achieved:

> Respecting the printed books, in the Welsh language, it is not necessary to say much, any further than to announce, that we have about one thousand volumes of them, upon various topics; some of which have gone through several editions. Our catalogue, to be sure is not large; but, arising from the spirit of reading, among the peasants of a small mountainous country, it must acquire some degree of importance in the opinion of strangers, to whom the circumstances may be hitherto unknown altogether, that we should have any books in our language.[225]

Although the development of cheap print was vitally important as a means of strengthening the Welsh language, it should not be forgotten that oral transmission was still of the utmost significance. Scriptural passages and parts of the Prayer Book were read aloud in church. People first heard sermons preached aloud, and only later did they read them at leisure. The catechism was inculcated by verbal question-and-answer modes, and within the household unit the content of didactic and devotional books was read aloud to the unlettered. Clearly a new and more pious vocabulary could be spread by print, especially among the literate middling sorts, but popular ballads, songs and interludes, chanted and sung by ballad-mongers, rhymesters and travelling players, catered for more plebeian tastes. In the last resort, however, it is impossible to tell to

---

[224] *Y Gowrain Gelfyddyd o Japannio neu Rodd meistr iw Brentis* (Bala, 1761).
[225] Pughe, *Dictionary*, I, Introduction, sig. C1r.

what extent pious or popular works shaped or reflected daily language, and we should not perhaps automatically assume that day-to-day patterns of speech were deeply influenced by available reading matter.

Recent studies have drawn attention to the distinctive role of the Welsh middling sorts in the cultural life of eighteenth-century Wales and to this we now turn. This was a period when increasingly articulate and assertive 'middle sorts of people' began to re-examine the nature of Welshness and create a new sense of identity based on the Welsh language.[226] Changing patterns in the distribution of landed wealth and a general sense of decay and decline in the cultural infrastructure prompted growing numbers of cultural patriots to conclude that neither social nor economic salvation would come from parasitic absentee landlords who drained the country of its resources. As the landed oligarchy distanced itself from the sociocultural life of Wales, much of the initiative passed into the hands of scholar-patriots who delighted in rediscovering the literary and historical treasures of the past and in championing the cause of the Welsh language. This was a period of linguistic innovation and gifted lexicographers and 'purists' introduced a remarkably large number of new words into the vocabulary. Languages, of course, are always in a state of change; old words lapse or acquire new meanings, and new words enter. But it is clear that linguistic change was much more apparent as the eighteenth century unfolded. There was a growing desire to see the language become 'masculine and bold'[227] and, in the absence of a national academy charged with the task of preserving linguistic purity and promoting the use of new words, amateur lexicographers shouldered the responsibility of stabilizing and enriching the language.[228] The standard historical dictionary, *Geiriadur Prifysgol Cymru*, reveals a dramatic increase in the number of new words entering the language from c.1770 onwards, and the fact that John Walters was able to produce his English-Welsh dictionary in two bulky volumes (published in successive parts) between 1770 and 1794 provides tangible proof of the manner in which the language had been successfully extended.[229] New words entering the vocabulary reflected vigorous social and economic activity – *cyfanwerthu* (to sell by wholesale), *mânwerthu* (to sell by retail) and *mantoli* (balance) (1770); scientific developments – *dyfeisgar* (inventive) (1771), *daearyddiaeth* (geography) (1793) and *disgyrchiant* (gravity) (1795); and the human personality – *dynoliaeth*

---

[226] Jenkins, *Making of a Ruling Class*, chapter 9; Jenkins, *The Foundations of Modern Wales*, pp. 386–9. See also Jonathan Barry and Christopher Brooks (eds.), *The Middling Sort of People. Culture, Society and Politics in England, 1550–1800* (Basingstoke, 1994).
[227] Gambold, *A Welsh Grammar*, sig. A2v.
[228] T. J. Morgan, 'Geiriadurwyr y Ddeunawfed Ganrif', *LlC*, 9, no. 1 and 2 (1966), 3–18.
[229] John Walters, *An English-Welsh Dictionary* (London, 1794).

(humanity) (1774), *hunan-adnabyddiaeth* (self-acquaintance) (1771) and *arddegau* (teens) (1794).[230] This was a period, too, which witnessed the publication of some of the most influential treatises on the Welsh language, notably Thomas Llewelyn's *Historical and Critical Remarks on the British Tongue and its Connection with other Languages* (1769) and John Walters' *A Dissertation on the Welsh Language* (1771), both of which loudly praised the antiquity, copiousness and 'grammatical perfection' of the Welsh language.

Nowhere was the obsession with the origin, nature and uses of languages and dialects more evident than in London. Towns in Wales were still woefully small and no urban community could hope to match London in terms of wealth, sociability, and the opportunity to acquire ideas. During his youth in rural Merioneth, William Owen Pughe believed that London was 'the primary point in the geography of the world',[231] and as the young and the ambitious sought their fortunes in one of the most colourful and cosmopolitan cities in Europe it acquired a reputation as the surrogate capital of Wales. The more educated among them forged alliances with London's bourgeoisie and their integration with such élites seriously affected the quality of the Welsh they spoke and wrote. As early as the Tudor period, for instance, the vivid chronicles and texts written by Elis Gruffydd, the multilingual soldier and chronicler from Flintshire, became Anglicized in vocabulary and syntax during his sojourn in London.[232] However, the formation of London-Welsh societies in the mid-eighteenth century provided a new lease of life for Welshness in the city by sharpening the consciousness of expatriates of being Welsh. The constitution of the Society of Cymmrodorion (1751), constructed by the indefatigable Morris brothers of Anglesey, spoke loudly of the need to cultivate the Welsh tongue (members were enjoined not even to 'whisper' English in meetings) and the correspondence of the three brothers were liberally sprinkled with references to opening new cultural avenues 'er clod ac anrhydedd i'n hiaith' (for the glory and honour of our language) and of the paramount importance of persuading men of influence to 'love and caress their language'.[233] Their profound belief in, and affection for, the Welsh language shines through in their celebrated letters and it is clear they possessed an extensive repertoire of linguistic styles and an enviable knowledge of local accents, vocabularies and syntax.

---

[230] Prys Morgan, 'Dyro Olau ar dy Eiriau', *Taliesin*, 70 (1990), 38–45.
[231] Pughe, *Dictionary*, I, Introduction, sig. b3r.
[232] NLW MSS 3054D, 5276D; Mostyn MS 158. See also Patrick K. Ford (ed.), *Ystoria Taliesin* (Cardiff, 1992), pp. vii–viii.
[233] *Gosodedigaethau Anrhydeddus Gymdeithas y Cymmrodorion yn Llundain* (Llundain, 1755); *ML*, II, p. 368.

But although the Morris brothers (and some of their more cultured correspondents) were brilliant conversationalists and linguistically self-conscious men, the same could not be said of the rank and file of the Cymmrodorion Society. The London gentry who associated themselves chiefly with the conviviality of the Society were disinclined to absorb the cultural blueprint of the Morrises, and from 1770 onwards the newly formed Society of Gwyneddigion became far more influential as a leader of Welsh opinion. Its lively and convivial members delighted in displaying their gift for loquacity, parody and badinage in smoke-filled taverns, and some of their goals were not dissimilar to those professed by members of literary clubs in America, France and Spain. 'Hir Oes i'r Iaith Gymraeg' (Long Life to the Welsh Language) was one of their popular toasts and it was on their initiative that the Welsh eisteddfod was revived and strengthened. In their meetings members seemed to have complied with the Welsh-only rule though, if Iolo Morganwg is to be believed, the dialect of these 'becockneyed Cambrians' was 'seal'd all over with the most uncouth anglicisms, and other barbarisms'.[234] Even a clerical scholar like Evan Evans felt obliged to use language which would have been 'a valuable acquisition to Billingsgate' among the tippling, pipe-smoking congeries of scholars and patriots who frequented the raucous taverns favoured by the Gwyneddigion.[235]

London also offered a congenial home for those with a taste for romantic fantasy, myths and legends. By encouraging creativity and spontaneity, romanticism played a significant role in reviving interest in one of the oldest living literary tongues in Europe. The outlandish forgeries, fantasies and dreams of the gifted stonemason, Iolo Morganwg (a man who reputedly spoke English more fluently than Welsh but who could construct a sentence of 116 Welsh words without a single verb in order to reveal the capacity of the language to 'express a pretty long sentence'[236]) helped to introduce into Welsh the language of revolutionary politics, of *sans-culottisme*, free-thinking and republicanism as a means of publicizing Jacobin thought and provoking a new sense of nationhood. Radical patriots at the end of the eighteenth century resisted efforts to embritish the Welsh and were agreed that the Welsh language lay at the heart of the distinctive national claims of Wales and the national character of its people. In an extraordinary (even by his standards) paean to the Welsh language, Iolo Morganwg declared:

---

[234] NLW MS 13121B, f. 478; NLW MS 21419E, f. 19.
[235] Jenkins and Ramage, *History of Cymmrodorion*, p. 98.
[236] Richard M. Crowe, 'Diddordebau Ieithyddol Iolo Morganwg' (unpubl. University of Wales PhD thesis, 1988), p. 36.

... we have more than a thousand printed books in the Language, probably near two thousand, we have ten presses at least in Wales employed in printing Welsh books, besides many that are printed in London. It has three or four periodical publications, or magazines, and is now equal if not superior to what English literature was in the Reigns of Elizabeth and James, everything considered . . . It has no loose immoral books of any kind, none that inculcate the pernicious doctrines of infidelity . . . It has no places, pensions, profitable trades, no offices, employment, and high Trusts to attain to that might lead it into temptation . . . There can be no doubt but that the preservation and retention of the Welsh Language will be the greastest [sic] blessing of all others to Wales.[237]

Nevertheless, not all romantics, however well meaning, succeeded in restoring dignity and status to the language. Their reverence for imagination, emotion and the extraordinary often led them astray. For instance, William Owen Pughe's notorious *A Grammar of the Welsh Language* (1803) was universally derided for its ludicrous orthographical quirks, and the *reductio ad absurdum* of the mania for 'inventing' words were futile monstrosities like 'anghyflechtwynedigaetholion' and 'gogyflechtywynedigaetholion' devised by Iolo Morganwg.[238] The energy poured into Welsh romanticism was not always well directed, and Dafydd Ddu Eryri had good cause to deplore the 'anfeidrol ynfydrwydd' (infinite madness) of its most wilful practitioners.[239] Even so, the flamboyant and eminently marketable ideas peddled by romantics proved a powerful means of raising the profile of the Welsh language. Many more voices were raised on behalf of the native tongue at the end of the eighteenth century than ever before. In many ways, optimism about its future was in vogue, and for this romanticism must be accorded its fair share of credit.

In general, therefore, it would be no exaggeration to claim that people were acutely conscious that the Welsh language had expanded in use during the eighteenth century. Certain localities, especially towns, had become progressively more Welsh. The appreciable expansion in the number of Welsh publications, the growth of evangelical religion and increasing literacy had led to greater confidence in the use of the vernacular as a written medium, not only for personal communication (as in correspondence) but also in permitting the displacement of English as the official language of record in many wills, in some parish vestry records, and even presentments at the Courts of Quarter Sessions. The use of Welsh in the crucial domain of religion had been established and

---

[237] NLW MS 13121B, ff. 474–5.
[238] Crowe, 'Diddordebau Ieithyddol Iolo Morganwg', p. 199.
[239] Glenda Carr, *William Owen Pughe* (Caerdydd, 1983), p. 94.

developed, while the great surge of scholarly and romantic activity had helped to identify the native language as a vital part of the national consciousness of the people. Above all, the sheer numbers of Welsh speakers had more than doubled in the early modern period and it is to their distinctive ways of speaking we now turn.

Genres

In the remainder of this chapter we shall examine the language of ordinary discourse — a task we undertake with some apprehension since lack of evidence renders the subject fraught with difficulties. Virtually all verbal exchanges in early modern Wales have, of course, vanished without trace. The earliest informants who assisted the pioneer O. H. Fynes-Clinton in accumulating data on the vocabulary of spoken Welsh in the Bangor district were monoglot speakers born in 1835 and 1839.[240] Tapes also exist in the sound archive of the Museum of Welsh Life of the natural speech of informants, the earliest of whom was born in 1840. Nothing comparable exists for the period before 1800. Actual speech patterns, therefore, remain hidden from the historian and we can no longer hope to know or reproduce the authentic accents, intonation, rhythm, pitch and delivery of our early modern ancestors let alone the subtle shades of meaning, hidden nuances and associations which characterized the spoken word. Although speech was of much greater importance in daily lives than the printed word, what we know of the spoken language is necessarily based on what was written at the time. While written language and printed materials can yield valuable and sometimes unexpected information about spoken modes of communication, it should always be borne in mind that the transcription of conversations, discourses or dialogues into some form of written record inevitably entails imposing a more formal and stylized gloss on the original.

The following discussion is based on an amalgam of documentary evidence which touches on linguistic matters. First, there are the writings of scholars who possessed extensive, first-hand knowledge of local dialects and vocabularies and these can be supplemented by the comments of travellers and observers. Letters have survived in some quantity from the eighteenth century and many correspondents clearly complied with Jane Austen's injunction: 'write as you would speak'. The celebrated *Morris Letters*, for instance, display remarkable verbal and written versatility. The 'epistles' brimmed with snatches of verbal exchanges, ejaculations and

---

[240] O. H. Fynes-Clinton, *The Welsh Vocabulary of the Bangor District* (Oxford, 1913), pp. iii–iv.

digressions, coded euphemisms and word-plays. Much can be gleaned, too, from the imaginative literature of the period, though this field is also beset with difficulties. It would be foolish to believe, for instance, that the language employed by Renaissance scholars or Puritan evangelists reflected ordinary discourse. Ellis Wynne's satirical work, *Gweledigaetheu y Bardd Cwsc* (1703) (Visions of the Sleeping Bard) reflects the scandalous language of the 'Cockney school' genre rather than daily patterns of conversation in late Stuart Merioneth. Conversely, Twm o'r Nant's gift for observation and ear for dialogue enabled his eighteenth-century interludes to engage the attention and sympathy of the unlettered peasantry. More often than not, too, the dialogue rings true in the mass of almanacks, ballads, *halsingod*, carols and chapbooks which reached the height of their popularity in the eighteenth century, although little is known about their production and circulation. Even more valuable is the intriguing evidence available from cases of slander and defamation preserved in the records of the civil and ecclesiastical courts.[241] Most of the evidence relating to language use is anecdotal but this corpus of some 2,000 cases provides glimpses of who was speaking what language, when, and in what place. These records contain the exact wording (either in English or in Welsh with an English translation) of colloquial speech as reported in the courts in the period 1543–1830, and sociolinguists believe that the evidence therein relating to the spoken language is generally 'natural and informal rather than literary and hypercorrect'.[242] Used sensitively, these records can provide details of some of the varieties of spoken Welsh. It is in the courts that we discover and hear the authentic voice of non-élite groups from all parts of early modern Wales.

It is sometimes suggested that Welsh is a classless language because spoken Welsh is dominated by regional variety rather than status-based speech patterns. The progressive Anglicization of the gentry has already been noted and we can be certain that wealthy and socially exclusive landowners conducted polite conversation in what Henry Rowlands called 'the genteel and fashionable Tongue'.[243] Since English was the language of polite taste and advancement, Welsh was associated with inferiority, penury and backwardness. On the other hand, scholars and clergymen, who were crucial in creating greater confidence in the vernacular language, presumably practised the civil, courteous modes of speech – in both Welsh and English in appropriate contexts – which humanist treatises

[241] Suggett, 'Slander in Early-Modern Wales', 119–53.
[242] G. M. Awbery, Ann E. Jones and R. F. Suggett, 'Slander and Defamation: A New Source for Historical Dialectology', *Cardiff Working Papers in Welsh Linguistics / Papurau Gwaith Ieithyddol Cymraeg Caerdydd*, no. 4 (Welsh Folk Museum, 1985), p. 3.
[243] Henry Rowlands, *Mona Antiqua Restaurata* (Dublin, 1723), p. 38.

recommended, and consequently their speech would have been more formal and precise than the colloquial forms employed by humbler folk.[244] Goronwy Owen emphasized the distinction between 'hard words' and 'market Welsh'.[245] The cultured 'better sorts' in Wales bemoaned the quality of Welsh spoken by the 'vulgar sorts' just as John Aubrey deprecated the imprecise locution which characterized the language of the people of north Wiltshire and the Vale of Gloucestershire.[246]

Even so, no one at the time was in a position to say what constituted 'correct' Welsh. Even after the publication of the Welsh Bible in 1588, there was no uniform standard for daily usage and it would be rash to assume that scriptural language permeated the daily speech of common people before the coming of the Sunday schools at the end of the eighteenth century. The absence of a natural focal point meant that socio-economic, linguistic and cultural patterns in Wales were centrifugal rather than centripetal, and given the absence of an overarching 'national' spoken language, a rich and colourful variety of local dialects prevailed. Welsh-speaking travellers within Wales were accustomed to a multiplicity of regional speech patterns, some of which would be difficult to understand. The shrewdest observers made valuable and perceptive comments. In 1573 Humphrey Llwyd echoed Gerald of Wales by designating the language of Cardiganshire 'ye finest, of al the other people of Wales', that of Gwynedd the purest, and that of south Wales the 'rudest, & coursest'.[247] Nearly two centuries later Lewis Morris asserted that since the natives of Anglesey, Caernarfonshire and Merioneth pronounced vowels 'more gaping & open than any other part of Wales' their dialect was probably closest to 'the antient pronunciation of ye British tounge'.[248] A radically different view was propagated by Iolo Morganwg at the end of the eighteenth century. He was able to identify three traditional dialects: Gwenhwyseg (Silurian), which was spoken in the counties of Glamorgan, Monmouth, south and east Brecon, and the Welsh part of Hereford; Dyfedeg (Demetian), which was spoken in the counties of Cardigan, Carmarthen, Pembroke, parts of Brecon, and parts of Gower; and Gwyndodeg (Venedotian), which was spoken in the counties of north Wales. On the basis of his extensive knowledge of

---

[244] Peter Burke, *The Art of Conversation* (Cambridge, 1993), chapter 4. See also Peter Burke and Roy Porter (eds.), *Languages and Jargons. Contributions to a Social History of Language* (Cambridge, 1995).
[245] *Letters of Goronwy Owen*, p. 141.
[246] David Rollison, *The Local Origins of Modern Society. Gloucestershire 1500–1800* (London, 1992), pp. 258–64.
[247] Humphrey Llwyd, *The Breuiary of Britayne* (London, 1573), f. 75v.
[248] Hugh Owen, *The Life and Works of Lewis Morris (Llewelyn Ddu o Fôn) 1701–65* (Anglesey Antiq. Soc., 1951), p. 145.

linguistic and cultural patterns in Wales and of data accumulated during exhaustive and exhausting tours of the country, Iolo also claimed that the finest exponents of the Silurian tongue were located in Aberdare, Defynnog, Gelli-gaer, Blaenau Gwent, Basaleg, Llancarfan, Margam and Ewias, that the Demetian tongue was to be heard at its best at Llanbadarn Fawr, Newcastle Emlyn, Whitland and Llandeilo Fawr, and that the most fluent practitioners of the Venedotian dialect were the natives of Aberffraw, Llannerch-y-medd, Beddgelert, Corwen, Llanidloes and Machynlleth.[249] Like beauty, the quality or purity of spoken Welsh lies in the eye (or more accurately the ear) of the beholder and it was natural for local patriots to champion their own pronunciation and style. For instance, in 1716 Myles Davies of Whitford in Flintshire claimed that 'the truest common Cambrian Idiom is best spoken in Denbighshire . . . but the British Atticisms are most frequent in Flintshire'.[250]

In assessing the value of evidence of this kind we should bear in mind the bitter rivalry which divided poets, linguists and scholars from north and south Wales. Goronwy Owen used to refer to 'Iaith Gwynedd ag Iaith yr Hwyntwyr' (The Language of Gwynedd and the Language of the Southerners)[251] and there were many who claimed at the time that the dialect and language of both areas were mutually incomprehensible. The publications of the Carmarthenshire Dissenter, Stephen Hughes, in the Restoration years are suffused with marginal glosses for the benefit of readers in north Wales, but his contemporary, Thomas Jones, wearily declared that Welsh and Hebrew had more in common than the speech of Gwynedd and of south Wales.[252] Goronwy Owen was convinced that the Welsh spoken in Glamorgan was 'uncouthest Gibberish', and Iolo Morganwg was equally certain that the Venedotian dialect was 'little better than that of a Hottentot'.[253] (It is worth noting that the term 'Hottentot', in eighteenth-century parlance, implied inferior intellect as well as 'clicking speech'.)[254] Authors from south Wales were far more self-

---

[249] Crowe, 'Diddordebau Ieithyddol Iolo Morganwg', pp. 257–8, 325; idem, 'Iolo Morganwg a'r Tafodieithoedd: Diffinio'r Ffiniau', *NLWJ*, XXVII, no. 2 (1991), 205–16.

[250] Myles Davies, *Athenae Britannicae* (6 vols., London, 1716–20), II, p. 191. For stimulating essays on patterns and functions of speech, see Richard Bauman and Joel Sherzer (eds.), *Explorations in the Ethnography of Speaking* (Cambridge, 1974).

[251] *Letters of Goronwy Owen*, p. 105.

[252] Thomas Jones, *Newydd oddiwrth y Seêr* (Llundain, 1684), sig. A2r.

[253] *Letters of Goronwy Owen*, p. 69; BL Add MS 15207, f. 79r. See also Peter Wynn Thomas, 'Dimensions of dialect variation: A dialectological and sociological analysis of aspects of spoken Welsh in Glamorgan' (unpubl. University of Wales PhD thesis, 1990), pp. 174–89.

[254] Geoffrey Hughes, *Swearing. A Social History of Foul Language, Oaths and Profanity in English* (Oxford, 1991), p. 128.

conscious about what Stephen Hughes called their 'poor anglicized Welsh'[255] than their counterparts in the north, and recent surveys have confirmed that a deep and abiding sense of inferiority regarding the quality of their spoken and written Welsh continues to afflict the people of Glamorgan.[256]

Those with a keen ear for variations in dialect noted some of the major differences in the speech patterns of the people of north and south Wales. Lewis Morris identified the use made by southerners of 'taw' rather than 'mai' (that), 'dere' rather than 'tyrd' (come), 'fe' rather than 'fo' (he), 'yn awr' rather than 'yrwan' (now), 'i bant' rather than 'o amgylch' (about), and many other similar examples which are not unfamiliar to Welsh speakers in our own day.[257] Iolo Morganwg detected among what he called the 'peculiarities' of speech patterns among the inhabitants of north Wales words like 'efo' (with), 'acw' (there), 'yrwan' (now), 'deud' (to say) and 'purion' (all right), as well as phrases like 'pur lew' (fair), 'pur dda' (quite good), 'abl deg' (quite able), 'myned ar led' (to spread abroad), 'yn dipie man' (in tiny pieces), and 'rheiol ffordd' (good road). He contrasted these with Silurian words like 'occo' (that one), 'gwedyd' (to say), 'ynawr' (now), and 'i bant' (away), and he also revelled in the local habit of hardening consonants, e.g. 'croci' (to hang), 'gweithretu' (to act), 'rhacor' (more), a practice which he claimed was not employed by better educated, polite middling sorts, especially Dissenters, in Glamorgan.[258] Court records relating to cases of slander and defamation reveal the interesting information that the use of the third-person singular verbal suffix -ws, e.g. 'gwelws' (he saw), 'tynnws' (he pulled), 'dygws' (he stole), was to be heard at least as early as the sixteenth century in south-east Wales and was current even in Breconshire and Radnorshire by the seventeenth and eighteenth centuries.[259]

The pace and processes by which English words and idioms infiltrated the daily speech patterns of Welsh speakers was probably extremely variable. A complex set of interrelated factors affected speech patterns and there was evidently much continuity as well as degrees of change and an awareness of change within that continuity. The Welsh language was

---

[255] Stephen Hughes (ed.), *Gwaith Mr. Rees Prichard* (Part IV, 1672), sig. a6r.
[256] Beth Thomas and Peter Wynn Thomas, *Cymraeg, Cymrâg, Cymrêg* . . . (Caerdydd, 1989), pp. 6–7.
[257] BL Add MS 14923, ff. 132v–134r. In a letter to Edward Richard in 1762, Morris claimed that 'the British of South Wales is notoriously mixed with English, and as the children learn it of their mothers they transmit it to their children. Who can help all this?' *ALM*, II, p. 547.
[258] NLW MS 13103B, f. 87; NLW MS 13130A, ff. 405–9; Crowe, 'Diddordebau Ieithyddol Iolo Morganwg', pp. 267–87.
[259] Awbery et al., 'Slander and Defamation', pp. 16–17.

continually obliged to respond and adapt to new and different social and economic requirements, particularly from the mid-seventeenth century onwards. John Aubrey believed that patterns of linguistic change were accelerated by the upheavals of the civil wars, but the swiftest developments probably occurred in the eighteenth century.[260] Thomas Llewelyn, an exceptionally well-informed Baptist minister, claimed that as a result of 'daily intercourse and reciprocation of [commercial] benefits, the English language had gained more ground in the first half of the eighteenth century than in any other period'.[261] Authors were acutely conscious of the changes in spoken Welsh and 'purists' among them complained loudly about the progressive corruption of vocabulary, syntax and idiom. In his popular dictionary in 1688, Thomas Jones distinguished by parentheses 'those words which the Britains had (so needlessly) borrowed of the English':

> . . . megis ag y mae'r saeson yn gwyllt serchu y Castiau Cyfnewidiol ar ddillad y ffraingeig-wyr, fellu i mae'r Cymry yn ynfydu am lediaith y Saesnaeg, yn gymmaint hyd oni ddaeth Iaith y Cymry yr awron mo'r llygredig ag ymmadrodd eu Cymmydogion.
>
> (. . . as the Englishman is enamoured with the tricks and quillets of the Frenchman's garments, so are the Britains enchanted with the Englishman's dialect, insomuch that the Britains own language is now become as barbarous as their neighbours.)[262]

The number of English words contained in Rees Prichard's *Canwyll y Cymru* suggests that daily speech, at least in his native Carmarthenshire, had been seriously corrupted,[263] though one suspects that words like 'attendio' (to attend), 'bildio' (to build), 'correcto' (to correct), 'cownto' (to count), 'ordro' (to order) and 'reparo' (to repair) were utilized for mnemonic reasons rather than because they reflected modes of discourse employed by people in humbler walks of life. Nonetheless, from the mid-seventeenth century onwards, Cymricized English verbs such as 'declario' (to declare), 'prefaelio' (to prevail), 'resolfo' (to resolve) and 'trafaelio' (to travel) were

---

[260] Clark, *'Brief Lives'*, II, p. 329.
[261] Llewelyn, *An Historical Account of the British or Welsh Versions and Editions of the Bible*, p. 86.
[262] Jones, *The British Language in its Lustre*, sig. a2v.
[263] Lloyd, *Cerddi'r Ficer*, pp. 177–214. Cf. Brinley Rees, *Dulliau'r Canu Rhydd 1500–1650* (Caerdydd, 1952), pp. 9–39, 64, 122–3.

freely used by translators of English books into Welsh,[264] thereby confirming Moses Williams's fears that the printing press could prove a double-edged sword by introducing a profusion of new English words into the Welsh vocabulary.[265] The anonymous translator of one of George Whitefield's letters in 1740 did not attempt to translate English words like 'balls' and 'motto', 'masquerades' and 'plays', and Timothy Thomas deliberately inserted English words in his *Traethiad am y Wisg-Wen Ddisglair* (1759) for the benefit of readers inhabiting border counties.[266] Like many grammarians, the eighteenth-century almanacker Siôn Rhydderch listened intently to the speech of common people and detected the increasing use of English verbs like 'iwsio' (to use), 'mendio' (to mend) and 'repento' (to repent),[267] and the same pattern was reflected in the list of 225 essentially English words, prepared by the scholar Alban Thomas, which he claimed had become an intrinsic part of the daily discourse of common people in the counties of Cardigan, Carmarthen and Pembroke.[268] Ironically, too, the widely admired Welsh interludes of Twm o'r Nant either introduced or popularized phrases like 'Do not talk nonsense' and 'O bless my soul', as well as words like 'bonnets', 'lottery', 'jockeys', 'ruffles', and 'suit'.[269]

Defamation cases confirm that the spoken Welsh of the period was riddled with loanwords, but these were by no means evenly distributed within the language. It is probably incorrect to view the process negatively in terms of lexical erosion, i.e. the replacement of Welsh words by English words. Borrowing was evidently selective and tended to occur in domains such as the law, commercial life and fashion, where English was dominant. A striking example of selective borrowing is provided by a slanderous accusation from Fishguard in 1796. Martha Phillips, wife of a mariner (who may, of course, have 'imported' English words and expressions into the locality) was accused of having said of John and Martha David: 'Fe fy Martha gwraig John David yn cysgu gyda modrib a fy; y gododd y lawr o'r gwely ag y agorodd fox mamgu a ddwgodd shugr candy o honof, a'g ath lawr y'r shop mamgu ag y ddwgodd ddau geiniog; ag y ddwgodd gorn o gatgut, hancichers o shop Mortmer, a penniff o shop Martha David' ('Martha, the wife of John David, slept with my aunt

---

[264] See, for instance, T. E. and E. E., *Cyngor i Ddychwelyd at yr Arglwydd* (Rhydychen, 1727–8); Simon Thomas, *Histori yr Heretic Pelagius* (Henffordd, 1735); [John Bunyan], *Y Rhyfel Ysprydawl* (Amwythig, 1744); William Roberts, *Ffrewyll y Methodistiaid* (no imprint, 1747).
[265] Moses Williams, *Pregeth a Barablwyd yn Eglwys Grist yn Llundain* (Llundain, 1718), p. 15.
[266] George Whitefield, *Llythyr oddiwrth y Parchedig Mr. George Whitefield* (Pontypool, 1740); Timothy Thomas, *Traethiad am y Wisg-Wen Ddisglair* (Caerfyrddin, 1759).
[267] Siôn Rhydderch, [*Almanac*] (Amwythig, 1726), sig. C8v.
[268] Bodleian Library, Ashmole MS 1820, ff. 145–6.
[269] Isaac Foulkes (gol.), *Gwaith Thomas Edwards (Twm o'r Nant)* (Lerpwl, 1874), pp. 5, 9, 12, 72, 73, 100, 156, 223.

and self; and got down from the bed and opened my grandmother's box and stole thereout sugar candy, and went down to the shop of my grandmother and stole two pence; and she stole a piece of catgut, handkerchiefs from Mortimer's shop, and a penknife from the shop of Martha David').[270] It should be noted that these loanwords (some of them carefully mutated) mostly refer to consumer items, and the loanword presumably arrived with the article. Much less is known of the borrowing process in monoglot Welsh-speaking communities. One wonders why particular words were borrowed (and not others), whether loanwords were actually recognized as English by monoglot Welsh speakers, and who were the Welsh agents of transmission whose speech carried prestige.

The manner in which Welsh was 'infected' by English words and pronunciation was often most discernible in urban communities or on the extreme eastern side of the border counties. Thomas Mills Hoare, vicar of Newport, maintained in 1771 that English was most commonly spoken in the town and parish, but that most of the inhabitants understood Welsh 'but it is the Welsh commonly spoken which is very corrupt'.[271] In heavily Anglicized parts of east Radnorshire, some inhabitants pronounced guttural Welsh words without realizing they were Welsh and some English words were said to combine 'Welsh peculiarity' with 'English vulgarity'.[272] Communities trading directly with England were especially liable to absorb loanwords. In the 1690s the vicar of Coychurch, Glamorgan, stated that the language spoken in the parish was 'p'tly English p'tly Welsh our tradeing being for ye most parte with Summer [Somerset] & Devon Shires wch spoiles our Welsh'.[273] In 1707 Edward Lhuyd referred to spoken Welsh in the border counties as heavily marked by loanwords: 'those [parts] of Wales, that border upon England, use a great many English words disguis'd with their own Terminations; but as such are only us'd by the Borderers.'[274]

There are signs, too, of a more radical consequence of language contact than borrowing. In some parts of eighteenth-century Wales a mixed or hybridized language was developing. In 1789 William Jones of Llangadfan claimed that people living on the eastern borders of Montgomeryshire were 'a sort of Mongrels that cannot speak Welsh or English correctly, having lost the one before they learnt the other'.[275] Such a one was Welch Franke, a ploughman who could 'speake neither good Welsh nor good

---

[270] NLW, Great Sessions 28/173–1/autumn 1796.
[271] NLW, LL/QA/5 (Newport).
[272] Williams, *History of Radnorshire*, pp. 276–7.
[273] Edward Lhuyd, 'Parochialia', *AC*, Supplements (1909–11), III, pp. 14–15.
[274] Edward Lhuyd, *Archaeologia Britannica* (Oxford, 1707), p. 32.
[275] NLW MS 13221E, f. 375.

English' when he married Martha Dudleston of Myddle.[276] So, too, was Dorothy George of Llandaff, a widow aged forty-five in 1718, who was described in the Court of Arches as 'a person that understands or at least speaks or pronounces neither Welsh nor English intelligibly, who might . . . pout out and utter a parcell of fragments of broken English & Welsh gibberish promiscuously and confusedly mixt'.[277] It is difficult to judge whether cases of this kind were examples of 'imperfectly learnt' languages, or dialects heavily penetrated by English words and phrases, or relatively short-lived hybridized Welsh-English 'pidgin'.

The complexity of the social situation relating to broken English can be illustrated by the case of 'Saesneg Llantwit', the 'barbarous English' spoken by the inhabitants of Llantwit Major in Glamorgan. The origin of the dialect may lie with the effects of the Anglo-Norman settlement of the Vale, together with strong trading connections with the West Country. With the exception of Llantwit Major, Welsh overwhelmed the English dialect in the Vale in the seventeenth and eighteenth centuries. The dialect was first mentioned by one of Edward Lhuyd's assistants in 1697: 'Saesneg Llhan Illtid is a proverb for broken English, for the old Natives were English, but Welsh encroaches very much.'[278] Throughout the eighteenth century there were conflicting reports about the dominant language at Llantwit Major, but the observations of Benjamin Malkin carry conviction: 'A late tourist is mistaken . . . in saying, that there is not a trace of the Celtic tongue among them; for though the inhabitants commonly converse with each other in a barbarous kind of English, yet they can all speak Welsh, and indeed make as much use of it among themselves as of the English.'[279] Clearly, Llantwit Major was a bilingual community using Welsh and 'barbarous English' in different contexts, and different situations of language selection are reflected in the apparently conflicting accounts of the speech of the inhabitants.

In most parts of Wales, however, many inhabitants understood little if any English. As we have seen, there were many monoglot Welsh speakers and many communities where Welsh dominated virtually all aspects of daily life from the cradle to the grave. Illiterate or sub-literate monoglot Welsh peasants proudly defended their own local forms of dialect, speech patterns and secret codes, and since little of it has been recorded in print it is impossible for the historian to gain access to their mental world. They

---

[276] Richard Gough, *Antiquities & Memoirs of the Parish of Myddle* (Shrewsbury, 1875), p. 63.
[277] Lambeth Palace Library, Court of Arches Records, process book D1930, Smith v Thomas (1719).
[278] John Fisher (ed.), *Tours in Wales (1804–1813) by Richard Fenton* (London, 1917), p. 348.
[279] Malkin, *The Scenery*, p. 622; R. F. Suggett, 'Some aspects of village life in eighteenth-century Glamorgan' (unpubl. University of Oxford BLitt thesis, 1976), pp. 157–8.

were clearly suspicious of 'literary Welsh' ('yr Enwau dyrys')[280] and it may well have been true, as an Anglesey curate insisted, that 'ye most illiterate Country fellow talks ye best, truest, prettiest Welsh'.[281] At this level, language was not merely a natural daily medium of communication; it was also a repository of a wide range of emotions, thoughts and perceptions and it served as a means of developing and sustaining human relationships. Men and women did not simply speak Welsh; they blessed, cursed, prayed, grieved and made love in Welsh. Benjamin Malkin observed that the daily conversation of the peasantry was littered with figures and metaphors relating to nature, life, birth and death, joy and sorrow.[282] Local communities possessed an extraordinarily rich vocabulary for agricultural practice and farm implements, customary tenure, weights, measures and prices, folk customs and recreations, ailments and remedies, food, drink and clothes. As an example we may note that the identification of sheep and cattle in a largely pastoral society depended on an elaborate system of artificial markings (slits and notches cut into the ear),[283] whose vocabulary was not easily translated when noted in legal records. Thus the markings of a lamb suspected to have been stolen in 1586 at Moylgrove, Pembrokeshire, included 'the top of the right ear cut and called "Bulch trithorrad"', i.e. 'bwlch tri thoriad' or a notch of three cuts.[284] When John Lloyd of Ystumanner in Merioneth wrote to Rowland Pugh of Mathafarn in 1614 he found it easier to describe the markings of stolen cattle in Welsh: 'torry blaen y glust ddehe a hollti/r/glust chwithig & thynny/r/garre ussa' (cropping the front of the right ear and slitting the left ear and pulling the lower lace).[285] The oxen were described as coloured black and 'gwin gole' ('light wine' or brown), a term of some interest since the categories used for colour discrimination in English and Welsh did not correspond exactly.[286] Farmers often identified animals in wills and inventories by their physical features; in Caernarfonshire, for example, some referred to 'y fywch fraith' (the speckled cow), 'bystach tallog' (lively bullock) and 'y fywch gorngam' (the crooked-horned cow).[287] Special calls were reserved for different kinds of domestic animals and varied from region to region.

---

[280] *Letters of Goronwy Owen*, p. 148.
[281] Emyr Gwynne Jones, 'Letters of the Rev. Thomas Ellis of Holyhead', *TAAS* (1951), 80.
[282] Malkin, *The Scenery*, p. 65. Cf. NLW MS 10B, f. 78.
[283] Dafydd Roberts, 'Sheep Ear and Body Identification Marks in Wales', *Folk Life*, 20 (1981–2), 91–8; William Linnard, 'Welsh Ear-marks', *BBCS*, XXXIV (1987), 78–86.
[284] NLW, Great Sessions 4/776/3/10.
[285] NLW, Great Sessions 4/144/2i/86.
[286] On colour terms in Welsh and English, see Edwin Ardener, *Social Anthropology and Language* (London, 1971), pp. xxii–xxiii.
[287] G. H. Williams, 'Caernarfonshire Probate Records', p. 401; UWBL, Gaianydd MS 1, ff. 4, 5, 23–4, 33; W. Llewelyn Williams, *'S Lawer Dydd* (Llanelli, 1918), p. 12. We owe this reference to Mr Emrys Williams.

The speech of 'y werin gyffredin ffraeth' (the witty common people) was replete with anecdotes, proverbs and sayings, and there was a rich oral culture of storytelling, poetry and singing. An early-seventeenth-century Protestant account of north Wales refers to hillside gatherings on Sundays and holidays when multitudes assembled to hear 'harpers and crowthers' sing of the valorous deeds of their ancestors and the traditions of the saints and the prophets.[288] It is clear from the brief memoranda collected in Edward Lhuyd's *Parochialia* that the landscape was rather like a 'memory surface' where place-names were reminders of a vast store of local traditions.[289] Little of this material has survived. Few oral genres had acquired 'literary' status although proverbs did appeal to humanists. William Salesbury's *Oll Synnwyr pen Kembero ygyd* (1547) was essentially literary, but many vernacular proverbs were included in James Howell's *Lexicon Tetraglotton* (1660). Protestant reformers were convinced that this genre was an effective didactic device and the wise sayings published by Rees Prydderch in *Gemmeu Doethineb* (1714) drew heavily on Welsh proverbial tradition. Few other genres were recorded in manuscript or print, although there were many clues regarding the extensive nature of these traditions. Edward Lhuyd's efforts to collect 'hen chwedlau' (old legends) for their historical interest met with disapproval from some correspondents who believed that oral traditions were irredeemably vulgar.

The memories of common people were heavily stocked with what James Owen derisively termed 'lying old tales' and 'monkish fables',[290] and listeners hung upon the words of accomplished storytellers. During his exile in Milan, the Catholic writer Gruffydd Robert fondly recalled how 'grey-haired old men' ('henafguyr brigluydion')[291] in his native Anglesey were widely admired as historical remembrancers. Some spellbinding storytellers became legends in their own times. Elis Gruffydd of Gronant in Flintshire, the Tudor soldier and chronicler who wrote a massive history of the world in Welsh, possessed consummate gifts as a spinner of tales: 'Bring him a stool to sit on', he wrote self-deprecatingly, 'and a mugful of beer warmed up and a piece of burnt bread to clear his throat, so that he can talk of his exploits at Therouanne and Tournay.'[292] In late Stuart times, the prose style of Thomas Jones the almanacker was so natural, spontaneous and readable that he must have often regaled his

---

[288] Ifor Williams, 'Hen Chwedlau', *THSC* (1946), 28.
[289] Lhuyd, 'Parochialia', passim.
[290] James Owen, *Trugaredd a Barn* (Llundain, 1715), sig. A4v.
[291] Gruffydd Robert, *Gramadeg Cymraeg*, ed. G. J. Williams (Caerdydd, 1939), p. 2.
[292] Prys Morgan, 'Elis Gruffudd of Gronant – Tudor Chronicler Extraordinary', *FHSP*, 25 (1971–2), 11.

employees at his printing-house in Shrewsbury with tales of how he outmanoeuvred pirate almanackers and punished unscrupulous apprentices.[293] In mid-eighteenth-century Montgomeryshire, William Jones entertained local people at Cann Office in the parish of Llangadfan with stirring tales of legendary Welsh heroes, risqué jokes and bawdy songs.[294] The Morris brothers of Anglesey marvelled at the capacity of their aged father – a carpenter by trade – to recount in detail hundreds of events which had occurred during his boyhood or which had been related by his own parents,[295] and Iolo Morganwg, who was determined to rescue traditional tales, proverbs and legends 'from that damnation with which they are threatened by Methodism', listened and recorded the recollections of the likes of Thomas Jones, an old Catholic from Llancarfan, who 'stored his memory with abundance of . . . fabulous accounts'.[296]

There were also tensions between 'high' and 'low' poetic traditions. Whenever they were confronted with the ancient strict metres or 'unintelligible jargon and gibberish', peasants would say: 'A choethi fyth inni ffrythoneg [sic]?' (Must you always prate this rigmarole to us?)[297] The old poetic tradition, sustained by professional bards, had been characterized by subject, complexity of metres, vocabulary, and access to patronage, but by the late Stuart period the Welsh gentry no longer shared the zeal of their forefathers for the preservation of the poetic craft.[298] Free-metre poetry began to flourish and the low tradition, associated with *y glêr* and unlicensed poets and vagabonds, thrived orally and appealed to those whom Gruffydd Robert called 'unskilled people' ('bobl annhechnennig').[299] Each locality had its poets, and although few of their compositions were published, their carols, lullabies and epigrams can sometimes be found on the flyleaves and other pages of books, ballads and almanacks. These humble rhymesters, who thrived on impromptu verses, recitations, songs and general ribaldry, ensured that historical and entertaining material did not vanish from memory. In the second half of the eighteenth century, for instance, the deaths of some ten poets were recorded by a diarist in the eastern vale of Glamorgan, near Cardiff. They included Zephaniah Jones, a Llantrisant tiler (d.1763) and 'a man given

---

[293] Geraint H. Jenkins, *Thomas Jones yr Almanaciwr 1648–1713* (Caerdydd, 1980), pp. 78–85.
[294] NLW, Llangadfan Parochial Records, no. 1, ff. 43v, 45r, 49v–50r.
[295] *ML*, II, p. 517.
[296] Ceri W. Lewis, *Iolo Morganwg* (Caernarfon, 1995), pp. 60, 146.
[297] *GPC*, s.v. 'brythoneg'.
[298] Jenkins, *The Foundations of Modern Wales*, pp. 227–8.
[299] Robert, *Gramadeg Cymraeg*, p. 279; T. H. Parry-Williams (ed.), *Canu Rhydd Cynnar* (Caerdydd, 1932), pp. lxxxiv–vi.

much to some vain Rhymes, and a greate diverter of vain folks in winter nights by telling y^m old stories'; Evan the Cooper of St Nicholas (d.1768), 'a Welch poet . . . and a great banterer'; John Evan of St Andrews (d.1770), another cooper and 'a Great Rhymmer'; the blind William Robert of Llancarfan (d.1771), 'a great Rhimister'; and many others.[300] Their compositions – essentially oral and often satirical – generally celebrated local events and the quirks and personalities of local inhabitants. Entertaining works such as almanacks, ballads, interludes and crudely-illustrated chapbooks, replete with allegories, dialogues, conversation pieces and satirical portraits, also strongly suggest that daily discourse was characterized by rich and earthy humour.

Most of the characteristic ways of speaking have disappeared forever. Nevertheless, some aspects of oral culture were preserved by intellectuals and antiquarians who were fascinated by the diversity of language and interested in linguistic curiosities and archaisms. In some ways, interest in language involved the 'discovery of the people', a process which Peter Burke has analysed elsewhere in Europe.[301] Edward Lhuyd was fascinated by dialect, place-names and folk traditions, and one of the key questions he asked of his Welsh correspondents in his celebrated questionnaire in 1696 was: 'What Words, Phrases, or Variation of Dialect in the Welsh, seems peculiar to any part of the Country?'[302] He believed that common people were the most reliable recorders of 'observables' and he possessed a rare talent for teasing out information from illiterate shepherds in 'mountainous and desert places'.[303] Shrewd and knowledgeable local people supplied Lhuyd with valuable collections of dialect words. In 1702 David Lewis of Llanboidy sent him a list of 'some British words' used in his district but 'not found in our dictionaries',[304] and Isaac Hamon, writing from Gower in 1697, noted that 'Old English' phrases and pronunciations which had been perfectly familiar to people born in Elizabethan times had disappeared and become 'strange to the people now that are under 50 years of age'.[305]

Antiquarians collected words for the light they shed on the past. William Baxter, a native of Llanllugan and a man who allegedly knew no language other than Welsh until he was sent to Harrow at the age of

---

[300] Cardiff MS 4.877, ff. 100, 385, 501, 518.
[301] Peter Burke, *Popular Culture in Early Modern Europe* (London, 1978), chapter 1.
[302] Lhuyd, 'Parochialia', p. xii.
[303] Frank Emery, *Edward Lhuyd F.R.S. 1660–1709* (Cardiff, 1971), p. 27.
[304] Ibid., p. 77.
[305] Idem, 'Edward Lhuyd and Some of his Glamorgan Correspondents', 84. See also idem, 'A New Reply to Lhuyd's Parochial Queries (1696): Puncheston, Pembrokeshire', *NLWJ*, X, no. 4 (1958), 395–402.

eighteen, believed that 'a good deal of druid philosophy may be guessed at from the names of plants', names like 'menig ellyllon' (foxglove), 'llygad y dydd' (daisy) and 'gedowrach' (burdock). He claimed that 'priests' had sought to disguise pagan names and that some plants were therefore known by dual names. Thus ground ivy was sometimes called by its 'druid name' – 'mantell y corr' – and sometimes by its Christian name – 'mantell Mair'.[306] Interest in linguistic curiosities also gathered pace in the eighteenth century. The following 'Popish prayer' was dictated to Dr Humphrey Foulkes (d.1737) by 'A Gentleman near Bala', who had memorized it on his grandmother's knee:

> Pan godwy'r boreu yn gynta,
> Yn nawdd Beino yn benna;
> Yn nawdd Kerrig [sic] nawdd Patrig,
> Yn nawdd gwr gwyn Bendigedig;
> Yn nawdd Owain ben lluman llu,
> Ag yn nessa yn Nawdd Iessu.[307]

(When I get up in the morning, under the protection of Beuno mainly; under the protection of Curig and Patrick, under the protection of a holy and sacred man; under the protection of Owain, the chief banner of an army, and next under the protection of Jesus.)

There are some oddities in this *lorica*, especially the reference to Owain, and the prayer may not be entirely genuine. Even so, it is probable that greetings and sayings in the seventeenth and eighteenth centuries were still saturated with references to God, Christ and the saints, and with appeals for their protection and blessing.

The words of customary salutations and blessings between travellers and those going about their daily tasks have been preserved in an eighteenth-century source as instances of 'agreeable effusions of benevolence' indicating 'civilization and philanthropy':

When a person is driving a herd of Cattle along the Road or oxen or horses in a team or plow, those who meet generally say, Rhad Duw ar y anifeiliaid (The Blessing of God be on the Cattle) [and] the owner of the Cattle answers Groesaw, or Welcome – and when one person passes by another who is employed in any work, the passer by says Rhad Duw ar y Gwaith – God's Blessing on the work, or God prosper the Work [and] the person employed replies in the same manner, Groesaw or Welcome; or if the traveller sees a

---

[306] Oxford, Bodleian Library, Ashmole MS 1814 (1), f. 270.
[307] Oxford, Bodleian Library, Ashmole MS 1815, f. 56; M. T. Burdett-Jones, 'Gweddi Anarferol', *Y Cylchgrawn Catholig*, III (1994), 35–6.

woman milking cows he says in the same manner Rhad Duw ar y Blith, The Blessing of God on their produce.[308]

By the end of the eighteenth century sayings of this kind were increasingly obsolete. In his miscellaneous writings, Iolo Morganwg remembered the time when 'the dawn the sunrising or the moonrising were never announced but in the following terms: Duw fendithio'r wawr – yr haul, y Golau, y Glaw, etc.' Such expressions, however, were deplored by reforming zealots and lost their currency. 'Puritanism began the work', wrote Iolo, 'and Methodism finishd it of exploding these expressions as relics of popery.'[309] Such losses prompted him to rescue, assemble and cherish traditional words, dialects and speech habits, and in his latter years he referred increasingly to the importance of establishing a Welsh academy to collect and preserve thousands of words which were swiftly dropping out of memory. He also made a point of travelling extensively through Wales and often boasted that he knew more than any other living person about the current state of the Welsh language:

> I have rambled deliberately over all Wales with all my ears open to every word and sound of the language of the Hwntwyr, the Deudneudwyr, Gwancwn Gwent, Adar Morganwg, a Brithiaid Brycheiniog – Cwn Edeirnion, Moch Môn, Dylluanod Ial, a Lladron Mowddwy.[310]

The blessings we have described were also an aspect of greetings. The manner in which people greeted one another, either orally or in correspondence, is a poorly researched but important subject. In parts of north Wales, for example, 'Wala hai' or 'wala' was used as a greeting among friends, and this could be coupled with more agitated cries of 'Wala, wala', 'Wawch' and 'Wala! wfft a dwbwl wfft' in conversation.[311] Much, of course, depended on the social context of the discourse. Within the domestic circle, at least among educated middling sorts, ties between parent and child and husband and wife were relatively formal and this was reflected in their correspondence. Writers invariably affirmed their love, constancy and obedience. In his letters to his mother, the Puritan Morgan Llwyd used the plural pronoun of address 'chi' (you) as a mark of respect, and John Thomas of Myddfai, the eighteenth-century evangelist, did

---

[308] NLW MS 6608E, ff. 49–50.
[309] NLW MS 21431E, f. 48.
[310] NLW MS 13224B, f. 32.
[311] *ML*, I, p. 288; ibid., II, pp. 171, 277.

likewise.[312] Richard Morris, one of the Morris brothers, greeted his father, 'Anrhydeddus Dad' (Honourable Father), and each of the sons used the plural pronoun when writing to him.[313] An interesting aspect of slanderous accusations, usually expressed in the 'ti' form, is that accusations against a person of high status were still sometimes expressed using the 'chi' form. In 1655 at Llandingad in Carmarthenshire, Rees Rudderch David called John Lloyd, gentleman, 'Llydir y gwydde ychi' (You are a thief of geese),[314] and three years later at Tre-lech David Philip Moris said to John Beynon, gentleman, 'Nyd ych chwi syr ond whiwgi' (You are nought but a filching dog, sir).[315]

More formal greetings between strangers or between those of different status involved using the pronoun of respect and addressing those of higher status by title. 'Maister', as in 'maister sheriff', was a common term of respect for office, and 'syr' was used long after the Reformation when addressing a parson or a poet. Greetings were usually accompanied by a physical gesture of respect such as bowing, removing one's hat or curtseying.[316] Failure to observe these proprieties was deemed an insult. Complaints against a Denbighshire man in 1635 included the allegation that he had called a justice of the peace, Robert Wynne esquire, simply Robert Wynne 'without an addition'.[317] Similarly, in 1596 a Montgomeryshire gentleman was scandalized by a social inferior for not 'pooting his hat to him'.[318] When the Quaker Richard Davies of Cloddiau Cochion violated codes of deference by appearing behatted before the high sheriff and magistrates of Montgomeryshire they were nonplussed by his temerity.[319] By refusing to doff their hats, bow, curtsey and acknowledge titles, Quakers incurred the wrath of their social superiors.

Elaborate modes of greeting were noticed by English visitors. Benjamin Malkin was struck by the 'unusually affectionate' modes of greeting, especially among women, 'who are constantly seen saluting each other at market, and on the most ordinary occasions of business'.[320] It is a commonplace that well-bred Englishmen despised and derided the demonstrative gestures which accompanied the speech of Mediterranean

---

[312] J. H. Davies (ed.), *Gweithiau Morgan Llwyd o Wynedd*, II (Bangor, 1908), pp. 243, 267–9; Ioan Thomas, *Rhad Ras*, ed. J. Dyfnallt Owen (Caerdydd, 1949), pp. 81–8.
[313] *ML*, II, pp. 260–2.
[314] NLW, Great Sessions 13/26/9.
[315] NLW, Great Sessions 13/26/11.
[316] Rees, *Dulliau'r Canu Rhydd*, pp. 12–13.
[317] NLW, Great Sessions 4/21/4/28.
[318] NLW, Great Sessions 4/137/4/6.
[319] Davies, *An Account of the Convincement*, p. 59.
[320] Malkin, *The Scenery*, pp. 66–7.

people, and it may well be true that the middle and lower classes in Wales also employed unrestrained gesticulative language.[321] One aspect of this behaviour was enquiry about health. According to Edward Pugh, common people in north Wales were extremely solicitous:

> On meeting their friends, the mode of salutation, 'Pa sut mae galon? or, How is thy heart? Pa sit mae yr wraig ar plant? How are thy wife and children?' is expressive of simplicity and affection.[322]

'Pa sut yr wyd ti?' is a greeting noted in William Owen Pughe's Dictionary, together with the reply, 'Yr wyv yn wych iawn' ('How dost thou do? . . . I am very bravely').[323] According to a Breconshire parson, those who had been ill would invite enquiries about the state of their health by signalling their indisposition: 'both sexes, if the slightest illness or pain affects them are constantly seen with handkerchiefs sound round their heads.' Failure to be solicitous was, of course, considered a serious affront. On the other hand, it was also claimed 'they seem to think they cannot pay you a higher compliment than to tell you that you look extremely ill'.[324] In winding up their letters, the Morris brothers used 'Byddwch wych' (Farewell) or 'Duw fo gyda chwi' (God be with you), phrases which were presumably also oral modes of leave-taking.[325]

Using names appropriately was a significant aspect of greeting and social relationships generally. Welsh men and women had several cognomens. There were 'official' names, descriptive names relating to occupation and status, and nicknames. Families among the lower classes, more especially in upland communities, continued to practise the peculiar system of Welsh patronymics, i.e. using the father's first name after 'ap' or 'ab' (the son of) or 'verch' or 'ferch' (the daughter of) in place of a surname. By the mid-eighteenth century, however, growing numbers of freeholders, yeomen and tenant farmers were following the example of the gentry and the middling sorts by replacing the Welsh model of patronymics with fixed permanent surnames, e.g. ab Evan became Bevan, ap Hywel became Powell, and ap Rice became Price.[326] Traditional baptismal names like Angharad, Lleucu, Ednyfed, Dyddgu and Llywelyn passed out of circula-

---

[321] Jan Bremmer and Herman Roodenburg (eds.), *A Cultural History of Gesture* (Cambridge, 1991), pp. 6, 9. See also Joan Wildeblood and Peter Brinson, *The Polite World* (Oxford, 1965), pp. 197, 199–200. We are grateful to Dr Michael F. Roberts for these references.
[322] Edward Pugh, *Cambria Depicta* (London, 1816), p. 131.
[323] *GPC*, s.v. 'gwych'.
[324] NLW MS 787A, f. 168.
[325] *ML*, I, pp. 18, 328; ibid., II, pp. 156, 333, 397, 444.
[326] T. J. Morgan and Prys Morgan, *Welsh Surnames* (Cardiff, 1985) and J. B. Davies, 'Welsh Names and Surnames', *South Wales Family History Society*, vol. 3, no. 1 (1979), 5–9.

tion among landowning families and were replaced by names such as Anne, David, Catherine and William. The rise of Dissent and Methodism ushered in biblical names, among them Daniel, Moses, Samuel, Rachel and Sarah, which were widely adopted by the pious.

Within the local community people were often known by their occupation or status. Craftsmen (Dic Tincer, Wil y Saer) were known by their trade, farmers (Hugh Maesgwyn, Tom Cefnpennar) by their farms, and servants (Tom gwas Hugh Maesgwyn) by their masters' names. The historian Theophilus Jones noted how the use of descriptive names confused judges and magistrates:

> When a complaint is made against a neighbour, his worship is entreated to grant a warrant against 'Twm o'r Cwm', i.e. Tom of the vale. 'Thomas of the vale (repeats the justice) what's his surname?' 'I never heard he had any other name', is the common reply.[327]

Neutral, descriptive names often merged into nicknames or aliases which involved amusing or controversial assessments of character. Some nicknames were bestowed for obvious physical reasons – 'Old William Jenkins, trwyn coch' (red nose) and 'Mary Rogers alias Bys bwtt' (stump finger) – and cases of 'tew' (fat), 'coch' (red), 'bach' (small) and 'moel' (bald) were legion.[328] Libidinous males were marked out for special treatment: John Evans (d.1696) of Llanfyllin was known as 'Carwr merch' (woman lover), although John Havard (d.1788) of Llandeilo Graban was probably dubbed 'Shôn y Cock' because of his 'cocked' hat.[329] Joseph Thomas (d.1703) alias Pobman (everywhere) of Llangatwg was presumably the Stuart equivalent of Harold Hare, the mentally retarded Mary Roberts (d.1764) of Wrexham was known as 'Moll Wirion', Ann John (d.1770) of Lower Penarth – 'a wild swearing bitter-tongued sort of a woman' – was called 'Nany y Gof Gwyllt', while Bessy Saesones (Betsy

---

[327] Jones, *A History of . . . Brecknock*, I, p. 290; D. E. Williams, 'A Short Enquiry into the Surnames in Glamorgan from the thirteenth to the eighteenth centuries', *THSC* (1961), 48, 78–84; G. P. Jones, 'A List of Epithets from Welsh Pedigrees', *BBCS*, III, part 1 (1926), 31–48. See also Goronwy Owen's manner of enquiring after the health and well-being of his relatives and acquaintances: 'Mae'ch nai Sion Owen fwynwr? Mae Parry o'r Mint? Mae'r Person Humphreys? Ai byw Tom Williams y Druggist o Lôn y Bais? . . . Ai byw Huwcyn Williams, Person Aberffraw?' (How is your nephew John Owen the miner? How is Parry the Mint? How is Parson Humphreys? Is Tom Williams the Druggist of Petticoat Lane alive? ... Is Huwcyn Williams, Parson of Aberffraw, alive?), *Letters of Goronwy Owen*, p. 198.

[328] J. A. Bradney, *A History of Monmouthshire* (4 vols., London, 1904–33), I, part 2, p. 342.

[329] McDonald, 'Parish Registers', 412; NLW, SD/CCB/59/3456.

the Englishwoman) (d.1785) was clearly judged a novelty even in south Monmouthshire.³³⁰

Nicknames shaded into name-calling and the language of insult. Names of disgrace were often linked to animals, especially dogs, which were widely thought of as noisy, quarrelsome and filthy, and there are many instances of 'corgi' (cur), 'chwiwgi' (filching dog), and 'wyneb-ci' (dog face) in court records and correspondence. Uncomplimentary epithets about 'rhyw lymgi o Sais' (some English rascal), 'llymgi ystrywgar' (a crafty rascal) and 'fflamgi drewllyd' (stinking rascal) abound in *The Morris Letters*, for each of the brothers 'wrote as they would speak'.³³¹ Their correspondence contains vivid but acerbic references to some of their less well-liked contemporaries, e.g. 'hurthgen' (blockhead), 'dyn bawaidd, drewllyd, di-ddaioni' (a filthy, smelly, useless man), and 'lloercan yslafan bendew' (a fat-headed laver moonlighter).³³² The most fascinating and evocative examples of the vocabulary of abuse, however, are to be found in cases of defamation and slander. Although the Welsh word 'anudonwr' (perjurer) was widely used, many accusatory words like 'wits', 'rog', 'villen', 'bastard', 'knaf', 'cuckwallt' and 'rhascal' were corruptions of English words. Colourful nouns with wounding adjectives were spat out during bitter quarrels: 'cornworwm brwnt' (foul cuckold), 'y bastard bingam' (thou spayfooted bastard), 'y scwlpin benglog brwnt' (thou scounder like filthy blockhead), 'yr hwch feddw' (drunken sow), 'scrwb gast' (scrub of a bitch) and 'yr hen puttain caglogg' (you old draggle whore).³³³

Oral exchanges were not only less formal than those found in conventional written texts but also more robust, colourful and vulgar. Although fastidious Puritans and Methodists favoured 'plain speech' and Quakers clung tenaciously to Christ's injunction 'swear not at all', reformers often peppered their vocabulary with virulent descriptions of the so-called Antichrist as 'the whore of Babylon' and 'the Devil's harlot', epithets which became common labels of abuse. Among the chattering middle-classes of eighteenth-century Wales, indelicate language was not

---

³³⁰ McDonald, 'Parish Registers', 412; Palmer, *Wrexham*, p. 277; Cardiff MS 4.877, f. 472; Bradney, *History of Mon.*, I, p. 342. The diarist William Thomas also referred to 'David the Sheepherd', 'John y Cwrw', 'John y Cymro', 'Ingenious Jack', 'Ann the bloodletter', and 'Jack the Weaver' (Cardiff MS 4.877, ff. 847, 852, 917, 955, 1062, 1070).

³³¹ *ML*, I, pp. 327, 388, 394, 400; ibid., II, pp. 41, 211, 587, 595. See also Keith Thomas, *Man and the Natural World* (London, 1983), p. 101.

³³² *ML*, I, pp. 61, 77, 159, 179, 346, 352. For more examples, see J. E. Caerwyn Williams, *Llên a Llafar Môn* (Llangefni, 1963), 137–58.

³³³ See the voluminous evidence in Richard Suggett, 'An Analysis and Calendar of Early Modern Welsh Defamation Suits' (2 vols., ESRC Project 1679), NLW Facsimile 271.

uncommon.[334] The edited version of *The Morris Letters*, for instance, is riddled with the footnote u.f.p. (unfit for publication), thereby depriving the modern reader of examples of curses, foul language and smutty references which were clearly in use in the eighteenth century. Coarse 'four-letter' words were deliberately excluded from contemporary Welsh dictionaries, but in convivial circles, where beer flowed freely and the muse excited unorthodox language, oaths, slurs and obscenities had a broad currency. Lewis Morris believed that eighteenth-century Welsh poets were 'naturally inclined to buffoonry, dirty language, and indecent expressions',[335] and the behaviour of members of Y Gymdeithas Loerig (The Lunar Society) in rural Merioneth was outrageous even by Grub Street standards.[336] In popular interludes, the Fool armed himself with a phallus and sometimes styled himself 'Ffowcyn Gnychlyd' (Copulating Foulke) or 'Tinanllad' (Lewd-arse).[337] However hard ardent religious reformers tried to eliminate cursing and swearing, nothing could stem the flow of coarse language. Many traditional English 'minced oaths' – Od Od! Ods Buds, Sbuds, Zownds, Sliffe, Ods Zooks – were absorbed in a corrupt and stilted form in the Welsh vocabulary.[338] Phrases such as 'For God's sake' and 'God damn you blockhead' were used by some of Twm o'r Nant's most colourful characters.[339] John Wesley discovered Welsh speakers in Anglesey whose daily conversation was laced with English oaths and curses, and one traveller in 1788 claimed that the Welsh were prone to scold in the vernacular but curse in English.[340] In monoglot Welsh-speaking communities, the most prevalent oaths and blasphemies were 'Myn Duw' (By God), 'Myn chwys Duw' (By the sweat of God), 'Duw'n farn' (As God is my judge), and 'Myn Crist' (By Christ).[341] Iolo Morganwg collected many earthy and foul aphorisms which were deeply

---

[334] See the marginal comments on a copy of *The British Language in its Lustre* (1688) (NLW W.S. 50); Emyr Gwynne Jones, 'Llythyrau Lewis Morris at William Vaughan, Corsygedol', *LlC*, 10, no. 1 and 2 (1968), 3–58; Rhiannon Thomas, 'William Vaughan: Carwr Llên a Maswedd', *Taliesin*, 70 (1990), 69–76; Dafydd Johnston, 'Sensoriaeth Foesol a Llenyddiaeth Gymraeg', *Taliesin*, 84 (1994), 10–23; Cynfael Lake, 'Puro'r Anterliwt', ibid., 30–9.

[335] *ALM*, II, p. 525.

[336] Jenkins, *The Foundations of Modern Wales*, p. 389.

[337] Lake, 'Puro'r Anterliwt', p. 30.

[338] James Owen, *Salvation Improved* (London, 1696), p. 23; Simon Jones, *Dr Wells's Letter to a Friend* (Amwythig, 1730), p. 18.

[339] *Gwaith Thomas Edwards*, p. 100.

[340] Williams, *John Wesley in Wales*, p. 47; Peter Oliver, 'Journal of a Voyage to England in 1776. And of a Tour through part of England (and Wales) in 1788' (BL Egerton MS 2672/3, vol. 2, f. 634). We owe this reference to Mr Peter Howell Williams.

[341] Henry Evans, *Cynghorion Tad i'w Fab*, ed. Stephen Hughes (Llundain, 1683), p. 58; Iaco ab Dewi, *Llythyr y Dr Well's at Gyfaill* (Amwythig, 1714), p. 14. On Welsh oaths in the legal record, see p. 175 below.

offensive to ardent Methodist evangelists, and noted with particular delight the coarse expressions and proverbs which the 'mongrel' inhabitants of Llantwit Major practised:

> Tis but zo zo, as the Devil zaid of his zupper, when he was eating turd.
> Well done my cock as the Devil zaid to old Harry (Harry 8th).[342]

Cases of slander and defamation provide unusually rich sources which can help us restore the authentic voices of humble people. Actions for slander were brought for damages for injuries to a person's reputation which might involve a financial loss. These were overwhelmingly accusations of theft, usually expressed by the phrase 'lleidr wyt ti' (you are a thief). Accusations of defamation, brought in the church courts, related to morals, particularly sexual morals, and the characteristic accusation was 'putain wyt ti' (you are a whore).[343] 'Whore' was a common term of abuse between women, both married and unmarried, and was applied by men to women. There are numerous examples often expressed in the most vivid language. In 1781 Rees Ellis, a labourer of Newborough in Anglesey, allegedly said of Jane Abraham, a mariner's wife: 'O'r hen hwr din-boeth, ni faswn i ddim yn mynd arnati heb cwlltwr poeth i fynd o 'mlaen, y mae dy afl wedi llosci fel cregin cocos' ('O thou old hot arsed whore, I would not have gone upon thee without a hot coulter to go before me, thy private parts are burnt like cockle shells').[344] Some of the most coruscating expressions were employed by women about women. In 1655 Mary Evans of Beaumaris, a yeoman's wife, was accused of calling Elizabeth Prichard a 'Hoore boith . . . pechod na loskyd hi rhyng ffagode, pechod na chertid hi' ('A burnt whore, it is a pity shee should not bee burnt between faggotts, it is pitty she should not be carted'),[345] while in 1743 Susan Rowland, a labourer's wife of Llangoed in Anglesey, was alleged to have said to Susan Owen, a carpenter's wife: 'God damn ar dy galon di hen scrwd boeth' ('God damn your heart, an old poxed or clapped scrub').[346] Quarrels between women seem frequently to have ended in public quarrels or 'scolding bouts' in which voices were raised loudly in order to bring neighbours from their houses to hear the accusations and

---

[342] NLW MS 13131A, f. 513. For similar Welsh witticisms, see NLW MS 13089E, f. 137; NLW MS 37B, f. 119; Thomas Jones (ed.), *Rhyddiaith Gymraeg, Yr Ail Gyfrol. Detholion o Lawysgrifau a Llyfrau Printiedig 1547–1618* (Caerdydd, 1956), pp. 48–52, 182–4. For the 'barbarisms' of the inhabitants of Llantwit Major, see Suggett, 'Some aspects of village life in eighteenth-century Glamorgan', pp. 157–8.
[343] Suggett, 'Slander in Early-Modern Wales', 136–8.
[344] NLW, Bangor Consistory Court, B/CC/G/252.
[345] NLW, Great Sessions 16/7, m. 7.
[346] NLW, Great Sessions P. 1347.

subsequently offer themselves as witnesses. 'Gwrandewch bawb o nifer y Brafen' ('Hearken all of Aberavan people'),[347] cried Elizabeth Mathew in 1727, before launching into a stream of accusations against Mary Hopkin.

Defamation ushers us into the realm of rumour, gossip and other speech acts, some of which were gender-specific or, at least, gender related. Since women do not figure prominently in the normal run of documentary evidence, we know very little about their speech worlds and to what extent they possessed a distinctive vocabulary. Many of the records – written by males – which portray women as sharp-tongued scolds, garrulous talebearers and evil mischief-makers exhibit some of the worst features of male attitudes towards women. Ellis Wynne bracketed together 'bawds' ('carn-butteiniaid'), 'gossip mistresses' ('Meistresod y chwedleu'), 'termagant rideabouts' ('Marchogesau') and 'scolds' ('Yscowliaid') in his 'Vision of Hell'; Howel Harris spoke ill of 'clacking wives'; Huw Jones of Llangwm likened female discourse to the sound of wasps or cockle shells ('Caccwn neu Swn Cregin Coccos'); Williams Pantycelyn vilified female gossipmongers who swept from house to house 'fel *Gazet* tros Satan' (like a *Gazette* for Satan), and the diarist William Thomas of Michaelston-super-Ely condemned the 'spiteful', 'scratching' and 'bitter-tongued' spinsters and widows in his area.[348] Only death would silence some women's tongues. 'Eist! Tewch a sôn Sian!!' ('Hush! Hold your peace, Jane!!'), wrote the vicar of Tregaron in the parish register after the burial of the local gossip Jane, wife of Edward Jones, in July 1749.[349]

Women of wealth and privilege, at least until early Stuart times, possessed a distinctive vocabulary and set of manners. Siân Mostyn of Gloddaith was described by Gruffudd Hiraethog as 'yr orav o'r Mamav ar sydd yn Traythv Iaith Gamberaec'[350] and servants and dependants benefited from her discourse. In Welsh-speaking communities authors would still rely on the wives of lesser squires to take them under their wing and pass comment on their literary labours.[351] The poet, Goronwy Owen, attributed the purity of his diction to the influence of his mother, who eliminated from his speech every 'uncouth, inelegant phrase, or

---

[347] NLW, Llandaff Consistory Court, Ll/CC/G/478.
[348] Wynne, *Gweledigaetheu*, p. 101; Huw Jones, *Dechrau owdl brith ddigri* (Y Bala, 1758), p. 3; *Gweithiau William Williams*, II, p. 206; Cardiff MS 4.877, ff. 293, 299, 401–2, 443. For the language of gender in English courts, see Jenny Kermode and Garthine Walker (eds.), *Women, Crime and the Courts in Early Modern England* (London, 1994).
[349] D. C. Rees, *Tregaron: Historical and Antiquarian* (Llandyssul, 1936), p. 41.
[350] D. J. Bowen, 'Siân Mostyn, "Yr Orav o'r Mamav ar sydd yn Traythv Iaith Gamberaec"' in J. E. Caerwyn Williams (ed.), *Ysgrifau Beirniadol XVI* (Dinbych, 1990), p. 112.
[351] Jenkins, *Literature, Religion and Society*, pp. 273–4; Lloyd, *Blodeugerdd Barddas o'r Ail Ganrif ar Bymtheg (Cyfrol 1)*, p. 366.

vicious pronunciation'.[352] Women members of Dissenting assemblies from the mid-seventeenth century onwards were highly esteemed for the piety, prudence and 'good stock of knowledge' which they imparted to their children.[353] Yet women were excluded from certain genres of oral culture. Only aggressive Quaker women asserted their right to preach the Gospel. For reasons which are not entirely clear, poetry was a male-dominated genre of popular culture. The satirical element in folk poetry was perhaps regarded by men as inappropriate for women, and hymns were almost always written by men.[354] Only one of the sublime hymns composed by Ann Griffiths of Dolwar Fach in the parish of Llanfihangel-yng-Ngwynfa has survived in her own hand, and had not Ruth Evans, her maidservant, committed her work to memory and transmitted them to her husband, the Revd. John Hughes of Pontrobert, some of the most remarkable hymns of the eighteenth century would have been lost forever.[355]

Cursing was a striking example of a gender-related genre of verbal abuse. Ritual cursing was a petitionary prayer to God, by those who considered themselves wronged, for retribution on the wrongdoer. The malediction was usually delivered in a kneeling posture of supplication, with the hands upraised to heaven as the curser called for the destruction of the wrongdoer's person and property. To be cursed could be a thoroughly alarming experience. Keith Thomas has suggested that ritual cursing was a significant feature of Welsh border life and this must have reflected the daily face-to-face linguistic situation in the March. In 1617 a revealing confrontation occurred at Westhide in Herefordshire when a churchwarden complained that Joanna Powell had 'cursed him in the Welsh language, kneeling down upon her bare knees and holding up her hands, but otherwise the words he could not understand'.[356]

Instances of ritual cursing are scattered throughout the legal record. In 1672, in the Brecon Consistory Court, Mary, wife of David Thomas, was accused of cursing Jane Powell several times, 'sometimes upon her knees' and saying 'she was the cause of making her husband ly from her'.[357] Katherine, wife of Oliver Rees ap Humffrey, was presented at the

---

[352] *Letters of Goronwy Owen*, pp. 61–2.
[353] E. D. Jones, 'Llyfr Eglwys Mynydd-bach', *Y Cofiadur*, 17 (1947), 3–50; idem, 'Llyfr Eglwys Pant-teg', ibid., 23 (1953), 18–70.
[354] Ceridwen Lloyd-Morgan, 'Oral Composition and Written Transmission: Welsh Women's Poetry from the Middle Ages and Beyond', *Trivium*, 26 (1991), 89–102; eadem, 'Ar Glawr neu ar Lafar: Llenyddiaeth a Llyfrau Merched Cymru o'r Bymthegfed Ganrif i'r Ddeunawfed', *LlC*, 19 (1996), 70–8.
[355] A. M. Allchin, *Ann Griffiths* (Cardiff, 1976), p. 13; Dyfnallt Morgan (ed.), *Y Ferch o Ddolwar Fach* (Gwasg Gwynedd, 1977), pp. 95–9.
[356] Keith Thomas, *Religion and the Decline of Magic* (London, 1971), p. 508.
[357] NLW, SD/CCB (G)/28.

Machynlleth Court Leet in 1655 for cursing a neighbour 'by prayeinge and wishing with her lifted hands to heaven that he shold not be worth an yearlinge sheepe'.[358] In 1681 it was reported at the Denbighshire Quarter Sessions that Elizabeth Parry fell down upon her knees and 'wished God would send from heaven wild fire' to consume her enemy's houses.[359] Examples of formal cursing tend to be found in seventeenth-century sources, but ritualized cursing was certainly performed even in the eighteenth century. In his graphic account of the growth of Methodism in north Wales, *Drych yr Amseroedd* (1820), Robert Jones of Rhos-lan told an extraordinary and perhaps embellished story of the persecution to his grave of John Owen, chancellor of the diocese of Bangor, by Dorothy Ellis (Dorti Ddu) of Llannor. Following a bitter quarrel, Dorti Ddu dogged the steps of the chancellor and interrupted his sermons with foul curses:

Gorchmynnai y canghellwr i'w wardeniaid ei llusgo allan: a thrafferth ddirfawr a fyddai ar y rheini yn cael y fath wiber ddychrynllyd o'r llan. Rhwymid hi weithiau wrth bost ym mhorth y fynwent nes darfod yr addoliad; ond yn y man y darfyddai y canghellwr â'i wasanaeth, byddai hithau ym mhorth y fynwent yn ei ddisgwyl allan, gan godi ei dillad a syrthio ar ei gliniau noethion i regi a melltithio â'i holl egni yn ddychrynllyd.[360]

(Ordered by the chancellor to drag her out, the wardens had great difficulty in ejecting such a frightful viper from the church. She was sometimes tethered to the post in the entrance to the graveyard until worship was over; but as soon as the chancellor had completed his service, she awaited him at the entrance of the graveyard, raising her clothes and falling on her bare knees to curse him frightfully with all her strength.)

Dorti Ddu continued to curse the chancellor until he pined away and, following his burial at Llanidloes in 1755, she gleefully defiled the grave. Some forty years later at Fishguard, a distraught woman publicly vilified and cursed the antiquarian Richard Fenton: 'you, Richard Fenton, are a villain, a robber of the fatherless and widow, a thief . . . I curse you; I curse your children; I curse your home. From the day you enter it, misfortune and trouble shall follow you.'[361] Cursers were almost always old and poor women whose only defence against slights and injuries were words. Cursing was thus a weapon used by the weak against the strong.

---

[358] NLW, E. A. Lewis Papers, Transcript of Machynlleth Court Leet Records, 1655.
[359] NLW, MS Chirk B38a/12.
[360] Robert Jones, *Drych yr Amseroedd*, ed. G. M. Ashton (Caerdydd, 1958), pp. 48–9; NLW, B/CC/G/54 (excommunication of Dorothy Ellis).
[361] Richard Fenton, *A Historical Tour through Pembrokeshire* (Brecknock, 1903), p. xxvii.

Very occasionally the actual words of a Welsh malediction have been preserved. In 1684 Jane, wife of Edward Lloyd of Llanynys, in a dispute about her house, cursed her opponents, saying, 'melltith Duw ir neb a ddelo i'm tu/i/om anfodd' (the curse of God on anyone who meddles in my house against my will) and solemnly prayed that her opponents would never prosper: 'Na chaffo byth gam rhwdd, na byth rhwydeb nag iechyd a gymero nhu i' (Those who take my house shall never have an easy step, prosperity, nor good health).[362] Although the voices of women are far less prominent in historical records than one would like, there are good grounds for believing that they were not necessarily passive victims in a world dominated by males.

To sum up. Throughout the early modern period the Welsh language exercised dominion over vast expanses of territory in Wales. Although English was the dominant language in key domains like government and administration, law, commerce, science and polite society, Welsh held sway on the hearth and in the workplace, in church and chapel, in literature and poetry, in recreation and popular culture. This meant that for most practical purposes people were able to live their lives fully in Welsh. The Welsh language was not only the sole medium of communication for the bulk of the population but also the most tangible and significant badge of national identity. In many ways, the language was stronger in 1800 than it had been in 1500. It is true that the gentry élite had become Anglicized, that there were fewer monoglot Welsh speakers, and that there were disturbing signs of corruption in the vocabulary and idiom of common discourse, but on the other hand the number of people speaking Welsh had doubled and a substantial number of them could read as well as speak their native tongue. Welsh was the language of religion and the vernacular Bible had become a source of spiritual sustenance for worshippers and a dignified literary model for writers. The Welsh book trade was flourishing and cultural activists, most of whom were also fluent in English and well versed in its literature, were keenly aware of the long and distinguished literary tradition of the native language and its links with other Celtic tongues. It is not an exaggeration to say that the Welsh language had survived its first crisis of identity.

---

[362] NLW, Great Sessions 4/32/4/22.

3

Tudor Legislation and the Political Status of 'the British Tongue'

PETER R. ROBERTS

TWO SEMINAL acts of parliament passed in the sixteenth century are generally believed to have changed the status of the Welsh language, first in a legal and then in a religious context, and in the process to have transformed the cultural development of the nation. The received opinion has been that the so-called 'Act of Union' of Wales with England in 1536 pronounced English to be the official language of public life in Wales, and that the native tongue was banished from the courts of law. The Elizabethan act of 1563 for the translation of the Bible and the Book of Common Prayer into Welsh is remembered as having conferred upon the language formal recognition as the appropriate medium for church worship in areas of the country where English was not spoken or understood. It would be foolish to consider these measures as expressing a consistent and single-minded 'Tudor policy towards Wales' or to assume that their cultural impact was invariably what was intended. Public attitudes to the status of the Welsh language were conditioned by the political, religious and intellectual values of the time, and in the period between 1536 and 1563 a discernible shift can be traced in these values as they impinged upon policy-making. The circumstances in which policy was enacted need to be examined rigorously if we are to identify the purposes that these acts were designed to serve and the motives of the reformers and the lawmakers. It appears that initiatives taken by the spokesmen of sectional interests in Wales, and by Welsh humanists moved by less worldly motives, were successful in persuading the regime to revise its priorities at critical junctures. In helping to frame the statutes that enshrined 'Tudor policy' on two significant occasions, a number of influential Welshmen were given a voice in deciding the place which their language was to occupy in the Reformation state and church.

Traditional accounts of the cultural and social consequences of the 'Act of Union' have focused on the Anglicization of the leaders of society. There is another dimension to be considered, for the period witnessed a two-way process of acculturation of Welsh and English elements, and significant traces of both an Anglicizing and a Cymricizing tendency can be detected in Welsh society before the union with England. Some of the settler families of the Middle Ages had, to some degree, already been Cymricized, a process that seems to have started earlier in some of the marcher lordships than in the lands of the principality.[1] While intermarriage between landed families of English and Welsh extraction could have a levelling effect, lingering attachment to distinctions of law and custom, together with the competition for land and offices, still formed a barrier to harmonious coexistence. At the beginning of the sixteenth century the burgesses of the 'plantation boroughs' of north Wales – Caernarfon, Conwy and Beaumaris – still clung tenaciously to the exclusive privileges granted to their predecessors by Edward I. The Welsh communities in the principality and the lordships in north Wales obtained a degree of parity with the burgesses in the royal charters of privileges granted late in the reign of Henry VII. The townsmen challenged the validity of these concessions, and though at least some of the charters were endorsed on the accession of Henry VIII, there remained some doubt about their legality. The burgesses of Conwy repeated their complaints to the young king in 1509 in terms which show that they still regarded themselves as English colonists in a frontier society:

> . . . it is no more meete for a welshman to beare any office in Wales, or especiallie in any of the Three englishe Townes then it is for a frinchman to be Officer in Calis, or a skotte in Barwicke.[2]

This exclusiveness was to be undermined in the following two decades by the infiltration of Welsh purchasers of burgage property, who ignored the uncertain legal status of the charter and thereby defied the prohibitions of the Lancastrian penal laws against the Welsh. The 'invasion' of the boroughs seems to have been facilitated by more frequent intermarriage between urban and county families.[3]

The most acute of these internal tensions between the inhabitants of town and country had disappeared before parliament ordained in 1536 that law and government in Wales should be assimilated to English forms and institutions. While communities of 'Welshry' and 'Englishry' persisted in the Marches, in the northern principality at least a degree of social assimilation had taken place even though the legal status of the Welsh was

---

[1] A. H. Dodd, 'Welsh and English in East Denbighshire: a historical retrospect', *THSC* (1940), 43–8.
[2] Robert Williams, *The History and Antiquities of the Town of Aberconwy and its Neighbourhood* (Denbigh, 1835), p. 49.
[3] E. A. Lewis, *The Mediaeval Boroughs of Snowdonia* (London, 1912).

still that of 'foreign inhabitants' in their own country. When the 'Act of Union' made the Welsh equal with the English before the common law, there was little in the way of a defensive reaction on the part of the inhabitants of the boroughs.[4] None of the responses to the changes, which were mostly favourable, reflected any residual distinctions of national identity within Wales. The prescription in the 'Act of Union' that English was to be the language of the law courts cannot be construed as a deliberate design on the part of the legislators to perpetuate these internal divisions or to revive an 'English ascendancy' in Wales.

The only direct contemporary reference in Welsh to the so-called 'Act of Union' is to be found in Elis Gruffydd's 'Cronicl': 'Ynnol hynn i pashiodd actt arall i orddeinio ac i wneuth[r] holl Gymru yn siroedd' (Subsequently he passed another bill to decree and divide the whole of Wales into counties).[5] That is all that the measure meant to him, or all that he gathered of its significance from his post in the garrison at Calais. The shire system introduced into the whole of Wales was based on the English model and the pattern of administration already operating in the three shires of the northern principality. Within this framework annual sheriffs were to be appointed and a new system of courts was to be established to administer the common law in the English language.[6] The imposition of a language qualification for the holding of judicial and fee-bearing offices is the most controversial of all the provisions of the first 'Act of Union'. It has gained a notoriety in modern Welsh historiography comparable to that of 'the Treason of the Blue Books'. A detailed reconstruction of the making of the act is not possible in the state of the surviving evidence, but the formulation of the clause merits careful scrutiny in the fuller context of the legislative programme proposed or enacted for Wales in the years 1533–6.

The essential key to understanding the significance of the 'language clause' of the act in its contemporary setting is the attitude of the Welsh to the prospect held out to them of equality with the English before the law in both countries. The gentry for the most part welcomed the alteration in status because of the legal and economic benefits it brought them. In spite of the prohibitions of the Lancastrian penal laws, a few favoured leading

---

[4] Richard Bulkeley of Beaumaris and John Salesbury were initially fearful for their offices in the exchequers at Caernarfon and Denbigh, but their interests were protected in the event.

[5] NLW Mostyn MS 158, f. 509v.

[6] The Lord Chancellor was given the right to appoint commissions of the peace for Wales in the act 27 Henry VIII, c.5. The Quarter and Great Sessions were in operation before the act of 1543 was passed. Ivor Bowen (ed.), *The Statutes of Wales* (London, 1908), pp. 67–9; Peter R. Roberts (ed.), '"A Breviat of the Effectes devised for Wales", c. 1540–41', *Camden Miscellany Vol. XXVI* (Camden, 14, 1975), 31–5.

Welshmen had since the mid-fifteenth century held offices of charge under the Crown in the principality and lordships, but they did so by royal favour and licence rather than as a birthright.[7] A substantial number of Welsh landowners in different parts of the country were anxious to secure the consolidation and perpetuation of their estates according to the rules of primogeniture and entail. It may be safely assumed that their voluntary adoption of English land law over several generations had accustomed them to understand its complexities, if not always the languages in which the law was couched, namely English, Norman French and Latin. The conditions on which the charters of enfranchisement were negotiated from Henry VII testify to the readiness with which Welsh landowners in the northern communities were prepared to abandon native customs to gain permanent immunity from their 'alien' status and equality with the burgesses of the 'walled towns'.

The timing of the introduction of the reforms of 1536–43 may well have been decided in part by a resumption of these overtures to the Crown. It was John Puleston, constable of Caernarfon Castle, who took the initiative in organizing a petition, probably early in 1536, 'to have the three shires of North Wales in like manner and condition and like laws as be used and accustomed within the realm of England'. The names of Puleston's fellow petitioners are not recorded, but if they were the representatives of country families (both his wives were Welsh), they could have been under no illusion about the implications of the changes involved. On the other hand, the petition presented by Puleston was opposed, on the grounds that they had not been consulted about it, by six landowners from the old shires of Anglesey and Caernarfon and two burgesses of Conwy and Beaumaris. They protested that it had been proposed out of malice for 'the poor commons', for they were apprehensive that English taxes would follow English law into the shires, to their impoverishment. Their caution therefore signified not an attachment to their native inheritance so much as a wariness about the extra burdens which the innovations might impose upon them.[8]

There is thus a sense in which the provisions of the 'Act of Union' were a response to an invitation for change emanating from Wales itself, though the evidence does not suggest a unanimous desire on the part of the gentry for the complete adoption of the English legal system. Nor should the 'Act of Union' be seen as an inevitable or progressive development from the charters of liberties. A list of measures drawn up by Thomas Cromwell for parliament late in 1533 included the resumption of all patents of offices

---

[7] Some also acted as stewards to the few remaining independent marcher lords.
[8] Puleston's petition has not survived but its tenor is rehearsed in the counter-petition. PRO SC8/115/5707, *n.a.*, but datable from internal evidence.

held by Welshmen, 'and that no Welsheman to be any officer ther according to the old lawes of this land'.[9] This prohibition was not revived and Cromwell was eventually to reverse it, but not before the severe laws of 1534 enacted in parliament against disorder in the lordships were enforced by Bishop Rowland Lee as President of the Council in the Marches. By the spring of 1536 this rigorous approach had succeeded in suppressing the worst excesses of marcher lawlessness, in Cromwell's judgement if not in Lee's, and it was decided that a radically different approach to government could safely be adopted as part of a general strategy for the integration of the realm. It would not have been possible to introduce the English shire system without the recruitment of the local landowners as officials and justices, and the common law could only be administered in the English language. Cromwell therefore overcame his initial reluctance to entrust Welshmen with offices under the Crown and he disregarded the advice of Rowland Lee, who continued to express his disapproval of the policy of permitting 'one thief to try another'. The prevalence of faction among the gentry was evidently no longer regarded as an insuperable barrier to fundamental reforms in law and administration. In these circumstances the 'language clause' represented the residual restraint on the holding of office by Welshmen, the price which had to be paid for a concession, as much as a qualification for office. The new structure of law and administration augmented the Crown's sources of patronage, which could be dispensed to underwrite loyalty to the regime and the royal supremacy in the church. This may indeed have been a deciding factor in the making of the new policy for Wales as well as of the scheme to dissolve the lesser monasteries later in the same year.

Welsh clerics and civil lawyers were already functioning in key ecclesiastical offices from the early stages of the Reformation. The most sedulous of those engaged in diocesan visitations are known to have tested the patience of their superior. In 1537 John Capon, the non-resident bishop of Bangor (1534–9), complained about the inconvenience caused by too frequent visitations of the clergy in the Vale of Clwyd by the commissioners, John Vaughan, priest, and the civilian Dr Elis Price:

> Ffor the nature of a Welsheman is ffor to bere office and to be in authoritie. He will not let to runne thorow the fyer of hell and sell and geve all he can make of his owen and his ffrends for the same.

---

[9] The bills 'for justices in Wales' on the list must refer to English justiciars such as those already operating in the northern and southern shires of the principality. BL Cotton MSS, B I, ff. 161, 453.

Capon was of the same mind as Bishop Rowland Lee that such fickle and unreliable people were not suited to hold offices of trust.[10]

Neither bishop could reverse the policy begun in 1536 or withstand the growing demand from Welsh gentlemen and clergy to hold responsible offices in the church and under the Crown in their own country. Sir John Price and Dr Elis Price were among the visitors of the monasteries in England and Wales respectively; other Welshmen served on various royal commissions before 1536. Indeed, the service rendered by such men as agents of the Reformation may well have been decisive in convincing Cromwell that the Welsh gentry were capable of shouldering greater administrative responsibilities. He may have been influenced by his familiarity with Sir John Price, who married his wife's sister in October 1534 and thereby became his brother-in-law. The wedding took place in Cromwell's house in Islington on 11 October 1534, and their first-born son was named after the latter's son, Gregory. Price took pride in his important connections on the distaff side, not only with Cromwell but with the Seymours. An entry in his Welsh commonplace book explains that his wife Joan, the daughter of John Williamson, 'whose sister was the wife of Thomas, Lord Cromwell, the mother of Gregory Cromwell, who married the sister of Queen Jane, the mother of Prince Edward' ('a oedd chwaer i wraic Thomas Arglwydd Crumwel mam Gregory Crumwel a briodes chwaer brenhines Siaen mam Bryns Edwart').[11] Cromwell's close association with Price may have been sufficient in itself to point out the anomaly of employing Welshmen in high offices in England while not involving them in offices of trust in their own communities. There is nothing in the extant records to connect Price with the so-called 'Act of Union', but he was clearly in a position to be consulted by Cromwell on the reforms for Wales in the crucial years from 1534 to 1536. Following Cromwell's fall and execution, Price was to be appointed secretary, first of the king's affairs in the Marches and then of the Council there, and in that capacity certainly played his part in implementing the settlement.[12]

---

[10] Letter of 20 December 1537 from the abbey of Hyde, which Capon held *in commendam*, to his steward in the diocese: BL Harleian MS 283, f. 153; *Letters and Papers, Henry VIII*, X, no. 330.

[11] These words in the commonplace book had been scratched out, by a resentful person, as is explained in a marginal note in a Tudor hand. 'Rhiw ddyn kenfigennus a tynodd y geiriay hyn allan.' Dr E. D. Jones comments that the occasion of jealousy was doubtless Price's connection with Cromwell and the royal court. Bodleian Library, Balliol College MS 353 (NLW MS 9048E is a facsimile); E. D. Jones, 'Llyfr Amrywiaeth Syr Siôn Prys', *Brycheiniog*, VIII (1962), 97–104.

[12] Roberts, *Camden Miscellany Vol. XXVI*, 42. As a humanist as well as Crown servant, Price's presence in Cromwell's circle may account for the note of conciliation that is struck in the preamble to the 'Act of Union' about the relations of the Welsh and the English.

The legislators had good reason to suppose that a significant section of Welsh landowners would be well disposed to the reforms and, as was not the case with the native Irish, that their attachment to indigenous customs would be no barrier to the reception of English law and all that that entailed. The political principle underlying the reforms of 1536 was the concept of the unitary state. English was established as the universal speech for all the king's subjects, though the policy was not uniformly applied. The draconian measures taken to suppress languages other than English in other parts of the king's dominions outside the realm, such as Calais and Ireland, contrasts with the conciliatory note struck in the preamble to the act for Wales.[13] The legislative intention was to bring the king's subjects in both countries to 'an amicable Concord and Unity' commensurate with equality before the law of England, and 'utterly to extirp all and singular the sinister Usages and Customs differing from the same'. This phrase has been interpreted by some modern commentators as embracing the Welsh language as well as the residual native laws. Others have suggested that it is not the language but the 'Usages and Customs' that are considered to be the anomaly.[14] The phrasing is admittedly ambiguous and, like so much else in the preamble, may have been deliberately vague. What is condemned is the slanderous logic of the 'rude and ignorant people' who made invidious distinctions between the king's subjects on the spurious grounds that the laws, customs and language of the former differ from those of England.

The first enacting clause proceeds to abolish the surviving native laws, though even this ban is qualified in later clauses. In the 'language clause' (number 20 in modern editions of the statute),[15] it is stipulated that the proceedings of the courts were to be in English, and no Welshman was to hold any judicial or fee-bearing office unless he was proficient in that language. Those who aspired to such offices were thus encouraged to become bilingual, and the suggestion that the Welsh language was banned is a misreading of the provision.[16] The laws of Hywel Dda, written in

---

[13] Peter R. Roberts, 'The Union with England and the Identity of "Anglican" Wales', *TRHS*, 22 (1972), 61–2.

[14] Bowen, *Statutes*, p. 76; *Legal Status of the Welsh Language: Report of the Committee under the Chairmanship of Sir David Hughes Parry* (London, 1965), p. 9.

[15] Bowen, *Statutes*, p. 87. The provision superseded, but did not rescind, the penal laws, which remained on the statute book until they were repealed in 1623: 21 James I, c.28. Ibid., pp. 167–8.

[16] The clause has not always been accurately represented in modern commentaries on the effects of the legislation on Welsh culture. The partial quotation in Raymond Garlick, *An Introduction to Anglo-Welsh Literature* (Cardiff, 1970), p. 14, distorts the meaning of the clause by truncating it, rehearsing the section which prohibits all Welsh speakers from holding any office or fees while leaving out the conditional qualification: '. . . unless he or they use and exercise the English speech or language'.

Welsh, had some time since ceased to be a vital force in the land, so that the loss of status for the language was the culmination of a long historical process bound up with the decline of the laws. Even so, it had long been evident that the Welsh language was not dependent on the native laws for its survival as a living tongue and it was certainly not abolished at the same time as those laws.

The ruling that English should be the official language of law and administration in Wales was to have an inescapable impact on the life of the community and on the standing of the Welsh language, but the evidence for this impact in the short term is sparse and problematic. Apart from the misgivings of Lee, the only reservations expressed about the act 27 Henry VIII, c.26, were those of existing office-holders, either in parliament or in the country.[17] If any objections were raised to the 'language clause', they have not left a trace in the records. The bards, who were not slow to comment on any Anglicizing trend in society, were reticent on this occasion, perhaps because the reforms as a whole were not perceived at the time to be a latent threat to the language. The new conditions of service under the Tudor Crown required the gentry to be resident in their own communities, and thereby better placed to exercise their duty of hospitality, but the apparent acquiescence of the bards in the new order may be explained by their concern for larger loyalties than the patronage dispensed in the country houses. In one of his odes to Henry VIII, Lewys Morgannwg praised the king's imperial qualities as the heir of Brutus and a second Charlemagne, and (possibly alluding to the acts of 1534 against disorder in the Marches) he paid tribute to him for imposing order on the Welsh.[18] After the fall of Anne Boleyn in May 1536, Lewys denounced her as a traitor, a second Alys Rowena who had corrupted the kingdom of the Britons with her sponsorship of the 'new religion'. In the same poem the poet urged the king not to appoint Englishmen of low rank to high office. The contentment and security of the kingdom, he averred, were best assured by elevating Welshmen from the locality. This

---

[17] Provisos were attached to the bill during its passage through parliament reserving the rights of existing office-holders like the earl of Worcester. Bowen, *Statutes,* pp. 91–3.

[18] y holl afreol Kymru a rolaist [reolaist]
herwyr ymladdwyr yma a luddiaist
wedy i holl drethau da y llywodraethaist
am i kywired mwyn i keraist.
(you imposed order on all the disorder of Wales, you stood in the way of outlaws and aggressors here, afterwards you ruled well over all their taxes, because of their honesty you loved them dearly.)
E. J. Saunders, 'Gweithiau Lewys Morgannwg' (unpubl. University of Wales MA thesis, 4 vols., 1922), I, pp. 204–12. Sir John Price copied the ode into his commonplace book: NLW MS 9048E [photostat of Balliol MS 353], f. 20.

may well be an oblique reference to the two measures of 1536 (27 Henry VIII, cc.5, 26), recently passed in parliament, which provided for the appointment of sheriffs and justices of the peace in the Welsh shires; if so, it seems to be the only bardic comment on the legislation of 'union'.[19]

That *gwrêng* as well as *bonedd* welcomed the new measures as enfranchisement rather than imposition may be gauged from the reaction of the countrymen of the lordship of Denbigh in May 1537. They clearly interpreted the 'Act of Union' as a final confirmation of the charter of 1506 when, 'by a man in a hood', they proclaimed in the market place of Denbigh that they were as free as Englishmen and need not pay stallage in the town.[20] In the event such privileges were to be paid for dearly by the monoglot majority who found that, in any action in the courts, they were not after all equal before the law with those of their compatriots who had a command – or even a smattering – of English. Only occasionally do the records of the courts and other sources reveal the difficulty which these disadvantaged litigants or defendants encountered in coping with the new dispensation.[21]

No special legislative or administrative provision was made during the period of transition to deal with the linguistic problems involved in the process of transforming a whole legal system. A dispute over lands held by native tenure in Caeo, Carmarthenshire, was settled according to the laws of Hywel in a Welsh document dated 8 June 1540. This may have been an extra-curial arbitration, but even if it arose out of an action in one of the commotal or hundred courts in the shire, it would still have been a valid transaction since it was determined a year before the final prohibition on Welsh laws came into effect. The statute 34 & 35 Henry VIII, c.26, was legislating retrospectively when it stipulated 24 June 1541 as the date from which all native tenures were extinguished.[22] Welsh units of landholding such as *gwely* and *gafael* were henceforth to be subject to English tenure, though a royal official still deemed it appropriate to use the Welsh language to survey and describe those belonging to the Crown

---

[19] In an elegy to Rhys ap Siôn of Glyn Neath, Lewys expressed his disapproval of the English influences which were creeping over Glamorgan and Gwent. The poetry of Iorwerth Fynglwyd, Lewys's contemporary among the Glamorgan bards, was less deferential to authority, though in condemning the persecution of the Welsh by corrupt English officials he may have been seeking to comfort a patron who had been ruined by litigation. E. J. Saunders, op. cit., I, pp. xvii, 63–4, 190–8; *DWB*, p. 565; G. J. Williams, *Traddodiad Llenyddol Morgannwg* (Caerdydd, 1948), p. 68.

[20] PRO SP1/120/50: Lee to Cromwell, 12 May 1537.

[21] For examples of some revealing exchanges (one of them in Welsh) in the Courts of Great Sessions as preserved in non-forensic sources, see Peter R. Roberts, 'The Welsh Language, English Law and Tudor Legislation', *THSC* (1989), 38–9.

[22] Bowen, *Statutes*, p. 122.

estate in Anglesey in a rental of 1549.[23] This was an exceptional instance, however, and the practice does not seem to have been repeated or emulated in other parts of the country where Welsh tenure continued as an extra-legal survival.

The language provision of the 'Act of Union' became a bone of contention on one occasion during the transitional period, when some confusion clearly remained over the jurisdictions of courts in the 'Welshries' of the marcher lordships. In a dispute over the possession of lands in the manor of Leighton in the new shire of Montgomery, Thomas Kerry, a London merchant who claimed to be the lord of the manor, accused the sheriff, Humphrey Lloyd, of assaulting two of the jurors at the manorial court held by Kerry's steward in 1541, 'bycause they gave their verdite in the Englysshe tonge accordyng to your graces lawes, for that as he pretendyd that the same was ayent the Welshe lawes'. If the charges against Lloyd were true, they cast a curious light on his conduct in office as the first sheriff to be appointed for the county and on his motives as a prominent agent of the new order in Wales. For he had been one of the signatories of the petition from Montgomeryshire urging that the provisions of the 'Act of Union' be fully implemented, and had also been entrusted with the task of formally presenting it to the king. Lloyd appears to have defied the operation of the 'language clause' in pursuit of his own private interests, and he may have escaped responsibility for his actions by taking advantage of the administrative delay in 'shiring' the Marches and erecting the new system of courts. Kerry failed to overturn the Chancery decree of 1544, which refuted his title to the property in dispute, and Lloyd retained his estate at Leighton and served as knight of the shire in 1545 and 1547.[24]

Under the new dispensation the official language of the law was to be English, but was it the intention of the act to forbid the use of the Welsh language in the courts completely? The eight proceedings stipulated in the

---

[23] T. Jones Pierce, 'An Anglesey Crown Rental of the Sixteenth Century', *BBCS*, X, part 2 (1940), 156–76, esp. 157, where attention is drawn to 'its rare character as an administrative document written in Welsh'. The prefatory note, however, is in Latin.

[24] PRO SP 1/144, ff. 83–4; Star Chamber 2/23/116, 167. S. T. Bindoff (ed.), *The History of Parliament: The House of Commons 1509–1558* (3 vols., London, 1982), II, pp. 540–1. Lloyd was steward of the lordship of Cause, Salop, under Henry, Lord Stafford, c.1554–62. Professor R. Geraint Gruffydd has suggested that Humphrey Lloyd of Leighton was the translator (from the Latin) of the medical treatises traditionally ascribed to Humphrey Llwyd, *The treasuri of helth* (c.1552), and *The jugement of vrynes* (1553). The latter work bears a dedication to Lord Stafford which indicates that the former was also translated at his request, but there is no independent evidence that his deputy was learned in either Latin or medicine, and it seems safer to stay with the traditional attribution. R. Geraint Gruffydd, 'Humphrey Llwyd of Denbigh: Some Documents and a Catalogue', *TDHS*, 17 (1968), 56.

'language clause' to be kept in English do not, in fact, exhaust all the proceedings of a court of law. The omission of 'pleadings' and enrolments from the list may be significant, for the surviving evidence suggests that in the case of English courts these may have been in Norman French and Latin respectively. Since the principal purpose of the act was the assimilation of the legal system to that obtaining in England, 'the particular intention of the language clause would presumably be to assimilate the linguistic practice of the courts in Wales to that of the courts in England'.[25] In the mid-sixteenth century pleadings in the assize courts of the west of England were still conducted in French, which the suitors did not understand.[26] If the same practice in respect of pleadings was observed in Wales after the 'union', the English litigants there must have been as confused as the Welsh, whether the latter were monoglot or bilingual. But the other model specified in the act 27 Henry VIII, c.26, for the procedures of the new courts of higher justice in Wales (which came to be known as the Great Sessions) was the court of the justice of north Wales, where the conventions may have differed from those of the English assizes. In the older counties of Cardigan and Carmarthen, which constituted the 'southern principality', it is known that advance notice of the holding of sessions before the king's justice had been proclaimed annually, by ancient custom, 'both in English and Welshe to th'entent that no man shuld be therof iugnorantt . . .'[27] It is probable that a similar practice was observed with respect to the sessions held by the justice of the northern principality. But we cannot tell the extent to which the procedures were understood by all the litigants or defendants who came before the courts under the new or the old dispensation.

The concessions made by the regime to those afflicted by the 'language barrier' were piecemeal and dilatory. The earliest evidence we have for the linguistic practices in the higher reaches of the new Welsh judicature dates from the 1550s. Evidence could be given in Welsh by monoglot witnesses and defendants, and interpreters were used to translate their testimony (and presumably to explain the procedures to them) in the court of the Council at Ludlow as well as in the Courts of Great Sessions.[28] In its administrative, as distinct from its judicial capacity, the Council was obliged to accord Welsh a quasi-official status to ensure that

---

[25] J. Goronwy Edwards, 'The Language of the Law Courts in Wales: Some Historical Queries', *CLR*, 6 (1975), 5–9.
[26] F. W. Maitland (ed.), *Year Books of Edward II: Selden Society, I* (London, 1903), p. xxxv.
[27] PRO Star Chamber 2/18/234.
[28] Roberts, 'The Welsh Language', loc. cit.; Murray Ll. Chapman, 'A Sixteenth-Century Trial for Felony in the Court of Great Sessions for Montgomeryshire' [at Welshpool, Feb. 1572], *MC*, 78 (1990), 167–70.

regulations were understood and obeyed in every corner of its jurisdiction. In the 1570s a council order for the appointment of 'overseers' in Merioneth to assist the justices of the peace in keeping order in the parishes was 'to be openly read and published in the Welsh tonge' at Quarter Sessions.[29]

In January 1576 Sir William Gerard, Vice-President of the Council in the Marches, explained to Sir Francis Walsingham the historical background to existing procedures in the Welsh judicature. In his summary of Henry VIII's legislation his gloss on the 'language clause' is particularly illuminating: it was a provision 'forbiddinge soe muche the use of Walshe speeche, as all pleadinges and proceedinges in sute to be in the English tong' in the courts. If this is taken literally as indicating the precise sense in which the provision of 1536 had been interpreted, it would follow that pleadings were conducted in English in the courts of higher justice from the beginning. In so far as this departed from the practice in England, it may denote a continuity of the procedures obtaining in the medieval principality. Acutely conscious that miscarriages of justice were inherent in the system, Gerard went on to recommend that it would be very convenient if at least one justice in each circuit of the Great Sessions should understand Welsh. His nominee as a second justice in the south-western circuit was Edward Davies, who 'is well learned and can speak the Wealche tonge but no Welcheman'. As a native of Shrewsbury, Davies was evidently considered a second-generation Englishman, but there were objections to his nomination on the grounds of his poverty and lack of learning in the law, though he had already served twice in parliament as a burgess for Cardigan boroughs.[30] An act providing for a second justice to be appointed in each of the Welsh circuits was passed in parliament within two months of Gerard's letter. The act 18 Elizabeth, c.8, did not stipulate that one of the justices in each circuit should know Welsh. The sticking point may have been an objection in principle to Welshmen serving as judges in their own country. A statute of 1542 (33 Henry VIII, c.24) had laid down that no justice of assize should serve in any country where he 'was borne or doth inhabyte'. This ruling must have applied to appointments in Wales as well as England, and there were to be few exceptions.[31] Only two justices

---

[29] Peter R. Roberts, 'Elizabethan "Overseers" in Merioneth', *JMHRS*, IV, part 1 (1961), 7–13; W. Ogwen Williams, 'The Survival of the Welsh Language after the Union of England and Wales: the First Phase, 1536–1642', *WHR*, 2, no. 1 (1964), 72.

[30] 'A note of such as desire to be placed Justices in Wales by the new statute, with their qualities and conditions etc.: 1576.' PRO SP12/110/13. P. W. Hasler (ed.), *The History of Parliament: The House of Commons 1558–1603* (3 vols., London, 1981), II, pp. 21–2.

[31] According to the preamble of the act 18 Elizabeth I, c.8, the appointment of second justices was granted in response to the petition of the Welsh, which may indicate a

known to be Welsh speakers seem to have been appointed in the sixteenth century.[32]

This policy of appointment differed markedly from that in the Elizabethan church, where a series of distinguished Welshmen served as bishops. Both the justices of Great Sessions and the bishops served ex officio on the Council in the Marches, whose other members included a number of Welsh gentlemen-lawyers like Sir John Wynn of Gwydir and Dr Elis Price of Plasiolyn. Such councillors and bishops would have easily understood the testimony of the monoglot Welsh suitors who appeared before them, but they were open to the charge of partiality. Having served as Vice-President of the Council at Ludlow when he was bishop of Worcester, Archbishop John Whitgift had mixed impressions about the capacity of the Welsh to dispense impartial justice in that high tribunal. He had disapproved of the indulgent attitude towards the Welsh held by the Lord President, Sir Henry Sidney. As a privy councillor from 1585, Whitgift took part in the drafting of the queen's instructions to the Council in the Marches. In 1592 he welcomed the proposal to appoint four lawyers to serve the Council, but advised that 'they neyther should be Welshmen nor dwelling within the Marches'.[33] 'The Dialogue of the Government of Wales', written by George Owen in the 1590s, contains no comment on the absence of Welsh-speaking judges in its analysis of the defects in the administration of justice. It is remarkable that the observation on the disadvantages suffered by Welsh litigants came from an Englishman – Sir William Gerard – and that, as far as is known, there were no complaints from the Welsh themselves on this score.[34]

The policy-makers and legislators of 1536 must have been confident that there would be sufficient numbers of English speakers among the gentry to administer the law, but that no special provision had been made for the future caused concern to at least one contemporary Englishman. William Barlow, bishop of St David's, complained to Cromwell late in 1536 that the clergy were unlearned and the people ignorant 'and the Englishe tongue nothinge preferred after the acte of parleamente'. His adversary, Thomas Lloyd, precentor of the cathedral, had obtained a royal

---

stirring of interest on the part of the Welsh members of parliament. *Statutes of the Realm*, III, pp. 864–5; IV, pp. 618–19; Bowen, *Statutes*, pp. 152–6; PRO SP12/110/14; Penry Williams, *The Council in the Marches of Wales under Elizabeth I* (Cardiff, 1958), pp. 263–4.

[32] Edward Davies, passed over two years previously, was in 1578 nominated as one of the deputies of John Puckering as justice of the Carmarthen circuit; while between 1576 and 1584 Simon Thelwall of Plas-y-ward acted as deputy and vice-justice of Chester and the north-eastern Welsh shires. W. R. Williams, *The History of the Great Sessions in Wales 1542–1830* (Brecon, 1899), pp. 70–1.

[33] BL Harleian MS 6995, f. 123: letter to Sir John Puckering dated 16 October 1592.

[34] Williams, *Council in the Marches*, pp. 82–3, 145–6.

licence even before the act was passed to establish a school in New Carmarthen, but it was not until 1543 that the site of the ruined friary there was acquired to build the King's School. In 1538 Barlow assured Cromwell that if provision were made for learning in grammar, the liberal sciences and knowledge of the Scriptures, 'the Welsche rudenesse wolde sone be framed to English cyvilitie and their corrupte capacyties easely reformed with godly intelligens'. Within three years he had obtained letters patent to found Christ's College, Brecon. The preamble to the school's charter explains the reasons for the foundation: because of their poverty and the lack of educational provision, both laity and clergy in south Wales were ignorant of their duty to God and their obedience to the king. They were even unacquainted with the common English tongue, and therefore unable to understand the obligations which the law imposed on them. For Barlow, if not for Lloyd, the foundation of a grammar school was a direct response to the act 27 Henry VIII, c.26. At the same time, both Barlow and Bishop Salcot of Bangor made more immediate provision for the spiritual needs of their flock: the gospel was to be preached in Welsh in the churches so as to dispel the 'superstitious' adherence to the old faith.[35]

For all the endemic disorder, Wales in the mid-1530s was not considered by the regime to be a frontier society, where attachment to the indigenous culture and language fostered a disaffected separatism which might resist the changes of the Reformation. If anything, the linguistic difference was believed to inhibit the spread of dissent and disobedience. Lee told Cromwell early in 1537 that the Welsh were quiet, 'and to my knowledge litle among them conceived of the matters in Englande, fforasmoche their language doth not agree to the advauncement therof'.[36] Lee was referring to the disturbances which had broken out late in 1536 in the north of England, where discontent had been stoked up by wild rumours into the armed 'pilgrimage of grace', but his comment applied equally to the prevailing lack of understanding of the religious reforms ushered in with the 'king's great matter'.

It was not until the end of the reign that two Welsh humanists set about to dissipate this ignorance with religious literature in print. The authority granted by the king to Lewys Morgannwg and two other commissioners in 37 Henry VIII (1545-6) to oversee the bardic order implied an official recognition of the formal standing of the native language in communal life

[35] PRO SP1/113, f. 114. Barlow to Cromwell, 16 August 1538: BL Cotton MSS, Cleopatra E iv, f. 316. William Dugdale, *Monasticon Anglicanum* (6 vols., London, 1817–30), VI, part 3, p. 1498. Glanmor Williams, '"Thomas Lloyd his Skole": Carmarthen's first Tudor Grammar School', *CA*, X (1974), 49–62.

[36] BL Cotton MSS, Cleopatra E v, f. 414: Lee to Cromwell, 15 January [1537].

if not in the courts of law.[37] The appearance of the first two printed books in Welsh in 1546–7 is further evidence that no general proscription of the language had been intended in the act of 1536. *Yny lhyvyr hwnn*, compiled by Sir John Price, was both a religious miscellany and a general vade-mecum of practical utility, in which the foremost defender of the British History paid tribute to the king's temporal gifts to the Welsh nation which were to be augmented and compounded by the spiritual gift of the gospel. In the same year William Salesbury produced his Welsh-English Dictionary. As a humanist, Salesbury feared that, if it failed to attain the status of a learned language in printed literature, Welsh would degenerate into a patois. He was responding to the challenges posed by the Reformation and the 'union', though his allusion to the act of 1536 in the dedication of the *Dictionary* addressed to Henry VIII refers to the preamble, not to the language provision. It had been ordained:

> that there shal herafter be no difference in lawes and language bytwyxte youre subiectes of youre principalytye of Wales and your other subiectes of your Royalme of Englande . . .[38]

That Salesbury subscribed to the prevailing belief in the advantages and convenience of a common language emerges from the royal licence, dated 13 September 1545, which he and John Waley obtained to print the *Dictionary*, so that 'our welbeloved subjects in Wales may the soner attayne and learne our mere englyshe tonge'. In the Welsh preface to the reader, Salesbury explains that he intended the *Dictionary* for literate Welshmen who were unfamiliar with English, though a Welsh-English word list was perhaps of limited value for such a purpose. He acknowledged that English was an honoured language for learned discourse and that it was important for the Welsh to attain a knowledge of it. These were sentiments which he was to repeat, in the context of a paean of praise to English monarchy, in *A briefe and a playne introduction* . . . (1550) to the Welsh language for Englishmen and others who wished to learn it. His book was designed to serve the needs of Englishmen, especially those from the border shires, who had occasion to converse with the monoglot Welsh in the course of their trades and professions, as well as the interest of foreign scholars and linguists. The publication was also aimed at Welsh emigrants in England who wished to consult their roots in Wales and make contact with their kinfolk, '& moost chiefely to edifie them, as well

---

[37] NLW Peniarth MS 194A.
[38] William Salesbury, *A dictionary in Englyshe and Welshe moche necessary to all suche Welshemen as wil spedly learne the englyshe tongue* (London, 1547), sig. A1v–A2r.

in ciuyle institutions, as in godlye doctryne'.[39] Such men were evidently expected to fulfil a secular as well as a religious mission, and this revealing phrase suggests that Salesbury paid at least lip service to the concept of 'English civility' that was entertained by advanced Protestant Englishmen. He expressed it with greater delicacy than did Bishop Barlow, and with greater fellow feeling towards his compatriots.

Behind this commitment to cater for the religious and worldly needs of his readers, there was an evident desire to recover the standards of Welsh as a spoken language. Salesbury was a man of his time with a transcendent mission to restore the reputation as a language of learning of the venerable 'British' tongue, which 'by continuall misnomer the recorder of the aunciente hostilitie is called Welshe'.[40] It was in this spirit that he launched his single-minded campaign to re-establish the standing of the language as a worthy vehicle for the Scriptures. Hence his lament in 1550 that so few fragments of early 'British' writings had been preserved from the age of the Celtic church when the ancestors of the Welsh had possessed the gospel in their own tongue, whereas codices of the laws of Hywel Dda, by contrast, had survived intact. That he found the contrast somewhat ironic is revealing of his scale of values: the old Welsh laws, it is implied, had declined and become obsolete. Even so, while he may not have felt any regret for their condition, he was to consult these texts to perfect his mastery of traditional Welsh idiom in preparing his Scriptural translations, which was his foremost priority.

There is a sense in which Salesbury displayed a greater confidence in the standing of English as a worthy language for learned discourse than did many of his English contemporaries. The argument for the English Bible had not been entirely won to the satisfaction of the leading reformers in the Church of England. Stephen Gardiner, the conservative bishop of Winchester, did not believe that the English language was sufficiently venerable to be a proper vehicle for the Scriptures; its attainment of a uniform standard had but shallow roots in the past and its future was far from secure.[41] Salesbury was conscious that his own language was vulnerable to similar questioning and wished to enhance its dignity so that it could be a fitting medium for God's Word. This was the challenge that he addressed in his second publication *Oll Synnwyr pen Kembero ygyd* (1547), a work which reveals that he had shifted his ground, largely because he was now convinced that the propagation of the gospel could

---

[39] Idem, *A briefe and a playne introduction, teachyng how to pronounce the letters in the British tong (now com'enly called Walsh)* (London, 1550), sig. A3v.

[40] R. Brinley Jones, *William Salesbury* (Cardiff, 1994), pp. 23–6. Cf. idem, *The Old British Tongue: the Vernacular in Wales, 1540–1640* (Cardiff, 1970).

[41] J. A. Muller (ed.), *Letters of Stephen Gardiner* (Cambridge, 1933), p. 121.

not wait until his countrymen were proficient in English. He warned his readers that if they did not preserve, correct and perfect the language in the present generation, it would be too late. In identifying a crisis in the condition of the Welsh language, he did not explicitly associate this with any recent change in its legal status. If he had in mind a threat to its integrity posed by recent legislation, this is perhaps less likely to have been an appraisal of the immediate impact of the 'language clause' of 1536 than of the implications of the Henrician and Edwardian measures for reforming church liturgy. The second royal injunctions to the clergy of 1538 and a royal proclamation in 1541 had provided for the placing of copies of the English 'Great Bible' in every parish church in Wales as well as England. On Edward's accession, injunctions were issued requiring the reading of the Epistles and Gospels in the pulpits in English rather than Latin.[42] To read them in any other language would have been to defy the authority of the supreme head of the church. Salesbury would have been deeply conscious of this, but he would also have been acutely aware, for all his acceptance of the need for the Welsh to become bilingual, that scriptural readings from the pulpit in English were unlikely, in the short term, to make much impression on Welsh congregations. These were surely the urgent concerns which elicited the *cri de cœur* in *Oll Synnwyr pen*: that if Welsh failed to match the advance in the use of English in church services, then all would be lost for the faith and the language in Wales.[43]

The status of Welsh as a language of religion was further jeopardized in January 1549, when the Act of Uniformity authorized the exclusive use of Cranmer's Book of Common Prayer in church services. Parliament thereby confirmed the action of royal prerogative in 1547 regarding the Litany: English was to be the language of public worship throughout the realm, and any departure from this practice would be an infringement of statute law.[44] In the event the principle of the vernacular Scriptures was not to be explicitly applied to Wales in any official instrument during this reign, when the Reformation attained its most advanced Protestant expression in England. Apart from the French versions of the Prayer

---

[42] H. Gee and W. J. Hardy (eds.), *Documents Illustrative of English Church History* (London, 1896), pp. 275–81; P. L. Hughes and J. F. Larkin (eds.), *Tudor Royal Proclamations, i: the Early Tudors, 1485–1553* (New Haven, 1964), pp. 296–8; John Strype, *Memorials of the Most Reverend Father in God, Thomas Cranmer* (3 vols., Oxford, 1848), II, pp. 442–60.

[43] Saunders Lewis has described the introduction to *Oll Synnwyr pen* as the 'manifesto of Welsh Protestant humanism'. Saunders Lewis, 'Damcaniaeth Eglwysig Brotestannaidd' in R. Geraint Gruffydd (ed.), *Meistri'r Canrifoedd: Ysgrifau ar Hanes Llenyddiaeth Gymraeg* (Caerdydd, 1973), p. 127. For a discussion of this claim in relation to the views advanced by Mr Lewis in *Tynged yr Iaith* (Llundain, 1962), see Roberts, 'The Welsh Language', 48–9 and n. 77.

[44] 2 & 3 Edward VI, c.1: *Statutes of the Realm*, IV, pp. 37–9.

Books of 1549 and 1552, translated under licence for the use of the king's subjects in Calais and the Channel Islands, there were to be no authorized exceptions to the exclusive provision made for the English-speaking subjects of the Crown in the two Edwardian acts of uniformity.[45] Undeterred, in 1551 Salesbury decided to print Welsh versions of the Epistles and Gospels, translated from the original Hebrew and Greek, in *Kynniver Llith a Ban*.[46] He may have regarded this as an interim measure to await a fuller version of the Litany, on which he himself may already have been engaged, to set beside Cranmer's Book of Common Prayer. In his Latin address he invited the five bishops to scrutinize the text so that, if it was found to be free of error, it might be sanctioned by their authority for use in public worship. This could be done even if they themselves were 'ignorant of the native language' by appointing six of the most learned men in each diocese to confer together as examiners of the text.[47] It is evident that in 1551 Salesbury caused his book to be printed without obtaining prior permission from the ecclesiastical authorities, though he did undertake not to distribute the work until it had been approved by the bishops or their nominees.[48] His request went unheeded, for no special dispensation was made for Wales when the revised English Book of Common Prayer was issued in the following year. There is no evidence that *Kynniver Llith a Ban* or any other Welsh version of the Litany was authorized for use in Welsh churches during the reign of Edward VI.

With the accession of the Catholic Queen Mary, Salesbury's hopes were eclipsed, and at the outset the Elizabethan regime appeared to be no more sensitive than its predecessors to the spiritual needs of the Celtic nations. Sometime between 1559 and the meeting of the Convocation of 1563, proposals were 'exhibited to be admitted to authority' prescribing punishments for those who could not recite the articles of the faith, the catechism, the Lord's prayer and the ten commandments. It was proposed that it might be 'lawful for such Welsh or Cornish children as can speak no English' to learn the rudiments of the faith in their own tongues.[49] There is no evidence that any comprehensive action was taken for Wales at this stage, but at the diocesan council of St Asaph on 12 November

---

[45] A. Owen Evans, *A Memorandum on the Legality of the Welsh Bible and the Welsh Version of the Book of Common Prayer* (Cardiff, 1925), p. 11.

[46] William Salesbury, *Kynniver Llith a Ban*, ed. John Fisher (Caerdydd, 1931), p. xxv.

[47] Translated in D. R. Thomas, *The Life and Work of Bishop Davies and William Salesbury* (Oswestry, 1902), pp. 71–2.

[48] Ceri Davies (ed.), *Rhagymadroddion a Chyflwyniadau Lladin 1551–1632* (Caerdydd, 1980), pp. 18–21.

[49] BL Egerton MS 2350, f. 54. (A later copy of miscellaneous items on religious reform; the context and its placing in the sequence of documents, some of which are dated, suggest a date of *c.*1560 for this item.) D. R. Thomas, op. cit., p. 15.

1561, it was declared that the Epistle and Gospel should be read first in English, then in Welsh, and it is possible that Salesbury's *Kynniver Llith a Ban* was adopted for the purpose. It was also decided that the catechism should be read every Sunday by the clergy 'aptly and distinctly' in Welsh as well as in English, and that the Litany be sung on other days. This development might have prompted Salesbury's erstwhile business partner, John Waley, to seek a licence for the printing of the Litany in Welsh in 1562–3. The bare entry in the accounts of the Stationers' Company is all that is known of this work, if indeed it ever issued from the press, but there is little doubt that the translator was William Salesbury.[50]

Over a period of sixteen years, Salesbury's determined campaign for the publication of authorized printed versions of the Scriptures in Welsh had elicited little response. Then, in the parliament of 1563, the act 5 Elizabeth I, c.28, was passed for 'the translating of the Bible and the Divine Service into the Welsh Tongue'. Four years later, when the New Testament and the Book of Common Prayer were published, Salesbury declared: 'Behold how the clemencye of God hath now heard my longe desired petition . . .'[51] His campaign had at last borne its first fruits in works of biblical scholarship largely of his own making. Even so, it is unlikely that he had been the only petitioner or that he was responsible for the legislative initiative in 1563. There survives a manuscript draft of one such petition addressed to authority. It is a fragment consisting of a single page, bearing corrections but lacking date, address or signature. In this rough draft the request is addressed to 'your lordship' at one point and 'your lordships' at another to search for and summon 'the godlyest & best learned men in divinitee or knowledge of the holy scriptures & the Walsh tong withall, whersoever [in the whole realme] their habitacion or abydyng shall hap to be'. These scholars and divines were to consult together to decide on the best remedy for expelling the miserable darkness which, given the lack of the strong light of Christ's gospel, still prevailed in Wales. If it be thought necessary or convenient that the people there should be 'ministred taught or preached unto in their vulgar understanded tong to their better edificacion . . . then it may please your good lordships to wyll, requyre & command the learned men to traducte the boke of the Lordes Testamentes into the vulgare Walsh tong' for the benefit of preachers as well as the people.

---

[50] Could it have been a new licence to issue another impression of *Kynniver Llith a Ban*? Ibid., pp. 72–3. E. Arber (ed.), *A Transcript of the Registers of the Company of Stationers of London* (5 vols., London, 1875–94), I, p. 209 (entered in the accounting year 22 July 1562 to 21 July 1563). Isaac Thomas, *Y Testament Newydd Cymraeg, 1551–1620* (Caerdydd, 1976), p. 138.

[51] *Statutes of the Realm*, IV, part 1, p. 2457; Bowen, *Statutes*, pp. 149–51.

The handwriting of the petition cannot be identified with any certainty; it evidently predates the act of 1563, but its precise relationship to it cannot be established.[52] The lords addressed in the petition may have been the five bishops of Wales and the borders, the Privy Council or the House of Lords. Its emphasis on a preaching and teaching ministry, for which the translation was to be a means for the spiritual deliverance of the Welsh, rather than on the use of the vernacular in church services, points to composition by a more advanced Protestant than even Salesbury had become by this time. Salesbury always insisted on the description 'the British tongue', which may be read as a pointer telling against his authorship of this petition.[53] The request was for the 'boke of the Lordes Testamentes' – presumably the Bible without the Apocrypha – to meet the urgent need to reveal to a benighted people 'the shynyng lyght of Christes Gospell'. This was the impulse which, together with a keen appreciation of what was feasible in the time allowed, must have moved the translators once they embarked on the work commissioned by authority of parliament in 1563.

The statute 5 Elizabeth I, c.28, provided for the translation into Welsh of both the Bible and the Book of Common Prayer. The work of translation was to be prepared under the supervision of the bishops of the Welsh dioceses and of Hereford; it was to be completed by 1 March 1567 (new style), and copies of each text were to be used in church services in all parishes where 'the British or Welsh Tongue' was spoken.[54] Thus Welsh was to acquire an official status as a language of worship in the services of the established Church. The act also contained the first formal indication that the feast of St David's was to be a recognized red-letter day in the new Protestant calendar.

A new version of the Prayer Book would require the sanction of parliament because it altered the provision of the Act of Uniformity of 1559. It is less certain that the translation of the Bible itself called for such authorization or for the emending of any previous statute. In the reign of Henry VIII the English Bible had been sanctioned by royal injunction and proclamation. Presumably the same instruments could have been used in this reign had the queen and her council so willed it. Why then was the Welsh Bible authorized by an act of parliament rather than by an order of the queen as supreme governor of the church? The explanation advanced

---

[52] The document is printed in Roberts, 'The Welsh Language', appendix I, p. 73.
[53] Some of the sentiments of the petition anticipate those expressed by John Penry, over two decades later, when he urged that preachers of the Word in Wales should gain a mastery of it in their own tongue. John Penry, *Three Treatises Concerning Wales*, ed. David Williams (Cardiff, 1960), pp. xvi, 55–6.
[54] Bowen, *Statutes*, pp. 149–51.

by a foremost modern authority on the Elizabethan translations of the Scriptures into Welsh is that implicit in the 'language clause' of the 1536 act was a ban on the use of Welsh in church services, and what had been decreed by statute could only be altered or qualified by parliament.[55] But this is to read too much into the Henrician language provision, which applied to the courts of common law and the holding of offices and fees under the Crown, not to benefices or services in the church. There had been an element of Welsh in the worship of the reformed church before Cranmer's Prayer Book of 1549, and its legality seems to have been taken for granted by Sir John Price in the reign of Henry VIII. Moreover, the right of the monarch to make laws for Wales independently of parliament in qualification of the legislation of 'union' had been recognized for three years in 1536 and made perpetual in 1543. In the event this exclusive discretion was never used by any monarch, but had it been the case that the 'language clause' required to be revised, the Crown possessed the constitutional right to do so without further reference to parliament.[56]

As it happened, the legislative initiative did not come from above, from the queen or the upper chamber, but from the members of the House of Commons. The preamble to the act of 1563 was concerned exclusively with the Prayer Book, which it acknowledged to be inaccessible to most of the inhabitants of Wales because they did not understand English. The Bible *per se* was ushered in only in the first legislative provision after the enacting formula. This may indicate that the preamble, which rehearsed the original rationale of the measure, was left unrevised as the scope of the bill was enlarged during its progress through parliament. When the bill was first read before the Commons on 22 February 1563, it was entered in the journal of the House as: 'The Bill that the Book of Service in the Church shall be in the Welsh Tongue in *Wales*'.[57] The first mention of the Bible occurs in the entry in the Commons journal for the second reading. This would seem to confirm the evidence of the preamble that the original intention was solely to authorize the translation of the Book of Common Prayer. The act was not printed among the sessional statutes at the end of the parliament, and must therefore have begun as a private bill, entered on payment of substantial fees to the officers of both Houses of

---

[55] Isaac Thomas, *Yr Hen Destament Cymraeg 1551–1620* (Aberystwyth, 1988), p. 175. Cranmer's Book of Common Prayer had been authorized by the Act of Uniformity of 1549.
[56] Peter R. Roberts, 'The "Henry VIII Clause": Delegated Legislation and the Tudor Principality of Wales' in T. G. Watkin (ed.), *Legal Record and Historical Reality* (London, 1989), pp. 37–49.
[57] *Commons Journals*, I, p. 66.

Parliament.[58] Ten days elapsed before the bill received its second reading in the lower house on 4 March; this time it was entered in the journal as 'for the Bible & Book of Services'. It was duly engrossed on the same day, but not apparently committed before it was sent to the upper house, which suggests that its provisions had been redrafted by its sponsors before the second reading in the Commons.[59] The petition for the 'boke of the Lordes Testamentes' could well date from this interval in the process of legislation, between 22 February and 4 March, or else it was drafted to accompany the engrossed bill on its delivery to the House of Lords in order to persuade 'your lordships' to agree to the Commons' decision to extend the purview of the bill to include the Bible.

The bill received three readings in the upper house, on 30 and 31 March and 5 April; on the last occasion a proviso was added by the Lords and given its three readings before being returned to the Commons. This proviso enjoined that copies of the Welsh Bible and Prayer Book were, on publication, to be placed alongside copies of the English versions in every parish church where literate parishioners could have access to them. In this way monoglot Welshmen 'maye by conferring both Tongues together, the sooner attain to the Knowledge of the English Tongue'. The recurrence of this old refrain reveals the main provision to have been a concession which had to meet certain conditions before it was reluctantly accepted in the Lords. These conditions were presumably laid down either to overcome active opposition or to allay doubts voiced late in the proceedings by some of the peers or bishops about the wisdom of conferring statutory recognition upon Welsh as a language of worship.[60] Another significant alteration made to the original bill in the Lords was to change the date for the completion of the translations from 1 March 1565 to 1 March 1566 (old style). Of the five bishops who were to supervise the

---

[58] G. R. Elton, 'Wales in Parliament, 1542–1581' in R. R. Davies et al., *Welsh Society and Nationhood: Historical Essays Presented to Glanmor Williams* (Cardiff, 1984), p. 119.

[59] *Commons Journals*, I, p. 67; *Lords Journals*, I, pp. 610–13; Simonds D'Ewes, *The Journals of all the Parliaments during the reign of Queen Elizabeth* (London, 1682), pp. 72, 88–9.

[60] Comparison of the text of the Welsh with the English Bible for the purpose of learning the latter language would have been possible only if they were exactly parallel translations. The English Prayer Book was based on the Great Bible, not the Geneva Bible, with its marginal glosses imbued with Calvinist doctrine, and soon the 'Bishops' Bible' would be the authorized version. The 1563 act decrees that the English Bible, with the Book of Common Prayer, 'as is now used within this Realm in English, [was] to be truly and exactly translated into the British or Welsh Tongue'. Dr Isaac Thomas reads this to mean that the original intention was for the Welsh text to be translated directly from the Great Bible. It is more likely that the phrase 'as is now used within this Realm in English' relates only to the Prayer Book, and that the ambiguity reflects the circumstances in which the Commons bill was redrafted for its second reading to include the Bible as well. Thomas, *Y Testament Newydd Cymraeg*, pp. 139–41.

work of translation, St Asaph and St David's were present for the first two readings, Hereford attended the second reading, but Bishop Richard Davies alone attended on the day the proviso was read. If Davies, as the person best able to appreciate the burdens involved, suggested the extension of the date of completion, it may have been because he had not been consulted at an early stage in the drafting of the original bill.

According to Gruffudd Hiraethog, the promoter of the bill in the Commons was the antiquary Humphrey Llwyd, the burgess of parliament for Denbigh:

> Pwy air gystadl pur gwestiwn
> Pert [*sic, recte* Perl] mewn ty Parlment yw hwn
> Peibl wyneb pob Haelioni
> A wnaeth yn act o'n Iaith ni . . .[61]

(Who is as good as his word? Fair question! A pearl in parliament is he. He, the face of all generosity, made the Bible in our language a statute.)

While there is nothing in the way of independent evidence on record to confirm this claim, there is no good reason to doubt the testimony of the bard. Three of Llwyd's fellow members from Wales had departed the Commons before the bill was returned from the Lords. Between 15 and 24 March, Dr Elis Price of Plasiolyn, Simon Thelwall and Morus Wynn, knights of the shires of Merioneth, Denbigh and Caernarfon respectively, were granted licences to be absent 'for their necessary affairs'.[62] That is all that can be gleaned from the parliamentary record or any other source about the passage of this act, which does not seem to have engaged the full attention of either the Welsh members or the bishops.

No provision was made in the act of 1563 for financing the work of translation. The costs of purchasing copies for each parish were to be divided between the incumbents and the parishioners.[63] *Lliver gweddi gyffredin* (folio) and *Testament Newydd ein Arglwydd Jesu Christ* (quarto) appeared in print on 6 May and 7 October 1567 respectively, a few months later than the revised date stipulated in the act. According to the title-page of the Welsh Prayer Book, it was 'vewed, perused and allowed' by the five bishops, and it is significant that by this time three of them were Welsh-

---

[61] R. Geraint Gruffydd, 'Humphrey Lhuyd a Deddf Cyfieithu'r Beibl i'r Gymraeg', *LlC*, 4, nos. 2 and 4 (1956–7), 114–15, 233.
[62] Simonds D'Ewes, op. cit., pp. 88–9.
[63] The bishops were to fix the price of the books and to pay a fine of £40 each if they were negligent in these tasks, though they do not appear to have incurred these penalties when in the event they failed to meet the prescribed deadline. Bowen, *Statutes*, p. 150.

speaking.[64] In the Register of the Stationers' Company, it was entered as authorized by Edmund Grindal, bishop of London, presumably acting on behalf of his fellow bishops at the printing stage.[65] Only one Welsh prelate was sufficiently gifted to engage in the work of translation: Richard Davies of St David's, who was already commissioned as one of the translators of the 'Bishops' Bible'.[66]

Official permission to produce the Scriptures in the vernacular was extended to the native Irish as well in the 1560s, following what appears to have been a general decision of policy to encourage the spread of Protestantism. In the case of Ireland there is more direct evidence than there is for Wales of the queen's approval of the principle that the Bible should be 'understanded of the people'. In 1567 the Archbishop of Armagh and the Bishop of Meath were reminded that Elizabeth had expended the considerable sum of £66.13s.4d. 'for the making of Caracter to print the New Testament in Irish', and they were admonished that the money should be reimbursed 'unless they do presently put the same into print'. The expense of casting a special typeface for the Irish language evidently called for a greater degree of royal patronage than was required for Wales, but this initial outlay was not maintained.[67] The Welsh translations of 1567 and 1588 had not required a printer versed in the language, and were seen through the press by their respective translators, Salesbury and Morgan. While Elizabeth and her Council were prepared to countenance the translations in both languages, their support fell short of a full commitment to finance the ventures.[68]

The act of 1563 had set a definite time limit for the task of translating the whole Bible. No formal action was taken subsequently to obtain separate authority for a Welsh translation of the Old Testament in order to complete what Davies and Salesbury had left unfinished, and to enable

---

[64] Melville Richards and Glanmor Williams (eds.), *Llyfr Gweddi Gyffredin 1567* (facsimile ed., Caerdydd, 1965).

[65] E. Arber, op. cit., I, pp. 336–7.

[66] Glanmor Williams, *Bywyd ac Amserau'r Esgob Richard Davies* (Caerdydd, 1953); idem, *Welsh Reformation Essays* (Cardiff, 1967), pp. 155–205.

[67] In August 1587 the English Privy Council advised the Lord Deputy and Council in Dublin to appoint a printer for the Irish New Testament. There continued to be difficulties in producing suitable 'characters' by a printer skilled in the language, and the New Testament in Irish was not in fact printed until 1602, and the Book of Common Prayer did not appear before 1608–9. Bruce Dickens, 'The Irish Broadside of 1571 and Queen Elizabeth's Types', *TCBS*, I (1949–53), 48–60. E. R. McC. Dix, *Printing in Dublin prior to 1601* (Dublin, 1932), pp. 27–8.

[68] Dr Isaac Thomas has pointed out that it was the Archbishop of Canterbury who bore the expenses of preparing the Bishops' Bible, and that the translators of the King James Bible received only their living expenses on those occasions when they met to confer. Thomas, *Y Testament Newydd Cymraeg*, p. 140 and n. 54.

church services to be held entirely in Welsh. William Morgan is assumed in some modern accounts to have embarked on the work without official sanction.[69] It is true that the time specified for the preparation of the translations had in fact expired, and this should have been renewed if normal parliamentary practice was to be observed. But to do so would have been unduly legalistic in the light of the powers vested in 1543 by parliament in the Crown, in addition to its general prerogative rights, to legislate for Wales. As it was, the special needs of Wales seem to have been catered for, not by prerogative action, but by the patronage of John Whitgift as Archbishop of Canterbury, whose encouragement was doubtless deemed to be sufficient warrant for Morgan's translation of the Old Testament.

The criticisms which came to be levelled at the rendering of the Scriptures into Welsh were not in the event advanced on grounds of legal technicality. In the reprinted revision of his *A playne and a familiar Introduction* in 1567, Salesbury included a letter to Humphrey Toy in which he referred to those who had opposed 'this godly enterprise' since the time Toy 'tooke in hand the doing of this our Countrey matter'. These critics had objected not only to Salesbury's curious orthography but also to the very project itself: 'Some saying wyth *Iudas* the Traitor, what needed thys waste?'[70] The sceptics' claim that the numbers of literate Welshmen (that is to say, the clergy) were too few to justify such an enterprise was to be countered by other Protestant apologists for the vernacular Scriptures. William Morgan was conscious of a residual opposition in Wales as well as England to a Welsh version of the Scriptures. This may explain why, in his letter of dedication to the queen, he went out of his way (as Salesbury had done before him) to commend that there should be one uniform language spoken by all her subjects, even as he too set about the task of ensuring that in his own country religious instruction would be available in the vernacular. The criticism of the translation of the Scriptures into Welsh that was voiced by a Welsh churchman in an 'eisteddfod', that is, an assembly of clerics such as convocation,[71] was to be denounced by Morris Kyffin in *Deffynniad Ffydd Eglwys Loegr* (1595).[72] In the course of deliberations on a proposal to license a printer to print books in Welsh ('pan grybwyllwyd am roi cennad i vn celfydd i brintio Cymraeg'), the

---

[69] Morgan refers to the act of 1563 in his dedication to the queen. Thomas, *Yr Hen Destament Cymraeg*, pp. 175–6.

[70] Cited by W. A. Mathias, 'William Salesbury – ei Fywyd a'i Weithiau' in Geraint Bowen (ed.), *Y Traddodiad Rhyddiaith* (Llandysul, 1970), pp. 47–8.

[71] Bedwyr L. Jones, 'Deddf Cyfieithu'r Beibl i'r Gymraeg, 1563', *Yr Haul a'r Gangell*, XVII (1963), 24.

[72] W. P. Williams (ed.), *Deffynniad Ffydd Eglwys Loegr* (Bangor, 1908), 'At y Darllenydd', p. xiv.

unnamed cleric objected on the grounds that he would rather the people learn English and lose their Welsh, adding that a Welsh Bible would do more harm than good. Kyffin condemned the objector out of hand as a dog in the manger who would permit souls to be damned by placing impossible hurdles for the people to acquire knowledge of the Word of God. This episode may relate to the attempt by Salesbury and Waley to obtain a joint patent for the 'sole printing' of the Bible, the Book of Common Prayer, and other religious works in Welsh, and the assembly in which it took place may have been the Convocation of Canterbury in 1563.[73]

That these doubting Thomases were not heeded by the English Protestant establishment may have been largely due to the support which the early translators seem to have received from the queen's principal secretary, Sir William Cecil, and Archbishop Matthew Parker. In their correspondence in the early 1560s, Parker, Salesbury and Richard Davies exchanged views on questions of British antiquity and the religion of the early Celtic church, and these views were to form the basis of the historical justification for the reformed faith advanced in the prefatory 'Epistol at y Cembru' in the New Testament of 1567.[74] In 1587 William Cecil, now Lord Burghley, noted in his memoranda certain good laws made in the queen's reign. Among the five 'statutes offensive to the papists' passed since 1558, he included the act 'for translating the Bible into the Welsh tongue'. Cecil was referring to the commitment of Tridentine Catholicism to the Vulgate and the Latin mass.[75] Catholic versions of the Scriptures certainly existed in the native languages of certain countries, but in 1546 the Council of Trent had declared the Vulgate alone must be used for public readings, sermons and disputations. No deviation from this ruling was to be allowed, and the Tridentine Index, published on 24 March 1564, included the rule prohibiting all Catholics, priests and laity, from reading the vernacular Scriptures without the permission of a bishop or an inquisitor.[76] Burghley's assessment of the significance of the measure of 1563 suggests that the Privy Council regarded the vernacular Scriptures as a potent weapon in the campaign to implement the Elizabethan settlement of the church. Since the survival of the regime and of reformed religion alike were at stake, it was doubly imperative to root out adherence to the old faith which seduced the

---

[73] Roberts, 'The Welsh Language', appendix II, 74–5.
[74] Robin Flower, 'William Salesbury, Richard Davies, and Archbishop Parker', with an appendix by D. Myrddin Lloyd, 'William Salesbury and "Epistol E.M. at y Cembru"', *NLWJ*, II, no. 1 (1941), 7–16.
[75] PRO SP12/199, f. 92.
[76] *New Catholic Encyclopaedia*, s.v. Council of Trent, Vulgate, Vernacular Scriptures.

queen's subjects from their true allegiance. The old order in Wales, which Henrician commentators like William Barlow believed to be inimical to the reception of Protestantism and to respect for the rule of law (alias 'English civility'), was not considered by the Elizabethan regime to be sustained by the continuance of the Welsh language. Once the advocates of the vernacular Scriptures had won the argument for the Welsh translations, the language was recognized as a means of converting the people from 'Romish superstition'. Religion rather than language was now generally acknowledged to be the principal divisive factor in society. Burghley was more able to appreciate this in 1587 than in 1563, and his comment was probably a reflection on Catholic reaction to the act rather than on the original legislative intention.

Welshmen were prominent among those Catholic exiles who were dedicated to the mission of the seminary priests, first to revivify the old faith in the mother country, and then to an enterprise of conquest and reconversion. Humanists in exile like Gruffydd Robert and Morys Clynnog were not moved to emulate the example of Gregory Martin, the translator of the Rheims New Testament in English, by producing a Welsh Catholic version of the Scriptures. There is no direct or unambiguous evidence on record of how these Catholics viewed the translations of 1567, although one of them clearly expressed alarm at the impact that Protestant Welsh printed books in general was making on the lives of Catholics living in Wales. In a letter dated 22 August 1579 to Cardinal Sirleto, Dr Owen Lewis, archdeacon of Cambrai, called for papal sponsorship for a programme of printed literature in the vernacular which he had in hand. His attitude to the role of language in the propagation of religious truths is significant:

> . . . there are thirteen shires in England where the Welsh language is spoken, which differs from the English language as Greek differs from Hebrew. The English have seen to it that their heretical books in their own language have been translated into Welsh, in order to contaminate with heretical disgrace these thirteen shires, which hitherto have been kept in a more healthy state through their ignorance of English heresies written in English. Against this fiendish treachery we are preparing deliverance, to save the souls of [the Welsh,] our brothers in the flesh, in those books which are to be despatched to those shires . . .[77]

---

[77] R. Geraint Gruffydd, 'Dau Lythyr gan Owen Lewis', *LlC*, 2, no. 1 (1952), 36–45. Transcripts of the Latin originals in the Vatican Library and Welsh translations of both letters are given in appendices, ibid., 43–5.

It is possible that *Lliver gweddi gyffredin* and *Testament Newydd* were among the Protestant translations that Owen Lewis had in mind. The Common Prayer Book was certainly believed by Catholics to be a heretical work and Richard Davies's 'Epistol at y Cembru', which prefaced the New Testament, was profoundly anti-Roman. To the post-Tridentine Catholics the English Bible, as translated by the Protestants, was full of heresies, as witness its disparagement by Richard Gwyn (Richard White) (d.1584), who is regarded by the Roman Catholic Church as its first martyr in Wales:

> Y Beibl Seisnig sydd chwym chwam,
> Yn llawn o gam ddychmygion . . .[78]

(The English Bible is whim-wham, full of erroneous conjectures.)

An earlier letter from Lewis to Sirleto mentioned three Welsh books which he claimed were ready for printing at Milan under the direction of Gruffydd Robert.[79] The Cardinal was asked to intercede with the Pope for a gift of a hundred or two hundred gold pieces towards the cost of printing the books in Milan and their distribution among the Welsh through a clandestine network of priests. No such works were published, but there is evidence that some of the Catholic books written in Italy after 1567 did reach Wales. In 1571 Lewys Evans, the earl of Leicester's agent in the lordship of Denbigh, reported the confiscation of a Welsh book written 'by some of Rome' and printed in Italy. At the request of the bishop of St Asaph he had translated it into English 'and soe doe aunswere yt'. The catechism by Morys Clynnog, *Athravaeth Gristnogavl*, with an introduction by Gruffydd Robert, was printed at Milan in 1568, and *A brief answer to a short trifling treatise of late set forth in the British tongue written by one Clinnock at Rome, and printed at Millain and lately spread secretly abroad in Wales* was duly published in London in 1571.[80] Of the few Catholic writings in Wales which sought to counter the claims and influence of the Elizabethan church before the end of the reign, a number were to circulate in manuscript form, and at least one – *Y Drych Cristianogawl*

---

[78] Quoted in Salesbury, *Kynniver Llith a Ban*, p. xxii, n. 2.
[79] The tracts concerned papal supremacy, the Eucharist, and the catechism of Canisius.
[80] G. Dyfnallt Owen (ed.), *HMC Manuscripts of the Marquess of Bath at Longleat, Vol. V: Talbot, Dudley and Devereux Papers 1533–1659* (London, 1980), p. 182. The place of publication is given by the editor as 'Avyllen', which looks to be a mistranscription of 'Myllen'. Evans had also seized written prophecies in Welsh which 'are marvauylous sediciouse and trayterouse'. Corpus Christi College, Cambridge, Parker MSS, no. 105, ff. 363–5.

(1587) – was printed in Wales at a secret press kept in a cave at Penrhyn Creuddyn.[81]

In an address in the form of a prosopopoeia in Gruffydd Robert's *Dosbarth Byrr ar y rhann gyntaf i ramadeg cymraeg* (Milan, 1567), the Welsh language apostrophizes its benefactor, Sir William Herbert, the earl of Pembroke, who held it in such estimation that he spoke it with his compatriots in the company of the highest in the land.[82] The expectation of Gruffydd Robert and Morys Clynnog that Pembroke and Cecil as privy councillors might have favoured the return of the country to the Roman obedience was misplaced. Neither the earl nor any of the other leaders of Welsh society had responded to Salesbury's plea for intercession with the king to have the Bible translated into the Welsh language. For all that has been claimed for Pembroke's protection of Welsh causes at court, there is nothing to connect him with the patronage of the language, apart from Gruffydd Robert's dedication. There is a note of unintended irony in the presentation of a work of grammar to a councillor who was reputed to be semi-literate, though this claim may have signified little more than that he was more proficient in Welsh than in English.[83] Pembroke was Lord President of the Council in the Marches from 1550 to 1558, and doubts must remain whether he could properly have held such high office had the 'language clause' of the act of 1536 been rigorously observed.

In 1567 Catholics had not yet despaired of the return of the realm to the Roman allegiance. Their attitude is reflected in a secret communication of the same year from Morys Clynnog to William Cecil. The letter which Clynnog wrote in Welsh on 24 May 1567 contained the confidential message that, unless Cecil repented and persuaded Elizabeth to embrace the Roman faith, he would be damned to perdition and the queen excommunicated. The warning took the form of a parable ('ar ddameg') that the Catholic powers were preparing a campaign against the heretical faith and its false laws ('y gam phydd ai gau deddfe').[84] Cecil was thus forewarned of the papal bull of excommunication which was promulgated by Pius V in 1570. It is possible that Clynnog regarded the act of 1563, the first fruits of which were not yet published when he wrote his letter, as one of the Protestant 'false laws'. Whatever Cecil made of the message, it

---

[81] R. Geraint Gruffydd, *Argraffwyr Cyntaf Cymru: Gwasgau Dirgel y Catholigion adeg Elisabeth* (Caerdydd, 1972).

[82] In the list of the branches of learning that could be rendered in the perfected language, godliness and divinity are included but not the Scriptures. *Dosbarth Byrr ar y rhann gyntaf i ramadeg cymraeg* (Milan, 1567), sig. B2r–v.

[83] For the case against the claim that Pembroke was illiterate in English, see N. P. Sil, *William Lord Herbert of Pembroke, c.1507–1570: Politique and Patriot* (Lewiston, New York, 1987), pp. 27–31.

[84] W. Llewelyn Williams, 'Welsh Catholics on the Continent', *THSC* (1901–2), 114–19.

is evident that by this stage the Council of Trent had made the vernacular Scriptures a closed book for most Catholics in every nation.[85] The queen's secretary may well have been apprised from the outset of the opportunities which this situation offered for the consolidation of the Elizabethan religious settlement in Wales as well as England.

A letter written in Welsh sent from Rome to London across a continent divided into hostile religious camps would retain its secrets as surely as if it had been couched in cipher. Morys Clynnog could write thus in the confident expectation that Cecil could call on the many Welsh speakers at court, including his chaplain, Gabriel Goodman, to translate it for him. Welsh Catholic humanists made their unique contribution in printed books to the refinement of Welsh as a language of piety and learning, but in terms of practical utility it was to be reduced to the condition of a private code during their exile on the Continent. In their letters to each other and to their co-religionists, the brothers Robert and Hugh Owen of Plas Du, Caernarfonshire, exchanged confidential instructions and code words in Welsh as well as in cipher.[86] But the resources at the disposal of ardent Welsh Catholics on the Continent were too slender to enable them to entertain realistic hopes of undermining the Protestant settlement in their native land.

The Welsh language was eventually saved by the transformation in religious culture that was to be wrought by the scriptural translations, which drew on bardic literature and lexicography as well as humanist scholarship. The occurrence of a 'decisive bifurcation'[87] in the cultural history of Wales should not be pre-dated, for the activities of these writers and translators delayed the effects of the Anglicization that was latent in the legislation of union. The linguistic crisis feared by William Salesbury and others did not materialize in the sixteenth century, thanks largely to their own achievements. Nevertheless there could be no guarantee that the respite was to be permanent, for the fate of 'the British tongue' would depend on the continuity of the Protestant settlement.

---

[85] The commission to revise the Pauline index was set up by the Council of Trent in February 1563 (new style). If its early deliberations were known in England, this may have influenced the Elizabethan regime's endorsement of the private bill in its revised form as it was presented for its second reading on 4 March.

[86] It was not an invariably foolproof method of secret communication, for some of the messages were intercepted and discovered. A. H. Dodd, 'Two Welsh Catholic émigrés discuss the accession of James I', *BBCS*, VIII, part 4 (1937), 355–8.

[87] Gwyn A. Williams, *Welsh Wizard and British Empire: Dr John Dee and a Welsh Identity* (Cardiff, 1980), pp. 21–5.

4

The Welsh Language and the Court of Great Sessions

RICHARD SUGGETT

THIS CHAPTER examines in detail the law as a domain of language use, paying particular attention to the work of the Court of Great Sessions, the principal royal court in Wales, created by the 1543 Act of Union and abolished by statute nearly three hundred years later in 1830. We now, of course, understand that the Court of Great Sessions was established as part of a broad strategy of Tudor state building. Towards the end of the sixteenth century, the Welsh experience of the Great Sessions was held up as a precedent to be followed for the reform of Ireland. Sir William Gerard, appointed Chancellor of Ireland after many years serving the Elizabethan state in Wales, explained to the lords of the Privy Council: 'Kinge E[dward] the first thought he had conquered all Walles . . . yet Walles contynued their Walshe disorders, untill Kinge H[enry] the viijth established Justices Itinerant to travell throughout all partes of Walles, by which travell onely I saye Walles was brought to knowe civilitie the same as in at this daye.'[1]

The new Welsh itinerant courts had extraordinary powers equivalent to the King's Bench, Common Pleas and assizes rolled into one. The resulting archive, a monument of the efficiency of Tudor record-keeping, is significant on a European scale for its sheer bulk, interest and continuity. On the civil side there is a majestic series of plea rolls, and the criminal records or 'gaol files' are more comprehensive than their English assize counterparts.[2]

The vastness of the archive of the Great Sessions has the capacity to overwhelm the researcher so it is important that the questions one seeks to answer from the record are clearly defined. There are several crucial

---

[1] Charles McNeill (ed.), 'Lord Chancellor Gerrard's Notes of his Report on Ireland', *Analecta Hibernica*, 2 (Dublin, 1931), p. 124; Ciarán Brady, 'Comparable Histories?: Tudor reform in Wales and Ireland' in Steven G. Ellis and Sarah Barber (eds.), *Conquest and Union. Fashioning a British State, 1485–1725* (London, 1995), pp. 64–86.

[2] The scale of the archive is now apparent from Glyn Parry's meticulous *A Guide to the Records of Great Sessions in Wales* (Aberystwyth, 1995).

subjects. First, procedure; i.e. how the Court of Great Sessions worked in practice, especially in relation to the notorious 'language clause' of the Act of Union of 1536. Second, the record. The records of the Great Sessions are an important source for learning about the language. A surprising amount of Welsh can be found in the otherwise Latin or English record of the court. We need to know what sort of words are preserved and why, and what they can tell us about the use of language. Third, reform. We need to understand the reforming activities of the Great Sessions and their relation to Welsh language and culture. More generally, too, there is the consideration: in what senses might it be said that Welsh people were alienated from the Court of Great Sessions?

Language and Personnel

Twice a year after the second Act of Union of 1543, in spring and autumn, for three hundred years the Sessions were held in twelve Welsh counties (Monmouthshire was not included). These were periods of very concentrated activity and a major domain of language use. It might perhaps have been expected that there would have been widespread alienation from the courts: they were largely conducted in a foreign language; they interfered in the routines of daily life; and despite inefficiencies, they were nonetheless bloody assizes. Those accused of capital felonies were tried at the Great Sessions (rather than at the Quarter Sessions), which therefore had a special significance as a court of life and death. It is estimated – although this is a somewhat rough-and-ready figure – that some 4,000 convicted felons were executed in the second half of the sixteenth century alone. For all these reasons, one might have expected widespread alienation from the court. However the reverse is true: throughout the second half of the sixteenth century and well into the seventeenth century the criminal and civil business of the Great Sessions increased in a way which suggests widespread acceptance rather than rejection of the court. Like other booming European courts of the period, the Great Sessions were popular because they represented royal justice standing above local faction to which, in theory at least, the weak could complain about the powerful. Only later, particularly after the civil wars, was there widespread disengagement from, and indifference or hostility towards, the court, and its business accordingly declined dramatically.

The Act of Union (1543) which established the Court of Great Sessions also swept away forever the customary law of the marcher lordships and their courts. Some of these courts were certainly held in Welsh and a few of their procedural terms have survived. In the lordship of Glasbury, for example, when a prisoner was arraigned for felony and asked how he would be tried, the answer was 'ar dduu ar wlad' (by God and the country) or 'ar dduu a deylad or wlad' (by God and free-tenants of the country). When judgement of death or outlawry was given in Glamorgan, it was 'gwynt a gwydden a phen blaidd a chrogi hyd farw' (wind and forest and wolf's head and hanging until dead).[3]

Undoubtedly the creation of the Great Sessions and subordinate courts (Quarter Sessions and Sheriffs' Tourns) involved a process of Anglicization. English law was regarded as having displaced Welsh and marcher law. The 'language clause' of the Act of Union (1536), despite some oddities of expression, made two things very clear: that from henceforward courts in Wales were to be kept in the English language; and that office-holders of the courts were to use English. There was clearly a period of some adjustment, if not confusion. It appears from a Star Chamber case that in 1541 the sheriff of the newly created county of Montgomeryshire caused an affray at a manorial court when the jurors gave their verdict in English instead of the customary Welsh.[4]

By restricting office-holding to those who could understand English, it was hoped to achieve uniformity of administration through an English-speaking Welsh élite. It is difficult to know how this worked out in practice. In reality, office-holding was linked with local status and influence (rather than language competence) because offices were a good source of profit for those acting as brokers between the state and their localities.

In the 1570s it was acknowledged by the Council in the Marches that a great number of justices of the peace were unfit to be in the commission, including some who were 'living by that office only'. A revealing late Elizabethan Star Chamber case (1594) apparently demonstrates that fifty years after the Acts of Union a barely literate Radnorshire landowner, Thomas Vaughan of Llowes, was able to hold office as a coroner and later a justice. He was described by his opponents as utterly unlearned and one that could neither write nor read and scarce speak the English language, but because he was powerful locally he was able to use his 'scabbed' offices (as he called them) to extort many bribes and rewards.[5] *Cymhortha*, the collecting of bribes and rewards, had been forbidden by statute in 1534, but the proliferation of offices with the Acts of Union provided new opportunities for extortion in relation to the legal process. Complaints

---

[3] NLW, Peniarth MS 408, f. 333; Rice Merrick, *Morganiae Archaiographia. A Book of the Antiquities of Glamorganshire*, ed. Brian Ll. James (South Wales Record Society, I, 1983), p. 34, with another version on p. 37: 'Crogi nes marw gwynt a gwydden a phen blaidd'.
[4] Cf. 'Gerard's Discourse', *Y Cymmrodor*, XIII (1900), 147; Peter R. Roberts, 'The Welsh Language, English Law and Tudor Legislation', *THSC* (1989), 31–2.
[5] 'Dr. David Lewis's Discourse', *Y Cymmrodor*, XIII (1900), 131; PRO STAC 5/B60/6.

against corrupt justices of the peace, sheriffs and coroners were made before the Council in the Marches and the Star Chamber.[6] Bailiffs and constables who regarded *cymhortha* as a perquisite of office were fined at the Great Sessions. From a grand-jury presentment in 1588, we learn that Breconshire bailiffs routinely extorted livestock (sheep or lambs), small sums of money, and grain in return for manipulating the legal process. It is presumably in the context of *cymhortha* that we should interpret the punishment of three Carmarthenshire hundred-bailiffs in 1558, who were each fined for the offence of 'not knowing or recognising (*non novit*) English law' when performing their office.[7]

Bailiffs and constables were among those relatively minor officials, drawn from the freeholding class, obliged by the Act of Union to 'use and exercise the speche or language of Englishe'. Welshmen might be excused from serving these offices if they convinced the justices at Quarter Sessions that they knew no English.[8] Still more far-reaching was the requirement, by no means theoretical, that jurors should understand English because the procedural language of the courts was English. In certain extrajudicial circumstances the use of Welsh towards juries might be authorized. When the Council in the Marches was anxious that a case of homicide should be properly investigated, the Flintshire coroner was instructed to read certain English examinations to the inquest jury but 'with suche interpretacion into their vulgar tongue as they may understaund the same'.[9] This dispensation was unusual, and possibly contrary to statute. In the context of the assizes it was expected that the principal presenting and trial juries should understand English. The evidence about linguistic competence, slight as it is, suggests that the majority of grand jurors and jurors of 'life and death' may have understood some English. In 1634 the deputy justice of North Wales established that nine of the twelve jurors in a difficult Anglesey murder trial could speak English.[10] Jurors who did not understand English could

---

[6] 28 Henry VIII, c. 6: Ivor Bowen (ed.), *The Statutes of Wales* (London, 1908), p. 57; Penry Williams, *The Council in the Marches of Wales under Elizabeth I* (Cardiff, 1958), pp. 27, 60–1, 307–8; Ifan ab Owen Edwards, *A Catalogue of Star Chamber Proceedings Relating to Wales* (Cardiff, 1929), passim, esp. pp. 40, 120.

[7] NLW, Great Sessions 13/18/4, unnumbered presentment (Brecs., 1588); NLW, Great Sessions 19/18, m. 23 (Carms., 1558).

[8] Several petitions to the Quarter Sessions survive, including the petition of Robert David of Llanfihangel, nominated as high-constable for Isaled, with certificate from his neighbours that he is 'a simple illiterate man and understandeth noe English', NLW, MS Chirk B15(b)/32–32/1 (Denbs. Quarter Sessions, 1659); J. Gwynfor Jones, *Law, Order and Government in Caernarvonshire, 1558–1640* (Cardiff, 1996), pp. 69–71.

[9] NLW, Great Sessions 4/970/3/33 (Flints., 1580).

[10] W. Ogwen Williams, 'The Survival of the Welsh Language after the Union of England and Wales: the First Phase, 1536–1642', *WHR*, 2, no. 1 (1964), 72.

be punished – as happened, for example, at Brecon in 1588 when Harry Edward of Llandyfalle was fined 40 shillings for not being able to speak English.[11] This was particularly harsh because jurors were not volunteers but had been summoned by the sheriff.

The principle that grand jurors should understand English was clearly restated in the mid-seventeenth century by an order on the Chester circuit which required that only 'such as understand the English tongue' among gentlemen and freeholders should serve on the great inquests.[12] In fact, a procedure developed that enabled non-English speakers summoned for grand-jury service to petition the court for a writ of exemption. Needless to say the petition had to be in English. In the earliest surviving petition (1615), two poor freeholders from Faenol (Denbs.) pleaded to be discharged from a fine of 20s. for non-appearance, describing themselves as being of 'weak capacity' and 'understanding noe worde of English'. There are half a dozen similar mid-seventeenth-century petitions from Flintshire and Denbighshire, all emphasizing illiteracy and the inability to understand English.[13]

In the late seventeenth century the Denbighshire grand jury expressed concern that jurors of the 'meanest and most ignorant sort' served in non-criminal trials.[14] Ignorance in this context seems primarily to have meant the inability to understand English. Grand jurymen may have been required to understand English, but it would have been hopelessly un-realistic to expect that all jurors should understand English. The necessity of empanelling numerous trial juries in civil actions meant that the language requirement had to be overridden and it must be assumed that many jurors understood little or no English. In linguistically divided counties (Glamorgan and Pembrokeshire, especially), juries might be composed of both monoglot Welsh speakers and monoglot English speakers. According to George Owen, in some Pembrokeshire juries 'there wilbe the one half that cannot vnderstand the others wordes; and

---

[11] Harry Edward appeared, but was probably unable to take the oath in English. The circumstances seem to have been unusual; the grand jury was apparently not sworn and Harry Edward was a member of the second jury: Great Sessions 13/18/4, unnumbered document (Brecs., 1588). For the second or hundred jury, see Parry, *Guide to the Records of Great Sessions*, p. lxvii.

[12] NLW, Great Sessions 14/70, f. 124 (Flints. Crown Book, 1653).

[13] NLW, Great Sessions 4/16/3/3 (Denbs., 1615). Other petitioners unable to speak or understand English included Thomas Jones of Whitford (Flints., 1655); Thomas ap Edward Raphe of Treithyn and Thomas Jones of Mertyn (Flints., 1656); Thomas ap Rees of Derwen, 'a meare Welshman' (Denbs., 1661); Edward Williames of Dolevechles (Flints., 1662); Edward Jones of Cyfnant (Denbs., 1669): NLW, Great Sessions 13/46/1; 13/46/3; P. 659; P. 327; P. 672.

[14] NLW, Great Sessions 4/31/4/42 (Denbs., 1681).

yett must they agree upon the truth of the matter, before they departe'.[15] It may be that an effort was made to select a literate, bilingual foreman who would have a special role in interpreting evidence and conveying the instructions of the judge to his fellow jurors. The crucial role of bilingual jurors is certainly suggested by an account of the composition of a mid-eighteenth-century Caernarfonshire jury which returned a verdict contrary to the directions of the judge. Thomas Hughes, a Bangor glazier, had taken it upon himself to inform the rest of the jury of the nature of the evidence and the direction of the judge. Hughes acknowledged that 'although he was not master of the English language, so as to understand it readily and clearly, yet he thought he understood it better than the rest of the jury (. . . many of them understanding none of that language)'.[16]

Welsh juries acquired an undeserved reputation for corruption and partiality. The fining of jurors for returning perverse verdicts was not uncommon in the sixteenth and early seventeenth centuries; in the eighteenth and early nineteenth centuries trials were sometimes transferred to the nearest English county because of the alleged partiality of jurors. In an influential eighteenth-century judgement which eroded the independence of the Great Sessions from the jurisdiction of the King's Bench, it was argued that 'it was very difficult to have justice done in Wales, for they are all related to one another'.[17]

It was common practice in the Great Sessions, especially before the Restoration, to challenge jurors on the grounds of kinship and alliance. In civil actions genealogical statements were made to show kinship between the plaintiff and the sheriff or coroner who had summoned the jury (challenge to the array) or kinship between jurors and litigants (challenge to the polls). *Practica Walliae*, the attorneys' vade-mecum, devotes many pages to the technicalities of the challenge to the array, but the principle was very simple: if the plaintiff failed to declare his kindred with the sheriff or coroner, then the defendant would make his challenge which, if successful, would lead to the quashing of the jury, involving the plaintiff in delays and expense as trial was deferred to the following session.[18]

Challenges were numerous in the first hundred years of the court but declined in importance after the Restoration. It is difficult to calculate the number of challenges in the Elizabethan and Jacobean record, but they probably numbered several thousand. The challenges were pedigrees in chart form which were filed among the prothonotaries' papers and later

---

[15] Owen, *Description*, I, p. 40.
[16] Affidavit of David Williams, attorney, NLW, Great Sessions P. 1591 (Caerns., 1742).
[17] Parry, *Guide to the Records of Great Sessions*, p. xvii.
[18] Rice Vaughan, *Practica Walliae; or the Proceedings in the Great Sessions of Wales* (London, 1672), pp. 38–44; Parry, *Guide to the Records of Great Sessions*, pp. xcix–c.

enrolled as a narrative pedigree in the plea rolls. The involvement of herald-bards and gentleman genealogists as compilers of pedigrees and expert witnesses is highly probable, although they are unnamed in the record.[19] Defendants in particular needed expert guidance to demonstrate the genealogical connections of the plaintiff, which were often traced through agnatic lines. Pedigrees showing cousinage to the fourth degree were routinely submitted, but challenges of up to eight generations in depth were suggested to the court. The early Tudor founders of great houses regularly appear at the apices of these pedigrees: for instance, Sir David Gam and Thomas Havard Hir in Breconshire; Pennant Abbas and Richard ap Howel alias Mosten in Flintshire; John Ayr Conway and Thomas Hen Salusbury in Denbighshire.[20] These pedigrees were generally submitted in Latin, sometimes in English, but the learning was essentially Welsh. Occasionally an untranslated Welsh challenge pedigree was filed among the prothonotary's papers: several six-generational pedigrees in Welsh have been preserved in the Breconshire papers which show the relationship between the petitioner or 'gofynnwr' and the sheriff and coroners.[21]

After the jury had been called, but before it was sworn, litigants were able to challenge individual jurors on the grounds of kindred with the other party. These challenges were not formally noted in the record of the court, but an account of a celebrated action for trespass in Glamorgan shows how expert witnesses might be involved in the process. In this action, the plaintiff, who was also sheriff, had revealed in his pedigree his relationship with the coroners. The defendant accepted that the coroner could return the jury, but challenged individual jurors for kinship with the plaintiff using expert witnesses. The defendant had provided himself with two heralds ('herehauts') at the bar of the court 'to trye pettigrees': John Gamage, 'a gentleman of good name', and Mericke David, 'rhymer'.

---

[19] The end of the tradition is indicated by the petition of William Griffiths of Melyney, 'sole antiquary' belonging to the counties of Cardigan, Carmarthen and Pembroke, asking to be released from appearing at any leet or court: NLW, Great Sessions P. 3088 (Cards., 1676). Cf. Francis Jones, 'Griffith of Penybenglog', *THSC* (1938), 143–4.

[20] NLW, Great Sessions 13/19/6–7 (Brecs., 1605); NLW, Great Sessions 13/39/8 and 13/41/3 (Flints., 1612 and 1623); NLW, Great Sessions 13/2/14 and 13/4/5 (Denbs., 1575 and 1590).

[21] The following Welsh challenge pedigrees have been preserved: (i) relationship between Edward ap Lewys, gofynnwr, and Edward Awbrae ap Wiliam, siryf: NLW, Great Sessions 13/18/7 (Brecs., 1591); (ii) relationship between Sion Gwnter ap Tomas, gofynnwr, and (a) Thomas ap Hywel, crwner, (b) Katrin ferch D[afyd]d Ifan, gwraig Sion Games, crwner, (c) Rosser Fychan ap Rosser Drydydd, siryf: NLW, Great Sessions 13/19/1 (Brecs., 1596); (iii) relationship between D[afyd]d ap D[afyd]d Morgan, gofynnwr, and same coroners and sheriff: NLW, Great Sessions 13/19/1. The pedigrees were enrolled in Latin.

According to the author of *The Storie of the Lower Borowes*, there were 'challenges and excepcions for sundry respectes of affinitie and kinred, as I never saw nor heard of the like'. But the gentleman-genealogist 'behaved himself so conceiptedly at the barr in derivinge pettegrees, as he caused all the court to laughe merilie'.[22]

The Courts of Great Sessions were incredibly busy. In one session there might be four or five hundred people involved as officers, jurors, suspects, litigants, prosecutors, witnesses and those on bail. Much of the procedure, especially the preliminary procedure, was taken up with reading lists of names of those who should appear. Again, petitions by those fined or imprisoned for non-appearance show that this was clearly a difficult time. The court might be crowded, the business was long, and the language unfamiliar. David Morris, committed to the gaoler's custody for non-appearance in 1663, explained in a petition for release that 'not being perfect in the English tongue' he could not answer when called.[23] There were moments of utter incomprehension when badly garbled versions of names were called. William Salesbury has a revealing story of Ednyfed ap Iorwerth failing to answer when his name was read out by an English clerk ('being but a yong beginner') in its abbreviated and Latinized form as Eden ap Iorum. In this instance the 'geste' was discovered at the last moment and there was 'no smale laughter' in the court at the confusion.[24]

Names were a continual problem for officials at the Court of Great Sessions. There is no documentary corroboration of Thomas Pennant's story about the origin of the Mostyn surname, but it is not implausible: it was said that the President of the Council in the Marches wearied of the lengthy recitation of the patronymics of the jurors as they were called and instructed that they should assume their last name or that of their residence as a surname. Thus Thomas ap Richard ap Howell ap Ieuan Fychan, lord of Mostyn, became Thomas Mostyn.[25] The courts certainly preferred (abridged) patronymics to the unofficial names by which people were often better known in their localities. However, numerous examples of occupational, descriptive and locational cognomens, as well as nascent surnames were noted in court records. David ap Llewelyn alias Benwyn of Cardigan, Jenkin William alias Glyncorrwg of Brecon and Ieuan Lewis alias Ieuan Gwyn Daliwr are characteristic examples. The naming process

---

[22] John Stradling, *The Storie of the Lower Borowes of Merthyrmawr*, eds. H. J. Randall and William Rees (South Wales and Monmouth Record Society, I, [1932]), pp. 70–1.

[23] NLW, Great Sessions P. 662 (Denbs., 1663).

[24] William Salesbury, *A briefe and a playne introduction, teachyng how to pronounce the letters in the British tong (now com'enly called Walsh)* (London, 1550), sig. Diiv; Roberts, 'The Welsh Language', 38.

[25] Thomas Pennant, *A Tour in Wales* (2 vols., London, 1778–83), I, p. 12; T. J. Morgan and Prys Morgan, *Welsh Surnames* (Cardiff, 1985), p. 169.

might generate several alternatives: Henry ap John alias Syr John alias Henry Parson of Llanrhidian, tailor, was indicted in Glamorgan in 1569.[26] Names and aliases were carefully recorded for fear of a misnomer which could prove fatal to an indictment. A Radnorshire suspect indicted by the singular name of Gelle Maen was discharged after successfully pleading that he had been called David ap Ieuan David Thomas from his baptism.[27]

At the Great Sessions we encounter the shadowy world of the outlaw and wanderer and others on the margin of society where official names meant little. Richard ap Hugh, a person of 'no constant place of abode' and a suspected horse-stealer, was indicted under his alias 'Coch y Cwrw'. We learn of the Montgomeryshire outlaw called 'Kig Eiddion' and his companion, the ironically named 'Ifan Torri Dim', and a Merioneth robber called 'Yr Ebol Gwyn'. A Montgomeryshire cutpurse who called herself 'Winter and Summer' told magistrates she would rather be hanged than answer any of their questions.[28] Suspects with multiple aliases continued to be indicted in the eighteenth century.[29]

Language and Procedure

This section examines some of the procedural details of language and the courts, particularly the life and death situation of the trial for felony. There was really a trilingual situation which related to different procedural stages. First, origination. This was the point of articulation between the court and the community. A Welsh language complaint was made to a justice of the peace which was then translated into a written English examination for the benefit of the court. Second, procedure. The language of the court was English. Certain procedural steps were absolutely required to be in

---

[26] NLW, Great Sessions 4/883/4/6 (Cards., 1556); NLW, Great Sessions 4/343/5/89 (Brecs., 1630); NLW, Great Sessions 4/14/1/33 (Denbs., 1605); NLW, Great Sessions 7/4, m. 10Dv (Glam., July 1569).

[27] NLW, Great Sessions 4/462/2/6 (indictment, 1557); NLW, Great Sessions 13/21/9/ [unnumbered] (plea, 1560); NLW, Great Sessions 4/463/4/44 (issue decided by the jury, 1561).

[28] NLW, Great Sessions 4/24/4/10, 52 (Denbs., 1648); NLW, Great Sessions 4/148/1/49, 4/152/1/49 (Mont., 1630 and 1662); NLW, Great Sessions 4/154/3/21 (Mont., 1654). Cf. also Hughe ap William alias 'yr Aer' indicted for burglary: NLW, Great Sessions 4/1/6/54 (Denbs., 1562); Richard Lewis alias 'Brenyne Baughe', labourer of Doley, indicted for housebreaking: NLW, Great Sessions 4/476/2/73 (Rad., 1598); Humphrey ap John alias 'Capten Towyn' convicted of rape with judgement of hanging: NLW, Great Sessions 23/26, Rex m. [unnumbered] (Mer., 1632); Edward ap Edward ap John Griffith alias 'Swaggarer': NLW, Great Sessions 4/18/3/14 (Denbs., 1627).

[29] At Brecon in 1726 bills of indictment were filed against William Evans alias Davies alias Powell alias Maesmyrddin, Llywel, weaver, and against Rees Thomas alias Jones otherwise 'Rees or Mynith, the famous horse stealer': NLW, Great Sessions 4/372/5 and 28/31 (September, 1726).

English, although the use of Welsh was permitted at certain points. Third, the record. The official record of proceedings was in Latin until 1732–3 and afterwards in English. In certain circumstances Welsh and English words were admitted into the Latin record.

The procedure in the trial for felony is important because it could send a man or (more rarely) a woman to the gallows and it raised problems in relation to language.[30] The arraignment and trial of a suspect took place after the grand jury had found a bill of complaint against him. The arraignment of the prisoner was a moment of great importance. The clerk of the court called the prisoner to the bar and he was instructed to hold up his hand. The clerk then addressed the prisoner in English: 'Thou art here indicted by the name of A.B. for that thou . . .' (the indictment was then translated from Latin into English and read). The clerk concluded: 'Art thou guilty therof or not guilty?' If the prisoner pleaded not guilty, as usually happened, the clerk then asked, 'Culprit, how wilt thou be tried?' The required response (and none other was allowed) were the English words 'by God and the country'.

There are a number of points here which need stressing. First, by holding up his hand, the suspect was considered to be acknowledging himself as the person named in the indictment; second, that the pleading, and subsequent verdict and judgement were in English. We have already considered the problem of names – official, unofficial and mangled. It was bad enough for a suspect to be indicted under a garbled version of his name but worse, we may suppose, that his life depended on proceedings that were in a language which was unintelligible or barely intelligible.

The Act of Union of 1536 required that the court was to be kept in English. This meant that the key procedural steps in a trial were in English. Presumably, special procedures were available for those unable to plead in English, possibly prisoners repeated the English words after the clerk. Occasionally Welshmen would not use English. The gaol calendar for a Montgomeryshire Sessions in 1635 records that Thomas Morgan was committed to the gaol 'for not answeringe the Court in English'.[31] Refusing to plead in English according to due form was a very dangerous course for suspects to take. The law required set answers to the question, 'How wilt thou be tried?' and they were in English. It was not sufficient to use the old formula 'ar Dduw a'r wlad' or some other words instead of the exact English formula, 'by God and the country'. If the prisoner

---

[30] This account is based on an Elizabethan formulary used on the Chester circuit, NLW, Great Sessions 35/18. Procedure at the English assizes was similar: cf. J. H. Baker, 'Criminal Courts and Procedure at Common Law 1550–1800' in J. S. Cockburn (ed.), *Crime in England, 1550–1800* (London, 1977), pp. 32–45.

[31] NLW, Great Sessions 4/150/3/128 (Mont., 1635).

refused to use the required words, this was equivalent to standing mute or refusing to plead. Refusal to plead (i.e. not acknowledging the authority of the court) carried the terrible and barbaric penalty of being pressed to death. Usually, one supposes, a reluctant suspect was eventually forced to plead, but there are several Elizabethan cases where Welsh suspects remained silent at arraignment. In 1578 John Treylo of Ackhill, near Presteigne, was pressed to death for refusing to plead; the year before, the mute Robert ap Hugh ap Ieuan ap William of Hope, Montgomeryshire, presumably suffered the same fate after a jury had decided that he was able to speak. Do any of these judicial victims include early language martyrs who preferred death to pleading in English? It is impossible to tell from the record, which merely records that a jury found the prisoner standing mute either from malice or from visitation of God, and judgement of death by compression was given accordingly.[32]

After the prisoner had pleaded, his shackles were removed and the trial began. (An inventory of Radnor gaol reveals that a large fetter was familiarly called 'Gwenllian Hir'.[33]) There are few contemporary accounts of trials. The most detailed is the trial of the future martyr Richard Gwyn in 1584, though this was an exceptional event recorded in an exceptional form.[34]

Because of the language barrier between judges and witnesses, particular importance seems to have been attached to written evidence. These were the initial statements taken on oath from witnesses and suspects, which were translated into English by the justices of the peace or their clerks. According to a sixteenth-century formulary from the Chester circuit, these English examinations or extracts from them were read aloud; passages which made most for the Crown against the prisoner were marked and presumably emphasized.[35] Witnesses and prosecutors had to confirm orally the written examinations. The account of a Montgomeryshire trial in 1632 reveals that the prosecutor was called to the bar and 'demanded in the Welsh tongue if he would justify his examination to be true'. The witness then answered in Welsh and his response was conveyed to the chief justice in English, 'by way of

---

[32] NLW, Great Sessions 4/469/1/62 (Rad., 1578); NLW, Great Sessions 4/128/5/52, 54, 85 (Mont., 1579). The likely reasons for standing mute were terror, and the intention to deny the Crown goods which would otherwise be rendered forfeit by conviction.

[33] '... one greate bolte called gwenllian here & sixe shackelles for the saide bolte': NLW, Great Sessions 26/48, m. 17 (Rad., 1573). Presumably the male felons regarded the shackle as 'female'.

[34] D. Aneurin Thomas (ed.), *The Welsh Elizabethan Catholic Martyrs* (Cardiff, 1971), pp. 84–131. Richard Gwyn's witticisms in three languages during arraignment and trial discomposed the judges and confused language categories normally kept apart.

[35] NLW, Great Sessions, 35/18, f. 7.

interpretation', who then asked further questions. In the same period on the North Wales circuit, the deputy justice recorded that 'the witnesses speak Welsh and English witnesses are interpreted in Welsh when it is required'.[36]

It is not clear who actually did the interpreting. References to professional, paid interpreters first occur in early-eighteenth-century court papers, and it is likely that before this period translations were made by officers of the court, attorneys or justices of the peace who understood both languages.[37] However, it is clear from other sources that interpreters, whatever their status, were specially sworn. In 1598 the practice in Wales of using sworn interpreters was recommended for the Irish courts, with the comment that if they interpreted untruly they were 'subject to every man's censure'. Few complaints about mistranslation have survived.[38]

After the evidence, the judge directed the jury in English and the jury retired to consider their verdict, which was also given in English. Before judgement was given on those suspects found guilty, the prisoners were brought to the bar and asked (presumably in English): 'Now what can you say for your selves why you should not have judgment to suffer death and execucion to be awarded accordinge to lawe.' The prisoner might claim a pardon, if a man plead benefit of the clergy, or if a woman plead pregnancy. More usually one supposes the prisoner made a futile plea for mitigation. If this was in Welsh, it was probably not translated – there was no point because the judge could not depart from the sentence of death laid down by statute. The sixteenth-century instructions for the clerk of the Crown are memorably blunt at this point: 'when they [the prisoners] can say nothinge, bid them stand aside'.[39]

This is an appropriate point to consider control and manipulation of the trial for felony. Although a great many people were hanged for felony, they were but a small proportion – less than a quarter – of those who were actually indicted. Acquittal rates were high and an unknown number of suspects were never tried because the grand jury rejected the draft bills of indictment against them. Although the Great Sessions appears as a very powerful institution, there was (for the first hundred years at least)

---

[36] Murray Ll. Chapman, 'A Sixteenth-Century Trial for Felony in the Court of Great Sessions for Montgomeryshire', *MC*, 78 (1990), 167–70; Williams, 'The Survival of the Welsh Language', 72.

[37] Fees paid to interpreters were noted in bills of costs. Fees rose from 2s. in the 1720s to 10s.6d. in the 1820s, with 2s. paid to the crier for swearing the interpreter: NLW, Great Sessions BC. 1–15. Interpreters were very occasionally named, perhaps in special cases; cf. 'Interpreting fee paid to Mr. Garnons upon tryal' in an action for slander: Humphrey v. Jones, NLW, Great Sessions P. 1632 (Caerns., 1762).

[38] Williams, *Council in the Marches*, p. 82.

[39] NLW, Great Sessions 35/18, ff. 7v–8.

widespread manipulation of it by people who used the processes of the court to get what they really wanted. People may have participated in the prosecution of suspected felons, but they did so with rather different conceptions from the judiciary of what outcome was desirable. By and large, the state wanted retribution and the exemplary punishment of felons through public executions; what people wanted was the restitution of stolen goods and compensation for thefts and other injuries. Prosecutors and their witnesses did not particularly want to see a thief hanged, although of course sometimes they might. It was better to have a live thief and compensation for a theft than a dead thief and the stolen goods gone forever. Compounding with a thief was actually a felony, but there are plenty of hints that the threat to prosecute was used as a lever to obtain compensation; and once this had been arranged prosecutions were abandoned.

George Owen provides a contemporary description of this process in his account of the abuses of the legal system. He explains that as the time of the Great Sessions drew near, the suspect 'falleth to talke for an end to be had with the partye pursuant' and in the end agrees with him so that the prosecutor will stop the cause as much as he may. The prosecutor was bound to prosecute, but did so half-heartedly in order to save his recognizance but producing no clear evidence against the suspect, who would be discharged at the end of the Sessions.[40]

There are strong hints that in parallel with the formal English-language courts, there was another less visible Welsh-language system of arbitration and compromise. Compensation or restitution for theft was achieved through intermediaries and go-betweens and sometimes by arbitration. Formal Welsh language arbitration procedures existed most clearly in relation to homicide and lesser injuries to the person, and even after the Acts of Union the ideas of *sarhaed* (insult), *galanas* (blood-price), and *rhaith* (compurgators) were embodied and sometimes actually named in formal arbitration documents. A Radnorshire arbitration of 1563 was to settle certain 'hurtes, soores, or in Welsh surrayed'.[41] The term *galanas* is not used, but there are several instances of the related word *glanastra*. A case in the plea rolls concerned the death of a servant of Christopher Turbervill of Glamorgan when 'all glanastra, bothers, murders and manslaughters' were

---

[40] Owen, *Description*, III, pp. 44–6. Cf. Nia M. W. Powell, 'Crime and the Community in Denbighshire during the 1590s: the Evidence of the Records of the Court of Great Sessions' in J. Gwynfor Jones (ed.), *Class, Community and Culture in Tudor Wales* (Cardiff, 1989), pp. 268–9; G. Dyfnallt Owen, *Wales in the Reign of James I* (London, 1988), p. 14.

[41] Robert John Thomas v. Roger ap Meredith, NLW, Great Sessions 13/21/18 and 26/32, m. 16 (Rad., 1565). The word 'svrrayed' in the original plea filed with the prothonotary has been scribally mangled as 'storrageg' on the plea roll.

to be settled by arbitrators.⁴² *Glanastra* seems to have had the meaning of a death crying out for revenge. Those dying from wounds inflicted by another would name the culprit and leave their death on them: a kind of curse. In two Denbighshire cases, the actual words are recorded: in 1676 Edward Hughes left his death on a neighbour by saying: 'yglanastra i ar Mrs Williams yn fyw ag yn farw' (My curse on Mrs Williams in life and in death). Again, in 1689, the dying John Vaughan, a Denbigh glover, named his assailant and declared: 'Fynglanastra i am plant a fo arno fe' (May my curse and that of my children be upon him).⁴³

The central feature of these arbitrated cases was the decision by arbitrators to compel the suspect to take a solemn oath with a certain number of oath-helpers that he had not committed the injury and in default to pay compensation to the injured party or his kin. Thus, in the Radnorshire case previously mentioned, Roger ap Meredith of Boughrood, yeoman, was ordered to appear at his parish church with eight persons and after divine service to swear upon the holy evangelist (i.e. the gospels) that Agnes ferch John at the time of the supposed affray had received neither hurts, sores or *sarhaed* from him. If Roger ap Meredith failed to produce his oath-helpers, then he was to give the arbitrators 13s.4d. to pass on to Agnes.⁴⁴

About half a dozen or so similar awards have survived; a small number perhaps, but enough to show that customary Welsh-language procedures for compensation for personal injury existed outside the Great Sessions in the second half of the sixteenth century. It is quite clear from Llinos Beverley Smith's work on arbitration that there was considerable continuity from the late-medieval period onwards.⁴⁵ It is difficult to know the exact importance of arbitrated settlements for personal injury, but the scale of settlements – apparently involving tens and sometimes hundreds of people willing to take oaths – suggests that they were highly significant. Some doubt has been expressed that the rules applying to large numbers of oath-helpers (the *rhaith*) specified in the various texts of the Welsh laws were ever applied. However, in the early modern period it is clear that arbitrators specified large numbers of oath-helpers for the denial of liability in serious cases of personal injury and these must have been very solemn and memorable occasions. In 1544 some fifty oath-helpers were required in a Brecon case to swear that Philip John had not rebuked or shamed

---

[42] Llinos Beverley Smith, 'Disputes and Settlements in Medieval Wales: The Role of Arbitration', *EHR*, CVI (1991), 849.
[43] NLW, MS Chirk B32(d)/10 (Denbs. Quarter Sessions, 1676); NLW, Great Sessions 4/34/1/39 (Denbs., 1689).
[44] NLW, Great Sessions 26/32, m. 16 (Rad., 1565).
[45] Smith, 'Disputes and Settlements', 835–60.

John Morgan and his sons from malice. In 1550 the suspects indicted at the Caernarfonshire Great Sessions for the murder of Robert ap Griffith ap John were to appear at their parish church with a hundred gentlemen to swear that his death was not premeditated.[46] Finally, in Glamorgan in 1558, the astonishing number of 360 oath-helpers were required by arbitrators in a case of homicide.[47]

These cases are illuminating because they show very sharply the different conceptions or models of justice which existed more generally at different points within the legal system. There was essentially tension between the retributive justice (the punishment of the guilty) of the state and the desire for compensation on the part of the victims of theft, assault and slander. Care is needed in expressing the difference between restitution and retribution. Arbitration was an alternative – presumably a Welsh-language alternative – to the formal procedures of the Court of Great Sessions. Nevertheless, it was not an alternative in the sense of being oppositional. Arbitration and compensation generally lay outside the formal framework of the courts, but they did in fact depend on willingness to use the processes of the court. Compensation for theft could only be obtained because of the threat to indict and following through a process which could eventually lead to the gallows. Arbitration took place only because the parties bound themselves by a bond whose penalty (£40–£100) could be recovered in the Court of Great Sessions if the arbitration was not performed. Despite the problems of language (or perhaps because of them), people were able to manipulate the legal system to obtain what they wanted. Using the law was an inducement to settle, to obtain what one really wanted, and the same was as much true of civil as criminal cases.

The Welsh Language in the Record of the Court

This section examines briefly examples of Welsh which have found their way into the record of the court. In an accumulation of documents as large as the archive of the Great Sessions, there are inevitably language 'strays'. Among the pen-trials, doodles and doggerel written by bored clerks on court papers, there are *englynion* as well as English verses.[48]

---

[46] NLW, Penpont Deeds and Documents (Supplementary) 94; NLW, Brogyntyn Deeds and Documents 3508.
[47] Howell ap Rees et al. v. Lewis Thomas, NLW, Great Sessions 22/30, m. 18 (Glam., 1561).
[48] *Englynion* in NLW, Great Sessions 4/7/5/41v (Denbs., 1588) and 4/125/5/17v (Mont., 1567), both written on examinations. Examples of English verse in NLW, Great Sessions 4/135/1/24v (Mont., 1592).

Extraneous material incorporated into the record includes an apparently unique copy of a patriotic broadsheet printed in Welsh, which was used as a file divider in the prothonotary's office during the Napoleonic wars.[49] These language strays are interesting, but of greater importance is the use of Welsh in the formal record of the court. The Welsh language has left very little trace in the record of the staple civil business of the court, mostly actions for debt, except in a few cases which involved customary measures and payments.[50] Welsh had no place in the formal parchment indictments for theft and other felonies,[51] but Welsh words were incidentally and haphazardly noted in the less formal paper examinations and depositions in criminal cases. However, in actions for slander and prosecutions for seditious words and perjury, the court required that Welsh words should be faithfully recorded and entered in the record.

The importance of pre-trial written examinations of suspects and witnesses has already been mentioned. Few examinations have survived among the English assize records; their preservation in the record of the Court of Great Sessions can be attributed, in part at least, to their greater significance in Wales, where the language of the court was English but the language of suspects and witnesses was by and large Welsh.[52] Examinations were the result of a translation process from Welsh into English by a magistrate or a clerk, although this was rarely made explicit in the document. Occasionally a non-Welsh-speaking justice of the peace noted the problem of language. William Fowler of Shropshire, who acquired an estate in Radnorshire, found that two of his servants were accused of cattle stealing in 1564. He examined some of those concerned

---

[49] NLW, Great Sessions P. 1717 (Caerns., 1805): *Attebion Eglur i Ymofyniadau Eglur mewn Ymddiddan rhwng John Bwl a Bonaparte*, printed by T. Roberts, 1803.

[50] Some examples: conditional bond concerning the payment of 'arrian ryngilt', 'arrian melyn' and 'Candlemasse penny' to the bailiff of Hopedale: Edward, Earl of Derby v. Edward Yonge, NLW, Great Sessions 30/52, m. 13 (Flints., 1550); agreement at Llanfrothen to buy a certain quantity of hay 'Wallice vocat gwrid o wair' measuring 2 yards in length, 4 yards in width, and 3 yards in height: Nicholas Owen v. Richard Rowland and John ap Robert, NLW, Great Sessions 23/30, m. 3d. (Mer., 1636); action concerning the lease of the fourth part of a parcel of tithes called 'Rhandir tyr y wlade' in the parish of Llanwnnws: Morgan Harbert v. Oliver Lloyd, NLW, Great Sessions 13/27/7 (Cards., 1649). Conditional bonds concerning acreage by 'lathe Lethins' or 'lathe Bleddyns' measure were litigated in Glamorgan, e.g., NLW, Great Sessions 22/45, m. 25 and 22/46, m. 11d.

[51] Only two indictments have been noted which specify a Welsh term for stolen goods: the indictment of Margaret ferch Rees for the theft of one and three quarter ells of woollen cloth called 'glannen', valued at 12d.: NLW, Great Sessions 21/58, m. 18 (Denbs., 1578); indictment of Morgan ap David Gogh for the theft of two ells of woollen cloth 'Wallice vocat les Gvrthban' valued at 6d.: NLW, Great Sessions 23/15, m. 9 (Mer., 1594; indictment referred from the Quarter Sessions).

[52] The survival of examinations is discussed by Parry, *Guide to the Records of Great Sessions*, pp. lxiv–lxv.

but, because he did 'not understande the language of the owner of the cattle and other[s]', he asked a neighbouring Welsh-speaking justice to examine them so that the evidence would be clear.[53]

Examinations were English-language documents, but they sometimes incorporated Welsh words for precision and for the faithful reconstruction of an event. The markings of stolen cattle and sheep were occasionally described in Welsh and English for greater certainty.[54] A sheep stolen from Llangadfan in 1590, for example, had an elaborate ear mark which was simply 'called in Welshe kynwyro'. In the early eighteenth century, a stolen horse was described as 'lear-eyed' or having 'llygaid brithion'.[55] Some quite ordinary objects were given their Welsh names to avoid ambiguity or when they were implements used in serious crimes. A new implement stolen from a Denbighshire fair was described as a 'spade iron called in Welsh pen rhaw ball'; 'cowblake' or 'dryed cowesheard' used as fuel or kindling by the poor was called 'gleyhaden'; tactics in a grazing dispute involved attaching 'cloffrwm' ('peeces of wood') to the tails of sheep. The word 'mingammu' glossed the account of housebreaking in which a robber was said to have mocked his agitated victim.[56]

Most crimes tried before the Court of Great Sessions were capital felonies, but cases of suspected murder were treated with exceptional seriousness, and witnesses were thoroughly examined. Occasionally these examinations preserve reported speech in Welsh. On the night in 1671 when Ellis Vaughan of Llanddulas (Denbs.) was murdered, a witness heard the suspects talking urgently: 'Dowch yma, dowch yma ar frys' ('Come hither, come hither quickly'). Someone answered, 'Deliwch fo, deliwch fo' ('Hould him, hould him'), and the response came, 'Gwn yn enw Duw' ('I will in the name of God'). Characteristically, the drama of a situation was recalled by the Welsh language imperatives which had been used in the event. 'Prockiwch!' ('thrust at him') was spoken immediately before a fatal shot was fired; 'Attogh, attogh' ('looke to you') was the warning given before a fatal assault in Ruthin churchyard; the challenge 'stande . . . in good sort' – 'mewn gweddeidd dra' – 'as it becometh you' was partially translated in 1605; 'Gwiliwch y pacen!' ('Beware the peece of wood') was shouted before an unfortunate woman was crushed by falling timber. A baby suspected of having been murdered was said by a witness

[53] NLW, Great Sessions 13/21/17 (Rad., 1565).
[54] See above, pp. 106–7.
[55] NLW, Great Sessions 4/134/2/58 (Mont., 1590); 4/372/2 (Breconshire examinations 1725, formerly in Wales 28/52).
[56] NLW, Great Sessions 4/23/1/10 (Denbs., 1639), 4/141/3/51 (Mont., 1607), 4/16/1/15 (Denbs., 1595), 4/38/1 [unnumbered] (Denbs., 1702). Cf. also 'a sicknesse called y vam Englished the fitts of the mother or spleen', NLW, Great Sessions 4/798/3/16 (Pembs., 1686).

to have been born 'yn lled fyw', that is scarcely alive.[57] The situation of death and the last words of the dying were sometimes recorded in Welsh: 'fom llas i' ('I am kylled'); 'O Duw, di am lleddest i' ('O God, thou hath killed me'). The solemn curse of the dying (*glanastra*) has already been mentioned.[58]

Welsh words in English examinations, while never common, are increasingly rare after the mid-seventeenth century. One supposes that with the progressive Anglicization of the gentry, a growing proportion of magistrates were unable to speak Welsh. Examinations were increasingly mediated through clerks and other interpreters who are rarely mentioned and never named. Robert Jones, accused of leading an immoral life with Lowri ferch John, was examined by a Denbigh magistrate in 1651. The magistrate noted that Lowri was Robert's 'lover' as 'the word out of ye Welch was expounded to me' and claimed that the unrepentant suspect expressed himself in Welsh 'in ye plainest & fowlest manner that could bee', without of course recording his actual words.[59]

Welsh words in English examinations were rather exceptional. The majority of examples of Welsh in the otherwise Latin or English legal record are provided by some 2,000 slander cases over a period of nearly three hundred years. These cases by and large record examples of ordinary, colloquial speech and provide a remarkable corpus of knowledge for those working on the history and distribution of the language. It should be emphasized that the Welsh slander cases are probably unique among sources which document the non-English languages of the British Isles. It seems that there are no Cornish slander cases in the English legal record, and actions for slander in Irish or Scottish Gaelic do not exist.[60]

Slander cases were brought for financial compensation by those who considered themselves wrongfully accused of a crime. Words spoken in court were considered privileged, so actions for slander often preserve the words of pre-trial accusations. Actions for slander in Welsh were first brought in the 1550s. In Denbighshire the earliest case on the plea rolls is actually a very exceptional racial insult: 'ffals scott brunt' ('fals harlott scott') spoken at Ruthin in 1555. The second case (1557) is, however,

[57] NLW, Great Sessions 4/28/4/61 (Denbs., 1671), 4/28/2/13 (Denbs., 1670), 4/12/1/13v (Denbs., 1601), 4/14/1/28 (Denbs., 1605), 4/14/2/5 (Denbs., 1606), 4/21/1/51 (Denbs., 1634).
[58] NLW, Great Sessions 4/13/4/32 (2) (Denbs., 1604); NLW, Great Sessions 4/33/6/11 (Denbs., 1687). Cf. also Hugh ap Ieuan from Llanrhaeadr 'uttering these w[i]th a submissive voyce in haec Wallica verba, viggelyn, vingelyn' (my enemy, my enemy), NLW, Great Sessions 4/10/1/16 (Denbs., 1595).
[59] NLW, Great Sessions 4/24/6/18 (Denbs., 1651).
[60] Richard Suggett, 'Slander in Early-Modern Wales', *BBCS*, XXXIX (1992), 119–53.

characteristic of a thousand others: 'Yr wyt ti yn garn lledyr', translated as 'Thou art an arrant theyf'.[61]

The majority of slander cases concerned accusations of theft and other felonies (some 80 per cent), followed by allegations of perjury (15 per cent); the remaining cases related to such matters as professional incompetence brought by attorneys and others.[62] Although allegations of perjury were common, prosecutions for the offence were not numerous at the Great Sessions. The Council in the Marches seems to have tried most cases of perjury, but following the abolition of the Council in the mid-seventeenth century a scattering of indictments at the Great Sessions relate to false oaths in a variety of contexts.

Perjury was a criminal offence and the indictment had to specify the words which had been spoken falsely on oath. Occasionally indictments preserve snatches of dialogue with an examining magistrate. In 1683 Peter Hughes of Ruthin, labourer, complained that he had been assaulted. The magistrate asked him, 'Pwy ach trawodd chwy?' (Who has struck you?) Peter Hughes answered, pointing to one Robert Jones, 'Dymma yr gwr am trawd i a charregg ag a dorodd fyngnoll i' ('This is the man [that] strooke me with a stone & broake my pate'). In another case involving an oath administered by a magistrate, Katherine John Lewis of Cathedin (Brecs.) perjured herself by accusing her neighbours of perjury: 'Constance gydda dy dad ay dwy whare tungeste nidon yn erbin a mam yee' ('Constance together with her father & two sisters did forsweare herselfe againste my mother'). More usually perjury involved false oaths at various courts of record, including the Great Sessions. In an action for trespass at the Radnorshire Great Sessions, Katherine Parry of Llanbedr Painscastle was accused of swearing falsely in court that 'Rees Morgan a spoilodd tree grown o wair wrth croppo onnen . . .' ('Rees Morgan hath spoiled three ridges of hay by cropping an ash [tree] . . .'); Thomas Humphreys of Llanfair was accused of perjury after he had sworn falsely at the Montgomeryshire Great Sessions about an arbitration: 'Ir oedd reference o flaen Mr Hall rhwng William Owens a Shone Meredith' (There was a reference before Mr Hall [for arbitration] between William Owens and Siôn Meredith).[63] Presumably these were particularly blatant cases of suspected perjury; they are also useful reminders that evidence was given orally in Welsh in open court before the justices of the Great Sessions.

[61] Atkynson v. Salysbury, NLW, Great Sessions 21/16, unnumbered membranes (Denbs., 1555); Mydelton v. Fulc ap Rees ap Kynnrick, NLW, Great Sessions 21/20, m. 7 (Denbs., 1557); Suggett, 'Slander in Early-Modern Wales', 128, 130–1.
[62] Suggett, 'Slander in Early-Modern Wales', 127.
[63] NLW, Great Sessions 4/32/1/50 (Denbs., 1683), 4/351/2/45 (Brecs., 1654), 4/505/3/22 (Rad., 1688), 4/165/3/65 (Mont., 1694).

Language, Culture and Social Control

This section examines some of the reforming activities of the Great Sessions itself in relation to Welsh language and culture. The state was concerned with order, civility and uniformity. Accordingly the Council in the Marches, through the Great Sessions, conducted campaigns against thieves, recusants, unlicensed alehouses, local weights and measures, and rogues and vagabonds.

Rogues and vagabonds were a diverse group who comprised pedlars, tinkers, and masterless men of various types, but they also included wandering bards and musicians. Bards and musicians were increasingly defined as vagabonds as a result of a successful petition to the Council in the Marches for the holding of an eisteddfod at Caerwys in 1567. The commission for the eisteddfod recited that it had come to the knowledge of the Lord President and others of the Council, that 'vagraunt and idle persons, naming theim selfes mynstrelles, rithmers and barthes, are lately growen into such an intollerable multitude . . . that . . . gentlemen and other[s] . . . are oftentymes disquieted in theire habitacions'. It added that the expert minstrels had become discouraged by this and not a little hindered in their living and preferment. As is well known, the commission for the eisteddfod provided that the expert bards and minstrels should be separated from the bad by a process of certification. Those not considered worthy and without certificates were liable to be taken up as rogues and vagabonds and treated according to the statute – that is branded or whipped unless someone could be found who would take them into service.[64] It is known that the eisteddfod was held and that certificates were awarded; is there any evidence that the bards and minstrels without certificates were taken up and prosecuted as rogues and vagabonds at the Court of Great Sessions?

The evidence suggests in fact that a campaign against the *clerwyr* had begun some years before. Eleven bards, musicians, and dancers were prosecuted in Flintshire in 1547. They included Richard and Hugh Downsior, Robert, John and Foulk Fiddler, Thomas Grythor, Richard y Prydydd Brith and Robin Clidro, poets. Several *cywyddau* are attributed to Robin Clidro and Richard y Prydydd Brith. Richard y Prydydd Brith was also presented at the Denbighshire Great Sessions in 1553, along with fifteen other 'vakabonds cawllyng them selyffs mynstrells'. This group included three fiddlers, two crowders, one Ieuan Brydydd who was

---

[64] J. Gwenogvryn Evans, *Report on Manuscripts in the Welsh Language* (2 vols., London, 1898–1902), I, pp. 291–2; Gwyn Thomas, *Eisteddfodau Caerwys: The Caerwys Eisteddfodau* (Caerdydd, 1968); D. J. Bowen, 'Y Cywyddwyr a'r Dirywiad', *BBCS*, XXIX, part 3 (1981), 465–7.

presented for going about with a harp, and Thomas Tyvie alias Brythyll Brych ('trout'), who was probably a dancer.[65] There were also other prosecutions. In 1578 Owen ap Thomas of Denbigh was taken up at Ysbyty Ifan on suspicion of leading an idle life. Asked what he was doing at Ysbyty Ifan Church, he explained that he was there 'because he can make songs or rymes, and for that is a rymer and wandreth abroad'.[66] Prosecutions were not confined to north-west Wales. There is evidence of a campaign against minstrels in Pembrokeshire. In the early seventeenth century, several minstrels were apprehended for wandering the country at 'shearing and seed time', and they included a piper, fiddler and crowder. In 1615 Rowland David was accused by the grand jury of wandering up and down the country with a fiddle and crowd and keeping two youths and training them as apprentices.[67]

These wandering minstrels may in fact have been victims of the state's concern about rumour, talebearing and sedition. Increasingly, the state was interested in words as well as deeds. This is clear from one of the recurring articles in the instructions issued to the Council in the Marches:

> ... divers Lewd and maliciouse persons have heretofore and of Late dayes more and more devised spread abroad reported or published many false and seditious tales newes sayeings ... which amongst the people have wrought and may worke greate mischieffe and inconveniences ...[68]

It is probable that prosecutions for contemptuous, scandalous, and seditious words were generally increasing in the late sixteenth and early seventeenth centuries. Certainly numerous actions for slander were prosecuted at the Court of Great Sessions and the book of fines of the Council in the Marches records cases of abusive words, slanderous rhymes and libels of various kinds in the first half of the seventeenth century.[69] The state was concerned with the written as well as the spoken word, particularly after about 1570. A mid-Elizabethan brief for the reform of the instructions given to the Council in the Marches recommended that the article giving the Council power to punish reporters of seditious tales

---

[65] NLW, Great Sessions 4/966/6/174 and 175 (Flints., 1547), 4/1/2/36 (Denbs., 1553).
[66] NLW, Great Sessions 4/4/5/247 (Denbs., 1576).
[67] NLW, Great Sessions 4/780/3/63, 4/781/4/28 (Pembs., 1615 and 1620).
[68] C. A. J. Skeel, 'The St. Asaph Cathedral Library MS. of the Instructions to the Earl of Bridgewater, 1633', AC, XVII (1917), 202.
[69] Eadem, 'Social and Economic Conditions in Wales and the Marches in the early Seventeenth Century', THSC (1916–17), 132; A. Fox, 'Ballads, Libels and Popular Ridicule in Jacobean England', PP, 145 (1994), 47–83; Pauline Croft, 'Libels, Popular Literacy and Public Opinion in Early Modern England', BIHR, 68, no. 167 (1995), 266–85.

should be extended to cover the publishers of seditious books, letters and libels.[70]

Growing literacy in late Tudor and early Stuart Wales was expressed by some illuminating incidents. In 1576 Rinald ap Gruffith refused to answer various interrogatories put to him and instead presented the justices with a 'scrowe of paper and said that all his knowledge and saings . . . was conteyned in the same'.[71] Scandalous rhymes were increasingly circulated in written form. A Star Chamber case concerned Richard Edwards of Soughton, a common libeller and maker of songs and rhymes in Welsh and English, whose slanderous libels were written in a 'table-book' which he carried in his pocket. These libels concerned Elizabeth I, James I, and various great men, including Scottish lords.[72] Suspects accused of sedition might be asked if their words had a written source. After Ieuan ap David ap Owen Goch had unwisely speculated about the death of the queen, his interrogators asked if he could read 'prynt or wryting hand' and if he had 'bookes of prophecyeng', either in English or Welsh.[73]

Searches for seditious books were sometimes ordered by the Court of Great Sessions.[74] The state was particularly concerned about Catholic books and papers. Those who owned suspect Welsh books might be closely investigated. A Welsh manuscript found in London in the possession of Henry Jones, formerly of Flintshire, was discovered to contain 'certain papisticall and erroneous thinges' and the owner was examined by the Archbishop of Canterbury. The Archbishop recorded that Jones maintained that 'he wrote out the same to the ende that [he] thereby might learne to reade Welshe' but claimed that 'hee neither understood it nor readd anything of it after hee had copied it out'. Jones conceded that he had not been 'forward in religion', but was now confident that he had 'attayned better knowledge in true Christian religion' after a sojourn in St Thomas's Hospital, Southwark, where he had been instructed by Mr Harrison, a preacher. The investigation of the origin of the Welsh book was referred to the chief justice of Chester, but subsequent enquiry in north-east Wales proved inconclusive.[75] Catholic books and opinions were not easily discovered in north Wales after the executions of Richard Gwyn and William Davies, but in south Wales

---

[70] PRO SP/12/75/176.
[71] NLW, Great Sessions 4/969/3/20 (Flints., 1576).
[72] PRO STAC 18/205/21/17, 27–8; J. Alan B. Somerset (ed.), *Records of Early English Drama: Shropshire* (Toronto, 1994), pp. 66–70.
[73] NLW, Great Sessions 4/136/4/9–11 (Mont., 1594).
[74] Order for a warrant to search the house of Hugh ap Edward of Picton, Flints., for seditious books: NLW, Great Sessions 14/79, March 1594.
[75] NLW, Great Sessions 4/972/4/30–31 (Flints., 1591).

there were occasional prosecutions for heretical and seditious words about religion.[76]

The state's interest in words which touched on religion had several further aspects. Under the Penal Act of 1623 profane swearing and cursing became punishable at the Sessions with a fine of a shilling for each curse. Accordingly there were prosecutions for swearing profane oaths which could result in expensive fines when the oaths were counted. John Howell of Crunwear was presented by the Pembrokeshire grand jury for swearing 'x or xii oathes within an hower and a halfe'. These were oaths 'not fit to be heard among Christians', let alone repeated, but occasionally they were set down in the legal record, as for example, 'Myn gwaed Christ' and 'Myn kig Dyw' (by Christ's blood; by God's body).[77]

Blasphemy and unbelief could also be prosecuted. Indeed, during the Commonwealth period, denials of scriptural authority, the Resurrection and the Trinity were made capital offences by the Blasphemy Ordinance (1648). Although there were prosecutions at the Great Sessions for blasphemy, it does not appear that anyone was actually executed for the offence. The blasphemies included statements that 'Jesus Christ is but a bastard', denials that there was a God and a Trinity, and claims that 'this world was not made by God'. John Stonne of Montgomery said he would prove 'theire is neyther heaven nor hell', and regularly used oaths 'ye like hath not bin heard amongst Christians', commonly saying, 'God damme him & teare him to peeces'.[78] The subversive view, uttered by John Meredith Walter of Llansbyddyd in 1606, that 'p[er]jurie is no sin before God', struck at the heart of legal procedure and anticipated Quaker opposition to oath-taking.[79] It would be very interesting to know more about the context of statements like these, and whether there was a tradition of unbelief. But all we have are sporadic prosecutions, which continued into

---

[76] Indictments from Breconshire: 'The pope is hedd of the univ[er]sall churche and I will stand thereunto', spoken at Brecon by John Jones of Llandeilo Bertholau, clerk, in 1569; heretical opinions about purgatory and transubstantiation maintained by Brian Brittane, clerk, at Brecon in 1590, as well as the view that Martin Luther had invented the religion now established within the realm; 'The pope is the head of the Church of England and of all Christendom and I will maintayne it', spoken by William Beavan of Alexanderston, gent, in 1625: NLW, Great Sessions 4/325/5/38; 4/329/5/20; 4/342/1/15. These opinions all seem to have been expressed in English.

[77] NLW, Great Sessions 4/786/3/43 (Pembs., 1636); NLW, MS Chirk B15(b)/29 (Denbs., 1659); cf. also 'Baw diawl i chwi' ('the devil's turde to you'): NLW, Great Sessions 4/20/2/34 (Denbs., 1632).

[78] NLW, Great Sessions 4/718/3/29 (Carms., 1655), 4/161/3/60 (Mont., 1680), 4/601/7 (Glam., 1700), 4/153/2/7 (Mont., 1648).

[79] NLW, Great Sessions 4/335/1/32 (Brecs., 1606). He continued: '. . . a p[er]juror is in as great favo[u]r w[i]th God as him that tell the truthe. And the first institution of an othe was in respect of some poynts in law and for shortninge of suits.' The speaker may have been an Anabaptist.

the eighteenth century. One of the last prosecutions was brought against an Anglesey farmer in 1732. He had apparently been reproved for uttering several profane oaths and responded: 'Duw! Pa beth ydiw Duw i mi? Nid ydiw fi yn cowntio yn Nhuw ddim mwy na blewyn o wellt!' ('God! What is God to me? I do not value [my] God more than a straw!')[80]

Seditious and treasonable words took many forms. One of the most interesting was the felony (1581) of prophesying or reporting falsely the queen's death. A case occurred in 1594: Ieuan ap David ap Owen Goch of Llanfair, in Montgomeryshire, announced in Welsh (though his words are given only in translation): 'The Queene will deye within these sixt yeares and then we shall have a newe world.' The prediction erred by three years, but this was a classic millenarian statement with its stress on a new world. There were other cases. In 1603 William Dolben was indicted for predicting that the newly crowned King James would live but six years and six months and that after his death there would be war for three years.[81] Again, in 1590, Elizabeth Bedowe of Crugion, a widow, repeated in Welsh a rumour that 'a certein nobleman of the realme, whom shee did name, shalbe kinge of this realme of England after the decease of the Quenes Ma[jes]tie'. Believing that the offence might be capital, the examining magistrate committed the woman to prison for uttering seditious words, noting that it was a dangerous time with the beacons being watched, and adding that it was 'intollerable in a com[m]on wealth that base people of her sorte shuld babble of such highe stakes'.[82]

The babble of the base sort, when it involved speculation about the death of the king or queen, was treated with great seriousness by the authorities. This was partly because, as we have already mentioned, justice was royal justice. The processes of the court were issued in the name of the Crown and when there was no monarch it was popularly believed that the law might not apply. The death of a monarch might initiate a peculiar period when it was thought that the law had been suspended. Although Wales did not experience an event like the so-called 'busy week' of the northern borderland after the death of Elizabeth I and before James I was crowned, when many took the opportunity to settle old scores and indulge in cross-border raiding, it was still a dangerous time, however, and the Brecon man who announced in 1603, following the death of the queen, that the 'lawe was not in force' was promptly gaoled.[83]

---

[80] Indictment of Henry Williams of Llanfwrog: NLW, Great Sessions 4/250/4/ [unnumbered] (Angl., 1732).

[81] NLW, Great Sessions 4/136/4/9–11 (Mont., 1594); NLW, Great Sessions 4/13/2/15 (Denbs., 1603). Cf. Powell, 'Crime and the Community in Denbighshire', pp. 273–4.

[82] A marginal note identifies the nobleman as William Strange; Elizabeth was whipped: NLW, Great Sessions 4/134/2/89, 207 (Mont., 1590).

[83] NLW, Great Sessions 4/334/1/99 (Brecs., 1603). On the 'busy week', see Penry

Most prosecutions for seditious words were concentrated in certain critical periods when the state was vulnerable. There were three periods of crisis: the end of the reign of Elizabeth, the civil wars and Restoration, and the death of James II. The end of the reign of Elizabeth was one of those periods when, apart from seditious statements, there were prophecies and visions. The civil wars, too, produced wild rumours, visions and radical political and religious statements. These were very frightening times, not least because the authority of the law became uncertain and the legitimacy of officials was challenged. According to a speaker in 1654: 'Hee and noe other had power to execute anie office since the kinge died.' With the Restoration a Breconshire labourer alarmingly announced that he 'had power from the . . . King's Majestie to kill, burne and quarter men'.[84]

It would be a mistake to suppose that seditious words were uttered only by radicals. The political divisions of the civil wars touched most people and anyone might be forced to declare an allegiance. A particularly interesting example of the way in which people were forced to declare where they stood was through the drinking of healths. In alehouses people raised their glasses to the king or to parliament to declare their allegiance and to test others. When the health of the king was drunk at Llanbedr Felffre after the Restoration Thomas Lewis tersely responded 'Crogy' (Hanging) and of course was later charged with sedition![85]

Explicitly hostile statements about the Crown can be found in the legal record before the civil wars, but they are very rare. There was, however, a sense in which the well-being of the country was thought to depend on the person of the monarch. The difficulties of the late sixteenth and early seventeenth centuries were sometimes blamed obscurely on the Crown. A Radnorshire cutler observed in conversation with a cleric: 'Wo to that Com[m]onwealth where children and women do beare rule, and who doth reigne now over us but a woman.' The news of the death of James I's eldest son, Henry, Prince of Wales, prompted Thomas David Moris of St Edrens to remark: 'Ny cheyson ni ddim byd da gwedy y ddowad ef yn frenin, a melltith ddyw yr awr y dayth ef yn frenin' ('Wee have had no

---

Williams, 'The Northern Borderland under the Early Stuarts' in H. E. Bell and R. L. Ollard (eds.), *Historical Essays 1600–1750 Presented to David Ogg* (London, 1963), pp. 6–7.

[84] NLW, Great Sessions 4/789/1/20 (Pembs., 1654); NLW, Great Sessions 4/353/5A/36 (Brecs., 1663).

[85] NLW, Great Sessions 4/787/3/51 (Pembs., 1666). On drinking healths to the Pretender ('Yechid y Prince o Wales'), cf. J. H. Matthews (ed.), *Cardiff Records* (6 vols., Cardiff, 1898–1911), II, p. 187.

good world since he came to be kinge, and God's curse be upon the houre that he came to be king').[86]

The king might also be blamed for the misbehaviour of officials appointed in his name. This seems to be the sense of some rather puzzling outbursts preserved in indictments which are otherwise without an adequate context. In 1614 Evan David ap Thomas of Saint Harmon, Radnorshire, was arrested at Llanidloes on suspicion of treason after he was heard to say: 'Dyma dre a ddyle fod yn boeth ac fe a loskyd yr brenyn pette fo yma' ('This town ought to be burned, and yf our Kinge weare heere he shoold be burnt'). Elsewhere the words are reported as: 'This is a towne of badd gov[er]nment.' In a somewhat similar incident in 1615, Humfrey ap Thomas of Machynlleth, weaver, was accused of uttering words against the sacred person of the king. An altercation with the mayor's serjeant-at-mace had ended with the words: 'Turde to thee, t[urde] to thy master, and t[urde] to the kinge for appoynting such officers as you to p[atr]owle the towne.' The serjeant and aghast bystanders immediately cried, 'God save the king', the officer adding, 'I will cutt of thy head for usinge suche words.'[87]

Protestations of confidence in the Crown and the law accompanied the determination to resolve a dispute through litigation. 'D[u]w a savo gida grase y vrenhynes ai kyfraydd' (God save with grace the queen and her law), exclaimed a Montgomeryshire man during a grazing dispute. Indeed, at the very mention of the king's name and laws, it was customary for loyal subjects to remove their hats out of deference. In 1606, when John ap Cadwalladr announced his intention to go to law in a land dispute, he removed his hat and said, 'God save the kinge', adding 'that he wold come there in his ma[jes]t[y']s name and by vertue of his lawes'. His adversary 'w[i]thout any dutyfull reverence to his ma[jes]ty by puting of or removinge his hatte', responded that no one would come onto his land unless it was on the point of his sword: 'Ney ddoy dy neb arall yma, ony ddowch y ar flaen arfe.'[88]

Litigation inevitably prompted disparaging words, but the Commonwealth was a watershed in people's perception of the law. Notions about the sacred person of the king and the idea of the just king were taken less seriously. After the Restoration there was less confidence in the Crown standing above faction and of royal justice protecting the weak

---

[86] NLW, Great Sessions 4/477/1/52 (Rad., 1601); NLW, Great Sessions 4/779/6/1 (Pembs., 1613).

[87] NLW, Great Sessions 4/143/li/68 (Mont., 1614); NLW, Great Sessions 4/143/3/37 (Mont., 1616).

[88] NLW, Great Sessions 4/139/1D/[unnumbered] (Mont., 1601); NLW, Great Sessions 4/141/2/110–12 (Mont., 1606).

from the strong. 'The king is a man like any other men' was a not infrequently expressed opinion. As Valentine Lewis of Gwersyllt exclaimed in 1678: 'Rwi yn gystall gwr ar Brenin', adding, 'a beth a wn i ond eiff i enaid ef i yffern' ('I am as good a man as the king and what doe I knowe but his soule may go to hell'). The king had a soul to save like other men and his actions might lack God's favour. Meredith Evans of Nantmel, Radnorshire, expressed this clearly: 'Y mae gras yth frenin wedy troy yn anrhas y wneythir kam y ddynyon sydd honestach yn y ddealinge nag ef' ('The kings grace is tournd withoutt grace to doe wronge to men more honeste in their dealings than hee').[89]

The speakers of these and similar words almost certainly were not religious or political radicals, although one claimed vividly to have been a Cromwellian soldier.[90] Nevertheless, despite their small numbers, the radical opinions of Puritans and Quakers and their less than deferential actions were probably influential, and there was some sympathy for the plight of Dissenters after the Restoration. 'They that killed the old king did the people of that fayth good service', declared Howell Phillipp of Brawdy after the prosecution of Presbyterians in Pembrokeshire. If actions speak louder than words, the refusal of Quakers to appear bareheaded in court must have left an indelible impression. Thirteen Quakers refused to remove their hats at one Pembrokeshire Sessions after the Restoration in what must have been a memorable display of lack of deference.[91]

Increasingly after the civil wars people distanced themselves from the Great Sessions and this can be seen in the decline in the number of cases – both civil and criminal – brought before the Sessions. This sense of dissociation and opposition to the court and its processes was expressed verbally by the phrase 'baw i'r brenin' (a turd for the king). In the sixteenth century this expression was almost unknown. Cases of contemptuous and reproachful words against the processes of the court became more common in the first half of the seventeenth century, especially on the eve of the civil wars. But the outburst 'baw i'r brenin' was likely to provoke a loyal 'God save the king' from bystanders. By the second half of the seventeenth century the phrase is ubiquitous. When David William of Bodran, Montgomeryshire, was presented with a

---

[89] NLW, Great Sessions 4/30/5/80v, 87 (Denbs., 1678); NLW, Great Sessions 4/496/2/8 (Rad., 1661). Cf. *Cardiff Records*, II, pp. 178–9, 250, for words against William III ('ffol o frenin') and George III ('Damno'r Brenhin George y trydidd . . .').

[90] Cf. 'My fym yn soldyer dan Oliver Cromwell ag mi olchais ym dwylo yng wad Charles y kynta . . .' ('I was a souldier under Oliver Cromwell and I washed my hands in the blood of Charles the firste'), spoken by Rees ap Evan of Llangynidr, labourer: NLW, Great Sessions 4/353/5A/27 (Brecs., 1663).

[91] NLW, Great Sessions 4/798/1/50 (Pembs., 1685); NLW, Great Sessions 4/791/5/55 (Pembs., 1662).

warrant in 1695, he exclaimed: 'Baw iti ag ith warrant ag ir brenin ag ir Parliament' (he paused, then continued) 'Baw iti ag ith frenin ag iw Gyfreth' (A turd to you and to your warrant and to the king and to the Parliament. A turd to you and to your king and to their law).[92]

It might have been expected that there would have been widespread alienation in Wales from the Court of Great Sessions: the Sessions were conducted in a foreign language, they were disruptive, and they were punitive. However, paradoxically, the reverse was true: the civil and criminal business of the court boomed throughout the second half of the sixteenth century and well into the seventeenth century. Despite the apparent difficulties created by the 'language clause' of the Act of Union of 1536, there was in fact widespread understanding and manipulation of the processes and procedures of the court. Behind the English and Latin legal record there was a concealed world of arbitration, settlement and compromise in the Welsh language. After the Restoration there is evidence of widespread disenchantment with, and rejection of, the courts and a long decline in the business of the Great Sessions. The courts were increasingly controlled by a non-Welsh-speaking magistracy; the appearance of paid interpreters in the eighteenth century marks the change. For monoglot Welsh speakers, appearance at the courts may have been an increasingly demeaning experience. Contempt for attorneys, bailiffs and other minor officials was often expressed, and the absurdities of arcane English-language procedural terms were satirized in popular literature.[93] Nevertheless, unlike religion, there does not seem to have been a sense in which the law was a contested domain of language use. In the earlier period, in fact, there had been widespread manipulation of the court; in the later period the Great Sessions simply became marginal to the lives of most Welsh men and women.

---

[92] NLW, Great Sessions 4/167/2/98 (Mont., 1699).
[93] Thomas Roberts, *Cwyn yn erbyn Gorthrymder* (Llundain, 1798); O. M. Edwards (ed.), *Gwaith Glan y Gors* (Llanuwchllyn, 1905), pp. 79–81; John Fisher (ed.), *The Cefn Coch MSS.* (Liverpool, 1899), pp. 232–6. (I owe this last reference to Daniel Huws.) Cf. Parry, *Guide to the Records of Great Sessions*, p. xxxi, n. 14.

5

The Welsh Language in Local Government: Justices of the Peace and the Courts of Quarter Sessions c. 1536–1800

J. GWYNFOR JONES

ON 12 MARCH 1536 Bishop Rowland Lee, President of the Council in the Marches of Wales, wrote to Thomas Cromwell expressing his disapproval of the government's intention to appoint justices of the peace in Crown lands in Wales. 'And allso for justices of the peace and off Gaole Delivery to be in Wales', he maintained, 'I think hit not moche expedient . . . For there be very fewe Welshmen in Wales above Brecknock that maye dispende ten pounde lande and, to say truthe, their discretion lesse then their landes.'[1] His view reflected two aspects of fundamental importance, namely his own personal aversion to the Welsh people and his poor view of the status of Welsh gentry. In fact, there was much truth in his words for, despite their pretensions, the Welsh gentry were not as wealthy as their counterparts in England, and two years' experience of governing Wales and the Marches had revealed to Lee some of their less commendable features.[2] His crude coercive policy seemed to be achieving positive results, but his jaundiced view of the government's decision to appoint magistrates did not impress his master, who was determined to unite Wales and England. An essential part of that policy was to introduce an official who was to assume a leading role in local administration. Lee was not the only administrator to protest at the appointment of magistrates because, in Gwynedd for example, Sir Richard Bulkeley of Beaumaris feared that the office might be used by his enemies as a convenient

---

[1] *Calendar of State Papers, Foreign and Domestic* (London, 1862–), X, 1536, no. 453, p. 182. For more general information on the magistracy, see W. Ogwen Williams (ed.), *Calendar of the Caernarvonshire Quarter Sessions Records: Vol. I, 1541–1558* (Caernarvon, 1956); Keith Williams-Jones (ed.), *A Calendar of the Merioneth Quarter Sessions Rolls. Vol. I: 1733–65* (Dolgellau, 1965); J. R. S. Phillips (ed.), *The Justices of the Peace in Wales and Monmouthshire 1541 to 1689* (Cardiff, 1975); J. Gwynfor Jones, *Law, Order and Government in Caernarfonshire, 1558–1640: Justices of the Peace and the Gentry* (Cardiff, 1996).

[2] *Calendar of State Papers*, XII (ii), 1537, no. 1237, p. 434.

weapon against him.[3] In his view, the introduction of a new and powerful official was considered an unnecessary intrusion. Other formal objections to the office in north Wales emphasized the inferiority of the Welsh gentry and described them as 'bearers of thieves', ignorant of English law, corrupt in legal affairs, and materially inadequate.[4]

The office of justice of the peace was introduced into Wales and Cheshire by legislation in February 1536 (27 Henry VIII, c.5), shortly before the first Act of Union (27 Henry VIII, c.26).[5] It was the first measure to create uniformity in the Crown lands in Wales, and it stipulated that these new officials were to exercise their duties in the same manner as magistrates in the English counties. The office, mainly entrusted to the landed gentry, was a central cog in local government and essential in maintaining law and order in the localities.[6] Its introduction into the principality, Flintshire and the lordships of Pembroke and Glamorgan added a new dimension to the establishment of royal control in its territories. The act did not set out details and duties of the office, nor did it stipulate in what language business was to be conducted in court. In view of government policy, however, it was to be expected that the emphasis in the preamble would be on the need to establish uniformity.[7]

This act was the first indication of the government's new policy. What followed would be in accordance with the aim to establish uniformity. The Act of Union of 1536 legislated that officers were required to 'proclaim and keep' sessions in English, implying that certain procedures were to be formally recorded.[8] Latin was still used for indictments, recognizances and recognizance rolls, writs, *nomina ministrorum*, present-ments, warrants and jury panels; and English for the oaths of officers and juries, inquests and affidavits, verdicts and wagers of law as well as informations, petitions, correspondence and other miscellanea. The Welsh language seems not to have been barred from the courts so long as it was not used to record any legal and administrative business. Indeed, since a large proportion of those who attended court were monoglot Welsh speakers there was no alternative but to use the vernacular. Most officers, including magistrates, were doubtless fluent in Welsh and able to use legal terms in that language where necessary. To what extent they were familiar with English is difficult to tell. When Sir Roger Mostyn

---

[3] Ibid., XI, 1536, no. 525, p. 213.
[4] Ibid., X, 1536, no. 245, pp. 88–9.
[5] Ivor Bowen (ed.), *The Statutes of Wales* (London, 1908), pp. 67–9, 75–93.
[6] See J. R. Lander, *English Justices of the Peace 1461–1509* (Gloucester, 1989); Bertram Osborne, *Justices of the Peace, 1381–1848* (Sedgehill, 1960).
[7] Bowen, *Statutes*, p. 67.
[8] Ibid., p. 87.

expressed, in a letter to his father-in-law, Sir John Wynn, his opinion that his heir should return home from the Continent to deal with estate affairs, he added: 'he hath seene ynough and more than ever any of his ancestors in the later ages hath, yet they lived in some esteeme in their countrey without any other language than their owne'.[9] While some *uchelwyr* spoke only Welsh, most heads of families who rose to power in the 1530s were familiar with Latin and English, and the surviving Caernarfonshire Quarter Sessions records between 1541 and 1558 imply that most of those involved in the court's business were Welsh-speaking, and doubtless many of those people brought before it were monoglot.[10] The absence of written Welsh in the records is hardly surprising since a burdened clerk of the peace would automatically record proceedings in Latin or English. Besides, he had to familiarize himself with legal formulae and procedural matters in English. A survey of the sources shows that legal and administrative business was conducted in English, for there is no mention of interpreters, although Welsh was used orally in the courts.[11]

It appears that some officials had difficulty in using the English language. In Radnorshire in 1594, for example, Thomas Vaughan, magistrate and coroner, was accused in Star Chamber of holding office although he was unable to speak, read or write English, and of using his position to advance his own interests.[12] There were, of course, English-speaking areas, especially the towns, the Anglicized parts of Pembrokeshire and the border lowlands in the Marches. Elsewhere, including the Vale of Glamorgan and large areas of Monmouthshire, Welsh was frequently the language of daily conversation. But even in the most conservative northern and western areas there had gradually been an inflow of English settlers, chiefly into the boroughs after the Edwardian Conquest and settlement of the principality. Members of some of these families had intermarried into Welsh stock and had acquired a knowledge of the native language, but the degree to which they had mastered Welsh sufficiently to use it in court is hard to judge.

The offices of magistrate and *custos rotulorum* were extended to include the twelve shires of Wales (excluding Monmouthshire) in the second Act

---

[9] Lord Mostyn and T. A. Glenn, *History of the Family of Mostyn of Mostyn* (London, 1925), p. 126.
[10] W. Ogwen Williams, 'The Survival of the Welsh Language after the Union of England and Wales: the First Phase, 1536–1642', *WHR,* 2, no. 1 (1964), 71–3. See John Wynn, *The History of the Gwydir Family and Memoirs,* ed. J. Gwynfor Jones (Llandysul, 1990), p. 26; NLW Cwrtmawr MS 21, f. 174; UWBL, Mostyn MS 4, f. 117r.
[11] Williams, *Calendar of the Caernarvonshire Quarter Sessions Records,* pp. xxiii–xxv.
[12] Ifan ab Owen Edwards, *A Catalogue of Star Chamber Proceedings Relating to Wales* (Cardiff, 1929), p. 136 (B 60/6 (36)).

of Union in 1543 (34–35 Henry VIII, c.26).[13] The poet Siôn Mawddwy, satirizing the town of Newtown and its fair at a time when the Great Sessions were being held, drew attention to changes in attitudes towards the Welsh language. There, he remarked, he saw Welshmen who had neglected their language and wished to emulate the English.[14] Problems doubtless arose in the Englishries of the old lordships where there had been a predominantly English-speaking population and a mixture of Welsh law and marcher custom. In the Welshries and in parts of the adjoining English counties, however, the native language was still widely spoken. In January 1537 Rowland Lee testified that Wales and the Marches were 'in as good towardness to do the King's service as any subjects living' and that most of their inhabitants were not aware of governmental changes in England 'for their language does not agree to the advancement thereof'.[15] In the 1570s Christopher Saxton, the famous map-maker, employed Welsh-speaking as well as English horsemen to conduct him through the Welsh counties so that he might survey the countryside.[16] The Welsh Bible was used in the western parts of the diocese of Hereford[17] and, in 1606, it was stated that 'in many of them [the Welsh Marches] the Welsh tongue, even to this day, is as frequent and usuall as in other shires in Wales'.[18] On the other hand, John Penry stated in the 1580s that there were regions where the English language was often spoken.[19] In 1598 Captain Richard Gwynn of Caernarfon wrote to Robert Devereux, second Earl of Essex, offering his service in Ireland and presumed that the earl would appoint those familiar with the native language to lead the Welsh contingents.[20] According to George Owen of Henllys, when Barthol visited Pembrokeshire in the 1590s after spending three weeks travelling through Wales where, excepting in 'good Townes, or of some gent'men in the Countrey', he had heard nothing but Welsh, he was glad to hear English spoken.[21] In view of Owen's interest in judicial procedures it is surprising that he did not mention in the 'Dialogue of the Government of Wales' (1594) that linguistic uniformity had been imposed in the courts.

---

[13] Bowen, *Statutes*, pp. 113–14.
[14] NLW Llanstephan MS 35, f. 251.
[15] *Calendar of State Papers*, XII (I), 1537, no. 93, p. 49.
[16] J. R. Dasent (ed.), *Acts of the Privy Council* (London, 1890–), 1575–7, p. 259.
[17] Bowen, *Statutes*, p. 150.
[18] G. Dyfnallt Owen, *Wales in the Reign of James I* (London, 1988), p. 49.
[19] John Penry, *Three Treatises Concerning Wales*, ed. David Williams (Cardiff, 1960), p. 37.
[20] HMC, *Calendar of the Manuscripts of the Marquis of Salisbury (Hatfield House)*, VIII (London, 1899), p. 525.
[21] Owen, *Description*, III, pp. 16, 18.

Any examination of language and the administration of law at local levels in Wales raises the question of literacy in English and Welsh. What proportion of the Welsh people could read and in what language? Broad estimates have suggested that between ten and fifteen per cent of the population of Wales had some grasp of letters by the mid-seventeenth century in English or Welsh or both,[22] but the situation is not at all clear. In his preface to his translation of *Basilikon Doron* (1604) by James I, Robert Holland suggested that there was a language difference between governors and governed so that 'the chiefest Gouernors know not their complaints'.[23] Davis ap Hugh ap Thomas of Llanenddwyn, Merioneth, complained in Star Chamber that he was almost hoodwinked into sealing a bond which would have deprived him of some of his property because he was 'a simple and illiterate man that can neither write nor read nor speak nor understand any language but only his natural tongue being Welsh'.[24] On the other hand, the Puritan writer, Evan Roberts, stated in 1649 that many people in Wales had a grasp of English but added that those who could read and were heads of families should instruct 'their Houshold, Friends, and Neighbours, who can reade neither English nor Welsh'.[25] One fact is clear: demography, topography, literacy and the social structure are significant aspects of any study designed to assess the degree to which government was justly conducted. Efficient government depended largely on the skills and cooperation of a variety of officials involved in managing routine matters and not exclusively on the landed gentry. Correspondence between members of the gentry was invariably conducted in English because their educational training had been exclusively in that language and in the classics. Although many gentlemen spoke Welsh, probably as a first language, in the sixteenth and early seventeenth centuries, they chose to write in English.[26] In Glamorgan in the 1630s William Gamage sent William Herbert of Cogan Pill a book described as 'the A.B.C. of our ancient copious learned Brittishe tongue' and urged him to learn the language so that he might administer his landed affairs more easily.[27] He

---

[22] Glanmor Williams, 'Dadeni, Diwygiad, a Diwylliant Cymru' in *Grym Tafodau Tân: Ysgrifau Hanesyddol ar Grefydd a Diwylliant* (Llandysul, 1984), pp. 75–6.
[23] James I, *Basilikon Doron*, ed. John Ballinger (Cardiff, 1931), [(a)3].
[24] PRO, Star Chamber 8 286/33. See Ifan ab Owen Edwards, 'A Study of Local Government in the Principality of Wales during the Sixteenth and Seventeenth Centuries' (unpubl. University of Wales MA thesis, 1925), p. 26; Edwards, *Star Chamber Proceedings*, p. 187.
[25] Merfyn Morgan (ed.), *Gweithiau Oliver Thomas ac Evan Roberts: Dau Biwritan Cynnar* (Caerdydd, 1981), pp. [231–2].
[26] Owen, *Description*, III, p. 36. See also Dillwyn Miles (ed.), *Description of Pembrokeshire* (Llandysul, 1994), p. 40.
[27] NLW, Bute Box 132 Parcel C. See also G. T. Clark (ed.), *Cartae et Alia Munimenta quae ad Dominium de Glamorgancia pertinent* (6 vols., Cardiff, 1910), VI, pp. 2220–1.

also referred to the opportunities afforded to the heir of the Fan estate in Caerphilly to learn Welsh, French and Latin.[28] The Cefnmabli heir intended to return to his estate and to learn the language[29] and, in 1660, Colonel John Bodfel of Llŷn decided to care for his grandson's education and to have him bred in Wales so that he might understand that language and be acquainted with the place and people 'where and among whom he must dwell'.[30]

There were trends to the contrary, of course. The privately endowed grammar schools set up in Wales encouraged young gentlemen to broaden their cultural horizons. Sons of gentry became familiar with the new learning[31] and Welsh-speaking gentry became increasingly aware of the benefits of learning English and the adoption of courtly graces. William Glyn of Glyncywarch in Merioneth, for example, urged his son Cadwaladr (c.1637) to take pride in being sent to 'Oxenford, a famous University, the fountayne and wellhead of all learning' and urged him to 'speak noe Welsh to any that can speak English' so that he 'may attaine . . . and freely speake [the] Englishe tongue perfectly'.[32] His instruction points to a change of attitude and a degree of opposition among leading gentry to the survival of the Welsh language, as Robert Gwyn, Morris Kyffin and Dr John Davies of Mallwyd testify in their writings.[33] In the late seventeenth century, Edward Morris of Perthillwydion deplored the increasing estrangement of the gentry from their native traditions ('Seisnigedd yw bonedd byd'), and remarked on the increased use of English and the slow processes of social reorientation.[34] The use of the English language could prove to be a distinct disadvantage, especially when translators failed to interpret correctly exact testimony given in court.[35] In the Exchequer Court in 1583, for example, it was complained that the suit of Hywel ap Gruffudd ab Ieuan, a Nefyn yeoman who was ignorant of English, had been grossly misrepresented by his interpreter.

---

[28] Ibid.
[29] Ibid.; G. T. Clark (ed.), *Limbus Patrum Morganiae et Glamorganiae, being the Genealogies of the Older Families of the Lordships of Morgan and Glamorgan* (London, 1886), pp. 42–53, 286–7, 392–3.
[30] A. H. Dodd, 'The Tragedy of Colonel John Bodvel', *TCHS*, 6 (1945), 16.
[31] H. Barber and H. Lewis, *The History of Friars School, Bangor* (Bangor, 1901), pp. 142–4.
[32] T. Jones Pierce (ed.), *Clenennau Letters and Papers in the Brogyntyn Collection* (Aberystwyth, 1947), pp. 126–7 (no. 444).
[33] Garfield H. Hughes (ed.), *Rhagymadroddion 1547–1659* (Caerdydd, 1951), pp. 53, 94; Ceri Davies (ed.), *Rhagymadroddion a Chyflwyniadau Lladin 1551–1632* (Caerdydd, 1980), p. 116.
[34] Hugh Hughes (ed.), *Barddoniaeth Edward Morris, Perthi Llwydion* (Lerpwl, 1902), p. 39. See also E. D. Jones, 'The Brogyntyn Welsh Manuscripts', *NLWJ*, VI, no. 1 (1949), 29.
[35] PRO C. 24, 562. See Owen, *Wales in the Reign of James I*, p. 149 (n. 108).

This reveals that Welsh, when occasion demanded, was used in the central London courts.[36]

In 1615, when Sir John Wynn of Gwydir was accused in the Council in the Marches of oppressive behaviour,[37] he defended himself by stating that his witnesses 'being illiterat simple people, not havinge the English tounge', were interrogated by the common examiner who, being an Englishman, 'was fayne to use an interpreter, and whether the same did interprett right is to be doubted'.[38] This evidence, which reveals that Welsh was used on occasions in the court at Ludlow, is further borne out in the memoranda drafted in 1641 by Sir Richard Lloyd of Esclusham near Wrexham, King's Attorney in north Wales. One of his proposals to save the Council in the Marches from abolition was that the use of the language within it would ease the plight of monoglot Welsh people who would otherwise have to travel to London to seek justice, and that in English: 'the Common people in Wales', he maintained, '. . . had rather forgoe their right then travell to London, beinge for want of being able to speake English dishartened to travell farr.' Although nothing came of Lloyd's proposals, his argument on this point shows that the Council did allow the use of Welsh by employing interpreters when they were required.[39] Most tenants in the heartland were dependent on the goodwill and advice of their landlord, given mostly in Welsh. On another occasion, Sir John Wynn admitted that he enjoyed direct control over his tenants at Gwydir and that it was their 'humour' to trust him and not accept any lease from him in writing.[40] Although interpreters were not at all times trustworthy in fulfilling their tasks, in a report on the 'imperfections' of the judicial government of Ulster published in 1598, interpreters in Wales were judged more efficient and competent than judges in that province.[41]

Welsh was used on certain occasions to publicize proclamations and other official communications in Welsh-speaking areas. Welsh was also heard in some of the minor courts. In Newport, Pembrokeshire, Welsh was spoken in evidence in the Hundred Court in 1611–12,[42] and in Carmarthenshire in 1611 opposition was voiced in the court leets of Caeo, Maenordeilo,

---

[36] Emyr Gwynne Jones (ed.), *Exchequer Proceedings (Equity) Concerning Wales, Henry VIII–Elizabeth* (Cardiff, 1939), p. 46.

[37] J. Gwynfor Jones, 'Sir John Wynn of Gwydir and his Tenants: the Dolwyddelan and Llysfaen Disputes', *WHR*, 11, no. 1 (1982), 1–30.

[38] Ibid., 25; NLW MS 9055E, f. 725.

[39] Huntington Library, San Marino, California, MS 7466, quoted in A. H. Dodd, *Studies in Stuart Wales* (Cardiff, 1952), pp. 66–7. See also Penry Williams, 'The Attack on the Council in the Marches, 1603–1642', *THSC* (1961), 19.

[40] NLW MS 9059E, f. 1188.

[41] *Calendar of State Papers: Ireland, 1598–9* (London, 1895–), no. CCII (part iv), p. 394.

[42] B. G. Charles, 'The Records of the Borough of Newport in Pembrokeshire', *NLWJ*, VII, no. 1 (1951), 44–5.

Ceithiniog and Malláen to English lessees of the office of Raglorship. It was stated that the aggrieved leaders 'used a Welsh fraze "Trech gwlad nag arglwith" which ys in English, a whole contrye ys to hard for a Lord'.[43] In Star Chamber in 1587 it was declared that the high constable of Llanfarthin, Monmouthshire, had executed a warrant from the sheriff in Latin, English and Welsh.[44] In the 1630s some ship money documents were issued in the Welsh language,[45] and petitions, depositions and similar records doubtless had to be prepared by minor officials in Welsh.[46]

Welsh is not scarce in the Quarter Sessions records. In 1630 information was given to Sir William Thomas of Coedalun and William Gruffudd, two Caernarfonshire justices of the peace, regarding Katherine Jeffrey, who had called Alice Price a 'dihirog bydrog' (slattern, harlot) and 'coegen (hoeden, strumpet, coquette) naughtipake' (a woman of bad character).[47] In the same year Harry ap Jeffrey of Caerhun in Arllechwedd Isaf, the prospective high constable, pleaded that magistrates had been misinformed about his rank and status. He described himself as a poor and illiterate man, who was unable to perform his duties.[48] Several similar petitions have survived, with the petitioners usually pleading poverty or ill health or both. Robert David of Llanfihangel Glyn Myfyr in Denbighshire, for example, was supported by fellow parishioners in his plea to be excused from being appointed high constable of Isaled because, apart from his poverty, he was 'illiterate and not having a word of English'.[49] In 1636 Harry Lloyd, described as 'wandering & going from one country to another' and accused of influencing local people, together with those who accused him, would surely have been disadvantaged in court if expected to defend himself in English.[50] Lucy Stoddart, a Caernarfon spinster, declared in Quarter Sessions in 1650 that since she considered herself to have suffered an injustice she would seek justice herself. Her exact words were: 'If I do not obtain justice I shall demand justice on some of them by my own hand' ('oni chav gyfraith my fynna gyfraith ar rhay ohonnint am llaw fy hyn').[51]

---

[43] PRO, Star Chamber 8 41/13. See Edwards, *Star Chamber Proceedings*, p. 159; Owen, *Wales in the Reign of James I*, p. 131.
[44] Owen, *Wales in the Reign of James I*, p. 108 (P23/31/(29)).
[45] Gerald Morgan, *The Dragon's Tongue* (Narberth, 1966), p. 42; Williams, *Calendar of the Caernarvonshire Quarter Sessions Records*, p. xxxvii.
[46] Benjamin Howell, 'Local Administration and Law Enforcement in Sixteenth-Century Monmouthshire, including a Calendar of the Quarter Sessions and Gaol Deliveries Roll of 18–19 Elizabeth (1576–77)' (unpubl. University of Wales Diploma in Local History Dissertation, Cardiff, 1991), pp. 16, 34, 60, 65.
[47] Gwynedd Archives Service, XQS/1630.
[48] Ibid.
[49] NLW Chirk Castle MS 51 (c) 32, 32/1. See also 14 (a) 35, 14 (c) 21, 15 (a) 19, 16 (b) 9.
[50] Gwynedd Archives Service, XQS/1636.
[51] Ibid., XQS/1650.

In the same year Ellen Jones, of the same town, was called a 'strumpet . . . whore and jade' ('jadan', a reprehensible woman in colloquial Welsh) and 'arant whore or carn bitten' (i.e. 'arrant whore or prostitute').[52] When the bailiffs of Caernarfon were attacked in 1659, the assailants, it was stated, laid 'hands violently upon them and clasped [one of the bailiffs] down to ye ground and upon [his] riseing clept him downe the second tyme . . . uttering these words: "Nid oes dym cyfraith yr rowan iw gael" [There is no justice now to be had].' This was doubtless an adverse verdict on the Puritan government of the day and represented resentful opinions expressed by the lower orders on the unpopular regime.[53] Griffith Jones of Castellmarch in Llŷn, a stern Puritan magistrate, fined William Charles of Llanbeblig 3s.4d. for using the Lord's name in vain by uttering the words 'Gwaed yr Arglwydd' (The Blood of the Lord).[54] Articles were preferred against Edward Williams who, while 'playinge at nine pinns' in Llangollen churchyard, had drawn a knife on one Edward Abraham and sworn 'seu'all oathes in the Welsh language (to witt) Myn gwaud Christ my ath rhwyga dye ar gillell, wch words are thus in Englishe, By the blood of Christ I will ripp thee wth the knife'.[55] In 1660 Ellis Rowlands, the Puritan vicar of Clynnog Fawr and Llanwnda, exhibited articles of misdemeanours against Benjamin Lloyd and David Evans, complaining that they had locked the church door and prevented him from entering because he used the Bible without the Common Prayer:

> That the said Benjamin Lloyd finding the said Ellis Rowlands to repair to the parish Church . . . on the second day of December last [1660] did enter into the Church and shut the doore . . . uttering these or the like words: '*Ni chei di ddyfod i mewn ymma*' [You shall not come in here] . . . That upon the said 30 day of December, the said David Evans tooke away the Bible of Grace vch Ffrancis and would not restore it, but uttered expressions about burning it saying these or the like words. (*Mi a fynnwn weled llosgi y Bibles fydd heb y Common Prayers ynddynt*) [I wish to see the Bibles that do not contain the Common Prayers burnt] or (*ni a gawn weled llosci yr holl fibles sydd heb y Common Prayer ynddynt*) [We shall see Bibles that do not contain the common prayer burnt] and haveing so said he opened and held up the said book, saying *dymma fo* [here it is].[56]

---

[52] Ibid.
[53] Ibid., XQS/1659. For further discussion on these cases, see J. Gwynfor Jones, 'Caernarvonshire Administration: the Activities of the Justices of the Peace, 1603–1660', *WHR*, 5, no. 2 (1970), 153–6.
[54] Gwynedd Archives Service, XQS/1659.
[55] NLW Chirk Castle MS 51 (b) 29.
[56] Gwynedd Archives Service, XCS/1660; Bob Owen, 'Some Details about the Independents in Caernarvonshire', *TCHS*, 6 (1945), 38–41.

Official references such as these suggest that Welsh was used whenever it was considered necessary. Its use evidently caused few problems in a court where the majority understood and spoke Welsh. The petition of Gwen ferch Pierce of Llanrwst in 1658 in a case of assault, for example, is one among countless examples which show that although details of the offences committed were recorded in the sessions files in English, initial enquiries to ascertain the facts as well as the evidence presented in petitions and depositions to the courts in English would invariably be conducted in Welsh.[57] It was insisted, however, that the formality of legal and administrative procedures was respected to facilitate the use of English common law, that legal and administrative procedures were maintained, and strict supervision exercised. Since that law was imposed universally for the first time throughout the whole of Wales, it was necessary to establish legal precedent. Therefore, the installation of justices of the quorum and one *custos rotulorum* for each shire in 1543 ensured that the law was upheld. Government officials, assize judges and commissioners would then be able to attend to all matters relating to the Quarter Sessions. Imposing English, therefore, meant adhering to a common legal form and doctrine.

What is known about the language competence of those who sat on the magistrates' bench at the Quarter Sessions? Eulogistic poetry in praise of justices of the peace in the period *c.*1540–1640 drew attention to their ability to meet the requirements of the government. Before the Acts of Union several poets had sung to a growing number of patrons who sought material rewards. But they had increasingly become part of a broader cultural scene and had firmly allied themselves with the monarchy. In the period before the civil wars most magistrates were closely attached to their kinsfolk and tenants, and controlled community affairs. Many of them supported the poets and some were themselves poets. Whether they fully understood and appreciated the content of inflated eulogies is questionable, but an extraordinarily large corpus of eulogistic poetry has survived during the period from the death of Elizabeth I to the outbreak of the civil wars. It clung to conventional themes but newer elements were added, particularly in a period of economic hardship and social change when poets began to criticize rapacious gentry who neglected traditional social values.[58] They were counselled to adhere strictly to legal principles, maintain their regional leadership and protect their dependants.

Alliterative poetry also concentrated on the role of those whose task it was to maintain good order. At the top of the social scale Sir William Herbert, earl of Pembroke, for example, was praised by Wiliam Llŷn for

---

[57] NLW Chirk Castle MS 51 14 (c) 22.
[58] D. J. Bowen, 'Y Cywyddwyr a'r Dirywiad', *BBCS*, XXIX, part 3 (1981), 453–96.

his willingness to speak his native tongue with his fellow-countrymen at Court ('Doedai ef . . . Gymraec wrth Gymro ai gar').[59] Gentry who served as sheriffs, justices of the peace and, after 1586–7, deputy-lieutenants – the most prestigious office of all – were also highly esteemed. At a time when hierarchical concepts of society were threatened, poets defended traditional values based on descent and public obligation. Part of that responsibility was the maintenance of the cultural heritage, and some magistrates were actively involved in safeguarding literary standards. William Mostyn, for example, was a commissioner for the second Caerwys Eisteddfod (1567), he and his ancestors having received the 'gyfte and bestowing of the sylver harpe appertayning to the Cheff of that facultie'. Among other commissioners were Sir Richard Bulkeley of Beaumaris, Sir Rhys ap Gruffudd of Penrhyn, Dr Elis Price of Plasiolyn, Ieuan Lloyd of Iâl, John Salusbury of Rug, Rhys Thomas of Caernarfon, Morus Wynn of Gwydir, William Lewis of Anglesey, Piers Mostyn of Talacre, John Lewis Owen of Dolgellau (eldest son of the famous Baron Lewis ab Owain who was murdered at Mawddwy in 1555), Simon Thelwall of Plas-y-ward, John Gruffudd of Cefnamwlch and Robert Puleston of Bersham – all of them justices of the peace. The commission was established to reform the bardic order and its members were regarded as 'men both of wysdome and vpright dealing and also of Experience and good Knowledg in the scyence' of the bardic craft. They were expected to weed out disreputable poets and to guard the reputation of the eisteddfod.[60]

Some years earlier Sir John Price of Brecon – landowner, lawyer, administrator and humanist scholar – expressed concern for his nation's spiritual needs and translated the creed, the Lord's Prayer and the Ten Commandments in *Yny lhyvyr hwnn* (1546).[61] It was probably with this achievement in mind, and because of his support for the Welsh language, that Gruffudd Hiraethog composed an ode in his honour:

> Er bod tro ar y byd rhwydd . . .
> Un ydych ni newidiwyd . . .
> Cymro a dawn Cymru deg,
> Cymroaidd eich Cymräeg . . .[62]

---

[59] J. C. Morrice (ed.), *Barddoniaeth Wiliam Llŷn* (Bangor, 1908), p. 73.
[60] J. Gwenogvryn Evans, *Report on Manuscripts in the Welsh Language* (2 vols., London, 1898–1902), I, pp. 291–5. See also Gwyn Thomas, *Eisteddfodau Caerwys: The Caerwys Eisteddfodau* (Caerdydd, 1968), pp. 83–109; D. J. Bowen, 'Ail Eisteddfod Caerwys a Chais 1594', *LlC*, 3, no. 3 (1955), 139–61.
[61] Neil R. Ker, 'Sir John Prise', *The Library*, X (1955), 1–24; R. Geraint Gruffydd, '*Yny lhyvyr hwnn* (1546): The Earliest Welsh Printed Book', *BBCS*, XXIII, part 2 (1969), 105–16.
[62] D. J. Bowen (ed.), *Gwaith Gruffudd Hiraethog* (Caerdydd, 1990), pp. 72–3.

(Although there is much change in this flexible world . . . You have not been changed . . . You are a Welshman possessed of the talent of Wales, and your native speech is fluent.)

Among the clergy who served as magistrates and supported Welsh cultural activity was William Evans, Chancellor and Treasurer of Llandaff, a native of Llangatwg Feibion Afel in Gwent. He was a staunch patron of poets and was addressed by Dafydd Benwyn (who described him as the 'Ifor Hael of Llandaff'), Sils ap Siôn and other south Wales poets. He employed Maredudd ap Rhosier as a household bard and, according to tradition, organized an eisteddfod at Llandaff in which several bards competed to achieve proficiency in the ancient craft ('i gany ar wawd am y vaistrola[eth]') and where Evans himself and Thomas Lewis of Llandaff – another magistrate and a member of the Lewis family of Y Fan, Caerphilly – adjudicated the *englyn*.[63] The celebrated scholar Dr John Davies of Mallwyd served on the Merioneth bench and was described by Rowland Vaughan of Caer-gai in the same shire as 'the only splendid Plato of our culture' ('vnig Plato ardderchawg o'n hiaith ni').[64] Edmwnd Prys, Archdeacon of Merioneth, and his son Ffowc Prys of Tyddyn-du, Maentwrog, were also magistrates and were highly regarded for their contribution to Welsh poetry, as Gruffudd Phylip eloquently testified in his elegy to the latter:

> Hwn a'i dad hynod odiaith
> Oedd yn help i naddu'n hiaith;
> Am ein hiaith o'u meirw weithion
> Amddifad yw'r hollwlad hon,
> Na bo o'r gri mewn bro Gred
> Fyth gellwair y fath golled.[65]

(He and his remarkably excellent father assisted to fashion our language which is destitute after their demise. May the bewailing of such a loss cause no derision in Christendom.)

At Gwydir Morus Wynn (d.1580) and his son, Sir John Wynn, were steeped in native culture. Several of Morus Wynn's estate accounts were kept in Welsh and he was often praised by the poets for his stalwart

---

[63] Ceri W. Lewis, 'The Literary History of Glamorgan from 1550 to 1770' in Glanmor Williams (ed.), *Glamorgan County History, Vol. IV, Early Modern Glamorgan* (Cardiff, 1974), pp. 546–7, 549.
[64] Hughes, *Rhagymadroddion*, p. 120.
[65] Glenys Davies, *Noddwyr Beirdd ym Meirion* (Dolgellau, 1974), p. 210.

contribution as magistrate.[66] As his letter to Sir William Jones of Castellmarch, Lord Chief Justice of Ireland, showed, Sir John Wynn possessed an intimate knowledge of Welsh antiquities[67] and, in 1594, he unsuccessfully petitioned with other prominent justices of the peace, including Piers Gruffudd of Penrhyn, John Conway, Edward Thelwall and Hugh Hookes of Conwy, for a third eisteddfod to be held at Caerwys.[68] Like Huw Nannau Hen, a Merioneth magistrate, Wynn was elegized by a large number of poets who had enjoyed his lavish patronage.[69]

John Conway III of Botryddan near Rhuddlan translated *Klod Kerdd davod a'i dechrevad*, a translation of John Case's *Apologia Musices* (1588) and *A Summons for Sleepers, a defence of the Protestant Church* (1589) by Leonard Wright, entitled *Definiad i Hennadirion*.[70] The second work was presented to his cousin Robert Salusbury of Rug – another Merioneth magistrate – and, as a consequence, Huw Pennant recorded his skills as a linguist ('ych rhagoriaeth aeth fal ieithydd').[71] Another member of the Merioneth commission of the peace was Robert Vaughan of Hengwrt, the famous genealogist and collector of books and manuscripts, who cultivated influential cultural contacts and whose services to Welsh antiquity were immeasurable.[72] Sir John Salusbury of Lleweni was a poet and patron of poets, and Henry Perri, in his preface to *Eglvryn Phraethineb* (1595), written at Salusbury's request, applauded him as a guardian of the language.[73] Siôn Dafydd Rhys highly esteemed Sir Edward Stradling's cultural skills,[74] and also commended Morgan ap Maredudd, a Radnorshire magistrate of Bugeildy, near Knighton.[75] Stradling was described as his Maecenas – a most cultured and gracious gentleman – in his preface to *Cambrobrytannicae Cymraecaeve Linguae Institutiones* (1592),[76] and Sir Thomas Wiliems of Trefriw, lexicographer and copyist, in his

---

[66] NLW Llanstephan MS 179B. See Enid Roberts (ed.), *Gwaith Siôn Tudur* (2 vols., Bangor, 1978), I, pp. 125–6.
[67] NLW MS 9058E, f. 1005.
[68] Thomas, *Eisteddfodau Caerwys*, pp. 109–17; Bowen, 'Ail Eisteddfod Caerwys a Chais 1594', 155–60.
[69] J. Gwynfor Jones, 'Priodoleddau Bonheddig yn Nheulu'r Wynniaid o Wedir', *THSC* (1978), 78 et seq.; Arwyn Lloyd Hughes, 'Rhai o Noddwyr y Beirdd yn Sir Feirionnydd', *LlC*, 10, no. 3 and 4 (1969), 160–2.
[70] Enid Roberts, 'Seven John Conways', *FHSJ*, XVIII (1960), 70–3; Gwendraeth Jones, 'Siôn Conwy III a'i waith', *BBCS*, XXII, part 1 (1966), 16–30.
[71] Gwendraeth Jones, op. cit., 26.
[72] E. D. Jones, 'Robert Vaughan of Hengwrt', *JMHRS*, I, part 1 (1949), 21–30; Richard Morgan, 'Robert Vaughan of Hengwrt', ibid., VIII, part 4 (1980), 397–408.
[73] Hughes, *Rhagymadroddion*, p. 87.
[74] Davies, *Rhagymadroddion a Chyflwyniadau*, pp. 71–8.
[75] Hughes, *Rhagymadroddion*, p. 81.
[76] Davies, *Rhagymadroddion a Chyflwyniadau*, p. 73.

Latin preface to *Thesaurus Linguae Latinae et Cambrobrytannicae,* described him as 'prime cherisher of our Welsh language in south Wales' ('prif ymgleddwr ein iaith Gymraec yn neheuwlad Gymru').[77] He also complimented Morus Wynn of Gwydir and his son Sir John Wynn, Sir John Stradling, Robert Pugh of Penrhyn Creuddyn, John Edwards of Chirk, Hugh Gwyn of Berth-ddu, Llanrwst, Edward Thelwall of Plas-y-ward, Ruthin, and Robert Holland, cleric and translator – many of them active magistrates and sheriffs – for their support in completing his task.

George Owen of Pembrokeshire, genealogist, antiquary and patron of poets, was deeply interested in the broader aspects of cultural activity and was an eminent author of topographical, social, legal and administrative works.[78] Another prominent magistrate, Peter Mutton of Llannerch in Denbighshire, whose maternal grandfather, Gruffudd ab Ieuan, was a poet, spoke Welsh as his first language, and it was in that language that he informed his mother by letter of his marriage to an orphan girl.[79] Simon Thelwall of Plas-y-ward in Denbighshire was appointed one of the Barons and Justices of the seven shires by Queen Elizabeth and also functioned as a prominent bardic patron whose legal books were highly praised. He was a competent poet in the strict metres and took part in a bardic debate with the cleric Sir Rhys Gruffudd and William Mostyn.[80] In Gresford parish church stands an alabaster tomb with an inscription written entirely in Welsh to commemorate John Trefor of Trefalun (d.1580), who built the house there in 1576. He was a justice of the peace and on his tomb the following words were inscribed: '. . . Ei ddiwedd-oes a gartrefodd ef yn llywodraeth a gwasanaeth ei anedigaeth wlad' (. . . in his latter days he settled to govern and serve the land of his birth), an indication that he was familiar with the native language.[81]

The years between the Acts of Union and the civil wars revealed distinct signs of changing social habits and attitudes and a growing disregard among members of some of the more prominent families for cultural tradition and responsibilities. Closer ties were established between the Welsh gentry and the centres where English codes of conduct were observed. The gentry obtained positions in government, acquired a good education, and became familiar with the royal court and its officials. Nevertheless, there remained a remarkably strong group of resident heads of senior and cadet families,

---

[77] Hughes, *Rhagymadroddion,* p. 115.
[78] For a study of Owen's antiquarian interests, see B. G. Charles, *George Owen of Henllys* (Aberystwyth, 1976).
[79] David Jenkins, 'Llythyr Syr Peter Mutton (1565–1637)', *NLWJ,* V, no. 3 (1948), 220–1.
[80] NLW MS 1553A, f. 759; *DWB,* pp. 932–3.
[81] A. N. Palmer, *A History of the Old Parish of Gresford* (Wrexham, 1905), p. 101; Phillips, *Justices of the Peace in Wales,* pp. 55–7.

particularly in the north and west who, owing to their attachment to the native soil, were actively engaged in local administration and continued to foster an interest in Welsh cultural affairs. Although the bardic output was prolific, there was a marked decline in the quality of compositions which were strictly controlled by convention.

The homes of privileged families (*plastai*) continued to be focal points where the traditional gentry displayed themselves as moral leaders of their household and people and where, particularly among the more conservative families, the Welsh language continued to flourish. In the late sixteenth century, however, changing circumstances caused the poets to upbraid the gentry for persistently forsaking their responsibilities, thereby depriving the community of cultural leadership.[82] Breaking out of their traditional mould, poets fulminated against what they considered to be the major obstacle to social development, namely the gentry's abandonment of their role as protectors of their regions. The court of Quarter Sessions represented the ethos of the county community, and bardic references to the office of magistrate emphasized that distinctive contribution. It was a means by which society was organized, order preserved and leadership respected. Although social changes had affected all sections of the community, ample references appear in bardic tributes to the adherence of community leaders to the Welsh heritage in the decades following the Tudor settlement. They do not refer to language usage in the courts of law, but they strongly imply that, in the case of diligent magistrates, proceedings were conducted for the good of all. Edmund Meyrick of Ucheldref near Corwen is a good example: Rhisiart Phylip praised him on his appointment as sheriff in 1632 and lavishly extolled his virtues as justice of the peace.[83] Although the poet does not refer specifically to his use of language as sheriff and magistrate, his background and authority made the law, as he practised it, more intelligible to those whom he served. Justice, the poet explained, can only be done when the community is made to understand and appreciate its meaning. It was not merely a means of achieving uniformity but of maintaining community values. There is strong evidence that, before 1640, a large proportion of justices of the peace and other officials used the Welsh language. According to Lewys Morgannwg, Lewis Gwyn, Constable of Bishopston, continued to speak Welsh and maintain an interest in the cultural tradition.[84] Cadwaladr ap Morus of Y Foelas in Denbighshire was also praised by Gruffudd Hiraethog for his Welshness:

---

[82] For further information on this theme, see J. Gwynfor Jones, *Concepts of Order and Gentility in Wales 1540–1640* (Llandysul, 1992).
[83] Davies, *Noddwyr Beirdd ym Meirion*, p. 215.
[84] NLW Peniarth MS 114, f. 5.

> Sylfaen o ustus haelfawr . . .
> Cymro gloyw Cymraeg lawen . . .[85]

(A magnanimous justice . . . A polished Welshman who gladly speaks his tongue.)

Rhys Cain addressed one of the Trefors of east Denbighshire as one who respected the needs of ordinary folk,[86] and, as Gruffudd Phylip testified, Richard Fychan II of Corsygedol was a keen student of the bardic craft.[87] Sir William Maurice of Clenennau, a country squire well-versed in the ancient antiquities of the nation, quickly defended the bardic order against the derogatory remarks of a discredited relative, and remarked:

> my cheefest purpose at this time is rather to expostulate with you for your unkinde . . . detraction of your owne countrey and countreymen . . . The other unkinde glance or rather nipping of our country *beirdd* (whoe are muche more beeholdinge to Lucane . . .) than to you theire owne (country)man . . . fowle is fowel that files his owne nest.[88]

In the 1680s, at a time when bardic fortunes were much bleaker, Sir Thomas Mostyn's house at Gloddaeth was described by Edward Morris as a foundation of the language.[89] In an ode to Owain Wynn of Glyncywarch, Phylip Siôn Phylip underlined discretion, learning and justice, the three prime qualities that characterized the honourable governor,[90] and those virtues were exemplified further in Siôn Cain's elegy to Sir James Prys of Ynysymaengwyn:

> Calon dewrion i'w diroedd,
> Cefn drws y cyfiawnder oedd . . .
> Cefnodd, cadwodd le cadarn,
> Cefn y fainc, cyfiawna'i farn.[91]

(A valiant heart in his lands; the firm door of justice . . . He supported and maintained a strong position; defender of the bench, just in his judgement.)

---

[85] Bowen, *Gwaith Gruffudd Hiraethog*, p. 126.
[86] NLW Peniarth MS 69, f. 99.
[87] Hughes, 'Rhai o Noddwyr y Beirdd', 147.
[88] Jones Pierce, *Clenennau Letters and Papers*, pp. 134–5 (no. 474).
[89] Hughes, *Barddoniaeth Edward Morris*, pp. 36–8.
[90] Davies, *Noddwyr Beirdd ym Meirion*, p. 86.
[91] NLW Peniarth MS 116, f. 813.

Social harmony ranked highest in the poet's mind and that could imply using language for the purpose of administering law and order. The poets increasingly complained about growing apathy towards the language among the privileged classes; so also did humanist scholars, both Catholic and Protestant, who, as equally shrewd commentators on the cultural scene, drew attention to the neglect and incompetence of the gentry in using the language.[92] Robert Gwyn, the recusant priest, allegedly the author of the preface to *Y Drych Cristianogawl* (1587), considered that although the gentry had only some grasp of Welsh they should give a better example to their dependants by using it more frequently.[93] Clear signs of neglect had appeared towards the end of the sixteenth century in several parts of Wales, as the poets amply illustrate. Meurig Dafydd, a worthy Glamorgan poet employed in the Lewis household at Y Fan, for example, appears not to have impressed William Bassett of Beaupre, 'the good ould squier' as he was called, 'with a cowydh, odle or englyn . . . containinge partelie the praises of the gentleman, and partelie the pettygrees and matches of his aunceistors'. He met with a discouraging response because, although the poet was given his customary fee for his effort, the poem was indifferently 'put . . . sure enough into the fier'.[94] Social and economic transition largely accounted for such a negative attitude but, during the period between the Acts of Union and the civil wars, the situation generally appeared to be that housekeeping gentry, who administered justice and their estates, continued to welcome poets and retain a good command of Welsh in many areas but, as Simwnt Fychan indicated, those who had sought employment and fortune elsewhere tended to ignore it:

> Maent wŷr ifanc mewn trefi
> Yn gwatwar gwaith ein hiaith ni.[95]

(Young men in towns deride the craftsmanship of our language.)

In 1651 John Edwards (Siôn Treredyn), a modest cleric from Caldicot in Gwent, published his translation of Edward Fisher's *Marrow of Modern Divinity*. In his preface he bemoaned the lack of interest which the Welsh

---

[92] Hughes, *Rhagymadroddion*, p. 53.
[93] Ibid., pp. 53–4.
[94] John Stradling, *The Storie of the Lower Borowes of Merthyrmawr,* eds. H. J. Randall and William Rees (South Wales and Monmouth Record Society, I, [1932]), pp. 70–1; Lewis, 'The Literary History of Glamorgan', pp. 539–40.
[95] Cardiff MS 4.101, f. 112r.

people took in their language in spite of its ancient heritage, and he also deplored the lack of Welsh printed books.[96] His complaint was similar to that voiced by other Welsh authors of his generation that leaders of local communities were not performing their cultural duties as assiduously as they might. The work was presented to some of the most prominent and well-endowed gentry families in south-east Wales, namely the Herberts of St Julians and Raglan, the Morgans of Tredegar, the Kemeyses of Cefnmabli and Williamses of Llangybi in Gwent and their satellites.[97] Judging by Edwards's comments, they were not ardent supporters of the Welsh language at that time but were descendants of notable forebears and were all well represented on the county commissions of the peace in Monmouthshire and Glamorgan:

> canys, fel y gwelwn ni beunydd, hwy nac yr elo na Chymro na Chymraes i Lundain, neu i Caerloyw neu i un fann arall o Loeger, a dysgu ryw ychydig o saesneg, hwy a wadant eu gwlad a'u hiaith eu hunain. Ac o'r Cymru cartrefol, ie ym mhlith y Pendefigion yscholheigiaidd, ie ym mysc y Dyscawdwyr Eglwysig, braidd un o bwmtheg a fedr ddarllen, ac yscrifennu Cymraeg.

> (Therefore, as we see daily, as soon as a Welshman or Welshwoman goes to London or Gloucester or any other place in England, and learns a little English, they deny their own country and language. And of the homekeeping Welshmen, yes, among the educated nobility, yes among the ecclesiastical teachers, barely one in fifteen can speak and write Welsh.)

It is significant that in south-east Wales in the mid-seventeenth century members of families who had, in the past, granted patronage and hospitality to the Welsh professional poets were still considered sufficiently familiar with the Welsh language to earn the respect of a country cleric. John Edwards severely criticized the learned gentry and churchmen of his day for neglecting the language and its culture in a period of crisis, and appealed to the heads of these named families to receive his work gracefully as a token of their affection for the language.[98]

The political and religious upheavals of the 1640s and 1650s were not the only reason for the gradual recession in cultural matters, especially among the more prosperous families which survived the Puritan regime and were restored to their old position in Welsh society. Social

---

[96] John Edwards, *Madruddyn y difinyddiaeth diweddaraf* (Llundain, 1651), sig. A4v; W. J. Gruffydd, *Llenyddiaeth Cymru: Rhyddiaith o 1540 hyd 1660* (Wrexham, 1926), p. 130.
[97] Phillips, *Justices of the Peace in Wales*, pp. 360–1.
[98] Gruffydd, *Llenyddiaeth Cymru*, p. 130.

reorientation had been apparent over the previous century when new trends and attitudes deeply affected the governing classes. Matters came to a head, however, in the mid-seventeenth century. Since Wales was predominantly royalist in sympathy during the civil war years and the Puritan decade that followed, the economic power of the gentry gradually deteriorated. The wars had disrupted trade, families were subjected to heavy fines, and the estates of several among them were sequestered. Deep resentment was also felt because individuals of inferior status had replaced them in positions of authority under Puritan governments. The circumstances of landed families changed after the Restoration and a deep rift appeared between, on the one hand, the more eligible gentry who became increasingly Anglicized and estranged from the Welsh countryside and who enjoyed the ascendancy in county society, and, on the other, the homekeeping native *uchelwyr*, hard hit by economic stringency during the 1640s and 1650s. They were unable to contest parliamentary seats but maintained their role in public government as members of the local commissions of the peace although, after 1733, property qualification for magistrates was to rise to £100 a year with the intention of curbing the ambitions of less substantial gentlemen who wished to serve as magistrates.[99] From the late seventeenth century onwards modest heads of households, who held office and who had some stake in land, became the backbone of Welsh society and were involved in supporting philanthropic enterprises, subscribing to Welsh religious publications and caring for the welfare of a rural community. While the wealthier gentry were able to provide enough capital to invest in land, exploit the matrimonial market well and obtain lucrative offices, the less well-endowed, often encumbered with heavy mortgages and at the mercy of London usurers, were unable to develop large-scale estates and were dependent on rents and the sale of agricultural produce and livestock to earn a living.[100]

Despite the deep recession in bardic activity and output in the late seventeenth and early eighteenth centuries, poetic tributes to middling and lower gentry continued to appear at a time when formal changes were introduced in the language of the courts in Wales and England. In November 1650 it was legislated that the 'Bookes of Law, and all Process and Proceedings in Courts of Justice' were to be in English, thus replacing Latin for the formal records,[101] although in 1660 Latin was restored. It was

---

[99] 5 George II, c.18 (1732); 18 George II, c.20 (1745). *The Statutes at Large*, VI, 1730–46 (1769), pp. 83–4, 610–12.

[100] For a discussion of the social cleavage and the activities of eighteenth-century magistrates in Wales, see Geraint H. Jenkins, *The Foundations of Modern Wales. Wales 1642–1780* (Oxford, 1987), pp. 165–72, 219–22, 323–5, 327–8, 333–41.

[101] C. H. Firth and R. S. Rait (eds.), *Acts and Ordinances of the Interregnum, 1642–1660* (2 vols., London, 1982), II, pp. 455–6.

not until 1733 (6 George II, c.14) that all courts – including those of Wales – were required to use English only, and record proceedings in 'a common legible hand and character',[102] thereby supplementing an earlier act in 1731 (4 George II, c.26) which only referred to England and Scotland.[103] In the first act it was stated that the records had been 'in an unknown Language' (i.e. Latin), and that 'those who are summoned and impleaded had no knowledge or understanding of what is alleged for or against them in the Pleadings of their lawyers and attornies . . .'[104] If the law was prepared to admit as much with regard to English courts, how much more confusion might be caused in Welsh courts where neither language was understood by many? Another interesting feature of the 1733 act is that a fine of £50 was imposed in the event of any other language being used, implying that the use of Welsh might be subject to penalty. Records of Quarter Sessions courts after 1733 are all in English and contain hardly any Welsh. However, several slander cases appear in the Glamorgan files.[105] In Cardiff in Michaelmas 1729 Ann Lewis, spinster, exhibited articles of misdemeanours against John David alias Bowen of Michaelston-super-Avan, labourer, for uttering the following: 'I have lain with [or have had carnal knowledge of] John Lewis ye High Constable's daughter's body a hundred times besides the first time' ('Mi fuo gan ferch Shôn Lewis yr High Constable gan waith heb yr un waith ddiwethaf').[106] Another interesting slander case was that heard again at Neath in July 1730, brought against Margaret, wife of John Richard, for speaking to Rachel William concerning William Williams of Llansamlet:

Rachell, Rachell, Rachell, ble may Will dy fâb dy y guattws yn yr Claudd ag y rheibws fy whech mochen i ag oedd ar y Maes, ble may ef, i mi gael y gwade ef rhag ofn iddo ddwad ith i rheibo mwy y forry etto, mi vynna y croggy ef gwnna beth y costa i mi.[107]

(Rachel, Rachel, Rachel, where is Will thy son who lay hid in the Ditch and that bewitched my six pigs that were on the Ground: where is he that I may have his blood for fear that he should come to bewitch them tomorrow again. I will have him hanged whatever it cost me.)

---

[102] *Statutes at Large*, VI (1769), pp. 119–20; III (1603–98) (1763), p. 146.
[103] Ibid., VI, pp. 65–6.
[104] Ibid., VI, p. 65.
[105] J. H. Matthews (ed.), *Records of the Borough of Cardiff* (6 vols., Cardiff, 1901), III, p. 198 et seq.
[106] Ibid., p. 202.
[107] Ibid., p. 203.

Scandalous words, it was reported, were spoken at Llangyfelach in 1733: 'Fi ddaeth gwraig ach o Languick a Mochin o Landeilo hyd y Pwll Brwnt dan Dregibe ag fe ddaeth dau ar ei ol hy ag a cymmerth ef i fynnydd oddiwrthi' (A little woman came from Llan-giwc with a pig from Llandeilo as far as the Pwll Brwnt by Tre-gib; and two men came after her and took it away from her). On being asked, 'Had she stolen it?' ('Daeth hi ag ef yn lleddrad'?), it was answered, 'Yes, she had' ('Do, fe ddaeth').[108] Whether the justices who heard such cases were familiar with Welsh or not is not the point at issue. The exact Welsh words had to be recorded in order to prove to the court that they had actually been spoken. According to B. Ll. James, Welsh was predominantly spoken in the uplands of Glamorgan in the eighteenth century and it was widespread in the Cardiff area as well.[109] In *A Walk through Wales in August 1797*, Richard Warner was impressed with the amount of Welsh spoken in Abergavenny,[110] while on his arrival at Newport in 1787, John Byng, later 5th Viscount Torrington, stated that he had heard 'as much Welsh spoken as English' and, on approaching Cardiff, that he came across 'several people who did not understand English'.[111] William Thomas of St Fagans, schoolmaster and diarist, recorded in his diary for 20 April 1763 that the 'Quarter Session ended at Cowbridge . . . There was licensed one Isaac that knew but little English, for a dissenting Minister'.[112] It is not known who this Isaac was, but it is evident that some of the justices were able to deal with his case without the use of an interpreter.

In Merioneth, in the summer of 1746, the case of the Methodist preacher Lewis Evan of Llanllugan in Montgomeryshire was heard before William Price of Rhiwlas. He was accused of preaching, 'cynghorio' and reading the scripture at Bala without a licence, 'speaking and uttering several profane and blasphemous words'.[113] These words presumably were expressed in Welsh and used in court as evidence against the defendant. Cases of this kind might well have been heard almost entirely in Welsh since Price – a notable antiquary – was Welsh-speaking, as were other court officials.[114] Evidence in the court rolls for Hilary (1782), Easter and

[108] Ibid., p. 210.
[109] Brian Ll. James, 'The Welsh Language in the Vale of Glamorgan', *Morgannwg*, XVI (1972), 22.
[110] R. Warner, *A Walk Through Wales in August 1797* (Bath, 1801), p. 37.
[111] John Byng, *The Torrington Diaries*, ed. C. B. Andrews (6 vols., London, 1934), I, pp. 278, 280.
[112] Cardiff MS 4.877. I wish to thank Mr Brian Ll. James for this information.
[113] Bob Owen, 'Cofnodion Chwarter Sesiwn Sir Feirionnydd am Lewis Evan, Llanllugan, 1746', *CCHMC*, XLIII, no. 2 (1958), 42–3; Richard Bennett, 'Lewis Evan, Llanllugan', ibid., VI, no. 3 (1921), 51–6; Williams-Jones, *Merioneth Quarter Sessions Rolls*, pp. xxii, 46–8, 285.
[114] *DWB*, p. 782.

Trinity (1785) and Easter (1786) for Merioneth suggests that Welsh was used in the courtroom.[115] In Llanuwchllyn Parish Vestry records and Register Book, entries are found in English and Welsh.[116] In Monmouthshire there is an entry for 25 March 1803 of the Treasurer's Account Book (1803–14) for payment to be made to court interpreters.[117] On 14 July 1778 John Jones of Cadoxton near Neath was fined £10 for bad behaviour and committed into the custody of the gaoler until it had been paid. The justices on that occasion heard the defendant declare in Welsh words which were recorded in English as follows: 'The Bench are a lot of Cheaters, I look upon them as dividing the spoils, particularly the old cheat and kite Gabriel' (namely Gabriel Powell of Swansea).[118] It was noted in 1793 that pleadings in the Court of Great Sessions at Dolgellau were held in Welsh, using interpreters.[119] Similar records for Pembrokeshire in 1801 contain a Welsh petition demanding a reduction in corn prices, and John Ladd, mayor of Newport in that county, led a march to Llwyn-gwair to solicit the support of George Owen, the local magistrate.[120]

Among the active magistrates in eighteenth-century Merioneth were Robert Vaughan of Hengwrt, great-grandson of the celebrated antiquary, and his son Hugh Vaughan, Hugh Hughes Lloyd of Gwerclas, William Wynn (son of Ellis Wynne of Y Lasynys, who, in his famous work *Gweledigaetheu y Bardd Cwsc* (Visions of the Sleeping Bard) in 1703 satirized the office and other officials associated with the court of Quarter Sessions),[121] William Price of Rhiwlas, and William Vaughan of Corsygedol and Nannau, the first President ('Penllywydd') of the Honourable Society of Cymmrodorion, who was regarded as the 'last of the Welsh *uchelwyr*'.[122] In Flintshire, Sir Thomas Mostyn, 2nd baronet

---

[115] Williams-Jones, *Merioneth Quarter Sessions Rolls*, pp. xxi (n. 5), xxii, 32 (n. 47), 64 (n. 107), 216, 265 (n.).

[116] Henry Thomas, 'An Old Vestry Book', *JMHRS*, II, part 1 (1953), 39–44; G. Bowen Thomas, 'Llanaber Vestry Records, 1726–54', ibid., II, part 4 (1956), 271–84. See also T. C. Mendenhall, 'A Merioneth Wage Assessment for 1601', ibid., II, part 3 (1955), 204–8.

[117] Gwent County Record Office. Treasurer's Account Book 1803–14.

[118] Glamorgan Record Office. Order Book 1778–81. See Thomas H. Lewis, 'Documents Illustrating the County Gaol and House of Correction in Wales', *THSC* (1946–7), 243–4.

[119] NLW MS 9854C. See Peter R. Roberts, 'The Merioneth Gentry and Local Government *circa* 1650–1838', *JMHRS*, V, part 1 (1965), 34.

[120] R. Thorne and R. Howell, 'Pembrokeshire in Wartime 1793–1815' in Brian Howells (ed.), *Pembrokeshire County History Vol. III. Early Modern Pembrokeshire, 1536–1815* (Haverfordwest, 1987), pp. 381–2; Francis Jones, 'Disaffection and Dissent in Pembrokeshire', *THSC* (1946–7), 226 (n. 1).

[121] Aneirin Lewis (ed.), *Gweledigaetheu y Bardd Cwsc* (Caerdydd, 1960), p. 120; Gwyn Thomas, *Y Bardd Cwsg a'i Gefndir* (Caerdydd, 1971), pp. 75–7.

[122] Peter R. Roberts, 'The Social History of the Merioneth Gentry *circa* 1660–1840', *JMHRS*, IV, part 3 (1963), 227.

(d.1700?) and the 5th baronet, Sir Roger Mostyn (d.1796) were keenly interested in Welsh literature and antiquities, the former being described as a 'great collector of Welsh MSS and much inclined to Welsh genealogy'.[123] The long list of subscribers to Thomas Richards's *Antiquae linguae Britannicae thesaurus* (1753) included William Price, Sir Thomas Mostyn, Robert Myddelton of Chirk Castle, Vincent Corbett of Ynysymaengwyn, John Vaughan, Cwrt Derllys, Carmarthenshire, John Lewis, Gernos, Cardiganshire, William Morgan of Tredegar, Thomas Lewis of Llanishen, Robert Gwynne of Glanbrân and Marmaduke Gwynne of Garth, all of them justices of the peace and holders of other offices in their respective counties.[124] John Vaughan was not only a subscriber to Welsh books but also supported their publication and marketing in conjunction with the SPCK, with which he was in close contact.[125] A translation by Moses Williams of William Viccar's *Companion to the Altar* (*Cydymmaith i'r Allor*, 1711) was financed by John Lewis of Gernos, Llangunllo, and Walter Lloyd, Coedmor, partly financed Alban Thomas's *Dwysfawr Rym Buchedd Grefyddol* (1722).[126] Of the 141 magistrates on the commission of Glamorgan between 1774 and 1782, at least a third, chiefly from the Blaenau, are likely to have been familiar with the Welsh language and in a position, if the need arose, to use it in court; they included John Bevan of Neath, William Jenkins of Welsh St Donat's, Edward Thomas of Tregroes (Coychurch), William Thomas of Llanbradach (Llanfabon) and George Williams of Aberpergwm.[127] It is known that Edmund Thomas of Wenvoe (d.1677) spoke Welsh to his family, but that his descendant and namesake in the 1750s needed an interpreter for the purpose.[128]

Many magistrates in mid- and late-eighteenth-century Cardiganshire also were Welsh speakers. Among them were Thomas Lloyd of Bronwydd, John and Sir Herbert Lloyd of Peterwell, and David Lloyd of Braenog. Some of them, such as Thomas Johnes and his son and namesake of Aber-mad, and George Jones of Rhoscellan, were notoriously bad public servants who were considered for dismissal from the bench, but it is the case of Sir Herbert Lloyd, baronet, John Lloyd's younger brother, as county magistrate which best reveals how oppressive some justices of the

---

[123] *DWB*, p. 674.
[124] Thomas Richards, *Antiquae linguae Britannicae thesaurus* (Bristol, 1753), [n.p.].
[125] Geraint H. Jenkins, *Literature, Religion and Society in Wales, 1660–1730* (Cardiff, 1978), pp. 113, 253, 269; Mary Clement, 'John Vaughan, Cwrt Derllys, a'i Waith', *THSC* (1942), 73–107.
[126] Jenkins, *Literature, Religion and Society*, p. 269.
[127] I am grateful to Mr Brian Ll. James for providing me with information on this point.
[128] Philip Jenkins, *The Making of a Ruling Class: the Glamorgan Gentry 1640–1790* (Cambridge, 1983), p. 194.

peace could be when their own personal interests were at stake. He was an imperious figure and, on several occasions, exercised his authority in a tyrannical and thoroughly disreputable manner. He was responsible for the famous dispute concerning the Esgair-mwyn lead mines near Ysbyty Ystwyth in 1753 when he opposed Lewis Morris, the famous Anglesey antiquarian, who was Deputy Steward of Crown Manors in Cardiganshire and whose duty it was to protect royal interests at Esgair-mwyn, where rich lead ore deposits had been discovered in 1751.[129] Morris was expected to prevent any interference on the part of local gentry who were bent on extending their properties in mid and west Wales, but Sir Herbert Lloyd, armed with a pistol and accompanied by his kinsman and co-magistrate, William Powell of Nanteos, led a riotous group of supporters to the site where he threatened to shoot the beleaguered agent. This was but one among many of Lloyd's attempts to assert his authority in the most arbitrary fashion. He was not the only one in office to disregard legal procedures and to act despotically for, in a close-knit rural community, men of power and standing could and did exceed their authority with impunity; their social standing and leadership were assured and, in public matters, they experienced little effective rivalry. The majority of magistrates, however, were modest, self-respecting country gentlemen, who performed their legal and administrative duties, often in monoglot Welsh communities, with the minimum of publicity and with a degree of responsibility that ensured that government in their localities was conducted with reasonable efficiency.

In rural counties Quarter Sessions were often held in the most unsophisticated surroundings and, since the court was often convened in inns, chiefly at Lampeter and Tregaron in Cardiganshire, for example, the vernacular was doubtless used regularly in conversation between officials and others who attended. Local surveyors of highways and bridges, overseers of the poor and people who frequented the court from remote country districts such as Llangeitho, Llanbadarn Odyn, Lledrod, Llandysul, Blaenpennal and Llangwyryfon would have been monoglot Welsh speakers. Constables in the county were often fined or reprimanded for not returning freeholders for jury service, possibly because they found difficulty in finding individuals familiar enough with English to sit on cases heard entirely in that language.[130] In Breconshire, it is likely that Howel Harris's forceful preaching in Welsh led to the

---

[129] Bethan Phillips, *Peterwell: the History of a Mansion and its Infamous Squire* (Llandysul, 1983), pp. 63–71; David W. Howell, *Patriarchs and Parasites: The Gentry of South-West Wales in the Eighteenth Century* (Cardiff, 1986), pp. 164–5; Jenkins, *The Foundations of Modern Wales*, pp. 164–72.

[130] NLW, Cardiganshire Quarter Sessions Records OB/1–4.

conversion in 1737 of Marmaduke Gwynne of Garth, a justice of the peace. Harris mixed freely with country gentry and, on one occasion, he 'discours'd in a Justice of the peace's house', namely the residence of John Morris of Carrog, Llanddeiniol.[131] Thomas Price of Watford, Caerphilly, (known as 'Price y Justis'), one of Harris's ardent early followers, visited assizes outside his own county to defend Methodist exhorters accused of seditious activity.[132]

Times were changing, however, and the wealthier families distanced themselves from the language and culture of the common people. In his preface to *Antiquae linguae Britannicae thesaurus*, Thomas Richards sounded a warning by deploring the views of affluent Anglicized gentry who desired the extinction of the language.[133] Pursuing the same theme John Evans, in *A Topographical and Historical Description of North Wales* (1819), spoke of a similar attitude towards things Welsh among the governing classes, especially those who had achieved ascendancy in county society and were in charge of local administration: 'The gentry of the country are principally educated in England', he declared, 'and consequently few of them speak it, and many of them wish for its extermination.'[134] Some years earlier Benjamin Heath Malkin recorded in his itinerary through south Wales in 1803 that the survival of the Welsh language could cause irreparable damage to defendants in courts of law when interpreters were employed to facilitate the conduct of legal procedures:

> This interpreter, however distinguished may be his skill, can never convey the exact meaning, the tone, the gesture, as it bears upon the verbal impact of the evidence, the confidence or hesitation of the witnesses. The consequence is, that property or even life may be endangered by a defective interpretation . . . Such an evil . . . appears to be irremediable at present, and likely to remain so, unless the language of the superior country shall eventually supersede the ancient tongue, and become universal.[135]

In this passage Malkin was referring to Cardiganshire and he probably also had the Carmarthen circuit of Great Sessions in mind rather than the Quarter Sessions in that region. Because the assize judge was an Englishman, such difficulties could adversely affect the defendant's case

---

[131] Gomer M. Roberts (ed.), *Selected Trevecka Letters (1742–1747)* (Caernarfon, 1956), p. 2.
[132] J. Price Williams, 'Plas y Watford a'i Berchennog', *CCHMC*, XXXIX, no. 3 (1954), 57.
[133] Richards, *Antiquae linguae*, pp. xv–xvi; Francis Jones, 'The Old Families of Wales' in Donald Moore (ed.), *Wales in the Eighteenth Century* (Swansea, 1976), pp. 36–40.
[134] John Evans, *A Topographical and Historical Description of North Wales* (London, 1819), p. 129.
[135] Benjamin H. Malkin, *The Scenery, Antiquities, and Biography, of South Wales* (2nd ed., 2 vols., London, 1807), II, pp. 29–30; Howell, *Patriarchs and Parasites*, pp. 155–6.

but, in Quarter Sessions, the situation was doubtless eased by the presence of Welsh-speaking magistrates and minor officials.

What, therefore, were the chief social factors that facilitated the use of the Welsh language in the courts of Quarter Sessions during the two and a half centuries after the Acts of Union? It must be conceded that the evidence is disappointingly sparse, but the argument that all the Welsh gentry by the eighteenth century had divorced themselves entirely from the conservative countryside and had adopted new habits and attitudes should not be pressed too far. Social change was gradual and it varied from family to family according to different circumstances. The abandonment of the language among the governing classes was a much more protracted process than is often realized.[136] The majority of the Welsh people preferred to have their business conducted in the vernacular and since Wales was a predominantly rural, sparsely populated and conservative country, it would appear that legal and administrative matters were, at least in part, often conducted orally in Welsh. The fact that hardly any references occur to the language may conceal the extent of its use, and to suggest that justices of the peace in eighteenth-century Wales were increasingly unable or unwilling to attend to their business in the Welsh language is unwarranted. While it is true that some magistrates – notably members of more economically advanced families – were inclined to associate themselves with social groups in privileged circles, homekeeping magistrates continued to administer their regions with reasonable competence and were able to use the Welsh language when it was required. Although there were instances of irresponsible behaviour in public duty on the part of some incompetent magistrates during the early modern period, the general impression is that a relatively small band of governors in each county diligently performed their duties to the best of their ability. As agents of the central government in the localities, they shouldered the multifarious administrative burdens in their hundreds and parishes, and were drawn from a broad social stratum in urban and rural communities. Some were wealthier, more self-assured and more zealous in conducting their affairs, but the most active justices of the peace were regularly concerned with maintaining law and order, frequently in predominantly Welsh-speaking areas, and were respected by the community for what they truly represented, namely good lineage and qualities of leadership.

---

[136] Bedwyr Lewis Jones, '*Yr Hen Bersoniaid Llengar*' (Gwasg yr Eglwys yng Nghymru, 1963), pp. 8–12; Herbert M. Vaughan, *The South Wales Squires* (Carmarthen, 1988), pp. 233–9.

6

Unity of Religion or Unity of Language? Protestants and Catholics and the Welsh Language 1536–1660

GLANMOR WILLIAMS

THE PRIMARY bond of unity within the medieval church, after the Christian faith itself, was the Latin language. It was the medium through which all official ecclesiastical proceedings were conducted: the language of public worship, the Bible, and the service books; of canon law, and legal and administrative record; of religious literature and theological scholarship; and of learned discourse and expression. Nevertheless, since the vast majority of the population knew little or no Latin, and many of the inadequately-educated parish priests had but scant acquaintance with it, the Church had perforce to make extensive use of the vernacular languages. It was in the mother tongue that confession had to be heard, basic instruction given and sermons preached, as well as more informal communication conducted.

During the Middle Ages the Welsh language was well equipped to perform such functions.[1] An extensive corpus of prose literature, translated into Welsh from Latin so as to help priests and laymen carry out their religious duties, still survives in numerous manuscripts. It contains items such as translations of key passages of scripture. The Welsh translation of the *Officium Parvum Beatae Mariae Virginis* (Gwassanaeth Meir), for example, contained more extracts from the Scriptures than any other Welsh medieval text.[2] There are also manuals of instruction, prayers, hymns, works of piety and devotion, saints' lives, and a miscellany of comparable works. In addition to this body of prose, there was a close connection between religion and Welsh poetry. Poets and priests often

---

[1] D. Simon Evans, *Medieval Religious Literature* (Cardiff, 1986); Glanmor Williams, *The Welsh Church from Conquest to Reformation* (2nd ed., Cardiff, 1976); J. E. Caerwyn Williams, 'Medieval Welsh Religious Prose', *Proceedings of the International Congress of Celtic Studies 1963* (Cardiff, 1963), pp. 65–97; idem, 'Rhyddiaith Grefyddol Cymraeg Canol' in Geraint Bowen (ed.), *Y Traddodiad Rhyddiaith yn yr Oesau Canol* (Llandysul, 1974), pp. 312–408.
[2] Brynley F. Roberts, *Gwassanaeth Meir* (Caerdydd, 1961).

received a part of their education in company with one another, and it was clerics like Einion Offeiriad (Einion the Priest) who usually wrote poetic grammars. Members of the clergy frequently composed poetry and were among the most generous patrons of the professional poets. There exists a large body of religious verse written by the earliest court poets of the eleventh to the fourteenth centuries, the *cywyddwyr* of the fourteenth to the sixteenth centuries, and other bards. Favourite subjects included praise of the Trinity, the merits of the saints, life's brevity and man's sinfulness, the attraction of pilgrimages, and other comparable themes.[3] It also seems probable that there may have existed a large body of religious verse in the free metres which has long since disappeared, since it never enjoyed sufficient status to be preserved in manuscripts. All in all, as long and venerable an inheritance lay behind the Welsh religious literature of the biblical translations of the sixteenth century as that which was inherited by the contemporary English translators.

In theory, every parish priest was enjoined to teach his people the Lord's Prayer, the Ten Commandments, the Creed, the Seven Works of Mercy, the Seven Deadly Sins, and the like, four times a year. The priest had the opportunity of expounding them to his congregation in his sermon – the only part of his service propounded in the vernacular. All these formulae exist in Welsh translation in contemporary manuscripts. Just how widespread these writings were among the clergy and laity it is impossible to tell with certainty; but it must be supposed that in Wales, as elsewhere, manuscript coverage was patchy and ineffective, and oral transmission may well have fallen far short of making good the deficiency. The author of the first Welsh printed book, Sir John Price of Brecon, was in 1546 pointedly critical of the priesthood for its failure to teach the people those things they ought to have known. The result was, he said, 'that the great part of my nation the Welsh are in incalculable darkness for want of knowledge of God and His commandments' ('vot rhan vawr om kenedyl gymry mewn tywyllwch afriuaid o eisieu gwybodaeth duw ae orchymineu').[4] This he attributed to the shortcomings of the clergy, the fewness of manuscripts, and the complete absence of printed books. It was to repair these shortcomings in some measure that he published his book, *Yny lhyvyr hwnn* (In this book).

By the time Price produced this book, Henry VIII had already introduced his Reformation into Wales. Because there had been little demand for reform there, the new regime had to be imposed from above.

---

[3] Henry Lewis, *Hen Gerddi Crefyddol* (Caerdydd, 1931); J. E. Caerwyn Williams, *Canu Crefyddol y Gogynfeirdd* (Abertawe, 1977); Williams, *Welsh Church*, pp. 106–13, 416–30.

[4] John Price, *Yny lhyvyr hwnn*, ed. John H. Davies (Bangor, 1902), introduction; Garfield H. Hughes (ed.), *Rhagymadroddion 1547–1659* (Caerdydd, 1951), pp. 3–4.

Although change was promulgated in English by statute, proclamation, sermon, and printed text, and consequently was properly understood only by the small minority of the population which spoke English, the Latin rite was preserved in the churches as before. Even at this stage, however, there were some aspects of policy which, indirectly, exerted a significant effect on the Welsh language and literature. The dissolution of the monasteries, 1536–40, removed from the scene a number of major centres where Welsh manuscripts had been copied and stored, and many abbot-patrons of the poetry.[5] The suppression of pilgrimage sites in 1538 meant a further loss of sources of literary patronage and inspiration. All this, surprisingly, provoked little expression of regret; one leading poet, Lewys Morgannwg, even applauded the king's actions.[6]

Henry VIII was, in general, conservative by inclination, and he retained intact most of the medieval doctrine and forms of worship; but he did allow some use of the vernacular language in religion. The Bible was translated into English and the populace encouraged to read it. Some parts of the service were also rendered into the native tongue. These gradual moves towards the use of the vernacular were pregnant with significance for the assumption that in the future there might be one law, one faith, and one language under the prince.[7] A tiny minority grasped their import and sought to adapt them to conditions in Wales. As early as 1538 William Barlow, bishop of St David's, ordered the prior and vicar of Cardigan to preach and declare (i.e. expound) the epistle and the gospel in the mother tongue.[8] Barlow's notorious antipathy to Welsh, and the fact that Cardigan is known to have had a considerable English-speaking population, both suggest that 'mother tongue' in this context most probably meant English. In 1542, however, Bishop Arthur Bulkeley of Bangor, following up the king's proclamation of 1541 calling on all his subjects to learn the Creed, Paternoster, Ten Commandments, and Ave in the vernacular, required the clergy, schoolmasters, and heads of households of his diocese to give religious instruction to their charges in Welsh – the first episcopal requirement for the use of Welsh certainly known to have been issued during Henry's reign.[9] Around this time, possibly even earlier and certainly before 1543, some anonymous cleric in south Wales was

---

[5] Catrin T. Beynon Davies, 'Y cerddi i'r tai crefydd fel ffynhonnell hanesyddol', *NLWJ*, XVIII, nos. 3 and 4 (1974), 268–86, 345–73.
[6] Williams, *Welsh Church*, p. 548.
[7] Peter R. Roberts, 'The Welsh Language, English Law and Tudor Legislation', *THSC* (1989), 26.
[8] T. Wright (ed.), *Letters relating to the Suppression of Monasteries* (Camden Society, 1843), p. 187.
[9] William Salesbury, *Kynniver Llith a Ban*, ed. John Fisher (Caerdydd, 1931), p. xxi.

translating from English into Welsh parts of William Tyndale's New Testament. These were included, together with translated extracts from Thomas Cranmer's English Litany and Order of Communion, in Hafod Manuscript 22.[10] The translation from the New Testament would seem to have been undertaken to help clerics in one or both of the south Wales dioceses to 'declare' the sense of the epistles and gospels as commanded by the king. In 1543, however, an act of parliament condemned Tyndale's translation and other versions of the English Bible.

The last years of Henry's reign were, nevertheless, marked by important developments for the religious and cultural life of Wales. In December 1545 William Salesbury and the printer, John Waley, obtained a royal licence to print a dictionary to help Welshmen to attain a better knowledge of English.[11] In the following year, there appeared Sir John Price's *Yny lhyvyr hwnn*, the first book to be printed in Welsh. It contained among other things Welsh versions of material such as the Creed and Paternoster. Its importance lay in Price's assertion that it would be the greatest sin to allow many thousands of Welsh people to fall into perdition for want of instruction in the only language they understood, and which many of them were able to read, though they could manage no other. The content of Price's work may have been slight; but its significance lay in its insistence upon the crucial need to publish literature in Welsh for the generality of the people if reform was to make any headway, and its perception of the immense benefit that effective use of the printing press could confer upon them 'so that knowledge of his blessed words may be multiplied . . . and that a gift as valuable as this should not be less fruitful to us than to others' ('er amylhau gwybodaeth y eireu bendigedic ef . . . val na bai ddiffrwyth rhodd kystal a hon yni mwy noc y eraill').[12]

Soon afterwards, early in the reign of Edward VI, there emerged on the cultural scene the most creative and energetic figure in sixteenth-century Welsh reforming humanism and book publishing – William Salesbury.[13] Rooted in the centuries-old literary tradition of Denbighshire, he had grafted onto it the seminal new strains of humanism and reform he had

---

[10] Henry Lewis, 'Darnau o'r efengylau', *Y Cymmrodor*, XXXI (1921), 193–216; R. Geraint Gruffydd, 'Dau destun Protestannaidd cynnar o lawysgrif Hafod 22', *Trivium*, I (1966), 56–66.

[11] W. Ll. Davies, 'Welsh books entered in the Stationers' Registers 1554–1708', *JWBS*, II, no. 5 (1921), 167–76.

[12] Price, *Yny lhyvyr hwnn*, introduction; cf. Hughes, *Rhagymadroddion*, p. 3.

[13] R. Brinley Jones, *William Salesbury* (Cardiff, 1994); W. Alun Mathias, 'William Salesbury – ei fywyd a'i weithiau' in Geraint Bowen (ed.), *Y Traddodiad Rhyddiaith* (Llandysul, 1970), pp. 27–53; idem, 'William Salesbury – ei ryddiaith', ibid., pp. 54–78; D. R. Thomas, *The Life and Work of Bishop Davies and William Salesbury* (Oswestry, 1902); Glanmor Williams, 'The Achievement of William Salesbury' in *Welsh Reformation Essays* (Cardiff, 1967), pp. 191–205.

acquired at the University of Oxford and in London. More decisively than any other contemporary individual, he proclaimed the need for a printed Welsh literature in prose and verse. In his second book, *Oll Synnwyr pen Kembero ygyd* (The Whole Wisdom of a Welshman's Head) (1547), fittingly described as the first manifesto of Welsh Protestant humanism, he passionately urged his countrymen 'to obtain the scriptures in your own language . . .' and 'Go barefoot on a pilgrimage to the King's grace . . . to have the holy scriptures in your own tongue' ('mynwch yr yscrythur lan yn ych iaith' . . . 'Pererindotwch yn droednoeth, at ras y Brenhin . . . y cael yr yscrythur lan yn ych iaith').[14] He voiced his urgent appeal at a critical juncture early in Edward's reign, when a Protestant Reformation, as opposed to a caesaro-papal revolution, was first being introduced into England and Wales. Added relevance was given to his plea in 1549, when the first English Book of Common Prayer was published and its use enforced in all Welsh parish churches. For a non-English-speaking people, the shift from Latin to English was one of seismic proportions, and created a religious and linguistic crisis of the first order. Neither the new creed nor the strange language would be acceptable to the Welsh. Since few of them were able to read, or even understand, the new Prayer Book, it seemed to many of them like the forced imposition of the heretical 'faith of Saxons' ('ffydd Saeson').[15] Salesbury had a unique appreciation of the dilemmas and the perils confronting Welsh speakers. Working under acute pressure, he hurried to complete his translation of the epistles and the gospels of the Prayer Book and published it in 1551 as *Kynniver Llith a Ban*.[16] Committed a reformer, dedicated a scholar, and accomplished a prose author as he was, his work achieved less success than might have been hoped for. It lacked official support, showed signs of haste, and gave evidence of its author's idiosyncratic views on orthography. Even so, it had established an invaluable precedent for the future, and had shown not only the indispensable need for such a translation but also the practicability of supplying it. *Kynniver Llith a Ban* probably appealed warmly to a man like Gruffudd ab Ieuan ap Llewelyn Fychan, the first Welsh poet to applaud Protestant principles in his verse;[17] and copies of Salesbury's book were certainly valued enough to survive the reaction of Mary's reign.

---

[14] William Salesbury, *Oll Synnwyr pen Kembero ygyd*, ed. J. Gwenogvryn Evans (Bangor, 1902); cf. Saunders Lewis, 'Damcaniaeth Eglwysig Brotestannaidd', *EFC*, II (1947), 36–55.

[15] L. J. Hopkin-James and T. C. Evans (eds.), *Hen Gwndidau, Carolau, a Chywyddau* (Bangor, 1910), p. 33.

[16] Salesbury, *Kynniver Llith a Ban*.

[17] J. C. Morrice (ed.), *Detholiad o Waith Gruffudd ab Ieuan ab Llewelyn Vychan* (Bangor, 1910).

Criticism of the changed order in religion was soon forthcoming, especially among the poets. In the free metres and in *cynghanedd* verse, they censured not only innovations in doctrine, practice, and ritual, but were also no less disapproving of the abandonment of Latin in favour of English. One poet went so far as to claim that it was impossible worthily to translate the Latin mass into English.[18] Poetic protest may have been muted during Edward's reign, but the accession of Mary and her restoration of the Roman faith gave critics the opportunity to express themselves in freedom. Not that some of the most ardent champions of Mary's policies were unaware on their side of the need to make increased use of the mother tongue in religion if the mass of the people were to be won over firmly to Rome. In his synod of 1555, Cardinal Pole called for a translation of the New Testament and more emphasis on vernacular preaching.[19] Signs of an appropriate response emanated from bishops in Wales, like Thomas Goldwell of St Asaph and William Glyn of Bangor, and especially from their up-and-coming lieutenants, Morys Clynnog and Gruffydd Robert, both to be distinguished Catholic authors in exile during Elizabeth's reign. It was during Mary's years in power that Arthur ap Huw translated George Marshall's *Compendious Treatise in Metre* into Welsh. About this time, too, the unknown translator of the texts in Hafod Manuscript 17, who rendered parts of Mary's primer into Welsh, and the compiler of Llansteffan Manuscript 117, a collection of religious texts, were at work.[20]

The accession of Elizabeth to succeed her half-sister in November 1558 brought with it another sharp turn in the wheel of religious change. In the spring of 1559 the new queen's determination to reinstate a Protestant settlement resurrected in Wales the most thorny problems of the reign of Edward VI. The Act of Uniformity of March 1559 once more imposed an English book of common prayer, based largely on Edward's second book, with all its attendant difficulties for Welsh speakers. The central issue for the tiny handful of convinced Welsh Protestant humanists was whether or not they could achieve a Welsh version of the Prayer Book and the Scriptures and induce Elizabeth's government to authorize their use for public worship. In order to bring that about, they had to overcome a series of stiff hurdles. First of all, there were many of the queen's subjects, including Protestants, who favoured the use of one official language throughout the realm and saw no reason for employing Welsh. Again, although Welsh publishing was not illegal, any Welsh texts would have to

---

[18] D. J. Bowen, 'Detholiad o Englynion Hiraeth am yr Hen Ffydd', *EFC*, VI (1954), 5–12.
[19] Wilhelm Schenk, *Reginald Pole, Cardinal of England* (London, 1950), pp. 142–4.
[20] Brynley F. Roberts, 'Defosiynau Cymraeg' in Thomas Jones (ed.), *Astudiaethau Amrywiol* (Caerdydd, 1968), pp. 99–110.

be printed in London by printers ignorant of the language, and at greater expense and inconvenience. Furthermore, illiteracy was rife in Wales, and the number of those able to buy books and desirous of doing so was small; many of the Welsh were depressingly apathetic towards their own language, according to contemporary Welsh authors. There were proposals that Welsh and Cornish children who spoke no English might learn the rudiments of the faith in their own language.[21] A diocesan council held at St Asaph in 1561 called for the catechism to be read in Welsh, and the epistle and the gospel to be read first in English and then in Welsh[22] – which suggests that copies of Salesbury's *Kynniver Llith a Ban* had safely survived the reign of Mary. A copy of an 'Appeal made to the Privy Council' at this time still exists. It urged that the 'godliest and best learned men' be convened to find a means for dispelling 'sooch miserable darknes for the lack of the shynyng lyght of Christe's Gospell' by translating 'the Lordes Testament into the vulgare walsh tong'.[23] In 1562–3, John Waley, Salesbury's former printing partner, sought a licence for the printing of the Litany in Welsh.[24] No copy of this work has survived, but the assumption generally made is that, if indeed it was translated, then it was Salesbury who was responsible for it. Behind all these initiatives there can, presumably, be traced at work the resourceful hand of William Salesbury. He may have been given fresh heart by the encouragement of Richard Davies, who was bishop of St Asaph in 1560–1. It was Salesbury, Davies (who had become bishop of St David's in 1561), and Humphrey Llwyd, MP for Denbigh, who were probably the prime movers in obtaining the passage of the private act of parliament of 1563 for the translation of the Bible and Prayer Book into Welsh by 1567.[25] No act may have been needed to legitimize the translation of the Bible, but parliamentary sanction would certainly have been required to authorize the modification of the Act of Uniformity (1559) so as to permit the use of a Welsh Prayer Book. The use of the translated texts was authorized in all those parishes where Welsh was normally spoken. In the meantime, from Whitsun 1563 onwards, the epistles and the gospels, Paternoster, Creed, Ten Commandments, and Litany were to be read in Welsh.

[21] BL Egerton MS 2350, f. 54.
[22] Thomas, *The Life and Work of Bishop Davies and William Salesbury*, p. 72.
[23] Jones, *William Salesbury*, p. 51.
[24] Thomas, *The Life and Work of Bishop Davies and William Salesbury*, p. 102.
[25] R. Geraint Gruffydd, 'Humphrey Lhuyd a Deddf Cyfieithu'r Beibl i'r Gymraeg', *LlC*, 4, nos. 2 and 4 (1956–7), 114–15, 233; Glanmor Williams, *Bywyd ac Amserau yr Esgob Richard Davies* (Caerdydd, 1953), pp. 72–3; 92–5. G. R. Elton, 'Wales in Parliament, 1542–1581' in R. R. Davies et al. (eds.), *Welsh Society and Nationhood* (Cardiff, 1984), pp. 108–21.

The securing of such legislation was a formidable achievement; it meant that the queen and her advisers had been persuaded to agree to an about-turn in policy relating to the language used in religion in Wales, though the terms of the act required a copy of the Welsh Bible to be set side by side with the English one in every church, so that by comparing the one with the other the people might the more easily acquire a knowledge of the English language[26] – a pious hope never fulfilled in practice. But much still remained to be done. Whoever had been responsible for the act of 1563 had been sublimely confident in supposing that all the works called for could be translated in the time allowed. To produce a Welsh version of the Bible from the best contemporary editions of the original texts demanded a high degree of scholarship and judgement in Latin, Greek, and Hebrew.[27] There would also need to be a sensitive deployment of the Welsh language itself; freed from medieval terms and usages; not over-dependent on any one dialect; flexible and intelligible; yet dignified, resonant, and preserving the classic qualities of strength, uniformity, and purity associated with the old literary tradition. Dealing with printers in London would require skill and patience; and financing the venture out of the private pockets of the translators and their patrons would represent a serious financial sacrifice. The enterprise demanded of the men prepared to embark on it clear vision, unremitting commitment, and a willingness to dedicate themselves to the service of God and the good of their countrymen. Wales was fortunate that in its hour of need, between 1551 and 1620, out of a nation numbering no more than about 300–400,000 people, men of the calibre of William Salesbury, Richard Davies, William Morgan, Richard Parry, and John Davies emerged to fill the role of scriptural translators.[28]

It seems very probable that Salesbury, although unable to publish anything during Mary's reign, had nevertheless continued with his work of translating after 1551, or else it would appear very unlikely that he could ever have completed as much as he did during the 1560s. To expedite the work, he was invited to Davies's episcopal palace at Abergwili for several months in 1564 and again in 1565–6 in order to cooperate with the bishop and, later, with Thomas Huet, precentor of St David's. Davies had earlier begun the translation of I and II Timothy, Titus, and Philemon, which still exists in Gwysane Manuscript 27; but he abandoned them all except I Timothy, the only one of the four he

---

[26] Ivor Bowen (ed.), *The Statutes of Wales* (London, 1908), pp. 149–51.
[27] Isaac Thomas, *Y Testament Newydd Cymraeg 1551–1620* (Caerdydd, 1976); idem, *Yr Hen Destament Cymraeg 1551–1620* (Aberystwyth, 1988).
[28] R. Geraint Gruffydd (ed.), *Y Gair ar Waith: Ysgrifau ar yr Etifeddiaeth Feiblaidd yng Nghymru* (Caerdydd, 1988).

translated for the New Testament published in 1567. It was Salesbury who undertook by far the greatest part of the work of translation. Although the Welsh Prayer Book of 1567 bore the name of no translator, Salesbury's style and content were unmistakable, and similarly in the translation of the Psalter, which the Prayer Book contained. He also translated most of the books of the New Testament, although Davies translated five and Huet one.[29] The Prayer Book appeared first in May 1567, and was followed soon after by the New Testament; both were printed by Henry Denham 'at the costs and charges of Humphrey Toy'. They were intended for widespread use in the parish churches of Wales and the border, and also in schools and private households, wherever the means and the will existed to purchase them.

The translations represented a remarkable scholarly and literary feat. Salesbury's purpose, in his own words, was that 'God's own word may remayn sincere and unviolate from generation to generation', and his fidelity to the original text remained unimpugnable throughout.[30] Much as the translation owed to Salesbury as a classical scholar and prose author, his work was flawed by serious shortcomings. His orthography was highly unusual, being closer to that of English or French, which spell words according to their origin rather than to their sound, as Welsh orthography does. As a result, it bore heavily the stamp of his admiration for the Latin language, which led him to present too many Welsh words in a Latinized form, e.g., 'eccles' for 'eglwys', or 'discipul' for 'disgybl'. He also tended to preserve initial and medial consonants without mutations, although in this, as in other respects, he could be disconcertingly inconsistent in his practice. His marginal variant forms, intended to assist his readers to overcome dialectal differences, were too numerous and confusing. Also, believing as he did that the virtue of a language resided in its copious wealth of ancient forms, he retained too many archaic and outmoded words and expressions. The peculiarities were all the more regrettable because Sir John Price had earlier pointed out how much more agreement there was among the Welsh about their language than there was among the English.[31] Whereas Salesbury kept his eye firmly on the scholarly public at large in Britain and Europe, his main collaborator, Richard Davies, kept his focused much more closely on the average priest and worshipper.[32] In the books he translated he wrote more naturally and readably than Salesbury. Davies also provided for the New Testament

---

[29] Davies translated I Timothy, Hebrews, James, and I and II Peter. Huet translated Revelation.
[30] Gruffydd, *Gair ar Waith*, pp. 51–3.
[31] Neil R. Ker, 'Sir John Prise', *The Library*, X (1955), 1–24.
[32] Williams, *Welsh Reformation Essays*, pp. 212–13.

what was to prove a highly influential introductory 'Epistol at y Cembru' (Letter to the Welsh Nation). It took the form of an historical survey, seeking to show how the initially pure Christianity of the ancient British ancestors of the Welsh was strictly based on the vernacular gospel that was common in their midst. This pristine Christian faith, introduced into Britain by Joseph of Arimathea soon after Christ's death, had become corrupted down the centuries by papal excesses. The new translation of 1567, therefore, took the form of the second flowering ('ail flodeuat') of the Gospel in their own tongue among the Welsh. This Protestant reinterpretation of British history was ideally fitted to answer the two main criticisms brought against the Reformation in Wales: first, that it was a new-fangled heresy, and second, that it was an alien English faith imposed on the Welsh from without.

Opinions differed to some extent among contemporaries as to the suitability of the translations for use in the parish churches. Two eminent Welsh Elizabethan authors, John Penry and Morris Kyffin, were sharply critical. Penry protested that they were 'most pitifully euill read . . . and not vnderstoode of one among tenne of the hearers';[33] while Kyffin maintained 'that the ear of a true Welshman could not bear to hear it' ('na alle clust gwir Gymro ddioddef clywed mo 'naw'n iawn').[34] Conversely, two leading clerics were decidedly complimentary. Bishop Nicholas Robinson of Bangor testified in 1576 to his pleasure at knowing that 'all things are done in Welsh',[35] and when William Morgan in 1588 came to dedicate his Bible to Queen Elizabeth he paid a remarkable tribute to Salesbury, 'who, above all men, deserved well of our church'.[36] Judging only by the eccentric outward appearance of the printed texts, it is not difficult to understand why inadequately-educated Welsh laymen and clerics, who were obliged to make use of them, might have found them complex and unmanageable. Yet those who remember how erratic and unstandardized sixteenth-century orthography can be at best, and who also have had occasion regularly to read the texts, will testify that with repeated practice they become much easier to cope with. A more serious criticism of Salesbury and Davies, perhaps, is that they failed to translate the whole Bible. They had expressed in print their intention of completing the Old Testament, but were alleged by Sir John Wynn of Gwydir to have quarrelled with one another, possibly around 1575,

---

[33] John Penry, *Three Treatises Concerning Wales,* ed. David Williams (Cardiff, 1960), p. 56.
[34] Morris Kyffin, *Deffynniad Ffydd Eglwys Loegr,* ed. W. Prichard Williams (Bangor, 1908), p. [x].
[35] Glanmor Williams, *Recovery, Reorientation and Reformation. Wales c.1415–1642* (Oxford, 1987), p. 315.
[36] *Y Beibl Cyssegr-lan* (1588), dedication.

apparently over the meaning of one word.[37] That is difficult to accept, unless it be supposed that some fundamental difference between the two men over the principles to be adopted in translating had come to a head over a single word. Davies then appeared to have had some intention of proceeding to a joint translation with his nephew, Siôn Dafydd Rhys, but the plan was never carried out.

It was left to a young Cambridge graduate, William Morgan, vicar of the remote parish of Llanrhaeadr-ym-Mochnant,[38] to complete the translation. No certainty exists when he began the work, but it can hardly have been later than 1579 for him to have had the work ready for publication by 1587. He completed his task with the enthusiastic encouragement of Archbishop Whitgift and the help of a number of friends from his Cambridge days, and published it in September 1588. Not until 1599 was he in a position to produce his version of the Prayer Book, revised in accordance with the text of his Bible. It represented a vastly more reader-friendly edition than anything which had preceded it, and proved to be a striking advance in making the reformed service intelligible to the people and endearing it to them.[39] He had also stated his intention of bringing out a new edition of the New Testament, which would contain fewer mistakes than the text of 1588, be smaller in size, and sell more cheaply. Alas! no such edition ever appeared; it seems to have been lost in the confusion in the affairs of Morgan's publisher, Thomas Salisbury, which followed the plague of 1603.

Morgan's Bible was recognized by competent judges soon after its first appearance as an incomparable triumph. As a scholar Morgan was extremely accomplished; as the editor of a Welsh text he was unsurpassed. Although he accepted some three-quarters of Salesbury's translations, he comprehensively revised and modernized the whole text of the New Testament and the Prayer Book as far as vocabulary and orthography were in question. Finally, his use of the Welsh language bore all the hallmarks of a superb writer, instinctively attuned to the genius of his own language, as well as of an erudite scholar. At a critical juncture for the language, when the bards, hitherto the guardians of its strength and purity, had entered upon a period of grievous and accelerating decline, Morgan embodied in his translation all that was best and most enduring in their tradition. As the Welsh prose writer, Huw Lewys, declared, Morgan restored 'the respect and dignity of a language which was decayed and

[37] John Ballinger (ed.), *The History of the Gwydir Family* (Cardiff, 1927), p. 64.
[38] R. Geraint Gruffydd, '*The Translating of the Bible into the Welsh Tongue*' by William Morgan in 1588 (London, 1988); Prys Morgan, *A Bible for Wales* (Cardiff, 1988); Glanmor Williams, *The Welsh and their Religion* (Cardiff, 1991), pp. 173–229.
[39] Williams, *The Welsh and their Religion*, pp. 215–22.

which had more or less collapsed'.[40] Contemporary bards and prose writers at once acknowledged instinctively what a priceless service Morgan had performed for the Welsh language and its literature. As early as Christmas 1588, the parson-poet, Thomas Jones of Monmouthshire, urged his hearers:

> Er mwyn prynu hwn rhag trais
> Dos, gwerth dy bais, y Cymro.[41]

(In order to buy this, without oppression, go, sell thy shirt, thou Welshman.)

Siôn Tudur hailed Morgan with delight:

> Dwyn gras i bob dyn a gred,
> Dwyn geiriau Duw'n agored . . .[42]

(Bringing grace to every man who believes, bringing God's words openly . . .)

and Morris Kyffin in 1595 referred to it in glowing phrases as 'an indispensable, masterly, godly, learned work, for which Wales can never repay and thank him as much as he deserves' ('gwaith angenrheidiol, gorchestol, duwiol, dyscedig; am yr hwn ni ddichyn Cymry fyth dalu a diolch iddo gymaint ag a haeddodd ef').[43]

The final instalment in the translation of the Bible into Welsh was the edition of 1620, the work of Richard Parry, bishop of St Asaph, and his brother-in-law, Dr John Davies of Mallwyd. Parry, who had succeeded Morgan as bishop, was deeply impressed by the merits of the Authorized Version of the English Bible (1611) and was anxious to see a comparable benefit conferred upon Wales. He was also aware that copies of William Morgan's Bible were in short supply. Therefore, with the indispensable help of John Davies, he produced his version of 1620. Davies, the greatest Welsh grammarian ever, had served his apprenticeship as a biblical translator working under Morgan's direction on the preparation of the Prayer Book of 1599 and the lost version of the Testament of 1603. He was mainly responsible for the 1620 revision of the Bible of 1588; basing his own work on the same Greek and Hebrew texts as the Authorized Version, he achieved for Wales what the latter had for England. His success may be gauged from the fact that the 1620 Bible was still in

---

[40] Morgan, *A Bible for Wales*, p. 27.
[41] *Hen Gwndidau*, pp. 187–92.
[42] Enid Roberts (ed.), *Gwaith Siôn Tudur* (2 vols., Caerdydd, 1980), I, p. 375.
[43] Kyffin, *Deffynniad Ffydd*, pp. [ix–x].

universal use until 1988, and in the minds of many Welsh individuals and congregations it has still not been supplanted by the new Welsh Bible! In 1621 came an updated edition of the Prayer Book, based on the Bible of 1620. This was the Prayer Book to be used for centuries in the Anglican churches in Wales. It also included Edmwnd Prys's metrical version of the Psalms, which came to be sung in Welsh churches and attained a phenomenal popularity. Some ten years later, in 1630, was published the first cheap, handy, and popular edition of the Welsh Bible – 'y Beibl Bach' (the Little Bible), selling at five shillings. Financed by two pious and prosperous London-Welsh merchants, Rowland Heylin and Sir Thomas Myddelton, it was intended for family use in household devotions and for private reading by individuals. Its sponsors urged the reader: 'it must dwell in thy chamber, under thine own roof . . . as thy friend, eating thy bread like a dearest companion and chief adviser' ('mae'n rhaid iddo drigo yn dy stafell di, tan dy gronglwyd dy hun . . . fel cyfaill yn bwytta o'th fara, fel anwyl-ddyn a phen-cyngor it').[44] Translating the Bible into Welsh had been the supreme challenge facing the Protestant humanists. Successfully overcoming it would, above all else, prove that the language was capable of meeting the most demanding calls made upon it and would simultaneously solve both the profoundest religious problem and the most harrowing cultural dilemma faced by the Welsh. Along with a number of European peoples, they were able to produce an epoch-making version of the Bible in their own tongue, but were the only one among the Celtic peoples to do so in the sixteenth century.[45] Among the other Celts, the translation came much later or not at all, and it never attained the same place in the people's affections that it did in Wales. It was the most important book in the Welsh language in W. J. Gruffydd's considered opinion,[46] and J. Lloyd Jones described it as 'the basis of all the Welsh prose written since'.[47]

Certainly, the Bible and Prayer Book opened up a whole new vein of Welsh prose in the years that followed. In many ways the most influential genre was the catechism, editions of which were published at intervals as separate publications as well as being included in every Prayer Book.[48] The pre-Reformation clergy had been severely criticized for their failure to instruct the people. The regular appearance of printed copies of the

---

[44] *Y Bibl Cyssegr-Lan* (1630), dedication to the reader.
[45] Glanmor Williams and Robert Owen Jones (eds.), *The Celts and the Renaissance. Tradition and Innovation* (Cardiff, 1990); Gruffydd, *Gair ar Waith*, pp. 150–8.
[46] *Geiriadur Beiblaidd* (Wrecsam, 1926), I, p. 209.
[47] J. Lloyd-Jones, *Y Beibl Cymraeg (The Welsh Bible)* (Caerdydd, 1938), p. 53.
[48] R. Geraint Gruffydd, 'Religious prose in Welsh from the beginning of the reign of Elizabeth to the Restoration' (unpubl. University of Oxford DPhil thesis, 1952); *Libri Walliae*.

catechism, many of which were published before 1660, points to the increased emphasis now being placed on systematically instructing parishioners, especially the younger ones, though, no doubt, catechisms were intended for lay folk hardly less than the clergy. The Book of Homilies, official sermons for the benefit of those clergy unlicensed to preach, which might have been expected to appear early in view of the dire shortage of clergy who could preach in Welsh, was not published until 1606 in a Welsh translation by Edward James.[49] In view of the excellence of its prose style, it might appear strange that it was not reprinted until the nineteenth century, unless it was that both its content and expression proved to be over the heads of many members of the congregations – and, conceivably, not a few of the clergy too.

Of the other religious prose works destined for publication during the years between 1588 and 1660, something like seven out of eight were translations into Welsh.[50] At first sight this might seem distinctly odd, since it is proverbially difficult for translators to avoid following too closely the idioms and speech rhythms of original authors. However, the prime purpose of these writers was less to enhance their own literary reputation than to promote the religious welfare of their readers. So they translated recognized classics which had already won an assured place in the esteem of the wider public – books like John Jewel's *Apologia Ecclesiae Anglicanae* or *The Practice of Piety* by Lewis Bayly, whose authors were described by Huw Lewys as 'powerful and effectual workers in the vineyard of the spirit' ('gweithwyr grymus nerthol, yn y winllan ysprydol').[51] Such a procedure made translators surer of themselves and of their readers; it became 'an accustomed practice to translate godly works of good and devotional men from one language to another in order to add to knowledge, enlarge understanding, and purify morals and Christian practice' ('peth arferedig yw cyfeithio a throi gweithredoedd duwiol gwyr da defosionol o r naill iaith i iaith arall er chwanegu gwybodaeth, er egorud deall, ac er pureiddio moesau da').[52] Few of those writing such books concerned themselves with the controversial aspects of religion; nearly all their works were aimed at raising the level of day-to-day belief and conduct. They were directed at the heads of households, the property-owners great and small, whose duty it was not only to accept religious obligations on their own account but also 'to be able to instruct

---

[49] Glanmor Williams, 'Edward James a Llyfr yr Homiliau', *Morgannwg*, XXV (1981), 79–99.
[50] Glanmor Williams, 'Religion and Welsh Literature in the Age of the Reformation', *The Welsh and their Religion*, pp. 158–61.
[51] Huw Lewys, *Perl mewn Adfyd* (1595), ed. W. J. Gruffydd (Caerdydd, 1929), p. [xvii].
[52] David Rowlands, *Disce Mori*; Hughes, *Rhagymadroddion*, p. 132.

their children and their households in the principles of the faith' ('i fedru dyscu eu plant a'u tylwyth gartref y ngwyddorion y ffydd').[53] Almost without exception, their authors expressed their intention of writing in a plain, unadorned style, as Robert Lloyd put it, 'contenting myself with such ordinary words as the commonalty of the country are familiar with and understand' ('gan ymfodloni ar cyfryw eiriau sathredig, ac y mae cyffredin y wlâd yn gydnabyddus a hwynt, ac yn yspys ynddynt').[54] Protestations of this kind ought not to let it be supposed that these authors wrote in a debased manner. On the contrary, the generation of the 1620s and 1630s — John Davies, Rowland Vaughan, Robert Lloyd and Oliver Thomas — expressed themselves with a singular sureness and felicity of touch. An even higher peak was attained by the most masterly of the Puritan authors of the 1640s and 1650s, Morgan Llwyd,[55] widely recognized as one of the two or three greatest exponents of Welsh writing. By this time, three or four generations of Welsh prose authors, building on the foundation laid by the Welsh Bible, had shaped a new, pliant, and virile prose, which conveyed to those of their countrymen who could read the core truths of the Reformation.

Welsh poetry, like the prose, had its own contribution to make to the expression of religious truth and sentiment. The classical *cynghanedd* poetry was too conservative and custom-bound to lend itself readily to the ideas of a new age. Conventional poets refused all overtures made to them by critics like Edmwnd Prys that they should abandon their customary ways and embrace a new role as poets of Christian learning and the printed book.[56] The *cynghanedd* verse was to play its part in the main through the medium of praise-poetry directed at the leading Protestant bishops and clergy, many of whom, by contrast with their predecessors of the medieval period, were resident, Welsh-speaking Welshmen. Some among them, notably Richard Davies at Abergwili, and William Morgan at Mathern and St Asaph, maintained households which were nerve centres of literary as well as religious activity. Nothing prompted fountains of ecstatic poetic greeting on anything like the same scale as Morgan's Bible.[57]

Much more telling than the part played by the *canu caeth* (fixed-metre verse) was that of the *canu rhydd*, the poetry of the free-metre poets. In

---

[53] Oliver Thomas, *Carwr y Cymry*, ed. John Ballinger (Caerdydd, 1930), p. 8.
[54] Robert Lloyd, *Llwybr hyffordd yn cyfarwyddo yr anghyfarwydd i'r nefoedd* (Llundain, 1630), sig. A10r; Hughes, *Rhagymadroddion*, p. 130.
[55] Hugh Bevan, *Morgan Llwyd y Llenor* (Caerdydd, 1954); M. Wynn Thomas, *Morgan Llwyd* (Caerdydd, 1984); idem, *Morgan Llwyd, ei Gyfeillion a'i Gyfnod* (Caerdydd, 1991).
[56] Williams, *The Welsh and their Religion*, pp. 162–3; Gruffydd Aled Williams, *Edmwnd Prys a Wiliam Cynwal* (Caerdydd, 1986).
[57] Gruffydd, 'The Translating of the Bible', passim.

cwndidau, *carolau* and *halsingod*, and, most of all, in Edmwnd Prys's *salmau cân* (metrical psalms) and Vicar Prichard's popular verses, they had a decisive function to fulfil. Free poetry, by its very nature, was far better adapted for religious teaching, and far easier for the illiterate and semi-literate to memorize, than verse written in *cynghanedd*. Nowhere was this more convincingly borne out than in the popular reaction to the work of Edmwnd Prys and Vicar Prichard. Prys contended, 'all children, servants and every unlearned person will learn a verse of a carol, whereas only a scholar could learn a *cywydd* or some other skilful song' ('pob plant, gweinidogion, a phobl annyscedic a ddyscant bennill o garol, lle ni allai ond ysgolhaig ddyscu Cywydd neu gerdd gyfarwydd arall').[58] The immediate, immense, and enduring success attendant upon his psalms, composed in simple metre and plain language, bore out his judgement: ninety-nine editions of them were published between 1621 and 1885. Similar success awaited Vicar Prichard's homely verses. They, as he said, aimed at no artistic composition:

> Ni cheisiais ddim cywrein-waith,
> Ond mesur esmwyth, perffaith,
> Hawdd i'w ddysgu ar fyr dro,
> Gan bawb a'i clywo deirgwaith.[59]

(I attempted no artistic composition but smooth and perfect metre, easily and quickly learned by everyone who hears it three times.)

Vicar Prichard had hoped to reinforce the success of his poems by reproducing them in print, but died before he could do so. They were, however, published by Stephen Hughes in 1658, and from then onwards exercised an extraordinary appeal for ordinary people; between 1658 and 1820 no fewer than 52 editions appeared.[60] The religious poetry simplified and made memorizable what was contained in more depth and detail in the prose texts. It paraphrased the content of the Bible; it repeated in verse the content of the Prayer Book, homily and catechism; and it summarized in concise, everyday language the prolix arguments of long theological works. As long as the large majority of the Welsh remained illiterate or barely literate, these poems were the most effective way of appealing to them.

It was not only the Protestants who appreciated the point of reaching their audience through the mother tongue; Catholics were hardly less

---

[58] T. H. Parry-Williams, *Canu Rhydd Cynnar* (Caerdydd, 1932), p. xxxvii.
[59] D. Gwenallt Jones, *Y Ficer Prichard a 'Canwyll y Cymry'* (Caernarfon, 1946), p. 50.
[60] R. Brinley Jones, *'A Lanterne to their Feete'* (Porth-y-rhyd, 1994), pp. 26–31.

aware of it.[61] Although the vernacular did not figure as centrally in Catholic worship and teaching, the medieval church had always been concerned to make use of it. The revived Roman church of the Counter-Reformation, perceiving what an effective instrument native speech was among Protestants, made considerable use of it for popular instruction of its adherents. In other respects, also, Welsh Catholics and Protestants, in spite of being irreconcilably opposed to one another in doctrine, had more in common than might have been supposed. Both groups were intensely patriotic and shared the same pride in what they believed to be the ancient, distinctive and illustrious history, language, and literature of the Welsh.[62] Each side also set great store by literacy and the printed book. In the effort to produce a printed literature they faced many of the same obstacles. Both experienced a comparable difficulty in finding generous patrons to provide money to meet the expense of printing; and neither could count on a large, enthusiastic, or literate public for their books. Catholics were, in addition, shut out from English printing presses by strict government censorship. They were, consequently, obliged to set up their own secret, and usually short-lived, printing presses, like the one in the cave at Rhiwledin near Llandudno,[63] or to print their books on the Continent, smuggle them in and distribute them clandestinely. Or else they had to depend on the painstaking labour and amazing devotion of Welsh manuscript copyists like Llywelyn Siôn.[64] A manuscript version of a Welsh text might be as much of a literary medium for its author as a printed book. Several manuscript copies of popular Catholic texts were often secretly circulating at the same time, and recusants encouraged their distribution 'as far as they will go', even though, if detected with such a manuscript in their possession, they might have to disavow all knowledge of how they had come by it. A young student like Robert Gwyn adopted the expedient of writing a Welsh letter to his family, in the expectation that many other Catholics would read it.[65] Recusant landowners like John Edwards of Chirk exercised their authority over their dependants and tenants by reading Welsh Catholic manuscripts to them when they met for worship in secret.[66]

[61] Geraint Bowen, 'Rhyddiaith Reciwsantiaid Cymru' (unpubl. University of Wales PhD thesis, 1978); idem, 'Llenyddiaeth Gatholig y Cymry (1559–1829): rhyddiaith a barddoniaeth' (unpubl. University of Liverpool MA thesis, 1952–3); see also *LlLlG*.

[62] The outstanding example was Gruffydd Robert. Gruffydd Robert, *Gramadeg Cymraeg*, ed. G. J. Williams (Caerdydd, 1939).

[63] R. Geraint Gruffydd, *Argraffwyr Cyntaf Cymru* (Caerdydd, 1972).

[64] G. J. Williams, *Traddodiad Llenyddol Morgannwg* (Caerdydd, 1948), pp. 157–60.

[65] Robert Gwyn, *Gwssanaeth y Gwŷr Newydd*, ed. Geraint Bowen (Caerdydd, 1970).

[66] Geraint Bowen, 'Gweithiau apologetig reciwsantiaid Cymru', *NLWJ*, XIII, no. 2 (1963), 174–8.

A number of the Welsh Catholic works written during this period seem to have been lost, while others have left only their titles. Of some thirty or so Catholic religious and devotional prose texts traced by Dr Geraint Bowen, only some half a dozen were printed, and four of these were catechisms.[67] The overwhelming majority of them, like the books written by Protestants, were translations of well-established classics. They were primarily intended to prop up the faith of loyal Welsh-speaking Roman Catholic minorities in an age of intensifying pressures. Their authors maintained that they were writing simply and clearly for the benefit of the unlearned, that is, for those who had no formal education in the classical languages, but were not necessarily illiterate or unwilling to listen to others reading to them. The books were the work of a tiny handful of dedicated individuals, mostly priests, writing in accordance with their own vision of the needs of their church, and not in conformity with any overall plan or direction, which simply did not exist. Indeed, their efforts, whether by writing or by word of mouth, may have suffered much because the English exiles, who chiefly directed Counter-Reformation enterprises, did not properly understand or take into account the national sympathies of the Welsh or the critical need to appeal to them through the medium of the Welsh language.[68] Many of the Welsh seminary priests found it difficult or impossible to venture back into districts where they were known, but priests who could not speak Welsh would have been of little use in such places.

Catholics seem to have been just as aware as Protestants of the value of Welsh verse as a means of religious instruction and inspiration. A considerable quantity of Catholic poetry was circulated among Welsh people; but, and not surprisingly in view of the persecution of Catholic believers, much less of it has survived than of corresponding Protestant verse. Most of that still extant appears to be content to urge a simple and generally acceptable Christian piety, punctuated with occasional outbursts against Protestants. However, some of the poems by Richard Gwyn, put to death in Wrexham in 1584 – the only Welsh poetry of the period ever to find its way into print although all of it has long since disappeared – were distinctly more combative and controversial in tone.[69] This may have been because his poems were sparked off by the growing strength of heresy, and even some of the more aggressive Puritan traits within it. Gwyn, for example, dismissed the English Bible as being full of false

---

[67] Williams, *The Welsh and their Religion*, p. 153.
[68] John Bossy, *The English Catholic Community, 1570–1850* (London, 1975), pp. 97–9.
[69] T. H. Parry-Williams (ed.), *Carolau Richard White [1537?–1584]* (Caerdydd, 1931); D. Aneurin Thomas, *The Welsh Elizabethan Catholic Martyrs* (Cardiff, 1971).

imaginings, and denounced with searing economy the sacrilege of Protestant services:

> Yn lle allor trestyl trist
> Yn lle Krist mae bara.[70]

(In place of an altar a pathetic trestle, instead of Christ, bread.)

In spite of the heroism of Richard Gwyn and other Catholic martyrs and sufferers at the hands of the Protestant state, the recusant community remained at all times a small, embattled minority. Nevertheless, in the centres of its strength, like parts of Flintshire and Monmouthshire, it continued to be remarkably tenacious and resilient, actually adding to its numbers down to the 1640s.[71] Its employment of the Welsh language no doubt helped to indoctrinate the faithful, stiffen morale, and create a tradition of Catholic literary activity in Wales which lasted until the eighteenth century. The Privy Council was apprehensive about such seditious pursuits, and from time to time came down heavily upon those who circulated their literary wares. The son of the famous historian, David Powel, claimed that his father had for many years acquainted the Council with news of such subversive Catholic writings and speeches against the queen.[72] Perhaps the surest testimony to the value which Catholic believers placed on Welsh recusant literature was the persistence with which they clung to it throughout the sixteenth and seventeenth centuries in spite of all the difficulties they encountered in producing and disseminating it.

Who were the primary targets of all this religious activity conducted through the Welsh language in the form of prose, poetry, services, sermons, catechizing, and other forms of instruction? True, there were some people in Wales who would have been perfectly capable of absorbing the message in English. There were English-speaking populations along the south Wales coast in places like south Pembrokeshire, the Vale of Glamorgan, the plain of Gwent, and along the eastern border with England. There were others in all the market towns and among many of the gentry, lawyers, trading classes, and a number of the clergy. William Salesbury was of the opinion that there were some English speakers in most parishes in Wales.[73] An indication of the spread of the English

---

[70] Parry-Williams, *Carolau Richard White*, p. 32.
[71] Williams, *The Welsh and their Religion*, p. 169.
[72] PRO, Star Chamber Proceedings, 5/P48/25.
[73] Thomas, *The Life and Work of Bishop Davies and William Salesbury*, p. 67.

language may be gleaned from the fact that more Welshmen wrote books in English than in their native tongue in the sixteenth century. Yet the fact remained that the large majority of the population of Wales could be successfully appealed to only in Welsh. Either they knew no language but their own, or were more comfortable in it than in any other. As the preamble to the act of 1563 for the translation of the Bible acknowledged: 'the English Tongue . . . is not understanded of the most and greatest Number of all her Majesty's most loving and obedient Subjects inhabiting within . . . Wales'.[74] That meant, as all the writers most sensitive to their countrymen's condition knew, that unless religion was brought to them effectively in their mother tongue, they were likely to go to perdition. There were ardent Protestants who were convinced that the whole point of the providential preservation of the Welsh language by the Almighty was to ensure that news of 'Christ's second birth'[75] or the 'second flowering of Christ's gospel' could be proclaimed to the people in Welsh. Moreover, the inculcation of religion in Welsh would have the additional advantage of keeping the language and its literature alive and healthy. This was a consideration of the utmost relevance to those leading humanists, on both sides of the religious divide, who were steeped in the traditions of the cultural past of Wales.

That being so, the champions of religion and language must have given careful thought to the question of those at whom they were primarily aiming. It would seem very probable that there were two groups in particular whom they wished to reach: the clergy and the heads of households. The clergy would have seemed both to Catholics and Protestants to have an essential 'knock-on' role in conveying to their flocks what they had themselves absorbed. Both parties were also agreed that the clergy were seriously in need of reform. Greater emphasis was placed on their formal education – in seminary, or in grammar school and university, though it must be admitted that none of those institutions made any provision whatsoever for studying the Welsh language. The Protestant community, however, paid special attention to ensuring that a vernacular Bible and Prayer Book were available. It also placed particular emphasis on preaching, providing printed homilies for clerics who were not licensed to preach their own sermons, and free-metre verses, *cwndidau,* or 'sermons in song', as well. Even so, improvement among the clergy was painfully gradual. The established Church was too poor to offer many comfortable livings for learned clergymen. Huw Lewys complained that the majority of the clergy were 'lazy in their office and calling, without

---

[74] Bowen, *Statutes,* pp. 149–50.
[75] Jones, *William Salesbury,* p. 38.

being accustomed to preach or expound the mystery of God's word to the people, but being dumb and without speech, like dogs without barking, bells without clappers, or a candle under a bushel' ('yn ddiog yn ei swydd ai galwedigaeth, heb ymarddel a phregethu ac a deongl dirgelwch gair Duw i'r bobl, eythr byw yn fudion, ac yn aflafar, fal cwn heb gyfarth, clych heb dafodeu, ne gannwyll dan lestr').[76] Well into the seventeenth century, complaints about their inadequacies continued to be plentiful.

The other strategically important group consisted of heads of households. In many European countries where Protestant doctrine took root, what was experienced was not so much the 'priesthood of all believers' as the 'priesthood of the *paterfamilias*'. Vicar Prichard, and others like him, had no doubts what functions a godly householder ought to discharge:

> Bydd Reolwr, bydd offeiriad,
> Bydd Gynghorwr, bydd yn Ynad,
> Ar dy dŷ, ac ar dy bobol,
> I reoli pawb wrth reol.[77]

(Be a ruler, be a priest, be a counsellor, be a justice, over thy house, and over thy people, to rule them all with law.)

Such heads of households included parish gentry, freeholders, clergymen, merchants, lawyers, and the like. At the lower end of the scale, also, were to be found substantial tenants and husbandmen; men of sufficient status to be expected to bear the responsibility of filling local offices such as that of parish constable or churchwarden. All were counted upon to combine under the greater gentry's direction to uphold the established religion and the social order. Hence the necessity of encouraging literacy among this group. A mild Puritan like Oliver Thomas tried to shame his compatriots into learning to read by comparing them unfavourably with the English, among whom, he claimed, even the poorest could read their Bibles.[78] Vicar Prichard sought to encourage them by assuring them, more in hope than expectation, that where the will existed they could manage the task of learning to read within a month.[79] It was all the more important that this group should not only be able to read and acquire godly religious opinions themselves, but also be in a position to instil them into others

---

[76] Lewys, *Perl mewn Adfyd*, introduction [xxi]; cf. Hughes, *Rhagymadroddion*, p. 101.
[77] Glanmor Williams, *Grym Tafodau Tân: Ysgrifau Hanesyddol ar Grefydd a Diwylliant* (Llandysul, 1984), p. 162.
[78] Thomas, *Carwr y Cymry*, pp. 23, 38, 39, 71, 100.
[79] Williams, *The Welsh and their Religion*, p. 45.

who came under their authority: wives, children, servants, sub-tenants, labourers, and even paupers and beggars. It need hardly be added that virtually all the latter groups would consist of monoglot Welsh speakers. There is reason to suppose, nevertheless, that this theory of a society peopled with God-fearing citizens setting a shining example to lesser mortals fell far short in practice. There was more preaching of duties than carrying them out, and far more exhortation than execution. Seventeenth-century Puritan critics would continue to rank Wales among the 'dark corners of the land'.[80]

For all that, the years from 1536 to 1660 witnessed profound shifts in the nature of religion and language in Wales. First of all, Wales became one of the Protestant countries of Europe, with all that that implied for the place of the mother tongue in worship and devotion. There is no doubt that, initially, it was the intention of the Crown that English should permanently replace Latin as the language of religion throughout the kingdom. That, to all intents and purposes, is officially what happened in the other Celtic-speaking parts of the realm, i.e. Cornwall, the Isle of Man, and Ireland. Yet that astute Welsh antiquary, George Owen of Henllys, shrewdly observed that English was as unintelligible to the Welsh (as it was, for that matter, to the other Celts) as Latin had been in what he described as 'the time of blindness'.[81] A similar cultural imperialism took place in Norway, where the Danes introduced the Reformation in Danish even though most of the Norwegians found it difficult to understand. Fortunately for the Welsh, there had always been, from the first introduction of the Reformation, a small but enlightened and resolute group who had perceived that the Reformation would never really take root unless it was presented in Welsh. They were also convinced that the language had the inherent resources to furnish an appropriate translation. To William Salesbury, and later, William Morgan, and the small but committed group of humanist scholars they inspired, Wales owes the fact that it was ultimately to embrace the Reformation in its own language and not an alien one. Admittedly, the progress of the Reformation among the mass of the Welsh people was very slow. As late as 1630 Robert Lloyd, vicar of Chirk, complained in the introduction to his translation of *The Plain man's pathway to heaven* that they were negligent of religion and given up almost entirely to 'the playground, bowls, taverns, football, and tennis' ('y twmpath chwareu, a'r bowliau, ar tafarnau, a'r bêl-droed ar denis'),[82] and over a century later, Griffith Jones, Llanddowror, described

---

[80] J. E. C. Hill, 'Puritans and "the Dark Corners of the Land"', *TRHS*, 13 (1963), 77–102.
[81] Owen, *Description*, III, p. 57.
[82] Lloyd, *Llwybr Hyffordd*, sig. A10r; cf. Hughes, *Rhagymadroddion*, p. 128.

in despairing tones 'the brutish, gross and general ignorance in things pertaining to salvation'. He identified the basic weakness: 'how deplorably ignorant the poor people are who cannot read, even where constant preaching is not wanting'.[83] The Protestant religion was a religion of a book; it was intended principally for literates, and was seriously undermined by people who were unable to read for themselves. Not until the second half of the eighteenth century, when successful campaigns had been launched for the large-scale conquest of illiteracy, could the Reformation really come of age in Wales.[84] Yet it would be a serious mistake to underestimate the success of the Anglican Church, relatively speaking, in Wales in the period before 1642. It had certainly won a secure place in the affections of many of those who were literate, and some who were not. Loyalty to it, moreover, survived the disasters and defeats of the civil wars largely unshaken. Among a minority, however, the fervent 'Church puritanism' of the early Stuart era, strongly reinforced by the State encouragement given to the Puritan sects in the 1650s, and the fiery preaching of their leaders, prepared the way for the relatively rapid spread of their opinions among some of the Welsh-speaking sections of the people. The Puritan stalwart, Walter Cradock, testified that he had seen 'in the mountains of Wales, the most glorious work that I ever saw in England . . . The Gospel is run over the mountains between Brecknockshire and Monmouthshire, as the fire in the thatch'.[85] These early harbingers of Puritanism were preparing the ground for a Nonconformity whose chosen tongue would be overwhelmingly Welsh.[86]

Because the Reformation gave Welsh a place of honour in religion, in so doing it conferred upon the clergy a role of enhanced relevance in relation to the language. Already, throughout the medieval period, clerics had tended to cherish the national speech and had done much to accord it status and dignity, even to the extent of making formal representations to the Pope that Welsh-speaking bishops ought to be appointed to Welsh dioceses.[87] From the sixteenth century onwards, the language would matter even more to them. Since it had now become the language of worship they had no choice but to put forth their best efforts to uphold it. It was all the more to their credit that they should have done so when the language found no place in the education they underwent at university or

---

[83] Glanmor Williams, *Religion, Language, and Nationality in Wales* (Cardiff, 1979), p. 202.
[84] Williams, *Welsh Reformation Essays*, pp. 27–30.
[85] Quoted in Thomas Rees, *History of Protestant Nonconformity in Wales* (London, 1861), p. 77.
[86] R. Tudur Jones, *Hanes Annibynwyr Cymru* (Abertawe, 1966); T. M. Bassett, *The Welsh Baptists* (Swansea, 1977); Derec Llwyd Morgan, *The Great Awakening in Wales*, translated by Dyfnallt Morgan (London, 1988).
[87] Williams, *Welsh Church*, pp. 126–7.

grammar school. The clergy were the only educated group in the country which had a professional and personal interest in using the Welsh language in the course of their calling and maintaining its honour. The native culture of gentry and lawyers, especially from the seventeenth century onwards, was becoming persistently eroded by Anglicized modes and manners; and in the process, the bards, hitherto 'the architects of the language' ('penseiri'r iaith'), as Salesbury had described them,[88] were fast losing credit. It was clerics who largely took their place. Over the coming centuries, the stars of the Welsh literary firmament, major or minor, whether prose authors like John Davies, Morgan Llwyd, or Charles Edwards, or poets as different from one another as Edmwnd Prys, Vicar Prichard, or Goronwy Owen, were nearly all to be clerics. Similarly, the outstanding pioneers of popular education and instruction – Stephen Hughes, Samuel Jones, Brynllywarch, and Griffith Jones – were also clerics. If from the fields of Welsh education, literature, and book-publishing, the names of clergy and ministers were removed, little of substance would be left. The fact that in the Tudor and early Stuart periods most of the bishops and higher clergy, especially in north Wales, were themselves Welsh-speaking, helped a great deal in creating this awareness of the essential place of Welsh in religion. Even a bishop with a somewhat doubtful reputation, like William Hughes of St Asaph, could be taken to court for his unwillingness to institute a clergyman who was unable to speak Welsh. In 1585 he was proceeded against for his refusal to admit one Bagshaw to the living of Whittington on account of the insufficiency of his Welsh.[89] At the other end of Wales, in Swansea, the vicar, John After, was prosecuted in the consistory court by his parishioners in 1593 for not conducting services in Welsh, and was obliged by the court to do so.[90]

From the first appearance of the Bible, poets and scholars had been quick to appreciate that it had nearly as much to contribute to the language as to the religion of Wales. What they did not, and could not, realize was just how portentous it was going to be. It would have been virtually unthinkable for them to envisage a situation in which Welsh was in danger of not being spoken by the large majority of the population of Wales. Indeed, one of the most compelling reasons why men like Salesbury and Morgan undertook their translations was that there was so little prospect of the Welsh being able to read the Bible or anything else in any language but their own. Making Welsh the language of public

---

[88] Jones, *William Salesbury*, p. 4.
[89] D. R. Thomas, *History of the Diocese of St Asaph* (3 vols., Oswestry, 1908), I, p. 100.
[90] W. S. K. Thomas, *The History of Swansea from Rover Settlement to the Restoration* (Llandysul, 1990), p. 181.

worship in all those parishes where it was normally spoken, and the consequent need to furnish a Welsh Bible, service book, and ancillary literature, was, in the long run, the most crucial single factor in ensuring the survival of the language. If English had continued to be used for worship, then every parish church in Wales, however remote or inaccessible, would have become a focus for familiarizing people with that language. It would have had the effect of creating a universal and permanent network of extraneous influences in Wales where otherwise they would rarely or never have penetrated. The Welsh language would certainly have been gravely weakened and might well have disappeared. Not at once, naturally; it would have been a slow process but an inexorable one. The Act of Union of 1536 had already made English the language of government, administration, law, and justice, and in so doing had given a decisive impetus to the Anglicization of the upper classes. It was the act of 1563 which undid much of the effect of the earlier legislation by making Welsh an official language of religion. After all, the contacts of the mass of the population with government and justice were sporadic and peripheral; but the law of the land required every subject to attend church on Sunday. If English had been the only language heard there, then every parish church would have become a focus for its dissemination. In addition, it is necessary to estimate what the effect would have been if the clergy, instead of seeing it as their function to conduct services for their parishioners, to instruct, catechize, and preach to them in Welsh, had concluded it was their responsibility to induce them to learn English as quickly as might be. In this respect, there is a marked contrast between the status accorded to Welsh in religion and the continuingly inferior position occupied by the other Celtic languages.[91] The failure to accord them an enhanced status had a profound effect on their chances of survival. As spoken languages, Cornish and Manx disappeared altogether in time. Even Irish, spoken in the sixteenth century by many more people than Welsh, has declined more rapidly than its kindred language. Even without the use of Welsh in churches, it has to be conceded that the language might well have continued to be spoken, but only as an assorted mass of peasant dialects, lacking dignity, correctness, or uniformity. It was the Bible, according to Siôn Dafydd Rhys, which had led to the cultivation of the language on the part of learned men in their own time: 'having been cultivated by learned men of our own time and that especially because of turning into Welsh the body of the holy Scripture' ('wedi dechrau "[c]affael peth gwrtaith gan wyrda dysgedig o'n hamser ni, a hynny yn enwedig o ran Cymreicáu corff yr Ysgrythur

---

[91] Williams and Jones, *The Celts and the Renaissance,* passim.

Lân" ").[92] It was this which had given Wales a standard language of distinction, which like the poetic language it replaced, was common to the whole country and intelligible to most of its people.

If Welsh had survived at all without achieving a new start of this kind, if it had dragged out an existence as a debased peasant patois, it could hardly, by any stretch of the imagination, have continued as a fitting medium for literature. Such a predicament would have been intensified by the sad and rapid decline of the bardic order from the end of the sixteenth century onwards. If the function of the bards had been extinguished without being replaced by an adequate substitute, the prospect for Welsh as a literary language would have been catastrophic. Not only was the bardic order in irreversible decline, but there were also seductively powerful temptations for Welsh authors to write in English, to which many yielded.[93] It was the Welsh Bible which, like Luther's Bible in Germany, constituted the standard and model for the work of all those subsequent authors who wrote in Welsh. The Bible and the works based upon it fulfilled the most eager aspirations of the sixteenth-century Welsh humanists.[94] It gave substance to their conviction that Welsh could meet all the demands that the new combination of Renaissance learning and Reformation theology imposed upon it. In the following centuries the greater part of what was written and published in Welsh – in prose especially – derived from a religious or moral purpose. Comparatively little of it was primarily motivated by literary ambition at all; its function was overwhelmingly didactic. Nevertheless, a virtually new prose tradition was created; and, in addition, the success of Prys's metrical psalms and Vicar Prichard's verses set the stage for the rich and fecund hymnology and the religious lyric verse of the eighteenth and nineteenth centuries. Limited the arena of this literature may have been, and its themes restricted, but within its own confines a remarkably rich and accomplished output was maintained. Welsh was the only one of the Celtic literatures which successfully spanned the transition from the oral and manuscript tradition of the Middle Ages to the printed literature of modern times.

Finally, the period from 1536 to 1660 witnessed an impressive interweaving of religion, language, and literature with a compelling sense

---

[92] Gruffydd, *Gair ar Waith,* p. 73.
[93] Glanmor Williams, 'Welsh authors and their books, 1500–1642' in M. B. Line (ed.), *The World of Books and Information* (British Library, 1987), pp. 187–96.
[94] Gruffydd, *Gair ar Waith,* pp. 87–112; Bowen, *Traddodiad Rhyddiaith,* passim; Thomas Parry, *History of Welsh Literature* (Oxford, 1955), chapter 8; G. J. Williams, *Agweddau ar Hanes Dysg Gymraeg* (Caerdydd, 1969), chapter 2.

of national identity among the Welsh.[95] This was as true in many respects of the Catholics in their midst as of the Protestants. The former, at home and in exile, showed themselves to be deeply patriotic, as their cogent criticisms of some of the enterprises sponsored by their fellow-Catholics among the English, and many references in their written works, brought to light. But their allegiance to a universal church and loyalty to a supra-national papacy inevitably imposed restraints on their pride in a nation and especially in that monarchy regarded by Protestants as a 'national' one. Protestants experienced no such inhibitions. They felt themselves to be identified with a regime whose rulers were sympathetic to their ideals. They applauded the supposed 'British' virtues of James I hardly less than those of the Tudors.[96] They even went to the extent of praising their ancient enemies, the English, whose demeanour had once been that of ravening wolves, for having become, since the Reformation, careful shepherds.[97] They plausibly represented the Reformation as a reversion to the pristine purity of the apostolically planted religion of the early Britons in the most splendid epoch of their history, 'the first of all the provinces to receive Christ's name openly' ('y gyntaf o'r holl daleithiau i dderbyn enw Crist yn agored').[98] That original faith was being resurrected in the sixteenth century as the fulfilment at its most sublimated level of the prophecy of the restoration of the ancient glories of Wales. Their pride in a unique blend of religiosity and Welshness, founded in the early modern period, continued for centuries afterwards. It encouraged among the Welsh a belief that they were an elect people, on a par with, and ultimately descended from the same stock as the Hebrews themselves. Nothing was better calculated to preserve their own sense of a separate and special identity.

---

[95] Gruffydd, *Gair ar Waith*, pp. 135–58; Williams, *The Welsh and their Religion*, pp. 169–72, 226–9.
[96] A. H. Dodd, 'Wales and the Scottish Succession 1570–1605', *THSC* (1937), 201–5.
[97] Charles Edwards, *Y Ffydd Ddi-ffuant*, ed. G. J. Williams (Caerdydd, 1936), pp. 209–10.
[98] Gruffydd, *Gair ar Waith*, p. 101.

7

The Established Church, Dissent and the Welsh Language c.1660–1811

ERYN M. WHITE

IN HIS preface to *Antiquae Linguae Britannicae* in 1621 Dr John Davies of Mallwyd claimed that God had preordained the Welsh people to communicate with Him in the Welsh language. He fervently believed that were it not for divine providence the language would never have overcome all the obstacles in the way of its survival.[1] Through the works of Davies and other humanists of the period, the Welsh were encouraged to believe that the Welsh language was a pure and sacred tongue presented to their ancestors by Gomer, the grandson of Noah. This legend proved to be a most enduring one and was vigorously upheld for many years by historians and scholars, including Charles Edwards and Theophilus Evans. It is true that the language merited a position of importance as a medium of worship. Since Elizabethan times, religious reformers had argued that the Welsh language was essential as a means of disseminating religious truths, since it was the only language understood by the majority of the Welsh people. In his preface to the 1588 Bible, William Morgan conceded that it would be most desirable for the Welsh to learn English, but he believed that it would be cruel and barbaric to condemn them in the meantime to perish for want of the Word of God by depriving them of the Scriptures in their own tongue.[2] In order to save souls, therefore, it was necessary to make use of the Welsh language among the monoglot Welsh. In a period when the language lacked any status in law and administration, religion was one of the few domains in which it could be

---

[1] Ceri Davies (ed.), *Rhagymadroddion a Chyflwyniadau Lladin 1551–1632* (Caerdydd, 1980), pp. 117–18.
[2] Ibid., pp. 68–9.

dominant.[3] In areas where the Welsh language seemed to be threatened by decline, religion frequently proved to be its most enduring stronghold.[4]

During the second half of the seventeenth century and throughout the eighteenth century, it was considered obligatory to conduct the services of the established Church through the medium of Welsh in Welsh-speaking areas, according to the principle established by the twenty-fourth article of the Anglican Church, and by the Act for the Translation of the Scriptures in 1563 and the Act of Uniformity of 1662. These statutes ordained that Welsh services should be conducted in Welsh-speaking parishes. In the 1760s Evan Evans (Ieuan Fardd) referred to the Act for the Translation of the Scriptures as the 'charter of our religious liberty' because he believed it established the legal right of the Welsh to have church services in their native tongue.

Although the vast majority of Welsh people at the end of the seventeenth century were loyal to the established Church in Wales, there is no doubt that the Church itself faced dire difficulties. It suffered from lack of leadership by its bishops. Its structure and administration were the legacy of the Middle Ages and were totally inadequate to meet the challenge of Dissent and the new industrial society. Most of the difficulties the Church faced, however, stemmed from sheer poverty. The condition of the Church in south Wales was particularly woeful since the right to collect tithes in a large number of parishes had fallen into the hands of lay impropriators following the dissolution of the monasteries. It was estimated that the dioceses of St Asaph and Bangor in the mid-eighteenth century were both worth £1,400 per annum, while St David's was worth £900, and Llandaff, the Cinderella of the dioceses, a mere £500.

Since Welsh sees were so poor, bishops tended to regard them as mere stepping stones to more lucrative appointments. Edward Cressett was an exception among the bishops of the period in that he rejoiced in his promotion to Llandaff in 1748. Such was his pleasure that he hoped he would never have to leave Llandaff, and his wish was granted when he died as incumbent of the see in 1755. The majority of his contemporaries, however, regarded a period of service in a Welsh bishopric as a penance to be endured for as short a period as possible. Many of them spent their time casting envious eyes towards the glittering prizes to be won over the border. 'Though I love Wales very much', said Thomas Herring, bishop

---

[3] In contrast, it has been suggested that English literature in the eighteenth century associated the English language with the law and the constitution in order to promote national consciousness. John Barrell, *English Literature in History, 1730–80* (London, 1983), pp. 110–75.

[4] Philip N. Jones, 'Baptist Chapels as an Index of Cultural Transition in the South Wales Coalfield before 1914', *JHG*, II (1976), 356; Colin H. Williams, 'Language Decline and Nationalist Resurgence in Wales' (unpubl. University of Wales PhD thesis, 1978), p. 103.

of Bangor, in 1742, 'I would not choose to be reduced to butter, milk, and lean mutton.'[5] John Gilbert gave thanks for a merciful release when he was translated from Llandaff to Sarum in 1748. Some bishops went so far as to request to be translated before the process of consecration had even been completed. It has been claimed that only bishops who fell from favour remained in Wales for any length of time. Richard Watson, for example, is said to have been obliged to remain in Llandaff throughout the period 1782–1816 as a result of political indiscretions.

Bishops complained not only of the lack of financial reward but also of the difficulties involved in attempting to travel to Wales to visit their flocks. Their presence was required in the House of Lords during the winter months in order to cast their votes for the government which had appointed them. It was only during the summer months that they were free to visit their dioceses and even then precious little enthusiasm was evident for the annual pilgrimage to Wales. Some preferred not to undertake the journey at all. Benjamin Hoadly, the lame bishop of Bangor (1716–21), won notoriety for not once visiting his diocese over a period of six years, although it is said that he attempted to travel there by sea from Bristol during the summer of 1719. His physical disability did not, however, prevent him from climbing the ecclesiastical ladder to gain wealth and influence as bishop of Sarum and later of Winchester.

The Church, therefore, suffered as a result of the absence and indifference of its spiritual leaders. Moreover, most of those leaders were Englishmen who displayed scant respect for Wales and its people. During the period immediately following the Restoration, a number of conscientious Welsh-speaking bishops were appointed, but even the likes of William Lloyd at St Asaph (1680–92) and Humphrey Humphreys at Bangor (1689–1701) proved unable to resist the temptation to cross the border to improve their lot. Humphrey Humphreys won respect and approval as a result of his patronage of Welsh publishers: in 1701 Ellis Wynne dedicated *Rheol Buchedd Sanctaidd*, his translation of Jeremy Taylor's *Holy Living*, to him as the person best suited to provide succour for the book. In dedicating to Humphreys his translation of John Fox's *Time and the End of Time* in 1707, Samuel Williams thanked him for all his kindness towards the country and its language, describing him as a foster-father and an excellent supporter of the ancient British tongue.[6] William

---

[5] Norman Sykes, *Church and State in England in the XVIIIth Century* (Cambridge, 1934), p. 94.
[6] Samuel Williams, *Amser a Diwedd Amser* (Llundain, 1707), sig. A2r–v; Owain W. Jones, 'The Welsh Church in the Eighteenth Century' in David Walker (ed.), *A History of the Church in Wales* (Penarth, 1976), p. 109; Geraint H. Jenkins, 'Bywiogrwydd Crefyddol a Llenyddol Dyffryn Teifi, 1689–1740' in *Cadw Tŷ Mewn Cwmwl Tystion: Ysgrifau Hanesyddol ar Grefydd a Diwylliant* (Llandysul, 1990), p. 138.

Lloyd also demonstrated his support for the language by ensuring that Welsh speakers were appointed to Welsh-speaking parishes in his diocese. Upon his translation to Lichfield in 1692, he urged the Archbishop of Canterbury to appoint a Welshman as his successor at St Asaph. William Beaw, bishop of Llandaff, believed that Lloyd's influence was responsible for his failure to gain the bishopric, and he complained subsequently that he suspected Lloyd had been whispering in the archbishop's ear the radical notion that any bishop appointed to Wales should be a Welshman.[7]

Despite the efforts of William Lloyd, this principle was not implemented. Between 1727 and 1870 no Welsh-speaking Welshman was appointed to a Welsh diocese and knowledge of the language was not considered necessary for such appointments. Bishops were selected on the basis of their political loyalty to the government rather than their suitability to serve Wales. The result was an estrangement between the shepherd and his flock. As Jenkin Evans said: 'How can the Sheep know the Shepherd's Voice, when they do not know the meaning of one Syllable he says?'[8] Many 'Esgyb Eingl' (Anglo Bishops) nursed a contemptuous attitude towards the Welsh language. Although Richard Smallbrooke, bishop of St David's (1724–31), was said to have learnt a smattering of Welsh, the majority of bishops displayed a profound lack of sympathy towards the country's language and culture and a number of them made no attempt to conceal their scorn. Edward Cressett's fondness for his diocese did not apply to the mother tongue of the majority of his parishioners.[9] Philip Bisse, bishop of St David's, refused to subscribe to Welsh translations since he believed they would prevent the spread of the English language.[10] The most uncompromising enemy of the Welsh language among the bishops, however, was Robert Hay Drummond (a 'poisonous Scotsman', according to William Morris), who was appointed bishop of St Asaph in 1748. During a dinner for the clergy and prominent laymen of the diocese he proclaimed publicly that it would be beneficial if the Welsh language were completely uprooted. In a sermon preached in 1753 he aired his opinion that the Welsh language should be eliminated and that the Welsh would benefit greatly from broadening their horizons

---

[7] A. Tindal Hart, *William Lloyd 1627–1717* (London, 1952), p. 85; Sykes, op. cit., pp. 363–4.

[8] Anon., *A Dialogue between the Rev. Mr. Jenkin Evans . . . and Mr. Peter Dobson . . . concerning Bishops, Particularly the Bishops in the Principality of Wales* (London, 1744), pp. 56–7.

[9] C. L. S. Linnell (ed.), *The Diaries of Thomas Wilson, D.D. 1731–37 and 1750* (London, 1964), p. 235.

[10] Mary Clement (ed.), *Correspondence and Minutes of the S.P.C.K. relating to Wales, 1699–1740* (Cardiff, 1952), p. 42.

and uniting with the English in language as well as government.[11] Such sentiments enraged the Morrises of Anglesey and their circle of cultured Welshmen. Evan Evans emerged as the most scathing critic of the bishops, composing a vitriolic essay around 1764–5 condemning the Church which he believed was in urgent need of reform. He attributed all the weaknesses of the Church to oppressive foreigners who cared little for the souls of the people and were motivated largely by pecuniary considerations. It was utterly unreasonable, he maintained, to expect the entire population to change its language in order to accommodate four English bishops.[12]

Despite the prejudices of the likes of Bishop Drummond, it remained necessary to conduct Welsh services throughout most of the country for the simple reason that so many worshippers could not understand any other language. The use of Welsh in the context of public worship remained essential in most parts of Wales throughout the eighteenth century. The language of church services therefore provides a valuable insight into the distribution of the Welsh and English languages. Each bishop was required to hold a visitation as soon as possible after his consecration and every three years subsequently. Prior to each visitation a list of queries was distributed to the clergy and churchwardens of each parish with questions relating to the services held, the condition of the buildings and the behaviour of the parishioners. The answers contain a wealth of detail and, most valuably, a statement regarding the language of public worship in the churches and chapelries.

The language question appeared in the diocese of Llandaff for the first time in 1771 and subsequently in the years 1774, 1781, 1784, 1788, 1791 and 1795 during the eighteenth century, as well as in 1802, 1805, 1809 and 1813 in the early nineteenth century. Fewer returns have survived from the diocese of St David's, by far the largest of the four Welsh dioceses. St David's consisted of the counties of Brecon, Cardigan, Carmarthen, Pembroke, Radnor, part of Montgomery, three parishes in Monmouth and the Gower Peninsula in Glamorgan. The returns of the clergy are only available for the years 1755 and 1799, and also for 1762 for the Archdeaconry of Brecon. In the early nineteenth century, returns are available for the years 1807, 1813 and 1828. In the diocese of Bangor the language question appeared for the first time in 1749 and subsequently in the queries for 1776, 1778, 1788, 1807, 1811 and 1817. No question was posed regarding language in St Asaph until 1791. Returns are also

---

[11] *ML*, I, pp. 237, 288.
[12] NLW MS 2009B, passim; Geraint H. Jenkins, 'Yr Eglwys "Wiwlwys Olau" a'i Beirniaid', *Ceredigion*, X, no. 2 (1985), 140–1.

available for 1795, 1799, 1806 and 1809. In addition, some of the reports of the rural deans of St Asaph from the mid-eighteenth century have survived and they throw considerable light on the language of public worship in the diocese prior to 1791.

One of the most common complaints against the bishops was that they appointed monoglot Englishmen to Welsh benefices, thereby preventing Welsh people from worshipping in the only language they understood. But the evidence of the visitation returns clearly shows that the clergy who served in Welsh-speaking parishes were usually able to conduct services in Welsh. There were many who would have echoed this statement by Owen Owen, vicar of Llanilar, in 1813: 'I am a Welshman born, a native of this Parish, and lived in this Parish and the Neighbourhood all my days.'[13] To a large extent, for practical reasons it was necessary to waive the principle that only graduates should be ordained in Wales. As Bishop William Lloyd explained to Archbishop Sancroft in 1686, there were more benefices than graduates in the country and it was more important to secure Welsh speakers for those benefices than to fill them with graduates.[14] In addition, the stipend was frequently too low to attract highly qualified candidates. In those parishes where the parish priest was not conversant with the Welsh language, it was customary to appoint a curate who did speak Welsh to minister on his behalf. In 1763 Neville Walter, rector of Llanwytherin in Monmouthshire, declared that since he was unfamiliar with the Welsh language he had installed a curate to serve the parish while he remained in his Hampshire benefice.[15] Thomas Mills Hoare, vicar of Newport, Monmouthshire, confessed in 1771 that he had never once crossed the threshold of his chapel in Betws although he had been appointed to the benefice in 1760. Since most of the inhabitants did not understand English and he could not understand Welsh, he thought it appropriate to appoint a Welsh-speaking curate.[16]

There were occasional instances of clergymen who endeavoured to learn Welsh in order to lead their flock in worship. David Pugh, rector of Newport, Pembrokeshire, explained in 1813 that when first appointed to the parish forty years earlier his inability to conduct services in Welsh had forced him to employ a curate to perform his duties. This arrangement continued for several years until Pugh decided that he was a 'tolerable master of the Welsh language' and was fit to conduct his own services.[17] Similarly, Dr James Phillips, rector of Llangoedmor and vicar of Nevern,

[13] NLW, Church in Wales Records, SD/QA/7.
[14] Tindal Hart, op. cit., p. 64.
[15] NLW, Church in Wales Records, LL/QA/2.
[16] NLW, Church in Wales Records, LL/QA/5.
[17] NLW, Church in Wales Records, SD/QA/2; SD/QA/7.

explained that he had employed an assistant until he had perfected his knowledge of the Welsh language. Dr Phillips was brought up in Blaenpant in Llandygwydd and was a keen antiquarian. When he stated in 1755 that he had not yet completely mastered the Welsh language, he had already served as rector of Llangoedmor since around 1738 and as vicar of Nevern since 1730.[18]

Although the need to minister through the medium of Welsh in Welsh-speaking parishes was acknowledged, the practice of appointing pastors who could not fulfil that obligation continued. The inhabitants of Betws Cedewain in Montgomeryshire, which had formerly been a bilingual parish, were forced to attend English services from 1795 onwards following the appointment of a curate who spoke no Welsh.[19] There is no record of a similar instance in the Bangor diocese, but the practice continued in the other three dioceses into the nineteenth century and, inevitably, the most valuable benefices attracted the largest proportion of clergy from across Offa's Dyke. Evan Evans was particularly caustic about this tendency: 'Nid oes yrawron ond offeiriaid anwybodus o'r iaith yn perchennogi'r lleoedd gorau ymhob Esgobaeth, pan i mae y Cymry cynnenid yn gweini danynt am ffiloreg' (There are now only clergy unfamiliar with the language taking possession of the best places in every Diocese, while the native Welsh serve under them for a trifle).[20] Evans was embittered by his lack of preferment and he probably had his own case in mind when he condemned the bishops for failing to reward the talents of Welsh-speaking clergy. Nevertheless, his accusations are borne out by J. R. Guy's study of the diocese of Llandaff, where the greatest number of Englishmen were to be found in the most lucrative benefices, such as Llanwenarth in Monmouthshire. This parish was served by nine rectors between 1662 and 1800 and it is significant that five of them, during the period 1734–80, were English. Throughout most of the eighteenth century alternate English and Welsh services were conducted in the church, but it was necessary to appoint a Welsh-speaking curate to undertake these duties, while the rector enjoyed the income from the benefice.[21]

Bishops were not the only ones responsible for such appointments, for the right to nominate clergymen to many benefices had fallen into the

---

[18] NLW, Church in Wales Records, SD/QA/1; SD/MISCB./39; NLW MS 9145F, ff. 99–100; *ML*, I, p. 189.
[19] NLW, Church in Wales Records, SA/QA/8.
[20] NLW MS 2009B, f. 19.
[21] NLW, Church in Wales Records, LL/QA/2; J. R. Guy, 'An investigation into the pattern and nature of patronage, plurality and non-residence in the old diocese of Llandaff between 1660 and the beginning of the nineteenth century' (unpubl. University of Wales PhD thesis, 1983), pp. 467–8.

hands of laymen who were unlikely to suffer pangs of conscience about the effects of appointing non-Welsh-speaking clergy. In the diocese of Llandaff, for example, the bishop could appoint to one parish only, namely Basaleg, with its associated chapelries of Risca and Bedwellte. The bishop reserved the right to refuse to permit the appointment of a cleric on the grounds that he was unable to conduct services in Welsh, a right which was confirmed by the Pluralities Act of 1838.[22] But this power was seldom exercised. It appears that employing a Welsh-speaking assistant was generally considered to be an acceptable compromise. Since the collection of tithes in several parishes was the prerogative of lay impropriators, in many cases only a pittance was set aside to pay the curate for fulfilling his various duties. In St David's around 60 per cent of tithes had fallen into the hands of lay impropriators. By the time they and the incumbents had received their share of the profits, only some £5 or £10 remained for the curate. Many curates were consequently forced to minister to the duties of three or four parishes in order to make ends meet. In 1809, for example, James Thomas acted as curate in the parishes of Llansanffraid, Llanfihangel-nigh-Usk, Kemeys Commander, Trostre and Monkswood in Monmouthshire, conducting one service every Sunday in each.[23] Although only a mile or two separated Kemeys Commander, Trostre and Monkswood, since Llansanffraid and Llanfihangel-nigh-Usk were around three miles further north the curate could hardly have had time to catch his breath while rushing to complete his circuit each Sunday. As a result, pluralism was widespread in Wales and the poverty of curates proverbial. In the north, where laymen had not managed to plunder the Church's coffers to a similar degree, the situation was more encouraging. Since better salaries were paid to the clergy in the north, parishes there had not suffered so acutely from the effects of pluralism and absenteeism, and Evan Evans believed that it was this fact which explained the comparative failure of Dissent in that region.[24]

Bishop William Lloyd of St Asaph was one of the few prelates to insist upon appointing Welsh-speaking clergy. Thomas Clopton, the nephew of Lloyd's predecessor, Isaac Barrow, was appointed rector of Castell Caereinion on the understanding that he could speak Welsh, but it soon became apparent that this was a stratagem in order to secure the benefice. Lloyd swiftly realized that the congregation would gain little spiritual benefit from Clopton's clumsy attempts to read Welsh sermons and he went to some trouble to be rid of him.[25]

[22] Ivor Bowen (ed.), *The Statutes of Wales* (London, 1908), p. 253.
[23] NLW, Church in Wales Records, LL/QA/123.
[24] NLW MS 2009B, f. 13.
[25] Tindal Hart, op. cit., pp. 84–5.

The most determined opposition to the appointment of Englishmen to Welsh benefices manifested itself in the diocese of Bangor, notably during the celebrated affair of Thomas Bowles. Bowles – an elderly, monoglot Englishman – was appointed to the parishes of Trefdraeth and Llangwyfan in Anglesey in 1766 despite the fact that Welsh was the only language of the vast majority of the inhabitants. At the time, only five of the five hundred parishioners could understand English. The appointment ultimately led to his prosecution by his own parishioners in the Court of Arches in 1773. The Act for the Translation of the Scriptures 1563, the Act of Uniformity 1662 and the twenty-fourth article of the Church of England were deployed against Bowles, and such arguments were also effectively and concisely used in John Jones's work, *Considerations on the illegality and impropriety of preferring Clergymen who are unacquainted with the Welsh Language to benefices in Wales* (1767). Bowles employed a number of subterfuges in an attempt to obtain evidence to persuade the court that he was able to officiate in Welsh, but he failed to deceive the judge, Dr George Hay, who indicated that his appointment did not comply with the statutes of 1563 and 1662 and was also contrary to the spirit of the twenty-fourth article of the Church of England, which stated that it was unacceptable for prayers and sacrament to be conducted in a language unintelligible to the congregation. He further implied that the decision by Bishop John Egerton to appoint Bowles to minister in a parish of monoglot Welsh speakers was an act of arrant folly. But although he condemned Bowles, he was not able to deprive him of his living. Technically, therefore, Bowles was victorious, but the case confirmed that, according to civil and ecclesiastical law, the Welsh language had a paramount role in the public worship of the established Church, and that inability to speak the language was sufficient cause to disqualify a clergyman from serving in a particular parish.[26] Following this *cause célèbre*, parishioners in the diocese of Bangor were unwilling to tolerate similar appointments. In 1820 William Gruffydd and Robert Williams, churchwardens at Llanbeblig, Caernarfonshire, refused to accept Trevor Hill as their incumbent until he had learnt to read the Scriptures in Welsh. Angharad Llwyd, the antiquarian from Caerwys in Flintshire, expressed her admiration for the churchwardens by presenting each of them with a silver cup, both of which were reputedly frequently filled in order to salute her generosity.[27]

---

[26] Geraint H. Jenkins, 'Y Sais Brych' in *Cadw Tŷ Mewn Cwmwl Tystion*, pp. 198–224; idem, '"Horrid Unintelligible Jargon": The Case of Dr Thomas Bowles', *WHR*, 15, no. 4 (1991), 494–523.
[27] NLW MS 1577C, ff. 32–5.

In churches and chapels where provision was unsatisfactory, some parishioners preferred to join with Church congregations in other parishes or with Dissenters. Edward Tenison, archdeacon of Carmarthen, noted during his visitation of 1710 that the introduction of Welsh sermons in Laugharne had succeeded in attracting several stray lambs back to the Church fold. Many parishioners had turned their backs on the Church when an English incumbent had been appointed to the parish. When that incumbent, however, employed a Welsh assistant the number of families attending meetings with the Dissenters fell from sixteen to four.[28] Tenison's report reveals that he was aware of the need to secure sufficient provision through the medium of Welsh and that he was also prepared to criticize those who failed in that respect. In his opinion Lewis Beddo, an Englishman who was appointed rector of Llanglydwen, was unsuitable for a parish which called for a Welsh-speaking clergyman. Beddo (reputedly a violent drunkard) visited his flock only once a year, and was happy to leave the parish in the hands of a Welsh curate who shouldered all the responsibilities for a miserly stipend of six pounds a year. The linguistic arrangements in the parish of Llanrhian also caused the archdeacon some concern. Since the officiating curate had no knowledge of Welsh, parishioners consequently chose to travel some three miles every Sunday in order to attend meetings conducted by a Welsh-speaking Dissenting preacher in Llangloffan.[29]

It was not uncommon for parishioners to desert their parish church in order to attend services conducted in their mother tongue. The four or five parishioners of St Woollo's Church in Newport who could not understand English attended Welsh services in the nearby church of Basaleg, with the blessing of their vicar, Thomas Mills Hoare, who was also rural dean for Newport in 1771.[30] In 1809 in Newmarket in Flintshire the morning service was conducted in Welsh and English on alternate Sundays and the evening service always in Welsh. Edward Davies, the curate, insisted that English services should be provided for those who did not speak Welsh, even though only two of the 250–300 parishioners understood no Welsh. As a result, a large proportion of the congregation chose to attend Dissenting meetings on those Sunday mornings when English services were held in their church.[31]

---

[28] G. Milwyn Griffiths, 'A Visitation of the Archdeaconry of Carmarthen, 1710', *NLWJ*, XVIII, no. 3 (1974), 307.

[29] Ibid., 302; ibid., XIX, no. 3 (1976), 324; S. R. Thomas, 'The Diocese of St David's in the Eighteenth Century: the working of the diocese in a period of criticism' (unpubl. University of Wales MA thesis, 1983), pp. 15–20.

[30] NLW, Church in Wales Records, LL/QA/5.

[31] NLW, Church in Wales Records, SA/QA/15.

Visitations by rural deans (who were appointed from the ranks of the clergy) meant that there was some measure of supervision over decisions made by the parish clergy regarding the language of service. In 1749 the bishop of St Asaph requested that rural deans take particular note of the language of service: 'I must intreat you to inform me as particularly as you can, what in this respect would be most for the Edification of the Generality of the Parishioners.'[32] In ten of the 116 places of worship examined, the clergy were criticized regarding linguistic provision. In each case, the dean judged that more Welsh was required in the services and frequent references were made to the parishioners' disquiet concerning lack of provision. The proportion may not appear high, but it is significant that those parishes which bore the brunt of the deans' criticism were located in bilingual areas in east Montgomeryshire, Denbighshire and Flintshire, areas where the relationship between the two languages was in a state of flux. The returns of the clergy for 1791 provided further evidence regarding the diocese of St Asaph. By then four places of worship (Berriew and Llangynog in Montgomeryshire and Nerquis and Holywell in Flintshire) used more Welsh in services, and five (Aberhafesb, Betws Cedewain, Llanfair Caereinion, Llanllwchaearn in Montgomeryshire and Ruabon in Denbighshire) used more English. The arrangement of Welsh and English services on alternate Sundays remained unchanged in Northop in Flintshire.[33]

Unfortunately, the reports of the rural deans regarding language of services have not survived to such an extent in other dioceses. It is, therefore, impossible to compare their comments with those of the parish clergy. Yet they do shed some light on the standard of some of the clergy. In 1733, for instance, the dean of Dungleddy noted that William Crowther, the incumbent at Maenclochog, Llangolman and Llandeilo, was not performing his duties in a satisfactory manner, although he believed that there was some hope for reform. Ten years later his hopes remained unrealized when fifteen of Crowther's parishioners, including the churchwardens, sent a petition to Edward Willes, bishop of St David's, complaining bitterly of his many failings.[34] Among his alleged sins were drunkenness, immorality, fathering two illegitimate children, profaning the Sabbath, and the inability to speak Welsh. It was alleged that during his thirteen years in the parish he had never once recited the service in a language intelligible to his congregation.

---

[32] NLW, Church in Wales Records, SA/RD/26.
[33] NLW, Church in Wales Records, SA/QA/7.
[34] NLW, Church in Wales Records, SD/MISC/1199; Thomas, 'The Diocese of St David's', pp. 191–2.

Although churchwardens were usually expected to testify to a clergyman's willingness to use the language, or combination of languages, best suited to the parish, very few of them used the opportunity to voice any criticism. In a number of cases, the returns do not bear the wardens' signature, but rather their mark, which suggests that the clergy wrote on their behalf. Thomas Powell of Battle in Breconshire was the only warden to express dissatisfaction about the language chosen for public worship; in 1804 he complained that most of the parishioners stayed away from church because so much English was used in the services. It is significant that the returns reveal a change in language from exclusively Welsh in 1799 to Welsh and English alternately in 1807. It appears that Thomas Powell's complaints had very little effect since the linguistic arrangement remained unchanged until 1813. It was only with the arrival of a new curate in 1828 that English services were confined to once a month only.[35]

It appears, therefore, that parishioners had very little opportunity to appeal against the language policy of the parish clergy. Yet, when the parishioners of Machynlleth sent a petition to Lewis Bagot, bishop of St Asaph, in 1800 urging him to permit more extensive use of English in their services, their request was granted. Bishop Bagot ordered that two services a month should be conducted in English, rather than one as before, and that the communion service should be conducted in English four times a year.[36] Even so, the language used in most parishes was, more often than not, determined by the officiating clergy, and church authorities seldom interfered with their decision. Local clergymen were naturally best suited to assess the linguistic needs of their parishioners. On numerous occasions clergy claimed to have taken the wishes of their flock into account before deciding upon the language of worship. The parishioners of Llangattock nigh Usk in Monmouthshire decided in 1809 that services should be conducted alternately in Welsh and English. At Newton Nottage in Glamorgan in 1781, the rector and his flock agreed to hold one service on a Sunday, during which the Psalms would be read in English, but the rest of the service, including the sermon, would be conducted in Welsh.[37] Some of the clergy would wait until their congregation had assembled before deciding which language or combination of languages would be appropriate for that particular service. This was a common arrangement in a number of bilingual parishes, including Trinity Chapel, Whitson and Bishopston in Monmouthshire, Llan-gors and Talach-ddu in Breconshire,

---

[35] NLW, Church in Wales Records, SD/QA/187; SD/QA/253; SD/QA/190; SD/QA/200.
[36] NLW, Church in Wales Records, B/MISC/10.
[37] NLW, Church in Wales Records, LL/QA/23; LL/QA/8.

Ruabon in Denbighshire, Fishguard in Pembrokeshire, and Pyle and Kenfig in Glamorgan. The disadvantage was that the parishioners had no way of knowing beforehand how much of the service would be conducted in a language intelligible to them, and it is quite possible that this uncertainty prevented some of them from attending regularly.

There is little doubt that the wishes of the most prominent parishioners usually prevailed. Edward Evans, curate of Diserth in Flintshire, agreed to conduct an English service once a month at the request of his 'most respectable' parishioners. Similarly, the most prominent parishioners of Oswestry managed to convince Bishop Lewis Bagot to limit the use of Welsh to one service a month in 1799.[38] It was common practice to use the English language in order to curry favour with the local gentry when they chose to attend services. This occurred even in parishes that would otherwise have been uniformly Welsh. The fifty or so Welsh speakers who attended the church of Llanfair Nant-y-gof in north Pembrokeshire were obliged to listen to an English service whenever the Vaughan family of Trecŵn were present.[39] Welsh services were conducted in Pendeulwyn in Glamorgan except on those Sundays when the Earl of Talbot and his family attended worship.[40] In stark contrast, the curate of Llandygái explained in 1811 that it was only in the absence of the Penrhyn family that he was permitted to conduct an English service. Following the death of her husband during the war in 1815, Lady Penrhyn insisted on maintaining this tradition. The English parishioners awarded the curate an additional fee for preaching in their language on alternate Sunday mornings when the Penrhyn family were absent.[41] But this situation was an exception to the rule and many loyal churchmen were infuriated by the fact that monoglot Welsh-speaking congregations were being deprived of Welsh services. For example, William Fleetwood, bishop of St Asaph, in his charge of 1710, roundly condemned the tendency to preach in English in order to placate the gentry:

> In some Place I understand there is now and then an English Sermon preached, for the sake of one or two of the best Families in the Parish, although the rest of the Parish understand little or nothing of English, and those few Families understand the British perfectly well, as being their native Tongue. I cannot possibly approve of this Respect and Complaisance to a few, that makes the Minister so useless to the rest, and much the greatest Number of his People.[42]

[38] NLW, Church in Wales Records, SA/QA/6; SA/QA/8; SA/QA/12.
[39] NLW, Church in Wales Records, SD/QA/129.
[40] NLW, Church in Wales Records, LL/QA/4.
[41] NLW, Church in Wales Records, B/QA/19; B/QA/22.
[42] William Fleetwood, *The Bishop of St. Asaph's Charge to the Clergy of that Diocese in 1710* (London, 1712), pp. 11–12.

Samuel Williams, Llandyfrïog, was greatly angered by parsons who were too 'puffed up' to preach in Welsh to monoglot Welsh speakers and his son, Moses, launched a fierce attack on 'idle priests' who continued, in the most shameless fashion, to conduct English services in the presence of Welsh-speaking congregations.[43]

Despite the occasional black sheep, however, the clergy were for the most part well aware of their obligations. This, after all, was the Church which produced men of vision, learning and culture like Moses Williams, Griffith Jones, Theophilus Evans, Daniel Rowland and William Williams, Pantycelyn. Some of the most brilliant and productive scholars of the period were in church orders and they endeavoured to provide religious literature which set sound moral and devotional standards for their parishioners. In order to compensate for his absence while undertaking the work of revising the Bible and the Book of Common Prayer, Moses Williams dedicated his catechism, published in 1716, to his parishioners at Llanwenog. Theophilus Evans published a number of translations of English works, including Thomas Bisse's *The Beauty of holiness in the Common Prayer* (*Prydferthwch Sancteiddrwydd yn y Weddi Gyffredin*) in 1722, for the edification of his monoglot countrymen. In 1710 William Stanley arranged a translation of his *The Faith and practice of a Church of Englandman* at his own expense for the benefit of his parishioners at Henllan. In 1730 Robert Roberts, vicar of Chirk in Flintshire, published *A Du-Glott-Exposition, of the Creed, the Ten Commandments, And the Lords Prayer*, specifically for the parishioners of Chirk 'whose Inhabitants are partly Welsh and partly English'. Such men were motivated by concern for the souls under their care, for, as David Maurice explained in 1700, preaching without knowledge was like building without a foundation, and the provision of religious literature was essential in order to establish that foundation. The written word, he maintained, would last long after a sermon preached from the pulpit had faded from memory.[44] Subscription lists appended to the printed books of the period contain the names of large numbers of clergymen. When Dafydd Jones of Trefriw published his *Blodeu-gerdd Cymry* in 1759, for instance, the 137 clergymen vastly outnumbered any other social group or occupation among the subscribers. The Church, therefore, was equipped with a large number of conscientious clergymen who were loyal to the language and likely to concur with the view of the Llandudno cleric who declared in 1811:

---

[43] Williams, *Amser a Diwedd Amser*, sig. A2r–v; Moses Williams, *Pregeth a Barablwyd yn Eglwys Grist yn Llundain* (Llundain, 1718), p. 14.

[44] David Maurice, *Cwnffwrdd ir Gwan Gristion, neu'r Gorsen Ysyg Mewn Pregeth* (Llundain, 1700), p. vi.

In Wales, it is a mockery to read the service in English where the Congregation dont understand it, or indeed dont wish to have the Language of their Forefathers abolished.[45]

On the whole, visitation returns reflect the language used by the parishioners. Among the 1,010 churches and chapelries which figure in the returns there are very few examples of clergy failing or refusing to minister through the medium of the language best suited to their congregation. Having said that, a number of problems arise from the use of the visitation returns as evidence. For a variety of reasons, information is not available for some areas in Wales. Some of the eastern parishes of Radnorshire were included in the diocese of Hereford and some of the parishes of north Wales were included in the dioceses of Chester and Lichfield, none of which made any linguistic inquiry. In addition, the area of Hawarden in the north-east was an ecclesiastical peculiar which did not fall under the jurisdiction of the local bishop. Even in the rest of the country, few returns have survived for certain years. For instance, returns are available for only 10 per cent of the parishes of Pembrokeshire in 1755. The question relating to language of service was not included in every set of queries and even when it was included the clergy would at times neglect to answer it in full. After completing the return for 1784, the vicar of St John's in Cardiff refused to answer any queries for the following three visitations, apart from recording the number of communicants.[46] Even when the clergy did their best, their responses were often vague and inconsistent. Keenly aware that they were reporting to the church authorities and of the importance of making a good impression, they naturally took care not to make statements which might have adverse effects on their careers and their hopes of promotion. Curates answering on behalf of absent incumbents were particularly wary of jeopardizing their position by offering answers which might reflect badly on the incumbents. The desire to please everyone and to employ discretion may well have been responsible for the ambiguity of some of their statements. For example, in 1771 Evan Thomas, curate of Trostre and Kemeys Commander in Monmouthshire, claimed that he preached 'very often in Welsh, but oftener in English' in both parishes.[47] In the parish of Llan-non in Carmarthenshire, the curate, John Jones, explained that he preached 'promiscuously' in English and Welsh in both 1810 and 1813.[48] The difficulty experienced by clergy in explaining their linguistic arrangements stemmed in part from the complexities of serving

---

[45] NLW, Church in Wales Records, B/QA/19.
[46] NLW, Church in Wales Records, LL/QA/10; LL/QA/12; LL/QA/14; LL/QA/16.
[47] NLW, Church in Wales Records, LL/QA/5.
[48] NLW, Church in Wales Records, SD/QA/66; SD/QA/68.

in bilingual parishes. The returns reveal the difficulties facing clergy ministering in parishes where two languages coexisted and their efforts to cope with the situation. The search for a suitable and satisfactory combination could in some cases result in an excruciatingly complicated system. In Oswestry in 1791, for instance, the vicar attempted to explain his language policy as follows:

> On every other Sunday in the Month it is all English service – on every other Sunday it is English and Welsh alternately in the Morning with the Exception of the first Lesson and second service in English on Welsh Sunday Mornings and all English Service in the Afternoons.[49]

It is important to bear in mind that the answers are statements of policy for individual churches and chapels rather than statements regarding the language of the parishioners. Yet that policy would have been adopted with the aim of meeting the needs of the linguistic situation which existed in the parish. In theory, therefore, one might expect the clergy's choice to reflect that situation. Not surprisingly, the vast majority of parishes in the counties of Anglesey, Caernarfon, Cardigan, Carmarthen, Denbigh, Merioneth and north Pembroke were exclusively Welsh-speaking. Other areas, including south Pembrokeshire and Gower were wholly Anglicized. Catering for the population in these areas was a simple matter, but the clergy faced more difficult decisions when seeking to determine the language of worship in bilingual parishes. In this context the word 'bilingual' denotes an area where both languages were used, but the entire population did not necessarily have knowledge of both. In areas where both languages were used fairly equally, the simplest arrangement was to conduct alternate Welsh and English services. But fulfilling the 'double duty' often proved too burdensome for the impoverished Welsh curate driven to pluralism because of his pitiful salary. One way of lightening the load was to conduct one service on a Sunday, using Welsh and English for different elements of that service. In Llanmihangel in Glamorgan in 1781, the Psalms, hymns, the first lesson and the litany were conducted in English and the rest of the service in Welsh. In Lavernock and Penarth in Glamorgan the whole service was conducted in English, with the exception of the sermon, which was preached in Welsh because the incumbent claimed the congregation were more conversant in that language. The adoption of mixed language services ensured that all members of the congregation heard at least some of their mother tongue every Sunday, even though they were deprived of an entire service

[49] NLW, Church in Wales Records, SA/QA/7.

through the medium of that language. Such services also provided an opportunity for people to familiarize themselves with the sound of the other language. When Welsh and English services were held on alternate Sundays, however, parishioners simply did not attend when the service was conducted in the language which was unfamiliar to them. As the incumbent of Llanfair-ar-y-bryn explained in 1813: 'But few, or none, of those who understand the English language attend the Welsh service and "vice versa".'[50]

On the basis of the answers given in the four dioceses, parishes have been divided into the following language categories:

NA   No answer

W1   Welsh
W2   Some English
W2a Some English for visitors/gentry
W3   English once a month
W3S English sermon once a month
W3M Mixed service once a month
W4   English every third Sunday
W4S English sermon every third Sunday
W5   3 services every Sunday – 1 English and 2 Welsh
W6   1 mixed service and 1 Welsh service every Sunday/
     English and Welsh services alternately and 1 Welsh service every Sunday
W6S English sermon once a fortnight
W7   Mixed service, with greater use of Welsh/
     Welsh and English alternately, but a consistent element of Welsh every Sunday

B1   Welsh and English alternately
B2   Welsh and English on alternate Sundays
B3   Mixed service with equal use of both languages
B4   Bilingual – unspecified
B5   English service and Welsh sermon

E1   English
E2   Some Welsh
E3   Welsh once a month
E3S Welsh sermon once a month

[50] NLW, Church in Wales Records, SD/QA/68.

E4	Welsh every third Sunday
E4S	Welsh sermon every third Sunday
E5	3 services on a Sunday – 1 Welsh and 2 English
E6	1 mixed service and 1 English service every Sunday/ Welsh and English services alternately and 1 English service every Sunday
E6S	Welsh sermon once a fortnight
E7	Mixed service, with greater use of English/ Welsh and English alternately, but a consistent element of English every Sunday

Since visitations were not held in the same year in each diocese, some difficulty arises in the case of counties with parishes in more than one diocese. The most complex instance is Montgomeryshire where thirty-nine places of worship were located in the diocese of St Asaph, seven in Bangor and two in St David's. Visitation returns from the closest possible years in the different dioceses have therefore been brought together in an attempt to produce a complete picture of the linguistic pattern of the county. For the purpose of this study, Gower has been treated separately from the rest of Glamorgan, not only because it was located in a different diocese but also because its linguistic situation contrasted so greatly with the remainder of the county. An additional problem is the fact that in each diocese the number of returns for certain visitations are insufficient to provide a representative sample, and figures for those years have therefore been discounted.

The results (see Appendices 1–3) reveal that areas to the west formed the strongholds of the Welsh language in this period. The highest percentage of exclusively Welsh parishes were to be found in the counties of Anglesey, Caernarfon, Cardigan and Merioneth. The county displaying least English influence was Merioneth, which remained almost wholly Welsh-speaking, with English being used only occasionally in the churches of Llanycil and Corwen, and in Rug Chapel. English elements were included in services at Corwen whenever the Rug family attended church[51] and services at Rug Chapel were also conducted mainly in English for their benefit.[52] Welsh was the daily medium of communication in the parish of Llanycil, but whenever the Assizes assembled at Bala English was used for the benefit of judges, justices and lawyers.[53]

---

[51] NLW, Church in Wales Records, SA/QA/6.
[52] NLW, Church in Wales Records, SA/RD/26.
[53] NLW, Church in Wales Records, SA/RD/21; SA/RD/23; SA/RD/26; SA/QA/12.

The evidence of the clergy concerning the importance of the Welsh language in west Wales is reaffirmed by the churchwardens' responses to the question regarding the language of the Bibles and Common Prayer Books used in parishes. This query was an attempt to ensure that all churches possessed an adequate supply of books. In north-west Wales, in Cardiganshire and north Pembrokeshire, as well as large areas of Carmarthenshire, the overwhelming majority of parishes possessed Welsh books only. In an attempt to justify the lack of English books, references were frequently made to the fact that they would be useless to the inhabitants since they had no knowledge of English. The churchwardens of Llangrannog explained courteously in 1820 that English books were not 'requisite' in the parish, but a number of churchwardens, including those at Aber-porth, Henfynyw and Eglwyswrw, answered curtly: 'English books not wanted here.'[54] Further confirmation of the belief that most of the communities of the rural south-west in the eighteenth century were inhabited by Welsh monoglots is found in the answers to the query set in the diocese of St David's in 1807: 'Do you read His Majesty's Proclamation against Vice, and for the encouragement of Virtue, at least once a Quarter in your Church or Chapel?'[55] A large number of the clergy in the south-west replied that they had no Welsh version of the proclamation and that to read the English version would be a futile exercise since it would be completely unintelligible to their congregations. This was the complaint, for instance, in Llanbadarn Fawr, where services were conducted exclusively through the medium of Welsh.

In the eastern borders, however, the English language was gaining ground. The boundary of Welsh Wales was slowly inching westwards under pressure from increasing English influence in the east. As the Welsh language gradually retreated, a bilingual area was created which acted as a buffer zone between the Welsh and English languages and which edged slowly towards the west. Both languages coexisted within this zone, although the balance between them was in a state of constant flux. By the eighteenth century there were no discernible traces of the use of the Welsh language in the Herefordshire parishes which were part of the diocese of St David's. The language held its ground somewhat better towards the north, and continued to be used consistently in a cluster of parishes in the vicinity of Oswestry in Shropshire. Welsh was still the only language of service in the parish of Llanymynech, located on the border

---

[54] NLW, Church in Wales Records, SD/QA/3; SD/QA/10; SD/QA/11; SD/QA/13.
[55] NLW, Church in Wales Records, SD/QA/5–6; SD/QA/65; SD/QA/124–5; SD/QA/187.

between Montgomeryshire and England.[56] Welsh and English services were conducted alternately in the nearby parish of Llanyblodwel and Welsh services were maintained once a month in Selatyn and Oswestry itself.[57] The bilingual zone cut through parishes in north-west Montgomeryshire such as Meifod and Llanfyllin, and ran along the border with Shropshire, via Llansilin and Llangedwyn in the lower reaches of Denbighshire, and thence through Wrexham and Ruabon. By 1809 the bilingual zone had reached as far as Llanfair Caereinion in Montgomeryshire, but Welsh continued to be the main language of worship in the majority of churches in the north-west of the county. In Denbighshire, Welsh was the main language of all the churches and chapelries to the west of Wrexham and Ruabon, apart from the town of Ruthin, where services were conducted in Welsh and English alternately. In Flintshire, the bilingual zone engulfed most of the county, with only a handful of parishes around Rhuddlan in the north-west conducting Welsh services. Yet only four of the Denbighshire parishes and not one of the Flintshire parishes used English as the main language of worship (although the majority of parishes in Flintshire were bilingual).

On the other hand, it was apparent by the mid-eighteenth century that the Welsh language was yielding ground to English in Radnorshire, despite Lewis Morris's emphatic statement in 1742 that church services were conducted in Welsh in every part of the county. Returns for Radnorshire in the eighteenth century are far from complete, but enough remain to reveal that the language was waning in the county, although a few parishes in the south and west still used Welsh until very late in the century. Not until 1799 did Welsh cease to be the language of public worship in the parishes of Boughrood, Llandeilo Graban, Glasbury and Llansteffan in the south, and Diserth and Cefn-llys in the west. By the early years of the nineteenth century, the only four parishes where Welsh could still be heard were Saint Harmon, Rhayader, Llansanffraid Cwmteuddwr and Nantmel. Occasional Welsh services were held at Rhayader and a Welsh sermon was preached once a month at Nantmel until 1807, when the language was finally abandoned in the parish. Between 1755 and 1828, therefore, only two parishes consistently used Welsh as the main language of service, namely Saint Harmon and Llansanffraid Cwmteuddwr in the north-west of the county. Forty parishes consistently used English as the language of worship during the same period and six parishes adopted the practice of conducting exclusively English services rather than bilingual ones.

[56] NLW, Church in Wales Records, SA/QA/10; SA/QA/12; SA/QA/15.
[57] Ibid.

The response of the cleric of Cwm-hir in 1813 is one of the most significant statements to appear in the visitation returns:

> Church service is performed always in English, & has been so for a great number of years; as the young people do not in general understand Welsh, but the Old People do understand English.[58]

By that stage everyone in the parish understood English, and Welsh was no longer essential as a means of communication. In such a situation, the strength of people's loyalty and commitment to maintaining the Welsh language would ultimately determine whether services would continue to be conducted in Welsh or not. The fact that only the older generation understood Welsh was a strong indication that English would be the language of the future in Radnorshire.

During the same period, the Welsh language retreated slightly in east Breconshire, and there was an increase in the use of English in fourteen places of worship in the area. Nonetheless, Welsh held its ground in the rest of the county, which bordered on the strongly Welsh-speaking counties of Cardigan, Carmarthen and Glamorgan. The advance of the English language was much more striking in Monmouthshire. In the eastern parishes of the county the Welsh language had disappeared as the language of public worship by the mid-eighteenth century. English was also the language of worship in most of the towns, including Newport and Usk. Monthly Welsh services continued to be held in Abergavenny in 1763, but by 1771 the Welsh language had relinquished its hold there also. A bilingual zone reached like an amoeba to engulf the central parishes of the county, edging constantly towards the west, where the only exclusively Welsh places of worship were located. Of the 128 places of worship mentioned in the returns, only eleven remained completely Welsh until the visitation of 1813, namely Llanddewi Fach, Pant-teg, Mamheilad, Aberystruth, Llanhiledd, Bedwellte, Mynyddislwyn, Henllys, St Bride's Wentlloog, Risca and Coedcernyw. Other parishes, such as Bedwas and Betws, might be included in this category, but there is insufficient documentary evidence to confirm this supposition. During the period 1771–1813 seven places of worship adopted bilingual rather than Welsh services and twenty-five parishes adopted English as their main language of service. By 1813 eighty-six places of worship (i.e. 67 per cent) in Monmouthshire employed English as the main medium of public worship. The conclusive testimony of the returns, therefore, is that the

---

[58] NLW, Church in Wales Records, SD/QA/190.

Welsh language was rapidly dying out as the language of the Church in Monmouthshire.

Certain areas in Wales, commonly known as Englishries, had long since been Anglicized, but there is no indication that such areas were extending their influence over neighbouring parishes during this period. South Pembrokeshire formed a lone island of Englishness in the far south-west and there was little or no change in the linguistic provision of the region. The striking contrast between the north and south of the county has often been noted: the boundary between Welsh and English, following the southern borders of the hundreds of Dewisland and Cemais, almost forms a straight line across the county.[59] To the north of this line were located forty-four places of worship which remained consistently Welsh in their language provision. A narrow strand of bilingual parishes along the borders of these hundreds separated the monoglot Welsh areas from the seventy-eight places of worship which used English as the main language of their services. The only parishes to the south of the line which continued to use Welsh were the Welsh parish of Llan-y-cefn and the bilingual parishes of Ambleston, Walton East, Llys-y-frân and Bletherston, which straddled the boundary between the hundreds of Cemais and Daugleddau.[60] In addition, a cluster of exclusively Welsh (Llanfallteg and Llan-gan) and bilingual (Llanddewi Felffre and Llanbedr Felffre) parishes were located along the eastern boundary of the county, and in reality bore a stronger natural association with the Welsh-speaking areas of Carmarthenshire than with south Pembrokeshire. The English language did not gain much ground in Pembrokeshire; indeed, it suffered greater losses than did Welsh during the period 1755–1828, with the churches of Llanbedr Felffre and Bletherston in the east becoming bilingual instead of favouring English services, and the church of Llanstinan in the north abandoning the English language in favour of Welsh. Very few parishes used both languages. Only fourteen places of worship provided bilingual services during the eighteenth century and by the early nineteenth century four of those had adopted Welsh as their main language of public worship. English influences penetrated to a certain extent along the coast from south Pembrokeshire to lower Carmarthenshire. English was the only language of service in the coastal parishes of Llansadyrnin and Pendine by the mid-eighteenth century. During the same century, the

---

[59] Brian S. John, 'The Linguistic Significance of the Pembrokeshire Landsker', *PH*, 4 (1972), 7.

[60] Brian John lists the parishes of Ambleston, Walton East, Llys-y-frân, Bletherston and New Moat, in which English services were conducted by the eighteenth century, as parishes which gradually returned to the use of Welsh after early colonization by Normans and Flemings. Ibid., p. 25.

nearby parishes of Eglwys Gymyn and Marros relinquished their custom of conducting bilingual services and only vestiges of Welsh remained in the parish of Laugharne by the first quarter of the nineteenth century.

The Gower Peninsula formed another long-established Englishry in south Wales. Once again, a striking contrast was evident between this region and the surrounding area. Most of the archdeaconry of Gower in the diocese of St David's was wholly English in language. A small cluster of bilingual parishes were located to the north of Swansea, bridging the gap between the English peninsula and the Welsh areas in the vicinity. Such striking contrasts between contiguous areas bear some relationship to the terrain.[61] In Gower, the coastal lowland was Anglicized, while the northern highlands remained Welsh-speaking. Similar patterns emerged in the differences between the Vale of Glamorgan and the hills to the north (*Bro* and *Blaenau*). In this area, too, the English language had penetrated the low-lying coastal plains, while Welsh continued to dominate in the mountainous area to the north. Such differences emerged in part as a result of the settlement pattern of the Norman invaders, who tended to be drawn to the flat, fertile land which proved more suitable for the manorial system of farming. They displayed little interest in the less productive highland regions and, consequently, the Welsh language was not displaced in those areas.

There is no evidence, therefore, to suggest that the influence of the traditional Englishries of south Pembrokeshire and Gower spread to neighbouring regions. But changes were afoot in another area which had long been Anglicized, namely the Vale of Glamorgan. A bilingual zone known as the Border Vale formed the northern edge of the Vale between Margam and the river Rhymni. To the north were the upland areas of the *Blaenau*, to the south the fertile, heavily populated Vale itself. By the end of the eighteenth century, a third of the population of Glamorgan was located in that area, which included the towns of Cardiff, Cowbridge and Bridgend. It is likely that the Welsh language regained lost ground in the area, partly as a result of an influx of Welsh speakers from the Border Vale and the *Blaenau*, and that it reached its zenith in the Vale during the century 1750–1850. A number of parishes along the southern coast continued to use English only, including Sully, Porthceri, Gileston, St Athan and Llantwit Major. But Welsh was gaining strength even in these areas, with St Donat's adopting Welsh as the sole language of service by 1802 and Merthyr Dyfan likewise by 1813. According to the evidence of

[61] V. A. Chesters, 'Studies in the linguistic geography of the Vale of Glamorgan, the Swansea Valley and the Breconshire hinterland' (unpubl. University of Wales MA thesis, 1971), p. 9; Brian Ll. James, 'The Welsh Language in the Vale of Glamorgan', *Morgannwg*, XVI (1972), 18–19; Michael Williams, 'The Linguistic and Cultural Frontier in Gower', *AC*, CXXI (1972), 62–5.

the visitation returns, eleven places of worship in the area made more extensive use of the Welsh language between 1771 and 1813. During the same period, however, twenty places of worship adopted a policy which entailed greater use of the English language. Fourteen of these adopted bilingual services rather than exclusively Welsh services, five adopted English services rather than bilingual ones, and one, Michaelston-le-Pit, adopted English instead of Welsh services. It is apparent, therefore, that south Glamorgan witnessed considerable language change in this period, with both tongues experiencing losses and gains. The language of services varied greatly, with exclusively English, exclusively Welsh, and bilingual parishes located within a few miles of each other. It is difficult to attribute such changes to any overriding geographical pattern, but, on the whole, the parishes which experienced an increased use of English were located on the northern edge of the Vale proper. English influences tended to spread in a north-westerly direction. For example, bilingual services replaced Welsh services in a cluster of parishes around Laleston and Merthyr Mawr.

In addition to the traditional Englishries, the towns of Wales on the whole formed pockets of English influence, even within virtually monoglot Welsh-speaking areas. As a rule the language of worship in the most important towns throughout Wales did not reflect the language of the surrounding areas. In Anglesey and Caernarfonshire, the towns of Beaumaris, Amlwch, Bangor, Conwy and Caernarfon contrasted sharply with the monoglottism of the rural hinterland. Aberystwyth, Cardigan and Lampeter were Anglicizing influences in Cardiganshire, as were Carmarthen, Newcastle Emlyn, Llandeilo and Llanelli in Carmarthenshire. Another important factor which helped promote acquaintance with English was the catechism employed in the churches. It was the clergy's duty to teach and examine the catechism regularly, but they complained time and again that parents neglected to send their children to church to be instructed. Judging by the clergy's responses, there was a definite tendency to catechize in English even in places such as Llaneugrad in Anglesey, Botwnnog in Caernarfonshire, Dolgellau in Merioneth and Eglwysilan in Glamorgan, where the language of worship was exclusively Welsh. A number of clergy admitted that it was necessary to explain the English catechism in Welsh so that congregations could comprehend it. In spite of the difficulties, however, they continued to favour the English version, possibly in an attempt to extend their parishioners' knowledge of English. In Gelli-gaer in Glamorgan in 1771, services were conducted in Welsh, but the children were catechized in English, and the catechism was explained in Welsh to the older inhabitants.[62] The commentary on the

---

[62] NLW, Church in Wales Records, LL/QA/4.

catechism most frequently mentioned in the returns from this period was William Wake's *The Principles of Christian Religion explained* (1699), of which there was no Welsh translation. Among the other most commonly used commentaries were *Catechism yr Eglwys wedi ei egluro* (1713), Ellis Wynne's translation of John Lewis's work; *Traethiadau ar Gatecism Eglwys Loegr* (1778), Thomas Jones's translation of Thomas Secker's commentary, and *Egwyddorion a dyledswyddau y grefydd Grist'nogawl* by Thomas Wilson, bishop of Sodor and Man, which was translated into Welsh in 1752. A number of clergymen also referred to the work of William Beveridge, bishop of St Asaph, which appeared in Welsh in 1708 under the title *Eglurhaad o Gatechism yr Eglwys*.[63] Surprisingly, Griffith Jones's catechism was rarely mentioned, despite the remarkable influence of his circulating schools. The language of the local school was clearly an important factor in deciding the language of the catechism. Some incumbents, including those of Merthyr Mawr and Peterston-super-Ely, noted that they used the Welsh catechism since the parishioners were already well versed in it following the visit of a Welsh circulating school. In 1771 the incumbent of Ystradyfodwg in Glamorgan bemoaned the fact that he was obliged to catechize in English because there was no Welsh school in the parish despite the pressing need for one.[64]

A number of other factors during this period contributed to language change. In the counties of the south-west in particular, the presence of non-Welsh-speaking parishioners made it necessary to adapt the linguistic provision to suit their needs. The Church was obliged to be flexible regarding language because of its responsibility to serve all its members. Therefore, if an English family moved into a Welsh area, the inevitable result was the introduction of a certain amount of English into church services, even though it was unintelligible to the vast majority of the congregation. This occurred even in remote rural areas such as Troed-yr-aur in Cardiganshire. This tendency became more and more apparent in the counties of Cardigan and Carmarthen by the time of the visitations of 1813 and 1828 in the diocese of St David's. In Gartheli, in mid-Cardiganshire, an element of English was included in the service for the benefit of an English family which had moved into the area in 1813.[65] In nearby Tregaron the custom of conducting public worship partly in both languages commenced in the same year following the arrival of two English families. The vicar estimated that about 200–300 of the 1,300

---

[63] Geraint H. Jenkins, *Literature, Religion and Society in Wales 1660–1730* (Cardiff, 1978), pp. 75–84; D. L. Davies, 'A Study of Selected Visitation Material in Glamorgan, 1763–1813' (unpubl. University of Wales MA thesis, 1988), pp. 42–7.
[64] NLW, Church in Wales Records, LL/QA/4.
[65] NLW, Church in Wales Records, SD/QA/7.

strong population regularly attended church. Even allowing for an element of exaggeration, this meant that a large number of Welsh speakers in the town heard English regularly in church. Several other parishes, including Llanwenog and Llangrannog in Cardiganshire, Cilymaen-llwyd, Llanfair-ar-y-bryn, Llanfynydd, Llanllawddog and Pen-boyr in Carmarthenshire, and Llanganten and Merthyr Cynog in Breconshire, noted the need to use English for the benefit of a small number of individuals. In some areas it proved possible in time to assimilate incomers into Welsh communities. In Llanbryn-mair, for example, it was claimed that many of the Welsh speakers in the parish were descendants of English people who had been absorbed into the local community with the passage of time, but it was also noted that this was an exceptional circumstance.[66]

The Church also endeavoured to provide for occasional seasonal visitors, particularly in some of the coastal areas which were beginning to attract tourists during the summer months.[67] During the second half of the eighteenth century visitors were attracted by the prospect of sea-bathing to Porthcawl in the parish of Newton Nottage, and the incumbent would preach the occasional English sermon for their benefit.[68] Although Llandudno and Rhyl were not yet fashionable resorts, Abergele was already popular and attracted many visitors, for whom it was considered necessary to provide English sermons during the summer months.[69]

Some of the changes witnessed in the language of public worship were the result of migration into industrial areas. The iron, coal and lead industries developed in north-east Wales from the mid-seventeenth century onwards and the area experienced improvements in communications which resulted in an influx of workers. A number of these were Welsh speakers who had migrated from the countryside, but there were also many Englishmen, whose presence caused changes in the language of worship. In Minera chapel in the parish of Wrexham, lead miners made a financial contribution in order to ensure that the incumbent preached in English on alternate Sundays.[70] Complaints were voiced in Llangynog in north Montgomeryshire at the beginning of the eighteenth century that the curate was unable to conduct English services for the benefit of workers connected with the lead mines. By 1749, however, the complaint was that the curate was still conducting alternate English and Welsh

---

[66] NLW, Church in Wales Records, SA/RD/27.
[67] W. T. R. Pryce, 'Language Areas and Changes, c.1750–1981' in Prys Morgan (ed.), *Glamorgan County History, Volume VI. Glamorgan Society, 1780–1980* (Cardiff, 1988), p. 284; Geraint H. Jenkins, *The Foundations of Modern Wales. Wales 1642–1780* (Oxford, 1987), pp. 288–9.
[68] NLW, Church in Wales Records, LL/QA/10.
[69] NLW, Church in Wales Records, SA/QA/6; SA/QA/8; SA/QA/11; SA/QA/15.
[70] NLW, Church in Wales Records, SA/QA/3–4.

services, even though the lead mines had closed and the foreign workers had long since departed.[71] With the onset of industrial activity, in-migration of workers from two different directions occurred: Welsh speakers from the west and non-Welsh speakers from the east. The two streams tended to converge at Offa's Dyke, a long-standing linguistic and cultural boundary.[72] In his work on the linguistic geography of the north-east, Rees Pryce has suggested that by the mid-eighteenth century the bilingual zone corresponded broadly with the extent of the coalfield.[73] By the end of the century, nevertheless, it had obviously expanded to engulf the greater part of Flintshire, except for a few parishes to the north.

The most notable example of the effects of the growth of industry on language is Merthyr Tydfil in Glamorgan, a town which became the cradle of the industrial revolution in south Wales. Although most in-migrants originated from neighbouring Welsh counties, those who hailed from beyond Offa's Dyke were sufficiently numerous to necessitate a change in the language of the church. John Davies, curate of Merthyr, noted in 1771 that he had recently begun to preach in English every other Sunday night at the request of English workers associated with the ironworks in the parish. By 1784, however, one of the two services held on Sundays was conducted in English every fortnight. This meant that a quarter of the services were now in English. By 1788 conducting English and Welsh services alternately – an arrangement which would continue into the nineteenth century – was the norm. Within twenty years, therefore, a fundamental change had occurred in the language of the parish.[74] Yet the Welsh language maintained a firm hold over the remainder of the extensive mountain parishes of the *Blaenau*. Welsh was the only language of the church in the parishes of Ystradyfodwg, Aberdare, Glyncorrwg, Llanwynno, Gelli-gaer and Eglwysilan throughout this period.

The evidence of the clergy of south Breconshire suggests that industrial growth created problems in that area. Although services in the parish of Vaynor continued to be exclusively Welsh in 1828, the curate was concerned about the provision for the village of Coedycymer, located some two miles from the parish church. The number of inhabitants had increased to two thousand as a result of the proximity of the village to the

---

[71] NLW, Church in Wales Records, SA/RD/5; SA/RD/26; David Jenkins, 'The Population, Society and Economy of Late Stuart Montgomeryshire, c.1660–1720' (unpubl. University of Wales PhD thesis, 1985), p. 38.
[72] A. H. Dodd, 'Welsh and English in east Denbighshire: a historical retrospect', *THSC* (1940), 52; Melville Richards, 'The Population of the Welsh Border', ibid. (1970), 94–5.
[73] W. T. R. Pryce, 'Approaches to the Linguistic Geography of Northeast Wales, 1750–1846', *NLWJ*, XVII, no. 4 (1972), 353–5.
[74] NLW, Church in Wales Records, LL/QA/4; LL/QA/10; LL/QA/12.

ironworks at Merthyr Tydfil. The curate suggested that it would be beneficial to build a church there, since Methodists were already gaining ground in the community. The curate of the parish of Llanelli also faced the same dilemma: how to cope with an influx of people located at some distance from the parish church. He also voiced his concern that the Church was likely to lose ground to Dissent unless it acted swiftly:

> And I most respectfully beg to add that while dissenting chapels are continually erected without difficulty wherever the increase of population seems to invite yet there are so many obstacles thrown in the way of building a new church as to render it in many cases a hopeless object. And while in default of chapels, dissenting ministers are able to preach in private houses wherever they can form a congregation – yet the regular Clergyman is obliged to confine himself to his Church however remotely or inconveniently it may be situated.[75]

One of the major problems facing the established Church was its inability to adapt the parish system to the needs of the new industrial communities. Parish churches such as Ystradyfodwg, Bedwellte and Aberystruth had been built for a scattered agricultural population and there was a pressing need to build churches close to industrial centres.[76] By the early years of the nineteenth century, a number of clergymen were conscious of the growing threat posed by Dissent. It was feared that parishioners might decide to attend Dissenting meetings in order to hear their mother tongue rather than because of their religious convictions. The bishop of St David's noted in 1811 that 'the Welsh Language is with the Sectaries a powerful means of seduction from the church'.[77] Because of the flexible nature of their organization, it was much easier for Dissenters to establish meeting places in response to the needs of the new centres of population. The Church was also losing ground because so many clergymen, especially in south Wales, were pluralists and therefore unable to conduct more than one service in their churches on Sundays. In 1771 John Walters, the celebrated grammarian who was also vicar of St Hilary, Llandochau and St Mary Church in Glamorgan, noted that it was impossible for him to conduct more than one service in any of his churches because of the weight of his pastoral duties.[78] Nor was he the

---

[75] NLW, Church in Wales Records, SD/QA/200.
[76] E. T. Davies, *Religion and Society in the Nineteenth Century* (Llandybïe, 1981), pp. 51–2; Sian Rhiannon Williams, 'Iaith y Nefoedd mewn Cymdeithas Ddiwydiannol: y Gymraeg a Chrefydd yng Ngorllewin Sir Fynwy yn y Bedwaredd Ganrif ar Bymtheg' in Geraint H. Jenkins and J. Beverley Smith (eds.), *Politics and Society in Wales, 1840–1922: Essays in Honour of Ieuan Gwynedd Jones* (Cardiff, 1988), p. 48.
[77] NLW, Church in Wales Records, SD/MISC/1085.
[78] NLW, Church in Wales Records, LL/QA/4.

most hard-pressed of clergymen, since others were known to have borne a much heavier burden.

However valuable the evidence of the visitation returns may be, there are a number of questions which remain unanswered. It is impossible, for instance, to know to what extent the congregation understood the language spoken in the pulpit. It is difficult to believe that the practice of preaching a Welsh sermon once a year in places such as Morton chapel and St Martin's in Shropshire in 1791 was anything more than a largely outworn tradition.[79] Nor did conducting public worship through the medium of one language necessarily mean that the congregation had no knowledge of the other language. In the diocese of St David's in 1811, Bishop Thomas Burgess suggested that many of the Welsh speakers under his care understood English 'in Common conversation', but preferred to hear prayers and sermons in their mother tongue.[80] There were signs that the Welsh language had not totally disappeared in those areas where it had ceased to be the language of the church. In 1771 Thomas Mills Hoare, vicar of Newport, explained that English was the language of his church because that was the language most commonly spoken and best understood. But, he continued:

> the Welsh Liturgy very few of them can join in; and when a Welsh Sermon is to be preach'd many of them usually leave the church before the Sermon begins; for our Neighbouring Welsh Preachers affect preaching a pure correct Welsh, which is here almost unintelligible.[81]

W. H. Rees has argued that visitation returns do not reflect the language of the inhabitants of the parishes because they tend to overemphasize the degree of Anglicization and that they should only be used in conjunction with Nonconformist records.[82] The evidence of some of the clergy does reveal that English services were conducted in certain places for the benefit of a very small proportion of the parish population, but this was an indication of the difficulties and dilemmas which the Church faced in seeking to satisfy the needs of bilingual societies. Extensive Dissenting records which would enable us to compare the linguistic arrangements in their meetings with those of the Church are not available for this period. Congregationalist and Baptist church records were either written in Welsh or English, often depending on the linguistic

---

[79] NLW, Church in Wales Records, SA/QA/7.
[80] NLW, Church in Wales Records, SD/MISC/1085.
[81] NLW, Church in Wales Records, LL/QA/5.
[82] W. H. Rees, 'The Vicissitudes of the Welsh Language in the Marches of Wales, with special reference to its territorial distribution in modern times' (unpubl. University of Wales PhD thesis, 1947), p. 45.

patterns of the area. For example, the records of Cilfowyr Baptist chapel in Pembrokeshire, a branch of Rhydwilym Church, were kept in Welsh during the eighteenth century, whereas English records were kept by the Baptist church at Llanwenarth in Monmouthshire during the same period.[83] Although the accounts and membership lists of the Independents at Rhayader are in English, the texts of sermons are noted in Welsh throughout, an indication, perhaps, that Welsh prevailed in their services.[84]

During this period, a number of prominent Dissenters were acutely conscious of the need for religious literature to satisfy Welsh speakers. Like members of the established Church, they were sensible of the capacity of the printed word to plant the principles of the Protestant faith in the minds and hearts of Welsh people. Works by Charles Edwards and Stephen Hughes were published under the aegis of the Welsh Trust during the second half of the seventeenth century, but it was not until the eighteenth century that a generation of Dissenters emerged who were eager to publish religious literature through the medium of Welsh. The aim of such works was to explain doctrines and beliefs, to remind readers of the importance of the four last things (death, judgement, heaven and hell), and to urge them to live blameless lives in order to prepare for the Day of Judgement. Many publications were translations of well regarded English works, including *Dydd y Farn Fawr* by Jenkin Jones (1727) and *Darluniad o'r Gwir Gristion* by Phylip Pugh (1748). Among the best-known translators was Iaco ab Dewi or James Davies, a Congregationalist under the ministry of Christmas Samuel, who was responsible for translating a number of pious works into Welsh, including *Tyred a Groesaw at Iesu Grist* (1719), a translation of John Bunyan's *Come and Welcome to Jesus*. One of the consequences of the use of the printing press by Dissenters was the creation of an eager and articulate reading public, many of whom were attracted to the Methodist movement in the mid-eighteenth century.[85]

To a considerable degree, English was the language of record and administration among the Methodists. It could be argued that this was because the Association, the governing body of the movement, included members from English-speaking areas such as south Pembrokeshire, and because English Methodist leaders like George Whitefield occasionally visited Wales. Although society reports were frequently written in fluent

---

[83] NLW MS 1110B; NLW MS Deposit 409B.
[84] NLW MS 395A.
[85] Garfield H. Hughes, *Iaco ab Dewi (1648–1722)* (Caerdydd, 1953), pp. 101–28; R. Tudur Jones, *Hanes Annibynwyr Cymru* (Abertawe, 1966), pp. 130–3; T. M. Bassett, *The Welsh Baptists* (Swansea, 1977), pp. 69–80; Jenkins, *Literature, Religion and Society*, pp. 174–8.

Welsh by the exhorters, they were generally translated prior to their inclusion in the official records. The translation was usually undertaken by Howel Harris and on occasions he took advantage of the opportunity to censor some of the original content. Moreover, the major figures of the eighteenth-century revival tended to correspond with one another in English, a custom which was common in that period. Howel Harris kept his diary in Latin for some years in the 1730s, before turning to English for the rest of his life. Only occasionally, when noting the main points of sermons, did he include Welsh entries in his diary, although he was quite capable of writing fluently in his mother tongue, as his few surviving Welsh letters reveal. The societies themselves were conducted in whichever language best suited the members, but care was taken to ensure that the Welsh-speaking societies had an adequate supply of exhorters fluent in that tongue. It was noted in 1743, for example, that James Beaumont was unsuitable to exhort in Llanfihangel Crucornau, near Abergavenny, because he had no Welsh.[86] The society members were constantly urged by their leaders to attend Griffith Jones's circulating schools in order to learn to read the Word in their native tongue.

R. T. Jenkins once suggested that one of the main paradoxes of the Methodist Revival was the fact that its greatest influence did not lie in the field of religion.[87] There is no doubt that the Revival – unwittingly – had a positive influence on the Welsh language. Neither the leaders nor the members were aware that Methodism was an intrinsically Welsh or Welsh-speaking movement. Unlike writers like Griffith Jones and Theophilus Evans, Methodists did not appeal to the past or refer to the traditional links between the Christian faith and the Welsh language.[88] They preferred to celebrate their connections with other evangelical movements across the world. Yet, in the second half of the eighteenth century, Howel Harris expressed affection and loyalty towards the Welsh language on more than one occasion, and rebuked the Welsh people for their folly in rejecting an ancient tongue presented to them by the Almighty: 'I was much here too for ye old Brittons not to swallow ye English Pride & Language & despise their own.'[89]

Methodists were confronted with the age-old problem of finding adequate means of expressing religious experiences which were seemingly beyond words. It has been suggested recently that one of George Whitefield's major

---

[86] NLW, CM Archives, Trefeca MS 3001.
[87] R. T. Jenkins, *Hanes Cymru yn y Ddeunawfed Ganrif* (Caerdydd, 1928), p. 103.
[88] Derec Llwyd Morgan, 'Y Beibl a Llenyddiaeth Gymraeg' in R. Geraint Gruffydd (ed.), *Y Gair ar Waith: Ysgrifau ar yr Etifeddiaeth Feiblaidd yng Nghymru* (Caerdydd, 1988), pp. 100–1.
[89] NLW, CM Archives, Diaries of Howel Harris, 262, 24 May 1770.

achievements was to use the language of commerce to popularize religion during the eighteenth century.[90] In a number of sermons and letters he made use of images such as 'investing' in Christ and 'buying shares' in his kingdom. No such use of the language and images of commerce are evident in the work of the Welsh Methodists, mainly because Wales had not partaken of the consumer revolution to the same extent as England and America. Harry S. Stout, the American historian who developed these ideas, has suggested that Howel Harris, in contrast to Whitefield, adapted the language of love and courtship for the purpose of his mission in Wales,[91] but it would be more accurate to claim that William Williams, Pantycelyn, was chiefly responsible for developing this idiom. In doing so, Williams drew heavily on the style of the Song of Solomon, and like the early Puritans all his literary work was deeply rooted in the Scriptures.

Devout Protestants believed the language of the Bible was the only language suitable for discussing religious experiences. Because of the constant borrowing from the Scriptural idiom, the kind of vocabulary used in the Methodist societies and in the spiritual diaries of men such as Howel Harris, Richard Tibbott and John Thomas was similar to that found in Puritan conversion narratives.[92] These movements called for a detailed analysis of the spiritual condition of the individual, for which it was necessary to develop a suitable vocabulary. Methodists were also obliged to choose their words carefully in order to avoid incurring the wrath of church authorities. Griffith Jones advised Howel Harris in the early stages of his career to be prudent when selecting words. He suggested, for instance, that he should employ the word 'repentance' if the word 'rebirth' proved to be a stumbling block for some of his listeners.[93] In some instances, Methodists deliberately chose not to adopt the terminology of the Church or of the Dissenters in order to avoid accusations of presumption or of attempting to create a new denomination. For this reason, the movement's lay preachers were called 'exhorters' in the

---

[90] Frank Lambert, 'Pedlar in Divinity: George Whitefield and the Great Awakening, 1737–1745', *JAH*, 77 (1990), 812–37; Harry S. Stout, *The Divine Dramatist: George Whitefield and the Rise of Modern Evangelicalism* (Michigan, 1991), passim; Frank Lambert, '*Pedlar in Divinity*': *George Whitefield and the Transatlantic Revivals, 1737–1770* (Princeton, 1994), passim.

[91] Stout, *The Divine Dramatist*, p. 69.

[92] See, e.g., George Lawton, *John Wesley's English* (London, 1962); Perry Miller, 'The Plain Style' in Stanley E. Fish (ed.), *Seventeenth Century Prose* (Cambridge, 1971), pp. 147–86; Owen C. Watkins, *The Puritan Experience* (London, 1972); Patricia Caldwell, *The Puritan Conversion Narrative: the Beginnings of American Expression* (Cambridge, 1982); Glyn Tegai Hughes, 'Pantycelyn a'r Piwritaniaid' in Derec Llwyd Morgan (ed.), *Meddwl a Dychymyg Williams Pantycelyn* (Llandysul, 1991), pp. 31–54; Eryn M. White, '*Praidd Bach y Bugail Mawr*': *Seiadau Methodistaidd De-Orllewin Cymru 1737–50* (Llandysul, 1995), chapter IV.

[93] Diaries of Howel Harris, 54, 9 March 1740.

hope of allaying the suspicions of the church authorities. Similarly, the first buildings erected by the movement were dubbed 'schoolrooms' or 'society houses' rather than meeting houses or chapels.

Devising appropriate theological and administrative terms was, nevertheless, simply a small part of the Methodist agenda. Rather more important was the need to develop a language of spiritual experience for use in the societies. Members were usually grouped according to their spiritual condition and there are numerous references to 'experienced' Christians, to members who were 'under the Law' or backsliding, to hearts 'melting' or 'burning', and to 'dry' or 'easy' souls. Many English words beginning with the prefix 'self-' were coined following the increasing emphasis on self-examination by Puritans in the seventeenth century,[94] and it is significant that *Geiriadur Prifysgol Cymru* notes that several Welsh words beginning with the word 'hunan' (self) appeared in print for the first time during the eighteenth century.[95] By then, several works by English Puritans had been translated into Welsh for the first time and Methodists were producing their own distinctive literature.

The Methodist movement did much to strengthen and enrich the Welsh language by providing a substantial literature in the form of sermons, devotional manuals, hymns and elegies. William Williams made the most notable contribution, although he has frequently been criticized for using colloquial forms and for disregarding the rules of standard Welsh grammar. Thomas Charles believed that Williams cared little for purity of language and Saunders Lewis claimed that he mangled and mutilated words with impunity.[96] The original editions of his hymns did indeed include many colloquialisms, although far fewer than the works of Vicar Prichard in the previous century. Williams used dialect words, particularly in his hymns, in order to emphasize the feeling of intimacy with his Saviour. For instance, he made extensive use of the word 'Dere' (the dialect form of 'Come') when greeting Christ. This practice was characteristic of what Derec Llwyd Morgan has referred to as Williams's 'affectionate boldness' towards his Lord.[97] But Pantycelyn was acutely

---

[94] Charles Lloyd Cohen, *God's Caress: The Psychology of Puritan Religious Experience* (Oxford, 1986), p. 20.
[95] For example, the word, 'hunanchwilio' (self-search, self-scrutiny) appeared for the first time in Jenkin Jones, *Llun Agrippa* (Caerfyrddin, 1723), a translation of Matthew Mead, *Almost a Christian Discovered* (1671); 'hunanymddiddan' (soliloquy, monologue) in William Williams, *Golwg ar Deyrnas Crist* (Caerfyrddin, 1764) and 'hunanymholiad' (self-examination) in Thomas Baddy, *Pasc y Christion neu Wledd yr Efengyl* (Llundain, 1703).
[96] Saunders Lewis, *Williams Pantycelyn* (Llundain, 1927), p. 32; Alwyn Roberts, 'Pantycelyn fel bardd cymdeithasol', *Y Traethodydd*, 127 (1972), 7; Derec Llwyd Morgan, *Williams Pantycelyn* (Caernarfon, 1983), p. 5.
[97] Morgan, *Williams Pantycelyn*, p. 19.

conscious of the inability of the Welsh language, and indeed of every other earthly language, to convey with any measure of accuracy the experiences of which he sang:

> Uwch pob geiriau i ddodi ma's
> Yw dy gariad, yw dy heddwch,
> Yw dy anfeidrol ddwyfol ras.[98]

(Your love, your peace, your infinite divine grace are beyond words.)

The audience that Pantycelyn and the other revivalists were striving to reach were not united by one particular dialect. In order to convey ideas in a language which would be intelligible to all, it was necessary to create a kind of 'pulpit language' which combined the spoken word with scriptural language to create a common religious dialect.[99] In his preface to the second part of his collection of hymns, *Aleluia* (1745), Williams explained that his aim was to compose hymns in the 'sound and language of the Scriptures', the language common to his entire audience.

The Methodist movement developed the use of biblical language as a form of shorthand in order to reveal the spiritual condition of members. When a superintendent described a society as a 'city on a hill' or as 'the seed on stony ground', or when he referred to a member 'searching for the pearl', he would remind his readers of New Testament parables with which they were entirely familiar. Such phrases would succeed in conveying a wealth of knowledge about the condition of members in a concise and convenient manner. Images based on the Scriptures were also widely used. Among the most common were those of the journey through the wilderness, of the Christian as a soldier fighting bravely under Christ's banner, and of the faithful being invited to feast with the Lord. Biblical idioms became part of the everyday language of the Methodists and a myriad biblical place-names were also popularized as Pantycelyn's hymns attuned the ear to references to Salem and Calvary. Some of these names could be used to denote a particular spiritual condition; for instance, the contrast between Sinai and Zion was believed to represent the difference between those who remained 'under the law' and those freed by their faith in Christ.[100]

---

[98] Saunders Lewis, op. cit., pp. 33, 222–3; Kathryn Jenkins, 'Motiffau Emynau Pantycelyn' in Morgan, *Meddwl a Dychymyg*, pp. 105–6.

[99] Alwyn Roberts, op. cit., pp. 10–11; Glyn Tegai Hughes, *Williams Pantycelyn* (Cardiff, 1983), pp. 86–7; idem, 'Charles Wesley a Williams Pantycelyn' in Owen E. Evans (ed.), *Gwarchod y Gair: Cyfrol Goffa Y Parchedig Griffith Thomas Roberts* (Dinbych, 1993), p. 177.

[100] See, e.g., Ralph Erskine, *Sinai a Seion: Neu Allwydd y Ddau Gyfamod, Gan mwyaf tan yr Enwau Deddf a Gras* (Caerfyrddin, 1745).

By the nineteenth century the traditional link between the Welsh language and religion had been strengthened by the growth of Methodism and Dissent in general. During that century the Dissenting denominations came to be regarded as staunch supporters of the Welsh language and the Church as an increasingly Anglicized institution. The records show quite clearly, however, that the language of Church services during the eighteenth century and the early nineteenth century continued to reflect the language of the population and are therefore a reliable means of assessing the comparative strength of Welsh and English. The evidence of the visitation returns reveals that Welsh was being gradually eroded in the border areas, with a bilingual zone edging slowly towards the west. Even in areas where the Welsh language remained in the ascendancy, English gained a foothold, as the attitude of the gentry and the influence of towns and centres of industry encouraged the spread of Anglicization. Yet, Welsh remained the sole language of the majority of people in large areas of the country and that plain fact is reflected in the language of worship of the Church throughout the eighteenth century. Although there were signs of decline in certain areas, Welsh was still very much 'the language of heaven' for the majority of people.

APPENDIX 1

Anglesey – Percentage of places of worship in each language category 1749–1814

Places of worship: 76

	1749	1776	1801	1814	
Number of returns	53	57	63	51	
	%	%	%	%	
W1	98	96	95	92	
W2a	0	0	0	2	Welsh as the
W3	0	0	0	2	main language
W4	0	0	2	2	
W4S	0	2	0	0	
W5	0	0	2	0	Bilingual, but with a
W6	0	0	2	0	greater use of Welsh
B1	0	0	0	2	Bilingual
E6	0	2	0	0	Bilingual, but with a
E5	2	0	0	0	greater use of English

Breconshire – Percentage of places of worship in each language category 1799–1828

Number of places of worship: 80

	1799	1813	1828	
Number of returns	71	77	77	
	%	%	%	
W1	62	55	42	
W2	0	3	3	Welsh as the
W3	4	9	13	main language
W3S	0	3	0	
W7	0	0	1	Bilingual, but with a greater use of Welsh
B1	10	8	6	
B2	0	1	10	Bilingual
B3	4	5	3	
B4	8	60		
E7	0	0	8	Bilingual, but with a greater use of English
E6P	1	1	0	
E6	0	0	1	
E1	10	8	10	English as the main language

Caernarfonshire – Percentage of places of worship in each language category 1749–1817

Number of places of worship in Bangor diocese: 69
Number of places of worship in St Asaph diocese: 2
Total number of places of worship: 71

St Asaph Bangor	1749	1776	1801	1809 1811	1814	1817	
Number of returns	54	57	58	57	53	50	
	%	%	%	%	%	%	
W1	93	96	96	93	94	90	Welsh as the
W2	0	0	0	0	2	0	main language
W2a	0	0	0	0	2	0	
W5	0	0	0	2	0	0	Bilingual, but with a
W6	0	0	0	0	2	0	greater use of Welsh
B1	0	4	2	2	0	4	
B3	2	0	2	2	2	2	Bilingual
B4	0	0	0	2	0	0	
E1	6	0	0	0	2	0	English as the main language

Cardiganshire – Percentage of places of worship in each language category 1807–1828

Number of places of worship: 73

	1807	1813	1828	
Number of returns	57	69	70	
	%	%	%	
W1	86	83	70	
W2	2	4	7	Welsh as the
W2a	0	0	3	main language
W3S	4	0	0	
W4	0	3	0	
W7	4	3	10	Bilingual, but with greater use of Welsh
B1	2	3	3	
B2	0	0	1	Bilingual
B3	0	1	4	
B4	2	3	0	
E5	0	0	1	Bilingual, but with greater use of English
E1	2	0	0	English as the main language

Carmarthenshire – Percentage of places of worship in each language category 1755–1828

Number of places of worship: 87

	1755	1810	1813	1828	
Number of returns	54	66	80	84	
	%	%	%	%	
W1	76	75	61	55	
W2	0	2	10	2	Welsh as the
W2a	0	0	0	2	main language
W3	0	5	5	5	
W3S	0	0	1	0	
W6	0	0	0	1	Bilingual, but
W6S	0	0	0	1	with greater use
W7	6	2	1	6	of Welsh
B1	0	3	4	6	
B2	0	0	0	1	Bilingual
B3	14	6	5	10	
B4	4	3	3	10	
E7	0	0	1	1	Bilingual, but
E6	2	0	0	1	with greater use
E5	2	0	1	0	of English
E2	2	0	1	1	English as the
E1	6	6	6	6	main language

Denbighshire – Percentage of places of worship in each language category 1749–1811

Number of places of worship in Bangor diocese: 16
Number of places of worship in St Asaph diocese: 46
Total number of places of worship: 62

St Asaph Bangor	1749 1749	1791	1795	1799 1801	1809 1811	
Number of returns	49	40	41	47	57	
	%	%	%	%	%	
W1	71	58	61	70	65	
W2	0	3	2	4	4	
W2a	0	5	2	2	2	Welsh as the
W3	2	10	5	2	4	main language
W3S	2	5	0	2	7	
W3M	0	3	0	0	0	
W4	0	0	5	0	0	
W5	0	0	2	2	4	Bilingual, but
W6S	0	3	0	0	0	with a greater
W7	0	0	7	4	0	use of Welsh
B1	4	3	2	4	3	
B2	2	2	0	0	0	Bilingual
B3	2	0	0	0	2	
B4	2	0	0	0	0	
E7	6	0	0	0	0	Bilingual, but
E6	2	3	5	2	4	with a greater
E5	2	0	0	0	0	use of English
E1	2	8	7	6	7	English as the main language

Flintshire – Percentage of places of worship in each language category 1749–1809

Number of places of worship: 25

	1749	1791	1795	1799	1809	
Number of returns	22	21	23	21	21	
	%	%	%	%	%	
W1	36	33	26	24	29	
W2	0	0	0	5	0	Welsh as the
W2a	9	0	4	0	5	main language
W3	9	14	13	24	24	
W3S	0	5	4	0	0	
W6	0	5	4	5	10	Bilingual, but
W6S	0	5	0	0	0	with a greater
W7	14	19	4	5	0	use of Welsh
B1	0	14	17	14	19	
B2	9	0	4	5	0	Bilingual
B3	9	0	0	10	0	
B4	0	0	0	5	14	
E7	9	5	4	0	0	Bilingual, but
E6	5	0	4	0	0	with a greater use of English
E2	0	0	4	0	0	English as the
E1	0	0	4	5	0	main language

Glamorgan – Percentage of places of worship in each language category 1771–1813

Llandaff diocese: 103 places of worship

	1771	1774	1781	1784	1788	1791	1795	1813	
Number of returns	97	82	89	79	81	83	82	69	
	%	%	%	%	%	%	%	%	
W1	46	44	40	42	51	52	57	43	
W2	4	2	3	5	4	2	1	4	Welsh as the
W2a	1	0	1	0	0	0	0	0	main language
W3	0	0	1	1	0	0	1	0	
W3S	0	0	0	1	0	0	0	0	
W6	0	1	1	1	0	0	0	0	Bilingual, but
W6S	1	1	0	0	0	0	0	0	with greater
W7	0	4	4	4	0	2	1	0	use of Welsh
B1	1	2	2	8	5	5	2	1	
B2	2	5	3	4	1	5	11	16	
B3	16	11	3	11	11	5	6	3	Bilingual
B4	8	7	4	3	10	8	5	1	
B5	0	0	4	1	0	1	0	0	
E7	3	2	0	0	0	4	0	0	Bilingual, but
E6S	0	0	1	1	1	2	4	3	with a greater
E6	0	1	0	0	0	0	0	0	use of English
E5	1	1	1	1	0	0	0	0	
E3S	0	0	3	4	1	0	2	0	
E3	0	0	0	0	0	1	0	1	English as the
E2	2	6	2	0	1	0	0	1	main language
E1	13	11	16	13	12	12	9	17	

Glamorgan: Gower – Percentage of places of worship in each language category 1807–1828

St David's diocese: 25 places of worship

	1807	1810	1813	1828	
Number of returns	21	21	17	22	
	%	%	%	%	
W1	14	14	29	9	Welsh as the
W2	5	0	0	5	main language
W7	0	5	0	0	Bilingual, but with a greater use of Welsh
B1	0	5	0	5	
B2	5	0	6	0	Bilingual
B3	0	0	0	5	
B4	5	5	6	0	
E1	71	71	58	77	English as the main language

Merioneth – Percentage of places of worship in each language category 1749–1811

Number of places of worship in Bangor diocese: 21
Number of places of worship in St Asaph diocese: 14
Total number of places of worship: 35

St Asaph	1749	1799	1809	
Bangor	1749	1801	1811	
Number of returns	32	33	30	
	%	%	%	
W1	94	97	100	Welsh as the
W2	0	3	0	main language
W2a	3	0	0	
B4	3	0	0	

Monmouthshire – Percentage of places of worship in each language category 1771–1813

Number of places of worship in Llandaff diocese: 125
Number of places of worship in St David's diocese: 3
Total number of places of worship: 128

St David's *Llandaff*	1771	1774	1781	1784	1788	1791	1799 1802	1807 1809	1813 1813	
Number of returns	114	107	109	85	86	59	59	69	88	
	%	%	%	%	%	%	%	%	%	
W1	15	14	15	15	15	12	7	15	9	
W2	4	2	3	2	0	0	2	0	0	Welsh as the
W2a	0	1	0	0	0	0	0	0	0	main language
W3	1	2	1	1	0	2	2	0	2	
W6S	0	1	0	0	1	0	0	0	0	Bilingual, but
W7	3	3	0	2	0	2	0	0	0	with a greater use Welsh
B1	4	3	3	4	7	5	0	3	1	
B2	6	0	4	4	1	7	14	13	10	Bilingual
B3	8	8	8	7	2	3	2	1	1	
B4	7	6	6	7	8	7	8	1	6	
E7	0	2	1	2	0	2	2	0	0	
E6S	0	0	2	0	0	0	0	0	0	Bilingual, but
E6	0	1	1	0	0	0	0	0	0	with a greater use
E5S	0	0	0	0	0	0	3	0	0	of English
E4	0	0	0	0	0	0	0	1	0	
E3S	2	3	0	1	0	0	0	0	0	
E3	3	4	2	0	2	2	0	0	2	English as the
E2	3	6	5	1	2	0	2	0	0	main language
E1	46	46	50	53	60	59	59	65	68	

Montgomeryshire – Percentage of places of worship in each language category 1749–1813

Number of places of worship in St Asaph diocese: 39
Number of places of worship in Bangor diocese: 7
Number of places of worship in St David's diocese: 2
Total number of places of worship: 48

St David's	1755				1813	
St Asaph	1749	1791	1795	1799	1809	
Bangor	1749			1801	1811	
Number of returns	46	37	38	41	45	
	%	%	%	%	%	
W1	26	32	34	34	38	
W2	0	3	0	0	2	
W3	4	5	5	2	2	Welsh as the
W3S	7	8	5	7	4	main language
W4	7	3	3	5	0	
W4S	0	3	3	0	0	
W5	0	0	0	0	2	Bilingual, but with a
W6	0	0	3	0	0	greater use of Welsh
B1	6	16	5	5	9	
B2	13	0	5	2	7	Bilingual
B3	0	0	0	0	0	
B4	2	0	0	5	0	
E7	9	0	0	0	0	Bilingual, but with a
E6S	0	0	0	7	0	greater use of English
E6	0	0	3	0	4	
E3M	0	3	3	2	0	
E3S	2	0	5	2	0	English as the
E2	9	8	3	2	0	main language
E1	15	16	24	22	29	

Pembrokeshire – Percentage of places of worship in each language category 1807–1828

Number of places of worship: 147

	1807	1810	1813	1828	
Number of returns	93	58	139	139	
	%	%	%	%	
W1	25	10	29	27	
W2	1	2	1	2	
W2a	0	0	1	0	Welsh as the
W3	2	0	1	0	main language
W3S	0	2	0	1	
W7	0	0	2	6	Bilingual, but with a greater use of Welsh
B1	2	2	2	2	
B2	0	2	0	0	
B3	5	7	4	6	Bilingual
B4	3	3	3	0	
B5	0	0	1	0	
E7	0	0	1	1	Bilingual, but with a greater use of English
E2	0	2	1	1	English as the
E1	62	71	55	55	main language

Radnorshire – Percentage of places of worship in each language category 1762–1828

Number of places of worship: 48

	1762	1799	1807	1813	1828	
Number of returns	20	23	21	34	45	
	%	%	%	%	%	
W1	0	0	10	0	0	Welsh as the
W3	0	0	0	6	4	main language
B1	5	0	0	0	0	
B3	10	0	0	0	0	Bilingual
B4	10	0	0	0	0	
E7	5	4	0	0	0	Bilingual, but with a greater use of English
E2	0	0	0	3	2	English as the
E1	70	96	90	91	93	main language

APPENDIX 2

Language of places of worship of the established Church
c.1750/1771–c.1820
North Wales

	No. of places of worship	W	WBW	WB	WE	B	BWB	BEB	BW	BE	E	EBE	EB	EW	?
Anglesey	76	71	0	1	0	1	0	0	0	0	0	0	0	0	3
%		93	0	1	0	1	0	0	0	0	0	0	0	0	4
Caernarfon	71	61	0	1	0	2	0	0	0	0	1	0	0	2	4
%		86	0	1	0	3	0	0	0	0	1	0	0	3	6
Denbigh	62	51	0	0	0	5	0	0	1	3	1	0	0	0	1
%		82	0	0	0	8	0	0	2	5	2	0	0	0	2
Flint	25	9	1	3	0	7	0	0	3	0	0	0	0	0	2
%		36	4	12	0	28	0	0	12	0	0	0	0	0	8
Merioneth	35	34	0	0	0	0	0	0	0	0	0	0	0	0	1
%		97	0	0	0	0	0	0	0	0	0	0	0	0	3
Montgomery	48	18	0	3	1	6	0	0	2	2	14	1	0	1	0
%		38	0	6	2	13	0	0	4	4	29	2	0	2	0

Language of places of worship of the established Church
c.1750/1771–c.1820
South Wales

	No. of places of worship	W	WBW	WB	WE	B	BWB	BEB	BW	BE	E	EBE	EB	EW	?
Brecon	80	46	0	9	2	13	0	0	1	3	5	0	0	0	1
%		58	0	11	2.5	16	0	0	1	4	6	0	0	0	1
Cardigan	73	60	0	3	0	5	0	0	0	0	0	0	1	0	4
%		82	0	4	0	7	0	0	0	0	0	0	1	0	5
Carmarthen	87	56	0	9	0	9	0	0	5	3	2	0	3	0	0
%		64	0	10	0	10	0	0	6	3	2	0	3	0	0
Glamorgan	128	37	7	13	1	10	4	3	7	7	30	3	2	2	2
%		29	5	10	1	8	3	2	5	5	23	2	1.5	1.5	1.5
Monmouth	128	11	1	7	6	8	0	1	1	19	58	3	2	1	10
%		9	1	5	5	6	0	1	1	15	45	2	1.5	1	8
Pembroke	147	44	0	1	0	9	0	0	4	1	78	0	2	1	7
%		30	0	1	0	6	0	0	3	1	53	0	1	1	5
Radnor	48	2	0	0	0	0	0	0	0	6	40	0	0	0	0
%		4	0	0	0	0	0	0	0	12	83	0	0	0	0

APPENDIX 3
Language of worship in the established Church over the period
c.1750/1771 – c.1820

Key

W	Main language consistently Welsh
WBW	Main language Welsh, but bilingual services for a period
WB	Change from Welsh as main language to bilingual services
WE	Change from Welsh as main language to English as main language
B	Services consistently bilingual
BWB	Bilingual services, but Welsh as main language for a period
BEB	Bilingual services, but English as main language for a period
BW	Change from bilingual services to Welsh as main language
BE	Change from bilingual services to English as main language
E	Main language consistently English
EBE	Main language English, but bilingual services for a period
EB	Change from English as main language to bilingual services
EW	Change from English as main language to Welsh as main language
?	Insufficient information or an inconsistent pattern

Anglesey, c.1750–c.1820
(76 places of worship)

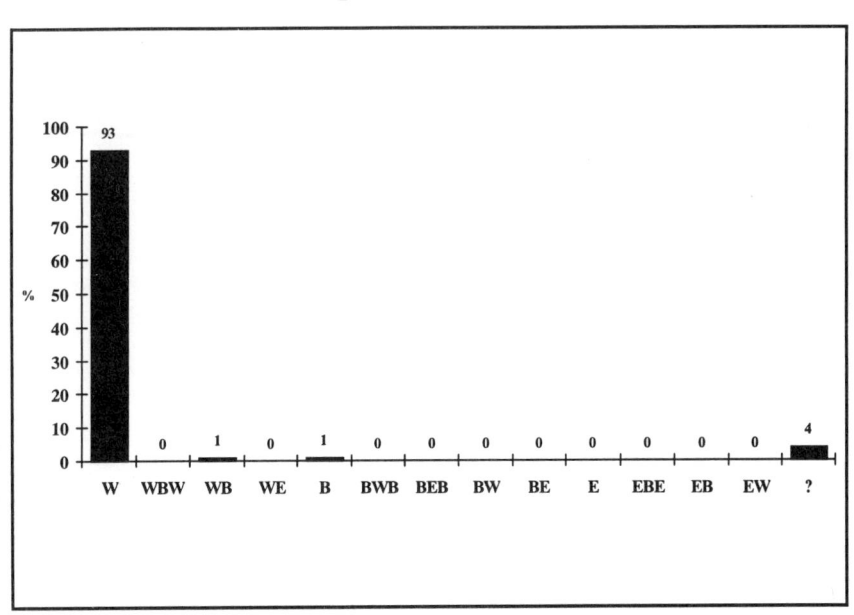

W	WBW	WB	WE	B	BWB	BEB	BW	BE	E	EBE	EB	EW	?
93	0	1	0	1	0	0	0	0	0	0	0	0	4

Breconshire, *c*.1750–*c*.1820
(80 places of worship)

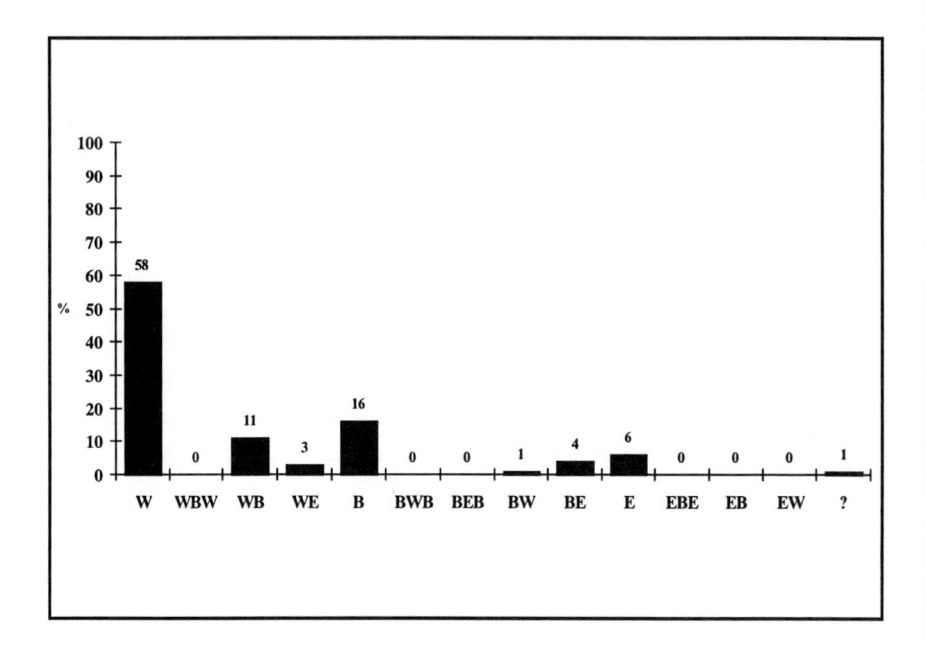

Category	%
W	58
WBW	0
WB	11
WE	3
B	16
BWB	0
BEB	0
BW	1
BE	4
E	6
EBE	0
EB	0
EW	0
?	1

Caernarfonshire, *c*.1750–*c*.1820
(71 places of worship)

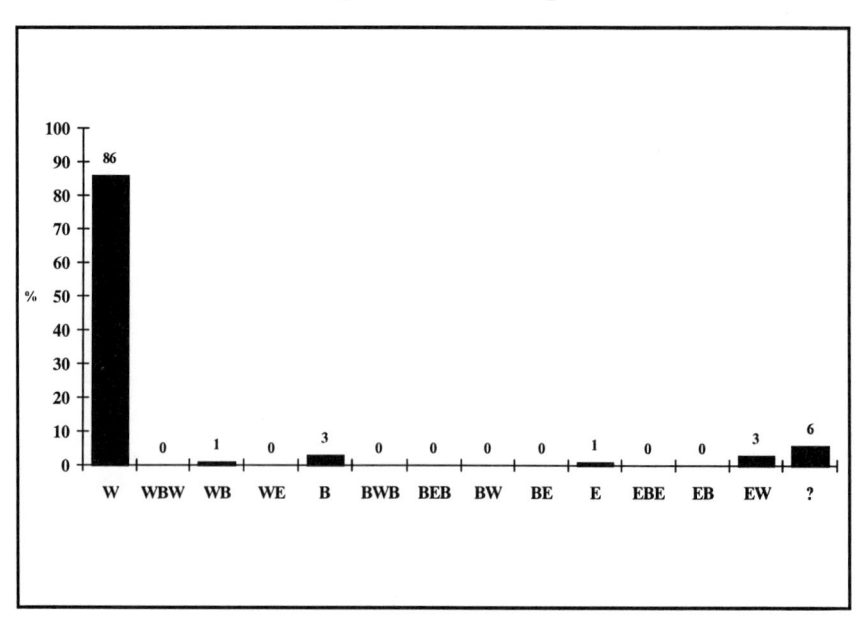

Category	%
W	86
WBW	0
WB	1
WE	0
B	3
BWB	0
BEB	0
BW	0
BE	0
E	1
EBE	0
EB	0
EW	3
?	6

Cardiganshire, c.1750–c.1820
(73 places of worship)

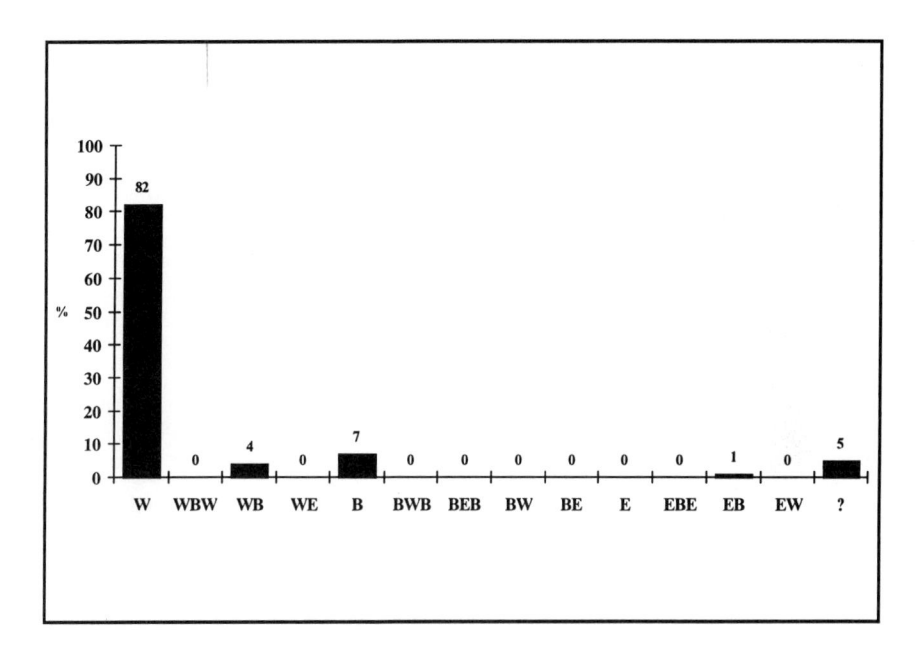

Category	%
W	82
WBW	0
WB	4
WE	0
B	7
BWB	0
BEB	0
BW	0
BE	0
E	0
EBE	0
EB	1
EW	0
?	5

Carmarthenshire, c.1750–c.1820
(87 places of worship)

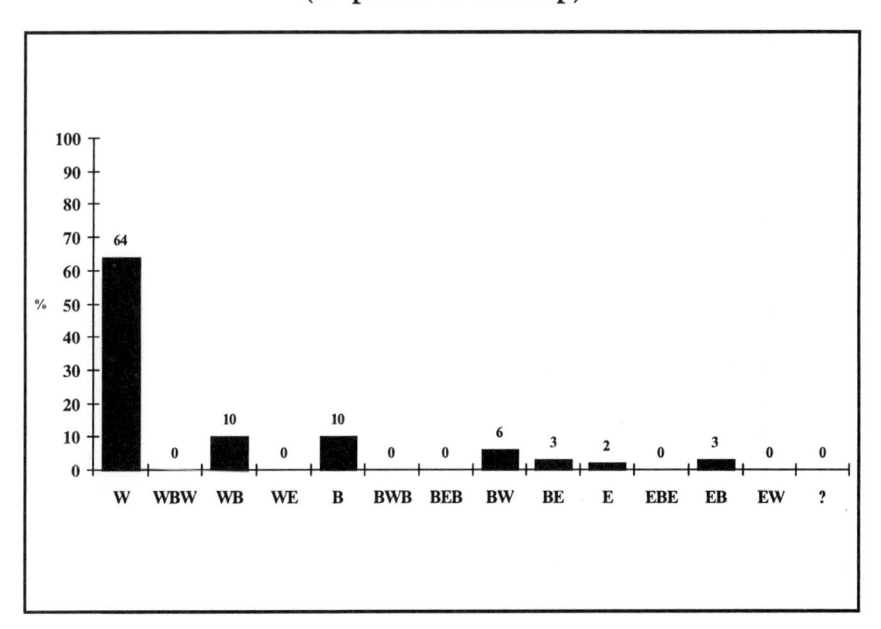

Category	%
W	64
WBW	0
WB	10
WE	0
B	10
BWB	0
BEB	0
BW	6
BE	3
E	2
EBE	0
EB	3
EW	0
?	0

Denbighshire, c.1750–c.1820
(62 places of worship)

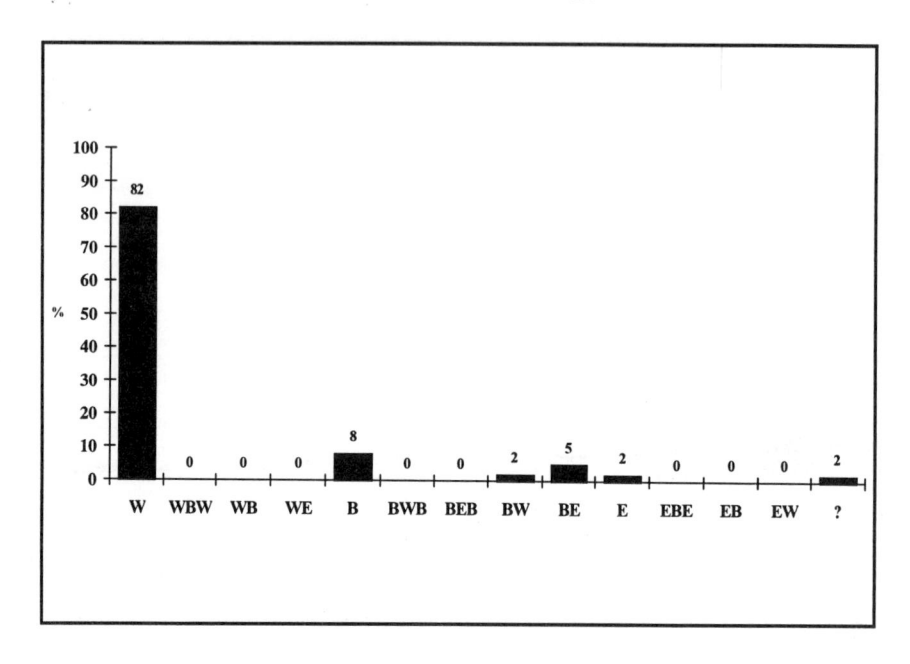

Category	W	WBW	WB	WE	B	BWB	BEB	BW	BE	E	EBE	EB	EW	?
%	82	0	0	0	8	0	0	2	5	2	0	0	0	2

Flintshire, c.1750–c.1820
(36 places of worship)

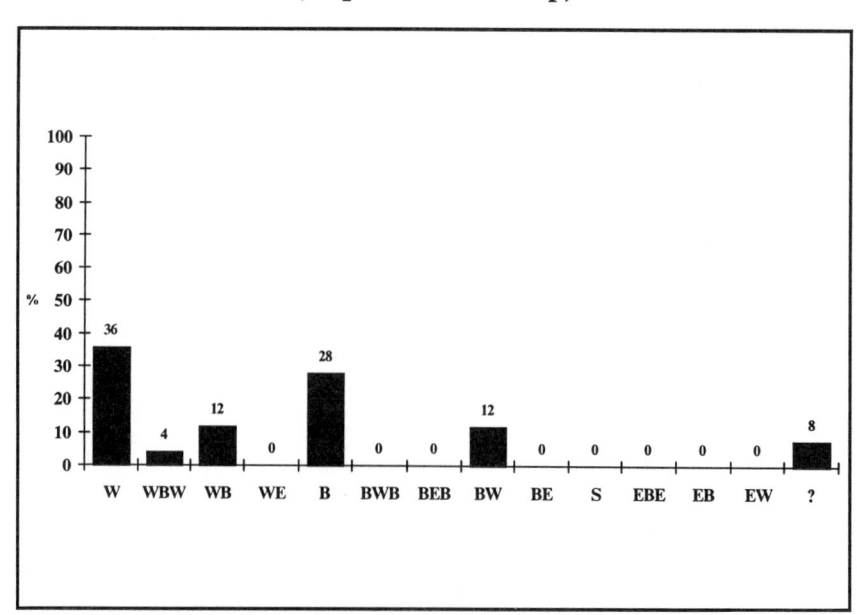

Category	W	WBW	WB	WE	B	BWB	BEB	BW	BE	S	EBE	EB	EW	?
%	36	4	12	0	28	0	0	12	0	0	0	0	0	8

Glamorgan, c.1750/1771–c.1820
(128 places of worship)

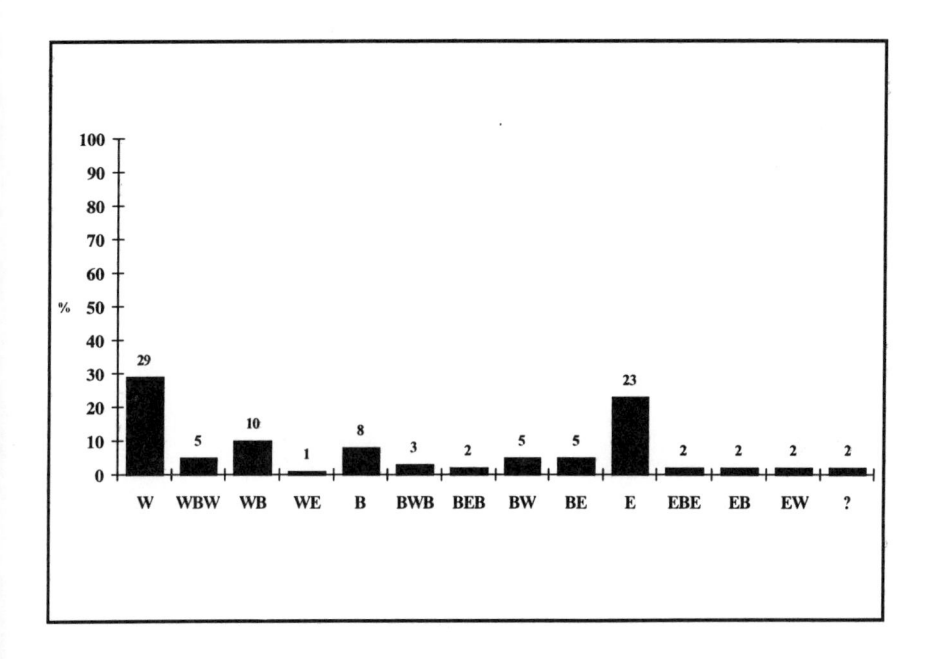

W	WBW	WB	WE	B	BWB	BEB	BW	BE	E	EBE	EB	EW	?
29	5	10	1	8	3	2	5	5	23	2	2	2	2

Merioneth, c.1750–c.1820
(35 places of worship)

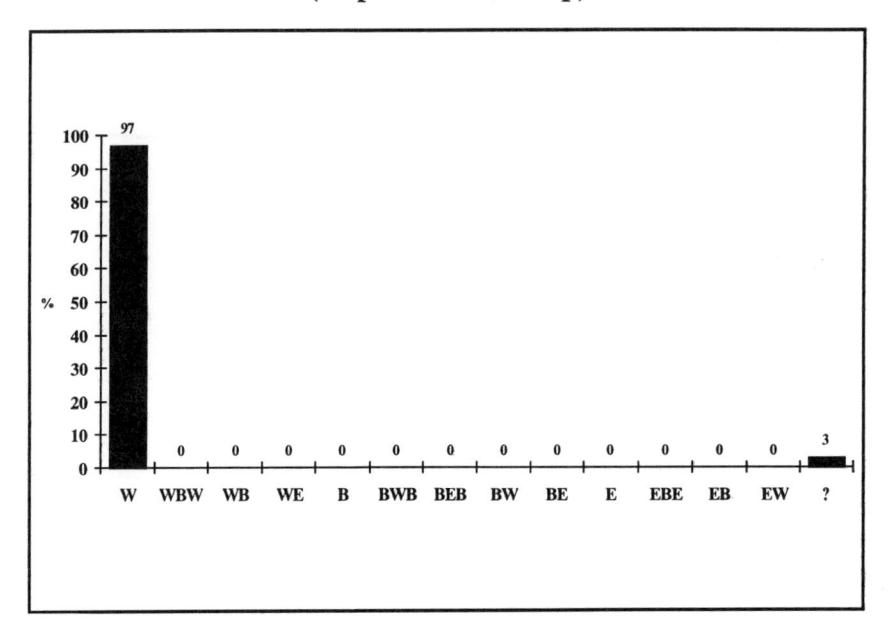

W	WBW	WB	WE	B	BWB	BEB	BW	BE	E	EBE	EB	EW	?
97	0	0	0	0	0	0	0	0	0	0	0	0	3

Monmouthshire, *c.*1750/1771–*c.*1820
(128 places of worship)

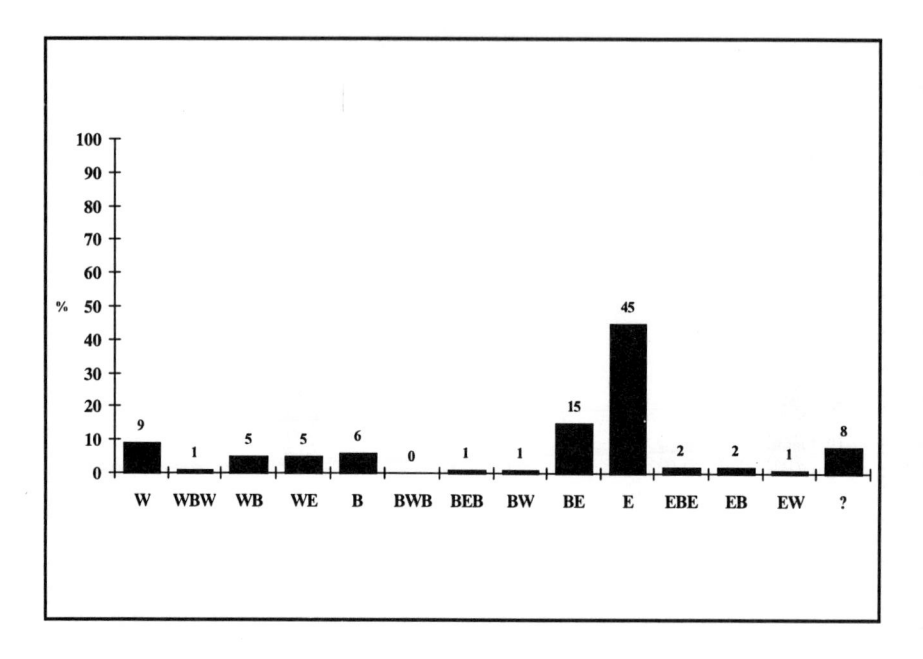

Category	W	WBW	WB	WE	B	BWB	BEB	BW	BE	E	EBE	EB	EW	?
%	9	1	5	5	6	0	1	1	15	45	2	2	1	8

Montgomeryshire, *c.*1750–*c.*1820
(48 places of worship)

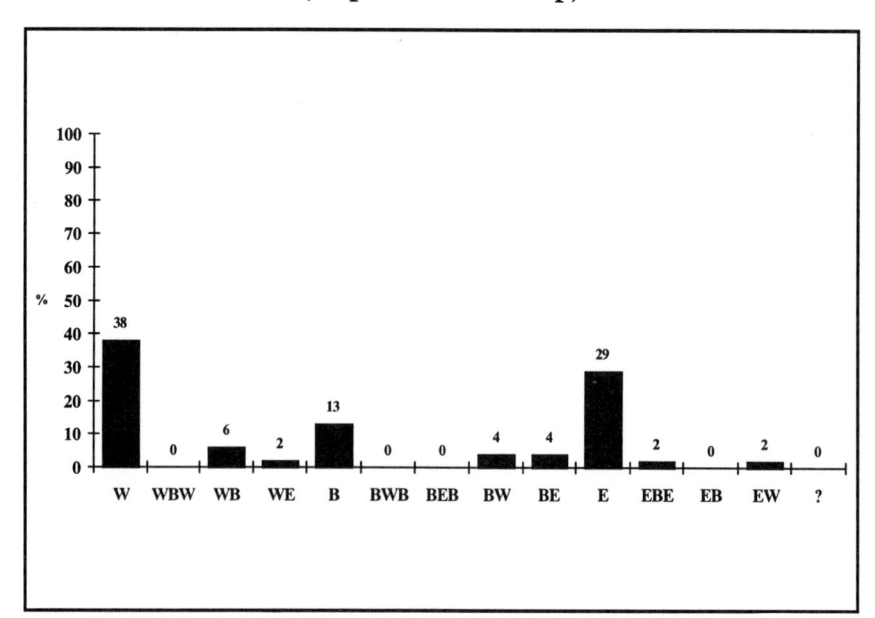

Category	W	WBW	WB	WE	B	BWB	BEB	BW	BE	E	EBE	EB	EW	?
%	38	0	6	2	13	0	0	4	4	29	2	0	2	0

Pembrokeshire, c.1750–c.1820
(147 places of worship)

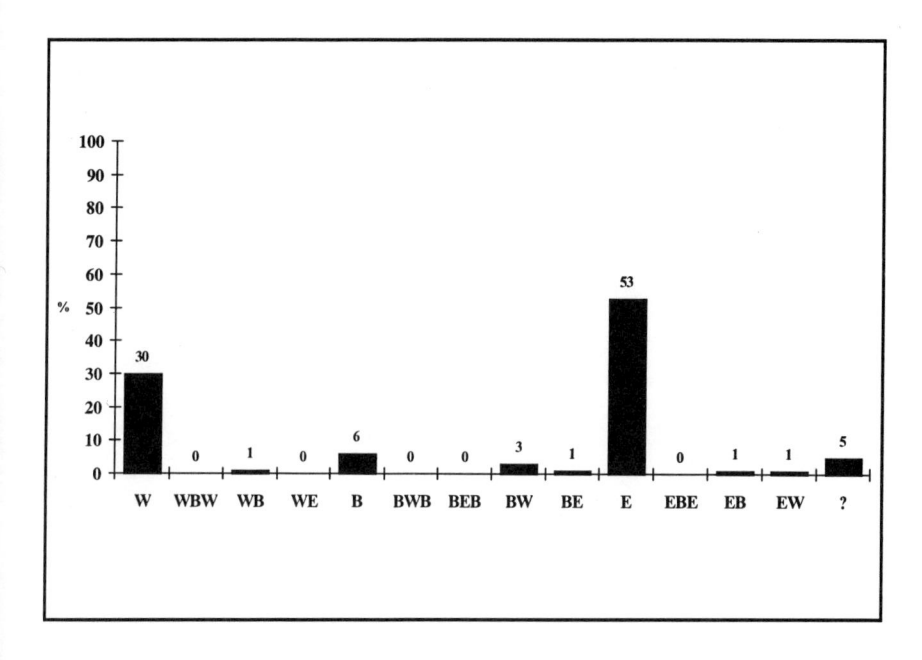

Category	%
W	30
WBW	0
WB	1
WE	0
B	6
BWB	0
BEB	0
BW	3
BE	1
E	53
EBE	0
EB	1
EW	1
?	5

Radnorshire, c.1750–c.1820
(48 places of worship)

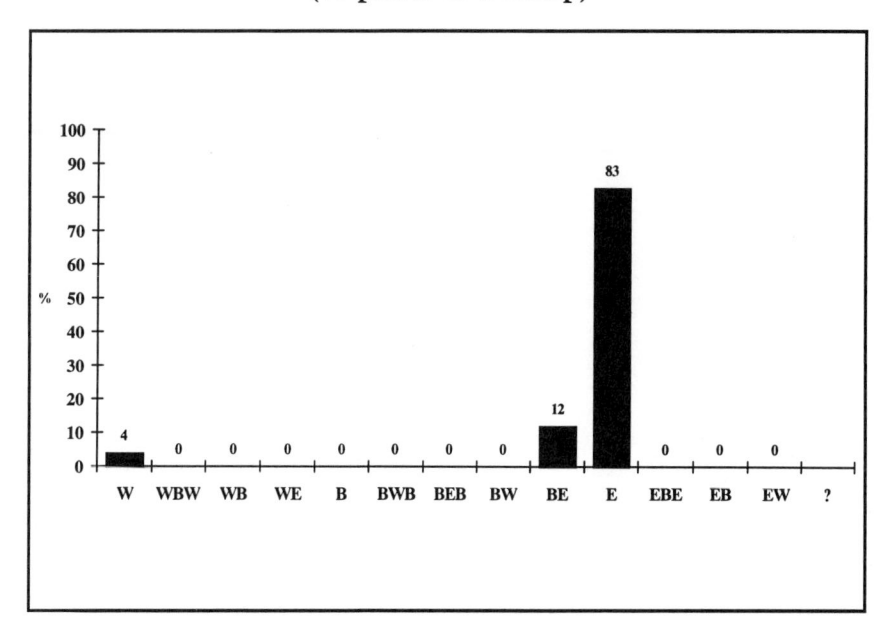

Category	%
W	4
WBW	0
WB	0
WE	0
B	0
BWB	0
BEB	0
BW	0
BE	12
E	83
EBE	0
EB	0
EW	0

8

Humanist Learning, Education and the Welsh Language 1536–1660

WILLIAM P. GRIFFITH

IT CANNOT BE claimed with any conviction that the Welsh language played a prominent part in the formal provision of education in Wales during the period between the Reformation and the Restoration. At best, the language was an informal conduit for instruction and there is evidence to suggest that it was actively ignored in the task of promoting humanist and Christian education among Welsh students. It is possible to say rather more about the role of the English language in Welsh education since, to a large degree, Welshmen derived their educational ideas at that time from England. Indeed, given the relatively limited urban growth in Wales and its assimilation into the English governmental structure, there was little scope to develop a fully independent Welsh perspective on education and its function, a perspective that might have given the language a prominent place in the dissemination of all good learning. This, indeed, was the dilemma which Welsh humanists fully appreciated, for they themselves were products of an anglophone education. In seeking to provide good cause as to why the vernacular should be employed as the vehicle for promoting education and learning, they were keenly aware that there were strong and persuasive reasons why English should be the preferred medium of education, and that due weight should also be afforded to the acknowledged classical tongues of Latin and Greek.

The influence of the English language and English values had become apparent long before the Acts of Union.[1] Sir John Wynn's ancestor, Maredudd ab Ieuan ap Robert, received a training in law, Latin and English at the Chancery for the principality of north Wales at Caernarfon in the late fifteenth century,[2] and the account of the courtly upbringing of

---

[1] Glanmor Williams, *Recovery, Reorientation and Reformation. Wales c. 1415–1642* (Oxford, 1987), pp. 144–5, 267–78.
[2] John Wynn, *The History of the Gwydir Family and Memoirs*, ed. J. Gwynfor Jones (Llandysul, 1990), pp. 49, 153.

Sir Rhys ap Thomas from south-west Wales also conveys the notion of the spread of English.[3] Similarly, the use of popularly available English grammar texts was apparent in north-east Wales at about the same time.[4] The increasing use of English in law and estate administration and the residence in Wales of English lawyers by the fifteenth century ensured that a degree of Anglicization must have occurred among some Welshmen, especially given the informal nature of legal training during that period.[5]

Nevertheless, these examples should not be exaggerated. The Welsh language still had a significant role to play among the upper echelons of Welsh society. The buoyancy of the poetic tradition among the household poets and their patrons and the increasing trend towards committing to manuscript antiquarian and poetic material for patrons to sample and savour were encouraging developments. The poetic grammar, 'y Dwned', derived from that of Donatus and revised during the Later Middle Ages, was a reminder of the classical associations possessed by Welsh culture and of the availability in Welsh of at least one powerful tool to access the fundamentals of learning and education.[6] The appearance of poets of gentle extraction like Hywel Swrdwal (*fl.* 1430–60) and gentleman poets like Ieuan ap Rhydderch (*fl.* 1430–70), who wrote for pleasure rather than payment, suggests that both Welsh and classical culture were permeating in informal educative ways across a broader range of society by the late fifteenth century.[7] Furthermore, such formal education as existed outside the courts of the most powerful of the Welsh *uchelwyr* seems to have been transmitted to the secular population by

---

[3] See Ralph A. Griffiths, *Sir Rhys ap Thomas and his Family* (Cardiff, 1993) for an ed. of Henry Rice, 'History of Sir Rhys ap Thomas', esp. pp. 182 et seq., 186–7, 196 for his royal, aristocratic and episcopal cultural links and martial education.

[4] Llinos Beverley Smith, 'The grammar and commonplace books of John Edwards of Chirk', *BBCS*, XXXIV (1987), 174–84, esp. 181. The use of English as a means of instruction leading to the classical languages was a novelty before the fifteenth century. Since the Norman Conquest education in England had been through the medium of French. See Nicholas Orme, *Education and Society in Medieval and Renaissance England* (London, 1989), pp. 4, 9–12. The impact of educational changes on the Cornish language is a theme which is not pursued in Orme's otherwise very thorough investigation, *Education in the West of England 1066–1548* (Exeter, 1976). That Cornish literacy and scholarship existed and persisted before 1500 in spite of the advance of English is clear from P. Berresford Ellis, *The Cornish Language and its Literature* (London, 1974), chapter 2.

[5] Based on the papers of Llinos Beverley Smith and A. D. Carr given at a conference on 'Literacy in medieval Celtic societies', held at University of Wales Bangor in 1994, and to appear in a forthcoming volume edited by Huw Pryce. See also Anthony Hopkins, 'The earliest written English in Monmouthshire? The Herbert bailiff's account. 1463', *MA*, XI (1995), 87–97.

[6] Thomas Parry, *A History of Welsh Literature* (Oxford, 1955), pp. 131–3, but cf. also p. 154; Williams, *Recovery, Reorientation and Reformation*, chapter 6.

[7] *DWB*, pp. 407 and 410.

means of the clerical profession, who were also often patrons of Welsh culture. In all probability there was an increase in Welsh literacy by 1500. Members of the regular orders and graduate clergy were probably responsible for teaching or at least introducing the Latin classics to their pupils through the medium of the Welsh tongue.[8] Often, moreover, the best-educated clerics were the only ones to have had the opportunity to share in the higher learning of the age by attending the continental or, more often, the English universities. Such experiences seem to have made them more enthusiastic to promote and advance their native culture when they returned to their homeland.[9] In the early modern period, however, a perception was created that England presented a superior set of norms and values in culture and education which it would be wise for the Welsh to emulate. In part, this was probably a response to the very considerable growth in literacy and in schooling provision which had occurred in England from the fifteenth century, and which outmatched provision in most other parts of Europe.[10]

The fact that a body of highly literate Welsh humanists emerged during the sixteenth and early seventeenth centuries to proclaim the status and antiquity of the Welsh language and the respectability of the Welsh cultural tradition confirms the persistence of that culture and its ability to modify, at least for some, the values acquired through the formal education system. Nevertheless, a dilemma, if not a crisis, prevailed in this period. This was encapsulated by Dr John Davies of Mallwyd in his introductory Epistle to *Antiquae Linguae Britannicae* (1621), in which he defended the language against its (unnamed) detractors and one in particular who had condemned the inconsistency of Welsh orthography. This had occurred, countered Davies, because the Welsh had been habitually reading and writing through the medium of English for the best

---

[8] Glanmor Williams, 'The collegiate church of Llanddewibrefi', *Ceredigion*, IV, no. 4 (1963), 336–52; L. Stanley Knight, 'Welsh Schools from AD 1000 to AD 1600', *AC*, XIX (1919), 276–87; F. Madan and H. H. E. Craster, *A Summary Catalogue of Western Manuscripts in the Bodleian Library at Oxford* (6 vols., Oxford, 1922–4), II, part 1, p. 171.

[9] Catrin T. Beynon Davies, 'Y cerddi i'r tai crefydd fel ffynhonnell hanesyddol', *NLWJ*, XVIII, no. 3 (1974), 278–84.

[10] W. Ogwen Williams, 'The Survival of the Welsh Language after the Union of England and Wales: the First Phase, 1536–1642', *WHR*, 2, no. 1 (1964), 68, 70; Nicholas Orme, *English Schools in the Middle Ages* (London, 1973), chapter 3; Rosemary O'Day, *Education and Society, 1500–1800* (London, 1982), chapters 1, 2; Lawrence Stone, 'The Educational Revolution in England, 1560–1640', *PP*, 28 (1964), 41–80; Victor Morgan, 'Approaches to the history of the English universities in the sixteenth and seventeenth centuries' in *Bildung, Politik und Gesellschaft: Wiener Beiträge zur Geschichte der Neuzeit*, Band 5 (München, 1978), 138–42, 144 et seq. Access to education tended to become increasingly status related; hence perhaps the enthusiasm of the Welsh gentry for English education.

part of a century.[11] Unfortunately, Davies did not expand on what had transpired during those hundred years. It might have been an oblique reference to the effects of the 'language clause' of the first Act of Union, or, alternatively, a reflection on the Anglicizing influences of the Reformation in Wales.[12] Certainly, Davies rejected the view that religious uniformity might be better secured by linguistic uniformity,[13] and it was his wish that his grammar would enrich the language competence of his fellow clergymen.[14]

What Davies may have had in mind, therefore, was the nature of schooling in Wales and the manner in which school foundations had developed. Grammar schools proper had begun to be established in Wales over the previous hundred years, and all of them had eschewed the Welsh language altogether, even though, as Davies knew as well as anyone, the vernacular embodied a long tradition of scholarly and educative discourse going back to antiquity.[15] Davies elaborated on developments in the sixteenth century in his Welsh dictionary, *Antiquae Linguae Britannicae . . . et linguae Latinae, Dictionarium Duplex* (1632), where he identified three types of educated groups in Wales who might wish to preserve their language but who, by directing their energies to acquiring a university education, had lost their language.[16] What other way was there for most sixteenth century Welshmen to reach university other than by first attending a grammar school?

The loss of the language among the leading gentry of Wales and to a degree among the clergy was a persistent theme among humanist writers. By implication, this was associated with education, since one of the principal causes of language erosion was the absence of good educative material in the Welsh language or in Latin to teach the Welsh language. Many such writers, therefore, sought to make amends by publishing material in Welsh. *Cambrobrytannicae Cymraecaeve Linguae Institutiones* (1592), by Siôn Dafydd Rhys, was intended as part of a programme of producing material for educative purposes centred around the vernacular and embodying ideals which Rhys had acquired as a schoolmaster in

---

[11] Ceri Davies (ed.), *Rhagymadroddion a Chyflwyniadau Lladin 1551–1632* (Caerdydd, 1980), p. 115.
[12] Discussed in Peter R. Roberts, 'The Welsh Language, English Law and Tudor Legislation', *THSC* (1989), 48–9.
[13] Davies, *Rhagymadroddion a Chyflwyniadau*, p. 117.
[14] Ibid., p. 121.
[15] Ibid., pp. 119–20.
[16] Ibid., pp. 125–6. The three groups consisted of those who had a deep love of the language and wished to preserve it from descending into barbarism; those who wished to ensure the survival of ancient writings in Welsh; and those who wished to see God's Word published in their own tongue.

Italy.[17] The appearance of Henry Salesbury's *Grammatica Britannica* (1593) and Henry Perri's *Eglvryn Phraethineb* (1595) reflected the aim of producing material of a standard which would enable Welsh grammar school masters, pupils and university students to pursue the close study of language structure.[18] Huw Lewys, too, shared their views on learning and the Welsh language[19] and their success in publishing scholarly Welsh material suggests that a coordinated attempt was made by north Wales clergymen centred on the diocese of Bangor to cultivate Welsh as a language of learning.[20] In so doing they were responding to ideas on the Welsh vernacular that had been circulating for at least two generations. In 1567 and 1584 the Catholic exile, Gruffydd Robert, had stressed the importance of making the Welsh tongue a medium for intellectual discourse but had also noted the obstacles which confronted those who sought to convey learning in the vernacular.[21] Earlier still, in 1547, William Salesbury had justified the publication of *Oll Synnwyr pen Kembero ygyd* by highlighting the dearth of Welsh language accounts of the fundamentals of west European education, the seven arts, as well as works derived from Erasmus and his imitators.[22]

All this reveals an anxiety to make the vernacular a language of modernity as well as honour its imagined glorious past, a past which had bestowed on the language as much antiquity and subtlety as those possessed by Latin, Greek and Hebrew, which were the very foundations of education and godly learning.[23] However, by the mid-sixteenth century the template for modern vernacular education was already being set by the English language. Salesbury himself conceded the educational value of learning English:

---

[17] Ibid., pp. 77–8, 88; Garfield H. Hughes (ed.), *Rhagymadroddion 1547–1659* (Caerdydd, 1951), pp. 66–7.
[18] Ibid., pp. 93, 99; Henry Perri, *Eglvryn Phraethineb*, ed. G. J. Williams (Caerdydd, 1930), pp. vii–ix.
[19] Henry Lewis (ed.), *Hen Gyflwyniadau* (Caerdydd, 1948), p. 9.
[20] What impact this was likely to have on Welsh scholarship and education must have been circumscribed by the print run. Only one edition of Perri's *Eglvryn Phraethineb* was ever published (prior to 1930), whereas there were many English and Latin editions and commentaries on Ramus' Rhetoric. See W. A. Jackson, F. S. Ferguson and K. F. Pantzer (eds.), *A Short-title Catalogue of Books printed in England, Scotland and Ireland* (2nd ed., 3 vols., London, 1976–91), II, p. 231, for Perri as 'Perry', and Bedwyr Lewis Jones, 'Testunau rhethreg y Dadeni' (unpubl. University of Wales MA thesis, 1961), chapter 4, and pp. 173 et seq. for the Ramist influence on one or two other Welsh scholars and poets.
[21] Lewis, *Hen Gyflwyniadau*, pp. 5–6; Thomas Jones (ed.), *Rhyddiaith Gymraeg, Yr Ail Gyfrol. Detholion o Lawysgrifau a Llyfrau Printiedig 1547–1618* (Caerdydd, 1956), p. 60.
[22] Hughes, *Rhagymadroddion*, pp. 11, 14.
[23] Davies, *Rhagymadroddion a Chyflwyniadau*, pp. 77, 81, 82, 84, 85, 98–9; R. Brinley Jones, *The Old British Tongue: the Vernacular in Wales 1540–1640* (Cardiff, 1970), introduction.

> Dyscwch nes oesswch Saesnec
> Doeth yw e dysc da iaith dec.[24]

(Learn so that you may lead your life in English, the knowing of it is wise, a good fine language.)

Other writers related their compositions to what was already being produced in England and also to the growing trend in Wales among the educated upper classes of depending mostly upon English texts. Sir John Price acknowledged his own ease with the English tongue and how natural it was to be bilingual.[25] The vernacular texts produced at the end of the century, such as Henry Perri's *Eglvryn Phraethineb*, were essentially translations or adaptations of popular English material.[26] By offering such works Welsh humanists hoped to modify the learning experience and counter the effects of Anglicizing influences.[27]

What gave the language a proper educative function was religion and the need to ensure a godly and well-informed population. During the sixteenth century Welsh humanists regarded the issue mainly as ensuring that there was a body of better educated, godly clergy competent to read the Scriptures in Welsh and preach in the vernacular. In other words, there were divine as well as scholarly functions to the language.[28] During the seventeenth century the stress was to shift more towards trying to secure popular literacy in the vernacular in order that the laity itself should be better able to study and meditate upon the Word of God.

That popular literacy of sorts in the vernacular existed even in the mid-sixteenth century was recognized by Sir John Price in 1546 when he claimed that it was not being catered for by vernacular Scripture.[29] Similarly, during the later 1580s, the Puritan, John Penry, made the assumption that there existed a vernacularly literate Welsh population which had nothing of value or spiritual worth to study.[30] How widespread was that literacy and how it had been achieved went unexplained by both Price and Penry, but presumably it was acquired mainly in an informal,

---

[24] Hughes, *Rhagymadroddion*, p. 8.
[25] Ibid., pp. 3–4; Davies, *Rhagymadroddion a Chyflwyniadau*, p. 37.
[26] Perri, *Eglvryn Phraethineb*, pp. vii–viii.
[27] Hughes, *Rhagymadroddion*, pp. 63–4; Jones, *The Old British Tongue*, pp. 48–51.
[28] Isaac Thomas, *Y Testament Newydd Cymraeg 1551–1620* (Caerdydd, 1976), pp. 58–9, 99–100; Roberts, 'The Welsh Language', 42, 47, 54–6, 67, 70, 71.
[29] Hughes, *Rhagymadroddion*, pp. 3–4.
[30] John Penry, *Three Treatises Concerning Wales*, ed. David Williams (Cardiff, 1960), pp. 34–5. Penry's ideal, of course, was that the Welsh should learn English but in the interim communication of scriptural truth in Welsh was essential (ibid., p. 37). See Glanmor Williams, 'John Penry: Marprelate and Patriot?' *WHR*, 3, no. 4 (1967), 376–8.

domestic manner rather than by the formal pattern of education and learning.[31] It was widely believed that formal learning was a major cause of Anglicization among local élites and among the common people.[32] Not having social leaders who were literate or adept in the Welsh language was considered especially harmful since it deprived the lower orders of spiritual and cultural exemplars, a point noted also by the Catholic, Robert Gwyn in 1585[33] and much later by the Puritan John Edwards (Siôn Treredyn) in 1650.[34] The answer was to try to encourage popular literacy at home by promoting self-didacticism as well as moral and spiritual duty. This theme, set out by Edward Kyffin and Thomas Salisbury in 1603,[35] became a constant one after 1620 when the new edition of the Welsh Bible under the aegis of Bishop Richard Parry, appeared.[36]

By promoting a popular edition of this Bible and encouraging the production of more devotional works in the vernacular, Puritan writers established new parameters for the language. None of them took for granted any longer that a vernacularly literate population existed in Wales, and they set about aiding language recovery among the Anglicized and promoting literacy among the monolingual, illiterate Welsh. Therefore, pious works were also required to have a didactic function. Some authors, in addition to wishing to polish reading skills and promote literacy within the home, took seriously the task of inculcating piety among those who might otherwise remain illiterate by encouraging the development of memory skills. Both Robert Lloyd in 1630[37] and David Rowlands in 1633[38] stressed the importance of being read to, and the latter also believed strongly in the mnemonic value of Welsh rhymes and verses. A similar approach was adopted by Richard Jones of Llanfair Caereinion in 1655, while Richard Jones of Denbigh in 1653 placed deliberate stress on perfecting mnemonic techniques.[39]

In a significant educative departure, in *Sail Crefydd Gristnogawl* (1649), Evan Roberts produced a Welsh (pronunciation) alphabet to enable Anglicized Welshmen to acquire a better grasp of Welsh words. Roberts had in mind literate Welshmen who, having been taught through the

---

[31] Both men were natives of Breconshire and it is interesting to speculate whether their comments were based on the experience of that county alone.
[32] Davies, *Rhagymadroddion a Chyflwyniadau*, p. 69.
[33] Hughes, *Rhagymadroddion*, p. 53.
[34] Lewis, *Hen Gyflwyniadau*, p. 27.
[35] Hughes, *Rhagymadroddion*, pp. 106, 108.
[36] Davies, *Rhagymadroddion a Chyflwyniadau*, p. 102.
[37] Hughes, *Rhagymadroddion*, pp. 127–9.
[38] Ibid., pp. 134–5.
[39] Ibid., pp. 137–8, 140–1.

medium of English, had become Anglicized. Having mastered the alphabet, they would be able to compare parallel texts and acquire the native tongue and become literate in it. In addition, and most importantly, such people would be in a position to instruct others: 'they may be better enabled to teach others, their Houshold, Friends, and Neighbours, who can reade neither English nor Welsh.' The dearth of material in Welsh was still a problem, according to Roberts:

> ... among twenty Families, there can scarce one Welsh Bible be found: As for the English Bible, in that Family where any is, it is but uselesse, in respect of the generalitie of those which know nothing, and understand nothing in that tongue.[40]

The inculcation of Welsh literacy, Roberts believed, would encourage the development of a more knowledgeable and moral public. These observations, and more, received the closest scrutiny from Robert's colleague, Oliver Thomas. In their joint edition of *Sail Crefydd Ghristnogol* (c.1640), which argued the case for extending popular literacy, they portrayed the vernacular as the vehicle for advancing piety among the populace. Hitherto, so it was claimed, no advance had been made in Wales in comparison with England.[41] This comparative element was a theme which Thomas had already examined in his *Car-wr y Cymru* (1631). The profusion of printed religious material in the English language had considerably aided popular piety among the English public, even among the servant classes, but there was a dearth of such material in Welsh. In addition, Welsh literacy was confined by fashionable attitudes which placed a greater emphasis on reading other languages, notably English. This led to a belief that it was sufficient to be able to read the Scriptures in that language alone. That was all very well for individuals or households who were acquainted with the English tongue, but the future of the Protestant faith depended on the growth of a Welsh reading public.[42] This was to be the recurring theme for the remainder of the century and beyond.

The realities of early modern education confirm that humanists and religious writers were not issuing statements for effect only. Although they might have been making assertions about language in order to justify

---

[40] Evan Roberts, *Sail Crefydd Gristnogawl* (Llundain, 1649), p. 2, in Merfyn Morgan (ed.), *Gweithiau Oliver Thomas ac Evan Roberts* (Caerdydd, 1981), p. 232.

[41] *Sail Crefydd Ghristnogol* (Llundain, c.1640), sig. A, in Morgan (ed.), op. cit., p. 161.

[42] *Car-wr y Cymru* (1631), pp. 4, 15, 38–9, 70–4, in Morgan (ed.), op. cit., pp. 34, 45, 100–4. On the situation in England, see Tessa Watt, *Cheap Print and Popular Piety 1550–1640* (Cambridge, 1991), pp. 322–6.

other aims or intentions, it is clear that Welsh educational aspirations and horizons were coloured by English presuppositions, values and prejudices. It must be re-emphasized at this stage that what was meant by education in this period, throughout western Europe, was that common core of values and ideas centred on classical literature and philosophy, on Latin and, increasingly, Greek learning. Similarly, that common education shared a lingua franca in that by far the greatest preponderance of books and texts were produced in the Latin tongue. This represented a central body of higher learning. In practical terms, it became the *sine qua non* for holding positions of professional, scholarly and administrative responsibility. Such learning existed over and above, or in addition to, national and regional vernaculars and whatever literature and culture were contained in those vernaculars. Obviously the manner in which the higher learning was disseminated had an impact on vernacular culture and the degree to which that vernacular was employed to teach the classical tongues and, by translation, to explain classical texts and sources. In addition to this came the impact of the religious and theological debates centred on the Reformation and Counter-Reformation. Although these, too, were conducted by means of a lingua franca – the Latin tongue – it was recognized that the vernaculars were essential to disseminating doctrinal and partisan ideas and crucial to instilling scriptural knowledge and values of piety. Education, therefore, came to combine a mixture of the classical and the religious ideas and beliefs transmitted by means of a combination of classical languages and vernacular languages. The precise balance in the combination varied from country to country, coloured by the attitude of the state, its prince, and the predisposition of the groups interested in endowing education, wanting its benefits, or seeking to promote literacy.

In Wales, changes in the status of the vernacular never occurred in a vacuum. Although a purely structuralist-functionalist explanation for the state of the language in this period is insufficient, there were undoubtedly features which suggest that it has some validity. The earlier assessment (pp. 123–52) of the status of the language has highlighted how, on the one hand, the growing importance of English in law at and before the Acts of Union detrimentally affected the language while, on the other, the need to advance and secure the Protestant faith in Wales gave firm value to the vernacular.[43] The first Act of Union of 1536, in stressing the disjunctions caused by the use hitherto of a different language from English and by further emphasizing that henceforth Welsh speakers holding

---

[43] More generally on the compulsions to promote education, see C. Arnold Anderson and Mary Jean Bowman, 'Education and economic modernisation' in Lawrence Stone (ed.), *Schooling and Society: Studies in the History of Education* (London, 1977), p. 9.

administrative office should be competent in, and employ, the English language and speech,[44] contributed over time to a particular view as to how education in Wales would be organized. In other words, there was an internalization of the merits of receiving an English-based or English medium education. Indeed, if Sir William Gerard's gloss on the 'language clause' of the act is correct, this internalization was apparent in Welsh support for the second and more detailed Act of Union of 1543:

> The likinge which bothe the kinge and the Subiectes of wales had of this chainge of all the walshe lawes and customes into the maner and order of the lawes of Englande, appereth by the acte the same kinge . . . pleased to passe.[45]

Undoubtedly, the reorganization of law and administration after 1536–43 reinforced the role of Ludlow as a regional capital and as a scholarly centre too, organized around the court and household of the lord president.[46] Gerard anticipated that as greater numbers of Welsh youths were trained as law clerks at Ludlow, greater benefits would accrue, in terms of order and civility, in all parts of Wales. In short, they would be conduits to convey English norms.[47]

The consolidation of a political centre in the Welsh Marches may help to explain the subsequent distribution pattern of Welsh grammar schools during the sixteenth and seventeenth centuries. These were concentrated around the eastern valley fringes of Wales, and all were accessible to Ludlow. The surviving evidence about the teaching and curricular arrangements of these schools indicates that they imitated arrangements in England without any allowance for the Welsh context. Indeed, the original statutes for Christ's College, Brecon (1542) aimed at dispelling the ignorance of the English language which existed among the local populace.[48] At other foundations, the central aim was to nurture pupils in comprehension and felicity of style in Latin and, to a lesser degree, Greek, but the newer pupils in the lower forms were to be taught through the medium of English exclusively. This was so at Bangor, Monmouth, Oswestry and Ruthin. At Ruthin, Dean Gabriel Goodman's statutes of 1590 forbade pupils in the senior forms from intruding English into the classical ambience in any way and in the junior forms Welsh was excluded

---

[44] William Rees, *The Union of England and Wales* (Cardiff, 1948), p. 70.
[45] D. Lleufer Thomas, 'Further Notes on the Court of the Marches', *Y Cymmrodor*, XIII (1900), 147; cf. Peter R. Roberts, 'The "Henry VIII Clause": Delegated Legislation and the Tudor Principality of Wales' in Thomas G. Watkin (ed.), *Legal Record and Historical Reality* (London, 1989), pp. 43, 45 for the first act.
[46] D. Lleufer Thomas, 'Further Notes', 109–10.
[47] Ibid., 163.
[48] Theophilus Jones, *A History of the County of Brecknock* (4 vols., Brecon, 1909–30), I, p. 46.

from the English ambience: 'if in one of the upper classes he speaks English and if in one of the lower Classes he speaks Welsh he shall be deemed faulty and an Imposition given him.'[49] Bangor's statutes, imitating those of Bury St Edmunds, declared that no scholar was to be admitted unless he was already fully literate in English, and while the normal medium of discourse was to be Latin, English played a significant secondary part in worship and doctrinal instruction.[50] Other school foundations in Wales, for example Defynnog, included in their statutes the requirements that their master or masters had to be Englishmen, and still others employed Englishmen by choice.[51]

Nor did the period of Puritan rule in the mid-seventeenth century offer much change in the pattern of education. Thomas Chaloner, ejected from Shrewsbury School in 1645, toured the schools of north Wales and the borders teaching the traditional classical arts subjects. At Hawarden, he was dismayed to discover that interest in education had permeated to the lower orders and that he was obliged to teach many of the 'lowest sort' English.[52] Notwithstanding the comments of those Welsh writers noted above about the importance of instructing through the vernacular, English Puritans nursed contempt for the Welsh language because of the apparent lack of religious zeal among the Welsh. The perceived need was to bring the country to godly order and uniformity with England by means of educational methods current in England. This was the sort of thinking which lay behind plans to establish a Puritan national seminary in Wales[53] and the guidelines behind the schools which emerged as a consequence of the Act for the Better Propagation and Preaching of the Gospel in Wales (1650). After 1650, all schools, both old and new, were to be ruled by masters whose qualities lay in their piety and learning rather than in their proficiency in the vernacular.[54]

Throughout the period schools were not only emulators of England in their organization and statutes but also in their reading material. Such

[49] L. S. Knight, *Welsh Independent Grammar Schools to 1600* (Newtown, 1927), p. 119; W. M. Warlow, *A History of the Charities of William Jones* (London, 1899), p. 358.
[50] Knight, *Welsh Independent Grammar Schools*, pp. 42, 97, 98; M. L. Clarke, 'The Elizabethan Statutes of Friars School, Bangor', *TCHS*, 16 (1955), 25–8. See O'Day, *Education and Society*, pp. 72–3, on the growing use of English to teach Latin.
[51] William P. Griffith, 'Schooling and Society' in J. Gwynfor Jones (ed.), *Class, Community and Culture in Tudor Wales* (Cardiff, 1989), p. 93.
[52] J. B. Oldham, *A History of Shrewsbury School, 1552–1952* (Oxford, 1952), pp. 49–50; also, O'Day, *Education and Society*, pp. 65–6 on the increase in English vernacular education.
[53] Geoffrey F. Nuttall, 'The correspondence of John Lewis, Glasgrug, with Richard Baxter and with Dr John Ellis, Dolgelley', *JMHRS*, II, no. 2 (1954), 130.
[54] Thomas Richards, *A History of the Puritan Movement in Wales, 1639–53* (London, 1920), chapter 15; Griffith, 'Schooling and Society', p. 108; J. W. Adamson, *Pioneers of Modern Education 1600–1700* (Cambridge, 1905), pp. 97–8.

evidence as survives makes no mention of any Welsh literature. The original library of Lady Hawkins's School at Kington on the Welsh borders in 1638 was composed overwhelmingly of Latin works, including grammar, literature, some natural philosophy and theology. The only exceptions were a few versions of the Scriptures and sermons in English.[55] A catalogue of the library at Beaumaris Grammar School, as it existed in 1662 following the convulsions of civil war and republican government, is even more indicative of the trends. Again, the majority of texts were in Latin, but it was noticeable that in practically all fields of learning the school also possessed English language volumes. Some attention was paid to French and German but nowhere, not even in the collection of Scriptures, was there any indication that Welsh was studied.[56] School libraries are also an indication of the pattern of learning available at university level in England, the logical line of progression from the schools. Again, from the limited evidence available, inventories belonging to Welsh students and university members reveal no Welsh material in their possession, only the same pattern as might be found at school.[57] Grammar schools, or at least the best of them, prepared their pupils for the sort of cultural life found at the English universities or inns of court. At Beaumaris during the 1650s, pupils participated in English plays, while some school statutes such as those of Ruthin encouraged pupils to rehearse Latin drama, activities which were outside the scope of normal Welsh cultural pursuits.[58]

The exclusion of the Welsh language from regular patterns of educational activity implied a desire to persuade Welsh pupils and students to conform to norms not only in learning but also in speech and behaviour appropriate to English students. Given the prevalence of English satirical views about the Welsh,[59] it is hardly surprising that the need to conform, or to be acceptable, entered the Welsh subconscious. In 1599 a proposed tutor for Robert Broughton of Lower Broughton, Flintshire, the son of a judge on the Chester circuit, expressed scorn for the Welsh tongue even though he was proficient in many other

---

[55] Penelope E. Morgan, 'The Library of Lady Hawkins' School, Kington, Herefordshire', *NLWJ*, XXIV, no. 1 (1985), 46–62.

[56] Anglesey County Record Office, Llangefni, David Hughes Charities, Box 13.

[57] See William P. Griffith, *Learning, Law and Religion: Higher Education and Welsh Society, c.1540–1640* (Cardiff, 1996), chapter 3.

[58] Knight, *Welsh Independent Grammar Schools*, p. 118; NLW, Annual Report 1978–9 (Aberystwyth, 1979), p. 60. I am grateful to Ms Nia M. W. Powell for this reference.

[59] T. Powell, 'The Welsh as pictured in old English jest books', *Y Cymmrodor*, III (1880), 107–16.

languages.⁶⁰ John Williams of Cochwillan reacted with embarrassment to the fun made of his Welsh 'tone' or accent when he first entered St John's College, Cambridge, in 1598:

> One thing put him to the blush, and a little Shame, that such as had gigling [sic] Spleens would laugh at him for his *Welsh* Tone. For those who knew him at his Admission . . . would often say, that he brought more *Latin* and *Greek*, than good *English* with him.⁶¹

Clearly, Williams's education at Ruthin Grammar School had been wanting in this respect. In order to acquire 'proper' standards, therefore, a Welsh student was expected to turn his back on the rough provincialism of his fellow countrymen and model his behaviour on better bred Englishmen:

> Speake noe Welsh to any that can speake English, noe not to your bedfellows, that therby you may attaine . . . Englishe tongue perfectly [sic]. I hadd rather that you shuld keepe company with studious, honest Englishmen than with many of your own countrymen who are more prone to be idle and riotous than the English.

So thought a Merioneth squire c.1637, in an oft quoted letter of advice to his son,⁶² expressing a view which was little different from that of Sir John Wynn in the early 1600s when he proposed to send his second son, Richard, to Lincoln's Inn, London: 'provyd hym a chamber with som good student an Enghleman [sic] as near the In as yow can.'⁶³

Even more revealing is the autobiographical account of Fr. Augustine Baker, who, as David Baker of Abergavenny, was brought up in the last quarter of Elizabeth's reign. In his case we see clearly the functional role of education and the perception that in order to obtain preferment it was essential to socialize with English scholars, learn English well and be able to pronounce it correctly. Although he had certainly learnt to read English (including polemical works) at Abergavenny, it appeared that his speech was flawed, partly because of the very Welsh ambience of the town and

---

⁶⁰ W. J. Smith (ed.), *Calendar of Salusbury Correspondence 1553 – circa 1700* (Cardiff, 1954), no. 55, pp. 40–1.

⁶¹ John Hacket, *Scrinia Reserata: A Memorial Offer'd to the Great Deservings of John Williams, D.D.* (London, 1693), part 1, p. 7; also discussed in Griffith, *Learning, Law and Religion*, p. 93. Cf. E. D. Snyder, 'The Wild Irish: a study of some English satires against Irish, Scots and Welsh', *MP*, 17, no. 2 (1920), esp. 165–8.

⁶² T. Jones Pierce (ed.), *Clenennau Letters and Papers in the Brogyntyn Collection* (Aberystwyth, 1947), pp. 126–7 (no. 444) and J. Gwynfor Jones, *Wales and the Tudor State: Government, Religious Change and the Social Order 1534–1603* (Cardiff, 1989), p. 153.

⁶³ NLW MS 9052E, no. 221.

the predominance of the vernacular. Therefore, at the age of eleven, he was removed from the local grammar school by his father and sent to London. There, at Christ's Hospital, he met the sons of the English gentry, attended English church services and Bible readings, and became so proficient in English that he forgot his Welsh. His proficiency in Welsh was only restored when, during the Armada crisis of 1588, he returned to Wales to rejoin his family.[64] Just as revealing as Baker's own account is the précis of his life made by his compatriot, co-worker and pupil, Fr. Leander Prichard. In particular, it conveys eloquently the unequal relationship between Welsh and English *vis-à-vis* contemporary notions of esteem:

> He got to speak English purely without any corruption from his mother tongue, which doth commonly infect men of our countrie, that they cannot speak English but that they are discovered by their vitious pronunciation or idiotisms. He tooke great care to remedy this in me; but it would not be, at least not perfectly. Now his father intended most especially, by sending him up to London, this acquiring of the English tongue, as most necessary for his advancement in the world.[65]

Daughters of gentlemen, as well as sons, received the benefit of an English education. Female education was largely organized by means of local private tuition. One of the daughters of the Brynkir household was taught at home to read fairy romances and to read English perfectly. However, in order to polish her English speech she too was dispatched specially to Chester, while her tutor moved on to another Welsh mansion.[66]

Schooling Welsh boys in England was not uncommon. Augustine Baker was merely following in his brother's footsteps when he was sent to London. A not inconspicuous minority of Welsh school pupils attended the larger or more important English foundations by the turn of the seventeenth century, notably Westminster, Winchester and Shrewsbury.[67] Shrewsbury's statutes stressed that all its entrants were expected to be fully

---

[64] Justin McCann and Hugh Connolly (eds.), *Memorials of Father Augustine Baker* (Catholic Record Society, XXXIII, London, 1933), pp. 30, 31, 75; cf. G. Dyfnallt Owen, *Wales in the Reign of James I* (London, 1988), p. 127, for the removal of a pupil from Carmarthen Grammar School to Hereford Grammar School for reasons of discipline and behaviour.

[65] *Memorials of Father Augustine Baker*, p. 58; cf. John Edwards (Siôn Treredyn) on the process of Anglicization in Monmouthshire a generation after Baker (Lewis, *Hen Gyflwyniadau*, pp. 27–8).

[66] John Ballinger (ed.), *Calendar of Wynn (of Gwydir) Papers 1515–1690* (Aberystwyth, 1926), no. 967. See also Williams, 'The Survival of the Welsh Language', 84.

[67] Griffith, 'Schooling and Society', pp. 98–100.

literate in English before admission. From an early stage its registrations reveal a clear and substantial Welsh presence, with boys who were drawn from around the border areas rendered distinctive by virtue of their patronymics. By the 1590s Welsh admissions were still a feature, according to the recorded places of origin, but by then most entrants possessed fixed surnames – a clear indication of the shift towards Anglicizing fashions.[68] During the 1630s, admissions from Wales (largely north Wales) at St John's College, Cambridge, included a significant number of students who had spent the year or so prior to admission at schools in England. It can be assumed that this occurred in order to refine the social and educational skills of those students prior to university life.[69]

Although the English universities did not offer the kind of social round found at the inns of court in London, they attracted increasing numbers of less academically committed, but socially motivated students, by the late sixteenth century. Although the majority of Welsh students were classed as plebeians or sizars, there was also a socially superior element which was readily drawn into the lifestyle and cultural pursuits of their English social equivalents. There and in the freer world of society within the inns of court there were attractions and pressures to conform to a more Anglicized life. Pressure to abandon the Welsh language was drawn out of the social relationships forged between young men of similar social background, friendships between Welsh and English students, such as those contracted by the sons of Sir John Wynn of Gwydir.[70] There were harsher pressures too, though how frequently felt it is hard to tell. The case of the generally recalcitrant Devonian student, Henry Leigh of Hart Hall, Oxford, in 1580, who took particular umbrage at students speaking Welsh, may be exceptional, but is worth noting for the sort of prejudice which might normally be concealed. Both Welsh and English students alleged that Leigh had produced libellous writings which included attacks upon four Welsh students. According to Griffith Hughes, Leigh had 'reade a certayne writinge agaynst the Welshmen terminge their speeche the vnlawfull Welshe tonge'.[71] The incident, it is true, had taken place at Christmas, when the custom of the Lords of Misrule prevailed and when all authority and normal behaviour could be overturned.[72] Nevertheless,

[68] E. Calvert (ed.), *Shrewsbury School Regestum Scholarium 1562–1635* (Shrewsbury, 1892), passim; Oldham, *History of Shrewsbury School*, p. 18.
[69] J. E. B. Mayor (ed.), *Admissions to the College of St John the Evangelist, Cambridge* (Cambridge, 1882), passim.
[70] Griffith, *Learning, Law and Religion*, pp. 403–5.
[71] Oxford University Archives, Hyp B.2. Depositions 1578–84; discussed also in Griffith, ibid., pp. 94, 173–4.
[72] Discussed in the context of schooling and keeping order in Griffith, 'Schooling and Society', p. 95.

the university authorities took Leigh's overall conduct sufficiently seriously to prosecute him at the Chancellor's Court. They were clearly not prepared to allow open hostilities between individuals or between ethnic groups.

Formal education and its social context, therefore, increasingly reflected the intrusion of English academic standards and mores. The inferiority complex identified with this assimilation of values was accompanied by the gulf which emerged between the educated upper classes and the rest of Welsh society as those upper classes learned to appreciate the merits of service to the English commonwealth. And, as Morris Kyffin noted, it was accompanied by the intrusion of English words into the native language.[73] This is especially the case in the transmogrification of English legal phraseology.[74] It was also reflected in the increasing tendency for letter-writing in Wales and between Welshmen to be transacted through the medium of English.

What was it, therefore, that enabled the language to persist within some sort of learning framework? First, it should be stressed that although English was important in the educational structure, priority in the period still lay with the classical tongues in such a way that the learning environment was only partially Anglicized. The social surroundings of education were, of course, different.[75] Second, although language competence in English became a much needed qualification, particularly following the Acts of Union, there was little or no outright government hostility to the Welsh language of the sort associated with English attitudes to Irish Gaelic, for example, in the act 28 Henry VIII, c.15, of the Irish Parliament.[76] Indeed, from the mid-sixteenth century onwards, it appeared for a while that there was a measure of acceptance, if not encouragement, for the Welsh vernacular and associated published works. The importance of William Herbert, first earl of Pembroke, a prominent Welsh-speaking courtier and patron of letters, in this context cannot be understated.[77] In addition, the importance of sympathetic English patrons such as Lord Lumley, Sir William Cecil, Sir Henry Sidney and Archbishop Parker was crucial in giving status to the language and psychological encouragement to those Welsh humanists who sought to elevate the vernacular as a scholarly and scriptural medium.[78] The acknowledgement given by

[73] Jones, *The Old British Tongue*, pp. 48–51.
[74] W. P. Griffith, 'Addysg a chymdeithas ym Môn, 1540–1640', *TAAS* (1985), 54n.; cf. Williams, 'The Survival of the Welsh Language', 73.
[75] Griffith, *Learning, Law and Religion*, pp. 400 et seq.
[76] Alan Ford, *The Protestant Reformation in Ireland 1590–1641* (Frankfurt am Main, 1985), p. 13.
[77] Davies, *Rhagymadroddion a Chyflwyniadau*, pp. 38, 95.
[78] Griffith, *Learning, Law and Religion*, p. 412; V. E. Durkacz, *The Decline of the Celtic Languages* (Edinburgh, 1983), pp. 33–5.

European scholars like Gesner and Montaigne to the language further established its validity,[79] reinforced as it was by the scholarly patronage of wealthy semi-aristocratic families like the Stradlings of St Donat's.[80] There was an incentive, therefore, for all those of a scholarly disposition to retain some intellectual grasp of the vernacular, particularly since it seemed as if the Welsh language bore phonic or structural similarities to highly prized languages like Greek[81] and Hebrew.[82]

An added incentive for retaining the vernacular or, in the case of Anglicizing gentry families, to learn some Welsh, was the very practical need to communicate directly with one's tenants and retainers. This featured in the early education of Edward, Lord Herbert of Chirbury, who, having been tutored at home in the classics, was sent, at the age of nine, to join the household of Edward Thelwall of Plas-y-ward, Denbighshire. Thelwall was a considerable scholar and linguist and doubtless would have succeeded in nurturing Herbert's Welsh had not illness curtailed the young boy's education.[83] Interesting correspondence between the Revd. William Gamage and William Herbert of Cogan Pill, Glamorgan, in the late 1630s reveals that Gamage extolled the virtues of multilingualism and reminded Herbert of the advantages of adding Welsh to the four tongues he knew already, namely Hebrew, Greek, Latin and especially English. To that end, he presented Herbert with a Welsh alphabet, of his own devising probably, and offered further tuition. The importance of learning this 'country language', he claimed, lay in that:

> you are a gentleman borne to good meanes in y^r native soyle and therefore not to deal in y^r affaires by interpreters wch oft are deceiptfull: but rather with METHRIDATES to answeare All in theire owne language . . .[84]

In drawing attention to the importance of learning Welsh, Gamage referred to the arrangement which a neighbour, Lady Beauchamp, had made on behalf of two youngish heirs to estates by employing three separate household tutors for three different languages, Latin, French and Welsh. How far the majority of gentry were able to afford tutors is a moot

---

[79] Griffith, op. cit., p. 391n.; John Florio (tr.), *The Essayes of Michael Lord of Montaigne* (3 vols., London, 1904–6), I, p. 196.
[80] Davies, *Rhagymadroddion a Chyflwyniadau*, pp. 72–4.
[81] *Memorials of Father Augustine Baker*, p. 40.
[82] Davies, *Rhagymadroddion a Chyflwyniadau*, pp. 108–9.
[83] *The Autobiography of Edward, Lord Herbert of Cherbury*, introduction by Sidney Lee (London, 1906 ed.), p. 21; also John Butler, *Lord Herbert of Chirbury (1582–1648)* (Lampeter, 1990), pp. 12–13.
[84] G. T. Clark (ed.), *Cartae et Alia Munimenta quae ad Dominium de Glamorgancia pertinent* (6 vols., Cardiff, 1910), VI, pp. 2220–1.

point. Most were not as wealthy as the Beauchamps, the Herberts or the Wynns of Gwydir. Where tutors were employed, it is doubtful whether they all taught or were able to teach Welsh. Attitudes no doubt varied towards a 'country language' in the same way that attitudes differed as to the respectability of 'country clergy'. By 1640, or later, some families no longer cherished the Welsh language and were not disposed to pass on the language to their offspring.

Nevertheless, it seems unlikely that the majority of Welsh gentry at this stage were wholly Anglicized; most were becoming or had become bilingual, indeed multilingual, within the context of the education of the time. For those gentry and middling orders who could not afford personal tutors, the alternative was the grammar school. As we have seen, school statutes usually required their entrants to be familiar with the English tongue and to be fluent in it. One must assume, therefore, that fluency in English was acquired gradually before the age of seven when admissions usually began. In the early stages of learning English it must have been necessary, for practical reasons, to have employed the Welsh language to instruct pupils. How far this might have been the work of dame schools or petty schools is as yet unclear in the Welsh context.[85]

There is some evidence of the presence of parish schools run by better-educated clergy.[86] Unfortunately, it is not always apparent to what standard or through the medium of which language that education was transacted. The reputedly Welsh-speaking Christopher Love of Cardiff received his early education during the 1620s in English because his clerical tutor possessed English textbooks only.[87] Other clergymen, such as the graduate Richard Gray at Llanfaethlu in Anglesey in the 1630s, may, because of their Welsh literary interests, have offered some Welsh teaching.[88] In the Vale of Clwyd in the later sixteenth century there were parish clergy who were knowledgeable in the classics and schoolmasters like John Wyn of Euarth who were Welsh and classical scholars.[89] Parish clergy at the very least were required to encourage scriptural literacy and there is some evidence, for example at Talach-ddu and Swansea, to show

---

[85] Griffith, 'Schooling and Society', p. 107 and cf. Williams, 'The Survival of the Welsh Language', 89 and n.1.
[86] Griffith, 'Schooling and Society', pp. 102–4.
[87] M. H. Jones, 'The life and letters of Christopher Love, 1618–51' (unpubl. University of Wales MA thesis, 1932), pp. 15–16.
[88] T. Gwynn Jones, 'Rhai o lawysgrifau Môn', *TAAS* (1921), 47–8; Griffith, 'Schooling and Society', p. 102.
[89] Discussed in Nia M. W. Powell, 'Robert ap Huw – a wanton minstrel of Anglesey', *Journal of the Society for Welsh Music History*, II (forthcoming).

that they kept in their parish chests for popular use devotional works in both Welsh and English.[90]

By the late sixteenth century, diocesans were certainly aware of the need to ensure that clergymen were competent in the native tongue and had the Scriptures in Welsh available for study or instruction.[91] Clerical ordination and recruitment policies, from what we know of the diocese of Bangor, were partially successful in getting better qualified clergymen who were natives of Wales and often drawn from the lower and middling ranks and therefore perhaps less prone to pursue Anglicizing trends.[92] Although there were still complaints about the linguistic competence of clergy in the mid-seventeenth century,[93] there were many who were undoubtedly competent instructors in the vernacular.[94] Efforts, albeit imperfect, had been made to create cathedral libraries and develop diocesan synodical systems in a bid to improve clerical quality.[95] Even the episcopal palaces became educational centres for a few clerics.[96] The better the clerical quality among graduates as well as among mere literati, the better the chance of schooling at parochial level, in a more popular vein and in the vernacular. Such parish schools were not hamstrung by statutes prescribing a set curriculum or the medium of instruction.

Even within the grammar schools the role of the vernacular was not entirely lost. It must have been difficult to deny entirely the use of Welsh at school, if the experience of John Williams of Cochwillan as a product of Ruthin is typical, and it may have been more blatant still if there were sympathetic masters, as is likely to have been the case at Ruthin both before and after its statutes were promulgated.[97] Siôn Dafydd Rhys taught at Friars' School, Bangor, and it is hard not to imagine that he applied his principles concerning the function of the vernacular during his mastership.[98] This may also have applied to other Welsh clergymen who became masters of Welsh grammar schools and who were fully bilingual. The letters testimonial for David Lloyd MA in 1665 declared him to be:

---

[90] Griffith, *Learning, Law and Religion*, p. 305; David Walker (ed.), *A History of the Church in Wales* (Penarth, 1976), p. 67.
[91] David Mathew, 'Some Elizabethan documents', *BBCS*, VI, part 1 (1931), 78; Davies, *Rhagymadroddion a Chyflwyniadau*, p. 79.
[92] Griffith, *Learning, Law and Religion*, pp. 285 et seq.
[93] Lewis, *Hen Gyflwyniadau*, p. 27.
[94] Griffith, *Learning, Law and Religion*, pp. 319 et seq.
[95] Ibid., pp. 312–13.
[96] Davies, *Rhagymadroddion a Chyflwyniadau*, p. 127.
[97] Powell, 'Robert ap Huw', noting Bishop Richard Parry in particular; also *DWB*, s.n.
[98] R. Geraint Gruffydd, 'The life of Dr John Davies of Brecon (Siôn Dafydd Rhys)', *THSC* (1973), 181.

a very Civill person, and a good preacher, both in Welsh and English, he hath laudably for Nine Yeares taught a grammar Schoole at Cowbridge and sent Sufficient grammar scholers from Thence to the university, he hath had the Tuition, and still hath, of many Gentlemen Sonns, which prosper very much under his Government.[99]

Similarly, it seems probable that private schoolmastering, for example under the recusant poet Richard Gwyn, would have employed the vernacular.[100] Perhaps, though, recusancy provides an additional reason for the insistence on language uniformity in educational endowments, for authorities disliked didacticism in a language they could not fathom. It should be recalled that once Augustine Baker had recovered his native tongue he did not lose it again and, in fact, he deliberately employed it as a secret language of communication.[101]

It is hard to explain how precisely Welsh literacy and scholarship survived and advanced in this period. If the formal pattern of education gave no regard to the Welsh language, how was it that there emerged a significant group of humanist writers, who, if nothing else, created such a fine Welsh prose tradition? How was it that the Welsh Church, notwithstanding all its failings, succeeded in advancing the Protestant faith through the vernacular? The answer lies in the tradition of literary patronage which had developed in Wales from the Middle Ages, accompanied by the tradition of manuscript collection and exchange, in which interest was aroused among a wide range of people. Although there was a body of poets and antiquaries who could be termed professional upholders of the bardic tradition and who were beneficiaries of the patronage of the gentry, this body was never self-contained. It was never a caste in the way that Irish Gaelic or Scots Gaelic poets were.[102] The body of Welsh poets was never defined by family tradition and there existed other interested parties, notably amateur poets – poets of their own living – who were drawn from the ranks of the lesser gentry, yeomen and clergy.[103] This meant that poetic and vernacular learning was quite broadly spread at the beginning of the sixteenth century and continued to be so for over a century despite cultural erosion. And although Welsh humanists complained that professional poets were

---

[99] UWBL MS 2693, transcript of Bodleian MS 28183 (Sheldon Papers), f. 118.
[100] Thomas Dempsey, *Richard Gwyn, Man of Maelor: Martyr or Traitor?* (Bolton, 1970), p. 16.
[101] *Memorials of Father Augustine Baker*, p. 58.
[102] John Bannerman, 'The MacLachlans of Kilbride and their Manuscripts', *SS*, 21 (1977), 1–34. See also Jenny Wormald, *Court, Kirk, and Community: Scotland 1470–1625* (London, 1981), pp. 60–5 for the two language cultures of Scotland, and D. B. Quinn, *The Elizabethans and the Irish* (Ithaca, N. Y., 1966), pp. 42–5 for the Irish poet class.
[103] For the poetic tradition, see Parry, *History of Welsh Literature*, pp. 135–6 and also 164–5 for the enthusiasm for free-metre poetry.

reluctant to compose on new themes and publish their output and other lexicographical information for the benefit of a wider audience, this did not mean that they were uncommunicative or wholly reluctant to share their knowledge. What is remarkable is the relative vibrancy of the tradition of manuscript collection and exchange, and of the discussions held in scholarly networks involving poets, gentry and clergymen at least into the early seventeenth century.

This interest often occurred in spite of the influence of formal education. Those who were adept at developing the vernacular were likely to have been immersed in Welsh culture before entering higher education and to have reinforced their vernacular during the course of their education.[104] The most likely scenario would appear to be that certain gentry and clerical households, in addition to hiring teachers and tutors, entertained the patronage of poets who, in the course of their hiring, were expected to provide household members with instruction in Welsh orthography, grammar and lexicography and to discuss the established poetical and musical metres and elaborate on matters of heraldry and pedigree.[105] Arguably, too, they might well have taught some elements of the classical *trivium* and *quadrivium*. Their own grammars were derived from the Latin, but at least some of them, most notably Gruffudd Hiraethog, were well aware of the different branches of learning.[106] When William Salesbury published his book of proverbs, *Oll Synnwyr pen Kembero ygyd* (1547), based on a collection by Gruffudd Hiraethog, he anticipated a learned audience of about a thousand people,[107] notably clergy and gentry who might benefit from and share in the scholarly pursuits which the Oxford-educated Salesbury had already enjoyed. Indeed, at that time the cultural network which centred on Gruffudd Hiraethog included individuals like Dr Elis Price, Dr Thomas Yale and Richard Mostyn, who were deeply sensible of the merits of formal classical education and Welsh learning.[108]

Those individuals who prized classical learning and Welsh learning were best placed to ensure the survival of the language as a scholarly

---

[104] D. J. Bowen, 'Canrif olaf y cywyddwyr', *LlC*, 14, no. 1 and 2 (1981–2), 27.
[105] Ibid., 23–4. See also the remarks of Lewys Dwnn about the poets and gentry from whom he acquired Welsh and heraldic material during the late sixteenth century. Lewys Dwnn, *Heraldic Visitations of Wales and part of the Marches*, ed. S. R. Meyrick (2 vols., Llandovery, 1846), I, p. 7, Dwnn's introduction of 1586.
[106] Griffith, 'Addysg a chymdeithas', 28, regarding poetry on the seven arts.
[107] Hughes, *Rhagymadroddion*, p. 9.
[108] D. J. Bowen (ed.), *Gwaith Gruffudd Hiraethog* (Caerdydd, 1990), pp. 10–15, 141–3, 160–1, 174–6, 291–3; idem, 'Siân Mostyn, "Yr Orav o'r Mamav ar sydd yn Traythv Iaith Gamberaec"' in J. E. Caerwyn Williams (ed.), *Ysgrifau Beirniadol XVI* (Dinbych, 1990), pp. 111–26, is a reminder of the importance of the educated gentlewoman in Welsh language maintenance on the hearth in the mid-sixteenth century.

medium. A lively tradition of poetic patronage, of translations of Latin and English material into Welsh and manuscript copying and collecting existed in Glamorgan, for example, centred on networks involving poets like Dafydd Benwyn and members of gentry families such as the Stradlings, the Mansels, the Lewises of Y Fan and the Jenkinses of Hensol.[109] The remarkable cooperation between poets, gentry and clergy in north Wales, especially in the Vale of Clwyd in the later sixteenth and early seventeenth centuries, represents a cultured and educative environment in which it became possible to merge the native and classical (including university) traditions and employ the vernacular thoroughly.[110] Although works by, for example, Dafydd Johns, vicar of Llanfair Dyffryn Clwyd, Richard Langford of Trefalun, John Conway III of Botryddan and, most notably, Roger Morris of Coed-y-talwrn remained only in manuscript, they represent efforts to produce educative material in Welsh.[111] That a fluent written Welsh style in communication had also matured may be seen in the letter addressed by the London law student, Peter Mutton of Llannerch and Rhuddlan, to his mother in 1605; both belonged to a highly cultivated Welsh family.[112]

Such scholarly interests were therefore maintained coterminously with formal patterns of education. Indeed, the element of autodidacticism was a significant one in the intellectual progress of many gentry families in these years, since it enabled them to select those Welsh and classical interests which fired their imagination. The Thelwalls of Plas-y-ward, the Lloyds of Henblas, Anglesey, or later on, Hugh Owen of Gwenynog, Anglesey and of Monmouthshire, are typical of the kind of gentry and minor gentry families who were interested in all manner of learning from an early stage.[113] It was from such a milieu that Welsh humanists who entered higher education in England sprang. Well grounded in the vernacular culture, they were able to form a bridge between Welsh learning and English-European higher learning and to produce scholarly and educative material which enriched their own vernacular.[114]

---

[109] G. J. Williams, *Traddodiad Llenyddol Morgannwg* (Caerdydd, 1948), chapters 3 and 5.
[110] Idem, 'Traddodiad Llenyddol Dyffryn Clwyd a'r Cyffiniau', *TDHS*, 1 (1952), 25–9; Enid Roberts, 'The Renaissance in the Vale of Clwyd', *FHSJ*, 15 (1954–5), 62–3; Nia M. W. Powell, *Dyffryn Clwyd in the time of Elizabeth I* (Ruthin, 1991), pp. 7–8, 12–15; see also eadem, 'Robert ap Huw', which includes a thorough bibliography.
[111] Jones, *Rhyddiaith Gymraeg II*, pp. 75, 76, 227–30; R. Alun Charles, 'Noddwyr y Beirdd yn Sir y Fflint', *LlC*, 12, no. 1 and 2 (1972), 7–8; Powell, 'Robert ap Huw'.
[112] Jones, *Rhyddiaith Gymraeg II*, pp. 209–10; Powell, *Dyffryn Clwyd*, p. 10.
[113] J. E. Caerwyn Williams, 'Anglesey's contribution to Welsh literature', *TAAS* (1959), 17–18; Butler, *Lord Herbert*, p. 12; Griffith, 'Schooling and Society', p. 110.
[114] Gruffydd Robert, *Gramadeg Cymraeg*, ed. G. J. Williams (Caerdydd, 1939), pp. xciv–xcviii; W. Alun Mathias, 'William Salesbury – ei fywyd a'i weithiau' in Geraint

Although the universities were portrayed by some Welsh scholars, for example by Thomas Wiliems, Trefriw,[115] as necessarily Anglicizing institutions, they nevertheless permitted some Welsh intellectual discourse. Without a doubt, the numbers of Welsh students at Oxford (over 2,000 enrolled between 1540 and 1640), and probably at the inns of court (700 in the same period), constituted a sufficiently large critical mass[116] to ensure that they were not likely to be overwhelmed by the Latin-English environment. Indeed, by congregating at the universities or the inns of court, Welsh students broke down the very real regional barriers they experienced at home and had the opportunity to forge a common Welshness. In addition to being able to employ the vernacular in conversation, there may have been occasions when it was used in tuition. Colleges sought to appoint tutors from students' own areas of origin and at several colleges, for example at Jesus and Queens' colleges, Cambridge, and Brasenose College, Oxford, Welsh students had Welsh supervisors. It would be surprising if tuition had not, at least in part, been held through the medium of Welsh.[117]

Jesus College, Oxford, of course, can also be assumed to have used some form of Welsh tuition, although this was never stated officially. Until 1589, the College possessed no real aim or direction even though it was dominated by Welsh students. The second set of letters patent in that year hinted that central government was poised to take a more serious attitude towards the College, probably in recognition of the importance of promoting the Protestant faith effectively in Wales.[118] This roughly coincided with efforts in Ireland to secure Protestantism through education which culminated in the creation of the University of Dublin and its Trinity College in 1593.[119] At Trinity, however, and despite the traditional hostility to Gaelic, it was found necessary to promote the faith through the vernacular by prescribing its instruction by statute. Nothing remotely like this occurred in the case of Jesus College and Wales.[120] Even in 1622, when Jesus College finally received its statutes of government, no

---

Bowen (ed.), *Y Traddodiad Rhyddiaith* (Llandysul, 1970), pp. 28–9; Gwyn Thomas, 'Rowland Vaughan' in ibid., p. 234.

[115] T. H. Parry-Williams (ed.), *Rhyddiaith Gymraeg, Y Gyfrol Gyntaf. Detholion o Lawysgrifau 1488–1609* (Caerdydd, 1954), p. 141; Griffith, *Learning, Law and Religion*, p. 394.

[116] Griffith, *Learning, Law and Religion*, chapter 1.

[117] Ibid., p. 69; cf. Anderson and Bowman, 'Education and economic modernisation', pp. 6–7.

[118] See a forthcoming article in *THSC* by William P. Griffith, 'Jesus College, Oxford and Wales: the first half-century'. For a more jaundiced view of the impact of the college on Welsh culture, see Parry, *History of Welsh Literature*, p. 162.

[119] Ford, *Protestant Reformation*, pp. 76–8.

[120] See William P. Griffith, 'Trinity College, Dublin and Wales' in *Hermathena* (forthcoming).

special clauses were inserted to specify the use of Welsh. This may have been because the authorities were confident of having enough native Welsh clergy to supply the Church, whereas in Ireland it was a matter of having to train immigrants or Anglo-Irish in the native tongue.[121]

In practice, instruction in Irish took place only irregularly, according to the outlook of whoever filled the provostship. Whether Welsh language instruction occurred with any regularity at Jesus College is even more difficult to detect. One suspects that some of the principals may have been more enthusiastic than others: John Williams, perhaps, since he had served benefices in Wales, or Griffin Powell, because of his interest as an instructor and as a devotee of the Church in Wales, or Eubule Thelwall, because of his roots in the culture of the Vale of Clwyd and his own commitment to the Welsh Church. Among the first stipendiary fellows and resident tutors in the 1590s was Edward James, later the Welsh translator of the Book of Homilies (1606).[122] It is possible that John Davies of Mallwyd might have been an early pupil of his. Although he took his higher degrees at nearby Lincoln College, Davies still retained some ties with Jesus. In 1630, one of the chief correctors of the new popular edition of Bishop Parry's revision of the Bible (accomplished with John Davies) was Michael Roberts, a leading Fellow at Jesus College, and, as it happens, a graduate of Dublin.[123] By the 1620s Jesus College, Oxford, had become widely regarded as the national seminary for Wales and, with its permanently resident body of fellows and scholars, it had the potential to teach through the medium of Welsh. Practically all the endowed members were Welshmen and were either in, or entering, holy orders. Even in the civil war and Commonwealth years – when Michael Roberts became head – the Welsh element remained formidable. Thus, there are some grounds for believing that the vernacular played its part in the teaching arrangements.

The actual recognition of the language in any formal way, however, was delayed until the Restoration period when a benefaction made by an English gentleman, William Backhouse, in 1661, established two new fellowships to be awarded to Welsh speakers.[124] Various glosses can be put on the benefaction. From one point of view, it could be interpreted as an

---

[121] See Philip Jenkins, 'The Anglican Church and the unity of Britain: the Welsh experience, 1590–1714' in Steven G. Ellis and Sarah Barber (eds.), *Conquest and Union: Fashioning a British State 1485–1725* (London, 1995), chapter 5, esp. pp. 118–22.

[122] Jesus College, Oxford MS, Memorandum by Griffin Powell 'Of the Estate of Jesus College in Oxon . . .' (1613), p. 2; cf. Ford, *Protestant Reformation*, pp. 76, 104–5, 124–5, 140–2. Trinity College Dublin never became a national institution in the same way that Jesus College did.

[123] R. Geraint Gruffydd, 'Michael Roberts o Fôn a Beibl Bach 1630', *TAAS* (1989), 31–3.

[124] E. G. Hardy, *Jesus College* (London, 1899), p. 143; NLW Nanhoron 573.

attempt to ensure some minimal provision for Welsh speakers when all other posts were falling into the hands of Anglicized Welshmen or non-Welshmen. But there is no evidence that such a trend was occurring. From another standpoint, it might be regarded as giving formal sanction to the role of Welsh-speaking fellows and tutors where none had existed before. Equally, it might be regarded as innovative by making linguistic facility the main or sole criterion for appointment. All other college benefactions relating to Wales stressed preferences for appointees who were related to benefactors by ties of kinship or who were associated with particular counties or districts or with certain grammar schools. Backhouse had no such axes to grind, for he was an Englishman with no ties with Wales and his generosity was in acknowledgement of the devoted service given to his family by the tutor Richard Lloyd (of Henblas, Anglesey), quondam fellow of Jesus College.[125]

At about this time, two Welsh writers acknowledged their debt to Oxford for impelling them to take up the pen. In 1658 Rowland Vaughan of Caer-gai, Merioneth, stressed how Oxford had drawn his attention to all good and seemly literature.[126] In 1661 Elis Lewis of Llwyn-gwern, Merioneth, conveyed the confidence he now felt about publishing *Ystyriaethau Drexelivs ar Dragywyddoldeb*, a Welsh adaptation of a meditative work, having received advice and editorial support from fellow-countrymen at Oxford.[127] Earlier, in 1632, Dr John Davies had praised the role of university-educated authors in elevating the language, though he regretted that not all members of the academic community had been prepared to share their learning with him.[128]

The academic community that was not Welsh shared some interest in the language and Welsh culture. Thomas Allen, head of Gloucester Hall, Oxford, in Elizabethan times, studied the Welsh laws. Many university and college libraries came to acquire Welsh manuscripts.[129] In London, the role of some of the Welsh civil lawyers in Welsh antiquarian studies in the early Elizabethan years, including Thomas Yale, stemmed in part from

---

[125] Hardy, op. cit., p. 143.
[126] Lewis, *Hen Gyflwyniadau*, pp. 20–1.
[127] Ibid., pp. 33–5.
[128] Davies, *Rhagymadroddion a Chyflwyniadau*, pp. 127, 154.
[129] Griffith, *Learning, Law and Religion*, pp. 409–10. See n. 8 above and also H. O. Coxe, *Catalogus Codicum MSS qui in Collegiis Aulisque Oxoniensibus* (Oxford, 1852), part 1, Balliol College, CCCLIII; King's College, CCLXXXVIII; part 2, Trinity College, X; Jesus College, XXVII, LVII, LXI, LXXXVIII, CXXXVII, CXXXVIII; R. A. B. Mynors, *Catalogue of the Manuscripts of Balliol College Oxford* (Oxford, 1963), pp. 349–51, and see also p. 280; M. R. James, *The Western Manuscripts in the Library of Trinity College, Cambridge. A Descriptive Catalogue* (4 vols., Cambridge, 1900–04), III, p. 324; *A Catalogue of the Manuscripts preserved in the Library of the University of Cambridge* (5 vols., Cambridge, 1856–67), IV, p. 213.

the scholarly and Renaissance values then emanating from the Doctors' Commons.[130] At the inns of court, too, an interchange of information occurred between Welsh students and English lawyers who were anxious to learn more about Welsh culture and language.[131] Moreover, manuscripts of Welsh material were prepared for Welsh exiles, notably at the universities, in the hope that they would retain an interest in the vernacular and traditional culture rather than succumb to the forces of classicism and Anglicization. Dr Theodore Price of Hart Hall, Oxford, was one who would have valued such material, and there must have been others.[132] The universities included scholars who were skilled in the poetic tradition or who, like Wiliam Bodwrda, became avid collectors and transcribers of manuscripts.[133]

Collecting proverbs in the vernacular and comparing words and phrases in different languages were among the commonest features of Renaissance learning.[134] Welsh students and academics clearly made use of, or were familiar with, them in their (mainly English) correspondence, for example, John Rogers, the Breconshire Puritan, George Stradling, the loyal Oxford Anglican, and Francis Mansell, the royalist principal of Jesus College.[135] That they pursued such interests as part of their academic studies is evidenced in the commonplace book of Thomas Ellis, Fellow of Jesus College, Oxford in the 1650s, where Welsh aphorisms were set alongside their English and Latin equivalents in some semblance of equality.[136]

But the totality of Ellis's information and the sources quoted emphasized how far a Welsh academic in reality had to depend on English material by the mid-seventeenth century. In the absence of a significantly separate and independent renaissance tradition, the intellectual curiosity of most Welshmen had to be satisfied by what was available in academic circles in England. Unlike the Irish experience, no large expatriate population of Welshmen was to be found abroad at the Catholic seminaries. Where they did exist, usually living alongside large numbers of English exiles under the same roof, it was never easy for them to express

---

[130] F. D. Logan, 'Doctors' Commons in the Early Sixteenth Century: a Society of Many Talents', *HR*, 61, no. 145 (1988), 151–65; see also J. Gwynfor Jones, *Wales and the Tudor State*, p. 288.
[131] Griffith, *Learning, Law and Religion*, pp. 408–9; Richard Ovenden, 'Jaspar Gryffyth and his books', *BLJ*, 20, no. 2 (1994), 116–18.
[132] Griffith, *Learning, Law and Religion*, pp. 393–4.
[133] Ibid., p. 395 and n. 82; Dafydd Ifans, 'Wiliam Bodwrda (1593–1660)', *NLWJ*, XIX, no. 3 (1976), 300–10.
[134] Jones, *The Old British Tongue*, pp. 81, 82.
[135] Bodleian MS D 273, f. 290; B109, f. 142v; Jesus College, Oxford MS I Arch. 18/5.
[136] Griffith, *Learning, Law and Religion*, p. 394.

or sustain their own identity.[137] Unlike the Irish, the Welsh therefore were unable to assert a sufficiently distinctive national presence which would have given them their own colleges and the opportunity to prepare learning in the vernacular.[138] On the other hand, the Welsh avoided the dilemma of the Scots in this period. Although the Scots had a distinctive political identity and a comprehensive framework of schools and universities, they were unable to reconcile fully the place of the Gaelic language.[139] Indeed, by 1600, Gaelic had already been relegated from any meaningful educative role in favour of English and in a way that was distinctly pejorative.[140] That did not happen to Welsh. Although the overriding ethos was one of encouraging a wider acquaintance with Latin or English, there was no overt hostility to the Welsh language and its culture. The vernacular was thus able to survive and in some ways develop in the interstices of the educational arrangements in Wales, to await a time when it would become the principal vehicle for popular evangelical learning.

---

[137] W. Llewelyn Williams, 'Welsh Catholics on the Continent', *THSC* (1901–2), 72–3.

[138] Mícheál Mac Craith, 'Gaelic Ireland and the Renaissance' in Glanmor Williams and Robert Owen Jones (eds.), *The Celts and the Renaissance: Tradition and Innovation* (Cardiff, 1990), pp. 57–89.

[139] John MacQueen, 'The Renaissance in Scotland' in Williams and Jones, *The Celts and the Renaissance*, p. 54; Durkacz, *The Decline of the Celtic Languages*, pp. 15–17.

[140] The impact of English on Scots culture was already marked by 1500, according to Gregory Kratzmann, *Anglo-Scottish Literary Relations, 1430–1550* (Cambridge, 1980). The undermining of Gaelic was a prolonged process and, unlike Wales, the later projects for evangelical education in the Highlands actually contributed to Anglicization. See Durkacz, *The Decline of the Celtic Languages*, pp. 18 et seq.; Glanville Price, *The Languages of Britain* (London, 1984), pp. 52–3; Charles W. J. Withers, 'Education and Anglicisation: the policy of the SSPCK toward the Education of the Highlander, 1709–1825', *SS*, 26 (1982), esp. 37–9.

9

Popular Schooling and the Welsh Language 1650–1800

ERYN M. WHITE

THIS PERIOD witnessed the first concerted efforts to teach substantial sections of the population of Wales to read. Most of these attempts were fuelled by a common motivation: the desire to save souls who were feared to be languishing in darkness and ignorance. The schools set up to achieve this end were mainly established by charitable organizations and funded by affluent well-wishers. The Welsh Trust (1674–81) and the Society for the Promotion of Christian Knowledge (1699–1737), Griffith Jones's Circulating Schools (1731–79) and the Sunday schools of Thomas Charles (1785–) each had their policy regarding the use of the Welsh language and that policy to a large extent determined the ultimate success of their endeavours. That the beginning of a breakthrough to mass literacy was achieved in this period was largely due to the decision, essentially taken in the 1730s, to use the Welsh language in order to teach a mainly monoglot population to read. Its use as a medium of instruction also helped to ensure that Welsh would survive in the long term as a language of the written as well as of the spoken word.

The recurring theme of each of these educational initiatives was the urgent and continuing need to explain the basic principles of the Protestant faith to the majority of the population. Protestantism was a religion of the book and implicit in its doctrines was the need for all believers to be able to read the Scriptures in their mother tongue. Education was regarded in this period as the means by which the Welsh would be freed from the shackles of popery, superstition and magic. During the Commonwealth period in the mid-seventeenth century, Wales was deemed by the Puritan regime to be such a 'dark corner of the land'[1] that it could scarcely be described as a Christian country. Concern about this deficiency was apparent in the preamble and content of the Act

---

[1] Christopher Hill, 'Puritans and "the Dark Corners of the Land"' in *Change and Continuity in Seventeenth Century England* (London, 1974), pp. 3–47; Geraint H. Jenkins, *Protestant Dissenters in Wales 1639–1689* (Cardiff, 1992), pp. 9–10; Christopher Hill, *The English Bible and the Seventeenth Century Revolution* (Harmondsworth, 1993), pp. 89–90.

for the Better Propagation and Preaching of the Gospel in Wales, which was passed on 22 February 1650. Its main aim was to appoint suitable preachers to proclaim sound Puritan doctrine to the people of Wales, but the Act also provided for the setting up of schools in order to improve standards of education. The existing grammar schools catered chiefly for the sons of the gentry and of well-to-do yeomen families, and no real provision existed for the lower orders in society. In an attempt to remedy this situation, sixty-three elementary schools were established in the major market towns of Wales. They were financed by funds sequestered from Church revenues and education was provided free for members of both sexes. The syllabus consisted of the 'three Rs' – reading, writing and arithmetic – through the medium of English. Thirty-seven schools were established in south Wales and twenty-six in the north. Since they tended to be located in areas where Puritan influence was relatively strong, they were more frequent in the border areas than in the mainly Welsh-speaking west. The use of English meant that the impact of the schooling could only be strictly limited, despite the good intentions that lay behind the Act.[2]

The initial term of the Propagation Act came to an end in March 1653 and, for a variety of reasons, it was not renewed by the Rump Parliament. Although many of the schools established under the terms of the Act continued to operate after 1653, suitably qualified schoolmasters were difficult to find and the last remaining schools were swept away after the Restoration in 1660. Thus ended the first attempt by the state to provide a system of primary education in Wales. Subsequent attempts in this period to instil literacy were the work of charitable organizations and of independent individuals. The first such endeavour was the initiative of the Welsh Trust, a voluntary movement founded in 1674 under the leadership of Thomas Gouge, who had been ejected from his living at St Sepulchre in Southwark. Although he was based in London he had developed a keen sympathy for the Welsh people and a passionate concern about their spiritual needs. Much of the inspiration for this interest stemmed from reading the biography of Joseph Alleine of Taunton, who had also yearned to improve religious conditions in Wales. Gouge established the Trust with funds collected from affluent and charitably-disposed Londoners, a number of whom were of Welsh origin. Support for the movement crossed religious divides and it was sustained by contributions from both Anglicans and Dissenters. The broad basis of its support reflected the Latitudinarian

[2] Mary Clement, 'Dechrau Addysgu'r Werin' in Jac L. Williams (ed.), *Ysgrifau ar Addysg: Y Bedwaredd Gyfrol* (Caerdydd, 1966), pp. 24–5; R. Tudur Jones, *Hanes Annibynwyr Cymru* (Abertawe, 1966), p. 49; Geraint H. Jenkins, *The Foundations of Modern Wales. Wales 1642–1780* (Oxford, 1987), pp. 53–4.

ideals of the age and was largely the result of the moderate and tolerant attitudes of its leaders, Thomas Gouge and Stephen Hughes. Like Gouge, Stephen Hughes had been ejected from his living, at Meidrim in Carmarthenshire, because of his Puritan tendencies. However, although an avowed Dissenter, he continued to preach in local churches and to take communion in the established Church. He displayed considerable tolerance towards all forms of religious beliefs, except for Catholicism, which he heartily despised.

The aims of the Welsh Trust were twofold: it sought to establish schools to teach children the principles of religion and to furnish people with copies of the Bible and devotional manuals. In its educational endeavours, the Trust initially had some notable success. Schools were established in the major market towns of each county, apart from Merioneth. They flourished particularly in the southern counties of Cardigan, Carmarthen, Pembroke, Glamorgan and Monmouth. By the summer of 1675 over eighty schools had been set up, with over two thousand children attending them. This proved to be the Trust's heyday; decline set in soon after and by 1678 only thirty-three schools remained open. Antagonism towards the Trust grew among those who suspected that a wish to reinstate Puritanism was its driving force. The initiative ended with the death of Thomas Gouge in 1681 and the Trust was wound up.[3]

The medium of instruction in the schools established by the Welsh Trust was English. Although little is known about the pupils, the schools tended to be located in areas where knowledge of English was more likely, namely in the major towns and along the borders. Even so, the use of English as the medium of instruction probably served to limit the impact of the schools. The choice of language would appear to have been a deliberate policy on the part of the Trust in order that the children might learn 'to be more serviceable to their country and to live more comfortably in the world'.[4] It may well have been expedient also in order to secure financial support from the gentry and the church authorities, neither of whom were enthusiastic supporters of the Welsh tongue. This decision was vehemently opposed by Stephen Hughes, who, in 1672, had already made clear his opposition to what he perceived as the folly of attempting to educate monoglot Welsh children through the medium of English:

---

[3] M. G. Jones, *The Charity School Movement* (Cambridge, 1938), pp. 277–89; E. T. Davies, 'The Church of England and Schools 1662–1774' in Glanmor Williams (ed.), *Glamorgan County History, Vol. IV: Early Modern Glamorgan* (Cardiff, 1974), pp. 452–4.

[4] Quoted in Jones, *The Charity School Movement*, p. 284.

Ac pyt fae dros lawer oes dri chant ar ddeg o Saeson dyscedig, cydwybodol, ar unwaith yn cadw ysgolion, yn nhair Shîr a'r ddeg Cymru, i ddyscu saesneg i'n cydwladwyr: er hynny ni byddei bossibl, i gyffredin bobl ein Gwlâd golli iaith eu mammau y pum can mlynedd ac a ganlynant, os parhaiff y Byd cyhŷd a hynny . . . Ac etto dymma'r fath beth y mae rhai yn ei phansio . . .[5]

(And if over many ages thirteen hundred educated, conscientious Englishmen, were to keep schools simultaneously in the thirteen counties of Wales, in order to teach our countrymen English; despite this it would not be possible for the ordinary people of our country to lose their mother tongue during the following five hundred years, if the world lasts that long . . . And yet, this is what some people fancy . . .)

Following the demise of the Welsh Trust, efforts to educate the Welsh continued primarily through the work of the Society for the Promotion of Christian Knowledge from 1699 onwards. The membership of the SPCK was drawn mainly from the established Church and it was fuelled by the same Pietist influences as a number of improving societies of the period, including the Society for the Reformation of Manners and the Society for the Propagation of the Gospel. It seems probable that what funds remained from the coffers of the Welsh Trust were used to found schools under the auspices of the SPCK. It is surely significant that thirty of the early schools established by the SPCK were located in places previously served by the schools of the Welsh Trust. A total of ninety-six schools were set up by the society between 1699 and 1740, sixty-eight of which were established by 1715. Again, the major successes were in the market towns of the south and only fourteen schools were established in the north of the country. The most prominent member of the Society in Wales was Sir John Philipps of Picton Castle in Pembrokeshire, who was responsible for establishing twenty-two schools in Pembrokeshire alone. A keen philanthropist, he took responsibility for all the expenses incurred in each of the schools he founded, including the salary of the teacher. He was concerned not simply with the schooling of the pupils, but also with providing them with adequate food and clothing. Other important patrons of the charity schools included Sir Humphrey Mackworth of Neath and John Vaughan of Cwrt Derllys, Carmarthenshire, whose daughter, Madam Bridget Bevan, later became a major benefactor of Griffith Jones's circulating schools.

The curriculum of the charity schools emphasized reading, writing and reciting the catechism. More advanced pupils went on to receive further instruction: the girls in needlework, knitting, weaving and spinning and

---

[5] Stephen Hughes (ed.), *Gwaith Mr. Rees Prichard* (Llundain, 1672), introduction.

the boys in arithmetic, navigation and agriculture. The language most commonly used in these charity schools was English. Some of those involved in establishing schools chose to exercise their own initiative to ensure that Welsh was used in lessons. Although there are no records of Welsh being used in south Wales, a number of schools in the north were conducted in Welsh. Dr John Jones, dean of Bangor, established twelve Welsh-medium schools in north Wales, and left money to some of the charity schools in his will on condition that the children were allowed 'to learn Welsh perfectly'.[6] Welsh was also taught in the British Charity School set up by prosperous members of the Society of Antient Britons in Clerkenwell Green in London. It would appear, therefore, that there was a certain amount of latitude permitted by the Society, although its clear preference was for the use of English.

Despite the promising start, the SPCK schools experienced a marked decline as a result of the political and sectarian conflicts of the Hanoverian age. Dissenters withdrew their support in the wake of the rancour caused by the Schism Act of 1714, which made cooperation with the Anglicans well-nigh impossible. The situation was further exacerbated by the political repercussions of the Jacobite rising of 1715. Despite its proclamations of loyalty to George I, the Society was suspected of fostering Jacobite ideas in its schools and lost the support of many patrons as a result. The benefits of education were not immediately apparent to all and it had never been an easy task to persuade poorer parents to permit their children to attend schools regularly. Many children were required at home to perform such humble tasks as herding animals and guarding crops against birds. Even mundane labour of this kind was of great value to poverty-stricken families and could ill be spared. These factors, combined with the language policy, severely restricted the influence and development of the SPCK in Wales.

Both the Welsh Trust and the SPCK in Wales remained committed to the use of English as a medium of instruction, despite the difficulties such a policy presented. A strong tradition of using English as the medium of education had already been established by the grammar schools and the schools of the Propagation Act. The early Puritans in Wales were also among those who subscribed to this trend. The Dissenting academies, established initially in an age of persecution to provide education for Dissenters banned from attending universities, followed in the same tradition. Among the first of these were Samuel Jones's academy at Brynllywarch and Rhys Prydderch's institute at Ystradwallter. Perhaps the best known was the Carmarthen Academy established in 1703 which later

[6] Mary Clement, *The S.P.C.K. and Wales, 1699–1740* (London, 1954), p. 10.

moved to Llwyn-llwyd under the direction of Vavasor Griffiths. The emphasis in these institutions lay firmly on the traditional university syllabus of the arts and the classics, with added instruction on oratory to prepare fledgling Dissenting ministers for their duties. The life of the academies was conducted in English; when William Williams, Pantycelyn, attended the academy at Llwyn-llwyd, for instance, he received instruction through the medium of English. This has been put forward as an explanation of the fact that his library was full of English works. In contrast, the Anglican school established at Ystradmeurig by Edward Richard used Welsh as the language of day-to-day life, work and play. The emphasis was on providing a thorough grounding in the classics, theology and Welsh poetry, so much so that in later years, Pryse Morris, the son of Lewis Morris, sought to excuse the inadequacy of his English on the grounds that he had been educated at Ystradmeurig: 'My none knowledge of the English tongue excuses my not writing in stile, you well know that Ystrad Meirig was but a Poor Englifying Colledge.'[7] The atmosphere and culture of the Dissenting academies was, however, essentially English.[8] It would appear, then, that there was much support from within and without the country, especially among prosperous people, for the notion that English should be established as the language of education.

Despite their reluctance to use Welsh as a medium of instruction, both the Welsh Trust and the SPCK were prepared to devote money and effort to the publication of religious literature in Welsh. Indeed, this provision may be regarded as their most substantial and abiding contribution to the growth of literacy. The Welsh Trust began by gathering together and overseeing the distribution of existing works, including 32 Welsh Bibles, 479 New Testaments and 500 copies of the perennial favourite, *Holl Ddyledswydd Dyn*, the translation of Richard Allestree's *The Whole Duty of Man*. The next step was to finance the publication of new books, new editions of old favourites and translations of English works. Stephen Hughes was especially active in this respect and was responsible for editing the works of Rees Prichard and John Bunyan, which proved exceptionally popular with the Welsh reading public. Most significant of all was the 1678 edition of the Bible, complete with Prayer Book and

---

[7] *ALM*, II, pp. 783–4; D. G. Osborne-Jones, *Edward Richard of Ystradmeurig* (Carmarthen, 1934), pp. 48–50. 'Englifying' refers to Edward Richard's interest in Welsh poetry and *cynghanedd*.

[8] G. Dyfnallt Owen, *Ysgolion a Cholegau yr Annibynwyr* (Abertawe, 1939), pp. 2–27; Dewi Eirug Davies, *Hoff Ddysgedig Nyth* (Abertawe, 1976), pp. 124–5; R. Tudur Jones, 'The Puritan Contribution' in Jac L. Williams and Gwilym Rees Hughes (eds.), *The History of Education in Wales*, 1 (Swansea, 1978), pp. 42–4.

Apocrypha, prepared by Stephen Hughes.⁹ Eight thousand copies were produced at an estimated cost of £2,000. Seven thousand of these were sold at a price of 4s.2d. each and the remainder were given to those who could not afford to pay for a copy. Following the collapse of the Trust, the SPCK inherited its mantle as patron of religious publications in Welsh. Again, the major achievement was the drive to meet the growing demand for Welsh Bibles. The success of the 1718 edition of the Bible was chiefly the result of the indefatigable efforts of Moses Williams, both in collecting subscriptions and in preparing the work for publication. Of the ten thousand copies produced, one thousand were distributed free to the poor.

The SPCK took a further step towards the promotion of literacy by establishing lending libraries stocked with Welsh books of a religious nature. Most libraries prior to this were private collections located in gentry households such as the library at Wynnstay and the collection held by the Mostyn family.¹⁰ The SPCK venture was primarily the brainchild of Sir Humphrey Mackworth, and it was as a result of his promptings that a committee was first set up to investigate the proposal. The outcome was the founding by 1711 of libraries in each of the four dioceses at Carmarthen, Bangor, Cowbridge and St Asaph. The libraries were funded by subscriptions from the Society's contributors in Wales. It was hoped to extend the provision to include libraries at a parish level and several parochial libraries were established during the early eighteenth century.¹¹ The Cowbridge library was open for two hours on market days for the benefit of any clergy or schoolmasters who resided within ten miles of the town, any of the library's trustees, and any person who contributed the sum of ten shillings in cash or the equivalent value in books. The extent of the library's influence is questionable: when it opened in 1711, although it stocked a number of sermons, works on philosophy and church histories, only one Welsh book – a copy of the 1689 Bible – was to be found on its shelves.¹²

This willingness to provide religious literature through the medium of Welsh may appear ironic in the light of the determination of the Welsh Trust and the SPCK to bar the language from their schools, but it has

---

⁹ Geraint H. Jenkins, *Literature, Religion and Society in Wales, 1660–1730* (Cardiff, 1978), pp. 58–60; idem, 'Apostol Sir Gaerfyrddin: Stephen Hughes c.1622–1688' in *Cadw Tŷ Mewn Cwmwl Tystion: Ysgrifau Hanesyddol ar Grefydd a Diwylliant* (Llandysul, 1990), p. 14.
¹⁰ Eiluned Rees, 'An Introductory Survey of 18th Century Welsh Libraries', *JWBS*, X, no. 4 (1971), 197–208.
¹¹ Clement, *The S.P.C.K. and Wales*, pp. 43–5.
¹² A copy of Edward Morris's translation, *Y Rhybuddiwr Cristnogawl* (3rd ed., 1706), was subsequently added to its collection. Ewart Lewis, 'The Cowbridge Diocesan Library 1711–1848', *JHSCW*, IV (1954), 39–43.

been suggested that this was largely an interim measure to cater for monoglot Welsh adults and that the long-term aim was the introduction of English.[13] Whatever the reasons, it must be acknowledged that the willingness of both movements to supply Welsh literature certainly helped pave the way for subsequent, and more successful, educational initiatives. In particular, copies of the Bible were made more readily available to the lower orders of society. Prior to 1660, a total of 15,000 copies of the Bible (or parts of it) were produced in Welsh, but 40,000 copies appeared in six separate editions between 1660 and 1730. The SPCK alone was responsible for printing at least 50,000 copies between 1718 and 1752.[14] In this way, these early charitable movements helped to lay the foundations for higher levels of literacy in Wales.

The principal breakthrough in terms of both Welsh-medium education and the growth of literacy came with the work of Griffith Jones and his circulating schools. Born in Pen-boyr in Carmarthenshire in 1684, Jones was rector of Llanddowror from 1716 to 1761 and had gained a reputation as a truly remarkable preacher of the gospel.[15] In defiance of Church practice, as a young man he had preached out of doors when his congregations proved too large to be contained in any church. When brought to task for his unconventional behaviour in 1714 by Adam Ottley, bishop of St David's, he argued that some of the inhabitants of south-west Wales knew less about Christ than several followers of Mohammed.[16] In the face of this ignorance, he felt compelled to continue to preach to them in their mother tongue in order to explain the basic principles of the Protestant faith. He also gained valuable experience for the future as a schoolmaster with the SPCK in Laugharne. His first school was set up in his own parish of Llanddowror in 1731 and by the time the first issue of his annual report, *The Welch Piety* (modelled on Hermann Francke's *Pietas Hallensis*), appeared in 1738 a system of circulating schools had been adopted.

Griffith Jones's educational enterprise was also motivated by the same pressing concern for the salvation of souls. Following a virulent outbreak of typhus in south-west Wales between 1727 and 1731, which had claimed the lives of many of his parishioners, he feared that many of them had died without knowledge of their Saviour and had inevitably been consigned to eternal damnation. He was compelled to act by a desire to

---

[13] Jenkins, *Literature, Religion and Society*, pp. 37–8.
[14] John Ballinger, *The Bible in Wales* (London, 1906), pp. 13–15.
[15] Geraint H. Jenkins, '"An Old and Much Honoured Soldier": Griffith Jones, Llanddowror', *WHR*, 11, no. 4 (1983), 455–7; Gwyn Davies, *Griffith Jones, Llanddowror: Athro Cenedl* (Pen-y-bont ar Ogwr, 1984), pp. 25–35.
[16] NLW, Ottley Papers 100, pp. 4–5.

rectify this pitiful situation. 'Ignorance', he claimed, 'is the Mother and Nurse of Impiety.'[17] In order to combat impiety, it was therefore essential to dispel ignorance. As far as his motivation was concerned, Griffith Jones had much in common with his predecessors. He differed quite radically from them, however, in his determination to use the Welsh language as the chief medium of instruction in his schools. His overriding aim was to ensure the salvation of souls, and this was an end which he felt could be attained most swiftly and effectively by using the language spoken and understood by the majority of the people of Wales.

Building on his experience with the SPCK, Griffith Jones adapted his schools to the needs of the poor and illiterate people of Wales. The primary goal was to introduce the basic principles of Christian knowledge and the moral imperative behind these endeavours inevitably influenced the methods and syllabus adopted. Since the essential aim was to learn to read God's Word, instruction in other subjects, including writing and arithmetic, was regarded as superfluous. By adopting such a narrow but effective syllabus, Jones believed that much could be achieved in a short space of time. In addition, the schools were to be held in the winter months to coincide with the slackest period of the farming calendar so that the greatest possible number of pupils would be able to attend. The schools, held mainly in parish churches and farmhouses, were established for periods of three months at a time, and were invited to return on a regular basis. There was little that was original about the scheme: Sir Humphrey Mackworth had urged the benefits of itinerant schoolmasters in 1719 and the SPCK had previously encouraged 'ambulatory' schools in the north of Scotland.[18] Griffith Jones's contribution, therefore, lay not in his originality but in his readiness to convert ideas into action and in his decision to use the Welsh language as the medium of education.

Griffith Jones defended his decision to teach through the medium of Welsh on the grounds of practicality and pragmatism. As he pointed out in one of the first issues of his annual report, *The Welch Piety*: 'Welsh is still the Vulgar Tongue and not English.'[19] On the basis of his experiences with the schools of the SPCK, he estimated it would take three years to teach a monoglot Welsh child to read in English but a mere three months for the same child to learn to read in his or her native tongue. Speed was of the essence wherever souls were in jeopardy. Jones also sounded a practical note by emphasizing how relatively few funds were required for an educational programme which could produce competent readers in a

---

[17] *The Welch Piety* (London, 1740), p. 12.
[18] Mary Clement, 'The Welsh Circulating Schools' in Williams and Hughes, op. cit., p. 61; Gwyn Davies, op. cit., p. 46; Jenkins, *The Foundations of Modern Wales*, p. 371.
[19] *The Welch Piety* (London, 1740), p. 44.

matter of weeks. On more than one occasion he boasted that he could educate six pupils for the cost of twenty shillings when they were taught in their native tongue. He countered the arguments that instruction in Welsh hindered people from learning English by pointing out that it was easier to teach English to those who were already literate in Welsh. Many pupils of the circulating schools, he declared, had subsequently learnt to read in English as well. There were, therefore, sensible utilitarian reasons for the use of Welsh. As men such as Bishop William Morgan had previously pointed out, however desirable the acquisition of English might be, could countless souls be permitted to remain in dire ignorance until it was acquired? Was it not better in the meantime to educate them through the medium of a language they could comprehend?

Griffith Jones's attitude to the language was not, however, solely governed by pragmatism.[20] In his apologia for the use of Welsh in his schools, he presented a spirited defence of the language which revealed his intense pride in and affection for the old British tongue. Although he claimed not to be concerned with the future well-being of the language as such, but rather with the salvation of the Welsh people, he defended it on the grounds of its purity and its antiquity. He took pride in the belief that the Welsh language was the purest and most chaste in Europe and maintained that it served to guard the people against the Catholic tendencies and the immoral influences which were to be found in the literature of other languages, including English. He argued that Welsh was akin to Hebrew and must indeed have sprung from it on the occasion of the confusion of tongues at the Tower of Babel. It had since remained unchanged from the days of Taliesin onwards. Not only did he believe it to be less reliant on loanwords than most other modern languages, but he also claimed that other languages had borrowed extensively from Welsh. He even quoted from Gerald of Wales's writings the account of Henry II and the Old Man of Pencader, which expressed the firmly held conviction that the Welsh language would still be spoken in Wales at the Day of Judgement. Nowhere, however, is his fondness for the language more evident than in the following extract:

> I pray, that due Regard may be had to *her great Age, her intrinsick Usefulness*; and that *her longstanding Repute* may not be stained by wrong Imputations: Let it suffice, that so great a Part of *her Dominions* have been usurped from Her; but let no Violence be offered to *her Life*: Let Her stay the appointed Time, to expire a peaceful and natural Death, which we trust will not be till the

---

[20] Prys Morgan, 'Welsh Education from Circulating Schools to Blue Books', *Education for Development*, 10 (1985), 35; Geraint H. Jenkins, 'Hen Filwr dros Grist: Griffith Jones, Llanddowror' in *Cadw Tŷ Mewn Cwmwl Tystion*, pp. 168–9.

POPULAR SCHOOLING AND THE WELSH LANGUAGE 327

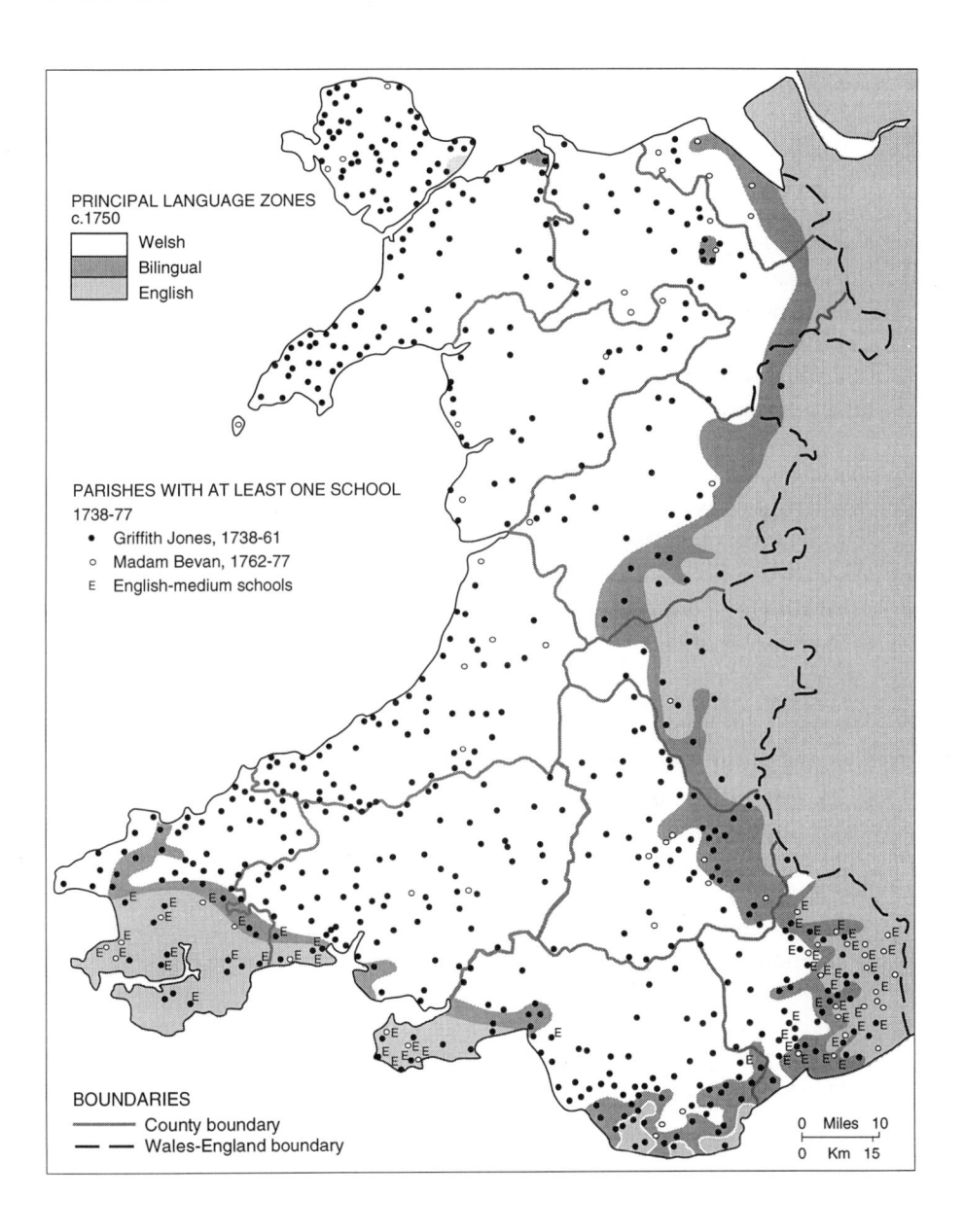

Principal language zones *c*.1750: parishes with at least one school 1738–77

Consummation of all Things, when all the *Languages* of the World will be reduced into one again.[21]

From the outset, the peripatetic schools flourished remarkably, especially in the counties of Cardigan, Carmarthen and Pembroke, where a total of ninety-two schools were held in the year 1741 alone.[22] They soon spread further afield, and had remarkable success in the counties of north-west Wales. In some of the north-eastern counties, however, the influence of the circulating schools was scarcely felt. In Flintshire, in particular, only thirty schools were established in eight parishes between 1751 and 1773. The situation was slightly more promising in Montgomeryshire, where eighty-seven schools were established in a total of twenty parishes between 1740 and 1776. In Radnorshire, also, the schools had only a limited impact with thirty-four schools located in fourteen parishes between 1739 and 1774.

Writing about the border counties, G. J. Lewis has suggested that the distribution of the circulating schools in a particular area may be taken as evidence of the continued presence of the Welsh language.[23] In the border counties of Denbigh, Flint, Montgomery and Radnor, where different sections of the population used Welsh and English, the circulating schools appear to have been conducted through the medium of Welsh and do indeed point to the continued presence of the language. In Flintshire, for example, circulating schools were held in the parishes of Caerwys, Cilcain, Y Cwm, Diserth, Halkyn, Llanasa, Meliden and Rhuddlan during the period 1751–73. These were all parishes where Welsh continued to be used as a major or significant part of public worship in the established Church. In Radnorshire the schools returned most frequently to the parishes of Llansanffraid Cwmteuddwr and Saint Harmon, two parishes where the use of Welsh in church services proved most enduring. There are, however, some instances in this county of Welsh circulating schools being held long after the language of public worship in the parish had become exclusively English. This is true in the case of Nantmel, where the language of services was said to be English from 1755 onwards, but a Welsh circulating school was established in the parish in 1766. There is also a record of one circulating school

---

[21] *The Welch Piety* (London, 1740), p. 51.
[22] Eryn M. White, '*Praidd Bach y Bugail Mawr*': *Seiadau Methodistaidd De-Orllewin Cymru 1737–50* (Llandysul, 1995), p. 30.
[23] G. J. Lewis, 'The Geography of Cultural Transition: The Welsh Borderland 1750–1850', *NLWJ*, XXI, no. 2 (1979), 134.

(presumably conducted in Welsh) held in Ffawyddog or Fwthog in Herefordshire in 1750.[24]

Even so, the presence of circulating schools cannot automatically be taken as proof of the use of the Welsh language in the vicinity, since an increasing number of schools employed the English language as a means of instruction. Ever the pragmatist, Griffith Jones realized the need to use English in those areas where English was the dominant language. In 1747 he explained that:

> ... in Compliance with very earnest, and repeated Importunities of many, I have set up of late some *English Charity Schools*, in such small Districts of this Country where the People speak the *English* Tongue, though very corruptly; and likewise some Schools of mixt *English* and *Welch* Scholars, on the Borders of these Districts. – *Many more such Schools are desired*; but at present I am not sufficiently provided with Means to encourage them.[25]

In the same issue of *The Welch Piety*, he included a letter from the vicar and some of the parishioners of Llangwm in Monmouthshire petitioning for an English-medium school on the grounds that 'the Welch Language is but very seldom used here in any Matter, and English is their Mother Tongue'.[26] This was doubtless done in order to confirm that the English schools were set up in response to genuine demands from local inhabitants. The majority of English schools, as might be expected, were to be found in the Anglicized areas of south Pembrokeshire, Gower and Monmouthshire. English schools were held, for example, in Pembrokeshire in Walton West ('where the Welch Language is not understood') in 1764 and 1773.[27] One of the mixed language schools that Griffith Jones referred to in 1747 was held in Eglwyswrw and was attended by fifteen Welsh and sixteen English scholars, although there is little evidence of the existence of other such bilingual schools. English-medium schools were also common in Monmouthshire, for instance, in the towns of Usk and Abergavenny. In 1769 *The Welch Piety* included for the first time the word 'English' in the title of its annual report on the circulating schools: *An Account of the Circulating and Catechetical Welsh and English Charity Schools*. This formula was used in each subsequent edition and references to English-medium schools appeared increasingly during the 1770s, by

---

[24] *The Welch Piety* (London, 1750), p. 97. Ffawyddog, although located in Herefordshire in the eighteenth century, became part of Monmouthshire in 1893. See Melville Richards, *Welsh Administrative and Territorial Units* (Cardiff, 1969), p. 70.
[25] *The Welch Piety* (London, 1747), p. 7.
[26] Ibid., p. 51.
[27] *The Welch Piety* (London, 1764), p. 22; ibid., (1773), pp. 25–6.

which time responsibility for the schools had passed to Griffith Jones's friend and patroness, Madam Bridget Bevan. The use of English seems to have caused disquiet in some circles and in 1761 Lewis Morris wrote to his brother Richard complaining about the:

> ... Circulating Charity Welsh Schools which are in Wales, which should be rather called English Schools, it being the English language they teach, contrary to the original design, and against the true intent of that Charity. For this kind of education as matters now stand only enables them, like the Irish, to crowd over in droves to England to the utter ruin of the place of their nativity, which by degrees must turn to a wilderness for want of hands.[28]

The Morris brothers were clearly extremely concerned about the importance of education through the medium of Welsh. Richard sent his daughter, Angharad, at the age of eight, to be educated in Welsh at a school in Beaumaris.[29] Lewis dispatched Lewis, John, William and Pryse, the four of his sons who survived infancy, to Edward Richard's school at Ystradmeurig to receive instruction in the classics.[30] William took pride in the fact that his niece, Peggy Owen, taught the local children in Welsh[31] and was moved to write to his brother Richard in 1752 deploring the attack by John Evans of Eglwys Gymyn on the circulating schools and their founder:

> Pa beth sydd yn darfod ir siaplan yna pan fo yn y modd echryslon yma yn ceisio taflu i lawr a llarpio mal llew rhuadwy ein hysgolion Cymreig ni. Y rhain ynhŷb pob Crist'nogaidd Gymro diduedd 'ynt dra mawr fendith i'n gwlad. Ai allan oi bwyll y mae'r dyn? Pam waeth pwy a yrro ymlaen y daionus orchwyl, bydded o Dwrc, Iddew brŷch, Pagan neu Fethodyst? Oni fyddai hyfryd gennych a chan bob Cymro diledryw weled yn yr ysgol yma, sef ymhlwy Cybi ond odid 40 neu 50 o blantos tlodion yn cael eu haddyscu yn *rhodd* ac yn *rhad* i ddarllain yr hen Frutanaeg druan ag i ddeall egwyddorion eu crefydd. Y rhai (pe nis cawsid drwy draul a diwidrwydd Mr Griff. Jones yr eluseni yma) a fasent mae'n ddigon tebyg bod ag un yn anllythyrennog ag ond odid yn anghrefyddol, h.y., heb na dysc na dawn.[32]

(What prompts that chaplain, in such a dreadful manner, to try to undermine and devour our Welsh schools like a roaring lion. These are in the opinion of every unprejudiced Christian Welshman a great blessing to our country. Is the

---

[28] *ML*, II, p. 368.
[29] Ibid., pp. 475, 487.
[30] *ALM*, II, pp. 540–1; Tegwyn Jones, *Y Llew a'i Deulu* (Tal-y-bont, 1982), pp. 94, 107, 115.
[31] *ML*, II, p. 477.
[32] *ML*, I, p. 197.

man mad? What does it matter who carries out this beneficial work, whether it be Turk, Jew, Pagan or Methodist? Would it not be delightful in your eyes, and those of every sincere Welshman, to see in this school in Cybi parish 40 or 50 poor children being taught without charge to read the poor old British tongue and to understand the principles of their religion. These children (if this charity had not been provided at the expense and through the industry of Mr Griffith Jones) would most likely all be illiterate and probably irreligious, i.e., without learning or talent.)

Estimates vary as to the actual numbers taught to read in the circulating schools. According to the reports of *The Welch Piety*, by the time of his death in 1761 Griffith Jones had established 3,495 schools in which 158,237 pupils had been educated. Historians generally agree that these figures need to be modified. Figures in the region of 3,325 schools, with a possible total number of adults and children of over 200,000, are cited as being more accurate.[33] Bearing in mind that the population of the country in the mid-eighteenth century was in the region of 480,000, this was a remarkable achievement and one of the most successful in Europe. Schooling was free and pupils of all ages were taught; farmers, craftsmen and labourers who were unable to attend during the daytime were taught in the evening and many carried fuel and candles to school in order to extend the hours of tuition. Affecting stories were recounted about the very young and the very old learning to read in their mother tongue for the first time. Tales of precocious children abound in the reports of the circulating schools. John Roberts of Margam marvelled to hear 'little Urchins, not seven years of Age' faultlessly reciting the responses to the catechism.[34] Rees Pierce, the incumbent of Llwyngwril in Merioneth, claimed to have been agreeably surprised when visiting a sick child in his parish to find a boy of thirteen at his bedside reading the Visitation for the Sick from the Book of Common Prayer as fluently as he himself might have done after forty-eight years as a clergyman.[35] In contrast, reports also dwelt on the sight of bespectacled and grey-haired elders, who, in their sixties and seventies, were being introduced to the wonders of the written word and who lamented the lost opportunities of their youth. Even the blind participated in some of the instruction, as this account from Gelligaer in Glamorgan reveals:

[33] Thomas Kelly, *Griffith Jones, Llanddowror: Pioneer in Adult Education* (Cardiff, 1950), pp. 45–7; Glanmor Williams, 'Religion, Language and the Circulating Schools' in *Religion, Language and Nationality in Wales* (Cardiff, 1979), pp. 207–8; Jenkins, 'Hen Filwr dros Grist: Griffith Jones, Llanddowror', p. 170.
[34] *The Welch Piety* (London, 1761), p. 3.
[35] *The Welch Piety* (London, 1755), pp. 42–3.

It may give you some Pleasure to be informed of a poor old blind Woman, above Eighty Years of Age, pretty near the School, that is now instructed in the Principles of Religion. This poor Creature, out of Curiosity at first, desired to be led into the School, to hear the Children; after she heard them catechised and their Answers, it had such an Effect upon her, that she also desired to be instructed.[36]

It was possible for the blind to attend and learn because of the phonetic and mnemonic methods employed in the schools. There are references to the instruction beginning with learning the alphabet, but much of the subsequent teaching was based on the repetition of sentences read aloud by the teacher. Learning by rote was a common trend in the early modern period[37] and Griffith Jones believed that this was a 'most rational Practice' which enabled pupils to read fluently.[38] The emphasis was on reciting and memorizing large portions of scripture as well as the responses to the catechism. Catechizing was an important activity in the schools, and it is worth recalling that they were referred to as Circulating and *Catechizing* Schools by their founder. This aspect of the teaching met with the approval of many of the parish clergy, who claimed that it rendered their obligation to catechize parishioners (usually at Lent) much easier, since the children were already familiar with the Welsh catechism.[39] Once the rudiments of learning had been acquired, it was then possible for teachers to develop the reading skills of the more advanced pupils on subsequent visits to an area. Another of the services performed by Griffith Jones was to help distribute reading material among pupils, usually at the request of the parish clergy. For instance, twelve copies of Griffith Jones's own work, *Galwad at Orseddfaingc y Grâs* (1738), were sent to the parish of Llanfair Talhaearn in Denbighshire in 1755, to be distributed among the poor parishioners.[40] In this respect the cooperation of the SPCK proved invaluable. Despite the decline of its schools, the Society continued to publish Bibles, Prayer Books, catechisms and devotional manuals and frequently provided them free of charge. Many Welsh books published during the eighteenth century also served as primers, since they contained the alphabet and a brief guide to reading words

---

[36] *The Welch Piety* (London, 1759), pp. 41–2.
[37] David Cressy, *Literacy and the Social Order* (Cambridge, 1980), pp. 20–1; Keith Thomas, 'The Meaning of Literacy in Early Modern England' in Gerd Baumann (ed.), *The Written Word: Literacy in Transition* (Oxford, 1986), p. 108; R. A. Houston, *Literacy in Early Modern Europe: Culture and Education 1500–1800* (London, 1988), pp. 56–7.
[38] *The Welch Piety* (London, 1752), p. 21.
[39] See, e.g., *The Welch Piety* (London, 1741), pp. 66–7; for comments on the parishes of Llantrisant, Newton Nottage, Peterston-super-Ely and Merthyr Mawr, see NLW, Records of the Church in Wales, LL/QA/4.
[40] *The Welch Piety* (London, 1755), p. 42.

containing varying numbers of syllables. Many of Griffith Jones's works contained such an introduction to reading, including the extremely popular *Cyngor Rhad yr Anllythrennog* (Free Advice to the Illiterate) (1737) and *Esponiad Byr ar Gatecism yr Eglwys* (A Brief Explanation of the Church Catechism) (1752). The advice in the former takes the form of a series of questions and answers. Griffith Jones's arguments for the use of Welsh are outlined again in response to the set question, 'Why do you wish to learn to read in Welsh?':

> Am mae'r Iaith Gymraeg fedraf i ddeall, rhaid llawer mwy o gost ac amser cyn dwad y ddeall saesnaeg nac allaf i, a dynion isel y hebcor; a chwedy treulio tair neu bedair neu whaneg o flynydde i'w dyscy, ni allaf gwedyn ddeall mo'r saesnaeg sydd mewn llyfrau yn agos cystal am Hiaith fy hun ... Mae Yscolion mewn Gieithoedd eraill, a pham na baent yn y Iaith Gymraeg? onid yw cyn reited yr Cymru gael Dysc y achub ei heneidau a phobl eraill? nid oes dim sôn am ûn wlâd na theyrnas yn y Bŷd oddiamgylch y ni, ond Cenhedl y Cymru, nad Iaith y wlâd lle bont mae pawb yn ddyscy yn yr yscolion, a rhai fo yn bwriady dyscy amriw Ieithodd, ei Hiaith ei hûn a ddyscant ei darllen gynta: a phwy feder feddwl mo'r resynnol yw'r trueni fod cnifer o'r tylodion a'r werinos gyffredin yn cael ei gadel y fynd mewn tywyllwch y Ddinistr, yn ein plith ni, o eisiau yscolion iw dyscy y ddarllen yn y Iaith a ddeallant.[41]

> (Because it is the Welsh language I understand, it would require much more cost and time to learn English than I, and lowly men, can spare; and having taken three or four or more years to learn it, I cannot then understand the English in books half as well as my own language ... There are schools in other languages, and why not in the Welsh language? Is it not as well for the Welsh, like other people, to have learning to save their souls? There is no other country or kingdom in the world around us, save the Welsh nation, that does not teach the language of the country to everyone in school, and those who mean to learn several languages begin by learning to read their own language first: and who can imagine how grievous is the misery that so many poor and ordinary people among us are left to go in darkness to destruction, for want of schools to teach them to read in a language they understand.)

Little is known about the schoolteachers employed by Griffith Jones, save that they were modestly paid for their labours. Salaries of £3.5s per annum were by no means unusual and compared unfavourably with the SPCK which paid up to £8 to schoolteachers in some cases.[42] Some of the teachers were themselves former pupils of the circulating schools and had received further training by Griffith Jones at *Yr Hen Goleg* (the Old

---

[41] Griffith Jones, *Cyngor Rhad yr Anllythrennog* (Llundain, 1737), p. 2.
[42] Clement, *The S.P.C.K. and Wales*, p. 7; Williams and Hughes, op. cit., p. 64.

College) at Llanddowror. A number of those whose names are recorded have been identified as having Methodist connections, including Howel Harris[43] and the hymn-writer, Morgan Rhys of Llanfynydd.[44] Several women were also employed as schoolmistresses, more so than has been hitherto realized.[45] There were at least twenty-eight instances mentioned in *The Welch Piety* of women being responsible for circulating schools, four of which were conducted in English.[46] These women, like their male counterparts, were described as being of unblemished life and conversation, and noted for their piety and industry. Such virtues were regarded as essential qualifications for all schoolteachers employed by Griffith Jones, for it was their solemn duty to instil a proper sense of morality among their pupils.

Despite the care with which Griffith Jones selected his teachers, both they and the circulating schools met with considerable criticism which served to check the growth of the movement. For a time in the 1740s, the schools experienced a period of decline which was probably the result of their alleged links with Methodism. The most scathing attack was launched by John Evans, the absentee rector of Eglwys Gymyn, in his *Some Account of the Welsh Charity Schools; and of the Rise and Progress of Methodism in Wales, through the Means of them* (1752). Although Griffith Jones wisely chose to ignore this jaundiced account, he was compelled to counter many of the criticisms he faced, in particular the charges that he employed Methodists as schoolteachers, that he sought to encourage the growth of Methodism, and that the use of Welsh in the schools hindered people from learning English. There is little doubt that the Methodist movement and the circulating schools helped to bolster one another and members of the Methodist societies were clearly urged to attend the schools to learn to read God's Word. Despite his links with the Methodist leaders, Griffith Jones felt obliged publicly to disassociate himself from the movement in order to placate his patrons. He relied entirely on well-disposed benefactors, such as his brother-in-law Sir John Philipps, as well as English gentry, doctors, bankers and scientists, to finance the schools. Close links with, and overt support from, early Methodism might have engendered hostility and reduced support from the gentry and local clergy

---

[43] Richard Bennett, *Howell Harris and the Dawn of Revival* (Bridgend, 1987), p. 139.

[44] Tom Beynon, 'Morgan Rhys a Chylch Cilycwm hyd at Ystrad Ffin', *CCHMC*, XX, no. 4 (1935), 145–7; Gomer M. Roberts, *Morgan Rhys, Llanfynydd* (Caernarfon, 1951), pp. 3–4.

[45] Jones, *The Charity School Movement*, p. 307.

[46] In some of these cases the same woman was employed in a different area in a different year. Lowri Owen, for example, took charge of schools in various places in Caernarfonshire, including Pwllheli and Llannor, and is described as being diligent and industrious.

and Griffith Jones was well aware that he could ill afford to alienate any potential sources of revenue. In the long term, however, much of the antagonism towards the circulating schools subsided as the benefits of the system became apparent. The parish clergy testified to the beneficial influence of the instruction received; as David Havard, curate of Llandysul in Cardiganshire, claimed in 1747: 'I may boldly say, that the *Welch Charity School* did more Good in our Parish than all our Preaching for many Years.'[47] John Owen, the incumbent of Llangefni in Anglesey, also bore witness to the success of the scheme in 1776: 'these Schools have a tendency to effect the Minds of People with a great Veneration for Religion and Piety, and to dispel the great Darkness that overspreads several Parts of our Principality.'[48]

It is difficult to assess the impact of the circulating schools on literacy through the medium of Welsh. Reading and writing were regarded as two completely separate skills during this period and it was usually only after attaining a certain degree of competence in reading that one went on to learn to write.[49] It is not clear how many pupils of the circulating schools took this step. Historians have generally accepted the ability to sign one's name as a measure of literacy, since it indicated a level of attainment in reading.[50] Keith Thomas argues, however, that emphasis on signatures might exclude large numbers of people who were able to read but had no skill in writing.[51] This may very well have been true of many pupils taught in the circulating schools. A further problem with this method is that a signature alone can give no indication as to the language in which the individual has attained literacy. It is evident, however, that there was a substantial growth in the reading public in Wales during the eighteenth century and that it was accompanied by an increase in the number of books available to them.[52] The reading public swelled to include elements of society who previously had little or no access to the written word. Some 2,500 works were published in Welsh during the eighteenth century and the subscribers of such publications increasingly

---

[47] *The Welch Piety* (London, 1747), p. 27.
[48] *The Welch Piety* (London, 1776), p. 30.
[49] Lawrence Stone, 'Literacy and Education in England, 1640–1900', *PP*, 42 (1968), 98; Cressy, op. cit., pp. 20–4; David Vincent, *Literacy and Popular Culture: England 1750–1914* (Cambridge, 1989), pp. 10–11.
[50] R. S. Schofield, 'The Measurement of Literacy in Pre-industrial England' in Jack Goody (ed.), *Literacy in Traditional Societies* (Cambridge, 1968), p. 319; Cressy, op. cit., p. 54; F. Furet and J. Ozouf, *Reading and Writing: Literacy in France from Calvin to Jules Ferry* (Cambridge, 1982), pp. 9–18; R. A. Houston, 'Literacy and Society in the West 1500–1850', *Social History*, 8 (1983), 270.
[51] Thomas, 'The Meaning of Literacy', pp. 102–3.
[52] Melville Richards, 'Yr Awdur a'i Gyhoedd yn y Ddeunawfed Ganrif', *JWBS*, X, no. 1 (1966), 18; Jenkins, ' "An Old and Much Honoured Soldier" ', 465.

included the middling sorts of society. No small part of the contribution of the circulating schools was that, for the first time, tenant farmers, craftsmen and labourers, and their wives and children, were given the opportunity to acquire literacy as part of the general desire to create a devout and God-fearing society in Wales.

There is little doubt that Griffith Jones made a highly significant contribution to the survival of the Welsh language by establishing it as a language of popular literacy. He has been called one of the nation's greatest benefactors and Glanmor Williams states that his schools did 'more than anything else to preserve and fortify the Welsh language and literature, of which the Bible was the corner-stone'.[53] In particular, the noticeable revival of the Welsh language in the Vale of Glamorgan during the eighteenth century has been attributed to the impact of the Welsh circulating schools in the area.[54] Iolo Morganwg believed that their influence was crucial in this respect, but the evidence to support his theory is not quite as clear and conclusive as he might have wished. The most reliable and systematic source of information regarding the linguistic geography of Glamorgan in the eighteenth century are the visitation returns of the established Church, which provide details of the language used in each parish from 1771 onwards. The parishes which were visited most frequently by circulating schools certainly tended to be those which used Welsh as the major language of public worship, such as Llangyfelach with a total of forty-one schools in the period between 1740 and 1773 and Aberdare with a total of thirty-four schools between 1740 and 1773. In the region of the Vale itself, however, the pattern is less obvious. The parishes of Colwinston, Radur and St Andrews were all visited by the circulating schools and also adopted a greater use of the Welsh language in church services by the late eighteenth century.[55] But not all parishes which experienced an increased use of Welsh received visits from the circulating schools. It may be significant, however, that of the thirteen parishes which changed from Welsh to bilingual services and the eight which adopted exclusively English services during the period 1770–1820, a substantial number made the change during the 1790s or the early nineteenth century, when the influence of the circulating schools was no

---

[53] Williams, 'Religion, Language and the Circulating Schools', p. 215.
[54] Brian Ll. James, 'The Welsh Language in the Vale of Glamorgan', *Morgannwg*, XVI (1972), 26.
[55] Circulating schools were held in Colwinston in 1746, 1749, 1750, 1757, 1759, 1760 and 1761; in Radur in 1755 and 1773; and in St Andrews Major in 1740, 1746, 1747, 1748, and twice in 1749. Colwinston adopted Welsh only services by 1791; Radur did the same by 1781, and St Andrews Major adopted bilingual rather than English services in 1795.

longer a factor in preserving the use of the Welsh language. In the parish of Laleston, for instance, where sixteen circulating schools were held in Welsh between 1740 and 1763, educating a total of 667 pupils, services were held chiefly through the medium of Welsh during the 1770s and 1780s, but by 1795 they were held in English and Welsh alternately. It is likely, therefore, that the work of the schools helped to maintain the use of the Welsh language in some parishes in the Vale during the mid-eighteenth century, although it is difficult to prove this conclusively. Visitation returns for the Vale with reference to language are not available before 1771 and, as a result, it is impossible to ascertain whether an increased use of Welsh coincided with the influence of the circulating schools or whether it was more closely associated with the rise of Methodism and Dissent.

Following Griffith Jones's death in 1761 the schools continued to prosper under the supervision of Madam Bridget Bevan, who proved to be an extremely active and accomplished manager. A bequest of £10,000 was intended to maintain the schools after her death in 1779, but the will was contested by her family and the money remained unavailable for many years. However, although the circulating schools to all intents and purposes collapsed during the 1780s, attempts to educate the people of Wales continued through the Sunday schools associated with Thomas Charles, a native of Llanfihangel Abercywyn in Carmarthenshire and a product of the circulating school system. The honour of being the first to introduce Sunday schools to Wales may actually belong either to Morgan John Rhys or Edward Williams of Oswestry, but it was Thomas Charles's influence which proved to be the most enduring and his name is inextricably linked with the development of education on the Sabbath in Wales. Biographers of Charles suggest that he was familiar with the work of Robert Raikes, who is generally accepted to have pioneered the Sunday school system in Gloucester from 1780.[56] Nevertheless, Charles's initial efforts in the field of education appear to have been modelled on the schools of Griffith Jones.[57] Charles had been converted through the preaching of Daniel Rowland, Llangeitho, who, in turn, had been converted by one of Griffith Jones's sermons. Like Jones, Charles was determined to win souls and to enable even greater numbers of children and adults to acquire reading skills. From around 1785 onwards – in an

---

[56] D. E. Jenkins, *The Life of the Rev. Thomas Charles of Bala* (3 vols., Denbigh, 1908), III, p. 366; Beryl Thomas, 'Mudiadau Addysg Thomas Charles' in Gomer M. Roberts (ed.), *Hanes Methodistiaeth Galfinaidd Cymru. Cyf. II. Cynnydd y Corff* (Caernarfon, 1978), p. 438.

[57] Derec Llwyd Morgan, '"Ysgolion Sabbothol" Thomas Charles' in *Pobl Pantycelyn* (Llandysul, 1986), pp. 90–1.

attempt to fill the vacuum left by the decline of the circulating schools – he began founding circulating day schools. The teachers were trained at his home in Bala; beginning with seven in 1786, the number steadily increased to twenty in 1794. It has been estimated that, by that time, forty schools had been established in north Wales.[58] From 1797 onwards, however, Charles became increasingly preoccupied with converting the day schools into Sunday schools.

There was little that was original or innovative about the curriculum of the Sunday schools. The emphasis remained firmly on learning to read and on catechizing. Like his predecessors, Charles came to realize that preaching was ineffective without a sound basis of knowledge on which to build. His major concern was not with education for education's sake, but with the promotion of Christian knowledge and the salvation of souls:

> Y mae'n drueni athrist i weled creaduriaid o berchen eneidiau anfarwol, yn cael eu magu a'u meithrin mewn hollol anwybodaeth o'r pethau a berthynant i'w tragywyddol heddwch! Os na thrysorwn ni eu meddyliau â gwerthfawr drysorau Duw, fe lanwa'r byd a'r diafol hwy â'r trysorau melldigedig a gloddir o uffern.[59]

> (It is a great shame to see creatures who possess immortal souls being reared and fostered in total ignorance of matters relating to their eternal peace! If we do not enrich their minds with the valuable treasures of God, the world and the devil will fill them with the damnable treasures which are mined in hell.)

With this aim always at the fore, Charles insisted upon the use of Welsh as the only feasible choice of language in which to educate Welsh-speaking pupils in his schools. Like Griffith Jones, he believed that literacy in Welsh was not an obstacle to acquiring similar skills in English. On the contrary, he believed that learning to read in one's mother tongue made it easier for pupils to proceed to achieve literacy in English as well. He made strenuous efforts to ensure that schools were adequately supplied with suitable textbooks in Welsh, including versions of the catechism and a major scriptural dictionary.[60] However, he did not confine his efforts solely to aiding Welsh speakers, for he was also deeply concerned with those for whom English was a first language. He published *An Evangelical*

---

[58] Jones, *The Charity School Movement*, p. 315.
[59] Thomas Charles, *Crynodeb o Egwyddorion Crefydd: neu Gatecism Byrr i Blant, ac Eraill, i'w Ddysgu* (Trefecca, 1789), p. ii.
[60] Charles, *Crynodeb o Egwyddorion Crefydd*; idem, *Hyfforddwr yn Egwyddorion y Grefydd Gristionogol* (Y Bala, 1807); idem, *Geiriadur Ysgrythyrol* (4 vols., Y Bala, 1805–11).

Catechism in 1797 and *A Short Evangelical Catechism* in 1801 for their benefit.

From their early beginnings in the late eighteenth century, the Sunday schools went from strength to strength. From the outset they had been closely linked to Methodism, but they also increasingly captured the imagination of Dissenters and even Anglicans in the nineteenth century. They managed to attract remarkable numbers and without doubt helped to improve standards of learning and levels of literacy simply by encouraging the reading habit. The returns of the Select Committee appointed to inquire into the Education of the Poor show that, by 1818, 315 Sunday schools attended by 25,000 pupils had been established in Wales.[61] Even those harsh critics, the Education Commissioners of 1847, had a high regard for the Sunday schools, whose achievements only served to underline the inadequacies of the day schools. Jelinger C. Symons, one of the three Commissioners, believed that most of the knowledge displayed by pupils in day schools was the consequence of their instruction in Sunday schools and he was emphatic about the value of their contribution: 'I must bear my cordial testimony to the services which these humble congregations have rendered to the community.'[62]

The Welsh language evidently fared better at the hands of the promoters of the educational movements of the late seventeenth and eighteenth centuries than did other Celtic languages within the British Isles. Charity schools elsewhere, in Scotland, Ireland and the Isle of Man, used English as the medium of instruction and, as a result, proved to be an Anglicizing force. The SSPCK (Society in Scotland for Propagating Christian Knowledge), for example, clearly stated that its aim was to 'wear out' the Gaelic language in Scotland. Even Griffith Jones saw little benefit in the preservation of Manx, Irish and Gaelic, although he foresaw practical problems in the elimination of those languages.[63] In his work on Gaelic, Charles Withers reveals that the concentration of the schools of the SSPCK along the borders of the Highlands reflected and even determined the geographic decline of the Gaelic language. In the more remote Highland areas, where there were comparatively fewer schools, Withers suggests that the native language was better able to survive. Although there were other factors involved in the decline of Gaelic, the

---

[61] John Williams, *Digest of Welsh Historical Statistics* (2 vols., The Welsh Office, 1985), II, pp. 201, 212.
[62] Gareth Elwyn Jones, 'Llyfrau Gleision 1847' in Prys Morgan (ed.), *Brad y Llyfrau Gleision* (Llandysul, 1991), p. 34. See also Prys Morgan, 'From Long Knives to Blue Books' in R. R. Davies et al. (eds.), *Welsh Society and Nationhood* (Cardiff, 1984), p. 207; Ieuan Gwynedd Jones, *Mid-Victorian Wales: The Observers and the Observed* (Cardiff, 1992), p. 132.
[63] *The Welch Piety* (London, 1740), pp. 51-3.

Anglicizing policy of the charity school movement without doubt had a detrimental effect.[64]

The Welsh language may have been viewed with a greater measure of tolerance because it was believed to be relatively free from the stigma of Jacobitism and Catholicism. Unlike Irish and Gaelic during this period, it was not associated in the public mind with rebellion and the need to ensure social control through the introduction of English may conceivably have been considered less essential in Wales as a result. M. G. Jones has pointed out that the charity school movements in Wales differed from parallel movements in England, Scotland and Ireland in that they sought to save the souls of the children of the poor, rather than to condition them for their lot in life.[65] In addition, the educational movements in Wales in the eighteenth century were not imposed from the outside, but were largely the work of Welshmen moved by concern for the welfare of their compatriots. The prime consideration was the spread of religious knowledge rather than pacifying a troublesome people.

Doubts remained, however, about the wisdom of teaching the lower orders to read. Unsupervised reading was considered potentially dangerous and there were fears that the possible consequences might include discontent and sedition which could ultimately lead to rebellion. Yet, religious reformers insisted that if standards of literacy were not improved, substantial numbers of people would be left in ignorance of the fundamental tenets of the Protestant faith. One of the sternest critics of education for the poor was Bernard de Mandeville, who advocated that the lot of the lower orders was to toil and that, for the good of the state, they should be kept in ignorance of civil and spiritual matters. His opinions struck a chord among several of the Welsh correspondents of the SPCK, who feared that the inevitable outcome of teaching the poor would be the creation of an idle and conceited lower class who would renounce manual labour.[66] Nevertheless, the powerful religious motivation behind the educational movements of the period for the most part prevailed over the doubts. It was hoped that the charity schools would promote a sense of morality, decency and obedience among their pupils. Griffith Jones even argued that education through the medium of the

---

[64] Charles W. J. Withers, *Gaelic in Scotland 1698–1981* (Edinburgh, 1984), pp. 131–3. See also T. C. Smout, *A History of the Scottish People 1560–1830* (London, 1969), pp. 461–6; Nancy Dorian, *Language Death: The Life Cycle of a Scottish Gaelic Dialect* (Philadelphia, 1981), pp. 20–3; V. E. Durkacz, *The Decline of the Celtic Languages* (Edinburgh, 1983), chapters 2 and 3.

[65] Jones, *The Charity School Movement*, p. 266.

[66] Clement, *The S.P.C.K. and Wales*, pp. 16–17; Thomas Walter Laqueur, *Religion and Respectability: Sunday Schools and Working Class Culture 1780–1850* (New Haven and London, 1976), p. 125; Vincent, *Literacy and Popular Culture*, p. 7.

Welsh language would help to preserve the social order rather than threaten it. He maintained that published works in the Welsh language contained none of the impiety and corruption that were so manifest in English literature. To teach the lower orders to read in Welsh would, therefore, serve to protect them against the forces of immorality, papism and atheism. In addition, he believed that it would make them more content with their lot since those who acquired English frequently aspired 'above their stations'. Griffith Jones feared that, if they were taught English, common labourers would hanker after preferment in England and desert their callings and their country. In the long term, however, the argument for education through the medium of Welsh had not been conclusively won. The need to combat ignorance was accepted, but the controversies of the nineteenth century revealed that uncertainty remained about which language could best achieve this end. In the opinion of many, English still had much to recommend it as a medium of instruction and as an instrument of social control.

10

The Welsh Language in Scholarship and Culture 1536–1660[1]

R. GERAINT GRUFFYDD

AT THE BEGINNING of our period there existed in Wales an outwardly flourishing guild of Welsh professional praise poets who represented a tradition that was then about a thousand years old. These poets were paid to praise the members of the Welsh élite for the virtues appropriate to their status in life, to lament their passing, to solicit gifts (promised beforehand) in verse, and occasionally to fashion love poems (an activity thought especially suitable for young poets) and religious poems addressed to God, the Virgin Mary and the saints. From time to time poets would engage each other in bardic controversy, often about mundane matters such as who had the best claim to a particular household's patronage, but sometimes about such lofty and fundamental questions as the source of their *awen* or poetic inspiration.[2] The latter question was crucial, because poets were believed to be invested with more than a tinge of supernatural power, derived from their pagan forebears, who were members of a priestly caste: it was thought they could foretell the future, which meant that at times of crisis they could play a powerful political role; and it was thought, too, that as their praise could materially uplift its recipient, so could their satire materially cast him down. Their verse was always composed in traditional strict metres, based on syllable count, with full *cynghanedd*, an intricate system of alliteration and internal rhyme, sometimes in combination; and it was declaimed by professional reciters to the accompaniment of harp or *crwth* played by professional musicians.

Welsh professional poets, in their role as political prophets or vaticinators, had played a significant part in rallying support within Wales

---

[1] I would like to record my general debt to the writings of Sir Glanmor Williams, particularly his *Recovery, Reorientation and Reformation. Wales c.1415–1642* (Oxford, 1987); for the latter part of the period Professor Geraint H. Jenkins's companion volume, *The Foundations of Modern Wales. Wales 1642–1780* (Oxford, 1987), has been similarly helpful.

[2] Bobi Jones, 'Pwnc Mawr Beirniadaeth Lenyddol Gymraeg' in J. E. Caerwyn Williams (ed.), *Ysgrifau Beirniadol III* (Dinbych, 1967), pp. 253–88.

for Henry Tudor during his progress to the Battle of Bosworth in 1485. Following Henry's victory at Bosworth, his government, and those of his successors, were naturally aware of the potential political power wielded by such vaticinators, and kept a watchful eye lest they be tempted to employ their gifts, for whatever reason, in opposition to the Crown.[3] In 1523 an eisteddfod (literally, a session) was held in the town of Caerwys in Flintshire before three gentlemen and two poets (one professional, the other amateur) in order to award degrees and grades to the professional poets and musicians and to regulate their activities: the instrument by which this regulation was to be achieved was a document named *Ystatud Gruffudd ap Cynan* (the Statute of Gruffudd ap Cynan), which purported to be the work of the twelfth-century king of Gwynedd of that name but which in fact was almost certainly drafted for promulgation at the eisteddfod.[4]

The leading figure at the Caerwys eisteddfod, apart from the powerful Flintshire gentleman Richard ap Hywel of Mostyn, was the great professional poet from Denbighshire, Tudur Aled. Unfortunately he died some three years after the eisteddfod was held, to be followed within a year or so by two fellow-poets of like eminence, Lewys Môn from Anglesey and Iorwerth Fynglwyd from Glamorgan.[5] With the single exception of Wiliam Llŷn, no other professional poet of comparable artistic achievement was to emerge during the one hundred and fifty years or so of life which the fraternity of professional poets was still destined to enjoy. In 1526–7, however, although the death of Tudur Aled in particular was much lamented, it by no means seemed the beginning of the end of a world. Lewys Morgannwg of Glamorgan stepped into the breach as Wales's leading professional poet, well supported by Siôn Brwynog of Anglesey.[6] In 1546 Lewys Morgannwg would grant at a marriage-feast in Radnorshire (in default of an eisteddfod) the degree of *disgybl pencerddaidd* to Gruffudd Hiraethog, a professional poet from Denbighshire who was to prove, among other accomplishments, an outstanding teacher of the next generation of professional poets.[7] At the

---

[3] Glanmor Williams, *Religion, Language and Nationality in Wales* (Cardiff, 1979), pp. 71–86.
[4] D. J. Bowen, 'Graddedigion Eisteddfodau Caerwys, 1523 a 1567/8', *LlC*, 2, no. 2 (1952), 129–34; J. H. Davies, 'The Roll of the Caerwys Eisteddfod of 1523', *TLWNS* (1904–5 – 1908–9), 85–102.
[5] Biographical detail will generally be found in *DWB* and *Companion*. Invaluable for bibliographical material are *LlLlG* and *LlLlG*².
[6] E. J. Saunders, 'Gweithiau Lewys Morgannwg' (unpubl. University of Wales MA thesis, 1922); Rose Marie Kerr, 'Cywyddau Siôn Brwynog' (unpubl. University of Wales MA thesis, 1960). Details of unpublished university higher degree dissertations relating to Wales will be found in Alun Eirug Davies (ed.), *Traethodau Ymchwil Cymraeg a Chymreig. Welsh Language and Welsh Dissertations 1887–1991* (Caerdydd, 1997).
[7] D. J. Bowen (ed.), *Gwaith Gruffudd Hiraethog* (Caerdydd, 1990), pp. xxvi–xxvii et passim.

beginning of our period, therefore, the venerable tradition of Welsh professional poetry appeared as if it might continue to flourish for another thousand years.

Even then, however, there were those who dissented from this optimistic assessment of the situation. These were the new Welsh humanists, mostly minor gentry who had been trained in the universities – of England, since Wales had none – and who had there become imbued with the ideals and values of Renaissance humanism.[8] These ideals and values not only assumed the primacy of classical, Greek and Latin, authors, as contrasted with those of the medieval period, but also included the desirability, if not necessity, of imitating those authors in the vernacular languages: Italian inevitably led the field in this respect, followed at some distance by French, Spanish, German and, belatedly, English. The Welsh humanists naturally wished to see their own language included in this beneficent process. They were sustained in this wish by their belief that the Welsh people were descended from Samothes or Gomer, one of two grandsons of Noah, and that they had been reinforced by the arrival in these islands of the remnants of the defeated population of Troy, led by Brutus, the great-grandson of Aeneas, some eleven hundred years before Christ; a further ingredient in their picture of the Welsh past was the introduction to Britain of the Christian faith by Joseph of Arimathea soon after the Crucifixion and Resurrection of Christ. As a result of this ancestry the Welsh language could claim a certain kinship with Hebrew, Greek and Latin – the three languages universally recognized as learned at that time. Not unnaturally it was thought that this high linguistic inheritance had given rise to a wealth of writing, but the Welsh humanists had to admit that of this wealth only fragments remained, a dearth which they sought to explain as the result of war, natural catastrophe and the activities of a malign priest named Ysgolan (who also, remarkably, turns up in Brittany). When the Welsh humanists looked at the professional poets of their own day, they in the main recognized them as the heirs of the *druides*, *bardi* and *vates* mentioned by classical authors and of the

---

[8] An account of Welsh humanism, with references, will be found in R. Geraint Gruffydd, 'The Renaissance and Welsh Literature' in Glanmor Williams and Robert Owen Jones (eds.), *The Celts and the Renaissance. Tradition and Innovation* (Cardiff, 1990), pp. 17–39. The basic documents for an analysis of the humanists' views are mostly collected in Henry Lewis (ed.), *Hen Gyflwyniadau* (Caerdydd, 1948); Garfield H. Hughes (ed.), *Rhagymadroddion 1547–1659* (Caerdydd, 1951); T. H. Parry-Williams (ed.), *Rhyddiaith Gymraeg, Y Gyfrol Gyntaf. Detholion o Lawysgrifau 1488–1609* (Caerdydd, 1954); Thomas Jones (ed.), *Rhyddiaith Gymraeg, Yr Ail Gyfrol. Detholion o Lawysgrifau a Llyfrau Printiedig 1547–1618* (Caerdydd, 1956); Ceri Davies (ed.), *Rhagymadroddion a Chyflwyniadau Lladin 1551–1632* (Caerdydd, 1980). See also R. Brinley Jones, *The Old British Tongue: the Vernacular in Wales 1540–1640* (Cardiff, 1970).

learned classes supposed to have been established by the descendants of Samothes. They recognized in them, too, an unusual mastery of their craft. But they were uneasy about them for two reasons, the one internal, the other external. Internally they did not match up to the humanist ideals of strict regard for the truth (always a delicate matter in panegyric), familiarity with the new learning of the Renaissance enshrined in printed books, eloquence (rather narrowly interpreted as knowledge of the art of rhetoric), and a willingness to make the secrets of their ancient art available to all. Externally the Welsh humanists detected in the population at large a tendency to disparage the Welsh language, and this was true not only of Welsh migrants to England but also, and crucially, of a growing number of the Welsh gentry, on whom the patronage of Welsh letters almost wholly depended. The humanists therefore urged the poets to desist from flattery, to acquire book-learning and add scientific and historical poetry to their repertoire (which might involve some metrical innovation), to familiarize themselves with the Renaissance art of rhetoric (manuals were provided by William Salesbury of Denbighshire and Henry Perri of Flintshire), and to allow the humanists themselves and the amateur poets of the Welsh Renaissance full access to the mysteries of their art: this last aim ideally involved the printing of a vast array of ancient and modern texts. (The two crucial documents in the interchange between the humanists and professional poets are the verse debate between Edmwnd Prys and Wiliam Cynwal, 1580–7, and the open letter addressed by Siôn Dafydd Rhys to the 'poets and learned men of Wales' in 1597.)[9] With regard to the gentry, whose allegiance to the language they saw as being undermined, the Welsh humanists on the one hand exhorted them to be mindful of their responsibilities, especially to the professional poets (William Salesbury and Siôn Dafydd Rhys, in particular, have moving passages on this theme),[10] and on the other hand sought to display to the gentry in their learned treatises the past and present glories of the Welsh people and language, in order to reinforce their attachment to their ancestral roots. We shall return briefly to this aspect of their work later.

The Welsh humanists signally failed to reform the practices of the professional poets, although a few of their number, especially Gruffudd Hiraethog and Siôn Tudur, were fully aware of the importance of the

---

[9] Gruffydd Aled Williams, *Ymryson Edmwnd Prys a Wiliam Cynwal* (Caerdydd, 1986); Jones, *Rhyddiaith Gymraeg II*, pp. 155–60. See also Gruffydd Aled Williams, 'Golwg ar Ymryson Edmwnd Prys a Wiliam Cynwal' in J. E. Caerwyn Williams (ed.), *Ysgrifau Beirniadol VIII* (Dinbych, 1974), pp. 70–109; Branwen Jarvis, 'Llythyr Siôn Dafydd Rhys at y Beirdd', *LlC*, 12, no. 1 and 2 (1972), 45–56.
[10] Hughes, *Rhagymadroddion*, pp. 15–16; Jones, *Rhyddiaith Gymraeg II*, pp. 156–7.

humanists' arguments.[11] Panegyric was the livelihood of these poets, and it was unrealistic of the humanists to expect them to modify the age-old conventions of the genre, and even more unrealistic to expect them to mix their praise with satire in order to conform with the humanists' notion of truth (the professional poets occasionally practised satire but were not supposed to do so). Nor was it realistic to expect them to abandon their traditional modes of training, essentially a nine-year apprenticeship, in favour of grammar school and university education, even if they possessed the means to follow the latter course. The professional poet Simwnt Fychan's response to the manual of rhetoric prepared by William Salesbury is on record and is not favourable: he argued, probably rightly, that figurative speech can better be learnt by imitation than from manuals.[12] Finally, the poets were naturally jealous of those parts of their learning which they had acquired by oral instruction during their apprenticeship and which were not included in the manuals of versecraft which had proliferated from the early fourteenth century onwards; and for whatever reason, few examples of their art, whether early or late, were printed during our period – a total of perhaps eleven *cywyddau* and three *awdlau*.[13] The effect of the Welsh humanists' efforts to arrest the decline of the gentry's patronage for Welsh letters is less easy to measure. These efforts almost certainly had some effect, but in the end social and political forces prevailed. Even before the Acts of Union, the Welsh gentry were rapidly acquiring English. Sir John Wynn of Gwydir testifies that his great-grandfather, Maredudd ab Ieuan, learnt English and Latin at a school in Caernarfon; and that this was a general tendency is implied in Dafydd Nanmor's tribute to Dafydd Llwyd ap Dafydd of Gogerddan, a man of substance in Cardiganshire in the mid-fifteenth century, although the poet asserts that his patron did not share in this tendency:

> Llawer ysgwier, dysg oedd,
> A draethant dair o ieithoedd.

---

[11] Bowen, *Gwaith Gruffudd Hiraethog*, pp. xcviii–cxxiii; Enid Roberts (ed.), *Gwaith Siôn Tudur* (2 vols., Caerdydd, 1980), I, p. 606; ibid., II, pp. 539–41.

[12] G. J. Williams and E. J. Jones (eds.), *Gramadegau'r Penceirddiaid* (Caerdydd, 1934), p. 130.

[13] Gruffydd Robert, *Gramadeg Cymraeg*, ed. G. J. Williams (Caerdydd, 1939), [349]–[354], [361]–[386] (*cywyddau* by Siôn Cent (2), Gruffudd Hiraethog, Siôn Tudur (4) and Dafydd ap Gwilym); NLW MS 727D, ff. 236–8 (a lost broadside containing a *cywydd* by Siôn ap Robert ap Rhys ap Hywel); Martial, *Martial to himselfe, treating of worldly blessedness* (London, 1571) (containing a *cywydd* by Simwnt Fychan); Richard Davies, *A funerall sermon* (London, 1577) (containing a *cywydd* by Huw Llŷn). Siôn Dafydd Rhys, *Cambrobrytannicae Cymraecaeve Linguae Institutiones* (London, 1592), pp. 235–46, has *awdlau* by Gwilym Tew, Lewys Morgannwg and Simwnt Fychan; he also prints passim numerous individual stanzas as examples of metres.

Mwy synnwyr a ŵyr o iaith
[Yn] naturiol no'i [*sic, recte* no'u] teiriaith.[14]

(Many an esquire, such is learning, speak three languages. He knows more sense by means of language, [his one] natural [tongue], than [they through] their three languages.)

As is fully explained elsewhere in this volume, the first Act of Union of 1536 required that all office-holders should henceforth know English and should speak it when carrying out their duties: English thus became the official language of administration in Wales. As a result, all the major gentry and the vast majority of the minor gentry rapidly became bilingual. It may be assumed that this was the normal state of affairs during the earlier part of our period, but towards the end of the period it seems likely that the major gentry at least were shedding their Welsh. Many of the minor gentry, however, retained theirs, and the great bulk of the population remained monoglot Welsh throughout the period.[15]

The decline in the use of the Welsh language among the gentry led inevitably to a gradual withdrawal of their patronage to the professional poets, a withdrawal of which the poets themselves were painfully aware.[16] The fact that they attempted to adapt to their patrons' changing self-image – they now saw themselves less as brave warriors than as skilful administrators – did nothing to stop the rot in the long run.[17] It must, however, be stressed that the guild of professional poets continued to flourish outwardly for more than a hundred years after the passing of the Acts of Union, and the forms and conventions employed by the professional poets continued to be put to use by gifted amateur poets until well into the eighteenth century (traces of them survive even in the nineteenth).[18]

---

[14] John Wynn, *The History of the Gwydir Family and Memoirs*, ed. J. Gwynfor Jones (Llandysul, 1990), p. 49; Thomas Roberts and Ifor Williams (eds.), *The Poetical Works of Dafydd Nanmor* (Cardiff & London, 1923), p. 71. Cf. Ralph A. Griffiths, *The Principality of Wales in the Later Middle Ages* (Cardiff, 1972), p. 446.

[15] W. Ogwen Williams, 'The Survival of the Welsh Language after the Union of England and Wales: the First Phase, 1536–1642', *WHR*, 2, no. 1 (1964), 67–93.

[16] D. J. Bowen, 'Agweddau ar Ganu'r Unfed Ganrif ar Bymtheg', *THSC* (1969), 284–335; idem, 'Canrif Olaf y Cywyddwyr', *LlC*, 14, no. 1 and 2 (1981–2), 3–51; idem, 'Y Cywyddwyr a'r Dirywiad', *BBCS*, XXIX, part 3 (1981), 453–96.

[17] Gwyn Thomas, 'Y Portread o Uchelwr ym Marddoniaeth Gaeth yr Ail Ganrif ar Bymtheg' in J. E. Caerwyn Williams (ed.), *Ysgrifau Beirniadol VIII* (Dinbych, 1974), pp. 110–29; idem, 'Golwg ar Gyfundrefn y Beirdd yn yr Ail Ganrif ar Bymtheg' in R. Geraint Gruffydd (ed.), *Bardos* (Caerdydd, 1982), pp. 76–94.

[18] A major research project supervised by Professor Emeritus D. J. Bowen on the patronage of poets in the old (pre-1974) Welsh counties is now virtually complete: there are unpublished dissertations on Anglesey (Richard Llewelyn Parry Jones, 'Arolwg ar y Traddodiad Nawdd yn Sir Fôn', 1975), Breconshire and Radnorshire (Tegwen Llwyd,

Thirty-one years after the first Act of Union, in 1567, a second eisteddfod was held in Caerwys in response to a commission from the Council in the Marches of Wales (of which Sir Henry Sidney was then President) to twenty-one gentlemen of north Wales, of whom the head of the house of Mostyn was again one of the most important. The main purpose of the eisteddfod was to protect the poets from the laws against vagrancy, and it bespeaks a concern for their well-being not only among the President and members of the Council but also among the commissioners (at least some of whom presumably petitioned the Council beforehand). It did not augur well that a petition for another eisteddfod in 1594 went unheeded, nor that Siôn Mawddwy's appeal to his patron George Owen to use his influence to secure such an assembly likewise fell on deaf ears. Gruffudd Hiraethog was three years dead when the second Caerwys eisteddfod was held, but four of his disciples achieved the highest grade for poetry, while three others achieved the highest grade but one; altogether some seventeen poets were awarded degrees as well as twenty-one harp players and sixteen players of the *crwth*.[19] Not surprisingly the history of professional poetry in north Wales during the next fifty years was dominated by the disciples of Gruffudd Hiraethog: Lewis ab Edward (who died soon after the eisteddfod was held), Wiliam Llŷn (d.1580), Wiliam Cynwal (d.1587), Owain Gwynedd (d.1601), Siôn Tudur (d.1602), Simwnt Fychan (d.1606) and Siôn Phylip (d.1620). Siôn Phylip's younger brother Rhisiart survived until 1641 and his sons Gruffudd Phylip and Phylip Siôn Phylip until 1666 and *c.*1677 respectively: this was the last of the great poetic dynasties. Roughly coeval with Rhisiart Phylip were Rhisiart Cynwal (d.1634) and Huw Machno (d.1637), both from the Conwy Valley. Wiliam Llŷn settled in Oswestry and schooled, as well as Siôn Phylip, two prolific poets who were also

'Noddwyr Beirdd yn Siroedd Brycheiniog a Maesyfed', 1988), Caernarfonshire (E. Mavis Phillips, 'Noddwyr y Beirdd yn Llŷn', 1973; John Gwilym Jones, 'Teulu Gwedir fel Noddwyr y Beirdd', 1975; Iwan Llwyd Williams, 'Noddwyr y Beirdd yn Sir Gaernarfon', 1986), Cardiganshire (D. Hywel E. Roberts, 'Noddwyr y Beirdd yn Sir Aberteifi', 1969), Carmarthenshire (Eurig R. Ll. Davies, 'Noddwyr y Beirdd yn Sir Gaerfyrddin', 1977), Denbighshire (Cledwyn Fychan, 'Astudiaethau ar Draddodiad Llenyddol Sir Ddinbych a'r Canolbarth', 1986), Flintshire (R. Alun Charles, 'Noddwyr y Beirdd yn Sir y Fflint', 1967), Glamorgan and Monmouthshire (Eirian E. Edwards, 'Noddwyr y Beirdd yn Siroedd Morgannwg a Mynwy', 1970), Merioneth (Arwyn Lloyd Hughes, 'Noddwyr y Beirdd yn Sir Feirionnydd. Casgliad o'r Cerddi i Deuluoedd Corsygedol, Dolau-gwyn, Llwyn, Nannau, Y Rug, Rhiwedog, Rhiw-goch, Rhiwlas ac Ynysmaengwyn', 1969; Glenys Davies, 'Noddwyr Eraill y Beirdd yn Sir Feirionnydd', 1972), Montgomeryshire (Robert Lewis Roberts, 'Noddwyr y Beirdd yn Sir Drefaldwyn', 1980) and Pembrokeshire (Euros Jones Evans, 'Noddwyr y Beirdd yn Sir Benfro', 1974). Articles based on these dissertations are listed in *LlLlG*, pp. 90–1 and *LlLlG*[2], pp. 86–9, but the only book is Glenys Davies, *Noddwyr Beirdd ym Meirion* (Dolgellau, 1974).

[19] See the articles cited in n. 4 above; see also Gwyn Thomas, *Eisteddfodau Caerwys: The Caerwys Eisteddfodau* (Caerdydd, 1968), and bibliography.

heralds (as, indeed, was Gruffudd Hiraethog), namely Rhys Cain (d.1614) and Lewys Dwnn (d.1616); they in turn instructed their sons Siôn Cain (d.*c*.1650) and Siams Dwnn (d.*c*.1660) in both poetry and heraldry (it should be noted that both Gruffudd Hiraethog and Lewys Dwnn held official posts in the College of Arms). In south-east Wales by far the most prolific professional poet of the latter sixteenth century was Dafydd Benwyn, who appears to have visited fairly modest gentry houses, but Meurig Dafydd (d.1595) and Llywelyn Siôn (d.*c*.1615) also made significant contributions. They were followed by Edward Dafydd, who did what he could to uphold the tradition until well into the seventies of the seventeenth century. An interesting contemporary of Llywelyn Siôn and Meurig Dafydd was Siôn Mawddwy (d.1613), who itinerated much more widely than most professional poets of his time. These names represent only a fraction of the professional poets practising in Wales between 1536 and 1660, although it is hoped the list includes the most important of their number. Together they produced several thousand *cywyddau* and *awdlau*, of which many remain unedited and hardly any have received close critical attention.[20] It may be repeated with some confidence, however, that of these poets only Wiliam Llŷn bears comparison with his great forebears of the later fifteenth and early sixteenth centuries: the rest of his sixteenth and earlier seventeenth century confrères were in the main simply competent literary craftsmen,

[20] The only published editions are of Gruffudd Hiraethog and Siôn Tudur (see n. 7 and n. 11 above) but there are dissertations on Lewis ab Edward (R. W. Macdonald, 'Bywyd a Gwaith Lewis ab Edward', MA University of Liverpool, 1960–1), Wiliam Llŷn (Roy Stephens, 'Gwaith Wiliam Llŷn', PhD University of Wales, 1983), Wiliam Cynwal (Sarah Rhiannon Williams, 'Testun Beirniadol o Gasgliad Llawysgrif Mostyn 111 o Waith Wiliam Cynwal ynghyd â Rhagymadrodd, Nodiadau a Geirfa', MA University of Wales, 1965; Geraint Percy Jones, 'Astudiaeth Destunol o Ganu Wiliam Cynwal yn Llawysgrif (Bangor) Mostyn 4', MA University of Wales, 1969; Richard Lewis Jones, 'Astudiaeth Destunol o Awdlau, Cywyddau ac Englynion gan Wiliam Cynwal', MA University of Wales, 1969), Owain Gwynedd (D. Roy Saer, 'Testun Beirniadol o Waith Owain Gwynedd, ynghyd â Rhagymadrodd, Nodiadau a Geirfa', MA University of Wales, 1961), the Phylip family (William Davies, 'Phylipiaid Ardudwy: with the Poems of Siôn Phylip in the Cardiff Free Library Collection', MA University of Wales, 1912), Huw Machno (Dan Lynn James, 'Bywyd a Gwaith Huw Machno', MA University of Wales, 1960), Dafydd Benwyn (Dafydd Huw Evans, 'The Life and Work of Dafydd Benwyn', DPhil University of Oxford, 1981), Meurig Dafydd and Llywelyn Siôn (T. O. Phillips, 'Bywyd a Gwaith Meurig Dafydd (Llanisien) a Llywelyn Siôn (Llangewydd)', MA University of Wales, 1937), Edward Dafydd (John Rhys, 'Bywyd a Gwaith Edward Dafydd o Fargam a Dafydd o'r Nant, a Hanes Dirywiad y Gyfundrefn Farddol ym Morgannwg', MA University of Wales, 1953) and Siôn Mawddwy (J. Dyfrig Davies, 'Astudiaeth Destunol o Waith Siôn Mawddwy', MA University of Wales, 1965). Articles on these poets and others are listed in *LlLlG*, pp. 93–121, 143–6 and *LlLlG*², pp. 89–105. A most useful anthology is Nesta Lloyd (ed.), *Blodeugerdd Barddas o'r Ail Ganrif ar Bymtheg (Cyfrol 1)* (Cyhoeddiadau Barddas, 1993). It should be noted that the pupil-teacher relationship is rather more complicated than is indicated in the text.

who could occasionally produce an exceptionally fine *cywydd*, but no more than that. Towards the end of the period a serious decline set in: poems became far too long, and the recital of pedigrees a far too prominent feature in them. In addition, mastery of the rules of *cynghanedd* became attenuated, and the traditional linguistic conventions of the genre became increasingly disregarded. The tradition was dying on its feet before the turmoil of the civil wars, and the social disruption which they caused, delivered the final *coup de grâce*. Following the passing of Gruffudd Phylip in 1666, it was no more than a pale shadow of its former self.

The ideal Renaissance gentleman could turn a sonnet as well as wield a sword, and the Welsh humanists naturally hoped that a body of gifted amateur poets would arise within their ranks, who would perhaps breathe new life into the moribund strict metres. This occurred to a limited extent only, although Thomas Prys of Plasiolyn in Denbighshire was able to list forty-nine such amateurs from the counties of Denbigh, Merioneth, Caernarfon and Anglesey between, say, 1560 and 1630.[21] These poets did indeed compose mainly (although not exclusively) in the strict metres, and it was presumably for their benefit that treatises on Welsh versecraft were published by Gruffydd Robert in Milan in 1584–94, by Siôn Dafydd Rhys in London in 1592 and by William Midleton, again in London, in 1593 (in the case of Gruffydd Robert and Siôn Dafydd Rhys those treatises formed part of a larger whole); Thomas Prys himself wrote a similar treatise which remained unpublished.[22] Of these amateurs Thomas Prys was by far the most prolific, but a not unsubstantial body of work also survives from the pen of Roger Kyffin, a Montgomeryshire gentleman, and 'Sir' Huw Roberts, an Anglesey clergyman.[23] Much of the work of these poets remained firmly within the panegyric tradition, although there was clearly less formality in the relationship between poet and patron, and versifying of pedigrees was often mercifully eschewed. Religion and love remained popular as subject matter for poems, depending on the inclination of the poets, but there was also a readiness from time to time to embark on themes not normally essayed by the professional poets, such as the description and criticism of contemporary life. The trouble with much

---

[21] J. Gwenogvryn Evans, *Report on Manuscripts in the Welsh Language* (2 vols., London, 1898–1910), II, p. 1093.

[22] Robert, *Gramadeg Cymraeg*, [205]–[332]; G. J. Williams (ed.), *Barddoniaeth neu Brydyddiaeth gan Wiliam Midleton yn ôl argraffiad 1593, gyda chasgliad o'i awdlau a'i gywyddau* (Caerdydd, 1930); Williams and Jones, *Gramadegau'r Penceirddiaid*, pp. lvii–lviii, lxi–lxxxviii, 189–91, 196–8.

[23] Many of Thomas Prys's poems are collected in J. Fisher (ed.), *The Cefn Coch MSS* (Liverpool, 1899); see also William Rowlands, 'Barddoniaeth Tomos Prys o Blas Iolyn' (unpubl. University of Wales MA thesis, 1912). Dyfed Rowlands is at present engaged in re-editing the *cywyddau*.

of this amateur strict-metre verse, however, is that the authors had not been to school with the masters. Welsh versecraft is so intricate that it demands a long apprenticeship, and subsequent sustained practice, before it can become a fit vehicle for high poetic vision. Of all these amateurs, only Edmwnd Prys even approaches this standard. Nevertheless, more of their work was printed than that of the professional poets: for example, a selection of the strict-metre poetry of Gruffydd Robert was printed both on a secret press in this country and in Milan in 1584–94. Similar selections by William Midleton were printed at Oxford c.1595 and (posthumously) in London in 1603, and a single *cywydd* by Huw Lewys was printed as an appendix to his *Perl mewn adfyd* of 1595.[24]

A simpler free-metre tradition ran parallel with the strict-metre tradition of Welsh verse.[25] In its original form, which is probably of great antiquity, it too employed traditional metres, but without *cynghanedd* and with less emphasis on syllable-count: indeed, with the passage of time, its basis tended to become accentual rather than syllabic. During the Middle Ages these 'free' metres were employed by a lower grade of professional poet than those who practised the strict metres, but their work has almost entirely disappeared.[26] During our period, apart from one or two survivors of the old order, free-metre verse was generally composed by members of the lower gentry, clergymen and the occasional craftsman: professional poets using the strict metres very rarely stooped to produce anything in the free metres. Not only was the linguistic register of the free-metre poetry markedly lower than that in the strict metres, but the scope of the topics treated was also much wider: apart from the two great staples of religion and love, there was a limited amount of panegyric, a fair amount of satire, a good deal of prophecy (some of it self-parodying) and considerable attention to contemporary events. English influence was everywhere evident, not least in the choice of tunes to which the poems were sung.[27] The quality of the verse was variable, although sometimes strikingly high. The audience for the free-metre poetry was much larger than that for poetry in the strict metres: indeed, the free-metre poetry may have been the kind of literature to which the bulk of the population was most exposed, and it is a useful index to the thoughts and feelings of the

[24] Robert, *Gramadeg Cymraeg*, [303]–[388], cf. *Libri Walliae*, no. 4382; ibid., nos. 465–9 (also Siôn Dafydd Rhys, op. cit., pp. 246–8); Huw Lewys, *Perl mewn adfyd*, ed. W. J. Gruffydd (Caerdydd, 1929), pp. [247]–[250].
[25] In general see Brinley Rees, *Dulliau'r Canu Rhydd 1500–1650* (Caerdydd, 1952); R. M. Jones, 'Mesurau'r Canu Rhydd Cynnar', *BBCS*, XXVIII, part 3 (1979), 413–41.
[26] See Cennard Davies, 'Robin Clidro a'i Ganlynwyr' (unpubl. University of Wales MA thesis, 1964).
[27] Brinley Rees, 'Tair cerdd a thair tôn', *BBCS*, XXXI (1984), 60–73.

common people.[28] Apart from the material which has been preserved, there was probably a good deal of anonymous free-metre verse circulating in the form of seasonal songs and *penillion telyn* (stanzas sung to harp accompaniment) which has been lost to us forever.[29] The Welsh humanists were so bewitched by the glories of the strict-metre tradition that they paid little attention to its humbler sister, although Gruffydd Robert, in his metrical treatise of 1584–94, advocated the use of Italian metres for the new scientific and historical verse, and it is likely that Edmwnd Prys and Siôn Dafydd Rhys also had such innovation in mind when they proposed new subject matter for Welsh poetry (Siôn Dafydd Rhys even tried his hand at Welsh hexameters, with dire results).[30] However, one who can plausibly be claimed as one of their number, Richard Hughes of Caernarfonshire, produced a number of delicate love lyrics which clearly reflect current courtly fashions.[31] The collections of free-metre verse which achieved print during our period – Richard Gwyn's *Carolau* (1600), Edmwnd Prys's *Llyfr y Psalmau* (1621) and Rees Prichard's 'Canwyll y Cymru' (1617, 1646?)[32] were all contributions to religious worship, instruction and controversy rather than to the progress of humanism, although all their authors had humanist credentials, and Prys, in particular, stands in the very front rank of Welsh humanists. The work of another fine free-metre poet, Morgan Llwyd of Wrexham (d.1659), was wholly inspired by his incandescent Puritan convictions.[33]

At a date not easy to determine, but probably well before the end of the sixteenth century, a new kind of free-metre poetry began to compete with the old. This new kind was based on popular English tunes rather than on traditional metres: words were composed to fit the tunes (sometimes echoing the popular songs with which the tunes were associated in England and Scotland) and then the lines so composed were invested with full *cynghanedd*. Both Edmwnd Prys and Richard Hughes composed early examples of the genre, and Hughes actually published one of his as a broadside *c.*1620.[34] The great masters of the new kind of free-

[28] Glanmor Williams, *Grym Tafodau Tân: Ysgrifau Hanesyddol ar Grefydd a Diwylliant* (Llandysul, 1984), pp. 140–63, 164–79.
[29] See, e.g., Meredydd Evans, 'Y Canu Gwasael yn *Llawysgrif Richard Morris o Gerddi*', *LlC*, 13, no. 3 and 4 (1980–1), 207–35, and Rhiannon Ifans, *Sêrs a Rhybana* (Llandysul, 1983).
[30] Robert, *Gramadeg Cymraeg*, [330]–[331], and the texts cited in n. 8 above.
[31] T. H. Parry-Williams (ed.), *Canu Rhydd Cynnar* (Caerdydd, 1932), pp. 1–20. Cf. ibid., pp. 21–9, for another remarkable series of love poems, possibly by Llywelyn ap Hwlcyn. See Bobi Jones, 'Wrth Angor', *Barddas*, no. 149 (September 1989), 8–9. Llywelyn's humanist connections have yet to be established.
[32] *Libri Walliae*, nos. 5179; 587; 1049; 4098.
[33] M. Wynn Thomas, *Morgan Llwyd: Ei Gyfeillion a'i Gyfnod* (Caerdydd, 1991); R. M. Jones, *Cyfriniaeth Gymraeg* (Caerdydd, 1994), pp. 39–77.
[34] Rees, 'Tair cerdd a thair tôn', 60–73; *Libri Walliae*, no. 2542.

metre verse, however, were Edward Morris (d.1689) and Huw Morys 'Eos Ceiriog' (d.1709), both of whom came from Denbighshire, albeit from opposite ends of the county.[35] Although both poets continued to use the conventional strict-metre forms for the purpose of panegyric before the end of our period and after it, their most important achievement was the perfecting of the new kind of free-metre verse which became known as *canu carolaidd* (carol-like song). At its best, in their hands, this new kind of verse achieved a union of words and music not dissimilar in effect, it may be surmised, to that produced by the marriage of strict-metre verse to traditional Welsh music in the Later Middle Ages. Most of the popular verse of the eighteenth and early nineteenth centuries, including the ballads and interludes (rudimentary peripatetic stage plays), was in this mode. Huw Morys was in fact a pioneer of the interlude, but his efforts in the genre appear to be later than the end of our period. The only play to survive from our period, *Troelus a Chresyd*, which may have been the work of the notable humanist Humphrey Llwyd of Denbigh (d.1568), creates its own metres based on English models but – very sensibly – without introducing *cynghanedd*.[36] *Troelus a Chresyd* is certainly a humanist undertaking, and its failure to beget progeny may be taken as symbolic of the relative failure of the humanist campaign to reform and revivify Welsh verse.

In the matter of Welsh prose the picture was very different. Here the Welsh humanists had a much freer hand. Welsh prose writing reached its apogee in the twelfth and thirteenth centuries and after that its story is one of relative decline, although much interesting work – most of it translation – continued to be produced during the fourteenth, fifteenth and early sixteenth centuries.[37] Throughout our period the fortunes of prose are bound up with the printing press to a far greater extent than those of poetry. The most ambitious prose writer of the first half of the sixteenth century, Elis Gruffydd of Flintshire and Calais (d.*c.*1552), who

---

[35] On Edward Morris, see Gwenllian Jones, 'Bywyd a Gwaith Edward Morris, Perthi Llwydion' (unpubl. University of Wales MA thesis, 1941), and on Huw Morys, see David Jenkins, 'Bywyd a Gwaith Huw Morys (Pont y Meibion) 1622–1709' (unpubl. University of Wales MA thesis, 1948). Articles relating to these poets are listed in *LlLlG*, pp. 144–5 and *LlLlG*^{2}, p. 115.

[36] W. Beynon Davies (ed.), *Troelus a Chresyd o Lawysgrif Peniarth 106* (Caerdydd, 1976); R. J. Stephen Jones, 'The authorship of *Troelus a Chresyd*', *BBCS*, XXVIII, part 2 (1979), 223–8.

[37] Excellent general accounts may be found in A. O. H. Jarman and Gwilym Rees Hughes (eds.), *A Guide to Welsh Literature Volume 1* (Swansea, 1976), pp. 189–276, and idem, *A Guide to Welsh Literature Volume 2* (Swansea, 1979), pp. 338–75. See also Ceridwen Lloyd-Morgan's important account, 'Rhai Agweddau ar Gyfieithu yng Nghymru yn yr Oesoedd Canol' in J. E. Caerwyn Williams (ed.), *Ysgrifau Beirniadol XIII* (Dinbych, 1985), pp. 134–45.

essayed a universal history of the world as he knew it, was never published and his work consequently remained almost unknown until the present century: Gruffydd can certainly be regarded as a proto-humanist at least. By the crucial fifth decade of the sixteenth century the Welsh humanists proper were ready to harness the printing press to advance their cause, which from the beginning – in common with most north European humanism – had acquired a predominantly religious complexion. As a result the greater part of the 160 or so books printed in Welsh between 1546 and 1660 were religious in character.[38] Because the religion of Wales, in common with England, was officially Anglican, most of these books are of that persuasion, but the voices of Roman Catholics and Puritans were also heard from time to time through the medium of the printing press. As it happens, the very first printed book, Sir John Price of Brecon's *Yny lhyvyr hwnn* (In this book) (1546), is a reforming Catholic rather than a Protestant text, but this is the exception that proves the rule; *Yny lhyvyr hwnn* was also a profoundly humanistic text because the bulk of it consists of extracts from the important thirteenth-century religious treatise 'Ymborth yr enaid' (Food of the soul), which Price regarded as a fragment of the ancient theological learning of the Welsh he now sought to make generally available.[39] Already in 1545, the fervent young Protestant humanist William Salesbury had contracted with the London stationer John Waley, under the protection of a royal patent, to print a dictionary and some religious translations, and the dictionary duly appeared in 1547.[40] Also, probably, in 1547, Salesbury set out his objectives in an impassioned preface to a collection of proverbs he had 'semi-filched' (his own term) from his friend Gruffudd Hiraethog; these objectives were: to have the Bible in Welsh and to have learning in Welsh, the one objective impossible to attain without the other.

The story of Salesbury's efforts in the field of Biblical translation has often been told and may be summarized briefly here. In 1551 he published, with the help of the reformer Robert Crowley, his own translation of the scriptural passages in the Book of Common Prayer, *Kynniver Llith a Ban*. In 1563, supported by his friends Bishop Richard Davies of St David's (d.1581) and Humphrey Llwyd, he succeeded in having an act of parliament passed which instructed the four Welsh bishops and the bishop of Hereford to have the Bible and Book of

---

[38] Glanmor Williams, *The Welsh and their Religion* (Cardiff, 1991), pp. 138–72.

[39] R. Geraint Gruffydd, '*Yny lhyvyr hwnn* (1546): the earliest Welsh printed book', *BBCS*, XXIII, part 2 (1969), 105–16; R. Iestyn Daniel, *Ymborth yr Enaid* (Caerdydd, 1995).

[40] For what follows see the chapter cited in n. 8 above; see also R. Geraint Gruffydd, 'The first printed books, 1546–1604' in Philip H. Jones and Eiluned Rees (eds.), *A Nation and its Books* (Aberystwyth, forthcoming).

Common Prayer translated into Welsh and published by St David's Day 1567. By 1567 he himself, with occasional help from Davies and Thomas Huet, precentor of St David's Cathedral, had translated the whole of the Book of Common Prayer and New Testament and these were published during that year, apparently at the expense of the London-Welsh stationer Humphrey Toy. Although Salesbury and Davies began work on a translation of the Old Testament, they could not see eye to eye and the partnership broke up. Salesbury was immensely learned and immensely opinionated – a not infrequent conjunction – and the orthography, in particular, which he adopted was largely determined by the humanistic principles of respect for antiquity and desire for variety; unlearned curates found it baffling and those with a feeling for natural Welsh found it intolerable. It was fortunate, therefore, that the translation of the whole Bible was eventually taken in hand by William Morgan (d.1604), then a parish priest on the borders of Denbighshire and Montgomeryshire, who published his work, with official support and approval, in London in 1588, just after the Spanish Armada had been defeated. Morgan built on Salesbury's strengths and eliminated most of his weaknesses, producing a generally acceptable and justly acclaimed version; he also revised Salesbury's translation of the Book of Common Prayer in 1599. Finally, Bishop Richard Parry of St Asaph (d.1623), with the crucial help of his brother-in-law Dr John Davies of Mallwyd (d.1644), produced a revision of Morgan's Bible in 1620 and of Salesbury and Morgan's Book of Common Prayer in 1621; these remained, without fundamental revision, the authorized versions of the Welsh Bible and Prayer Book until this century.[41]

Recent research has shown conclusively that the translators of the Bible into Welsh were both splendid Biblical scholars and supreme masters of the Welsh language, notwithstanding Salesbury's orthographic idiosyncrasies.[42] It remains to be demonstrated to what extent the syntax adopted by the versions reflected contemporary spoken and written usage; but even if it did so only partially, it was perhaps no bad thing that the register of these exalted texts should be somewhat heightened as compared with that of ordinary speech. (I am aware that there are powerful arguments to the contrary.) These translations are important in the first instance because of their religious import and impact, but from our point of view two further aspects of their importance may be identified. In the first place they

[41] For a general survey, see R. Geraint Gruffydd (ed.), *Y Gair ar Waith: Ysgrifau ar yr Etifeddiaeth Feiblaidd yng Nghymru* (Caerdydd, 1988); see also Williams, *The Welsh and their Religion*, pp. 173–229.

[42] Isaac Thomas, *Y Testament Newydd Cymraeg 1551–1620* (Caerdydd, 1976); idem, *Yr Hen Destament Cymraeg 1551–1620* (Aberystwyth, 1988).

provided for later prose writers a model of eloquent, regular and mellifluous prose encompassing a large variety of literary genres. In the second place — and in the context of these studies this is perhaps more important — they ensured that the great majority of the population was regularly exposed to activities bearing the highest possible prestige which were conducted in the Welsh language. If, as seemed likely in the period 1539–49, the people of Wales had been forced to attend divine service conducted wholly and solely in English, the effect of such attendance on the fate of the language might well have been catastrophic.[43] The debt which the language owes to the Protestant principle that each individual has the right of access to God's Word in his or her own language, the principle which directly underlay the Act of 1563, is incalculable.

As hinted above, a body of Welsh Anglican prose works clustered about the translations of the Bible.[44] Richard Davies's long introduction to Salesbury's New Testament of 1567 pleaded eloquently for the theory, almost universally accepted by Welsh humanists, that Britain had first been evangelized by St Joseph of Arimathea rather than by St Augustine of Canterbury, the emissary of the bishop of Rome. After that, prose works by Welsh Anglicans were nearly all translations and included such acknowledged classics as Morris Kyffin's translation of Bishop John Jewel's *Apologia Ecclesiae Anglicanae* (1595), Huw Lewys's translation (by means of an English version by Miles Coverdale) of Otto Werdmüller's *Ein Kleinot* (1595), Edward James's translation of the official Anglican books of homilies (1606), Rowland Vaughan's translation of Bishop Lewis Bayly's *The Practice of Piety* (1629), Robert Lloyd's translation of Arthur Dent's *The Plain man's pathway to heaven* (1630) and John Davies of Mallwyd's translation of Edmund Bunny's Protestant version of Robert Persons SJ's *The First booke of the Christian exercise, appertayning to resolution* (1632).[45] Towards the end of the Commonwealth period there was a resurgence of Anglican publication, to which Rowland Vaughan, much embittered by his experiences during the civil wars and afterwards, contributed no fewer

---

[43] Peter R. Roberts, 'The Welsh Language, English Law and Tudor Legislation', *THSC* (1989), 44–54.

[44] The field is surveyed in R. Geraint Gruffydd, 'Religious Prose in Welsh from the Beginning of the Reign of Elizabeth to the Restoration' (unpubl. University of Oxford DPhil thesis, 1952–3).

[45] There are modern editions of Morris Kyffin, *Deffynniad Ffydd Eglwys Loegr*, ed. W. Prichard Williams (Bangor, 1908), Huw Lewys, *Perl mewn adfyd* (see n. 24 above), and Lewis Bayly, *Yr Ymarfer o dduwioldeb . . . wedi ei gyfieithu i'r Gymraeg gan Rowland Vaughan*, ed. John Ballinger (Caerdydd, 1930). The others are *Libri Walliae*, nos. 1162 (James), 1682 (Lloyd) and 3869 (Davies). For a study of Lloyd, see Branwen Heledd Morgan, 'Arolwg o Ryddiaith Gymraeg, 1547–1634 gydag Astudiaeth Fanwl o *Dysgeidiaeth Cristnoges o Ferch* (1552) a'r *Llwybr Hyffordd* (1632)' (unpubl. University of Wales MA thesis, 1969).

than six titles, all translations and all probably published in 1658.[46] These Anglican translations served to consolidate the prose tradition already established by the Welsh version of the Bible. An early uncertainty concerning correct usage gave way to a broad consensus. Most translators, within the constraints which the practice of their art imposed upon them, aspired to as plain a style as possible in order to reach the maximum number of readers, and it is fairly clear also that they expected their books to be read aloud in company as well as privately (Edward James's homilies were, of course, designed from the first to be read aloud in church). In this way it is likely that the message of these books, as well as that of the Bible and Book of Common Prayer (essentially the same message), reached some of the four-fifths or more of the population – admittedly the lower strata of it – who still could not read but who attended church.[47] In spite of their populist aims, however, the translators remained humanists almost to a man, and their writings display an awareness of the resources of the Welsh literary tradition on which they drew and to which they contributed. Rowland Vaughan, for example, was educated at Oxford, and was a prolific poet in both the strict and the free metres as well as a translator of Anglican books. As a translator, however, he did not match up to Morris Kyffin, Edward James, Robert Lloyd and John Davies. Davies's *Llyfr y resolusion* (1632), in particular, shows him at the height of his powers as a writer of prose, and because of his unrivalled prestige as a reviser of the Welsh Bible and Prayer Book and as the author of the standard grammar and dictionary of the language, the translation quickly attained the status of an exemplar. Of the few Anglican writers after Richard Davies who attempted to produce original works, Robert Holland of Pembrokeshire stands out, particularly for his sparkling pamphlet against witchcraft, which he published in 1600.[48] Holland was later to be associated with the London-Welsh stationer Thomas Salisbury in his ambitious scheme to expand greatly the publication of Welsh books, a project which was thwarted by the plague of 1603.[49]

---

[46] *Libri Walliae*, nos. 708–9, 1874, 3526, 4150 and 4988.

[47] Williams, *Recovery, Reorientation and Reformation*, p. 437. The study of the surviving manuscript sermons of the period has not yet reached the point that will permit generalization, but there are pioneering dissertations by Glyn Morgan, 'Pregethau Cymraeg William Griffith (?1566–1612) ac Evan Morgan (*c*.1574–1643)' (unpubl. University of Wales MA thesis, 1969), and Ruth Elisabeth Jones, 'Y Bregeth Gymraeg 1558–1642 (gan fanylu ar y pregethau yn llsgrau. NLW 5982A, NLW (Add.) 73A, BL Add. 15058 ac NLW CM (Bala) 769)' (unpubl. University of Wales MA thesis, 1979).

[48] Jones, *Rhyddiaith Gymraeg II*, pp. 161–73; Stuart Clark and P. T. J. Morgan, 'Religion and magic in Elizabethan Wales: Robert Holland's dialogue on witchcraft', *JEH*, XXVII (1976), 31–46.

[49] R. Geraint Gruffydd, 'Thomas Salisbury o Lundain a Chlocaenog: ysgolhaig-argraffydd y Dadeni Cymreig', *NLWJ*, XXVII, no. 1 (1991), 1–19.

A number of Anglican prose translations remained unpublished, in particular the translation by John Conway of Flintshire (d.1606) of Leonard Wright's *A Summons for Sleepers*, the translation of Christopher Sutton's *Disce Mori* by Dafydd Rowland (d.1640) of Caernarfonshire, and the translation of both John Mayer's *English Catechism Explained* and Thomas Sorocold's *Supplications of Saints* by William Powell (d.1654 x 1660) of Wrexham, as well as other material the source of which cannot at present be identified.[50] None of the three was a great master of Welsh prose, although Powell was more accomplished than Rowland, and Rowland better than Conway whose command of the language was far from complete. Even so, Conway was a particularly interesting author: a wealthy Flintshire gentleman and a patron of professional poets, he also (as we shall see) translated a humanistic treatise on music; his wife, Margaret Mostyn, was a Roman Catholic recusant, and Conway's translation of the *Summons* may have been an attempt to establish his Anglican credentials.

This consideration points us towards the Roman Catholic literary effort during our period.[51] The campaign was much hampered by the effective prohibition, from 1559 onwards, of Roman Catholic printing in Wales. Roman Catholics sought to overcome the crippling effects of prohibition in three ways: by printing openly in Roman Catholic countries on the Continent; by printing secretly at home; and by the circulation of manuscript copies. As early as 1568, one of the Roman Catholic exiles in Rome, Morys Clynnog (d.1581) of Caernarfonshire, published his translation of a small catechism on Christian doctrine which was later said to be the work of Juan Alfonso de Polanco SJ; a fellow Welsh exile, Gruffydd Robert (d.1605?), also from Caernarfonshire, saw it through the press in Milan; it is clear that Clynnog's work reached this country because Lewis Evans set about refuting it in 1571.[52] Early in the

---

[50] On Conway, see Gwendraeth Jones, 'Astudiaeth o Definiad i Hennadirion, Cyfieithiad Siôn Conwy o *A Summons for Sleepers* gan Leonard Wright gyda Rhagymadrodd, Nodiadau a Geirfa' (unpubl. University of Wales MA thesis, 1963); on Rowland, see Beryl Dorothy Williams, '*Addysg i Farw*. Dafydd Rowland. NLW Add. MS. 731B: Plas Power 16: 1633. Astudiaeth Destunol, Hanesyddol a Llenyddol' (unpubl. University of Wales MA thesis, 1961), and on Powell, see Goronwy Price Owen, 'Cyfieithiadau William Powell yn llsgr. Ll.G.C. Peniarth 321' (unpubl. University of Wales MA thesis, 1988). Articles on Conway are listed in *LlLlG*, pp. 91, 140.

[51] The field is surveyed in Geraint Bowen, 'Llenyddiaeth Gatholig y Cymry (1559–1829): Rhyddiaith a Barddoniaeth' (unpubl. University of Liverpool MA thesis, 1952–3); idem, 'Rhyddiaith Reciwsantiaid Cymru' (unpubl. University of Wales PhD thesis, 1978). For Margaret Mostyn's recusancy, see Peter Roberts, *Y Cwtta Cyfarwydd: 'The Chronicle written by the famous clarke, Peter Roberts', notary public, for the years 1607–1646*, ed. D. R. Thomas (London, 1883), p. 118.

[52] *Libri Walliae*, no. 4020. Articles on Clynnog are listed in *LlLlG*, pp. 133–4; note esp. Geraint Bowen, 'Ateb i *Athravaeth Gristnogavl* Morys Clynnog', *NLWJ*, VII, no. 4 (1952), 388.

seventeenth century a third exile, Roger Smyth (d.1625) from Flintshire, published in Paris both a truncated and a full version of St Peter Canisius's catechism *Summa Doctrinae Christianae* (1609, 1611), and also a translation of Robert Southwell SJ's *An Epistle of a Religious Priest unto his father* (1612),[53] as well as a humanist work of moral philosophy to which we will return briefly later. The translation by Richard Vaughan (d.1624) of Denbighshire of St Roberto Bellarmino's *Dottrina Christiana* was likewise published in St Omer in France in 1618, probably through the agency of the Welsh Jesuit superior John Salisbury.[54] By contrast, the first part of *Y Drych Cristianogawl* (the Christian Mirror) was produced on the first secret press known to have operated on Welsh soil, that set up in a cave at Rhiwledin near Llandudno early in 1587; although the book, primarily a work of religious exhortation, is now thought to be the work of Robert Gwyn, a notable missionary priest from Caernarfonshire, the book itself claims that it was written by Gruffydd Robert and seen through the press by Roger Smyth in Rouen in 1585. The press was discovered on 14 April (Good Friday) 1587, and its personnel scattered, but an attempt was made late in the same year to set up another press in the house of Siôn Dafydd Rhys in Brecon in order to print the remaining two parts of the book: this attempt also was foiled by the vigilance of the authorities. There was talk of another secret press on the Flintshire-Shropshire border in 1590, and there survives one copy of a small collection of Gruffydd Robert's verse which must be the product of such a press; furthermore, we have a clear reference, as we have already seen, to the publication of St Richard Gwyn's controversial 'carols' in 1600.[55] Much the most substantial products of the Counter-Reformation literary effort in Wales, however, remained unprinted: these include the complete *Drych Cristianogawl*, a work of controversy entitled 'Nad oes vn Ffydd ond y wir Ffydd' (no Faith but the true Faith), a treatise forbidding attendance at Anglican services 'Gwssanaeth y Gwŷr Newydd' (the Liturgy of the New Men), an apologetic work 'Coelio'r Saint' (Faith in the Saints) and a

---

[53] *Libri Walliae*, nos. 3955–6. On Canisius, see John Ryan, 'Seventeenth-century Catholic Welsh Devotional Works, with Special Reference to the Welsh Translation of the Catechism of Petrus Canisius and Robert Bellarmine's *Summary of Christian doctrine*' (unpubl. University of Liverpool MA thesis, 1966); see also John Ryan, 'The sources of the Welsh translation of the Catechism of St. Peter Canisius', *JWBS*, XI, nos. 3–4 (1975–6), 225–32. The translation from Southwell was recently discovered in the Bibliothèque Mazarine, Paris; see A. F. Allison and D. M. Rogers, *The Contemporary Printed Literature of the English Counter-Reformation between 1558 and 1640* (2 vols., Aldershot, 1989–94), II, p. 144 (no. 725.5).

[54] *Libri Walliae*, no. 332; Allison and Rogers, op. cit., II, p. 148 (no. 747); Geraint Bowen, 'Richard Vaughan, Bodeiliog, ac *Eglvrhad Helaeth-lawn*, 1618', *NLWJ*, XII, no. 1 (1961), 83–4.

[55] R. Geraint Gruffydd, *Argraffwyr Cyntaf Cymru* (Caerdydd, 1972).

treatise on moral theology which may have borne the title 'Drych Ufudd-dod' (Mirror of Obedience). The second and third of those titles are certainly the work of Robert Gwyn, and Dr Geraint Bowen, the leading authority in the field, has argued consistently that the other three should be attributed to him also.[56] 'Coelio'r Saint' exists in two manuscript copies, a holograph and a transcript, which illustrates both the method by which these books were circulated and the limitations of that method. No Welsh Roman Catholic book was printed between 1618 and the end of our period, although a handbook on confession entitled *Drych cydwybod* (Mirror of Conscience) was apparently published in 1661, all copies of which have now disappeared.[57]

Puritans, too, used literature as well as the pulpit to promulgate their views. The earlier Puritans were mostly loyal churchmen, among whom we may number Rowland Puleston, later described as vicar of Wrexham, who, in 1583, wrote his substantial but linguistically uncouth 'Llyfr o'r Eglwys Gristnogaidd' (Book of the Christian Church), and Oliver Thomas, vicar of West Felton near Shrewsbury, who, in 1631, published a well-crafted exhortation to his fellow-countrymen to make good use of the Welsh family Bible which had appeared the previous year; Thomas later published other, less substantial, pieces.[58] Two of the most prominent leaders of Welsh Puritanism during the Interregnum, Vavasor Powell and Morgan Llwyd, had Welsh books published, but whereas those of Powell were translations into Welsh of his own original English works (there were two of these, both probably published in 1653), Llwyd's seven books and pamphlets in Welsh consisted of five original works and two translations (these are extracts from the writings of the Lutheran mystic Jacob Boehme, both published in 1657).[59] Llwyd, who came of gentle Merioneth stock but had to be content with a grammar school education at Wrexham (where he later ministered), was a man of profound spiritual experience, with a restless questing intellect and a great poet's way with words. Convinced that the events of his own day presaged Christ's early

---

[56] Geraint Bowen, *Y Drych Cristianogawl: Astudiaeth* (Caerdydd, 1988); idem, 'Ysgol Douai' in Geraint Bowen (ed.), *Y Traddodiad Rhyddiaith* (Llandysul, 1970), pp. 118–48. See also idem, *Y Drych Kristnogawl* (Caerdydd, 1996).

[57] *Libri Walliae*, no. 1718.

[58] Merfyn Morgan (ed.), *Gweithiau Oliver Thomas ac Evan Roberts: Dau Biwritan Cynnar* (Caerdydd, 1981).

[59] *Libri Walliae*, nos. 4056–8, 3400–18. Llwyd's works have been collected in T. E. Ellis (ed.), *Gweithiau Morgan Llwyd o Wynedd* (Bangor, 1899); J. H. Davies (ed.), *Gweithiau Morgan Llwyd o Wynedd Cyf. II* (Bangor a Llundain, 1908); J. Graham Jones and G. Wyn Owen (eds.), *Gweithiau Morgan Llwyd o Wynedd Cyf. III* (Caerdydd, 1994). Reference should also be made to M. Wynn Thomas, *Morgan Llwyd* (Cardiff, 1984) and Goronwy Wyn Owen, *Morgan Llwyd* (Caernarfon, 1992), both of which include valuable bibliographies. See also *LlLlG*, pp. 148–9 and *LlLlG*², pp. 115–16.

return to rule on earth, he sought to direct his fellow-countrymen to prepare themselves for that event by listening to the voice of the Spirit within themselves and obeying His promptings. His prose, profoundly figurative, is sometimes obscure but always compelling. In the book and two pamphlets he published in 1653 – *Llyfr y Tri Aderyn* (the Book of the Three Birds), *Llythyr i'r Cymru cariadus* (a Letter to the Beloved People of Wales) and *Gwaedd Ynghymru yn wyneb pob cydwybod euog* (a Cry in Wales confronting every guilty conscience) – his writing is at its most passionate and piercing. In the book and pamphlet he published in 1656 and 1657 respectively – *Gair or Gair* (a Word from the Word) and *Cyfarwyddid ir Cymru* (Advice for the People of Wales) – there is evidence of a more settled and speculative frame of mind. There is some dispute about Llwyd's basic orthodoxy, but of his towering eminence as a prose writer there can be no doubt. It is likely that he was also a highly effective preacher. None of the other Puritan writers of prose can even begin to compare with him, although several of his contemporaries were perfectly competent literary craftsmen: of these one might perhaps single out Richard Jones, a Puritan schoolmaster of Denbigh, who translated Richard Baxter's *A Call to the unconverted* in 1659 and who was later to help Stephen Hughes with the work which laid the foundations for the Welsh Trust.[60]

The humanist commitment of the authors of the religious prose works we have been discussing varied widely: to generalize somewhat rashly, it was strong in the case of the Anglicans, weaker in the case of the Roman Catholics, and weaker still in the case of the Puritans. There can be little doubt, however, about the devotion to humanistic ideals of a small group of prose writers who attempted to treat learned subjects (other than the language and history of Wales itself) through the medium of Welsh. William Salesbury's 'Llysieulyfr Meddyginiaethol' (Medicinal Herbal) is a shining example, based as it is on the latest authorities in England and on the Continent; unfortunately, it remained unpublished until the twentieth century.[61] Less innovative, but earlier (1552), was the translation by Richard Owen, about whom nothing is known, of the Spanish humanist Juan Luis Vives's *De Institutione Feminae Christianae*; this too remained unpublished.[62] In the same broad category of moral philosophy was Roger Smyth's translation of the Breton humanist Pierre Boaistuau's *Le*

---

[60] *Libri Walliae*, no. 310.
[61] See Iwan Rhys Edgar, 'Llysieulyfr William Salesbury: testun o lawysgrif Ll.G.C. 4581, ynghyd â rhagymadrodd ac astudiaeth o'r enwau llysiau Cymraeg a geir ynddo' (unpubl. University of Wales PhD thesis, 1984); idem, *Llysieulyfr Salesbury* (Caerdydd, 1997).
[62] It is discussed in the dissertation by Branwen Heledd Morgan (see n. 45), and in articles listed in *LlLlG*, p. 140 and *LlLlG²*, p. 112.

théâtre du monde; this, however, did achieve publication, either in Paris or surreptitiously in Britain, in 1615.[63] Two theoretical treatises on music were also translated during this period: John Case's *Apologia Musices* (1588) by John Conway towards the end of the sixteenth century, and Andreas Ornithoparcus's *Musicae activae micrologus* (1517) by the royal harper Robert Peilin early in the seventeenth century.[64] These remained in manuscript, happily in Conway's case because his Welsh is painfully inept, less happily in the case of Peilin because his translation is of much interest in the context of the history of music in Wales during this period. Conway remains, nevertheless, a fascinating figure: he may well be the highest-ranking Welsh gentleman after Sir John Price actually to write in Welsh during the period – although it is certain that many of his fellow-gentry would hotly contest that statement! – and both his desire so to write and his weak command of the language says much about its ambivalent status in the minds of its traditional patrons, at least in north-east Wales, towards the end of the sixteenth century. Conway's son remained a generous patron of the professional poets, but after that the family appears largely to have renounced its responsibilities in this regard.[65]

The category of prose just discussed must have had a very limited readership indeed. One wonders if even the religious writings, granted that they were read aloud in company as well as privately, ever commanded as wide an audience as the old tales described in a celebrated account of 'The state of North Wales touching religion' found among the Burghley papers and probably to be dated fairly late in the sixteenth century. It has been much quoted but will bear quoting again:

> Upon the Sondaies and hollidaies the multitude of all sortes of men woomen and childerne of everie parishe doe use to meete in sondrie places either one some hill or one the side of some mountaine where theire harpers and crowthers singe them songs of the doeings of theire auncestors, namelie, of theire warrs againste the kings of this realme and the English nacion, and then doe they ripp upp theire petigres at lenght howe eche of them is discended from those theire ould princs. Here alsoe doe they spende theire time in hearinge some part of the lives of Thalaassyn, Marlin, Beno, Kybbye, Jermon, and suche other the intended prophetts and saincts of that cuntrie.[66]

---

[63] Rhosier Smyth, *Theater du Mond (Gorsedd y Byd)*, ed. Thomas Parry (Caerdydd, 1930); *Libri Walliae*, no. 579: cf. Allison and Rogers, op. cit., II, p. 141 (no. 710).
[64] On Conway, see the references in n. 50 above. A dissertation on Peilin's treatise, Cardiff MS Hafod 3, is being prepared by Irwen Cockman.
[65] R. Alun Charles, 'Noddwyr y Beirdd yn Sir y Fflint', *LlC*, 12, no. 1 and 2 (1972), 3–11.
[66] Ifor Williams, 'Hen Chwedlau', *THSC* (1946–7), 28–58, esp. 28, n. 2. Sir Ifor's corrections have been incorporated in the quotation.

'That cuntrie', as Sir Ifor Williams has persuasively demonstrated, was almost certainly the area which had as its focus the parish of Clynnog Fawr, some ten miles south-west of Caernarfon. One suspects that the whole account was deliberately alarmist, and that little reliance can therefore be placed on its detail, but it is difficult to deny its main thrust. It seems that the medieval Welsh tradition of storytelling was still alive to some extent, at least in some parts of the country, up until the end of the sixteenth century. It will be recalled that Gruffydd Robert's testimony in the prologue to the first part of his Welsh grammar, published in Milan in 1567, is to the same effect:

> Os mynnych chwithau glowed arfer y wlad yn amser yn teidiau ni, chwi a gaech henafgwyr briglwydion a ddangossai iwch ar dafod laferydd bob gweithred hynod, a gwiwglod a wneithid trwy dir cymru er ys talm o amser.[67]

> (If you wished to hear the custom of the country in the time of our ancestors, you would find hoary-headed elders who would show you by word of mouth every remarkable and praiseworthy act performed in the land of Wales this long time.)

Although the standpoint is quite different, the prevalence of oral storytelling was again emphasized the following year in Robert's dedication of Clynnog's translation of the Polanco catechism, in which he urged his fellow-countrymen to abandon vain old tales, and flattering lying *cywyddau* ('gadael i ffordd henchwedlau coegion, a chywyddau gwenieithus celwyddog').[68]

The final aspect of the work of the Welsh humanists, in so far as that work impinged on learning and culture, is their activity in the field of Welsh language studies and Welsh history. As suggested earlier, this activity had as its objective not only disinterested scholarly research but also the demonstration to the Welsh gentry, especially those who were tempted to abandon their roots, of the richness and regularity of the Welsh language and the glories of the Welsh past. William Salesbury's first printed work was his Welsh-English dictionary of 1547, modelled on John Palsgrave's *Lesclarcissement de la langue francoyse* of 1530, and intended to help Welshmen to learn English (as Salesbury himself had done relatively late in his youth), although it could of course be put to other uses.[69] Salesbury was followed by a number of leading Welsh humanists

---

[67] Robert, *Gramadeg Cymraeg*, pp. 2–3.
[68] Lewis, *Hen Gyflwyniadau*, p. 6.
[69] W. Alun Mathias, 'William Salesbury a'r Testament Newydd', *LlC*, 16, no. 1 and 2 (1989), 40–68; the footnotes to this article serve as an index to Mr Mathias's many important contributions on Salesbury.

whose dictionaries were not published and are now lost, including David Powel, Henry Perri and William Morgan.[70] Two valuable and ambitious dictionaries have survived in manuscript: Thomas Wiliems's 'Trysor yr iaith Ladin a'r Gymraeg' (Treasury of the Latin and Welsh languages) of 1604–8, a Latin-Welsh dictionary based on Thomas Thomas's *Dictionarium linguae Latinae, et Anglicanae*; and Henry Salesbury's 'Geirfa Tafod Cymraeg' (a Vocabulary of the Welsh Language), a Welsh-Latin dictionary which is extant in two versions and on which its author was still working late in life (he probably died *c*.1635).[71] The only dictionary, apart from that of William Salesbury, to achieve print during our period was John Davies of Mallwyd's remarkable *Antiquae Linguae Britannicae . . . et linguae Latinae, Dictionarium Duplex* of 1632, which included a Welsh-Latin dictionary by Davies and a truncated version of Thomas Wiliems's Latin-Welsh dictionary – an extraordinary achievement by the greatest pure scholar produced by the Welsh Renaissance.[72] In the field of grammar, pride of place must go to Gruffydd Robert's *Gramadeg Cymraeg* of 1567–94, not only because it was the first grammar-book to appear but also because it was written in fluent and elegant Welsh prose; the first two parts of the grammar deal with orthography and morphology respectively, with some slight attention to syntax, and are notable for their emphasis on the validity of spoken usage, an emphasis almost certainly derived from the Sienese school of philologists led by Claudio Tolomei.[73] Reference has already been made to the latter parts of the book which deal with metrics, but its two appendices should also be mentioned: a fine translation of part of Cicero's *De Senectute* and an anthology of Welsh verse by Robert and others. The three other grammars of Welsh published during our period were all written in Latin, so that the learned world as well as the humanistically inclined Welsh gentry might be persuaded of the worth of the language. Siôn Dafydd Rhys published his *Cambrobrytannicae Cymraecaeve Linguae Institutiones* in 1592, with the moral and financial support of his patron Sir Edward Stradling; as already mentioned, it included a long section on metrics as well as sections on

---

[70] For an invaluable general survey, see J. E. Caerwyn Williams, *Geiriadurwyr y Gymraeg yng Nghyfnod y Dadeni* (Caerdydd, 1983).
[71] Idem, 'Thomas Wiliems, y Geiriadurwr', *SC*, XVI–XVII (1981–2), 280–316; Ceri Davies, 'Y berthynas rhwng *Geirfa Tafod Cymraeg* Henry Salesbury a'r *Dictionarium Duplex*', *BBCS,* XXVIII, part 3 (1979), 399–400; M. T. Burdett-Jones, 'Dau Eiriadur Henry Salesbury', *NLWJ*, XXVI, no. 3 (1990), 241–50.
[72] *Libri Walliae*, nos. 1551–2.
[73] For an edition, see n. 13 above. For discussions, see T. Gwynfor Griffith, 'A borrowing from the *Cortegiano*' in O. Feldman (ed.), *Homenaje a Robert A. Hall, Jr.* (Madrid, 1977), pp. 149–52, and Heledd Hayes, 'Claudio Tolomei: a major influence on Gruffydd Robert', *MLR*, LXXXIII (1988), 56–66.

phonology and morphology: the section on phonology is especially valuable.[74] Henry Salesbury's *Grammatica Britannica* of 1593–4 was a much slighter effort, as he himself confessed (it was written in 1587, long before the appearance of the *Institutiones*), but it is still of considerable interest.[75] All these works, however, were decisively superseded by the appearance of John Davies of Mallwyd's *Antiquae Linguae Britannicae . . . rudimenta* in 1621, a work which presented a meticulous analysis of the language employed by the professional poets, whom Davies, in common with his fellow humanists, rightly regarded as the chief custodians of the literary language.[76] Davies's grammar, even more than his dictionary, is the crowning achievement of Welsh humanist scholarship.

In the historical field, the efforts of the humanists were chiefly directed towards two objectives: the discovery, preservation and publication of ancient records of the Welsh past, and the defence of the mythical accounts of that past, which they all more or less believed and which enhanced their self-esteem as Welshmen and validated their scholarly and cultural activities.[77] With regard to the first objective, it was Humphrey Llwyd and David Powel who made the most significant contribution. In 1559 Llwyd produced a manuscript English translation of the medieval 'Brut y Tywysogyon' (Chronicle of the Princes) – the most important single source for the history of twelfth and thirteenth century Wales – and in 1584 Powel published this translation with his own addition and annotations as *The Historie of Cambria*. Throughout our period Welsh humanists also collected, transcribed and collated whatever ancient sources they could find, with John Jones of Gellilyfdy in Flintshire and Robert Vaughan of Hengwrt in Merioneth supreme among them: it is in fact tragic that Vaughan, the owner of the finest private library that Wales has ever seen, did not see fit to publish more of his discoveries.[78] With regard to the second objective mentioned above, the defence of the mythical accounts of the Welsh past, particularly those dependent on

---

[74] *Libri Walliae*, no. 4282; Glyn E. Jones, 'Central Rounded and Unrounded Vowels in Sixteenth Century Welsh', *Papurau Gwaith Ieithyddol Cymraeg Caerdydd / Cardiff Working Papers in Welsh Linguistics*, no. 2 (Amgueddfa Werin Cymru, 1982), pp. 43–52.

[75] *Libri Walliae*, no. 4558.

[76] *Libri Walliae*, no. 1550 (no. 1557 is a ghost).

[77] Ieuan M. Williams, 'Ysgolheictod hanesyddol yr unfed ganrif ar bymtheg', *LlC*, 2, nos. 2 and 4 (1952–3), 111–24, 209–23.

[78] On Vaughan, see T. Emrys Parry, 'Llythyrau Robert Vaughan, Hengwrt (1592–1667)' (unpubl. University of Wales MA thesis, 1961); and on Jones, see Nesta Jones, 'Bywyd John Jones, Gellilyfdy' (unpubl. University of Wales MA thesis, 1964) and Nesta Lloyd (née Jones), 'Welsh Scholarship in the Seventeenth Century, with Special Reference to the Writings of John Jones, Gellilyfdy' (unpubl. University of Oxford DPhil thesis, 1970); articles on Vaughan and Jones are listed in *LlLlG*, pp. 153–4 and *LlLlG*^{2}, p. 119.

Geoffrey of Monmouth's *Historia Regum Britanniae* (1138), Sir John Price with his *Historiae Britannicae Defensio* (written 1547–53, published 1573) led the field, followed by Humphrey Llwyd with his *Commentariolum* of 1572 and David Powel with various tractates in 1585; John Davies of Mallwyd, too, devoted much of the lengthy introduction to his *Dictionarium* of 1632 to arguing the claims of the traditional British history. Many of the most remarkable defences of Geoffrey remained, however, in manuscript: they were by Siôn Dafydd Rhys in 1597, by John Lewis of Llynwene during the years 1603–12, and by Robert Vaughan of Hengwrt and William Maurice of Llansilin during the last decade of our period.[79] The work of Lewis, Vaughan and Maurice are all in English, but that of Siôn Dafydd Rhys is in Welsh, and it is certainly the most important Welsh Renaissance text to remain unpublished. In it he examines at length, with great learning and in fine humanist style, four of the chief objections brought against Geoffrey's narrative, demolishing them all to his own complete satisfaction! These were: the fact that hardly anyone had mentioned Brutus except Geoffrey; the fable of the oracle of Diana which led Brutus to this island; the existence of the giants whom Geoffrey claims inhabited the island when Brutus landed; and the seemingly impossible feats of arms performed by some of Geoffrey's heroes.[80] There are two other historical texts in Welsh remaining in manuscript, by Roger Morris and Ifan Llwyd ap Dafydd respectively, and they too uphold the traditional view of the Welsh past, but without Siôn Dafydd Rhys's controversial thrust and certainly without the verve with which he wrote.[81] The trend of the times was against Geoffrey, however: Rowland Vaughan, who had defended him staunchly in 1629, had abandoned his cause as hopeless by 1655, and was sharply rebuked by his kinsman Robert Vaughan for having done so.[82]

What we witness in the period 1536–1660 with regard to the role of the Welsh language in learning and culture is thus a twofold movement. By the last third of the period at least, the allegiance of the major gentry, traditionally its most powerful patrons, to the language had been seriously weakened, and the profound social upheaval of the civil wars dealt it

---

[79] On Siôn Dafydd Rhys, see n. 80; on Lewis, see the articles listed in *LlLlG*, p. 153; on Vaughan and Maurice, see the thesis by T. Emrys Parry cited in n. 78.

[80] R. Geraint Gruffydd, 'Dr. John Davies, "the old man of Brecknock"', *AC*, CXLI (1992), 1–13.

[81] On Morris, see Robert Isaac Denis Jones, 'Astudiaeth Feirniadol o Peniarth 168B (tt. 41a–126b)' (unpubl. University of Wales MA thesis, 1954), and on Ifan Llwyd, see Nia Lewis, 'Astudiaeth Destunol a Beirniadol o "Ystorie Kymru neu Cronigl Kymraeg" (Ifan Llwyd ap Dafydd)' (unpubl. University of Wales MA thesis, 1967); see also D. J. Bowen, 'Ifan Llwyd ap Dafydd', *LlC*, 2, no. 4 (1953), 257–8.

[82] E. D. Jones, 'Rowland Fychan o Gaer-gai a Brut Sieffre o Fynwy', *LlC*, 4, no. 4 (1957), 228.

another damaging blow. In parallel, the guild of professional poets, traditionally the Welsh men of letters *par excellence*, went into steep decline, although it proved extraordinarily difficult to kill it off altogether. The bulk of the population below the gentry class, however, remained pretty solidly monoglot and still found intellectual enrichment in free-metre verse and oral storytelling, whatever impact the various religious movements of the period made upon them (and this is not to deny that they did make an impact). But there was also another contrasting movement. The minor gentry who became Renaissance humanists brought about the translation of the Bible and Book of Common Prayer into Welsh and thus ensured that the language would from then on dominate a crucial area of Welsh life. To reinforce the message of the Bible they produced a fine series of prose works (and a splendid metrical psalter). They succeeded also in describing the grammar of Welsh and in recording its vocabulary, so as to enhance its status as a learned language in the eyes of the European intelligentsia and, so they hoped, in the eyes of their own people who had been attracted by the ideals and objectives of humanism. In the light of these successes, their failure to produce a large body of Welsh humanist prose, and the probably inevitable frustration of their attempts to reform Welsh professional verse, can to some extent be discounted. By 1660 the language was certainly better equipped than it was in 1536 to face the continuing challenge of the times.

11

The Cultural Uses of the Welsh Language 1660–1800

GERAINT H. JENKINS

DURING THE second half of the seventeenth century writers who were concerned about the future of the Welsh language as a literary medium were plagued by a deep sense of pessimism, hopelessness and despair. 'To Languages as well as Dominion', wrote Thomas Jones the almanacker, 'there is an appointed time; they have had their infancy, foundation and beginning . . . and their old age, declinings and decayes.'[1] The malaise coincided with what the historian Paul Hazard called 'la crise de la conscience européenne',[2] although the bone of contention in Wales was cultural torpor rather than the secularization of thought. Wales lacked a thriving, populous capital city, a national cultural centre, literary clubs and academies. There were no universities to foster erudition and critical enquiry and the established Church was not disposed to use its revenues to promote Welsh scholarship or encourage its gifted servants. As late as 1795 Walter Davies (Gwallter Mechain) wearily confessed that Wales was never likely to rear 'a philosophic Bacon, an experimental Boyle, or an historic Gibbon',[3] and the crisis of identity was compounded by the antagonistic attitude of officialdom. In the eyes of the state and its governors, the Welsh were a marginal, barely visible people who dwelt beyond civilized social life. English was a 'polite' language and Welsh was a 'jargon' or a 'patois'. 'The duties of kings and Judges and Lay and Ecclesiastical Governors', wrote Ellis Wynne ruefully in 1701, 'besides being extensive and intricate are also, unfortunately, irrelevant to the Welsh language because such people are more learned in and more familiar with other languages.' ('Dyledswyddau Brenhinoedd a Barnwyr a Llywodraethwyr Gwledig ac Eglwysig, heb law eu bod yn faith ac yn ddyrus, maent hefyd yn ammherthynol sywaeth i'r Iaith Gymraec am fod

---

[1] Thomas Jones, *The British Language in its Lustre, Or a Copious Dictionary of Welsh and English* (London, 1688), sig. A3r.
[2] Paul Hazard, *La Crise de la Conscience Européenne 1680–1715* (Paris, 1935).
[3] *CAR*, I (1795), 282. For similar comments by William Owen Pughe, see ibid., III (1818), 127.

y cyfryw rai yn hyddyscach ac yn gynnefinach ag Ieithoedd eraill.')[4] In scholarly circles in England, too, there was a general feeling that the Welsh language was an appropriate target for ridicule and scorn, and no one was prepared to argue that Welsh literature was anything other than inferior, dull and conventional.

The Welsh, moreover, were increasingly prone to lament the cultural deficiencies of their native land. A host of authors described the Welsh language as 'regardless', 'enslaved', 'winnowed' and 'grown aged'.[5] The tradition of prose writing, especially in fields other than religion, was relatively weak, and most Welsh printed books tended to be translations or adaptations of pious works by 'affectionate practical English writers'.[6] Although high-calibre literary works like *Y Ffydd Ddi-ffvant* (1677), *Gweledigaetheu y Bardd Cwsc* (1703) and *Drych y Prif Oesoedd* (1716) were published in the early part of this period and were highly acclaimed, the feeling persisted that Welsh did not seem to be an appropriate medium for conveying subtle and complex intellectual ideas. In an international context it was easily brushed aside. When James Howell published his *Lexicon Tetraglotton, An English-French-Italian-Spanish Dictionary* in 1660, the English language was celebrated among 'the Civill'st Toungs of Christendom' and on the frontispiece the 'British' language lurked in the shadows behind four voluptuous and rather grand ladies representing the four major languages.[7] To many, Welsh was a worthless provincial barbarity, leading 'to no matter of moment; and, who will care to carry about that key, which can unlock no Treasure?'[8] Bewailing the decline of the professional bards, the drover-cum-poet Edward Morris of Perthillwydion, hankered after the golden age of Welsh poetry:

> Mae iaith gain Prydain heb bris,
> Mae'n ddiwobrwy, mae'n ddibris;
> Darfu ar fath, dirfawr fodd,
> Ei 'mgleddiad, ymgwilyddiodd.[9]

---

[4] Ellis Wynne, *Rheol Buchedd Sanctaidd* (Llundain, 1701), pp. 145–6.
[5] Jones, *The British Language*, sig. A4r; Thomas Williams, *Ymadroddion Bucheddol ynghylch Marwolaeth* (Llundain, 1691), sig. A2r; Gwenllian Jones, 'Bywyd a Gwaith Edward Morris, Perthi Llwydion' (unpubl. University of Wales MA thesis, 1941), p. 202; John Pritchard Prŷs, *Difyrrwch Crefyddol* (Amwythig, 1721), sig. A4r.
[6] Richard Baxter, *A Christian Directory* (London, 1673), part 3, p. 922.
[7] James Howell, *Lexicon Tetraglotton, An English-French-Italian-Spanish Dictionary* (London, 1660), sig. A1r.
[8] Thomas Fuller, *The Church-History of Britain* (London, 1655), Book 1, p. 65.
[9] Thomas Parry, *Hanes Llenyddiaeth Gymraeg* (Caerdydd, 1944), p. 175. For the translation, see idem, *A History of Welsh Literature*, tr. H. Idris Bell (Oxford, 1955), p. 221.

(Britain's bright tongue today despised
Lies unrewarded and unprized;
Men pass it by with scornful brow,
And none will bring it succour now.)

Family bards had given way to 'hangdog rhymesters', who practised poetry as a hobby rather than a serious professional craft.[10] Few people seemed to be aware of the past greatness of the literary and historical tradition of Wales. Indeed, there was a very real fear that the ancient literary tongue had been allowed to decay so alarmingly that it could easily slip irrevocably from the grasp of the Welsh people. Welsh was confronted by so many powerful and hostile pressures that the struggle to repair the damage promised to be long and arduous.

Yet, paradoxically, the imminent prospect of the extinction of Welsh as the language of culture helped to concentrate the minds of writers and prod them into action.[11] Out of the general mode of pessimism there emerged a burning desire to revive the language and literature of Wales. Especially by the eighteenth century, notable changes were under way which changed the climate of opinion and encouraged a sense of optimism. In the long run, these changes brought to the language and its literature an enhanced sense of self-esteem and respect. One of the principal engines of change was the printing press. The proliferation of printing presses on Welsh soil from 1718 onwards and the development of subscription ventures, book clubs and circulating libraries led to an extraordinary increase in book production and much wider access to printed material.[12] The following figures (which do not include miscellaneous publications such as almanacks, ballads and chapbooks) reveal the striking growth in the number of Welsh printed books as the eighteenth century unfolded:[13]

1660–1699	:	112
1700–1749	:	614
1750–1799	:	1907
TOTAL	:	2633

[10] Francis Jones, 'An Approach to Welsh Genealogy', *THSC* (1948), 402; Geraint H. Jenkins, *The Foundations of Modern Wales. Wales 1642–1780* (Oxford, 1987), pp. 227–30.
[11] See, in particular, Prys Morgan, *The Eighteenth Century Renaissance* (Llandybïe, 1981) and idem, 'The Hunt for the Welsh Past in the Romantic Period' in E. Hobsbawm and T. Ranger (eds.), *The Invention of Tradition* (Cambridge, 1983), pp. 43–100.
[12] Geraint H. Jenkins, *Literature, Religion and Society in Wales 1660–1730* (Cardiff, 1978); Eiluned Rees, 'Developments in the Book-Trade in Eighteenth Century Wales', *The Library*, XXIV (1969), 33–43; eadem, 'Pre-1820 Welsh Subscription Lists', *JWBS*, XI, nos. 1–2 (1973–4), 85–119; Geraint H. Jenkins, 'The Eighteenth Century' in Philip H. Jones and Eiluned Rees (eds.), *A Nation and its Books* (Aberystwyth, forthcoming).
[13] *Libri Walliae*.

Printing became a major business in leading Welsh towns and the power of the printed word exercised a greater influence than ever before on the minds of people. Articulate, lively and energetic middling sorts were also significant agents in the campaign to promote literary activity in Wales and, in many ways, their drive and ingenuity were responsible for what has recently been called 'the remaking of Wales in the eighteenth century'.[14] Cultural patriots associated with London-Welsh societies helped to rediscover the literary riches of the past and encouraged the belief that Welsh was a language which deserved serious scholarly study. Both Welsh language and literature, moreover, had cause to be grateful to the Methodist movement which produced literary works of enduring value and in the person of William Williams, Pantycelyn, a hymnologist and prose writer of a very special quality. Finally, a wave of romantic learning, which created bizarre and extravagant fantasies, helped to remind the wider scholarly world of the existence of the language and culture of one of the forgotten peoples of Europe. All these factors injected new life into the Welsh cultural scene and created in particular passionate concern about the condition and fate of the literary language.

The first priority of those who believed that the Welsh language was a cherished possession of noble, perhaps even sacred, lineage was to discover precisely from where the language had sprung. Since the fragile world of scholarship in Wales had yet to be disenchanted by the rise of science and reason, the subject of the genesis of languages was cloaked in mystery. There was no reliable chronological framework in which to incorporate literary or archaeological evidence, and, not surprisingly, people turned to the Scriptures.[15] Such was the reverence for the Bible that it stood as the sole and largely unchallenged frame of reference. In 1650 James Ussher, Archbishop of Armagh, had calculated, on the basis of genealogical evidence in the Scriptures, that the world had been created at 8 a.m. on 22 October 4004 BC. From the 1650s onwards sizeable editions of the Welsh Bible were made available to the growing reading public and a marginal note in the first chapter of the Book of Genesis served as a reminder of the year in which God had created the heaven and the earth.[16] Biblical narratives also told of how hubris had led to a fall from grace at the Tower of Babel and how the consequences proved traumatic and long-lasting. As a God-given punishment, the world was recolonized in the post-Diluvial period by Noah's son Japhet and his progeny. In the

---

[14] Trevor Herbert and Gareth E. Jones (eds.), *The Remaking of Wales in the Eighteenth Century* (Cardiff, 1988).
[15] Stuart Piggott, *Ruins in a Landscape* (Edinburgh, 1976), p. 4.
[16] John Ballinger, *The Bible in Wales* (London, 1906).

process, languages were dispersed to different parts of the earth. Different kinds of evidence reveal the degree to which the account of the Deluge and the repeopling of the world captured public imagination. In Sir John Vanbrugh's play *Aesop*, first performed at Drury Lane, London, in 1697, a Welsh-born herald (called 'Quaint') declared:

> Sir, I cou'd tell my Mothers Pedigree before
> I could speak plain: which, to shew you
> the depth of my Art, and the strength of my
>
> Memory, I'll trundle you down in an instant.
> Noah had three Sons, Shem, Ham and Japhet . . .[17]

During the same decade the Celtic scholar Edward Lhuyd told John Lloyd, a Ruthin schoolmaster, that human skulls had been discovered in a limestone quarry in Radnorshire and that the man who had dug them up had said that they were there since the world sank in the time of Noah ('bôd nhw yno erpan sincoddy byd yn amser Noe').[18]

In particular, three matters fascinated the Welsh: the alleged Hebrew origins of the Welsh language; the colonization of Britain following the Flood; and the new Celtomania. In the Latin prefaces to his celebrated Grammar and Dictionary, John Davies, Mallwyd, had argued persuasively that a strong affinity existed between Hebrew and other Oriental 'mother' languages, including Welsh.[19] His case was strengthened by the richly gifted Dissenting writer Charles Edwards, whose interest in the historical and spiritual identity of the Welsh inspired his much acclaimed classic *Y Ffydd Ddi-ffuant* (1677). Edwards claimed that the pronunciation of Welsh was akin to that of Hebrew: 'Mae ei llefariad yn aml fel yr Hebraeg yn dyfod oddiwrth gyffiniau y galon, o wraidd y geneu, ac nid fel y Saesonaeg oddiar flaen y tafod' (Like Hebrew its speech often comes from the vicinity of the heart, from the root of the mouth, and not, like the English, from the tip of the tongue).[20] Two years earlier, in *Hebraismorum Cambro-Britannicorum Specimen*, Edwards had revelled in the affinity between Welsh and Hebrew, 'the mother of Welsh', and had listed

---

[17] Bonamy Dobrée and Geoffrey Webb (eds.), *The Complete Works of Sir John Vanbrugh* (4 vols., London, 1927), II, Act 3.
[18] R. T. Gunther (ed.), *Early Science in Oxford, Vol. XIV, Life and Letters of Edward Lhuyd* (Oxford, 1945), p. 200.
[19] G. J. Williams, *Agweddau ar Hanes Dysg Gymraeg* (Caerdydd, 1969), p. 78.
[20] Charles Edwards, *Y Ffydd Ddi-ffuant* (Rhydychen, 1677), p. 150. For the background, see Derec Llwyd Morgan, 'A Critical Study of the Works of Charles Edwards (1628–1691)' (unpubl. University of Oxford DPhil thesis, 1967) and idem, *Charles Edwards* (Caernarfon, 1994), pp. 28–31.

phrases which offered proof of the sacred rather than the classical roots of Welsh:[21]

Latin	Hebrew	British
Usque ad quercum Moreh Gen. 12.6	Had eloun Moreh	Hyd lwyn Mre
Ab increpatione ejus Job 26.11	Im gaharathvo	Am gerydd fo
Quid profuit Chabbac. 2.18	Mah hounil	Mae ynnill

The recognition of the Welsh language as an honourable, sacred tongue, maintained since the earliest times by divine providence, enhanced its status considerably. Thomas Jones the almanacker, with characteristic impishness, asked of those who scoffed at the Welshman's God-given tongue: 'Can a man own God, and yet be ashamed of that language which God himself chose first?'[22]

The second matter which occupied the attention of antiquarians and scholars who 'adventured through some of the darkest Tracks of Time'[23] was the colonization of prehistoric Britain. Since contemporaries had no means of knowing that a period of two thousand years had elapsed between the immediate post-Diluvial age and the immediate pre-Roman age, some preposterous theories were advanced. In 1646 the brilliant French philologist, Samuel Bochart, published *Geographia Sacra*, in which he claimed that the commercial and maritime interests of the celebrated Phoenicians had brought them to Britain.[24] His view was enthusiastically endorsed and popularized by Aylett Sammes, an egregious lawyer who was neither a field archaeologist nor a philologist. In a numbingly tedious and muddle-headed folio volume entitled *Britannia Antiqua Illustrata* (1676), Sammes argued that the Phoenicians were the founding fathers of

[21] Charles Edwards, *Hebraismorum Cambro-Britannicorum Specimen* (London, 1675), unpaginated; Nigel Smith, 'The Uses of Hebrew in the English Revolution' in Peter Burke and Roy Porter (eds.), *Language, Self, and Society* (Cambridge, 1991), pp. 51–71.
[22] Thomas Jones, *Newydd oddiwrth y Seêr* (Llundain, 1684), sig. A7v. 'I verily believe', declared a curate Jenkin Evans, 'that Adam spoke something of the Welsh Tongue in Paradise.' Anon., *A Dialogue between the Rev. Mr. Jenkin Evans ... and Mr. Peter Dobson ... concerning Bishops, Particularly the Bishops in the Principality of Wales* (London, 1744), p. 42. In 1795 the dramatist Richard Cumberland wrote: ''tis well known that the first man Nature ever made was a Welshman' (*The Wheel of Fortune*, London, 1795, p. 25).
[23] Henry Rowlands, *Mona Antiqua Restaurata* (Dublin, 1723), sig. A1r.
[24] T. D. Kendrick, *British Antiquity* (London, 1950), p. 132; Stuart Piggott, *Ancient Britons and the Antiquarian Imagination* (London, 1989), p. 100.

Britain.²⁵ With hindsight it is clear that Sammes' profusely illustrated work was a piece of folly, but it heavily influenced early-eighteenth-century antiquarians, including Henry Rowlands and William Stukeley.

Of much greater interest to cultural patriots in Wales were accounts by Sammes and others of a tribe known as the Cimbri. One of the most memorable features of Sammes' volume was a remarkable map depicting the procession of the ancient Cimbri (wearing tall hats and travelling in covered wagons) from the Black Sea to Britain. But Sammes did not accept that the 'Cimbri' were the descendants of Gomer, son of Japhet, son of Noah, and it is unlikely that his reluctance to concede this point endeared him to Welsh readers. For as early as 1586 the brilliant antiquarian, William Camden, had argued in *Britannia* that the peoples of Britain were an offshoot of the Gauls, who were themselves the descendants of Gomer.²⁶ Camden's view was revived and considerably strengthened by the publication of *L'Antiquité de la nation et de la langue des celtes* (1703), the work of Paul-Yves Pezron, an ardently patriotic Breton monk. When Pezron's work was translated into English by David Jones and published in 1706, readers were reminded of Camden's notion that Britons and Gauls were the same Celtic people. Pezron not only became the most influential figure in the formation of what historians have called 'Celtomania' but he also confirmed that Gomer was the father of the Celts:

> The Language therefore of the Celtae, that fixed in Gaul, was from the first Ages of the Postdiluvian World, the Language of the Gomarians, who were seated originally in the Higher Asia, towards Hircania and Bactriana; and 'tis not to be doubted but the Language of the Gomarians was that of Gomer, who was the Head and Founder; and if it was the Language of Gomer, it must necessarily have been one of those formed at the Confusion of Babel.²⁷

Initially at least, Edward Lhuyd, the most learned Celtic scholar in late Stuart times, was enthusiastic about Pezron's work, but his ardour turned to suspicion (and perhaps even scorn in private) as the Breton scholar's theories achieved wider currency.²⁸ As Keeper of the famous Ashmolean

---

²⁵ Aylett Sammes, *Britannia Antiqua Illustrata* (London, 1676), p. 17.
²⁶ Kendrick, op. cit., pp. 108–9.
²⁷ David Jones, *The Antiquities of Nations; More particularly of the Celtae or Gauls, Taken to be Originally the same People as our Ancient Britains* (London, 1706), p. 144. See also Prys Morgan, 'The Abbé Pezron and the Celts', *THSC* (1965), 286–95; idem, 'Yr Abbé Pezron a'r Celtiaid', *Y Traethodydd*, 120 (1965), 178–84; idem, 'Boxhorn, Leibniz, and the Welsh', *SC*, VIII–IX (1973–4), 220–8.
²⁸ Gunther, op. cit., p. 489.

Museum in Oxford, Lhuyd moved in erudite circles and was at the hub of a constant and invigorating traffic and exchange of ideas.[29] Those who knew him and worked with him testified to the extraordinary range and depth of his knowledge, and they learnt too that no longer could academic study of the past be based solely on literary evidence. All received knowledge in Lhuydian circles was subjected to critical scrutiny and this had important implications for Celtic philology. In order to acquire a clearer understanding of the origin and nature of the Celtic languages, he embarked on a four-year voyage of discovery through Ireland, Cornwall, Scotland and Brittany, and he also learnt the major Celtic languages tolerably well. He set his sights on publishing major grammars and dictionaries which would effectively prove the affinity of the Celtic languages. His celebrated *Archaeologia Britannica* (1707) was part of a grander design and was simply a foretaste of his monumental researches. Yet it was a work of the highest importance and it won him the respect and gratitude of the scholarly world. Within the volume, Lhuyd had undermined Pezron's spurious theories by detecting the common origin of the Celtic languages and by formulating the Celtic *p* and *q* languages theory. He had also broken new ground by discovering the significance of Old Welsh and recognizing the continuation of the orthography from the earliest days of the inscriptions.[30] The conclusions of this extraordinary Celtic philologist marked a seminal advance in Welsh scholarship and it is a tragedy that his sudden and unexpected death in 1709 deprived the nation of a much richer harvest of published works. Had Lhuyd lived longer, his preliminary studies of comparative philology would undoubtedly have been greatly extended and refined, and his influence on succeeding generations would have been of enduring importance. Even so, the great virtue of *Archaeologia Britannica* lies in the astonishing scope of the achievement and the brilliance with which material relating to the Celtic countries was interrelated and interpreted.[31]

Although the multi-talented group of young Welsh scholars whom Lhuyd attracted to Oxford had cause to be grateful to him for mapping out the way, few of them followed his footsteps. The publication of *Archaeologia Britannica* had been hailed as the beginning of a new era in Welsh scholarship, but in reality it proved a false start. Only Moses

---

[29] G. J. Williams, 'Edward Lhuyd', *LlC*, 6, no. 3 and 4 (1961), 122–37; Frank Emery, *Edward Lhuyd 1660–1709* (Cardiff, 1971); Brynley F. Roberts, *Edward Lhuyd: The Making of a Scientist* (Cardiff, 1980).

[30] Brynley F. Roberts, 'Edward Lhuyd Y Cymro', *NLWJ*, XXIV, no. 1 (1985), 63–83; idem, 'Edward Lhuyd – Welshman', *Nature in Wales*, II (1984), 42–56.

[31] Edward Lhuyd, *Archaeologia Britannica* (Oxford, 1707). This volume, which was part of a grander design, was divided into ten parts, six of which included original material.

Williams showed any true desire to realize Lhuyd's ambitions. He set his heart on publishing 'A collection of writings in the Welsh tongue, to the beginning of the sixteenth century', but he failed to acquire 250 subscriptions, the minimum number necessary for the successful publication of the volume.[32] Williams had lost credit with wealthy Welsh gentlemen who had either heard or read some of his outspokenly patriotic sermons and he was also subsequently victimized by bishops who were hostile to his Welshness.[33] Others of Lhuyd's protégés displayed a greater appetite for alcohol than academic study, while those who had previously corresponded with him no longer seemed to share his fastidious regard for accuracy and honesty. William Baxter of Llanllugan, whom Lhuyd had suspected was 'too apt to indulge fancy',[34] published *Glossarium Antiquitatum Britannicarum* (1719), a dictionary of place-names and their derivations, which was replete with woolly philological speculations. Lewis Morris subsequently took Baxter to task for 'murdering and dismembering old British words'.[35] Henry Rowlands, another of Lhuyd's correspondents,[36] also went astray by publishing *Mona Antiqua Restaurata* (1723), in which he not only argued that Japhet was the progenitor of the European nations and that Anglesey had been the principal seat and academy of the British Druids, but also embarked on a series of philological forays which led him to proclaim that Apollo the Hyperborean derived his name from ap Rees, that Prasulagus was probably ap Rees leg and that Arviragus was ap Meyric.[37] Although the publication of *Mona* stiffened the pride of Anglesey patriots, it proved calamitous for the cause of philological and archaeological scholarship.[38]

As Welsh antiquarians, poets and romantics distanced themselves from Lhuyd's ideas, the wild theories of Paul Pezron became ever more popular. Indeed, they lay at the heart of virtually everything written on Welsh and Celtic origins in eighteenth-century Wales. In *Drych y Prif Oesoedd* (1716 and 1740), the most successful history book written in

---

[32] William Baxter, *Glossarium Antiquitatum Britannicarum* (London, 1719), sig. b4v; *Libri Walliae*, II, p. xxvii.
[33] Geraint H. Jenkins, *Cadw Tŷ Mewn Cwmwl Tystion. Ysgrifau Hanesyddol ar Grefydd a Diwylliant* (Llandysul, 1990), pp. 104–5.
[34] Gunther, op. cit., p. 476. Cf. Arthur Percival, 'William Baxter (1649–1723)', *THSC* (1957), 58–86.
[35] *ALM*, II (1949), p. 396.
[36] Gunther, op. cit., pp. 480–3.
[37] Rowlands, *Mona Antiqua*, p. 76.
[38] See the strictures in *CAR*, I (1795), 384. Iolo Morganwg believed that *Mona* contained 'the most incoherent jumble of mistakes, absurdities, of every thing that ever profaned the sacred name of History' (NLW MS 13089E, f. 460). For the background, see J. Gareth Thomas, 'Henry Rowlands The Welsh Stukeley', *TAAS* (1958), 33–45, and Tomos Roberts, 'Campwaith y "Derwydd"', *Y Casglwr*, 23 (1984), 19.

Welsh until late Victorian times,[39] Theophilus Evans gave wide currency to the views of Camden and Pezron in associating the Welsh with the Cymbri and the Celts, and captured the imagination of his readers by claiming that no people could trace their language to an earlier period than the Welsh:

> A phwy oedd yn siarad Cymraeg y dybiwch chwi y pryd hwnnw ond Gomer, mab hynaf Japhet, ap Noah, ap Lamech, ap Methusala, ap Enoch, ap Jared, ap Malaleel, ap Cainan, ap Enos, ap Seth, ap Adda, ap Duw?[40]

> (And who do you think spoke the Welsh language at that time, but Gomer, the eldest son of Japheth, son of Noah, son of Lamech, son of Methuselah, son of Enoch, son of Jared, son of Mahalaleel, son of Cainan, son of Enos, son of Seth, son of Adam, son of God?)

In 1718 Simon Thomas's *Hanes y Byd a'r Amseroedd* bore the stamp of Pezron's romantic lucubrations[41] as did his *The History of the Cymbri (or Brittains)* (1746), a work which did much to acquaint English readers with the dramatic story of the glorious origins of the Welsh.[42] Although he interpreted the Babel narrative in the Book of Genesis as a tirade against imperialism and the oppression of national languages, Griffith Jones Llanddowror also enthusiastically endorsed the ideas of Pezron in one of his most spirited apologiae for the Welsh language.[43] Similarly, Lewis Morris was happy to declare in his *Celtic Remains* that the Welsh language was 'the principal branch and chief remains of the ancient Celtic tongue'.[44] But Celtomania soon began to generate even more false prophets by the mid-eighteenth century. Bullet's *Mémoires sur La Langue Celtique* (3 vols., 1754–60) seductively claimed that Celtic was a sister dialect of Hebrew and that it had been spoken by God to Adam in the Garden of Eden. The lexicographer John Walters not only quoted extensively from Pezron's work but was also fulsome in praise of 'the

---

[39] Geraint H. Jenkins, *Theophilus Evans (1693–1767). Y Dyn, Ei Deulu, a'i Oes* (Llandysul, 1993), pp. 35–40.

[40] Theophilus Evans, *Drych y Prif Oesoedd* (Amwythig, 1740), p. 7. The English translation is taken from George Roberts, *A View of the Primitive Ages* (Ebensburg, 1834), p. 17.

[41] Simon Thomas, *Hanes y Byd a'r Amseroedd* (Amwythig, 1718), p. 51. For similar views, see Jeremy Owen, *The Goodness and Severity of God* (London, 1717), p. 10, and William Wotton, *A Sermon preached in Welsh before the British Society in . . . London* (London, 1723), sig. Alv.

[42] Simon Thomas, *The History of the Cymbri (or Brittains)* (Hereford, 1746), passim. See also Richard Rolt, *Cambria. A Poem in Three Books* (London, 1749), pp. 26–7.

[43] Griffith Jones, *The Welch Piety* (London, 1740), pp. 30–53.

[44] Lewis Morris, *Celtic Remains* (Cambrian Archaeological Association, London, 1878), p. xix.

exqisitely [sic] learned and amazingly industrious M. Bullet'.[45] Walters' disciple, Iolo Morganwg, believed that Pezron had done much to sustain a sense of national identity within Wales and a wider sense of Celticism, while Walter Davies (Gwallter Mechain) was so taken by the theories of the Breton monk that he transcribed substantial portions of the English translation of *L'Antiquité de la nation et de la langue des celtes*.[46] Even as late as 1818 William Owen Pughe believed that Pezron was still 'very plausibly ingenious'.[47] In many ways, therefore, the untimely death of Edward Lhuyd had calamitous consequences. From 1709 onwards Welsh scholarship found itself in the doldrums at Oxford, and within Wales no one was able to halt the retreat from intellectual rigour.

Yet it would be misleading to leave this subject without referring briefly to the distinctive, and lasting, contribution to language and philology of an intellectual giant who once described himself as 'half a Welchman'.[48] Sir William Jones – often called 'Oriental Jones' or 'Harmonious Jones' – was the London-born son of a brilliant mathematician (who bore the same name) from Llanfihangel Tre'r-beirdd in Anglesey.[49] Although Jones's command of Welsh was frail, he was a wonderfully gifted linguist and a major authority on Hindu law. In his celebrated address to the Asiatic Society in Calcutta in 1786 he made a startlingly innovative pronouncement concerning the historical kinship of Sanskrit with Latin, Greek, and the Germanic languages.[50] This was the first public statement of the fundamental principles of modern comparative linguistics, and it clearly repudiated the spurious linguistic theories peddled by Pezron and his disciples. Sir William Jones laid the foundations for the new philology propounded by Franz Bopp, Rasmus Kristian Rask and Jacob Grimm in the early nineteenth century and he also deeply enriched the field of

---

[45] John Walters, *A Dissertation on the Welsh Language* (Cowbridge, 1771), pp. 20–1. See also the views of his colleague Thomas Richards in *Antiquae linguae Britannicae thesaurus* (Bristol, 1753), sig. br, and of Rhys Jones in *Gorchestion Beirdd Cymru* (Amwythig, 1773), sig. B1v–B2r.

[46] Edward Williams, *Poems Lyric and Pastoral* (2 vols., London, 1794), II, pp. 8–9; NLW MS 1641Bii, ff. 383–433.

[47] *CAR*, III (1818), 146. See also the praise which the Cymreigyddion showered on Pezron (NLW MS 13221E, f. 166).

[48] Garland Cannon (ed.), *The Letters of Sir William Jones* (2 vols., Oxford, 1970), I, p. 81.

[49] Thomas A. Sebeok, *Portraits of Linguists. A Biographical Source Book for the History of Western Linguistics, 1746–1963* (2 vols., Bloomington and London, 1966), I, pp. 1–57; Garland Cannon, *The Life and Mind of Oriental Jones* (Cambridge, 1990); Caryl Davies, '"Romantic Jones"; The Picturesque and Politics on the South Wales Circuit, 1775–1781', *NLWJ*, XXVIII, no. 3 (1994), 255–78.

[50] R. H. Robins, *A Short History of Linguistics* (2nd ed., London, 1979), p. 134; David Crystal, *The Cambridge Encyclopaedia of Language* (Cambridge, 1987), p. 296.

linguistic science.[51] It is worth noting that Iolo Morganwg was familiar with the work of 'the father of modern linguistics' and the manner in which he had deepened people's understanding of the evolution of languages and of the common links which bound them together. He drew great encouragement from Jones's 'Asiatic researches' in his tireless campaign for national cultural institutions for the Welsh:

> Sir William Jones has very recently shown us what lights may be derived from the study of ancient languages, the general history of the world and mankind cleared up by them, new evidences of the Truth of divine Revelation obtained of gigantic strength. A College has lately been Instituted at Calcutta for the acquisition and study of the ancient India, and other Asiatic Languages; when will such an establishment appear in Europe for the study of the ancient Languages of Europe? Never! for money and money only, is the great object of acquisition. Pluton the God of Riches is adored by one half of the Christian World, (Blasphemously so called) and Mars the God of War by the other . . .[52]

Iolo Morganwg was more keenly aware than most of his fellow Welshmen of the vital influence universities and academies could play in the cultural life of nations. In the absence of major intellectual institutions, spurious knowledge about the historical origin and kinship of languages was bound to prosper.

It would be foolish to pretend, however, that all eighteenth-century writers were obsessed with the language of Gomer son of Japhet son of Noah or with the way in which Celtic languages derived from a common source. With the startling rise of Methodism in the counties of south and mid-Wales from the mid-1730s onwards, there emerged groups of spiritual pilgrims in this world who were less troubled by the fate of the language than by the salvation of souls. Methodism drew at least some of its impetus from a deep dissatisfaction with the immobility of the established Church and the slow rhythm of parochial life. Led by remarkably bold and hyperactive young men, it set its sights on wholescale spiritual renewal. Ablaze with missionary zeal, Methodist evangelists believed that they had been personally singled out by God to revitalize the established Church. In their eyes, Wales was still very much a *pays de mission*, and their army of travelling exhorters was nothing if not energetic. Champions of Methodism were never shy about publicizing their aims and achievements and, whether they wrote in Welsh or English, they never tired of emphasizing that

---

[51] Hans Aarsleff, *The Study of Language in England 1780–1860* (Princeton, New Jersey, 1967), pp. 159–61; David A. Thorne, *Cyflwyniad i Astudio'r Iaith Gymraeg* (Caerdydd, 1985), p. 37.
[52] NLW MS 13121B, ff. 481–2.

enthusiasm was the language of the heart. The inward experience of Christ filled them with joy, hope and love, and impelled them to spread the Gospel as widely as possible. Set alongside the outpouring of the Holy Spirit, the discord of Babel paled into insignificance. In a letter to George Whitefield, Howel Harris claimed that the spirit of Christ 'comes either as a Spirit of Wisdom to enlighten the Soul, to teach and build up, and set out the Works of Light and Darkness, or else a Spirit of Tenderness and Love, sweetly melting the Souls like the Dew, and watering the Graces; or as a Spirit of hot burning Zeal, setting their Hearts in a Flame, so that their Eyes sparkle with Fire, Love, and Joy'.[53] In their vigorous field sermons, Methodist preachers spoke in a declamatory style and made little effort to impress (or baffle) hearers by quoting from learned authorities. Like many poets and dramatists in early modern Europe,[54] they improvised readily and effectively, and extempore sermons were well received, especially in rural communities and private gatherings.[55]

It followed, therefore, that Methodists were not much interested in the genesis of languages and etymological niceties. Methodist tongues were expected to sing the praise of God and discussion within society meetings was largely confined to the experience of salvation. Nothing mattered more than the 'letters of the pure name of Jesus' ('Ac mae llythrennau dy enw pur / Yn fywyd ac yn hedd'),[56] for only His atoning grace could rescue degenerate men and women from their wicked and corrupt state. But since Methodism was quintessentially a religion of the heart, its leaders found the task of expressing the inexpressible well-nigh impossible. Having heard a sermon delivered by Daniel Rowland at Llangeitho in 1742, Howel Harris confessed that the 'light' and 'power' which was generated 'can't be expressed'.[57] The stupors and prostrations which characterized Methodist meetings provide ample testimony of a movement which could not discover adequate 'words to utter'.[58] When less well-educated exhorters did put pen to paper, they wrote at white-hot heat, swiftly and carelessly as they would in oral delivery. Even experienced authors groped for appropriate language to convey the life-

[53] Eifion Evans, 'The First Published Correspondence between Harris and Whitefield', *CCHMC*, 4 (1980), 32–3. See also J. E. Wynne Davies, 'Llythyrau ac Adroddiadau Thomas William, Eglwysilan', *CCHMC*, 18 (1994), 25.
[54] Peter Burke, *Popular Culture in Early Modern Europe* (London, 1978), pp. 142–4.
[55] Geraint H. Jenkins, 'The New Enthusiasts' in Herbert and Jones, *The Remaking of Wales*, pp. 49–50; Eryn M. White, '*Praidd Bach y Bugail Mawr*': *Seiadau Methodistaidd De-Orllewin Cymru 1737–50* (Llandysul, 1995), pp. 42–78.
[56] E. G. Millward (ed.), *Blodeugerdd Barddas o Gerddi Rhydd y Ddeunawfed Ganrif* (Cyhoeddiadau Barddas, 1991), pp. 152, 154.
[57] Gomer M. Roberts (ed.), *Selected Trevecka Letters (1742–1747)* (Caernarfon, 1956), p. 66.
[58] Ibid., p. 81.

enhancing significance of words like 'goleuni' (light), 'tân' (fire), 'grym' (power), 'bywyd' (life) and 'melyster' (sweetness).[59]

In many ways, enthusiasm was a wordless phenomenon which stirred passions rather than honed the intellect. It encouraged leaping, dancing, laughing, singing, groaning and weeping. Public demonstrations of praise were the hallmark of Methodist centres of worship and all matters were interpreted in the light of personal experience. Since God had endowed born-again Christians with the gift of the language of revivalism, they set little store by theological subtleties or intellectual thought. To be a Methodist was an intensely non-intellectual experience. They were deeply suspicious of 'head knowledge'. In his account of the spiritual odyssey of a Methodist convert, *Bywyd a Marwolaeth Theomemphus* (1764), William Williams, Pantycelyn, emphasized the novelty of the Methodist message and the dull predictability of traditional learning:

> Eu hiaith sydd oll o newydd, nid geiriau Babel ga'th,
> Ond iaith Caersalem newydd, na feder daer o'i bath;
> Rhyw ymadroddion hyfryd o foliant ac o glod,
> Mawr fo enw'r Oen fu farw fyth heddiw fel erio'd.
> . . .
> A raid cael gwybod ieithoedd, – Groeg, Lladin hen a'u sain,
> Caldeaeg, Hebraeg a Syriaeg, a llawer gyda['r] rhain
> Cyn gallo neb anturio i 'nganyd gair o'i ben
> O bulpud am drysorau haelionus nefoedd wen?[60]

(Their language is completely new, not the words of Babel, but the language of the new Jerusalem, the like of which an earnest person does not know; pleasant sayings of eulogy and praise, let the name of the Lamb who died be as great today as ever.
. . .
Is it necessary to know languages, – Greek, old Latin and their sound, Chaldean, Hebrew, Syrian, and many more besides, before one can venture to utter a word from a pulpit about the generous treasures of heaven?)

But the elevation of warm, affectionate spirituality above learning and erudition earned Methodists a reputation for philistinism and bigotry. In wickedly satirical vein, Lewis Morris derided the Methodist preacher in 'Young Mends the Clothier's Sermon':

---

[59] Derec Llwyd Morgan, 'Rhyddiaith Pantycelyn' in Geraint Bowen (ed.), *Y Traddodiad Rhyddiaith* (Llandysul, 1970), pp. 302–6.
[60] Gomer M. Roberts (ed.), *Gweithiau William Williams Pantycelyn Cyfrol 1* (Caerdydd, 1964), pp. 204, 377.

O ye Oxford & Cambridge, Eaton and Westminster and all Great Schools, Shut your doors, and weep at your downfall, for the Spirit hath Overcome you. The Spirit Can Expound all the dark Texts of Scripture even those which are Incomprehensible; and tho' the Spirit is Illiterate in Human Learning, Yet the Spirit Literally understands what is wrote in ye Greek, Hebrew, Syriack arabick & Chaldean, If he can but get them translated into his own mother Tounge – Great is the Vertue of ye Spirit.[61]

But although evangelical reformers generally paid no heed to the colour, culture or language of those who were potential cases for conversion, they knew well enough that their aims and objectives could best be achieved by employing the mother tongue. The fortunes of Methodism were intimately tied to the Welsh language and its leaders were expected to preach in the language of the people whom they addressed on their 'rounds'. Paradoxically, too, Methodism played a significant part in stimulating and satisfying the demand for Welsh books. William Williams, Pantycelyn, claimed, with pardonable exaggeration, that Methodism had been responsible for distributing over a hundred thousand books and tracts during his lifetime.[62] The intense spiritual experiences of evangelists were transmitted in a remarkable range of sermons, prose epics, hymns, elegies and works of practical divinity and inward scrutiny. If the preaching ministry had a vital role in introducing people to the language of revivalism, so too did the printed word.

Unquestionably the best introduction to the earnestness, passion and ecstasy which informed Welsh Calvinistic Methodism is the extraordinary literary output of William Williams, Pantycelyn. Williams published around ninety books and pamphlets and composed over a thousand hymns (some in English but the vast majority in Welsh), which earned him the sobriquet 'Y Pêr Ganiedydd' (The Sweet Singer).[63] His literary contribution to the success of the movement and to Welsh culture in general is of incalculable significance. In the words of Derec Llwyd Morgan: 'Dychmygwch y Diwygiad heb ei lyfrau ef, ac fe welwch mor ddistaw fyddai, mor enbyd o fud' (Imagine the Revival without his books, and you will see how silent it would have been, so awfully dumb).[64] A farmer's son from Carmarthenshire, Williams was the only Methodist

---

[61] NLW MS 67A, f. 69.
[62] Derec Llwyd Morgan, *The Great Awakening in Wales,* translated by Dyfnallt Morgan (London, 1988), p. 108.
[63] Gomer M. Roberts, *Y Pêr Ganiedydd [Pantycelyn] Cyfrol 1. Trem ar ei Fywyd* (Aberystwyth, 1949); idem, *Y Pêr Ganiedydd [Pantycelyn] Cyfrol II. Arweiniad i'w Waith* (Aberystwyth, 1958).
[64] Derec Llwyd Morgan, *Williams Pantycelyn* (Caernarfon, 1983), p. 14.

leader of his generation with a genuine love of learning and literature. He read avidly and his passionate curiosity took him into the fields of anatomy, astrology, history, mathematics, medicine, psychology and science.[65] Unlike his colleagues, who were generally hostile to the Renaissance ideal of culture and dubious of any language or dialect which did not sing the praise of the Lord, Williams was receptive to innovative intellectual ideas and endeavours. One of his epics, *Golwg ar Deyrnas Crist* (A View of Christ's Kingdom) (1756), a poem of 1,367 verses, revealed his interest in scientific curiosities, mathematical theories, planets and comets, while *Pantheologia, neu Hanes Holl Grefyddau'r Byd* (A History of all Religions of the World), published in parts between 1762 and 1779, was a compendium of general knowledge relating to the geography of the world and world religions. In all his works, however, the language deployed by Williams was scriptural, theological and evangelical. His principal aim was to persuade readers and hearers 'i garu Tywysog mawr ein Iechydwriaeth' (to love the Great Prince of our Salvation),[66] for only the atoning grace of Christ could rescue degenerate men and women from their wicked and corrupt state. In his prose works and hymns (which were sung with great fervour), Williams deployed a remarkable range of vocabulary, allusions and images in order to express the rich spiritual experiences of Methodist converts and his greatest service was probably to teach his followers the 'language of self-knowledge and self-expression'. By adopting established literary forms and plundering local idioms and dialects, he succeeded in developing a poetic diction which was at once novel and attractive.[67] He was conscious of breaking new ground in his published works and no one could match his ability to convey the sheer ecstasy of the experiential religion called Methodism. Purity of language counted for little in his work and some of his colloquialisms and English borrowings have been deplored by austere literary critics. But his literary gifts and profound Christian conviction helped to make the language of enthusiasm attractive and successful in Welsh-speaking circles. It is in the work of William Williams, more than any other, that we hear the distinctive voice of Welsh Calvinistic Methodism.

Not all lovers of Welsh language and literature, of course, were enamoured of Methodism. Believing that its devotees were 'religiously mad',[68] many heartily despised it. None were more contemptuous of the

---

[65] Alwyn Prosser, 'Diddordebau Lleyg Williams Pantycelyn', *LlC*, 3, no. 4 (1955), 201–14; D. Myrddin Lloyd, 'Rhai Agweddau o Feddwl Pantycelyn', *EA*, XXVIII (1956), 54–66; Derec Llwyd Morgan (ed.), *Meddwl a Dychymyg Williams Pantycelyn* (Llandysul, 1991).
[66] Roberts, *Gweithiau William Williams*, I, p. ix.
[67] Glyn Tegai Hughes, *Williams Pantycelyn* (Cardiff, 1983), p. 117.
[68] *ML*, I, p. 83.

'vital religion' than leading members of the Society of Cymmrodorion, founded in London in 1751. Led by Lewis and Richard Morris, sons of an Anglesey cooper, this Society set itself the goal of becoming the principal leader of opinion in cultural circles in Wales. Its founders fervently hoped that the Society would demonstrate that the loyalty of exiles to their native land and culture could be no less deep than that of Welsh speakers resident in Wales. The grandiose manifesto of the Society, drawn up by Lewis Morris in 1755, called for unswerving commitment to 'yr hen Iaith wir orchestol hon' (this truly ancient and noble Language) in the monthly meetings, and it was expected that the more affluent members would pay nostalgic homage to their native land by financing Welsh publications.[69] In the event, however, the Society did not become a focus for vigorous intellectual activity. The motley groups of drones, philistines and tipplers who frequented Cymmrodorion meetings preferred wine, women and song to cultivating the Welsh language for literary purposes, and it is an indisputable fact that the corresponding members who lived far from London proved much more active and successful in promoting the cause of Welsh letters. In particular, it was left to members of the Morris Circle, a coterie of like-minded scholars, antiquarians and poets – among them Lewis, Richard and William Morris, Evan Evans (Ieuan Fardd), Hugh Hughes, Goronwy Owen, Edward Richard and William Wynn – to collect, transcribe and preserve Welsh poetry and literature. Members of the Circle were determined to play their part in the urgent task of standardizing the orthography of the Welsh language and purifying its vocabulary. Richard Morris edited reprints of the Welsh Bible and Prayer Book with scrupulous care, while his brother Lewis, the unquestioned leader of the Circle, established a proprietorial attitude towards young writers and poets. An arrogant and often ill-tempered man, Lewis Morris liked to believe that he had the power to make or break the literary reputation of Welsh scholars, but although some of his protégés resented his overbearing style and wounding criticisms, the most talented among them responded enthusiastically to his advice. To many of his friends and acquaintances, Morris was omniscient. He was an astonishingly versatile man and his encyclopaedic mind was stored with facts both great and small. Although cursed by ill health, he was blessed with the energy and curiosity of Ezra Pound. He was well versed in antiquarianism, lexicography, history, medicine, music, philosophy, philology, place-names,

---

[69] *Gosodedigaethau Anrhydeddus Gymdeithas y Cymmrodorion / Constitutions of the Honourable Society of Cymmrodorion* (London, 1755), pp. 10–11. See also R. T. Jenkins and Helen M. Ramage, *A History of the Honourable Society of Cymmrodorion* (London, 1951).

science and technology.[70] He was the first to establish a printing press in north Wales (at Holyhead in 1735) and he spent the best part of forty years collecting and editing manuscripts. There was hardly a topic on which he was not prepared to pontificate and in many ways he believed that he was the true heir of Edward Lhuyd.

To the compilation of *Celtic Remains*, a massive scholarly work which remained unpublished until 1878, Lewis Morris brought all the gifts which made him the most erudite and influential scholar in Wales in the period between the death of Moses Williams in 1742 and the publication of Evan Evans's *Some Specimens of the Poetry of the Antient Welsh Bards* in 1764. In his introduction to *Celtic Remains*, Morris devoted twelve pages to a diatribe against William Camden, the Elizabethan antiquary whose 'wild fancies' and 'lame guesses' were, at least in Morris's eyes, plainly nonsensical.[71] In his view, Camden's errors had shown once and for all that to be without a thorough knowledge of the Welsh language was an insuperable handicap for all who ventured into the field of Welsh philology. As it happens, we now know that Lewis Morris's own forays into etymology were not especially successful,[72] but he had an almost religious obsession with words and an extraordinary ear for idiosyncrasies of dialect. 'The art of writing and speaking any language seems to me a bottomless pit', he wrote to Edward Richard in August 1760, 'I see no end of it . . . and I think the confusion of Babel is acted over and over every day'![73] Words tumbled from his lips and ran from his pen in great profusion, and often he would confess that Welsh words (or the lack of them) kept him restlessly awake at night.[74] So anxious was he to impress English scholars in London that he urged his brother William to coin Welsh equivalents for his beloved collection of fossils:

> You must make your cregyn Welsh names if they have none, there is no if in the case. You must give them names in Welsh. I'll send you a catalogue of ye English names of some sales here, which are all foolish whims, and it is an easy matter to invent new names, and I warrant you they will be as well received as Latin or Greek names. Tell them they are old Celtic names, that is enough. They'll sound as well as German or Indian names, and better.[75]

---

[70] For a list of books in his library, see *ALM*, II (1949), pp. 794–807. See also *ML*, I, pp. 87, 97–8, and Frank R. Lewis, 'Lewis Morris the Bibliophile', *JWBS*, V, no. 2 (1938), 67–83.
[71] *Celtic Remains*, p. lxxv.
[72] Williams, *Agweddau ar Hanes Dysg Gymraeg*, p. 119.
[73] *ALM*, II (1949), p. 482.
[74] *ML*, II, p. 5. See also his fascinating attempt to explain the origin of the word 'priodas' (marriage). *ALM*, I, pp. 296–9.
[75] Ibid., I, p. 347. Cf. pp. 108–15, 440.

Morris loved wrestling with words and dialects, and would pursue arcane solecisms, epigrams, proverbs and *bons mots* with childlike enthusiasm. His manuscripts are littered with Welsh words which he coined for a variety of shells, seeds, plants, ores, tools and machines, and some of his most memorable letters were devoted to the correct use and spelling of words relating to science, mathematics and technology.[76] Yet, as was the case for many gifted eighteenth-century Welshmen who rarely or never published, his was a life of partially-fulfilled talent. Rather than publish his own works, he preferred to supervise and counsel young authors. But he clearly had a natural talent for writing and his entertaining Rabelaisian satires — in prose and verse — were pure Grub Street. Some of his humorous character sketches and drinking songs (including, in English, 'The Fishing Lass of Hakin') display unusual zest and extravagance.[77] Few were as appreciative as he of the beauties of traditional *penillion telyn* (harp tunes), and although he preferred to correspond with men of taste and learning he also assisted the endeavours of humble poets and antiquarians like Dafydd Jones, Trefriw, Huw Jones, Llangwm, and Robert Hughes (Robin Ddu o Fôn).[78] Convinced that only he was equipped to take up 'the labouring oar',[79] Lewis Morris was determined to keep the language and literature of Wales buoyant in Welsh localities.

The celebrated letters (over a thousand of which have survived) which circulated among members of the Morris Circle and which enabled them to 'ymgyfrinachu . . . o hirbell' (eavesdrop . . . from afar)[80] prove that they were the unchallenged masters of letter-writing in eighteenth-century Wales. Their 'itch for scribbling'[81] has left a rich diversity of material for the social historian and linguist, and one cannot read the letters without marvelling at their mastery of the Welsh language. The Morris brothers in particular delighted in playing on words and interspersing Anglesey idioms with the colloquialisms of Billingsgate and Cheapside. All of them handled

---

[76] See his wonderful letter to his brother Richard (*ML*, I, pp. 108–15). See also Branwen Jarvis, 'Lewis Morris, Y "Philomath Ymarferol"' in Geraint H. Jenkins (ed.), *Cof Cenedl X* (Llandysul, 1995), pp. 61–90.

[77] Bedwyr Lewis Jones, 'Rhyddiaith y Morrisiaid' in Bowen, *Y Traddodiad Rhyddiaith*, pp. 276–92; Saunders Lewis, *A School of Welsh Augustans* (Wrexham, 1924), pp. 33–4; Emyr Gwynne Jones, 'Llythyrau Lewis Morris at William Vaughan, Corsygedol', *LlC*, 10, no. 1 and 2 (1968), 43; Raymond Garlick and Roland Mathias, *Anglo-Welsh Poetry 1480–1990* (Bridgend, 1982), pp. 90–2; A. Cynfael Lake (ed.), *Blodeugerdd Barddas o Ganu Caeth y Ddeunawfed Ganrif* (Cyhoeddiadau Barddas, 1993), pp. 24–31.

[78] Geraint H. Jenkins, '"Dyn Glew Iawn": Dafydd Jones o Drefriw, 1703–1785', *TCHS*, 47 (1986), 71–95.

[79] *ML*, II, p. 192.

[80] Ibid., I, p. 197.

[81] *ALM*, II, p. 423; J. E. Caerwyn Williams, 'Cymraeg y Morrisiaid', *Y Traethodydd*, 25 (1957), 69–82, 107–21.

words, especially unusual words, with reverence and enthusiasm. They invariably wrote as they spoke, putting words to paper in short, breathless bursts, and moving with disconcerting speed from subject to subject, pausing only to embellish the narrative with stylistic devices.[82] They clearly wrote to inform, instruct and entertain.

A central feature of the letters are the idealistic though sometimes practical plans regarding the future of the Welsh language and scholarship in general. Richard Morris drooled over 'yr Iaith odidoccaf dan y ffurfafen' (the finest language in the firmament),[83] while Goronwy Owen, who was fluent in Welsh, English, Greek and Latin and who possessed a fair reading knowledge of Arabic, Chaldean, Hebrew and Irish, insisted that 'our language excells most others in Europe'.[84] Owen believed that, as a poet who prized the Augustan ideals of clarity, smoothness and restraint, he could help to retrieve 'the antient splendor of our Language'.[85] His friends certainly expected him to reveal the copiousness of Welsh by composing a Christian epic of Miltonic proportions, but although his output revealed admirable craftsmanship his feckless ways condemned him to a life of alcoholism and penury. A classic under-achiever, Goronwy Owen wrote sparsely and never fulfilled his ambitions.

A second feature of the letters, and indeed the general labours of this literary coterie, is the reverence for Welsh manuscripts. Here again, the major driving force was Lewis Morris. It was he who coaxed, inspired or bulldozed timid antiquaries into investigating texts and documents. In August 1758 Morris sharply rebuked Edward Richard for neglecting the study of manuscripts relating to 'the old British tongue'. 'This is not fair', he ranted, 'your ancestors lost their blood as well as others in defence of their country and language, which they have handed down to us, why don't we keep what they have left us?'[86] Evan Evans's principal aim in collecting and transcribing Welsh manuscripts was 'to vindicate our language and poetry from ruin and oblivion' and when he stumbled across a manuscript containing the epic poem Y Gododdin he judged the discovery as significant 'as that of America by Columbus'.[87] 'One ancient British Ms. be it ever so despicable to ye sight and ragged', wrote Lewis Morris to Dafydd Jones in February 1757, 'is of greater value than all the

---

[82] Jenkins, *The Foundations of Modern Wales*, pp. 405–6.
[83] *ALM*, I, p. 264.
[84] J. H. Davies (ed.), *The Letters of Goronwy Owen (1723–1769)* (Cardiff, 1924), p. 7. See also pp. 38, 54, 103, 140.
[85] Branwen Jarvis, *Goronwy Owen* (Cardiff, 1986), p. 28.
[86] *ALM*, I, pp. 350–1.
[87] NLW MS 2024B, f. 90r; *ALM*, I, p. 349.

English Historians put together.'[88] It was claimed, probably correctly, that Goronwy Owen would sooner part with his wife than permit a friend to borrow some of his beloved manuscripts.[89] Determined to place Welsh scholarship on a sound foundation, such scholars spent their leisure hours travelling around Wales in search of priceless 'old writings on vellum' and transcribing them with loving care. In a letter to Rice Williams, Evan Evans legitimately claimed that only three other Welshmen 'understand the old British Language better than myself'[90] and the publication of his outstandingly impressive *Some Specimens of the Poetry of the Antient Welsh Bards* (1764) was not only an ideal riposte to the fabricated Ossian poems peddled by James Macpherson but also a confirmation of his standing as a major Celtic scholar.

The third feature of the correspondence of the Morris Circle was the growing interest in the development of Welsh lexicography. Lewis Morris, for instance, could easily have echoed the famous solecism of Dr Samuel Johnson, made in the preface of his *Dictionary of the English Language* (1755): 'We have long preserved our constitution, let us make some struggles for our language.'[91] Although eighteenth-century lexicographers acknowledged their enormous debt to Dr John Davies's famous dictionary, published in 1632, they were conscious that the linguistic resources and material at his disposal had been limited and that the growth of commerce, technology and literacy, as well as the proliferation of English dictionaries, had greatly expanded the Welsh vocabulary and made it necessary to find appropriate Welsh equivalents for specialized or unusual English words. As one of William Gambold's friends had confessed in 1727: 'We still want Words to make us Welshmen through.'[92] The discovery of valuable Welsh manuscripts and the growing number of Welsh printed books had furnished collectors with ever lengthening word lists and this had encouraged wider discussion and analysis of the potential of the vernacular. Long before the formation of the Morris Circle, of course, aspiring lexicographers had drawn freely and uncritically on the monumental work of Dr John Davies. In 1688 Thomas Jones the almanacker brought to the world of lexicography the zeal of the popularizer and the plunderer. His *Y Gymraeg yn ei Disgleirdeb* was a popular and inexpensive Welsh-English Dictionary designed to 'ail

---

[88] *ALM*, I, p. 301.
[89] Ibid., I, p. 293.
[90] Aneirin Lewis (ed.), *The Correspondence of Thomas Percy and Evan Evans* (Louisiana State University, 1957), p. 159; Aneirin Lewis, 'Ieuan Fardd a'r Gwaith o Gyhoeddi Hen Lenyddiaeth Cymru', *JWBS*, VIII, no. 3 (1956), 120–47.
[91] Samuel Johnson, *A Dictionary of the English Language* (London, 1755), Preface. See also T. J. Morgan, 'Geiriadurwyr y Ddeunawfed Ganrif', *LlC*, 9, no. 1 and 2 (1966), 3–18.
[92] William Gambold, *A Welsh Grammar* (Carmarthen, 1727), sig. A2r.

sefydlu'r Gymraeg, ac i'n llwybreiddio i ddysgu Saesnaeg' ('the re-establishing of the Welsh tongue, and for our conduct in learning of English').[93] Further editions followed in 1760 and 1777. Siôn Rhydderch – another almanacker and printer – published in 1725 a dictionary in order to enable readers to translate words from English into Welsh.[94] Others worked more silently and self-effacingly: Thomas Lloyd, a cultivated gentleman from Plas Power, near Wrexham, added around 100,000 words to his copy of John Davies's *Dictionarium*,[95] and William Gambold, rector of Puncheston and Llanychâr, completed, but never published, 'Lexicon Cambro-Britannicum' in 1721–2, a manuscript from which others borrowed heavily thereafter.[96]

The fascination with lexicographical work, however, was best illustrated in the ambitions and activities of scholars associated with the Morris Circle. Deeply alarmed by the decay, if not the disintegration, of old words, and fired by a desire to give currency to new ideas and topics, they were determined to enrich and improve their mother tongue. Lewis Morris nursed a burning ambition to publish a considerably enlarged edition of John Davies's *Dictionarium* and, conscious of Samuel Johnson's achievement and of similar lexicographical contributions by members of the Académie Française and the Accademia della Crusca, he disparaged all other Welsh dictionaries, including Thomas Richards's generally well-regarded *Antiquae linguae Britannicae thesaurus* (1753) (a work of 488 pages which included many words which had been heard or collected in Glamorgan) as 'mere trash and Jack-a-lanthorns'.[97] Without a national academy, lexicographers were unable to call upon acknowledged experts to pronounce upon linguistic matters, and even the opinion of Lewis Morris and his colleagues, especially regarding publications emanating from south Wales, was not entirely reliable or without prejudice. Indeed, the outstanding lexicographical work of the eighteenth century was by a native of Glamorgan. John Walters, rector of Llandough, published *An English-Welsh Dictionary* in fourteen instalments at Cowbridge from 1770 to 1783 and in two hefty volumes in London in 1794. This *tour de force* proved a marvellous storehouse of information. It introduced words of 'daily speech' and also a variety of 'invented' words like 'amaethyddiaeth' (agriculture), 'bytholwyrdd' (evergreen), 'canmoliaethus' (compliment-

---

[93] Jones, *The British Language in its Lustre*, sig. A4r.
[94] Siôn Rhydderch, *The English and Welch Dictionary* (Shrewsbury, 1725).
[95] E. D. Jones, 'Thomas Lloyd y Geiriadurwr', *NLWJ*, IX, no. 2 (1955), 180.
[96] NLW Llanstephan MSS 189 and 190; John Walters, *An English-Welsh Dictionary* (London, 1794), p. vi. See also Helen Emanuel, 'Geiriaduron Cymraeg 1547–1972', *SC*, VII (1972), 141–54.
[97] *ALM*, II, p. 513; Allen Reddick, *The Making of Johnson's Dictionary 1746–1773* (Cambridge, 1990), p. 14.

ary), and 'tanysgrifio' (subscribe), which were designed to meet contemporary needs and which have stood the test of time.[98] In Walters' work, lexicographical activity in Wales reached an admirably high level of achievement. Following this outstanding publication, one can well imagine that the merits of newly coined words as well as the expansion of languages were discussed not only in English-speaking coffee houses and salons but also in literary circles frequented by Welsh-speaking savants.

The publication of Walters' dictionary was partly the consequence of a deepening sense of crisis perceived by Welsh scholars from around the mid-1760s. In April 1765 Lewis Morris, the uncrowned king of Welsh cultural affairs, died, and the Society of Cymmrodorion sank into decline despite the heroic efforts of its President, Richard Morris. There was much resentment and anger among the Welsh literati towards the 'Great Leviathans', the tiny but powerful non-Welsh landowners who despised and disparaged the cultural inheritance and historic identity of the Welsh people. There was a widespread feeling that the 'new' gentry had grown vain, cynical and arrogant in their selfish pursuit of land and wealth.[99] Not only were they increasingly indifferent to the plight of tenant farmers and the labouring poor, but they also mocked the glorious historical legends and linguistic ideals which had sustained a sense of Welshness among their landed forebears. The notion of *noblesse oblige* was foreign to them. 'Go out away! Get ye off' was their surly response to itinerant bards who sought patronage.[100] By severing such ties with the past, several Welsh authors claimed that landowners had forfeited their right to the respect and allegiance of their inferiors. Evan Evans did not mince his words in telling some home truths to Sir Watkin Williams Wynn about his fellow landowners: 'They glory in wearing the badge of their vassalage, by adopting the language of their conquerors, which is the mark of the most despicable meanness of spirit.'[101] Poets and ballad-mongers, too, became increasingly hostile towards 'fat-bellied' Englishmen who were no longer prepared to fulfil their cultural obligations to the Welsh-speaking community.[102] Siôn Powell, a Llansannan weaver, bitterly chastised the new brood of behemoths:

---

[98] Walters, passim; Morgan, *The Eighteenth Century Renaissance*, p. 72.
[99] Jenkins, *The Foundations of Modern Wales*, pp. 265–9.
[100] Lake, *Blodeugerdd Barddas o Ganu Caeth y Ddeunawfed Ganrif*, p. xv.
[101] Evan Evans, *Casgliad o Bregethau* (2 vols., Amwythig, 1776), I, sig. b2v. Evans also warned of the dangers of permitting Edward Lhuyd's precious manuscripts to fall into the hands of the English 'who know no more how to value it than the dunghill cock in Aesop that of the jewel'. D. Silvan Evans (ed.), *Gwaith y Parchedig Evan Evans (Ieuan Brydydd Hir)* (Caernarvon, 1876), p. 245.
[102] *ALM*, II, pp. 745, 749–50.

> Hyll anwyr ni bu llawnach,
> Y cybyddion crinion crach,
> Yn trin y byd, ddybryd ddig,
> A charu pridd a cherrig.
>
> (There was never so many ugly scurvies,
> Scabby, withered misers,
> Dealing with the world, so full of woe,
> And loving earth and stones.)[103]

'Mae'r llafur yn feinach', wrote Hugh Hughes from Holyhead to Richard Morris in February 1767, 'y meistred tirodd yn dyblu a threblu eu hardreion i gael arian er porthi eu cyrph moethus efo chwi yn y ddinas anrhydeddus yna, ar Trethi yn chwannegu beunydd ar Saeson yn arglwyddiaethu yn y Tyddynod mwyaf yn y wlad yma, ar Cymru Truain megys Caeth Weision i blant Alis Rhonwen' (Labour is slimmer . . . landowners double and treble their rents to acquire money to feed their luxurious bodies with you in that honourable city, and taxes increase daily, and the English exercise dominion over the largest cottages in this land, and the poor Welsh are captive slaves to the children of Alice Rhonwen).[104] Amid the bustling action, comedy and obscene gestures which characterized the rough and ready and highly popular interludes composed by the likes of Twm o'r Nant, Jonathan Hughes and Ellis Roberts (Elis y Cowper) were lampoons of avaricious gentlemen such as 'Rinallt Ariannog' (Reginald Money-bags) and 'Siôn Llygad y Geiniog' (John Eye-of-the-Penny),[105] and many popular almanackers, poets and rhymesters also began to expose examples of gross injustices and tyrannies inflicted upon the vulgar sorts by 'the offspring of Hors' and 'the children of Alice'.[106] 'A raid i ni adael ein iaith i ddilyn *Rhonwen?*' (Must we abandon our language to follow Rowena?) cried Dafydd Jones, Trefriw.[107]

A second cause of disaffection was the potentially alarming long-term consequence of appointing non-Welsh prelates to Welsh dioceses. By the

---

[103] Bobi Jones and Gwyn Thomas, *The Dragon's Pen. A Brief History of Welsh Literature* (Llandysul, 1986), p. 50.

[104] *ALM*, II, pp. 685–6.

[105] T. J. R. Jones, 'Welsh Interlude Players of the Eighteenth Century', *Theatre Notebook*, 2, no. 4 (1948), 62–6; G. G. Evans, 'Yr Anterliwt Cymraeg', *LlC*, 1, no. 2 (1950), 83–96; ibid., 2, no. 4 (1953), 224–31; G. M. Ashton (ed.), *Anterliwtiau Twm o'r Nant* (Caerdydd, 1964).

[106] *ALM*, II, pp. 534, 717, 745, 749–50; Hugh Jones, *Gardd y Caniadau* (Amwythig, 1776), p. 71. Alice (or Alys) was the daughter of Hengist, the allegedly treacherous Anglo-Saxon chieftain who duped Vortigern and perpetrated the Treachery of the Long Knives. Even as late as the nineteenth century, the English were often called 'plant Alys'.

[107] Dafydd Jones, *Cydymaith Diddan* (Llundain, 1766), p. vi.

mid-eighteenth century the old canard, much deployed in Elizabethan times, that linguistic diversity endangered national unity, was resuscitated. At St Asaph bilious anti-Welsh prejudices were aired by Robert Hay Drummond (1748–61) and Thomas Newcome (1761–9), while at Bangor Dr George Harris, chancellor of the diocese from 1766 and author of *Observations upon the English Language* (1752), made no secret of his contempt for the 'uncouth' tongue of the Welsh people. Indeed, he viewed his appointment as an opportunity to 'civilize' ignorant country bumpkins in one of the dark and penurious corners of the land.[108] At St David's Bishop Samuel Squire (1761–6) flatly refused to permit Evan Evans to dedicate his magnificent volume of Welsh poetry to him,[109] and one of his successors, Robert Lowth, a man of refined conversation, used to refer to 'the *genius* of the [English] tongue' with such relish that champions of the Welsh tongue could not fail to sense his disapproval of the vernacular.[110] Country curates were convinced that bishops were conspiring to ensure that English-speaking place-hunters and sycophants were improving their positions and prosperity at the expense of deserving Welsh-speaking clergymen. In an inflammatory essay, which remained unpublished during his lifetime, Evan Evans thundered and raged against the 'Esgyb Eingl' (Anglo Bishops) for adopting a crude Anglicizing strategy which threatened to transform the mother church into 'an house of Merchandise and a den of thieves'.[111] He believed strongly that the implications of their policy for the future use of the Welsh language as the medium of the Protestant faith were dire:

> Nid oes achos ini er mwyn boddhau yr Esgyb Eingl, golli ein Hiaith a myned yn Saeson, ped fai hyny bossibl. Oherwydd nid oes dim a ddylai fod mor anwyl a gwerthfawr gennym a chaffael mwynhau gair Duw yn ein jaith ein hunain; a ffiaidd ag atgas ydyw'r bwriad hwnnw o'n difuddio ni o'r rhagorfraint hon. Ein lles ni am hynny yn ddiammau yw coledd a mawrhau ein Hiaith, er mwyn adeiladaeth Eglwys Dduw, a phur wybodaeth o'r efengyl dragywyddol.[112]

(There is no reason, in order to satisfy the Anglo Bishops, why we should lose our language and become English, if that were possible. Because nothing

---

[108] Robert Hay Drummond, *A Sermon preached before the Incorporated Society for the Propagation of the Gospel in Foreign Parts* (London, 1754), p. 22; *ML*, I, p. 236–7; G. D. Squibb, *Doctors' Commons. A History of the College of Advocates and of Law* (Oxford, 1977), p. 192; Lambeth Palace, Records of the Court of Arches, no. 10002, G 139/95.

[109] Lewis, *The Correspondence of Thomas Percy*, pp. 170–1.

[110] Robert Lowth, *A Short Introduction to English Grammar* (London, 1762), p. iii; John Barrell, *English Literature in History 1730–80* (London, 1983), p. 123.

[111] NLW MS 2009B, f. 37.

[112] Ibid., f. 30. See also Evan Evans, *The Love of our Country* (Carmarthen, 1772), pp. 27–8; Evans, *Gwaith y Parchedig Evan Evans*, pp. 34–41.

should be more dear and valuable to us as being able to enjoy the word of God in our own language; and the aim of robbing us of that privilege is loathsome and odious. Therefore it unquestionably behoves us to cherish and honour our language, for the edification of God's Church, and pure knowledge of the eternal gospel.)

His writings, strongly tinged with self-pity as well as hatred for English-speaking interlopers, became more overtly patriotic, though his poor health, alcoholism and penury dogged him at every step. Yet he continued to rail against 'estroniaid gormesawl' (oppressive foreigners)[113] until his dying day and it is a matter for regret that this extraordinarily gifted man should have spent his latter years in embittered emotional disarray. Having exposed acts of linguistic injustice within the established Church, no opportunities of climbing the ladder of preferment came his way and, long after his death, the 'Anglo Bishops' continued to exert their blighting influence over the mother church.

Fears that English might triumph at the expense of the native tongue were not confined to ecclesiastical circles. The Welsh literati were deeply concerned about efforts to glorify and propagate the English language. By the latter years of the eighteenth century English was a self-confident language spoken by eight million people in England alone, and the first edition of *Encyclopaedia Britannica*, published in 1768–71, referred to it as 'the language of a great and powerful nation'.[114] The growth of merchant capitalism, swelling Atlantic trade, and glorious military and naval victories over the common 'Popish' enemy abroad served to generate a greater sense of national pride and self-confidence among the English people. Linda Colley has argued that there were powerful incentives to be British at this time,[115] but although the term 'Great Britain' had been invented in 1707 and the words of 'Rule Britannia' composed in 1740, few people in Wales (save perhaps the ruling gentry families, who themselves were not Welsh) thought in terms of 'Great Britain'. Welsh scholars knew well enough that those who spoke Welsh were the authentic Ancient Britons and they were more concerned about the cultural imperialism implicit in the glorification of English. The pride and conceit of swaggering little Englanders irked them and they viewed with growing alarm claims that the English language was 'the Language of

---

[113] NLW MS 2009B, f. 16.
[114] Paul Langford, *A Polite and Commercial People. England 1727–1783* (Oxford, 1989), p. 306.
[115] Linda Colley, *Britons. Forging the Nation 1707–1837* (New Haven and London, 1992), pp. 364–75.

the bravest, wisest, most powerful, and respectable Body of People upon the Face of the Globe'.[116]

In view of these considerations, it is hardly surprising that Welsh writers rallied strongly to the support of the native tongue and spelled out its manifest superiority over the English language. By the mid-1760s Wales was taking part in the general discussion, current among many intellectuals in Europe, about the relative superiority or inferiority of languages as well as their nature and functions.[117] Antonio Gramsci has reminded us that whenever the *questione della lingua* appears, fundamental changes are occurring within society, and there is no doubt that cultural patriots in Wales were keenly exercised by the cultural and political implications of the language question. In a dissertation on Welsh versions of the Bible, published in 1768, Thomas Llewelyn spoke of his veneration for 'an ancient, expressive, and sonorous language' and his contempt for the notion of bringing about uniformity of language between the English and the Welsh.[118] A year later, in a spirited work dedicated to the Prince of Wales, Llewelyn surveyed the current condition of the language and analysed its 'genius'.[119] In 1770 a new periodical, *Trysorfa Gwybodaeth, neu Eurgrawn Cymraeg*, published in Carmarthen, offered valuable literary, historical and political articles. In his *Dissertation on the Welsh Language* (1771), John Walters endorsed the traditional belief that Welsh was one of the Oriental mother tongues, before launching into a fulsome paean to the antiquity, copiousness, elegance, expressiveness and grammatical perfection of his native language. Unlike the 'mongrel' English tongue spoken by 'aliens . . . that have by intrusion . . . got footing in the country', he believed that Welsh was 'diledryw' (unsullied) and suffused with 'soul-enchanting sounds'.[120] 'It is a language', he rejoiced, 'which I greatly admire, and "cujus amor mihi crescit in horas", for which my affection encreases every hour!'[121] The publication in 1773 of *Gorchestion Beirdd Cymru*, a selection of the masterpieces of the Poets of the Nobility, was designed, according to its editor, Rhys Jones of Blaenau, to display some of the most excellent authors of all time in the Welsh language ('rhai o'r Awduriaid ardderchoccaf, a fu erioed yn yr Iaith Gymraeg').[122] All

---

[116] James Buchanan, *The British Grammar* (London, 1762), Dedication.
[117] Jonathan Steinberg, 'The Historian and the *Questione Della Lingua*' in Peter Burke and Roy Porter (eds.), *The Social History of Language* (Cambridge, 1987), pp. 198–209.
[118] Thomas Llewelyn, *An Historical Account of the British or Welsh Versions and Editions of the Bible* (London, 1768), pp. 70, 89–90.
[119] Idem, *Historical and Critical Remarks on the British Tongue and its Connection with other Languages* (London, 1769), p. 118.
[120] John Walters, *A Dissertation on The Welsh Language* (Cowbridge, 1771), pp. 52, 60.
[121] Ibid., p. 63.
[122] Jones, *Gorchestion Beirdd Cymru*, title-page.

these publications exemplified the growing commitment to Welsh as a literary medium.

Sentiments of this kind dovetailed neatly with Johann Gottfried Herder's view that language was the principal hallmark of nationhood. In *Über den Ursprung der Sprache* (1772), Herder argued that language could either arouse or reawaken a sense of identity within a nation and also shape the character of its people.[123] In the long run, his notions had far-reaching social and political consequences, but even in the 1770s writers like Evan Evans and Iolo Morganwg clearly believed that there was an obligation to nurture and strengthen the association between language and national identity. From 1770 onwards, too, the largely moribund Cymmrodorion Society was overshadowed by the Gwyneddigion Society (also based in London), whose members were less cliquish and much more self-consciously Welsh. Although members of the Gwyneddigion set great store by heavy drinking, ragging, mock duels and boisterous merry-making, they also encouraged intense literary activity and the interchange of ideas.

Among the most affable – and gullible – of the Gwyneddigion was William Owen Pughe, a lexicographer and grammarian whose chequered career bore witness to the manner in which romantic self-expression and creativity could easily wreak havoc with the authentic literary tradition of Wales. Pughe fell under the spell of Rowland Jones, a native of Llanbedrog in Caernarfonshire, who had settled in London and become a wealthy barrister. Between 1764 and 1773 Jones published a series of weird and wonderful volumes which usher us into the 'cosy world of lunatic linguistics'.[124] For the modern critic, his work is as useless as a ceiling fan in an airless room, but even in his own day reputable Welsh scholars were justly sceptical of his theories and ready to cast doubt on his sanity. Lewis Morris believed him to be 'touched in the head' and Iolo Morganwg despaired of the 'blind and wildly rambling' ideas of 'Rowland Jones of insane notoriety'.[125] Even Jones himself admitted that the ideas he canvassed in works like *The Origin of Language and Nations* (1764), *Hieroglyfic* (1768), *The Circles of Gomer* (1771) and *The Io-Triads* (1773) were described by critics as 'a heap of the most unintelligible jargon that

---

[123] F. M. Bernard, *Herder's Social and Political Thought: From Enlightenment to Nationalism* (Oxford, 1965); George Steiner, *After Babel. Aspects of Language and Translation* (2nd ed., Oxford, 1992), p. 81; Peter Burke, *The Art of Conversation* (Cambridge, 1993), p. 70.

[124] Stuart Piggott, *The Druids* (London, 1968), p. 171.

[125] *ALM*, II, p. 616; NLW MS 13150A, f. 144. Evan Evans's response to Jones's *The Origin of Language and Nations* (1764) was '... a shame to common sense! O fie! O fie!', Lewis, *The Correspondence of Thomas Percy*, p. 15. Richard Morris called him 'a strange, whimsical fellow' (*ML*, II, p. 525).

ever filled the human pericranium'.[126] His bizarre claims would not normally merit scrutiny were it not for the fact that his theory that the primitive language of mankind had developed from root words of one syllable and that every other language comprised compounds of those root words heavily influenced the thinking of William Owen Pughe.

Pughe was so enchanted by the notion that languages could be broken down into particles or atoms that he adopted it as the fundamental principle of his study of Welsh orthography. Spurred on by a burning desire to breathe new life into 'a nearly expiring language',[127] Pughe began work on a new dictionary of the Welsh language in 1785. The first part was published in June 1793 and the complete edition, containing over 100,000 words, in 1803. Unlike John Walters, who remained firmly attached to well-established lexicographical and orthographical principles, Pughe believed that self-expression, creativity and even fabrication were required in order to prove to the Welsh themselves and the world at large that the Welsh language was virile, flexible and strong. His dictionary, therefore, was riddled with the most grotesque orthography which kept printers and proof-readers on their toes and almost totally baffled the common reader. In place of the letters ch, dd, f, ff and ph, Pughe had substituted ç, z, v, f and ḟ. Such orthographical horrors were compounded by the inclusion of strange-sounding words like 'cynnorthwyolion', 'gwrthymchwelogion', 'llewyrchiannawl', and 'ymddygymmysgiad'. Not all words, of course, were uncongenial, and it should not be forgotten that it was Pughe who coined words like 'alaw' (tune), 'awyren' (aeroplane), 'dathlu' (celebrate), and 'diddorol' (interesting), which are widely used in our own times.[128] Pughe and his ally, Iolo Morganwg, genuinely believed that his orthography was erudite and impressive. In reality, however, it was dangerous bunkum which was greeted at the time with a torrent of vituperation. The dictionary – and the even more unreadable *Cadóedigaeṫ yr Iaiṫ Cẏbraeg* (1808) – mystified and infuriated the ordinary reader. More critically, the bizarre orthography, bogus archaisms and turgid sentences which informed all his works made them a minefield for the unsuspecting scholar and especially for those who sought to emulate him. Even with the best will in the world, it is hard not to conclude that Pughe's lexicographical and orthographical enterprise was a colossal waste of time, effort and money.

---

[126] Rowland Jones, *The Philosophy of Words* (London, 1769), p. 45.
[127] William Owen Pughe, *A Dictionary of the Welsh Language, explained in English* (2 vols., London, 1803), I, sig.b1r.
[128] Glenda Carr, *William Owen Pughe* (Caerdydd, 1983), pp. 82–95; eadem, *William Owen Pughe* (Caernarfon, 1993), pp. 32–3.

A much more central role in the campaign to redefine, enrich and enhance the native language was taken up by Edward Williams, the outstandingly gifted Glamorgan stonemason who was better known at the time by his bardic *nom de plume* Iolo Morganwg. No eighteenth-century Welshman has been the subject of as much passionate and violent controversy as he. Myth-making, fantasy and fabrication figured prominently in Iolo's career and made him quite unlike anyone else in the whole history of Wales. Those who encountered him knew they were in the presence of an extraordinary person. He was a prodigiously learned authority on the language and literature of Wales, a historian of great subtlety and imagination, and a highly skilful romantic poet. To these gifts and attributes might be added encyclopaedic knowledge, elephantine memory, egoism, volatility, demonic energy and caustic wit. Nothing was of greater importance to him than 'yr hen ddywenydd' (the old happiness) i.e. the study of Welsh language, literature and history.[129] He dedicated around sixty years of his life to recovering – and embellishing – the literary history of his native land and his name is greatly honoured to this day as one of the most successful literary forgers in the history of Europe. His great friend Elijah Waring believed that his mind was akin to 'an old curiosity shop'[130] and his unbelievably chaotic cottage at Flemingston in the Vale of Glamorgan was strewn with manuscripts and books in cluttered profusion. Many papers were unfinished essays which he knew in the depth of his heart that he would never complete or publish. But there was also a mass of triads and bruts (many of them bogus), proverbs and vocabularies, free- and strict-metre poetry in the 'anialwch dyrus' (bewildering wilderness)[131] which surrounded him as he read and wrote with passion and commitment. He was so deeply attached to his manuscripts that he once described them as 'my own children' and expressed a desire for them to be placed, at the time of his death, in an enormous coffin and dragged by six horses to his place of burial![132]

Although Iolo's command of spoken and written English was much sounder than his grasp of Welsh, he believed strongly that the Welsh language was the touchstone of national identity. Two leading Welsh lexicographers – Thomas Richards and John Walters (both natives of the Vale of Glamorgan) – had awakened his interest in Welsh proverbial and dialectical wisdom and from then onwards he never tired of extolling the virtues of the Welsh language. In his treatise on 'Bardism', published in

[129] Ceri W. Lewis, *Iolo Morganwg* (Caernarfon, 1995), p. 158.
[130] Elijah Waring, *Recollection and Anecdotes of Edward Williams, The Bard of Glamorgan* (London, 1850), p. 11.
[131] NLW MS 13221E, f. 11.
[132] Ibid., f. 119.

The Heroic Elegies and other Pieces of Llywarch Hen (1792), one of his triads runs as follows: 'Tri anhepgor Iaith: purdeb, amledd, ac hyweddiant' (The three indispensables of Language: purity, copiousness, and aptness).[133] He strongly believed that a Golden Age of Welsh-language learning was at hand and to herald that new dawn he christened his first-born son 'Taliesin'.[134] In one of his most challenging moods, he once wrote:

> The Welsh with their language, retain in its words and phrases, independently of written memorials, a tolerable history of their progress in arts, literary knowledge and civilization. They are, I believe, the most tenacious, the Jews, perhaps, excepted, of ancient customs and usages, and national peculiarities, of any civilized people in Europe and the English are the least so.[135]

His writings were far less plaintive and fatalistic than those of his predecessors, and by the 1790s he had emerged as the most forward-looking and strident cultural nationalist in Wales.

Iolo Morganwg's remarkable gifts for inventing or forging literary and historical texts have made him one of the most controversial figures in the history of Wales.[136] Although he took a roguish, childlike pleasure in teasing his contemporaries, he was not at bottom a cheat. His desire to tamper with old manuscripts, edit out uncongenial passages and replace them with his own literary creations was not born of either mischief or malevolence. Part of the explanation lies in his unattractive appearance, his sheltered upbringing, his deeply rooted sense of inferiority (he was known locally as Ned Williams the stonecutter), and his own perception of himself as a penurious and unprized outsider. His personal quirks and eccentricities were also significant factors, as was his bitter resentment over the neglect of the literary and historical traditions of his native Glamorgan, an injustice he was determined to remedy. The most critical factor, however, was his dependence for fifty-three years on laudanum (a liquid extract of opium normally taken with alcohol), which consigned him to an Orwellian world of fantasy, forgery and deception. Like Coleridge, de Quincey, Shelley and many other romantics, Iolo became an opium addict. This gave rise to dreams, hallucinations and visions which fed his imagination, sharpened his

---

[133] William Owen Pughe, *The Heroic Elegies and other Pieces of Llywarch Hen* (London, 1792), p. lxxiv.
[134] Richard M. Crowe, 'Diddordebau Ieithyddol Iolo Morganwg' (unpubl. University of Wales PhD thesis, 1988), p. 74.
[135] NLW MS 13097B, f. 207.
[136] See the views of G. J. Williams, *Iolo Morganwg – Y Gyfrol Gyntaf* (Caerdydd, 1956); idem, *Iolo Morganwg* (London, 1963); Prys Morgan, *Iolo Morganwg* (Cardiff, 1975); Brinley Richards, *Golwg Newydd ar Iolo Morganwg* (Abertawe, 1979); Ceri W. Lewis, *Iolo Morganwg* (Caernarfon, 1995).

intellect, and enabled him to interconnect images and ideas in stimulating and often totally unexpected ways. Most of all, it led him to produce works which were a mixture of fact and fiction. He came to believe — not without good cause — that he could emulate and perhaps even surpass the works of Dafydd ap Gwilym and in 1789 he had no difficulty in passing off his material as the poetry of his late-medieval forebear. His material seemed so plausible and convincing to members of the Gwyneddigion, many of whom were deeply impressed by the erudition of this dazzling, almost mythical figure, that it is not surprising his work was widely admired. In some ways he seems to have succeeded in popularizing his forgeries as much by force of personality as by the fertility of his imagination. His conversation was so uniquely rich and knowledgeable that he became to the London-Welsh what Samuel Johnson was for the English — a fount of impeccable wisdom. None of his contemporaries (especially after the death of Evan Evans in 1788) was sufficiently learned to cast doubts on his material or challenge even his wildest assertions. His forgeries therefore survived scrutiny for well over a century. Not until the period after the First World War did the remarkable researches of Griffith John Williams, later Professor of Welsh at Cardiff, reveal the extent to which generations of Welsh scholars had been hoodwinked by a forger whose gifts far surpassed those of Chatterton and Macpherson.

Iolo was shrewd enough to realize that there was a considerable market for romantic fantasy in his day. He also understood better than most that the Welsh language could not be restored to its former glory without appropriate national institutions. Confident of public support, he therefore devised the compellingly attractive Gorsedd Beirdd Ynys Prydain (The Gorsedd of the Bards of the Island of Britain).[137] Iolo believed that until the 1780s Druidomania had been characterized by excessive zeal and insufficient critical scrutiny. In view of the fact that he believed that to be born in north Wales was the greatest misfortune that could befall any Welshman, it is hardly surprising that he had nothing but scorn for scholars from the north who had contributed to the study of druidism. He loudly disparaged Henry Rowlands for claiming in *Mona Antiqua Restaurata* (1723; second ed. 1766) that Anglesey had been the headquarters of British Druidism and mocked his 'jumble of mistakes [and] absurdities'.[138] Lewis Morris fared no better: in Iolo's jaundiced

---

[137] Geraint Bowen, *Hanes Gorsedd y Beirdd* (Cyhoeddiadau Barddas, 1991); Dillwyn Miles, *The Secret of the Bards of the Isle of Britain* (Dinefwr Press, 1992); Geraint H. Jenkins, 'Cyffesion Bwytawr Opiwm: Iolo Morganwg a Gorsedd Beirdd Ynys Prydain', *Taliesin*, 81 (1993), 45–57; idem, 'Iolo Morganwg and the Gorsedd of the Bards of the Isle of Britain', *Studia Celtica Japonica*, 7 (1995), 45–60.

[138] NLW MS 13089E, f. 460. Cf. NLW MS 13130A, f. 292.

view, his literary and philological observations were not 'worth a single *damn*'.[139] Delighting in 'the Silurian pronunciation and orthography',[140] he believed that only the bards of Glamorgan had been the privileged recipients of 'Cyfrinach y Beirdd' (Secret of the Bards) and that they had preserved, against all the odds, a continuous tradition of poetry, literature and wisdom from the days of the prehistoric Druids to the late eighteenth century. His beloved Glamorgan was given pride of place in the druidic myth and Iolo never tired of proclaiming that he and Edward Evan of Aberdare were the last living representatives of the druidic bards.[141] Often he would append the letters BBD (Bardd wrth Fraint a Defod Beirdd Ynys Prydain / Bard by the Privilege and Rite of the Bards of the Island of Britain) to his name, and he would loudly declare that only he was capable of conveying the essence of 'the divine revelation given to mankind' in the form of druidic religion and lore.[142] On 21 June 1792, in the company of a handful of Welsh patriots, he convened a druidical moot on Primrose Hill, London, where it was resolved 'in the eye of the sun and in the face of the light' to cherish the poetic tradition, practise the principles of pacifism, and instil into the people of Wales an enduring sense of pride in their language, literature and history. The subsequent addition of tangible insignia and quasi-masonic rituals to the stone circles and bardic garb made the Gorsedd a stirringly attractive institution. Iolo believed that a glorious past, even an invented one, could provide a solid foundation on which to build a national future. Although the Gorsedd was enacted as a theatrical event, he hoped that it would enable a people who had for so long belonged to a non-historic nation to gain a new and enhanced sense of their worth.[143] As a modern national institution, the Gorsedd would epitomize the Welshman's self-pride and dignity, and in July 1819, at the Ivy Bush Inn in Carmarthen, Iolo triumphantly realized his ambition of incorporating the Gorsedd in the official activities of the Eisteddfod. At the age of seventy-two, he publicly voiced his delight at being present on 'the resurrection-day of learning in our greatly beloved native language'.[144]

---

[139] NLW MS 13221E, f. 109.
[140] Ibid., f. 25.
[141] NLW MS 4582C; NLW MS 13128B, f. 302; *The Gentleman's Magazine*, LIX (1789), Part 2, p. 976.
[142] NLW MS 21401E, f. 14.
[143] Gwyn A. Williams, 'Druids and Democrats: organic intellectuals and the first Welsh nation' in *The Welsh in their History* (London, 1982), pp. 31–64; idem, 'Romanticism in Wales' in Roy Porter and Mikuláš Teich (eds.), *Romanticism in National Context* (Cambridge, 1988), pp. 9–36.
[144] Hywel Teifi Edwards, *Yr Eisteddfod* (Llys yr Eisteddfod Genedlaethol, 1976), p. 39.

With the support of the Gwyneddigion, Thomas Jones, an exciseman from Clocaenog in Denbighshire, had revived the flagging eisteddfodic tradition from 1789 onwards. For most of the eighteenth century local Welsh eisteddfodau had been gimcrack affairs, attended by small numbers of inebriated poets who exchanged poems of dubious quality over cheese and ale. Jonathan Hughes earnestly urged the London-Welsh to support the efforts of enthusiastic patriots in Merioneth and Denbighshire to 'extend the bounds of the old Welsh language' ('helaethu terfynau yr hen Iaith Gymraeg'),[145] and the Gwyneddigion responded in a positive and encouraging manner. Sustained by their patronage, robust and sometimes acrimonious eisteddfodau were organized in the market towns of north Wales, and their success (as well as that of the Gorsedd) prompted William Jones of Llangadfan to campaign on behalf of a truly national eisteddfod of Wales. He believed that the estranged 'old brothers' from the south should be encouraged to return to the fold to invigorate the proceedings and transform the eisteddfod into a major national institution.[146] His ambition was entirely consonant with many of the ideals of Iolo Morganwg. Both men dreamed – in vain in their own day – of establishing a Welsh academy and a national library to guard the literary treasures of the nation.[147] But at least the importance of creating national institutions to sustain the native language and literature had been emphasized. Moreover, the Gwyneddigion had responded positively to the demand for scholarly works, even though parts of those works are best understood as pieces of historical fiction. Thanks to the munificence and business acumen of Owain Myfyr (Owen Jones), first President of the Society and a wealthy currier, it became possible to publish *Barddoniaeth Dafydd ap Gwilym* (1789), a work which, as we have seen, bore the heavy imprint of Iolo Morganwg's bogus scholarship.[148] Even more seminal was the publication of *The Myvyrian Archaiology* (3 vols., 1801–7), edited by Iolo Morganwg, Owain Myfyr and William Owen Pughe, an invaluable collection of Welsh historical and literary work from the sixth to the fourteenth centuries. Although the *Myvyrian* was deeply flawed by Iolo's fabrications, at least it brought many important texts into the public domain for the first time.

Finally, the romantic myth-makers and cultural patriots of the 1790s were also clearly determined to propagate the language of political

---

[145] G. J. Williams, 'Llythyrau ynglŷn ag Eisteddfodau'r Gwyneddigion', *LlC*, 1, no. 1 (1950), 30; idem, 'Eisteddfodau'r Gwyneddigion', *Y Llenor*, XIV–XV (1935–6), 11–12, 88–96.
[146] NLW MS 1806E, f. 777.
[147] G. J. Williams, *Iolo Morganwg*, pp. 70–2; NLW MS 168C, f. 292; NLW MS 1806E, f. 783.
[148] G. J. Williams, 'Owain Myfyr', *LlC*, 8, no. 1 and 2 (1964), 42–7.

radicalism and nationalism in the native tongue. John Walters had invented the word 'gwladgarwch' (patriotism) in the year of the Declaration of American Independence and by 1798 the word 'cenedligrwydd' (nationality) had also entered the vocabulary.[149] By that time the language of political radicalism was being preached, notably by Unitarians, Baptists and other heterodox groups who appreciated the revolutionary powers of the printed word. Before 1789 most Welsh books had been unambiguously apolitical in their aims and content, but the fall of the Bastille heralded the construction of a new political discourse in the Welsh language which was fervently radical and patriotic. A spate of political pamphlets and journals, written with vigour and scurrilous zest, deplored the damaging effects of monarchical government, political jobbery, tithes and rack-rents, absentee landlordism, evangelical religion and creeping Anglicization. Like Tom Paine and Horne Tooke,[150] Welsh radicals believed that the King's English had been used to defend the traditional rights and monopolies of the ruling classes. By celebrating the ideals and achievements of Jacobins, *sans-culottes* and followers of Tom Paine in the Welsh language, they affirmed the special identity of the free-born Welshman.

In the case of Iolo Morganwg, the much-publicized Gorsedd did not simply epitomize a cultural vision. He believed that the ancient Druids had 'breathed the invincible Spirit of Liberty'[151] and there was no reason to think that their modern counterparts could not ignite the political imagination of the Welsh. As befitted a man who claimed descent from Oliver Cromwell, Iolo assiduously cultivated the image of 'The Bard of Liberty' and manipulated successive Gorseddau on behalf of Jacobin ideology. Just as Thomas Gray's 'The Bard' had exemplified heroic Welsh resistance to English oppression, so did 'Iolo, the Bard of Glamorgan' embody the ideals of Welsh republicanism during William Pitt's 'Reign of Terror'. His poem 'Breiniau Dyn' (The Rights of Man) revealed that, to him, 'peraidd iaith' (pure language) meant freedom, fraternity and peace,[152] and strains of 'God save Great Thomas Paine' rang out whenever he visited London. In May 1795 he invited William Owen Pughe to join him 'to talk of Politics, republicanism, Jacobinisms, Carmagnolism, Sanculololisms [*sic*], and a number of other wicked and trayterous *isms* against the peace of the Lords Kingism and Parsonism, their Crowns and dignities',[153] and although the authorities kept him under close

---

[149] *GPC*, s.v. 'gwladgarwch', 'cenedligrwydd'.
[150] Barrell, *English Literature*, p. 174.
[151] NLW MS 21401E, f. 14.
[152] Millward, *Blodeugerdd Barddas o Gerddi Rhydd*, pp. 242-7. See also NLW MS 13148A, f. 300.
[153] NLW MS 13221E, f. 49. See also NLW MS 21396E, ff. 3, 11, 13, 20, 34.

surveillance he vowed to champion the Jacobin cause 'oni chanwyf yn iach i'r byd hwn' (until I bid farewell to this world).[154]

Seditious and scurrilous talk was not confined to gorseddau and eisteddfodau in the 1790s, for disaffected democrats also began to cudgel Old Arrogance in Welsh-language publications. The last decade of the eighteenth century witnessed an explosion of Welsh printed books, many of which were so unashamedly partisan and polemical that they served to enlarge the political vocabulary of the Welsh. Popular radicals, several of whom had risen from relatively humble backgrounds, produced works which were less abstract and demanding than the philosophical writings (in English) of Welshmen like Richard Price and David Williams. In a powerful assault on Old Corruption, the Anglo-Norman yoke, English bishops, and tithe-grabbing clergymen, Thomas Roberts, Llwyn'rhudol, urged his fellow countrymen to stand up for their rights:

> Yn lle amddiffynu yn wrol, ac yn galonog eu breintiau, hefyd freintiau eu plant a'u hwyrion, maent mewn math o hunglwyf yn goddef yn rhy fynych yr hyn oll y mae eu Gorthrymwyr annhrugarog yn ei osod arnynt, heb unwaith feddwl, nad yw pob peth yn ei le.[155]

> (Instead of bravely and enthusiastically defending their rights, and the rights of their children and grandchildren, they are afflicted by a kind of sleeping sickness which too often makes them tolerate everything their merciless oppressors impose upon them, without ever thinking that everything is not right.)

John Jones (Jac Glan-y-gors), a committed republican and pacifist, published forthright Welsh paraphrases of Tom Paine's best-selling *The Rights of Man*,[156] and was also instrumental in founding in 1795 the Cymreigyddion, a London-based society whose strong radical bias was coupled with a fierce desire to promote the Welsh language. The refrain of the Society's song ran as follows:

> A d'wedwn i gyd, hardd frodyr un fryd,
> Ein hiaith a barhao a llwyddiant ai cadwo,
> Heb loes, trwy bob oes, tra bo byd![157]

> (And so say we all, handsome brothers at one, our language will survive and its success will keep it uninjured throughout the ages till the end of the world.)

---

[154] Edward Williams, *Salmau yr Eglwys yn yr Anialwch* (2nd ed., Merthyr, 1827), p. v.
[155] Thomas Roberts, *Cwyn yn erbyn Gorthrymder* (Llundain, 1798), pp. 42–3.
[156] John Jones, *Seren tan Gwmmwl* (Llundain, 1795) and *Toriad y Dydd* (Llundain, 1797). See also Albert E. Jones, 'Jac Glan y Gors, 1766–1821', *TDHS*, 16 (1967), 62–81.
[157] NLW MS 13221E, f. 167.

In *Y Cylchgrawn Cynmraeg* (1793), the first political journal in the Welsh language, Morgan John Rhys sought to inject some dynamism into the moribund political life of Wales by celebrating the ideals of liberty and equality,[158] while in the fastnesses of mid-Wales William Jones of Llangadfan, the Welsh Voltaire who scandalized local inhabitants with his blasphemous conversation and biting comments about tyrants, oppressors and fleecers, composed a robust Welsh national anthem – the first of its kind – as an antidote to the militant Englishness of 'God Save the King' and 'The Roast Beef of Old England'.[159] Thomas Jones the exciseman admiringly dubbed him 'the hottest-arsed Welshman' ('a'r mwya' tinboeth a'r welais I erioed') of his day.[160] The flinty Unitarian Thomas Evans (Tomos Glyn Cothi) was just as outspoken, and he was incarcerated in Carmarthen prison for allegedly singing in Welsh a seditious song 'to the Tune of the Marcellais hymn' at a 'cwrw bach' (bid-ale) in Brechfa.[161] Public displays of sedition and insolence, couched in the Welsh language, infuriated non-Welsh-speaking authorities and the political backlash which followed the lamentable French invasion of 1797 involved a relentless pursuit of cultural and political activists. Nevertheless, the tradition of radical discourse through the medium of Welsh had been firmly established.[162]

Although ardent champions of Welsh language and literature of the calibre of Edward Lhuyd, Lewis Morris and Iolo Morganwg had, for reasons largely beyond their control, fallen short of the lofty goals they had set for themselves, much had been achieved during the eighteenth century. No longer did it appear that Welsh culture was inextricably bound up with a way of life which was irrevocably decaying. Lost or forgotten manuscripts had been rescued, transcribed, preserved and

---

[158] Gwyn A. Williams, *The Search for Beulah Land. The Welsh and the Atlantic Revolution* (London, 1980), pp. 60–1; Hywel M. Davies, '"Very Different Springs of Uneasiness": Emigration from Wales to the United States of America during the 1790s', *WHR*, 15, no. 3 (1991), 368–98.

[159] NLW MS 13221E, f. 369.

[160] NLW MS 13221E, f. 256; Jones often spoke of his undying love for his 'heniaith friglwyd' (ancient language) (NLW MS 170C, f. 11).

[161] G. J. Williams, 'Carchariad Tomos Glyn Cothi', *LlC*, 3, no. 2 (1954), 120–2; G. Dyfnallt Owen, *Tomos Glyn Cothi* (Darlith Goffa Dyfnallt, 1963), p. 32. See 'Cân Rhyddid' in Millward, *Blodeugerdd Barddas o Gerddi Rhydd*, pp. 265–6.

[162] For English (and British) parallels, see Hugh Cunningham, 'The Language of Patriotism, 1750–1914', *History Workshop*, 12 (1981), 8–33; Jeannine Surel, 'John Bull' in Raphael Samuel (ed.), *Patriotism: The Making and Unmaking of British National Identity, vol. III, National Fictions* (London, 1989), pp. 3–25; Linda Colley, 'Whose nation? Class and national consciousness in Britain, 1750–1830', *PP*, 113 (1986), 97–117.

published, and printing presses were thriving as never before. A flurry of lexicographical and grammatical works had revealed that it was possible to use the Welsh language for a wide variety of literary, scientific and technological purposes. On behalf of the language of Christian praise, William Williams had written with a brilliance never equalled in his day, while small bands of radical writers had embarked on a new tradition of polemical and partisan literature. Although the spurious theories of Pezron were still warmly embraced, the study of Celticism achieved striking vitality in this period and served to enhance the prestige of vernacular languages. Most crucial of all, cultural patriots and romantic myth-makers had responded to the malaise of the times by inventing or reviving institutions which, in the long term, served to sustain a profound and inspiring belief in the resources of the Welsh language and its literature.

12

The Celtic Languages of Britain

BRYNLEY F. ROBERTS

ON THE basis of the available evidence, it appears that from the earliest times the native languages of the British Isles have been Celtic languages.[1] It is fruitless to surmise what languages may have been spoken previously since there is virtually no evidence to be examined. There are a few inscriptions extant in north-east Scotland, but they have so far defied attempts to decipher them. They may represent a Pictish language, but other better attested Pictish languages appear to be Celtic. The Celtic languages, as they first appear on the stage of British history, fall into two well-defined groups, the one a Goidelic family in which *c/k* (earlier *q*) corresponds to *p* in the other, British, family. There is, of course, a wider range of phonetic variation than this simple but useful categorization, and over a period of time the two groups diverged with the result that, to the ear, and in their written forms, they often appear to have little in common. From the Goidelic *c/k* group developed Common Gaelic which spread in the fifth and sixth centuries AD from Ireland to Scotland and the Isle of Man, and indeed to parts of north and south-west Wales where it did not survive. The Celtic languages of the whole of mainland Britain, from the Clyde and Forth southwards, and probably the Pictish languages to the north, were part of the other, British, group. The advent of Germanic tribes from the Continent towards the middle of the fifth century and their subsequent expansion marked the beginning of the long period of the waning of these native Celtic languages.

Place-names provide the only witness to the Celtic language(s) of most of present-day England, but the British kingdoms of Gododdin, Strathclyde and Rheged in southern Scotland and Northumbria, with their centres at Edinburgh, Dumbarton ('the citadel of the Britons') and

---

[1] There are historical and linguistic descriptions of these languages in Glanville Price, *The Languages of Britain* (London, 1984); Donald Macaulay (ed.), *The Celtic Languages* (Cambridge, 1992); Glanville Price (ed.), *The Celtic Connection* (Gerrards Cross, 1992); Martin J. Ball (ed.) with James Fife, *The Celtic Languages* (London, 1993); Paul Russell, *An Introduction to the Celtic Languages* (London, 1995).

perhaps Carlisle, survived long enough to inspire the oldest Welsh poetry and for the wars of these peoples against Saxons and Angles and amongst themselves to become the heroic age in the Welsh consciousness of the Middle Ages. Edinburgh fell in 638 and it appears that south-east Scotland was in the hands of the Angles by mid-century. By around 650–70 the Angles of Northumbria had overrun lands in the south-west, but Strathclyde enjoyed a period of resurgence with the result that it remained a British kingdom until 1092 when it became part of the kingdom of Scotland and the present boundary was established.[2] Its British language may have survived until the end of the eleventh or beginning of the twelfth century. The Cumbrian of Strathclyde probably represented the northern form of British – the evidence is too tenuous to describe the language in detail – but the western form of British is found in Welsh and Cornish, which began to diverge from one another around 600 AD, possibly following the battle of Dyrham (577), which severed the link between the western Britons and their compatriots in the south-west.

Wessex expanded swiftly to the west and had overrun Devon by the end of the seventh century. The river Tamar, a natural barrier, prevented, or at least hindered, further widespread expansion after 710, but the Anglo-Saxon chronicle and the *Annales Cambriae* record much fighting between the Saxons and the 'Wæst Wealas' along this border throughout the eighth century. As a result, this area of eastern Cornwall must have been home to a mixed population of Britons and increasing numbers of immigrants. Under Egbert (802–39) the expansion intensified from 815 onwards and he was able to make grants of lands in Cornwall to the west of the Tamar to the bishopric of Sherborne. The conquest was completed under Athelstan, the tenth-century 'imperator' who claimed the overlordship of the whole of Britain, 'the first of the Saxons to wear the crown of Britain', in Geoffrey of Monmouth's words, and whose powerful hegemony inspired the pan-British alliance which the author of the Welsh poem *Armes Prydein Vawr* so ardently supported.[3] Athelstan established the river Tamar as the border and brought the old Celtic 'kingdom' and its provinces into the administrative pattern of shire and hundred. The royal line of Cornwall lapsed and in 994 Cornwall was placed under the ecclesiastical jurisdiction of Bishop Ealdred.

There is no record evidence which would reveal the effects of English subjugation on Cornish, but one must assume that the English language spread gradually and increasingly from the settlements along the Tamar.

[2] Kenneth Jackson, *Language and History in Early Britain* (Edinburgh, 1953), pp. 218–19; Price, *The Languages of Britain*, p. 146.
[3] Ifor Williams (English version by Rachel Bromwich), *Armes Prydein* (Dublin, 1972), pp. xvii–xviii.

Place-name evidence confirms this assumption. In the north-east English place-names predominate and had superseded native forms even by the eighth and ninth centuries. Where Cornish names survive, they reflect the oldest forms (*quite, nant*, 'wood', 'stream'). In central Cornwall English and Cornish forms are found in approximately equal numbers, but the great majority of place-names in the west are Cornish and show late phonetic changes (*coos, cos, nance, nans* for older *quite, nant*).[4] The place-names confirm what might be expected in the pattern of expansion and immigration and Jago's claim[5] that Cornish was in use from the Tamar to Land's End in 1547 can scarcely be accepted.

Athelstan's conquest made Cornwall part of England, whatever ethnic or cultural differences existed between them. In administrative and political terms it was an English shire, a development which would have encouraged the spread of English not only geographically but also even more crucially in a sociolinguistic sense. In the Doomsday Book survey of 1086 three manors only, in the west, were held by men bearing Cornish names. Most landowners, i.e. the sector which wielded power and influence, were Anglo-Saxons and, not surprisingly, the Bodmin Manumissions (940–1040; BL Add MS 9381) record that 98 of the 122 serfs freed bore Cornish names, twelve Anglo-Saxon names, twelve Latin or biblical names, and that twenty-four of the thirty-three manumittors had Anglo-Saxon names, while five only were Cornish.[6]

English expansion was not to be so powerful, nor such an effective combination of political, administrative, economic and social factors, in any of the other Celtic countries as it was in Cornwall until the seventeenth and eighteenth centuries. A variety of languages was one of the features of British society throughout the Middle Ages. Latin was the western European language of literate culture and Christianity and could not be claimed by any state as its vernacular medium of communication. It was a school language which had to be learned through much effort and with varying degrees of success by successive generations of pupils who would need Latin in their professional occupations. It was not a community language which could be passed from one generation to another. But within those broader communities there could exist a wide diversity of languages and dialects and the concept of linguistic uniformity within a single kingdom or lordship was not a familiar one in the Middle

---

[4] P. A. S. Pool, *An Introduction to Cornish Place-names* (Penzance, 1971); Martyn F. Wakelin, *Language and History in Cornwall* (Leicester, 1975), pp. 74–6; O. J. Padel, *Cornish Place-name Elements* (Nottingham, 1985); idem, *A Popular Dictionary of Cornish Place-names* (Penzance, 1988), pp. 7–10.

[5] F. W. P. Jago, *An English-Cornish Dictionary* (London, 1887), p. ii.

[6] Wakelin, *Language and History in Cornwall*, p. 67.

Ages. Language might be an ethnic marker and individual groups used their own languages for their own purposes, but those languages coexisted with those of other groups or functions so that the multilingual nature of society, and to a lesser extent of individuals, was a common feature in many areas. There were Norse settlements in Wales, although the linguistic evidence, apart from place-names and some borrowings, is not abundant, but in Ireland the Scandinavian presence was a predominant element around Dublin and along the southern seaboard from the ninth century up to the battle of Clontarf in 1014. Anglo-Norman was the native language of one section of society in Wales and Ireland, and since that section comprised the governing class their language – of law and administration, and frequently of entertainment – penetrated native society. In a later period English, the language of commerce and many kinds of interaction, would become increasingly common, especially in the towns, with the result that speakers of the Celtic languages of Wales, Ireland, Cornwall and Scotland could not avoid coming into contact with it, even if they wished to, in those areas of their lives which impinged upon its functions, and a degree of bilingualism was no doubt common.

Nevertheless, the multilingualism of society did not lead to linguistic instability. One element in maintaining the linguistic equilibrium was the predominant numbers of native speakers as compared with the numbers of immigrants or users of special languages. Although Irish and Norse had lived closely together and intermingled to the extent that even by 856 there are references to the Gall-Gaídil – people who were neither Irish nor Norse but both – they were a small element within the total population.[7] But numbers were not the paramount factor; equally important was the range of activities within the community for which the native languages were used – from government and law to literature, culture and all the multifarious aspects of everyday living – and the fact that these languages were part of the unifying fabric of society. With the exception of Cornish, they were languages utilized to the full with few restrictions on their domains; limitations in use were more a feature of the incoming languages. The native languages enjoyed the stronger position in their own lands in the Middle Ages, and when reference was made to threatened languages, it was not so much the Celtic languages as the minority languages of Anglo-Norman or English which felt themselves under siege. Throughout Irish history following the Anglo- (or Cambro-) Norman incursions which began in 1170, there appeared a regular call for legislation prohibiting the

---

[7] Kenneth H. Jackson, 'The Celtic Languages during the Viking period' in Brian Ó Cuív (ed.), *The Impact of the Scandinavian Invasions on the Celtic-speaking Peoples, c.800–1100 A.D.* (Baile Atha Cliath, 1975), p. 4.

use of Irish in the courts and boroughs and enjoining the use of English in its own territory – the Kilkenny Statutes of 1366 are the most comprehensive example – but such legislation was generally ineffective given the dominant position of Irish and since a number of powerful families descended from the first invaders had become Irish, some of whom could speak neither French nor English. The position was changing, however, and by the beginning of the early modern period there were trends at work which would completely change the situation in all the Celtic countries. These trends were diverse, but the crucial change was the determination of Tudor government, and the English Crown thereafter, to create a unified British state with a single and uniform legislation, religion and language. A concept of the identification of language and state was created which gave rise to centralist and uniforming policies which altered the long-standing linguistic balance, with the result that all the Celtic languages faced challenges to their existence as comprehensive community languages in the seventeenth and eighteenth centuries. This had already occurred in the case of Scottish Gaelic within the Scottish context and those changes were to be intensified in the British context in the seventeenth century. In Cornwall these developments were well advanced before the seventeenth century and it is not surprising that Cornish had perished before the end of the eighteenth century: indeed, that it survived so long is remarkable. The history of the death of Cornish is a microcosm of the circumstances which were to affect the other languages and to lead to their decline.

Cornish[8]

Broadly speaking, it appears that the area around Truro had become the linguistic border by the fifteenth century: the eastern part of the county was English, but the two western hundreds, Penwith and Kerrier, were Cornish or bilingual. The letters and register of John de Grandisson, bishop of Exeter, reveal that the language was to be found 'in extremis Cornubiae', i.e. in the far west, in 1328–9, but there is also evidence that a substantial number of the inhabitants were monoglot Cornish since there was a need in some parishes for priests who could preach and hear confession in Cornish. When Andrew Borde's *The Fyrst Boke of the Introduction of Knowledge* was published in 1547, the position remained the

---

[8] In addition to the books noted above in n. 1, see esp. P. Berresford Ellis, *The Cornish Language and its Literature* (London, 1974); P. A. S. Pool, *The Death of Cornish* (Penzance, 1975); Wakelin, *Language and History in Cornwall*; Brian Murdoch, *Cornish Literature* (Cambridge, 1993); D. Simon Evans, 'The Story of Cornish', *Studies*, LVIII (1969), 292–307.

same. After noting the various languages of England 'and vnder the dominion of England', such as French, Welsh, Irish, he remarked:

> In Cornwall is two speches: the one is naughty Englyshe, and the other is Cornyshe. And there be many men and women the which cannot speake one worde of Englyshe, but all Cornyshe.[9]

This was confirmed by the directive of John Veysey, bishop of Exeter, in 1538 that priests should ensure that parishioners in those parishes where English was not spoken should be taught the Ten Commandments, the Credo, *Pater Noster* and *Ave Maria* in Cornish and that children should be taught the Seven Works of Mercy in that language. It must be doubted how far this order was enforced since no provision was made to have this material translated and, as far as can be judged, carrying out the bishop's instructions was left to the conscience, enthusiasm and skills of individual priests. Certainly, there were priests who could preach in Cornish, but whether this was sufficient qualification to translate the main articles of faith, and especially parts of the Gospel and Epistle of the day, as Veysey had called for, is open to question. Little Middle Cornish literature has been preserved, which may suggest that, lacking any institution which could nurture it and ensure the continuation of its language and context over a long period, the literary tradition had declined and died by the fourteenth and fifteenth centuries. Old Cornish shared the same ecclesiastical and secular culture as did Old Welsh and, while native governing structures and society remained, one might have expected the culture of Cornwall to enjoy similar support to that which its counterpart received in Wales. One of the consequences of absorption into the administrative mainstream of England was the loss of this cultural support, and the continuity and development which are the hallmarks of a living culture were lost. It is significant that the few Middle Cornish texts extant are popular religious poetry and plays: *Pascon agan Arluth* (The Passion of our Lord), the *Ordinalia* in three parts, and *Beunans Meriasek* (The Life of Meriasek) in two parts. These, and perhaps other miracle plays which have not survived, would have been the means of instruction in the tenets of Christianity to a greater extent than translations of the Scriptures and other articles of faith, as is suggested by the *plenys an gwary*,[10] the open-air theatres, which are a feature of a number of villages in western Cornwall.

---

[9] Quoted in Wakelin, *Language and History in Cornwall*, p. 89. See also Maria Palermo Concolato (ed.), *Andrew Borde: Gli itinerari d'Europa* (Napoli, 1992), pp. 20–7.

[10] See Sydney Higgins, 'Medieval Theatre in the Round', special issue of *Laboratorio degli studi linguistici* (1994), esp. pp. 23–40.

According to Richard Carew's description in 1602, these were a popular attraction:

> The guary miracle (in English, a miracle play) is a kind of interlude compiled in Cornish out of some scripture history with that grossness which accompanied the old Roman comedy. For representing it, they raise an earthen amphitheatre in some open field, having the diameter of it enclosed plain some 40 or 50 foot. The country people flock from all sides, many miles off, to hear and see it; for they have therein devils and devices to delight as well the eye and the ear.[11]

These appear to have been social 'folk' events which entertained and educated ordinary people, although the literature itself originated in ecclesiastical centres such as Glasney College near Penryn.[12] Whether traditional oral literature continued to flourish is not known. Oral culture must have existed, but the nature of the plays is revealing in the way English, French and Cornish were consciously utilized. Divine and virtuous characters speak Cornish, as do the wicked when they wish to create a favourable impression, but the devils use more English. This is clearly a dramatic device, but it would have been pointless were it not a recognizable indicator of linguistic attitudes. The audience, it appears, was aware of the unequal status of the two common languages, although there persisted some degree of commitment to Cornish in the face of the encroachment of 'foreign' or 'gentle' English, which could be expressed in the plays in a light-hearted way. The Welsh interludes of the eighteenth century reveal similar attitudes to the use of Welsh and English. But more important than this dramatic use of language is the language of discourse in general, and here the comparison with the Welsh interludes is invalid. The interludes use a rich, fluent language which reflects a register of literary conventions as well as drawing on a vibrant spoken language; the Cornish of the plays, on the other hand, is full of unadapted English borrowings, both words and phrases. There is no awareness of a literary tradition, and if the register reflects the language of the audience, one must assume that Cornish was rapidly losing its lexicon, although it retained its basic grammar. The macaronic features are even more apparent in *Gwreans an Bys* (The Creation of the World) by William Jordan, which may have been composed *c*.1530–50, although the only copy is dated 1611. Audiences may have been technically bilingual, but lexical interference had become overwhelming and there is little doubt that the language of 'monoglot' speakers contained a fair amount of

---

[11] Quoted in Ellis, *The Cornish Language and its Literature*, p. 36, but contrast Murdoch, *Cornish Literature*, p. 43.
[12] James Whetter, *The History of Glasney College* (Padstow, 1988), pp. 102–14.

English. Lacking the awareness and element of commitment to standard forms and conventions which a literary tradition provides, it must be doubted whether Cornish could have faced successfully the challenge of translating a range of texts for private devotion or public worship.

The Prayer Book Rebellion of 1549 probably reflects the way in which language and religion had become interrelated. This was, however, a protest against a new order of service: the language was one of its emblems. It was less a campaign in favour of Cornish than evidence of religious conservatism: 'We will not receive the new service because it is but like a Christmas game. We will have our old service of matins, Mass, evensong and procession as it was before.' One element in the argument was the claim that 'we Cornishmen, whereof certain of us understand no English, utterly refuse the new English'.[13] In his sarcastic response, which typified a government that could not comprehend the social and extra-utilitarian functions of a language, the archbishop enquired whether old Latin was more intelligible to Cornishmen than new English, and when the rebellion was put down the decrees of the 1549 Act of Uniformity were reconfirmed. What the protest revealed was that neither the church in Cornwall nor the bishop in Exeter was conscious of any need to translate the Bible or the Prayer Book: nor was there any appeal to cultural history. There was no antagonism towards Cornish as such, for the rebellion did have some effect. In 1560 the bishop of Exeter ordered that the catechism be taught in Cornish to such as were ignorant of English. At about the same time John Tregear undertook the translation of twelve homilies from the Catholic Edmund Bonner's *A Profitable and Necessary Doctrine and Certain Homilies Adjoined thereto* (1555) but, even if his translations were circulated and used, their Anglicized and inelegant language would scarcely have made them popular. When Richard Carew claimed in 1602 that the Lord's Prayer, the Apostolic Creed and the Ten Commandments were 'much used in Cornish beyond all remembrance', he was surely referring to recent local efforts. Unlike the situation in Wales, no one called for translations of the Bible or Prayer Book into Cornish, for there were none among the gentry or the leading clergy who were inspired either by the ideal or the necessity. The consequence was that the Protestant Reformation, through its new order of service, became one of the major channels for the dissemination of English.

---

[13] Quoted in Julian Cornwall, *Revolt of the Peasantry 1549* (London, 1977), p. 115; and cf. Wakelin, *Language and History in Cornwall*, p. 98 and Ellis, *The Cornish Language and its Literature*, p. 61.

Richard Carew's *The Survey of Cornwall*, based on work carried out by 1594, was published in 1602. He noted how English was continually spreading, forcing Cornish 'into the uttermost skirts of the shire':

> Most of the Inhabitants can no word of Cornish; but very few are ignorant of the English: and yet some so affect their owne, as to a stranger they will not speake it: for if meeting them by chance, you inquire the way or any such matter, your answere shalbe, *Meea nauid[n]a cowzasawzneck,* I can speake no Saxonage.[14]

The answer Carew received was actually 'I will not speak English', but although this may reflect a linguistic attitude (or a personal response to the enquirer), it does not affect his evidence which agrees with statements made by John Norden in his survey, *Speculi Britanniae Pars: A Topographical and Historical Description of Cornwall* (1610), based on the results of a visit made in 1584. Cornish, he maintains, was the language of the community only in Penwith and Kerrier, but even there all could speak English, 'vnless it be some obscure people, that seldome conferr with the better sorte', adding: 'But it seemeth that in few yeares the Cornishe Language wilbe by litle and litle abandoned.'[15] Scattered occasional references throughout the seventeenth century do not alter this picture of a language restricted to the two westernmost and most remote hundreds and of increasing bilingualism. In 1695 Edmund Gibson, in his remarks on Cornwall in his new English edition of William Camden's *Britannia*, noted: 'The old Cornish is almost quite driven out of the Country, being spoken only by the vulgar in two or three Parishes at the Lands-end; and they too understand the English.'[16] In *Nebbaz Gerriau dro tho Carnoack* (*c.*1700), Nicholas Boson expanded on this,[17] but Edward Lhuyd, who spent four months in Cornwall in 1701, provided the most detailed account of the linguistic situation. Cornish was the community language in the parishes of St Just, St Paul, Sennen, St Levan, Madron, Sancreed, Morvah, Towednack, St Ives, Lelant, Ludgvan, Gulval, and along the coast from Land's End to St Keverne near the Lizard.[18] Everyone,

---

[14] Richard Carew, *The Survey of Cornwall* (London, 1602), f. 56r.

[15] Wakelin, *Language and History in Cornwall*, pp. 90–1; John Norden, *Speculi Britanniae Pars. A Topographical and Historical Description of Cornwall* (repr. Newcastle upon Tyne, 1966), p. 21.

[16] Wakelin, *Language and History in Cornwall*, p. 92. Edward Lhuyd was responsible for the additional notes.

[17] See O. J. Padel (ed.), *The Cornish Writings of the Boson Family* (Redruth, 1975), pp. 24–37.

[18] Edward Lhuyd, *Archaeologia Britannica* (Oxford, 1707), p. 253. See also Derek R. Williams, *Prying into every hole and corner: Edward Lhuyd in Cornwall in 1700* (Redruth, 1993), esp. pp. 11–23.

however, could speak English and some were ignorant of Cornish. It appears that villages such as St Buryan and Mousehole in south-west Cornwall were the last home of Cornish. It is fruitless to search out the very last speaker, but individuals like Dolly Pentreath (a native speaker who died in 1777), William Bodinar (who had learned the language as a child and died in 1789) and a few others were the last to use Cornish as a natural medium of conversation. Notwithstanding a great deal of antiquarian activity at the end of the seventeenth century, which was valuable as a means of recording Cornish and of creativity in the language, the gentry who were involved in these pursuits were well aware that they were dealing with the dying language of the lower sorts. William Bodinar's exemplary letter of 1776 is the last piece of written Late Cornish: in his English version, he claimed: 'There is not more than four or five in our town can talk Cornish now, old people four score years old. Cornish is all forgot with young people.'[19]

In spite of its impressionistic nature, the evidence which these surveys present is revealing and there is no mistaking the picture which they provide. By around 1600 Cornish was restricted to the two hundreds west of Truro and its geographical area was to shrink gradually thereafter to the coastal settlements. It declined rapidly over the century as monoglot speakers virtually disappeared and bilingualism became the norm. There was no linguistic persecution: none was needed since so many factors were leading to the extinction of Cornish. Many of these factors were noted by seventeenth-century observers. Norden remarked that Cornish was the language of the home, but he observed also that it was used between 'Master and Servantes', a suggestion, perhaps, that it was the servants who used Cornish most commonly. The majority of the gentry had long since rejected the language as their social medium, as is suggested by the representation made by the leading parishioners of St Buryan in 1336, thirteen of whom used English and French, the rest Cornish;[20] the context and nature of other records relating to the use of Cornish point to a language which was used mainly by workers and cottagers. Gibson referred to it as the 'vulgar' tongue and Lhuyd observed that apart from the patriotic scholars who assisted him, few of the gentry could speak the language. By and large, native speakers were illiterate in Cornish. In 1662 John Ray claimed that only one person could write Cornish, while Gibson stated: "Tis a good while since, that only two men could write it, and one of them no Scholar or Grammarian, and then blind with age.'[21]

---

[19] P. A. S. Pool and O. J. Padel, 'William Bodinar's Letter, 1776', *Journal of the Royal Institution of Cornwall*, VII, 3 (1975–6), 234.
[20] Wakelin, *Language and History in Cornwall*, p. 88.
[21] Quoted in Wakelin, *Language and History in Cornwall*, p. 92.

Granted the restricted, anecdotal nature of the evidence, it nevertheless adds weight to the significance of the lack of Cornish literature and that little was rescued by antiquarian scholars at the turn of the seventeenth century. Native speakers failed to transmit the language to their children. John Ray remarked that few children spoke Cornish and Nicholas Boson's statement, 'We find the young Men to speak it less and less, and worse & worse',[22] points to the same conclusion. All these are familiar signs to modern sociolinguists and confirm that social factors, rather than legislation and persecution, led to the death of Cornish. The decline cannot be accurately mapped and traced in statistical terms but, according to estimates produced by Ken George,[23] 61 per cent of the population spoke Cornish in 1400, 54 per cent in 1450, 48 per cent in 1500, 40 per cent in 1550, 26 per cent in 1600, 15 per cent in 1650, 5 per cent in 1700; the figures cease to be statistically computable by 1750.

The Protestant Reformation may have been the catalyst which hastened the process of decline, but in his *Observations on an Ancient Manuscript entitled Passio Christi, written in the Cornish Language* (1777, but written in 1680), William Scawen ventured sixteen reasons for the decline of Cornish. He identified key issues.[24] He complained that the gentry gave the language no support and that this had led to common folk aping them lest they might be scorned for using Cornish. He saw that such people had lost their chief source of entertainment in Cornish when the plays came to an end after 1600 and that there existed virtually no religious or secular literature nor any standard literary tradition. The oral tradition also appears to have become much weaker by this time. In his own day Scawen saw an increasing number of immigrants, craftsmen and merchants who did not learn Cornish, 'so they were more apt and ready to let loose their own tongues to be commixed with ours, and such for the novelty sake thereof, people were more ready to receive, than to communicate ours to any improvement to them'. There is no doubt that the process of absorbing Cornwall into the government and administration of England was completed in the reign of the Tudors and that this, in turn, led to the expansion of industry and commerce and improved facilities for travel by land and sea. The 'new religion' was a powerful Anglicizing influence which had in addition an indirect effect on the status of Cornish. There had been much traffic between Cornwall and Brittany since the fifth and

---

[22] Quoted in Padel, *The Cornish Writings of the Boson Family*, p. 24.
[23] This summarizes a more extensive discussion: see Ken George, 'Cornish' in Ball, *The Celtic Languages*, pp. 410–15.
[24] For Scawen's evidence and discussion, see Wakelin, *Language and History in Cornwall*, pp. 91–2, Ellis, *The Cornish Language and its Literature*, pp. 82–5, Pool, *The Death of Cornish*, pp. 14–16.

sixth centuries – a form of British had been taken to Armorica, 'Little Britain', from south-west Britain – and Cornish ports and harbours had long been familiar with Breton fishermen and merchants who were accepted as cousins who spoke a similar language. The link was severed following the Reformation and it is interesting that Scawen notes this as one of the main causes for the decline of Cornish: 'The great loss of Armorica, near unto us, by friendship, by cognation, by interest, by correspondence . . . We can understand words of one another, but have not the benefit of conferences with one another in our ancient tongue.'[25] Increasingly Cornish became an isolated, unique language used by an ever declining group who felt more and more uncertain of its value and status. As the despised medium of an illiterate sub-group, a language lacking both learning and literature, and one which had no practical purpose, its end was inevitable. Scawen's term for this was 'general stupidity', the lack of faith of the Cornish in their language and their lack of regard for it. The factors which created this situation are not unique to Cornish. In broad terms, it completed its course at a time when the other Celtic languages of Britain were beginning to face similar pressures.

Welsh and Cornish represent two old dialects of British, or *p* Celtic: similarly, Irish on the one hand, and Scottish Gaelic and Manx on the other, are sister languages descended from *q* Celtic, the Goidelic of Ireland. A major difference, however, in the development of the two branches is that the separation into individual languages was comparatively late in the case of Goidelic.[26] An Irish kingdom was established towards the end of the fifth century AD in Argyll (*Airer Gáidel*, 'the coast of the Gael') by settlers from Dál Ríada (Antrim) in north-east Ireland. From these beginnings Scotland to the north of the rivers Clyde and Forth was conquered and a unified Irish kingdom was set up by the end of the ninth century. Subsequently Irish spread southwards, displacing British and English languages in those areas, at least as the speech of the highest level of society. Until the thirteenth century the language of Ireland and most of Scotland was one, although with some dialect variations: the gap between Scottish Gaelic and Manx became apparent by the fifteenth century. But the literary language of Ireland and Scotland (there is no Manx literature extant before the seventeenth century), used as the medium of classical poetry and of prose, continued up to the seventeenth and eighteenth centuries in what remained a single culture province. The basic cultural unity of these lands was expressed at a deeper level by a

---

[25] [William] Scawen, *Observations on An Ancient manuscript, entitled, PASSIO CHRISTI, Written in the Cornish Language, and now preserved in the Bodleian Library. With an account of The Language, Manners, and Customs of the People of Cornwall* ([London], 1777), p. 14.

[26] Kenneth Jackson, 'Common Gaelic', *PBA*, XXXVII (1951), 74, 92–3.

shared tradition of aristocratic patronage of native learning in all its various aspects. The same poets visited the leading families and they shared common standards, traditions and usages. The leading families intermarried and gave support to this common Irish culture. In both countries one of the major causes of the change in the status of native culture, and of the decline in the fortunes and form of the language which was its medium, was the loss of the involvement of the gentry as they were robbed of power in the wake of political and social upheaval.

Irish[27]

The story of Irish lies at the opposite end of the spectrum from Cornish. For most of the historical period from the ninth century onwards, Cornish was a language under siege, a minority language in a bilingual situation, lacking both the support of the gentry and any official status. It died from apathy, not oppression. Irish, however, has been the language of the overwhelming majority of the population for most of its history, the main language of the community and government. But although the catastrophic decline occurred in the nineteenth century, planned antagonistic pressures had been apparent since the seventeenth century and were to become increasingly evident.

Irish had been in competition with other languages in Ireland for centuries. The Norse incursions which began towards the end of the eighth century (the earliest record is 795) were initially raiding expeditions, but gradually they became permanent settlements along the coast,[28] especially in the south where the most important colonies – Dublin, Waterford, Wexford, Limerick – became leading towns and trading centres. But although such Norse raids and settlements were important as part of the process of Irish history and especially as a literary theme, in the context of the whole of Ireland their influence was restricted. There was, furthermore, a measure of intermingling and intermarriage, with the result that the Norse kingdoms were gradually losing their power even before the battle of Clontarf in 1014 which sealed the supremacy of the Gael in Ireland. The Norsemen influenced the shape of native society, but

---

[27] In addition to the books noted in n. 1, see esp. Brian Ó Cuív, *Irish Dialects and Irish-speaking Districts* (Dublin, 1951); Daniel Corkery, *The Fortunes of the Irish Language* (Dublin, 1954); Seán de Fréine, *The Great Silence* (Dublin, 1965); Brian Ó Cuív (ed.), *A View of the Irish Language* (Dublin, 1969); ibid., 'The Irish Language in the Early Modern Period' in T. W. Moody, F. X. Martin, F. J. Byrne (eds.), *A New History of Ireland, III, Early Modern Ireland 1534–1691* (Oxford, 1976), pp. 509–45; Reg Hindley, *The Death of the Irish Language* (London, 1990).

[28] D. Simon Evans, *Historia Gruffudd vab Kenan* (Caerdydd, 1977), p. lxx; Jackson, 'The Celtic Languages during the Viking period', p. 4.

ultimately they became Hibernicized and, apart from the borrowings from the language into Irish, they were not to be a direct threat to Irish society.

That threat came in 1169 with the advent of the Anglo-Normans as a new element in Irish politics. By 1172, following the incursions first of Richard FitzGilbert de Clare, 'Strongbow', and then of Henry II, the Normans, clearly new permanent lords and not mere raiders, were masters of the east and south-east of the country. Their grip tightened over the following century or so as the followers of Henry II and John received grants of lordship and lands which were further strengthened as they raised their castles and established towns across Ireland; by around 1250 some two-thirds of the country was under their authority. Save for the legal context, English had replaced French and Anglo-Norman as the language of the conquerors and their families, and it appeared that English would soon become the predominant language.

This was not to be. The thirteenth and fourteenth centuries saw such a remarkable resurgence of Irish language and culture that native life re-established itself almost completely. The Anglo-Norman (or better, perhaps, Anglo-Irish) institutions may not indeed have had an all-pervasive influence. The use of English would have been restricted to castles and towns, leaving the rural hinterland, and thus the bulk of the population, Irish-speaking. Some of the 'new' families intermarried with the Irish aristocratic families and many became 'Irish' both in language and culture. They retained their social and political power, but in cultural terms many were absorbed into native society to such an extent that they lost their language and became patrons of, and even participants in, Irish culture. To foreign eyes in England they could not be differentiated from native gentry, and in Ireland a new term – 'Old English families' – had to be coined to define them. English was the community language of a layer of society within a narrow strip of land of some sixty by thirty miles in the east. There were many attempts in the thirteenth and fourteenth centuries to impose English in the Pale and to prevent integration, but it is clear that the occasional legislation was ineffective and that Irish had regained its position in the country and even to some extent in the towns where there remained a significant bilingual element. It is worth quoting once more the well-known description of the position of Irish by Edmund Curtis:

> In 1250 it was only one of the several languages of the country; by 1500 it was almost without a rival in literary cultivation, in the extent over which it was spoken, in the attraction it had even for the colonists. It had swallowed up French, and seemed about to make a final conquest of English.[29]

[29] Edmund Curtis, 'The spoken languages of medieval Ireland', *Studies*, VIII (1919), 250; cf. Tomás Ó Fiaich, 'The language and political history' in Ó Cuív, *A View of the Irish Language*, p. 103, and Corkery, *The Fortunes of the Irish Language*, p. 65.

An idea of the extent of the 'Irelandization' (the term used in official records is that the Pale was being 'Irelandized') can be gained from a survey carried out in 1515 in an attempt to improve the situation. The ninety chief families were listed, sixty of whom were Irish leaders who were not subject to the king of England and thirty 'of thEnglyshe noble folke, that folowyth the same Iryshe ordre'. In thirteen counties the authority of the king was not recognized and 'All thEnglyshe folke of the said countyes ben of Iryshe habyt, of Iryshe langage, and of Iryshe condytions, except the cyties and the wallyd tounes'. The only counties where English law prevailed were half of counties Uryell, Meath, Dublin, Kildare and Wexford, and even in these eastern parts the majority of common folk were 'of Iryshe byrthe, of Iryshe habyte, and of Iryshe langage'.[30] Throughout the reign of Henry VIII many decrees and statutes were passed which indicate a new determination to eliminate Irish language and culture as part of an effective policy to establish English law and to confirm the king's authority. The king gained a significant opportunity to extend his authority with the fall of the house of Kildare and the execution of its chiefs in 1537. He was proclaimed king of Ireland by the Dublin parliament in 1541, but this was not followed by a fierce policy of extermination but rather by the legal ploy of 'surrender and re-grant', which allowed the Irish and Old English lords to continue to hold their lands as a grant, and thus by legal right, from the king. At the same time the policy declared that the Crown of Ireland was 'united, annexed, and knit for ever to the Imperial crown of the realm of England'. The authority of the Crown increasingly extended *de jure* and *de facto* over Ireland – by the displacement of native lords, or by contracts with them, and by means of direct government by deputies and lieutenants. Lords were encouraged to send their sons to court to be instructed and nurtured, but more specific was the legislation against any expression of Irish culture in order that English and its 'civility' might be enthroned as the language and usage of the new union. In the words of Curtis: 'Ireland was to be made if possible a second England through the compleasant bishops and nobility, and no provision was made for the recognition of Irish and Gaelic tradition.'[31]

All was not lost, however. Since the nature of Irish (and Celtic) lordship was fundamentally different from the Tudor concept of kingship, loyalties could not be lightly changed and traditional law could not be replaced overnight by a new system. The Gaelic rebellions came to a peak in the

---

[30] Ó Cuív, *Irish Dialects and Irish-speaking Districts*, pp. 10–11; cf. Corkery, *The Fortunes of the Irish Language*, pp. 64–5.

[31] Edmund Curtis, *A History of Ireland* (6th ed., London, 1950), p. 170.

battle of Kinsale in December 1601 when the armies of O'Neill and O'Donnell were defeated by Elizabeth's lieutenants, Sir George Carew and Lord Mountjoy. The outcome can rightly be regarded as fateful, for had O'Neill and O'Donnell won the day the trend towards English would have been halted and Irish would have continued as the language of government and society for a further period. The consequence of the victory of Carew and Mountjoy was to ensure that Ireland would be united under the English Crown and its administrative and linguistic systems, but more directly influential on the future shape of the vernacular culture was the 'flight of the earls' in 1607. The loss of Irish leaders and the increasing number who followed them heralded the beginning of the end of the social structures which had always supported native culture. The period between 1200 and 1650 is one of linguistic resurgence, the period of Classical Irish, the language of court poetry, its praise and elegy of noble families. As in the case of the Wales of the princes, bardic learning safeguarded the standard literary language which was used throughout Ireland and Gaelic Scotland. Fourteenth-century Wales succeeded in adapting the tradition of literary patronage and was able to transmit it to a new generation of ambitious and astute leaders who remained Welsh, however eager they may have been for office and status under the Crown. They needed the praise of the poets as much as the poets needed their patronage. Ireland suffered a traumatic transition in the seventeenth century and gradual (even intentional) transfer was not possible, partly because the language and its culture had become elements in, or at least symbols of, militant and political upheaval.

The seventeenth century was a century of rebellion and strife. The 'flight of the earls' was followed by plantation policies which established new immigrants in Ulster, Antrim and Down, and subsequently by the confiscation policies of 1653 which cleared Leinster and Munster to pay Cromwell's war debts, and which strengthened the English presence in the towns and cities. Only in Clare and Connaught, where many were replanted, were Irish gentry able to hold land. At the beginning of the century 90 per cent of Ireland was held by Catholics; the efficiency of the planting of Ulster reduced the figure to 59 per cent, and by 1685 to 22 per cent. The years between 1641 and 1650 saw many uprisings and rebellions, but none was more far-reaching in its consequences than the attempt by James II to regain his Crown in 1689. His Catholic armies were defeated by William of Orange at the battle of the Boyne in 1690, and at Aughrim in 1691, and when the Treaty of Limerick was signed in 1691 existing anti-Irish policies intensified. A million acres were confiscated, thereby reducing Catholic landholding to 14 per cent, and the anti-Catholic Penal Laws were strictly enforced. When they began to be relaxed in the 1770s only 5 per cent of the land was held by Catholics.[32] If the battles of the seventeenth century were for the land of Ireland, they were nevertheless symbolic of loyalty to different languages, cultures and religious convictions, with the result that society became divided into two unequal camps, the one a Protestant English governing, landowning and urban sector, the other rural, Catholic and Irish. The bards were fully aware of the changes and lamented the passing of the old pattern. Just as the 'flight of the earls' had robbed the community of its Irish leaders at the beginning of the century so, too, in the wake of William's victories at Limerick and the Boyne, did many thousands of gentry families and soldiers, 'the wild geese', flock to the Continent to seek better fortune, thereby dealing the final blow to a cohesive native society in which Irish was an integral element. By the beginning of the eighteenth century the old aristocracy had yielded its place to a new English class.

The consequences of planting and the loss of the gentry on the fortunes of the Irish language were not immediately apparent: the bulk of the Irish-speaking population remained in their old areas. What was lost with the destruction of the social framework was the concept of a common linguistic standard and, in time, familiarity with that register. The dialects began to become more prominent in literature,[33] as was to be expected in a society where the native culture was part of 'the hidden Ireland',[34] lacking both status and formal education. True, some bardic schools (and 'courts') and hedge schools continued, but it was inevitable that the literary tradition should weaken and that new forms of writing and styles should begin to appear. Literary activity would be more local than national henceforth, and common folk under the tutelage of priest and schoolmaster found solace in composing hopeful poems about the return of the king and the restoration of the old order.[35]

A century earlier Protestantism and the literature of the Counter-Reformation might have contributed to the continuation of the literary language. A number of Catholic books were published on the Continent in the first half of the seventeenth century – historical works as well as books of devotion and doctrine. Irish was sufficiently strong at the beginning of the century for Elizabeth I to appoint priests to parishes on the grounds of their ability to speak the language, and a press and type

---

[32] Ruth Dudley Edwards, *An Atlas of Irish History* (London, 1973), pp. 165–6.
[33] Ó Cuív, *Irish Dialects and Irish-speaking Districts*, p. 44.
[34] See, in general, Daniel Corkery, *The Hidden Ireland: A Study of Gaelic Munster in the Eighteenth Century* (Dublin, 1924, repr. 1967); P. J. Dowling, *The Hedge Schools of Ireland* (Dublin, [1935]).
[35] For education and literature in this period, see J. E. Caerwyn Williams and Patrick K. Ford, *The Irish Literary Tradition* (Cardiff, Belmont, 1992), chapter 5.

were set up to print the Bible which she had commanded should be translated. The New Testament appeared in 1603 and the Book of Common Prayer in 1608, but although the value of the language for the reformers continued to be advocated,[36] progress was painfully slow and the Old Testament was not published until 1685 and the complete Bible until 1690.[37] Unlike Wales, the efforts of the reformers met with little success. Official support for the language was lukewarm, and the use of Irish and the translations were insufficient to undermine the perception of Irish/Catholic – English/Protestant, which became ever more apparent. When the Catholic mission was re-established from the Continent in the eighteenth century, its medium was English.

Anti-Irish legislation was not required by the end of the seventeenth century. There was no sudden change following the Treaty of Limerick and 'the flight of the wild geese'; nor was there any single event which would explain the linguistic catastrophe of the nineteenth century. Yet it is clear that a number of factors contributing to the decline were in place by 1700. Outside Leinster and east Ulster, Irish remained the predominant language for the majority, but it became apparent that the policies of plantation, confiscation and clearing had proved more effective than the anti-language laws, since these policies affected the pattern of society and its cultural and linguistic unity. It is not possible to detail the decline statistically, but the plantations and the imposed school system established an English colony in every part of the country. English was given high status and authority, features which would impact upon the language of tenant and landowner and which would widen even further the divide between servants and masters. The pressure on Irish landowners to use English increased, as it did upon merchants and craftsmen, and bilingualism spread gradually from the towns in the east to the rest of the country.

The pace of bilingualism seems to have quickened in the second half of the eighteenth century. The relaxation of the Penal Laws in the 1770s opened new doors of opportunity for Catholics and, as the country began to enjoy a period of calm and greater prosperity, improved conditions for transport and commerce offered a better market for labour and craft. For many, Irish became the badge of poverty and illiteracy, the language of those who had not succeeded in the new contemporary world. Some two-thirds of the population spoke Irish in 1731; an estimated 2,400,000 – 800,000 monoglots, 1,600,000 bilinguals, i.e. around half the

---

[36] V. E. Durkacz, *The Decline of the Celtic Languages* (Edinburgh, 1983), pp. 31–3.

[37] For an account of the translations of the Bible, see J. E. Caerwyn Williams, 'Y Beibl yn yr Ieithoedd Celtaidd' in Owen E. Evans (ed.), *Gwarchod y Gair: Cyfrol Goffa Y Parchedig Griffith Thomas Roberts* (Dinbych, 1993), pp. 98–122; and Durkacz, *The Decline of the Celtic Languages*, passim.

population – spoke Irish in 1799. By 1800 it appears that Irish monolingualism was rare in the east and that parents in Leinster and Ulster were not transmitting the language to their children; the hedge schools, whose initial aim had been to protect Irish culture, were already teaching English.[38] In 1810 the Board of Education Commissioners could claim that the parish schools which had been established 'for . . . the introduction and diffusion of the English Language in Ireland' had achieved their goal. In the words of Reg Hindley:

> The Union of 1800 was probably irrelevant to language, for it made no difference to the role of English in the state, but it nevertheless broadly coincided in date with the time when the majority decided that collectively it needed English for its own utilitarian purposes.[39]

The new century would see the transformation of the linguistic situation partly as a consequence of a coercive education system and also of new national politics which generally were English-medium, but mainly in the wake of disastrous periods of famine and emigration which almost bled Irish society to death.

Scottish Gaelic[40]

Common Gaelic was brought from Ireland to Scotland with the forming of the Irish kingdom of Dál Ríada in Argyll towards the end of the fifth century AD. These Irish (*Scotti*) spread to the north and north-west from Kintyre along the coast to the isles and across the highlands to the east. The native Picts were overcome and drawn into the sovereignty of the *Scotti* not only by military power but also through dynastic intermarriage under Kenneth MacAlpin, with the result that the whole country north of the Clyde and Forth was a Gaelic kingdom, at least among the ruling classes, by 844. (The language of the immigrants was Irish, but to avoid confusion the Irish of Scotland is termed Gaelic in this chapter.) The Scots continued to expand. They had taken Edinburgh by the mid-tenth century and had won extensive lands from the Angles of Lothian by 973. The Britons of Strathclyde in the south-west succeeded in retaining their

---

[38] Maureen Wall, 'The decline of the Irish language' in Ó Cuív, *A View of the Irish Language,* p. 82.
[39] Hindley, *The Death of the Irish Language,* p. 12.
[40] In addition to the books noted in n.1, see esp. Durkacz, *The Decline of the Celtic Languages*; Charles W. J. Withers, *Gaelic in Scotland 1698–1981: The Geographical History of a Language* (Edinburgh, 1984); Kenneth MacKinnon, *The Lion's Tongue: the story of the original and continuing language of the Scottish people* (Inbhirnis, 1974).

lands in an ebb and flow of supremacy up to the beginning of the eleventh century. By defeating the Angles of Lothian in the battle of Carham in 1018, Malcolm II established a Gaelic kingdom as far as the Solway and Tweed. The king of Strathclyde died in the same year, to be followed by Malcolm's grandson Duncan, whose claim to the throne derived from the dynastic marriage of the two royal lines. When Duncan succeeded to the throne of Scotland in 1034, the bounds of his kingdom were extended even further.

The Norsemen were another group of settlers in Scotland. There had been many local incursions since the first raids in western Britain and eastern Ireland in the eighth and ninth centuries, but over the centuries the Norse had become a strong permanent presence in their settlements in north-east Scotland – Caithness, Sutherland – and in the northern and western isles. Orkney and Shetland were to remain Scandinavian colonies until the fifteenth century and Gaelic was not reintroduced there, but the western isles were regained for Gaelic, as also was the mixed colony in the south, Gall-Ghoídhil, which gave its name to Galloway. With these exceptions, Gaelic was the predominant language from the southern border to the north by the eleventh century, and also the language of court and government, learning and culture. The other, more localized, languages were not wholly displaced and English and Cumbrian were to persist, but it is reasonable to assume that Gaelic was the lingua franca throughout the kingdom.

Duncan's stormy reign came to an end in 1040 when Macbeth seized power. In turn, he was killed by Duncan's son, Malcolm III, in 1057 and the descendants of Kenneth MacAlpin regained the throne of Scotland. Malcolm had been brought up and educated in exile in England. In 1069 he married Margaret, who had fled to Scotland with her brother Edgar Atheling of Wessex, whose ambitions had been thwarted by the Norman conquest of 1066. The English-educated Malcolm, who had won his Crown with the aid of troops from Northumbria, probably shared his wife's unsympathetic response to the unfamiliar style and fashion of the Scottish court, which must have appeared uncivil and boorish to both. Under the direction of the queen, ecclesiastic structures were reformed and a new, more 'civilized' Anglo-Norman culture introduced into the court which migrated south to Lothian. In both geographical and conceptual terms, the centre of government and cultural life approached English life, although the actual numbers of Anglo-Normans who held office in church and court may have been small. The impact of the changed attitudes was not immediately obvious, but although there was some resistance to them after Malcolm's death in 1093, foreign influences were to increase significantly during the reign of his son David between

1124 and 1153. He, too, had been raised and educated in England and through his marriage he had a status in the English baronage. He created a court-centred administrative and social system and through his grants of lands he established a quasi-feudal order and a number of new bishoprics in the south. A new Anglo-Norman, French-speaking aristocracy came into being which intermarried with the native leadership, thereby affecting the latter's mores and fashions. As cross-border trade developed, a number of towns were given burgh status and privileges; by the time of David's death the 'Celtic' social order had been replaced in the south by Anglo-Norman institutions and models.

These changes in attitude and in structures were to be a turning point not only in the history of Gaelic but in the concept of Scotland, which in turn became a powerful factor in anti-Gaelic prejudices. Within two or three generations at the turn of the eleventh century, the door was opened wide for Anglo-Norman influences to flow into social and ecclesiastical structures and the number of immigrants, following changes in commercial and urban centres, increased to such an extent that the culture of southern Scotland changed its character. The concept of loyalty to chieftain and kin disappeared and the native aristocracy was absorbed into the new. Native learning lost its status when faced with the strength of new literary fashions and Gaelic was displaced as the language of high status at court and among the gentry by French and then by English. Gaelic did not die overnight — in some areas the evidence suggests that it survived for long periods — but the decline which is a consequence of restricting language to lower social groups, or to those with least influence, had begun. One of the remarkable features of Scottish cultural history is how thoroughly and how swiftly an awareness of Gaelic culture disappeared in the lowlands.

At the same time other political changes occurred which reinforced the position of Gaelic and also intensified the differences between the two cultures which were becoming even clearer in the thirteenth century. The chiefs in the Highlands had a long history of rebellion against the Scottish kings and the lords of the Isles were accustomed to claiming independence of the Crown and loyalty to the king of Norway. Not until the thirteenth century, when Scotland and England enjoyed a period of relative peace, did the Scottish kings have an opportunity to face these continuous threats. In 1263 Hakon of Norway was defeated by Alexander III and, according to the terms of a treaty agreed with his successor Magnus, Orkney and Shetland were ceded to Norway while the lordship of the Isles — the Hebrides, the Isle of Man, and the north-west area of the mainland — was transferred to the Scottish Crown, a powerful lordship which remained in effect an independent kingdom until 1493. The regaelicization of this wide area proved an important and far-reaching reinforcement of Gaelic culture since it was given political force, both locally and internationally, and also a high social status. In the isles and the highlands a unified and comprehensive culture in which all levels of society shared was safeguarded, and links with the learned orders and bardic system in Ireland ensured the continuance of Classical Gaelic as the formal literary language. The lordship of the Isles, a Gaelic state, was crucial for the safeguarding of Gaelic, but in the context of Scotland as a whole it brought about even greater polarization of its cultures. 'Inglis', the language to the south of the Clyde and Forth and from Lothian to the north-east and along the coast, gradually spread and although it is difficult to draw a precise language boundary, it appears to have displaced Gaelic in Dunkeld, much of Fife, Kinross and Clackmannan by around 1350, and only in a few parishes in south Perth and in Angus was Gaelic spoken.[41] Two Scotlands had come about, both of which claimed their languages as emblems of national identity. In the Lowlands (no longer simply a geographical term) and along the north-east coast, Inglis triumphed; in the Highlands and Islands Gaelic held its ground. Culturally, however, the dichotomy was more complex. The difference could be expressed in geographical terms by regarding the eastern edge of the Grampians as the boundary of the Highlands; thus the dichotomy of language could be stated as Highlands/Lowlands, Gaelic/Inglis. But Inglis – or Scots, Scottish – was now the language of government, Crown, administration, civility and style and, as a national language, it was driving Gaelic to the margins of national life. Negative attitudes towards Gaelic developed, not simply as a subordinate language, but as a barbaric one. John Fordun in the 1380s was the first to give a qualitative value to the dichotomy (although Gaelic had not yet lost its status as the 'Scottish' tongue):

> The people of the coast are of domestic and civilised habits, trusty, patient, and urbane, decent in their attire, affable, and peaceful, devout in Divine worship . . . the Highlanders and people of the Islands, on the other hand, are a savage and untamed nation, rude and independent, given to rapine, ease-loving, of a docile and warm disposition, comely in person, but unsightly in dress, hostile to the English people and language, and owing to diversity of speech, even to their own nation, and exceedingly cruel.[42]

It was inevitable that attitudes such as these would have an effect on the status of Gaelic in its own country, for Fordun's words are a characteristic

---

[41] Withers, *Gaelic in Scotland*, p. 25.
[42] Quoted in Withers, *Gaelic in Scotland*, p. 22: cf. Price, *The Celtic Connection*, p. 109.

expression of a foreign, imperialistic view of native culture. Such words have been spoken and written over the centuries, from the comments of Gerald of Wales to those of the travellers and visitors of the Victorian age and later. This is the attitude of a 'superior' culture towards 'the barbarian across the border', but with the important difference that Fordun was observing a section of the population of his own country with which he failed, or chose not, to identify himself. Gaelic ceased to be a national language and its continuing existence was deemed to be a threat to the governing sector in the south. It is not without significance that the fashion of referring to Gaelic as 'Yrish', 'Ersch', and then 'Irish', persisted to modern times.

It was only to be expected that such antagonistic views of the Highlands would be reinforced when a Protestant ecclesiastical order was established in 1560. In Scotland, as elsewhere in Britain, Protestantism demanded the imposition of one religion, which expressed a single system of values in the same language and culture. The statutes of 1561 and 1562 established an education system with primary schools in every parish, grammar schools in the towns, and universities. These were not specifically anti-Gaelic, nor did they have much effect on the language, but the only 'cultural' institution common to both parts of the country was being threatened. The Lowlands turned to Protestantism, but while the Highlands retained their Catholicism, their 'barbaric' culture and religion, mirroring the situation in Ireland, remained a two-edged threat to the political order. Over the following three centuries these were constant themes expressed in legislation relating to the Highlands – the need to save and to civilize the inhabitants, i.e. to ensure their Anglicization. Anti-Gaelic attitudes hardened with the union of the two Crowns, and the accession of James VI to the English throne in 1603 saw proscriptive legislation towards Highland culture as he sought policies which would strengthen the central authority of the Crown in London and remove the dangers which he perceived on the borders of his kingdoms. He had already given an indication of his attitude in his book of advice to his son Henry, *Basilikon Doron*, in 1598–9. He saw that the Isles were the Gaelic stronghold and that a policy of plantations was the most effective way of undermining it.[43] His opportunity came with his accession to the throne, at a time when the battle of Kinsale (1601) and the 'flight of the earls' (1607) had not only affected the strength of Gaelic culture in Ireland but had also destroyed the unified world-view which had linked the eastern and western parts of the Irish culture region. Although it was true that the two languages, Irish and Gaelic, had developed separately since the

---

[43] MacKinnon, *The Lion's Tongue*, p. 33.

thirteenth century, the classical language remained and Gaelic speakers were conscious of a culture broader than their own territory and which derived its strength from the west. Henceforth, culturally as well as in the fields of economics and religion, the Gaidhealtachd was to be drawn towards the centre of Scottish power and authority in the Lowlands, thereby ensuring that the seventeenth century would be a crucial period in the history of the language.

For the first time specifically anti-Gaelic legislation appeared in church and state. Previous measures had ignored the existence of the language and little effort had been made to prepare religious books in Gaelic: a translation of Knox's *Book of Common Order* had been published in 1567, but no other title appeared until the catechism in 1631, followed by the psalms produced by the Synod of Argyll in 1659 and the Psalter in 1684. James VI governed from London through his directives to the Privy Council in Edinburgh; but this was not effective in the Highlands where chiefs continued to ignore the authority of the king and where each sought to gain his own position of power in the disorder which followed the abolition of the Lordship of the Isles. James was able to use the struggle for power for his own ends by setting chief against chief. In 1608 he took a more decisive step to impose his own authority. He invited twelve chiefs from the Highlands and Isles to one of his ships, ostensibly to hear a sermon, and proceeded to imprison them for a year, releasing them in 1609 only when they signed the Statutes of Icolmkill (Iona) as a guarantee of their future loyalty. Some of the statutes were more symbolic than real, e.g. the reduction in the number of followers ('war bands') and restrictions on the bearing of arms, but others were of deeper significance. The reception of bards and other channels of the praise tradition was proscribed, as was begging and traditional hospitality. Poets and members of the learned orders became *de facto* beggars and wanderers, two groups proscribed by the statutes, and a blow was struck at the very heart of the cultural life of aristocratic society, and thus the status of the language, by putting an end to two essential elements in the oral culture – generous patronage and the basis of the tradition of praise. The sixth statute went to the roots of the policy when it was directed that all persons worth at least sixty head of cattle should send their eldest son or daughter to the Lowlands to learn to speak, read and write English:

> . . . it being undirstand that the ignorance and incivilitie of the saidis Iles hes daylie incressit be the negligence of guid educatioun and instructioun of the youth in the knowledge of God and good letters . . .[44]

[44] Withers, *Gaelic in Scotland*, p. 29; MacKinnon, *The Lion's Tongue*, pp. 34–6.

The need for ministers in Highland parishes was also emphasized. The terms of the statutes were strengthened in a Privy Council Act of 1616 which began as follows:

> Forsameikle as the Kingis Majestie having a speciall care and regaird that the trew religioun be advanceit and establisheit in all the pairtis of this kingdome, and that all his Majesties subjectis, especiallie the youth, be exercised and trayned up in civilitie, godliness, knawledge, and learning, that the vulgar Inglishe toung be universallie plantit, and the Irische language, whilk is one of the cheif and principall causes of the continewance of barbaritie and incivilitie amongis the inhabitantis of the Ilis and Heylandis, may be abolisheit and removeit.[45]

The attitude expressed by John Fordun at the end of the fourteenth century had developed into a concept which linked godliness, learning and civility with the English language. It followed, therefore, that the greatest need of the barbarians in the Highlands, as well as their fellow Gaels in Ireland in the same period, was for schools where they might learn to read and be instructed in the Christian religion. Education in the name of religion was to be the chief medium for the Anglicization of the Highlands, as the 1695 Act 'for rooting out the Irish language, and other pious uses' made clear.[46]

The seventeenth century witnessed a great deal of legislation designed to enforce the policies of setting up English schools in every parish, but its success was only partial in the Highlands. Nor does it appear that the Icolmkill education statutes were effectively enforced (as the continuing call for legislation suggests). Nevertheless, the effectiveness of the policies is not to be assessed by this direct result, but rather by the attitudes towards Gaelic and its culture which they engendered in the longer term and which took root among Highlanders themselves. English was regarded as the acceptable social language, a view which would guide future educational policies. Attitudes cannot be measured statistically, but it is not hard to believe that they prepared the ground for more direct influences.

There were some, like James Kirkwood, in the 1680s and 1690s who had drawn attention to the folly of attempting to teach religion in a language which was unintelligible to pupils and who had called for the use of Gaelic as a means of teaching them to read. Kirkwood and Robert Kirk sought to obtain a supply of Irish Bibles, reset in Roman type, for use in

---

[45] Withers, *Gaelic in Scotland*, p. 29; Macaulay, *The Celtic Languages*, p. 144.
[46] Withers, *Gaelic in Scotland*, p. 30.

the Highlands by 1690, but the plan failed for a number of reasons – shortage of ministers, the unfamiliarity of the language used, and the reluctance of the authorities to distribute the Bibles[47] – and the opportunity to create literate Gaelic speakers was missed. There was a danger that literacy would be equated with English. By the end of the century, however, the General Assembly of the Church of Scotland had become increasingly aware of the necessity of using Gaelic-speaking ministers and catechists in Highland parishes and the Act 'anent Planting of the Highlands' was passed in 1699, to be followed by other Acts which aimed to ensure the education and supply of Gaelic-speaking ministers. But the Church did not change its view that English was to be the language of parish schools, with the result that although it increased its efforts to provide a Gaelic ministry it insisted that English should be the medium of education.

The explanation for the apparent paradox is that Gaelic was seen as the language of missionary efforts, necessary in the short-term period of change before English became common. The introduction to the Welsh Bible of 1588 makes a similar point in order to justify the translation of the Scriptures. This view explains also the change in attitude in the schools of the Society in Scotland for Propagating Christian Knowledge (SSPCK), which was established in 1709 with the aim of making the inhabitants of the Highlands 'usefull to the Commonwealth' by instructing them in their duty to God, the king and the country, and 'rooting out their Irish language'.[48] Although the intention remained unchanged, as the work developed it became clear that English reading could not be taught without some explanation in Gaelic. Gradually, translation into Gaelic was allowed (1723), and in 1766 reading in both languages was accepted, although the prohibition on speaking Gaelic and its use as a medium of instruction or conversation in the schools was not lifted.[49] The Gaelic New Testament appeared in 1766, the Old Testament in 1801. Although these versions were in Classical Gaelic and not wholly intelligible (or in an unfamiliar register) to the majority of Gaelic speakers, they were, nevertheless, important means of nurturing Gaelic literacy and of encouraging writing and publishing in the language.[50] The influence of the schools could not be undone, but Gaelic was given a specific domain as the language of preaching and extempore prayer and as the medium of worship and devotion. The field and the literature produced were narrow,

---

[47] Ibid., pp. 43–5.
[48] Ibid., p. 122; Price, *The Languages of Britain*, p. 53.
[49] Withers, *Gaelic in Scotland*, pp. 127–8.
[50] See Williams, 'Y Beibl yn yr Ieithoedd Celtaidd'; Durkacz, *The Decline of the Celtic Languages*, pp. 61–8, 112–18.

but the existence of the Scriptures in Gaelic and the development of a literary corpus were a means of protecting and strengthening the spoken language and its literature. The bond between Gaelic and religion was so close that Gaelic services continued to be held in many areas when the language had disappeared from all other contexts and English had become the general medium.

The spirit of the Highland inhabitants together with their traditional lifestyle were destroyed in the wake of the 1745 rebellion. The external signs of the social order and the clan system disappeared. The clearances began in 1782 when large parts of the Highlands were depopulated to allow the introduction of a new agricultural system. The language lost its strongholds and many of its speakers were scattered to other parts of the country and overseas. Many factors had encouraged the decline of Gaelic since the beginning of the seventeenth century. The combination of practical politics and religious zeal was perhaps the most influential of these factors and in the longer term the schools were the most effective agents of Anglicization. Economic conditions – roads, markets, burghs, seasonal emigration – together with the attraction of the south and the British economy all undermined the position of Gaelic. Superficially, the south-eastern boundary of the Gaidhealtachd changed very little between 1698 and 1806: essentially it remained the geographical boundary of the Highlands. But it was steadily retreating westwards. In 1698 it ran to all intents and purposes from Nairn to Dumbarton along the edge of the Grampians; in 1745 it ran from Nairn to Dumbarton via Carron, Dunkeld and Crieff; in the 1790s Gaelic was in retreat in Speyside, Avonside, Deeside and Tay.[51] It was claimed that there were 230 Gaelic-speaking parishes at the beginning of the seventeenth century; the figure was 180 in 1690, and 162 by 1765.[52] More difficult to assess is the level of bilingualism and its effect on the density of the use of Gaelic in the Highlands. The south-eastern parishes were not so much a linguistic boundary as linguistically mixed areas, channels for further encroachment. Some knowledge of English was perhaps fairly common in the Highlands by the eighteenth century, but the process gained momentum after 1745 as the Highlands became less remote and were opened up to trade, tourism and all the influences from the south. But important as these political and economic factors are, the single overarching element in the history of Gaelic was that it had remained unacceptable to the governors of Scottish society since the fourteenth century. The schism in attitudes towards Irish

---

[51] Price, *The Languages of Britain*, p. 56; Durkacz, *The Decline of the Celtic Languages*, pp. 215–16; Withers, *Gaelic in Scotland*, maps 6–15 provide a valuable summary.
[52] See Withers, *Gaelic in Scotland*, chapter 4.

appeared far later in Ireland. In the seventeenth and eighteenth centuries Irish was a mark of separateness from English governors, but much of the history of Gaelic and its culture hinged on the effort to bring the Highlands into the mainstream of national life. It became a language of low esteem for those outside its own culture area. Moreover, the confidence of those who spoke Gaelic was undermined by an education system and by a church which at best offered it only lukewarm support. Many Highland gentry had already rejected Gaelic, and this impression is confirmed by contemporary observations that English services were held in some Gaelic parishes only when gentry were present or that Gaelic was spoken by the lower classes. But new pressures were placed upon Scottish culture in the second half of the eighteenth century as the gentry of both the Lowlands and Highlands were inexorably drawn into a British system and sought to adopt an English lifestyle. Scots was replaced by English as the socially acceptable language, a development which could not fail to affect the status of Gaelic.

Gaelic was a peripheral language, not simply in geographical terms but also in the consciousness of most of the population. It had lost its role as a national language, and for the majority it was, if not a barbaric tongue, at least the language of incivility. It was spoken by a lower class, conditioned by education to regard it as of no value except as the medium of religion. It is estimated that around half the population of Scotland spoke Gaelic around 1500; by 1700 the proportion had dropped to around 26 per cent and to 22 per cent by 1800, a decline which was to continue to around 8 per cent by 1900.[53]

Manx[54]

Common Irish was brought to the Isle of Man by the same expansion from Ireland which introduced the language to Scotland at around the same period. The original language of the island may have been a form of north British. The proximity of Man to mainland Scotland makes this likely and the possibility is given a measure of support by the admittedly uncertain evidence of an ogham inscription of around 500 AD which reveals British elements in personal names. Political links between Man and Gwynedd seem to have persisted over the centuries, since 'Merfyn

---

[53] Ibid., p. 253.
[54] In addition to the books noted in n. 1, see esp. R. L. Thomson, 'The study of Manx Gaelic', *PBA*, LV (1969), 177–210; J. J. Kneen, *A Grammar of the Manx Language* (Oxford, 1931); Reg Hindley, 'The decline of the Manx language: a study in linguistic geography', *Bradford Occasional Papers* (School of Modern Languages, University of Bradford), 6 (1984), 15–39.

Frych o dir Manaw' (Merfyn Frych from the land of Manaw) gained the kingship of Anglesey and then of Gwynedd in 825 and established the powerful line of Rhodri Mawr. It is possible that CRUX GVRIAT, an inscription of the ninth century from Port y Vullen, commemorates Gwriad, Merfyn's father.[55] But if the language of Man was a form of British and if Gwriad's ancestors were a British/Welsh family, it cannot be claimed that British institutions occupied a predominant or even leading position in the island since there is no evidence for British in the place-names or in the lexis of Manx. The evidence of ogham inscriptions, with the exception of the one already referred to, is that a Goidelic language was predominant from the fifth century onwards and Irish cultural influence is confirmed by church dedications, e.g. Columba, Brendan, Ninian, Patrick, Bridget. The Isle of Man formed part of the same cultural province which extended across the Irish Sea from Ireland to the Highlands and Islands.

Man was on the path of the same Norse raids which led to the establishing of Norse kingdoms and settlements in Ireland and the Isles. Man became subject to Norse rule in the ninth century and the kingdom of Man and the Isles achieved stability and power in the reign of Godred Crovan in 1079. After his death in 1095 some 150 years of confusion ensued as Man became a pawn in the struggle for power between England and Norway. As Norwegian power weakened and the role of Scotland became more significant, Alexander III, already referred to, succeeded in curbing the authority of the unruly lords of the Isles, and bringing them and Man under the jurisdiction of the Scottish Crown in 1266 when the Lordship of the Isles was created. Man continued to be a strategic element in Anglo-Scottish contention and the lordship of Man was finally granted by the English Crown to a succession of English gentry from 1334 until 1405, when it was granted to Sir John Stanley. The Stanleys (later to be the earls of Derby) and the dukes of Atholl were lords of Man until the lordship was sold to the English Crown in 1765.

During the hegemony of the Norsemen, trade developed on the island and towns were established. It can therefore be assumed that Norse and Manx coexisted throughout these centuries. Norse is a prominent element in both place and personal names and the Manx vocabulary has many words of Norse origin relating to trade and sailing, although bilingualism may have been restricted to these narrow areas since Gaelic was neither displaced nor fundamentally altered. Manx (which had developed over the period from the thirteenth to the fifteenth century, as seen above) was

---

[55] Bedwyr Lewis Jones, 'Gwriad's Heritage: links between Wales and the Isle of Man in the early Middle Ages', *THSC* (1990), 29–44.

the predominant language, perhaps reinforced from time to time by immigrants from Galloway; after 1266 there can be no doubt that Gaelic/Manx was the main language of the island. Had Man remained a Scottish province it might well have been drawn more closely into the orbit of the life and society of the Lowlands, given its proximity, and the links with Highland culture might have weakened. It is conceivable that it might have become an extension of the Lowlands and that the Anglicizing influences of the Scottish court might have overwhelmed the Manx Gaelic culture. Following the transfer of power to the English Crown and English lords in 1334, government was exercised by deputies and although these were Anglicizing factors, it is possible that their effect on the language and its culture was not as strong as might have been the case had Man remained Scottish. Be that as it may, the Isle of Man remained a part of Irish and Highland culture although politically separate from both.

There is no direct evidence for the fortunes of the language over these periods. Even if Manx was being used in civil and ecclesiastical administration, the records are in Latin and English; after 1334 it is probable that English was the language of government. More information becomes available in the seventeenth century as observers begin to make comments and to record their impressions in surveys and accounts of visits. James Challoner noted in *A Short Treatise of the Isle of Mann* (1656) that few spoke English, but the relative positions of Manx and English are better exemplified in John Speed's comment in *Theatre of the Empire of Great Britaine* (1611): 'The wealthier sort, and such as hold the fairest possessions do imitate the people of Lancashire, . . . howbeit the commoner sort of people, both in language and manners, come nighest unto the Irish.' The difference in the status of the two languages was apparent and it is not difficult to appreciate the significance of Edmund Gibson's remarks in his notes to Camden's *Britannia* (1695) – 'Their gentry are very courteous and affable, and are more willing to discourse with one in English than in their own language' – probably because that was their usual medium. Bilingualism was not uncommon, but it may have been restricted to buying and selling in English: 'Not only the gentry, but likewise such of the peasants as live in the towns, or frequent the town markets, do both understand and speak the English language.'[56]

John Phillips, bishop of Sodor and Man, translated the Book of Common Prayer into Manx around 1625, a sign that the language was a necessary medium in church services, but since his version was not published (until 1895) it is difficult to assess the use made of it. In spite of the attempts of Bishop Isaac Barlow (1663–71) to establish parish schools to

---

[56] Kneen, *A Grammar of the Manx Language*, p. 7; cf. Price, *The Languages of Britain*, p. 73.

teach English, these do not seem to have affected the linguistic pattern, and at the end of the century Manx still held a strong position among common people. One of the chief advocates for the use of Manx in church was Bishop Thomas Wilson (1698–1755), who realized that the majority of his flock could not be reached except through Manx, 'for English is not understood by two-thirds at least of the Island, though there is an English school in every parish, so hard is it to change the language of a whole country'.[57] As a result of his advocacy and that of other bishops, as well as the efforts of the SPCK, a number of translations of books of devotion and sermons were published during the eighteenth century.[58] The Book of Common Prayer appeared in 1765 and the Bible, in parts, between 1763 and 1773, possibly a sign of the same practical attitude as that being shown by the SSPCK at the time. Five editions of the Prayer Book by 1842 and three of the Bible by 1819 suggest that these Manx versions were necessary for church services, whatever may have been the needs of individual readers. But although these translations and publications were a response to the needs of congregations, they were not universally supported. Bishop Hildesley's zeal for the Manx Scriptures in 1763 earned him the description 'poor wrong-headed bishop' and in 1789 John Wesley bitterly opposed any attempt to use Manx: 'On the contrary', he urged, 'we should do everything in our power to abolish it from the earth.'[59] (In fact, Manx versions of Wesley's hymns appeared in 1795 and 1799, and the Rules of the Societies in 1800.)

There is no reason to believe that Manx was any more fervently supported than the other Celtic languages. It was not a threat to the political order, it did not have any negative connotations, and the religious activity simply suggests that the number of monoglot Manx speakers was great enough to merit attention. In fact, however, its position was not unlike that of Cornish in Penwith and Kerrier some centuries earlier. It was the language of the monoglot majority (unlike Cornish in the sixteenth century) and, as was true of Cornish, its speakers were conscious of being part of a wider linguistic community, Breton in the case of Cornwall, Gaelic in the case of the Isle of Man. (At the end of the nineteenth century fishermen informed Sir John Rhŷs that they understood Gaelic better than Irish and that they would never speak of private matters in Manx when they landed on the Islands.) But neither had been the language of administration for centuries; Cornwall was an English county, Man a lordship under the English Crown. The gentry had turned

---

[57] Kneen, *A Grammar of the Manx Language*, p. 8.
[58] There is a list of Manx publications in Kneen, *A Grammar of the Manx Language*, pp. 10–14; for the Scriptures, see Williams, 'Y Beibl yn yr Ieithoedd Celtaidd'.
[59] Price, *The Languages of Britain*, pp. 75–6.

their backs on the language, choosing to use Manx only in dealing with servants; market towns, and later tourism, were Anglicizing factors. There must have been a Manx oral literature, but written literature did not appear before Bishop Phillips's Prayer Book. There remain some Manx ballads but the old Gaelic learning and culture disappeared (as did the native culture of Cornwall), perhaps around the same time that the native social order disintegrated in Ireland and in the Highlands. As a result, by the beginning of the modern period Manx was the language of fishermen and smallholders; and although it had appeared in print since the eighteenth century, literature in the language was very restricted in its range. The Highlands and Islands enjoyed a buoyant oral culture which the translation of the Bible and religious activities could reinforce linguistically, and that oral culture was to become a favourite theme among antiquaries and those with a romantic view of the past in the eighteenth and nineteenth centuries. Such advantages were not shared by Manx and it never developed a body of literate speakers. Bilingualism spread and the fortunes of the languages declined rapidly from the mid-nineteenth century. When Sir John Rhŷs visited the island on several occasions between 1886 and 1891 in order to learn Manx and analyse its phonology, he found only middle-aged and elderly speakers, 'in prime of life or past it'. English was the home language and he found only one child who could speak Manx, and she lived with a grandparent. Manx survived rather longer than Rhŷs predicted, but the last native speaker died in 1974.[60]

The Celtic countries of Britain do not have a common history and the fortunes of their languages differ so much that their history cannot be set within the same frame. Nevertheless, there are shared threads in the pattern and some common themes can be discerned.[61]

All the languages suffered a sharp decline from the closing years of the eighteenth century, but the causes of that decline can be detected much earlier, sometimes as traumatic events, sometimes as insidious influences. The main aim of all governments and central authority towards the Celtic languages in this period was to encourage the assimilation of 'provincial' cultures and their absorption into a 'national' (English) culture. The beginnings of the process are to be found in the sixteenth century when each of these countries faced similar threats to its traditional society and culture in the name of uniformity and the desire to create a unified state.

---

[60] John Rhŷs, *The Outlines of the Phonology of Manx Gaelic* (Oxford, 1894), p. 163; Price, *The Languages of Britain*, pp. 81–2.
[61] See Durkacz, *The Decline of the Celtic Languages*, pp. 214–26; Hindley, *The Death of the Irish Language*, pp. 3–12.

At times the threat to language and culture was implicit, at other times legislation was consciously linguistic or anti-cultural, but the effect, whether in the political, military, social, economic, educational or religious domain, was the same. Not infrequently, a number of these elements were combined within the same legislation.

In the case of Cornish the assimilation had begun centuries previously and neither legislation nor military intervention was necessary. The language was of so little relevance that it could be largely ignored by church and state; and although the 'Prayer Book Rebellion' reminded the reformers of its existence, it was in no position to insist on a translation of the Scriptures. It could be ignored since it posed no threat. In contrast, as Irish swiftly became a political emblem in Ireland and a symbol of cultural separateness in the Highlands, concepts associated with language – treasonable (and at times rebellious) Catholicism and ethnic barbarity – were judged a threat to civil order and authority. In both countries military campaigns were reinforced by antagonistic social and cultural policies. The attack was two-pronged, upon the political leadership, the chiefs who upheld the economic system and who were the patrons of the culture, and upon the learned orders, who were responsible for its transmission. By the end of the seventeenth century, and after 1745, a society in which Irish and Gaelic had expressed an integrated comprehensive way of life had been shattered. The tension between the demands of political and religious uniformity and the pragmatism of accepting the vernaculars as the medium of evangelism and mission remained, but even where the language was given a role, it was no more than temporary recognition which did not change educational policies in the schools.

Many consequences followed from military and social supremacy. Peace and stability led to improved roads for trade and industry, commercial opportunities widened and the roles of market towns and villages were enhanced; the call for labour, craftsmen and seasonal work increased. The remoteness of the coastal parishes of western Cornwall and the Highland line ceased to provide protection for the languages as doors were opened for incomers (and emigrants) and for visitors. Some bilingualism was not uncommon in the seventeenth century, but in the following century the level must have increased as many more people regarded their mastery of English as a precondition (and sign) of prosperity.

Some of these changes could have been accommodated within a new social structure, as happened in Wales after 1282, in the sixteenth century and more radically in the eighteenth century, had the will to do so been stronger. The racial prejudice which is commonly revealed when the conquerors' culture comes face to face with that of the conquered is seen most clearly in Ireland and the Highlands. The distinguishing mark of Gaelic culture was believed to be its uncivil character and it was only a matter of time before native society accepted this view of itself, nurtured as it was by the educational system. In all the Celtic countries it was the gentry who bowed first to the pressure to adopt an English way of life. This could be voluntary or the consequence of government policy, but the result was that these languages lost social status and were seen as inferior tongues and a hindrance to social advancement. They lost their practical use and became badges of poverty and failure among the unprivileged sectors of society. When these attitudes were fortified by the absence of literature (as was the case in Cornwall and the Isle of Man) or the lack of civilized literature acceptable to polite English and Anglicized society (as was the case in Ireland and the Highlands), native society swiftly lost confidence in the value of its own culture and began to doubt the relevance of its language in the contemporary world. English schools were a long-term stratagem which were perhaps not fully effective until parents and children themselves sought to learn English, but their insistence that literacy in English was the only true literacy could not but deepen uncertainty regarding the value of native culture. Increasing bilingualism restricted even further the domains of the mother tongues: education and social divisions would have similar consequences. In many areas the language ceased to be the medium of a full and comprehensive culture and the next step would be its weakening as a community language.

The position of Welsh at the beginning of the nineteenth century was far stronger than that of its sister languages. It had not suffered the flight of its leaders in society, even after 1282, and it had never endured large-scale persecution similar to that wrought in Ireland and the Highlands. A key element in its survival was that Wales proved more able to adapt social patterns and to create new classes to sustain and support its culture as society changed from time to time. Since new literary genres and styles developed from what previously existed and from sub-literary forms, there was always a continuity of language. When Protestantism took root in a country where language was not a political emblem for factions antagonistic to the Crown, the translation of the Scriptures and the Book of Common Prayer was deemed an acceptable activity rather than a stumbling block. Unlike all the other Celtic cultures in Britain, Welsh was able to combine the learning of the Renaissance with the ideals of the reformers. Schools, the church and later the chapels provided the basis for popular literacy and ensured that the language maintained a high cultural status in its own land.

Index

Abbas, Pennant 157
Aberdare 101, 261, 336
Aberffraw 101
Abergavenny 76, 89, 301, 329
Abergele 259
Aberhafesb 245
Aber-porth 253
Aberystruth 255, 262
Aberystwyth 21, 76, 258
Abraham, Edward, Llangollen 189
Abraham, Jane 118
academies
   Carmarthen 321–2
   Rhys Prydderch, Ystradwallter 321
   Samuel Jones, Brynllywarch 321
Act for the Better Propagation and Preaching of the Gospel in Wales (1650) 299, 317–18
Act for the Translation of the Bible and Book of Common Prayer (1563) 123, 141–7, 231, 234, 236
Act of Uniformity
   1549 139, 414
   1559 142, 212, 213
   1662 236, 241
Acts of Union 62–3, 123–37, 182–4, 297–8
   'language clause' 17, 42, 62, 63, 125, 132–7, 154, 155, 298
Adam of Usk 40
Adam, Gruffith 71
Adventures of Roderick Random, The (Tobias Smollett) 65
Aesop (John Vanbrugh) 373
After, John, vicar of Swansea 230
Aleluia (William Williams) 268
Alleine, Joseph, Taunton 318
Allen, Thomas, Oxford, head of Gloucester Hall 313
Ambleston 256
Amlwch 258
Andrews, Thomas, vicar of Llandaff and Whitchurch 83
Anglesey 47, 51, 100, 117, 118, 156, 252

Annales Cambriae 408
Antient British Bard's Toast. Ffwrdd Ddieithryn, The (William Williams) 66
Antiquae Linguae Britannicae (John Davies) 235, 291, 366
Antiquae Linguae Britannicae . . . et linguae Latinae, Dictionarium Duplex (John Davies) 45, 292, 365, 367, 390
Antiquae linguae Britannicae thesaurus (Thomas Richards) 203, 205, 390
Antiquité de la nation et de la langue des celtes, L' (Paul-Yves Pezron) 375, 376, 379
Apologia Ecclesiae Anglicanae (John Jewel) 220, 357
Apologia Musices (John Case) 193, 363
arbitration 15, 27, 41, 44, 166–7
Archaeologia Britannica (Edward Lhuyd) 376–7
Armes Prydein Vawr 408
Arthur ap Huw 212
Aston 17
Athelstan 408, 409
Athravaeth Gristnogavl (Morys Clynnog) 150, 359
Aubrey, John 100, 103

Backhouse, William 312
Bagot, Lewis, bishop of St Asaph 246, 247
bailiffs 156
Baker, Father Augustine 67, 301–2, 308
Bala 111, 252
Bangor
   diocese 51, 72, 239, 241, 243
   district 98
   town 258
Barddoniaeth Dafydd ap Gwilym (1789) 402
Barlow, Isaac, bishop of Sodor and Man 436
Barlow, William, bishop of St David's 135, 136, 149, 209
Basaleg 101, 242
Basilikon Doron (James I) 78, 185, 429
Bassett, William, Beaupre 197
Baxter, Richard 84
Baxter, William, Llanllugan 110–11, 377

Beaumaris 75, 124, 258
Beaumont, James 265
Beaw, William, bishop of Llandaff 238
Beddgelert 101
Beddo, Lewis, rector of Llanglydwen 244
Bedo Brwynllys 35
Bedowe, Elizabeth, Crugion 176
Bedwellte 255, 262
Berriew 245
Bestiaire d'Amour 30
Betws Cedewain 241, 245
Beunans Meriasek ('Buchedd Meriadog') 412
Bevan, Madam Bridget 320, 337
Bevan, John, Neath 203
Beynon, John 113
Bible
 1588 82, 83, 100, 217–20, 356
 1620 218, 356
 1630 219
 1678 322–3
bilingualism 129, 139, 294, 305, 307, 348
 and religion 241, 246–7, 250–1, 253–6, 336
 communities 34, 35, 37, 57, 75, 76, 158, 245, 260, 263, 269
bishops 135, 236–9
 Anglo bishops 86, 238, 239, 240, 393
Bishopston 246
Bisse, Philip, bishop of St David's 238
Blaenau Gwent 101
Blaenpennal 204
Bletherston 256
Blinman, Richard 84
Blodeu-gerdd Cymry (Dafydd Jones) 248
Bodfel, Colonel John, Llŷn 186
Bodinar, William 416
Boehme, Jacob 361
Bokenham, Osbert 40
Book of Common Order (Knox) 430
Book of Common Prayer see Prayer Book
Book of Homilies, The (trans. Edward James) 220, 312
Book of Husbandry, The (Walter of Henley) 24
Book of St Chad 15, 44
Boson, Nicholas 415
Botwnnog 258
Boughrood 254
Bowles, Thomas, rector of Trefdraeth and Llangwyfan 243
Braose, Mary de 27
Braose, William de 27, 28
Brecon 120, 157, 166
 Christ's College 136, 298
Breconshire 47, 57, 100, 102, 114, 156, 159, 204–5, 255
'Breiniau Dyn' (The Rights of Man) (Iolo Morganwg) 403

Breton 48
Bridgend 89, 257
brief answer to a short trifling treatise . . ., A (1571) 150
briefe and a playne introduction, A (William Salesbury) 137
Britannia (William Camden) 375, 415, 436
Britannia Antiqua Illustrata (Aylett Sammes) 374–5
British language 407
British Language in its Lustre, The (Thomas Jones) 103, 389–90
Brittany 38
Broughton, Robert 300–1
Brut y Tywysogyon (The Chronicle of the Princes) 23
Builth 89
Bulkeley, Arthur, bishop of Bangor 209
Bulkeley, Sir Richard 181–2, 191
Bunyan, John 322
Burgess, Thomas, bishop of St David's 263
Byng, John, later 5th Viscount Torrington 201
Bywyd a Marwolaeth Theomemphus (William Williams) 382

Cadoedigaet yr Iait Cybraeg (William Owen Pughe) 397
Cadwaladr ap Morus 195–6
Caeo, commote 44
Caernarfon 31, 75, 124, 258
Caernarfonshire 47, 51, 100, 107, 158, 167, 183, 252, 258
Caerwys
 circulating schools 328
 eisteddfod
  1523 344
  1567 172, 191, 349
  third eisteddfod 193
Call to the unconverted, A (Richard Baxter) 362
Cambrobrytannicae Cymraecaeve Linguae Institutiones (Siôn Dafydd Rhys) 193, 292, 365–6
Camden, William 65, 386
'Cân Cymhortha' (Begging Song) (Thomas ap Ieuan ap Rhys) 59
Cantilupe, Thomas, bishop of Hereford 17, 18, 27, 28, 37
Canwyll y Cymru (Rees Prichard) 85, 103, 353
Capon, John, bishop of Bangor 127–8
Cardiff 76, 89, 257
Cardigan 40, 76
Cardiganshire 47, 51, 76, 100, 104, 133, 203–4, 252, 258, 319
 see also Ceredigion

INDEX

Carew, Sir George 422
Carew, Richard 413, 415
Carmarthen 76, 258
Carmarthenshire 26, 43, 47, 51, 76, 100, 103, 104, 133, 187–8, 319, 328
Carolau (Richard Gwyn) 353
Car-wr y Cymru (Oliver Thomas) 296
Casnodyn 22
Castlemartin 16, 54
Catechism yr Eglwys wedi ei egluro (trans. Ellis Wynne) 259
Catholic recusants 67
Catholics 148, 152, 222–5, 359–61
Catlyn, John, vicar of Kerry 87
Cecil, Sir William 148, 151–2, 304
Cefn-llys 254
Celtic Remains (Lewis Morris) 378, 386
Ceredigion 22, 43
  see also Cardiganshire
Chaloner, Thomas 299
Chanson de Roland 30
Charles, Thomas, Bala 90–1, 267, 337–8
Charles, William, Llanbeblig 189
Cheshire 19
Chestrook 17
Chirbury 20
Chirk, lordship 26, 28
Churchstoke 20
Cilcain 328
Cilfowyr 264
Cilymaenllwyd 261
Cimbri 375
Circles of Gomer, The (Rowland Jones) 396–7
clerics 240–5
clerwyr 172–3
Clopton, Thomas, rector of Castell Caereinion 242
Clun, lordship 17
Clynnog, Morys 149, 151–2, 212, 359
Coedcernyw 255
Coedycymer 261
'Coelio'r Saint' 361
Collins, Thomas, Swansea 87
Colwinston 336
Come and Welcome to Jesus (John Bunyan) 264
Commentariolum (Humphrey Llwyd) 367
commerce
  see trade and commerce
Companion to the Altar (William Viccar) 203
Compendious Treatise in Metre (George Marshall) 212
Considerations on the Illegality and Impropriety of Preferring Clergymen . . . (John Jones) 243
Conway, John, Botryddan 192, 193, 310, 355
Conway, John Ayr 159

Conwy 28, 124, 258
Copeland, William, Scottish packman 50
Corbett, Vincent, Ynysymaengwyn 203
Cornish 47, 170, 231, 402–3, 408–9, 411–19
Corwen 101, 252
Council in the Marches 155, 156, 172, 173–4
Court of Great Sessions 48, 70, 71, 153–80
  culture and social control 172–80
  personnel 154–61
  procedure 161–7
  record of the court 167–71
Cowbridge 76, 257
Coxe, William 58
Coychurch 105
Cradock, Joseph 75
Cradock, Walter 228
Cressett, Edward, bishop of Llandaff 236
Cromwell, Thomas 126–7, 128, 135, 136, 181
Crowley, Robert 355
Crowther, William, incumbent 245
Croyland, chronicler 39–40
cursing 120–2
Curton, Humphrey, Guilsfield 76
Cwm, Y 328
Cwm-hir 255
Cydymmaith i'r Allor (trans. Moses Williams) 203
Cyfarwyddiad i Fesurwyr (1715) 93
Cyfarwyddid ir Cymru (Morgan Llwyd) 362
Cylch-grawn Cynmraeg, Y (1793) 405
Cyngor Rhad yr Anllythrennog (Griffith Jones) 333

Dafydd ap Gwilym 21, 400
Dafydd ap Llywelyn 32
Dafydd Benfras 22, 32
Dafydd Benwyn 79, 192, 310
Dafydd Ddu Eryri 97
Dafydd Llwyd, lord of Abertanad 32
Dafydd Llwyd ap Dafydd, Gogerddan 347
Dafydd Llwyd Fychan 20
Dafydd Nanmor 35, 347
Dafydd, Edward 350
Dafydd, Meurig, bard 197, 350
Dalby, Alexander, dean of Chester 39
Darcy, Ann 80
Darluniad o'r Gwir Gristion (Phylip Pugh) 264
David ap Ieuan David Thomas 161
David ap Llewelyn alias Benwyn, Cardigan 160
David, John and Martha 104–5
David, Mericke 159
David, Rees Rudderch 113
David, Robert, Llanfihangel Glyn Myfyr 188
David, Rowland 171

Davies, Edward, burgess 134
Davies, Edward, curate of Newmarket 244
Davies, John, curate of Merthyr Tydfil 261
Davies, Dr John, Mallwyd 45, 53, 65, 78, 91, 186, 192, 214, 218, 221, 230, 291–2, 312, 313, 356, 358, 389, 390
Davies, Myles, Whitford 101
Davies, Bishop Richard 82, 91, 145, 146, 213, 214, 215, 221, 355–6, 357, 358
Davies, Richard, Cloddiau Cochion 68, 113
Davies, Walter (Gwallter Mechain) 51, 369, 379
Davies, William 173
Davis ap Hugh ap Thomas, Llanenddwyn 185
De Institutione Feminae Christianae (Juan Luis Vives) 362
De Senectute (Cicero) 365
defamation 56, 59–60, 71, 99, 102, 104, 116, 117, 118
Deffynniad Ffydd Eglwys Loegr (trans. Morris Kyffin) 147, 357
Definiad i Hennadirion (trans. John Conway III) 193
Defynnog 101
Demetian 100, 101
Denbigh, lordship 25, 27, 131
Denbighshire 47, 57, 101, 113, 157, 166, 169, 254, 328
Descriptio Kambriae (Gerald of Wales) 21–2
Devereux, Robert, second Earl of Essex 184
dialects 21–2, 31, 91, 95, 96, 98–105, 112, 214, 232, 268, 384
Dialogue of the Government of Wales, The (George Owen) 135
Dictionarium linguae Latinae, et Anglicanae (Thomas Thomas) 365
Dictionary of the English Language (Samuel Johnson) 389
Disce Mori (Christopher Sutton) 359
Diserth 254, 328
Dissenters 84–6, 262, 263–9, 321–2
Dissertation on the Welsh Language, A (John Walters) 95, 395
Dolben, William 176
Dolgellau 258
Dosbarth Byrr ar y rhann gyntaf i ramadeg cymraeg (Gruffydd Robert) 151
Dottrina Christiana (St Roberto Bellarmino) 360
drovers 34, 74
Drummond, Robert Hay, bishop of St Asaph 86, 238–9, 393
Drych Cristianogawl, Y (1587) 150–1, 197, 360
Drych Cydwybod 357
'Drych Ufudd-dod' 361
Drych y Prif Oesoedd (Theophilus Evans) 370, 377–8
Drych yr Amseroedd (Robert Jones) 121
Du-Glott-Exposition, of the Creed, the Ten Commandments . . ., A (Robert Roberts) 248
Dudleston, Martha, Myddle 106
'Dwned, Y' 290
Dwnn, Lewys 350
Dwnn, Siams 350
Dwysfawr Rym Buchedd Grefyddol (Alban Thomas) 203
Dydd y Farn Fawr (Jenkin Jones) 264

Ealdred 408
Ednyfed ap Iorwerth 158
Edward ap Rhys 42
Edward Gruffydd ap Ednyfed, Garthgarmon 50
Edward, Harry, Llandyfalle 157
Edward, Lord Herbert, Chirbury 79, 305
Edwards, Charles 230, 235, 264, 373
Edwards, John (Siôn Treredyn) 197, 295
Edwards, John, Chirk 26, 35–6, 194, 223
Edwards, John, rector of Tredynog 58
Edwards, Richard, Soughton 174
Edwards, Thomas (Twm o'r Nant) 392
Egbert 408
Egerton, John, bishop of Bangor 243
Eglurhaad o Gatechism yr Eglwys (William Beveridge) 259
Eglvryn Phraethineb (Henry Perri) 193, 293, 294
Eglwys Gymyn 257
Eglwysilan 258, 261
Eglwyswrw 253, 327
Egwyddorion a dyledswyddau y grefydd Grist'nogawl (Thomas Wilson) 259
Ein Kleinot (Otto Werdmüller) 357
Einion Fychan 34
Einion Offeiriad (Einion the Priest) 208
eisteddfod
see Caerwys
Elen, wife of Robin Nordd 21
Elgu ap Gelli 15, 44
Ellis, Dorothy (Dorti Ddu), Llannor 121
Ellis, Rees, Newborough, labourer 118
Ellis, Thomas, Fellow of Jesus College 314
English Catechism Explained (John Mayer) 359
English Litany and Order of Communion (Thomas Cranmer) 210
English-Welsh Dictionary, An (John Walters) 390–1
Epistle of a Religious Priest unto his father . . ., An (Robert Southwell) 360
'Epistol at y Cembru' 148, 150, 216
Erbery, William 84

Esponiad Byr ar Gatecism yr Eglwys (Griffith Jones) 333
established Church 86–8, 235–87
  incumbents 87, 240–64
  services 245–64
Evan David ap Thomas, Saint Harmon 178
Evan the Cooper, St Nicholas 110
Evan, Edward, Aberdare 401
Evan, John, St Andrews 110
Evan, Lewis, Llanllugan, Methodist preacher 201
Evangelical Catechism, An (1797) 338–9
Evans, Arise, Llangelynnin 67
Evans, David 189
Evans, Edward, curate of Diserth 247
Evans, Evan (Ieuan Fardd) 96, 236, 239, 241, 242, 385, 386, 388, 389, 391, 393, 396, 400
Evans, Jenkin 238
Evans, John 61
Evans, Revd John 55
Evans, John, Eglwys Gymyn 330
Evans, Lewis 359
Evans, Lewys, agent of the earl of Leicester 150
Evans, Mary, Beaumaris 118
Evans, Meredith, Nantmel 179
Evans, Ruth 120
Evans, Theophilus 90, 235, 248, 265
Evans, Thomas (Tomos Glyn Cothi) 68, 405
Evans, William, Chancellor and Treasurer of Llandaff 192
Evans, William, translator 71
Ewias 101
Ewias Harold 56
Ewias Lacy 56

Faith and practice of a Church of Englandman, The (William Stanley) 248
Fenton, Richard 55, 121
Ffawyddog 329
Ffydd Ddi-ffvant, Y (1677) 370, 373
First booke of the Christian exercise. . ., The (Robert Persons) 357
Fishguard 104–5, 121, 247
'Fishing Lass of Hakin', 'The (Lewis Morris) 387
Fleetwood, Charles, major-general 84
Fleetwood, William, bishop of St Asaph 247
Flemish 27, 44
Flintshire 50, 57, 101, 156, 172, 182, 254, 328
Fordun, John 431
Fouke le Fitz Waryn 30
Foulkes, Humphrey 111
Fowler, William, Shropshire 168
Fox, George, Quaker 67

Foxwist, Richard 43
French 16, 26, 27–30, 32, 34, 35, 40, 44, 126, 133, 139–40, 186, 215, 300, 305, 345, 411, 412, 413, 416, 420, 427
Fychan, Richard II 196
Fychan, Simwnt 197, 347
Fynes-Clinton, O. H. 98
Fyrst Boke of the Introduction of Knowledge, The (Andrew Borde) 411

Gair or Gair (Morgan Llwyd) 362
Gall-Gaídil 410
Galwad at Orseddfaingc y Gras (Griffith Jones) 332
Gam, Sir David 159
Gamage, John 159
Gamage, William 185, 305
Gambold, William 63, 389, 390
Gardiner, Stephen, bishop of Winchester 138
Gartheli 259
Garway in Archenfield 17
'Geirfa Tafod Cymraeg' (Henry Salesbury) 365
Gelli-gaer 101, 258, 261
Gemmeu Doethineb (Rees Prydderch) 108
gentry 28–36, 78–81, 195–7
Geographia Sacra (Samuel Bochart) 374
George, Dorothy, Llandaff 106
Gerald of Wales 27, 32, 100, 326
Gerard, William, Vice-President of the Council of the Marches 70–1, 134, 135, 153
German 40, 300, 345
Gibson, Edmund 415, 416
Gilbert, John, bishop of Llandaff 237
Gileston 256
Glamorgan 16, 47, 59–60, 66, 76, 79, 100, 101–2, 109–10, 157, 159, 167, 201, 319, 336
glanastra 165
Glasbury 254
Glossarium Antiquitatum Britannicarum (William Baxter) 377
Glyn, Cadwaladr, Glyncywarch 186
Glyn, William, bishop of Bangor 212
Glyn, William, Glyncywarch 186
Glyncorrwg 261
Goidelic 407, 418, 435
Goldwell, Thomas, bishop of St Asaph 212
Golwg ar Deyrnas Crist (William Williams) 384
Golwg ar y Byd (Dafydd Lewys) 93
Goodman, Gabriel 152, 298
Gorchestion Beirdd Cymru (ed. Rhys Jones) 395
Gorsedd Beirdd Ynys Prydain (The Gorsedd of the Bards of the Island of Britain) 400

Gouge, Thomas 318-19
Gower 47, 54, 55, 84, 100, 110, 257
Gower Anglicana (Isaac Hamon) 55
Gramadeg Cymraeg (Gruffydd Robert) 365
Grammar of the Welsh Language, A (William Owen Pughe) 97
Grammatica Britannica (Henry Salesbury) 293, 366
Gray, Richard, Llanfaethlu 306
greetings 111-14
Griffiths, Ann, Dolwar Fach 120
Griffiths, Vavasor 322
Grindal, Edmund, bishop of London 146
Gruffudd ab Ieuan ap Llywelyn Fychan 194, 211
Gruffudd ap Hywel ap Dafydd 20
Gruffudd Hiraethog 119, 145, 195-6, 309, 344, 346, 349, 350, 355
Gruffudd, John, Cefnamwlch 191
Gruffudd, Piers, Penrhyn 193
Gruffudd, Sir Rhys 194
Gruffudd, William, justice of the peace 188
Gruffydd, Elis, soldier and chronicler 95, 108, 125, 354-5
Gruffydd, William, warden of Llanbeblig Church 243
Guto'r Glyn 32
Gwaedd Ynghymru yn wyneb pob cydwybod euog (Morgan Llwyd) 362
Gwassanaeth Meir 207
Gweledigaetheu y Bardd Cwsc (Ellis Wynne) 99, 202, 370
Gwen ferch Pierce, Llanrwst 190
Gwenhwyfar, daughter of Rhys ab Einion 25
Gwentian speech 22
    see also Silurian
Gwreans an Bys (William Jordan) 413
'Gwssanaeth y Gwŷr Newydd' 360
Gwyn, Hugh, Berth-ddu 194
Gwyn, John, preacher 83
Gwyn, John Jankyn 71
Gwyn, Lewis, constable of Bishopston 195
Gwyn, Richard (Richard White) 150, 163, 224, 308, 353, 360
Gwyn, Robert 186, 197, 295, 360, 361
Gwynn, Richard, captain 184
Gwynne, Marmaduke, Garth 203, 205
Gwynne, Robert, Glanbrân 203
Gymdeithas Loerig, Y (The Lunar Society) 117
Gymraeg yn ei Disgleirdeb, Y (Thomas Jones) 103, 389-90

Halkyn 328
Hamon, Revd Isaac 55, 110
Hanes y Byd a'r Amseroedd (Simon Thomas) 92, 378
Harris, Dr George 393

Harris, Howel 88, 119, 204-5, 265, 266, 334, 381
Harry ap Jeffrey, Caerhun 188
Havard, David, curate of Llandysul 335
Hawarden 299
Hay, Dr George 243
Hebraismorum Cambro-Britannicorum Specimen (Charles Edwards) 373-4
Henfynyw 253
Henllys 255
Henry ap John alias Syr John alias Henry Parson of Llanrhidian 161
Herbert, Lord Edward, Chirbury 79, 305
Herbert, William, Cogan Pill 185, 305
Herbert, Sir William, earl of Pembroke 79, 151, 190-1, 304
Hereford
    county 48, 56, 100, 120
    diocese 17-18, 184, 249
Heroic Elegies and other Pieces of Llywarch Hen, The (1792) 399
Herring, Thomas, bishop of Bangor 236-7
Heylin, Rowland 219
Hieroglyfic (Rowland Jones) 396-7
Higden, Ranulph 38
Hildesley, bishop 437
Hill, Trevor 243
Historia Regum Britanniae (Geoffrey of Monmouth) 367
Historiae Britannicae Defensio (John Price) 367
Historical and Critical Remarks on the British Tongue . . . (Thomas Llewelyn) 95
Historie of Cambria, The (David Powel) 366
History of the Cymbri (or Brittains), The (Simon Thomas) 378
Hoadly, Benjamin, bishop of Bangor 237
Hoare, Thomas Mills, vicar of Newport 105, 240, 244, 263
Holl Ddyledswydd Dyn 322
Holland, Robert 78, 194, 358
Holy Living (Jeremy Taylor) 237
Holywell 245
Hookes, Hugh, Conwy 193
Hopkin, Mary 119
Howell, John, Crunwear 175
Hucks, Joseph 65
Huet, Thomas, precentor of St David's 214, 356
Hugh de Smethynton 31
Hughes, Hugh 385, 392
Hughes, Revd John, Pontrobert 120
Hughes, Jonathan 392, 402
Hughes, Peter, Ruthin 171
Hughes, Richard 353
Hughes, Robert (Robin Ddu o Fôn) 387
Hughes, Stephen 85, 102, 222, 230, 264, 319, 362

INDEX

Hughes, Thomas, glazier, Bangor 158
Hughes, William, bishop of St Asaph 230
Humfrey ap Thomas, Machynlleth, weaver 176
Humphreys, Humphrey, bishop of Bangor 237
Humphreys, Thomas, Llanfair 171
Hutton, William 50
Huw Machno 349
Huw Nannau Hen 193
Hywel ap Gruffudd ab Ieuan 186
Hywel ap Gruffudd Fychan, Aber-erch 27
Hywel Prains 21
Hywel Swrdwal 290

Ieuan ap David 76
Ieuan ap David ap Owen Goch 174, 176
Ieuan ap Gruffith ap Hoell 26
Ieuan ap Hywel Swrdwal 35
Ieuan ap Rhydderch 29, 290
Ieuan ap Wilkoc 26
Ieuan Fardd *see* Evan Evans
Ieuan Lewis alias Ieuan Gwyn Daliwr 160
Ifan Llwyd ap Dafydd 367
insults 116–18
interpreters 17, 23, 70–1, 164, 183
Io-Triads, The (Rowland Jones) 396–7
Iolo Goch 35
Iolo Morganwg 47, 60, 63, 68, 73, 102, 109–12, 336, 379, 380, 396, 398–404, 405
Iorwerth Fynglwyd 344
Ireland
  history 16, 419–25
Irish 40, 48, 54–5, 63, 90, 170, 231, 312, 339, 340, 408, 419–25
  Bible 1690 424
  Book of Common Prayer 1608 424
  New Testament 1603 424
  translating the Scriptures 146

James, Edward, Oxford 312, 358
Jeffrey, Katherine 188
Jenkin William alias Glyncorrwg 160
Jenkins, Sir Leoline 68
Jenkins, Lewis, Michaelchurch Escley 56–7
Jenkins, William, Welsh St Donat's 203
Jervis, John 77
John ap Cadwalladr 178
John David alias Bowen, labourer 200
John de Grandisson, bishop of Exeter 411
John, Philip 166
Johnes, Thomas, Aber-mad 203
Johns, Dafydd, vicar of Llanfair Dyffryn Clwyd 310
Jones, Dafydd, Caeo 74
Jones, Dafydd, Trefriw 387, 388, 392
Jones, Ellen 189

Jones, George, Rhoscellan 203
Jones, Griffith, Llanddowror 73, 89–90, 228–9, 230, 248, 265–6, 324–8, 339, 340–1, 378
Jones, Griffith, magistrate 189
Jones, Henry, Flintshire 174
Jones, Huw, Llangwm 69, 119, 387
Jones, Jane, Tregaron 116
Jones, John (Jac Glan-y-gors) 71
Jones, Colonel John 84
Jones, John, barrister-at-law 51
Jones, John, Cadoxton 202
Jones, John, clerk 83
Jones, John, curate of Llan-non 249
Jones, Dr John, dean of Bangor 321
Jones, John, Gellilyfdy 366
Jones, Owen (Owain Myfyr)
  see Owain Myfyr
Jones, Colonel Philip 84
Jones, Richard, Llanfair Caereinion 295
Jones, Richard, schoolmaster 362
Jones, Robert 170
Jones, Rowland, Llanbedrog 391
Jones, Samuel, Brynllywarch 230
Jones, Theophilus 58, 115
Jones, Thomas, almanacker 103, 108–9, 369, 374, 389–90
Jones, Thomas, Clocaenog, exciseman 402, 405
Jones, Thomas, Llancarfan 109
Jones, Thomas, Monmouthshire 218
Jones, Sir William, Castellmarch 193
Jones, Sir William, Llanfihangel Tre'r-beirdd 379–80
Jones, William, Llangadfan, 'The Welsh Voltaire' 68, 81, 105, 109, 405
Jones, Zephaniah, Llantrisant, tiler 109–10
Jonson, Ben 65
jurors 156–7
justices of the peace 181–206

Kenfig 247
Kerry, Thomas, merchant 132
Kilkenny Statutes, 1366 411
Kirk, Robert 431–2
Kirkwood, James 431–2
Klod Kerdd davod a'i dechrevad (trans. John Conway III) 193
Knighton 16, 76
Knucklas 16
Kyffin, Edward 295
Kyffin, Morris 186, 216, 218, 304, 358
Kyffin, Roger 351
Kynniver Llith a Ban (William Salesbury) 140–1, 211, 213, 355

Ladd, John, mayor of Newport 202

Laleston 337
Lampeter 258
Landsker 54–5
Langford, Richard, Trefalun 310
language
  decline 46–8, 104, 269
  oral 21–2, 93–4, 98–122
  swearing 115–16
  written 15, 22–3
Latin 16, 17, 28, 31, 32, 33–6, 41, 42, 70, 73, 81–2, 133, 162, 183, 186, 188, 199–200, 207, 228, 289, 297, 299, 300, 409–10
Laugharne 244, 257
Lavernock 250
law 24, 26, 38, 44, 63, 69–73, 122, 153–80, 298
Laws of Hywel Dda 44, 129–30, 166
Lee, Bishop Rowland 127, 128, 130, 136, 181, 184
Leigh, Henry, Hart Hall, Oxford 303
Lesclarcissement de la langue francoyse (John Palsgrave) 364
Levellers 70, 71
Lewis ab Edward 349
Lewis, Ann, spinster 200
Lewis, David, Little Newcastle 50
Lewis, David, Llanboidy 110
Lewis, Elis, Llwyn-gwern 313
Lewis, John, Gernos 203
Lewis, Katherine Jones, Cathedin 171
Lewis, Dr Owen, archdeacon of Cambrai 149
Lewis, Thomas, Llanbedr Felffre 177
Lewis, Thomas, Llandaff 192
Lewis, Thomas, Llanishen 203
Lewis, Valentine, Gwersyllt 179
Lewis, William, Anglesey 191
Lewys Glyn Cothi 20, 21, 35
Lewys Môn 344
Lewys Morgannwg 130, 136, 195, 209, 344
Lewys, Huw 217, 226–7, 352
lexicography 389–91, 396–7
'Lexicon Cambro-Britannicum' (William Gambold) 390
Lexicon Tetraglotton (James Howell) 108, 370
Leyland, John 36
Lhuyd, Edward 55, 105, 106, 108, 373, 375–7, 405
libraries 300, 307, 313, 323, 366
literacy 42, 174, 185, 227, 291, 294–6, 308, 317–41
Llanasa 328
Llanbadarn Fawr 101
Llanbadarn Odwyn 204
Llanbedr Felffre 256
Llanbryn-mair 260

Llancarfan 101
Llandaff
  diocese 239, 242
Llanddewi Fach 255
Llanddewi Felffre 256
Llandeilo 76, 258
Llandeilo Fawr 101
Llandeilo Graban 254
Llandingad 113
Llandochau 262
Llandudno 260
Llandysul 204
Llanelli 258
Llaneugrad 258
Llanfair-ar-y-bryn 251, 260
Llanfair Caereinion 245, 254
Llanfair Nant-y-gof 247
Llanfallteg 256
Llanfarthin 188
Llanfyllin 50
Llanfynydd 260
Llan-gan 256
Llanganten 261
Llangattock nigh Usk 246
Llangeitho 204
Llan-gors 246
Llangrannog 251, 260
Llangwyryfon 204
Llangyfelach 336
Llangynog 245, 260
Llanhiledd 255
Llanidloes 101
Llanllawddog 260
Llanllwchaearn 245
Llanmihangel 250
Llannerch-y-medd 101
Llanrhidian 32
Llansadyrnin 256
Llansanffraid Cwmteuddwr 254, 328
Llansteffan 254
Llanstinan 256
Llantwit Major 257
  dialect 106
Llanwenarth 264
Llanwenog 260
Llanwynno 261
Llanyblodwel 254
Llan-y-cefn 256
Llanycil 252
Llanymynech 253
Llewelyn, Thomas 51, 53, 103, 395
Lliver gweddi gyffredin (1567) 145, 150
  see also Prayer Book
Lloyd, Benjamin 189
Lloyd, David MA 307–8
Lloyd, David, Braenog 203
Lloyd, Edward, Llanynys 122

INDEX

Lloyd, Harry, wanderer 188
Lloyd, Sir Herbert, Peterwell 203–4
Lloyd, Hugh Hughes, Gwerclas 202
Lloyd, Humphrey, sheriff 132
Lloyd, Ieuan, Iâl 191
Lloyd, Jane, Llanynys 122
Lloyd, John 113
Lloyd, John, Peterwell 203
Lloyd, John, Ruthin, schoolmaster 373
Lloyd, John, Ystumanner 107
Lloyd, Richard, Henblas 313
Lloyd, Sir Richard, Esclusham 187
Lloyd, Robert 221, 228, 295, 358
Lloyd, Thomas, Bronwydd 203
Lloyd, Thomas, Plas Power 390
Lloyd, William, bishop of St Asaph 237, 238, 240, 242
Llwyd, Angharad, antiquarian of Caerwys 243
Llwyd, Humphrey 56, 82, 100, 145, 213, 355
Llwyd, Morgan 72, 84, 85, 112, 221, 230, 353, 361–2
Llyfr Coch Hergest 23–4
Llyfr Cyfnerth 24
Llyfr Hwsmonaeth (Walter of Henley) 24
Llyfr Iorwerth 24
Llyfr Meddyginiaeth a Physygwriaeth (William Williams) 93
'Llyfr o'r Eglwys Gristnogaidd' 361
Llyfr y Psalmau (Edmwnd Prys) 353
Llyfr y resolusion (trans. John Davies) 357, 358
Llyfr y Tri Aderyn (Morgan Llwyd) 362
'Llysieulyfr Meddyginiaethol' (William Salesbury) 362
Llys-y-frân 256
Llythyr i'r Cymru cariadus (Morgan Llwyd) 362
Llywelyn ap Gruffudd 17, 34, 38
Llywelyn ap Iorwerth 39
Llywelyn ap Llywelyn 28
Llywelyn Siôn 223, 350
local government 181–205
London 60–1, 74, 95–7
Love, Christopher, Cardiff 67, 306
Lowth, Robert, bishop of St David's 393
Ludlow 75, 298
Lumley, Lord 304

Machynlleth 101, 121, 244
Mackworth, Sir Humphrey 77, 320, 323, 325
Madruddyn y difinyddiaeth diweddaraf (John Edwards) 58
Malkin, Benjamin 55, 58, 106, 107, 113, 205
Mamheilad 255
Mandeville, Bernard de 340

Mansell, Francis, principal of Jesus College 314
Manx 47, 48, 231, 339, 418, 434–8
Maredudd ab Ieuan ap Robert 31, 289, 347
Maredudd ap Rhosier 192
Marescalh, Thomas 28
Margam 101
markets 53
Marros 257
Marrow of Modern Divinity (Edward Fisher) 197–8
Martin, Gregory 149
Mathew, Elizabeth 119
Maurice, David 248
Maurice, Sir William, Clenennau 196
Maurice, William, Llansilin 367
Meliden 328
Mémoires sur La Langue Celtique (Bullet) 378
Meredith ap Llewelin 26
Meredith, Siôn 171
Merfyn Frych 434–5
Merioneth 47, 51, 99, 100, 134, 202, 252
Merthyr Cynog 261
Merthyr Dyfan 257
Merthyr Tydfil 77–8, 261
Methodists 87–9, 109, 112, 116, 118, 262, 264–9, 334, 380–5
Meylor, William, St David's 50
Meyrick, Edmund, Ucheldref 195
Michaelston-le-Pit 258
Midleton, William 351, 352
migrants 76–7
miners 77
Mona Antiqua Restaurata (Henry Rowlands) 377
Monmouthshire 47, 58, 100, 116, 183, 198, 202, 255–6, 319
monolingualism 32, 33, 45, 48, 50, 62, 63, 69, 98, 122, 137, 243, 317, 319–20, 324, 325, 348, 368
  and religion 83, 85, 89, 144, 228, 235, 247–8, 255, 256, 257, 261
  communities 105, 106, 115, 253
  English monoglots 240, 241
  in the courts 69–70, 131, 133, 135, 158, 180, 182–3, 187, 204
  location 48–53, 251, 252–3
Montgomeryshire 47, 109, 113, 132, 155, 162, 163, 241, 328
Morgan ap Maredudd, magistrate 193
Morgan, Abel, Baptist 61
Morgan, Jenkyn, Rhos-meirch 71
Morgan, John, Brecon 167
Morgan, John, Tredegar 66
Morgan, Rees 171
Morgan, Thomas 162
Morgan, William, Tredegar 203

Morgan, William, bishop of St Asaph 66, 82–3, 146, 147, 214, 216–18, 221, 230, 235, 356, 365
Moris, David Philip, Tre-lech 113
Moris, Thomas David, St Edrens 177
Morris Letters 69, 95, 98–9, 113, 117, 387–92
Morris, Angharad 330
Morris, David 160
Morris, Edward, Perthillwydion 74, 186, 196, 354, 370
Morris, John, Carrog 205
Morris, Lewis 51, 58, 81, 100, 102, 117, 204, 322, 377, 382, 385, 386–7, 388, 391, 400–1, 405
Morris, Pryse 322, 330
Morris, Richard 113, 330, 385, 388, 392
Morris, Roger, Coed-y-talwrn 310, 367
Morris, Valentine, Piercefield 66
Morris, William 238, 330, 385, 386
Morys, Huw (Eos Ceiriog) 354
Mosten, alias Richard ap Howel 159
Mostyn, Margaret 359
Mostyn, Piers, Talacre 191
Mostyn, Richard 309
Mostyn, Sir Roger 182–3, 203
Mostyn, Siân, Gloddaith 119
Mostyn, Sir Thomas 196, 202, 203
Mostyn, Thomas (Thomas ap Richard ap Howell ap Ieuan Fychan) 160
Mostyn, William, commissioner 191, 194
Mountjoy, Lord 422
Musicae activae micrologus (Andreas Ornithoparcus) 363
Mutton 17
Mutton, Peter, Llannerch 194, 310
Myddelton, Robert, Chirk Castle 203
Myddelton, Sir Thomas 219
Myles, John 84
Mynyddislwyn 255
Myvyrian Archaiology, The 402

'Nad oes vn Ffydd ond y wir Ffydd' 360
names 114–15
  baptismal names 114
  nicknames 115
  occupational names 160–1
  patronymics 75, 112, 160–1, 303
  place-names 19
  plant names 111
  surnames 114, 160–1
Nantmel 254, 328
Nebbaz Gerriau dro tho Carnoack (Nicholas Boson) 415
Nerquis 245
New Testament 86, 210
  1567 24, 83, 145, 148, 150, 214–16, 356
  1603 218

Newcastle Emlyn 101, 258
Newcome, Richard, bishop of Llandaff 86
Newcome, Thomas, bishop of St Asaph 393
Newmarket 244
Newport (Mon.) 87, 105, 244, 254
Newport (Pembs.) 187
Newton Nottage 246
Northop 245

Observations on an Ancient Manuscript entitled Passio Christi . . . (William Scawen) 411
Observations upon the English Language (George Harris) 393
Officium Parvum Beatae Mariae Virginis 207
Ogmore, manor 21
Oliver Rees ap Humffrey 120
Oliver, Ieuan David Lloyd, curate of Gwnnws 72
Oll Synnwyr pen Kembero ygyd (William Salesbury) 108, 138–9, 210–11, 293, 307–8
Origin of Language and Nations, The (Rowland Jones) 396–7
Oswestry
  lordship 18
  town 18–19, 87, 250, 254
Ottley, Adam, bishop of St David's 324
Owain ap Llywelyn ab y Moel 20
Owain Glyndŵr 39, 40
Owain Gwynedd 349
Owain Myfyr (Owen Jones) 402
Owen ap Thomas, Denbigh 173
Owen, George, Henllys 16, 30–1, 33, 34, 38, 41, 43–4, 54, 165, 184, 194, 228
Owen, Goronwy 87, 100, 101, 119–20, 230, 385, 388, 389
Owen, Hugh, Gwenynog 67, 309
Owen, Hugh, Plas Du 67, 152
Owen, James 108
Owen, John, chancellor of the diocese of Bangor 121
Owen, John, incumbent of Llangefni 335
Owen, John, Ystumcegid 28
Owen, John Lewis, Dolgellau 191
Owen, Owen, vicar of Llanilar 240
Owen, Peggy 330
Owen, Robert, Plas Du 152
Owen, Sir Robert, Porkington 79
Owen, Susan 118
Owens, Griffith, Pwllheli 78
Owens, William 171
Oxford 376
  colleges 311–14

Pantheologia, neu Hanes Holl Grefyddau'r Byd (William Williams) 384
Pant-teg 255

Paris, Matthew 38
Parker, Archbishop Matthew 148, 304
Parochialia (Edward Lhuyd) 108
Parry, Elizabeth 121
Parry, Katherine, Llanbedr Painscastle 171
Parry, Richard, bishop of St Asaph 214, 218, 295, 312, 356
Pascon agan Arluth ('The Passion of Our Lord') 412
Pembroke 75
Pembrokeshire 27, 30–1, 33, 38, 47, 50, 54, 100, 104, 157, 173, 183, 184, 202, 256, 319, 328
Penarth 250
Pen-boyr 260
Pendeulwyn 247
Pendine 256
Peniarth MS 30 (Llyfr Colan) 24
Pennant, Thomas 36
Pennsylvania 61
Penry, John 75, 184, 216, 294
Pentreath, Dolly 47, 416
Perl mewn adfyd (trans. Huw Lewys) 352, 357
Perri, Henry 346, 365
Pezron, Paul 90, 375, 376, 379
Philipps, Sir John, Picton Castle 320, 334
Phillipp, Howell, Brawdy 179
Phillips, Dr James, rector of Llangoedmor 240–1
Phillips, John, bishop of Sodor and Man 436
Phillips, Martha 104
Philpot ap Rhys 20
Phylip, Gruffudd 80, 192, 196, 349, 351
Phylip, Phylip Siôn 196, 349
Phylip, Rhisiart 195, 349
Phylip, Siôn 349
Pierce, Rees, incumbent of Llwyngwril 331
Pigot, Richard, Denbigh 83
Plain man's pathway to heaven, The (1630) 228, 357
playne and a familiar Introduction, A (William Salesbury) 147
poetry
  free-metre 352–4
poets 22, 33, 109–10, 195, 199, 212, 221–5, 290, 308–10, 343–54
Polish 39
politics 56, 62–9, 81, 82, 123–52, 402–3
population 46–7
Porthcawl 260
Porthceri 256
Powel, David 56, 225, 365, 367
Powell, Gabriel, Swansea 202
Powell, Griffin, Oxford 312
Powell, Joanna 120
Powell, Siôn, Llansannan 391–2
Powell, Thomas, Battle 246

Powell, Vavasor 84, 361
Powell, William, Nanteos 204
Practice of Piety, The (Lewis Bayly) 220, 357
Prayer Book 81–3, 86
  1567 145, 150, 213, 215, 217, 355–6
  1599 218
Presteigne 76
Price, Alice 188
Price, Dr Elis 127–8, 135, 145, 191, 309
Price, Joan 128
Price, Sir John 128, 143, 191, 208, 210, 215, 294, 355, 363
Price, Richard 404
Price, Dr Theodore, Hart Hall, Oxford 314
Price, Thomas, Watford 205
Price, William, Rhiwlas 201, 202, 203
Prichard, Elizabeth 118
Prichard, Father Leander 302
Prichard, Rees 222, 227, 230, 232
Principles of Christian Religion explained, The (William Wake) 259
printing press 91–3, 371–2
Profitable and Necessary Doctrine . . ., A (Edmund Bonner) 414
Prydferthwch Sancteiddrwydd yn y Weddi Gyffredin (Thomas Bisse) 248
Prys, Edmwnd, archdeacon of Merioneth 192, 219, 221, 222, 230, 346, 353
Prys, Ffowc, Tyddyn-du 192
Prys, Sir James, Ynysymaengwyn 196
Prys, Thomas, Plasiolyn 351
Pugh, David, rector of Newport 240
Pugh, Edward 114
Pugh, Robert, Penrhyn Creuddyn 194
Pugh, Rowland, Mathafarn 107
Pughe, William Owen 90, 93, 95, 114, 379, 396–7, 402, 403
Puleston, John, constable of Caernarfon Castle 126
Puleston, Robert, Bersham 191
Puleston, Rowland, vicar of Wrexham 361
Puritanism 83–4, 112, 116, 198, 299, 361–2
Pyle 247

Quakers 67–8, 71, 113, 116, 175, 179
Quarter Sessions 181–205
Queste del Saint Graal 30

Radnor 16
Radnorshire 47, 58–9, 76, 102, 105, 155, 165, 183, 254, 328
Radur 336
Raikes, Robert 337
Ray, John 417
Rees, Katherine 120–1
Renaissance 63, 91, 99, 232, 345–6, 351, 366–8, 384

Res ap Eignion Vyghan 25
Res ap Jollyn 25
Res ap William 27
Rhayader 254, 264
Rheol Buchedd Sanctaidd (trans. Ellis Wynne) 237
Rhisiart Cynwal 349
Rhiwledin 222, 360
Rhuddlan 328
Rhydderch ab Ieuan Llwyd 29, 35
Rhydwilym 264
Rhyl 260
Rhys ab Einion Fychan 25
Rhys ap Gruffudd, Sir, Penrhyn 191
Rhys ap Thomas, Sir 290
Rhys Cain 196, 350
Rhŷs, Sir John 437, 438
Rhys, Morgan, Llanfynydd 334
Rhys, Morgan John 61, 337, 405
Richard, earl of Arundel 26
Richard ap Hywel, Mostyn 344
Richard y Prydydd Brith 172
Richard, Edward, Ystradmeurig 385, 386, 388
Richard, John 89
Richard, Margaret 200
Rights of Man, The (Thomas Paine) 403
Risca 255
Robert ap Griffith ap John 167
Robert ap Hugh ap Ieuan ap William, Hope 163
Robert, Gruffydd 108, 109, 149, 212, 293, 351, 352, 360, 364
Robert, William, Llancarfan 110
Roberts, Ellis (Elis y Cowper) 392
Roberts, Evan, Puritan writer 85, 185, 295
Roberts, Huw, an Anglesey clergyman 351
Roberts, John, Margam 331
Roberts, Michael, Fellow of Jesus College 312
Roberts, Robert, vicar of Chirk 77
Roberts, Thomas, Llwyn'rhudol 71, 404
Robin Clidro 172
Robin Nordd 21
Robinson, Nicholas, bishop of Bangor 216
Roger ap Meredith, Boughrood 166
Rogers, John, Brecon 314
Rogers, William, warrener 50
Roman de la Rose 30
Roose 16, 54
Rowland, Daniel, Llangeitho 248, 337, 381
Rowland, Susan, Llangoed 118
Rowlands, David 295
Rowlands, Ellis, vicar of Clynnog Fawr 189
Rowlands, Henry 99, 375, 377
Ruabon 245, 247, 254
Rug Chapel 252

Ruthin 31, 254

Sail Crefydd Ghristnogol (Oliver Thomas and Evan Roberts) 296
Sail Crefydd Gristnogawl (Evan Roberts) 295–6
Saint Harmon 254, 328
St Andrews 336
St Asaph
  diocese 72, 239, 242, 245
St Athan 256
St Bride's Wentlloog 255
St David's
  diocese 237, 240
St Donat's 257
Salcot, John, bishop of Bangor 136
Salesbury, William 24, 82, 83, 91, 137–42, 148, 210, 213, 214–17, 225, 228, 230, 293–4, 346, 347, 356, 365
Salisbury, Thomas 217, 295, 358
Salusbury, Sir John, Lleweni 193
Salusbury, John, Rug 191
Salusbury, Robert 25
Salusbury, Robert, Rug 193
Salusbury, Thomas Hen 157
Sancroft, William, Archbishop of Canterbury 240
Saxons 16, 17
Saxton, Christopher 184
sayings 110–12
schools
  Beaumaris Grammar School 300
  circulating schools 89–91, 317, 324–7
  Edward Richard, Ystradmeurig 322
  grammar schools 186, 292, 307–8
  King's School 136
  Lady Hawkins's School, Kington 300
  parish schools 306
  Ruthin Grammar School 301
  Shrewsbury 302–3
  Sunday schools 90–1, 317, 337–8
science 92–3, 122
Scotland 425
Scottish Gaelic 38, 47, 90, 170, 315, 339, 340, 418, 425–34
  decline 433–4
scriptorium 23, 24
Selatyn 254
sheep and cattle markings 107, 169
Short Evangelical Catechism (1801) 339
Short Treatise of the Isle of Mann, A (James Challoner) 436
Shrewsbury 75, 302
Shropshire 19
Sidney, Sir Henry 135, 304, 349
Sigons, William de 28
Sils ap Siôn 192

Silurian 100, 101, 102, 401
    see also Gwentian speech
Simwnt Fychan 349
Sion ap Hywel ap Tomas 20
Siôn Brwynog 344
Siôn Cain 196, 350
Siôn Dafydd Rhys 79, 91, 193, 217, 231, 307, 346, 351, 353, 360, 367
Siôn Mawddwy 184, 349, 350
Siôn Rhydderch 104, 390
Siôn Tudur 217, 346, 349
Sirleto, Cardinal 149, 150
slander 36, 58, 59–60, 99, 102, 104, 113, 116, 118–19, 167, 168, 170–1, 173, 200–1
Smallbrooke, Richard, bishop of St David's 238
Smyth, Roger 360
Society for the Promotion of Christian Knowledge 89, 317, 320–4, 332, 340
Society for the Propagation of the Gospel 84, 320
Society for the Reformation of Manners 320
Society of Cymmrodorion 95, 203, 385, 391, 396
Society of Friends 84
Society of Gwyneddigion 96, 396
Some Account of the Welch Charity Schools . . . (John Evans) 334
Some Specimens of the Poetry of the Antient Welsh Bards (Evan Evans) 386, 389
Speculi Britanniae Pars: A Topographical and Historical Description of Cornwall (John Norden) 415
Squire, Samuel, bishop of St David's 393
Stanley, Sir John 435
Star Chamber 155, 156, 185, 188
state of North Wales touching religion', 'The 363
Stoddard, Lucy, Caernarfon 188
Stonne, John, Montgomery 175
Storie of the Lower Borowes, The (John Stradling) 160
Stradling, Agnes 79
Stradling, Sir Edward 79, 193, 365
Stradling, George, Oxford 314
Stukeley, William 375
Sully 256
Summa Doctrinae Christianae (St Peter Canisius) 360
Summons for Sleepers, a defence of the Protestant Church, A (Leonard Wright) 193, 355
Supplications of Saints (Thomas Sorocold) 359
Surexit 15
Survey of Cornwall, The (Richard Carew) 415
Swansea 27, 28, 32, 306
Swift, Jonathan 50
Symons, Jelinger C. 339

Talach-ddu 246, 306
Tenison, Edward, archdeacon of Carmarthen 244
Testament Newydd ein Arglwydd Jesu Christ (1567) 145, 150
    see also New Testament
théâtre du monde, Le (Pierre Boaistuau) 362–3
Theatre of the Empire of Great Britaine (John Speed) 436
Thelwall, Edward, Plas-y-ward 193, 194, 305
Thelwall, Eubule, Oxford 312
Thelwall, Simon, Plas-y-ward 145, 191, 194
Thesaurus Linguae Latinae et Cambrobrytannicae (Thomas Wiliems) 194
Thomas ab Ieuan 21, 33, 34
Thomas ap Rosier, Hergest 35
Thomas Havard Hir 159
Thomas, Alban 104
Thomas, David 120
Thomas, Edmund, Wenvoe 203
Thomas, Edward, Tregroes 203
Thomas, Evan, curate of Trostre 249
Thomas, Hugh, historian, Brecon 76
Thomas, James, curate 242
Thomas, John 266
Thomas, John, Myddfai 112–13
Thomas, Mary 120
Thomas, Oliver 85, 221, 227, 361
Thomas, Rees 72
Thomas, Rhys, Caernarfon 191
Thomas, Sir William, Coedalun 188
Thomas, William, Llanbradach 203
Thomas, William, St Fagans, schoolmaster and diarist 61, 119, 201
Tibbott, Richard 266
Time and the end of Time (John Fox) 237
Tir Telych 15, 44
Topographical and Historical Description of North Wales, A (John Evans) 205
topography 50–3
towns 27–8, 75–8, 289, 319, 320
Toy, Humphrey 147, 356
trade and commerce 21, 30, 34, 50, 57, 60, 62, 73–8, 84, 93, 103, 104, 105
Traethiad am y Wisg-Wen Ddisglair (Timothy Thomas) 104
Traethiadau ar Gatecism Eglwys Loegr (trans. Thomas Jones) 259
translators 70–1
treason 176
Trefor, John, Trefalun 194
Tregaron 119, 259
Tre-lech 113
Trevisa, John 27
Treylo, John, Ackhill, 163
Troed-yr-aur 259

Troelus a Chresyd [Humphrey Llwyd?] 354
Trysor yr iaith Ladin a'r Gymraeg (Thomas Wiliems) 365
Trysorfa Gwybodaeth, neu Eurgrawn Cymraeg 395
Tudfwlch ap Llywyd 15, 44
Tudur ab Ednyfed 34
Tudur Aled 19, 35
Tudur Penllyn 33, 34
Twm o'r Nant 72, 104
Tyred a Groesaw at Iesu Grist (Iaco ab Dewi) 264

Über den Ursprung der Sprache (J. G. Herder) 396
Usk 255, 327
Ussher, James, Archbishop of Armagh 372

Vale of Glamorgan 20, 31, 60, 183, 257, 336
Vaughan, Ellis, Llanddulas 169
Vaughan, Hugh, Hengwrt 202
Vaughan, John, Cwrt Derllys 203, 320
Vaughan, John, priest 127
Vaughan, Robert, Hengwrt 193, 366, 367
Vaughan, Robert, Hengwrt [great-grandson of the antiquary Robert Vaughan] 202
Vaughan, Rowland, Caer-gai 192, 221, 313, 357, 358, 367
Vaughan, Thomas, Llowes 155, 183
Vaughan, William, Corsygedol 66, 202
Venedotian 22, 100, 101
Veysey, John, bishop of Exeter 412

Waley, John 137, 141, 148, 210, 213, 355
Walk through Wales in August, A (Richard Warner) 201
Wallography (1682) 46
Walsingham, Sir Francis 134
Walter, John Meredith, Llansbyddyd 175
Walter, Neville, rector of Llanwytherin 240, 262
Walters, John 94, 262, 378, 397
Walton East 256
Walton West 329
Waring, Elijah 398
Watson, Richard, bishop of Llandaff 237
Welch Piety, The 90, 324, 325, 329–30, 331, 334
Welsh Trust 84, 85, 317, 318–20, 323, 362
Welshpool 40
Wesley, John 89, 437
Wessex 408
Westminster 302
Whitefield, George 104, 264, 265–6, 381
Whitgift, John, archbishop 135, 147, 217
Whitland 101
Whitson, Monmouthshire 246

Whittington 30
Whole Duty of Man, The (Richard Allestree) 322
Wiliam ap Dafydd ap Gruffudd 20
Wiliam Bodwrda 314
Wiliam Cynwal 346, 349
Wiliam Llŷn 190–1, 344, 349
Wiliems, Thomas, Trefriw 193, 311, 365
Willes, Edward, bishop of St David's 245
William ap Rhys 27, 28, 32
William de Sigons 28
William, Rachel 200
Williams, David 404
Williams, David, Bodran 179
Williams, Edward, Oswestry 337
Williams, Edward, Llangollen 189
Williams, George, Aberpergwm 203
Williams, John, Cochwillan 301, 307
Williams, John, Oxford 312
Williams, Jonathan 58
Williams, Moses 51, 61, 104, 248, 323, 376–7
Williams, Rice 389
Williams, Robert, warden of Llanbeblig Church 243
Williams, Samuel 248
Williams, William, Llansamlet 200
Williams, William, Pantycelyn 88, 93, 119, 248, 264, 266–7, 322, 372, 382–4, 406
wills 41, 42, 71–2
Willym ap Rees ap Eynon 26
Wilson, Thomas, bishop of Sodor and Man 437
Winchester 302
Windsor, Thomas 67
women
  speech patterns 119–22
  see also cursing
words
  coining new words 386–7
  dialect 110, 215, 268
  loanwords 26, 30, 35, 85, 88, 102–5, 326, 386–8
Wrexham 75, 84, 260
Wyn, John, Euarth 306
Wyndham, Thomas 66
Wynn, Sir John, Gwydir 25, 28, 31, 80, 135, 183, 187, 192, 193, 194, 216, 301, 303, 347
Wynn, Morus 145, 191, 192, 194
Wynn, Owain, Glyncywarch 196
Wynn, Sir Richard 80, 301
Wynn, Sir Watkin Williams 391
Wynn, William 202, 385
Wynne, Ellis 72, 73, 119, 202, 237, 369
Wynne, Robert 113

Yale, Dr Thomas 303–4, 309, 313

Yny lhyvyr hwnn (John Price) 137, 191, 208, 210, 355
'Young Mends the Clothier's Sermon' (Lewis Morris) 378
Young, Samuel 64

Ystatud Gruffudd ap Cynan 344
Ystradyfodwg 261, 262
Ystyriaethau Drexelivs ar Dragywyddoldeb (Elis Lewis) 313